Bankruptcy

ANNE LAWTON

Professor of Law
Michigan State University College of Law

GILBERT

The publisher is not engaged in rendering legal or other professional advice, and this publication is not a substitute for the advice of an attorney. If you require legal or other expert advice, you should seek the services of a competent attorney or other professional.

Gilbert Law Summaries is a trademark registered in the U.S. Patent and Trademark Office

© 2019 LEG, Inc. d/b/a West Academic
    444 Cedar Street, Suite 700
    St. Paul, MN 55101
    1-877-888-1330

West, West Academic Publishing, and West Academic are trademarks of West Publishing Corporation, used under license.

Printed in the United States of America

ISBN: 978-1-64020-121-7

Table of Contents

Capsule Summary

I. INTRODUCTION

A. GOALS OF THE FEDERAL BANKRUPTCY LAWS

One of the main purposes of bankruptcy is to relieve an honest debtor of debts, thereby providing an opportunity for a *fresh start.* The bankruptcy laws also benefit creditors by (i) providing a forum for either an orderly liquidation of a debtor's estate or a judicially confirmed plan for full or partial repayment of creditors, (ii) protecting unsecured creditors from preferential or fraudulent transfers of the debtor's property, and (iii) requiring adequate protection of secured creditors' interests in collateral under certain circumstances.

B. LEGISLATIVE HISTORY

Article 1, Section 8 of the United States Constitution empowers Congress to enact uniform laws on bankruptcy. Under this grant of authority, Congress passed the *Bankruptcy Act of 1898* (the "Act"), which the Chandler Act of 1938 substantially amended. The Bankruptcy Reform Act of 1978 repealed the Bankruptcy Act of 1898, and created the *Bankruptcy Code,* which became effective on October 1, 1979. The Code substantially expanded the jurisdiction of the bankruptcy court to enable the bankruptcy judge to hear practically all matters arising in or related to the bankruptcy case, thereby eliminating some of the logistical problems of litigation under the Bankruptcy Act. In 2005, Congress passed the *Bankruptcy Abuse Prevention and Consumer Protection Act* ("BAPCPA"), which made substantial changes to the Bankruptcy Code that affected, among others, individual consumers by erecting an entry barrier to Chapter 7 with the "means test."

C. ORGANIZATION OF THE BANKRUPTCY CODE

With the exception of Chapter 12, the Code is organized into *odd-numbered chapters.* Chapters 1, 3, and 5 contain provisions generally applicable to the filing chapters and include definitions, rules on eligibility for relief, provisions on the automatic stay, and what constitutes property of the bankruptcy estate. The filing chapters are 7 (liquidation), 9 (municipalities), 11 (reorganization), 12 (family farmers and family fishermen), 13 (reorganization for individuals only), and 15 (cross-border insolvency). This study guide does not cover Chapters 9 or 15.

D. RULES OF CONSTRUCTION

1. "After Notice and a Hearing"

This statutory language requires notice and an opportunity for a hearing. However, the statutory language authorizes an act without an actual hearing if proper notice is given and: (i) no hearing is requested by a party in interest; or (ii) there is insufficient time for a hearing and the court authorizes the act.

2. "Order for Relief"

Entry of an order for relief occurs automatically by the filing of a voluntary petition or upon court determination in an involuntary case that the debtor is generally not paying his debts as they become due. Entry of an order for relief merely means that the case can proceed.

E. TERMINOLOGY

1. Claim

A claim is a right to payment, even if it is unliquidated, unmatured, disputed, or contingent. It also includes the right to an equitable remedy for breach of performance if the breach gives rise to a right to payment. Congress intended a broad definition of "claim."

2. Current Monthly Income

Current monthly income is the debtor's *average monthly income* from all sources during *the six-month period* that ends on the last day of the calendar month immediately before the debtor's bankruptcy filing. The term is used in the Chapter 7 financial eligibility test that Congress created in BAPCPA and also for determining disposable income in Chapter 13 cases.

3. Debt

A debt is a liability on a claim. A *consumer debt* is one incurred by an individual for a personal, family, or household purpose.

4. Entity

This term includes persons, trusts, estates, governmental units, and the United States trustee.

5. Insider

An insider is defined in terms of whether the debtor is an individual, a corporation, or a partnership, and generally includes the debtor's relatives and persons such as directors, officers, control persons, partners, and relatives of such persons.

6. Insolvent

An entity is insolvent when its debts total more than the aggregate value of all of its property, excluding property fraudulently transferred and exempt property.

7. Lien

A *lien* is a charge against or an interest in property to secure payment of a debt or the performance of an obligation. A *judicial lien* is a lien obtained by judgment, levy, sequestration, or other legal or equitable proceeding or process. A *security interest* is a lien that is created by agreement

8. Person

Individuals, corporations, and partnerships are persons; governmental units are not (with one exception for eligibility of certain governmental units to serve on a Chapter 11 creditors' committee).

9. Transfer

A transfer is any voluntary *or* involuntary disposition of property or interest in property.

F. BANKRUPTCY PETITION PREPARERS

A *bankruptcy petition preparer* is a person, other than the debtor's attorney or an employee under the direct supervision of the debtor's attorney, who prepares for compensation a document, such as the petition, for filing. A bankruptcy petition preparer cannot give a potential debtor legal advice. The Code provides for damages, fines, and injunctive relief against a bankruptcy petition preparer who violates the Code's rules.

II.   JURISDICTION AND PROCEDURE

A.   BANKRUPTCY COURT

The bankruptcy court in each federal judicial district constitutes a unit of the respective district court and receives its authority to hear cases and proceedings *by referral* from the district court. Bankruptcy judges are appointed for a judicial district by the United States court of appeals for the circuit in which the district is located. The judge's *term is for 14 years.* The bankruptcy judge is authorized to implement the provisions of the Bankruptcy Code by issuing *any necessary or appropriate order, judgment, or process* and is expressly authorized to take action *sua sponte* if necessary or appropriate to enforce court orders or prevent an abuse of process. The court also may hold *status conferences* and issue orders to expedite the case.

1.   Contempt

Most courts have held that the bankruptcy court has the authority to issue *civil* contempt orders to coerce compliance with a court order. The courts are split, however, as to *criminal* contempt orders issued to punish the violator.

2.   Sanctions

The bankruptcy court may impose sanctions on attorneys, law firms, or parties who sign, file, or submit pleadings or other documents, or advocate for positions that (i) are *not well-grounded in fact or in law* or (ii) are filed for any *improper purpose.*

B.   PERSONAL JURISDICTION

The Bankruptcy Rules provide for *nationwide service of process* by first class prepaid mail, except for subpoenas, in adversary proceedings and contested matters. Courts typically do not use the "minimum contacts" test. Service of process on an insured depository institution generally requires certified mail, rather than first class mail.

C.   SUBJECT MATTER JURISDICTION

1.   District Courts

District courts have *original and exclusive* jurisdiction over all bankruptcy cases. They have *original but not exclusive* jurisdiction over all civil proceedings, which are controversies arising under the Code, or in or related to a bankruptcy case. The district courts are vested with *exclusive jurisdiction* over all of the debtor's property, regardless of its location, as of the filing of a bankruptcy petition, as well as all property of the estate.

2.   Referral to Bankruptcy Courts

Each district has its own rule automatically referring all bankruptcy cases and proceedings to the bankruptcy judges in the district. Almost all cases and proceedings (with the exception of *trials* of personal injury tort and wrongful death claims) have been referred by district courts to the bankruptcy courts. Bankruptcy judges can hear and decide all referred **cases *and core proceedings*** and can issue final orders and judgments, which are appealable to the appropriate district courts. However, in *non-core matters,* bankruptcy judges may hear the proceedings and then must submit proposed findings of fact and conclusions of law to the district court for final disposition, and if an objection is filed, de novo review.

D. CORE VERSUS NON-CORE PROCEEDINGS

There are three categories of proceedings in a bankruptcy case: proceedings that (i) *arise under* title 11; (ii) *arise in* a bankruptcy case; or (3) *are related to* a bankruptcy case. Whether the bankruptcy court may enter *final judgments and orders* in a proceeding depends on whether the proceeding is a *statutory core or non-core proceeding* and, if the former, *whether it is a* **Stern** *claim.*

1. Core Proceedings

Core proceedings are those that *arise under title 11* or *arise in a bankruptcy case.* In a *core proceeding,* the bankruptcy court has the *statutory authority* to enter *final judgments and orders,* subject to regular appellate review. Core proceedings include matters regarding administration of the debtor's estate, allowance or disallowance of property exemptions and creditors' claims, counterclaims by the estate against claimants, the automatic stay, fraudulent transfers, preferences, use or sale or lease of estate property, and other matters listed in 28 U.S.C. § 157(b)(2). In its decision in *Stern v. Marshall,* the Supreme Court made clear that while a bankruptcy court may have *the statutory authority under § 157(b)(2)(C)* to enter a final judgment, it *may not have the constitutional authority* to do so.

2. Non-Core Proceedings

In a *non-core* proceeding, the bankruptcy court must submit *proposed findings of fact and conclusions of law* to the district court, which enters a final judgment or order, after conducting a *de novo review* on all matters on which a party has timely and specifically objected. If all the parties *consent,* however, the bankruptcy court may enter final judgments and orders, subject to appellate review, in a *non-core* proceeding.

3. Guidelines

- If the proceeding falls into one of the statutory categories of core proceedings and is not a *Stern* claim, then the bankruptcy court may enter a final judgment or order.

- If the proceeding falls into one of the statutory categories of core proceedings and is a *Stern* claim, then the bankruptcy court may enter a final judgment or order only with the parties' consent.

- If the proceeding falls into one of the statutory categories of core proceedings and is a *Stern* claim but the parties do not consent to the bankruptcy court entering a final order or judgment, then the bankruptcy court must submit proposed findings of fact and conclusions of law to the district court to review *de novo.*

- If the proceeding is non-core, then the bankruptcy court may enter a final judgment or order with the parties' consent.

- If the proceeding is non-core but the parties do not consent to the bankruptcy court entering a final order or judgment, then the bankruptcy court must submit proposed findings of fact and conclusions of law to the district court to review *de novo.*

E. JURY TRIALS

The Supreme Court has held that a party is constitutionally entitled to a jury trial of a bankruptcy proceeding if (i) the action would have been brought at law prior to the merger of law and equity courts, (ii) the remedy sought is legal in nature, and (iii) the proceeding involves a private right. In a case in which the right to a jury trial exists, Congress has authorized bankruptcy judges to conduct jury trials if the district court has *specially designated the exercise of this jurisdiction* and *all parties expressly consent.*

F. WITHDRAWAL OF THE REFERENCE

1. Permissive Withdrawal

The district court, *for cause,* may withdraw, in whole or in part, a case or proceeding that has been referred to the bankruptcy court either on its own motion or on the timely motion of a party.

2. Mandatory Withdrawal

On a timely motion, the district court must withdraw a proceeding from the bankruptcy court if *its resolution* requires consideration of *both* the Bankruptcy Code *and* a *nonbankruptcy federal statute* "regulating organizations or activities affecting interstate commerce." While the statute says that withdrawal is mandated when resolution requires consideration of *both* the Code and a non-Code federal statute, the vast majority of courts have interpreted § 157(d) to mandate withdrawal if resolution of the dispute requires "*substantial and material*" consideration of the *non-Code federal statute* and that statute has *more than a de minimis impact* on interstate commerce.

G. ABSTENTION

1. Permissive Abstention

The district court may abstain from hearing a *particular* proceeding arising under the Code or arising in or related to a bankruptcy case when *justice, comity with state courts, or respect for state law* favors resolution of the matter in a state forum.

2. Mandatory Abstention

On a timely motion, a district court must abstain from hearing a particular proceeding if it is based on a state law claim or cause of action *related to the bankruptcy case,* but *not arising in the bankruptcy case or under the Code,* if the proceeding: (i) could not have been brought in federal court without bankruptcy jurisdiction; (ii) already has been filed in an appropriate state court; and (iii) is capable of being timely adjudicated in that forum. Personal injury tort and wrongful death claim proceedings are not subject to mandatory abstention.

3. Proceeding Versus Case

It is important to differentiate between the court's abstaining from hearing a *single proceeding* that is only one component of the bankruptcy case and abstaining from hearing the *whole bankruptcy case.* The bankruptcy court may, at any time, abstain from hearing *an entire case* by dismissing it or by suspending all proceedings if it finds that abstention would better serve the interests of creditors and the debtor. But, the court is "limited to abstaining from a particular proceeding" under 28 U.S.C. § 1334(c).

4. Appeals

With one exception, a bankruptcy court's order in favor of or against abstention, whether permissive or mandatory, from hearing a particular proceeding may be appealed to the district court or bankruptcy appellate panel. An abstention decision by the district court or bankruptcy appellate panel, however, may not be appealed to the court of appeals or the Supreme Court.

H. REMOVAL

1. Civil Actions

A party may remove any claim or cause of action in a civil proceeding from a nonbankruptcy court to the federal district court for the district where the civil action is pending, if there is proper jurisdiction. *Note:* Tax court proceedings and civil actions by governmental units to enforce police or regulatory powers are *not* subject to removal.

2. Remand

The court to which a claim or cause of action has been removed has the power, based on the equities, to remand the action to the forum where it was pending. A bankruptcy court's order to remand or not to remand a removed proceeding is reviewable by the district court, but a remand decision by the district court is not reviewable by the court of appeals or the Supreme Court.

I. VENUE

1. Bankruptcy Case

Venue for the filing of a bankruptcy petition is in the federal district where the debtor has maintained her *residence, domicile, or principal place of business or assets* in the United States during or for the longest portion of the *180 days* immediately prior to filing. Venue is also proper in a district where a bankruptcy case concerning a general partner, partnership, or affiliate of the debtor is pending.

2. Bankruptcy Proceeding

For bankruptcy proceedings, venue lies in the district where the case is pending.

a. Exceptions

With the exception of certain post-petition claims, a bankruptcy trustee must file a proceeding *arising in or related to* the bankruptcy case in the district where the *defendant resides* if the proceeding is to recover (i) *money or property* worth less than *$1375;* (ii) *a consumer debt* of less than *$20,450;* or (iii) a *non-consumer debt against a non-insider* of less than *$13,650.*

b. Post-Petition Claims Against Estate

The trustee may bring a proceeding *arising under the Code, or arising in or related to* a bankruptcy case based on a claim that arises *post-petition from the operation of the debtor's business* only in the district where the action could have been filed under applicable nonbankruptcy venue law. This rule applies even if the trustee's claim is for a small amount that, otherwise, would qualify for an exception described above.

3. Post-Petition Claims Against Estate

A proceeding *against the trustee* based on a cause of action that arises post-petition from the operation of the debtor's business may be brought either in the district where the case is pending *or* in the district where the action could have been commenced under applicable nonbankruptcy venue law.

4. Change of Venue

A case may be transferred by one district court to another "in the interest of justice or for the convenience of the parties." The bankruptcy court can order a transfer, since motions to change venue generally are treated as core proceedings.

a. Improper Venue

If a case was filed in the wrong district, i.e., venue is improper, the bankruptcy court, upon motion of a party in interest or *sua sponte,* may transfer the case to another district if transfer is in *the interest of justice* or for the *convenience of the parties.* It is unclear whether the court may *dismiss* the case. It also is not clear whether the bankruptcy court may retain the case and not transfer it.

J. APPEALS

1. Appeals from Bankruptcy Court

An appeal may be taken from the bankruptcy court to the federal district court or to a bankruptcy appellate panel, if the jurisdiction has such a panel. Under certain limited circumstances, a party may appeal directly to the court of appeals.

a. District Court

The appellate jurisdiction of the district court and the bankruptcy appellate panel includes appeals from final orders, judgments, and decrees of the bankruptcy court, and from interlocutory orders extending or shortening the debtor's exclusivity period for filing a plan. Appellate jurisdiction over interlocutory orders is by leave of the district court or the bankruptcy appellate panel.

b. Bankruptcy Appellate Panels

The judicial council of each circuit must establish a bankruptcy appellate panel, comprised of bankruptcy judges from that circuit, to hear appeals *unless* (i) there are *insufficient judicial resources* or (ii) the procedure would cause *undue delay or increased cost* to parties in bankruptcy cases. Each appeal is to be heard by three members of the bankruptcy appellate panel who are not from the district where the appeal arises. Unless the appellant elects at the time of the appeal or any other party elects, no later than *30 days* after service of the appeal notice, to have the district court hear the appeal, the bankruptcy appellate panel will hear the appeal.

(i) Precedential Value

Decisions of the bankruptcy appellate panel bind the parties to the dispute before the court. Whether the panel's decisions are binding on bankruptcy courts within the circuit is unclear.

c. Direct Appeal to Circuit Court

In 2005, Congress provided for a direct appeal to the circuit court, under certain circumstances. The orders from which a direct appeal may be taken are those described in § 158(a): (i) final orders, judgments, and decrees; (ii) interlocutory orders expanding or shortening the exclusivity period under B.C. § 1121; and (iii) other interlocutory orders and decrees. The process for securing a direct appeal involves several steps.

d. "Clearly Erroneous" Standard

On appeal, the reviewing court must use the "clearly erroneous" standard with regard to the bankruptcy court's findings of fact, but the bankruptcy court's conclusions of law are subject to *de novo* review.

e. Interlocutory Orders

The district court or bankruptcy appellate panel may grant leave to appeal an interlocutory order of the bankruptcy court, but leave to appeal is justified only under *exceptional circumstances.*

f. Time for Appeals

With certain limited exceptions, a party must file a notice of appeal *14 days* after entry of the bankruptcy judge's order, judgment, or decree being appealed.

2. Appeal from District Court or Bankruptcy Appellate Panel

An appeal may be taken to the circuit court from a *final decision, order, or judgment* of: (i) the district court, in its *appellate capacity,* or (ii) the bankruptcy appellate panel. The Supreme Court has held that appeals from *interlocutory orders* of the district court sitting in its appellate capacity are governed by the general standard for review of interlocutory orders.

3. District Court as Court of Original Jurisdiction

If the district court functions as a court of original jurisdiction, rather than as an appellate court, *e.g.,* in *non-core or Stern-claim* proceedings in which the parties do not consent or in proceedings that have been *withdrawn,* the general standard for an appeal to the circuit court of the district court's final decision governs.

4. Automatic Stay Orders

The circuits that have addressed the issue all have held that a bankruptcy court's order lifting the automatic stay is a final order. The vast majority of courts also have ruled that a bankruptcy court order refusing to the lift the automatic stay is a final order.

K. SOVEREIGN IMMUNITY

1. Waiver

Bankruptcy Code § 106 waives the sovereign immunity of governmental units with respect to a number of bankruptcy issues. This waiver is intended to apply to monetary recoveries, other than punitive damages awards, as well as to declaratory or injunctive relief.

2. Offset Against Governmental Claims

If property of the estate includes a claim against a governmental unit that would be barred by sovereign immunity, the trustee can offset that claim against a claim of the governmental unit, e.g., an unrelated tax claim, but only up to the amount of the government's claim, *regardless of whether a claim of the governmental unit has been filed or allowed.*

3. Compulsory Counterclaims

If a governmental unit has filed a proof of claim in the bankruptcy case, then it is deemed to have waived sovereign immunity with regard to a compulsory counterclaim to its claim that arose out of the same transaction or occurrence.

4. State Sovereign Immunity

The Supreme Court has concluded that the States, by giving Congress the power to make uniform laws on bankruptcy, agreed "not to assert any sovereign immunity defense they might have had in proceedings" created by Congress under the Bankruptcy Clause.

III. COMMENCEMENT AND ADMINISTRATION OF THE CASE

A. ELIGIBILITY: ALL CHAPTERS

1. Person

Only a person (individual, corporation, or partnership) who *resides* or has a *domicile, place of business, or property in the United States* can be a debtor under the Code. Insolvency is **not** required. The term "corporation" includes business trusts and most companies or associations with corporate attributes. A limited partnership is not a corporation under the Code.

2. When a Debtor May Not File for Relief

In 2005, Congress added a pre-bankruptcy credit counseling requirement for individual debtors. With limited exceptions, an individual may not file for bankruptcy until she has satisfied this credit counseling requirement. An *individual* or a *family farmer* also is not eligible to file a petition under any chapter of the Bankruptcy Code if she has been a debtor in a case that was *dismissed in the preceding 180 days,* either because of the debtor's willful failure to obey court orders or "to appear before the court in proper prosecution of the case," *or* because she requested a voluntary dismissal of the case following a party's request for relief from the automatic stay.

B. ELIGIBILITY: CHAPTER-SPECIFIC REQUIREMENTS

1. Chapter 7: "Liquidation"

Chapter 7 relief is available to *any person* that *resides or has a domicile, a place of business, or property in the United States except* (i) individual debtors with primarily consumer debts who fail the "means test"; (ii) railroads; (iii) domestic savings institutions and insurance companies; (iv) certain small business investment companies; (v) foreign insurance companies engaged in such business in the United States; and (vi) foreign banks, savings and loan associations, and other similar financial institutions that have a branch or agency in the United States. Stockbrokers and commodity brokers may be debtors under special provisions of Chapter 7.

2. Chapter 11: "Reorganization"

Only individuals, partnerships, and corporations eligible for Chapter 7 relief can be debtors under Chapter 11. Stockbrokers and commodity brokers cannot be Chapter 11 debtors, but *railroads* are eligible for relief under special provisions of Chapter 11.

a. Business or Consumer Debtors

Designed mainly for business reorganizations, Chapter 11 may also provide relief for consumer debtors. Relief usually entails debtor reorganization by means of a confirmable plan, but the Code also provides for a liquidating plan.

3. **Chapter 12: "Family Farmer or Family Fisherman with Regular Annual Income"**

A *family farmer or family fisherman* whose *yearly income* is sufficiently *stable and regular* to fund a Chapter 12 plan may file a *voluntary* petition under that chapter. Certain individuals, individuals and their spouses, corporations, or partnerships may qualify as a family farmer or a family fisherman.

4. **Chapter 13: "Adjustment of Debts of Individuals with Regular Income"**

Chapter 13 relief is available *only to an individual who has regular income,* whose *unsecured debts* total less than *$419,275,* and whose *secured debts* total less than *$1,257,850.* The indebtedness used for these calculations must be noncontingent and liquidated liabilities, determined as of the date of the filing of the petition. An individual with regular income and his spouse may file a joint petition under Chapter 13, provided that their *aggregate unsecured* indebtedness is less than *$419,275* and their *aggregate secured* indebtedness is less than *$1,257,850.* Stockbrokers and commodity brokers do not qualify for relief under Chapter 13. A Chapter 13 case may be commenced only by the debtor's *voluntary* petition.

C. VOLUNTARY CASE

1. Filing the Petition

A voluntary case commences upon an eligible debtor's filing of a petition under Chapter 7, 11, 12, or 13. At that time, the filing fee must be paid unless the court has approved installment payments. Commencement of a voluntary case automatically constitutes an *order for relief.*

a. Notice

Notice of the order for relief is sent to all parties in interest.

b. Joint Case

Spouses can file jointly, thereby avoiding another filing fee. The debtors must be legally married; a joint petition may not be filed if they merely cohabitate. After the Supreme Court's decision in **Obergefell v. Hodges,** same-sex couples may legally marry; thus, they are eligible to file a joint bankruptcy petition. Joint filing is available only in a voluntary case.

c. Corporation

State law determines who has authority to file a voluntary bankruptcy petition on behalf of a corporation or a limited liability company. If the person or entity filing the petition lacks authority to do so under state law, then the bankruptcy court must dismiss the petition.

d. Partnership

A petition filed by fewer than all the general partners in a partnership is treated as an involuntary petition.

2. Schedules and Statements

In addition to the petition, a debtor under Chapter 7, 11, 12, or 13 must timely file a list of creditors and addresses, a schedule of assets and liabilities, a schedule of current income and expenditures, a schedule of executory contracts and unexpired leases, and a statement of the debtor's financial affairs. BAPCPA created a number of new filing obligations for individual debtors, including filing a statement showing compliance with the credit counseling requirement. A debtor's failure to file certain forms or paper work, or to perform certain statutory duties may result in dismissal of the case or lifting of the automatic stay. In addition, there are chapter-specific filing requirements with which the debtor must comply.

3. Debtor Duties

In addition to filing the required schedules and statements, the debtor must cooperate with the trustee and relinquish estate property and relevant records, and keep her address current. An individual debtor must appear at the discharge hearing, if one is held. In a Chapter 7 case, an *individual debtor with secured consumer debts* must file a statement of intention to retain or surrender and, if applicable, to exempt, redeem, or reaffirm debts secured by the collateral, and must perform such intention in a timely manner.

4. Automatic Stay

Once a voluntary or involuntary petition is filed, the automatic stay becomes effective against *all entities* to protect the debtor, his property, and property of the estate.

D. INVOLUNTARY CASE

1. Eligibility

An involuntary petition may be filed only under *Chapter 7 or Chapter 11* (not under Chapter 12 or Chapter 13) against a person who qualifies as a debtor under the applicable chapter. Even if filed under Chapter 7 or Chapter 11, an involuntary petition may *not* be filed against (i) a farmer, (ii) a family farmer, or (iii) a nonprofit or charitable corporation.

2. Filing the Petition

If there are *at least 12 creditors* (excluding the debtor's insiders and employees, and transferees of voidable transfers) holding claims against the debtor that are neither contingent as to liability nor the subject of a bona fide dispute as to liability or amount, *three or more of these entities* may file an involuntary petition provided that at least *$16,750* of their claims, in the aggregate, are *unsecured, noncontingent, and undisputed.* If there are *fewer than 12 creditors* (excluding the debtor's insiders and employees, and transferees of voidable transfers) holding noncontingent, undisputed claims against the debtor, one or more of these entities may file an involuntary petition provided that at least *$16,750* of the claims, in the *aggregate, are unsecured, noncontingent, and undisputed.*

3. Answer

Only the debtor, or in the case of a partnership debtor a non-petitioning general partner, may file an answer to the involuntary petition. In the answer, the debtor tries to controvert the allegations made in the petition.

4. Entry of an Order for Relief

The court will enter an order for relief against the debtor if (i) a timely answer is not filed; (ii) the court finds that the debtor is *generally not paying undisputed debts as they become due;* or (iii) a *custodian* was appointed or took charge of debtor's property within *120 days* before the petition was filed.

5. Gap Period

Between the filing of the petition and the entry of an order for relief (the "gap period"), the debtor can remain in possession of his property, continue business operations, and use, acquire, or dispose of assets, unless the court denies these privileges or appoints an interim trustee.

a. Transfers During Gap Period

If the debtor makes a transfer during the gap period, the transfer is not subject to the trustee's avoiding powers *to the extent of post-petition value given in exchange for the transfer* by the transferee.

b. Priority for Gap Creditors

Any creditors whose claims arise in the ordinary course of the debtor's business or financial affairs before the *earlier of* the appointment of a trustee or entry of the order for relief are entitled to *second priority status* in the order of distribution to claimants.

c. Interim Trustee

During the gap period in a Chapter 7 case, on request by a party in interest and after notice to the debtor and a hearing, the court may direct the United States trustee to appoint an interim trustee if the court finds that such an appointment is needed to *preserve property of the estate* or to *avoid loss.*

6. Dismissal of Involuntary Petition

If the court dismisses an involuntary petition other than on the consent of all the petitioning entities and the debtor, and if the debtor has not waived her right to damages, then the court may award a judgment to the debtor and against the petitioners for costs and/or reasonable attorneys' fees. When the court dismisses an involuntary petition, and finds that a petitioning entity filed the petition in *bad faith,* the court may award the debtor damages proximately caused by the involuntary petition, as well as *punitive damages.* BAPCPA added certain protections for *individual debtors* whose involuntary petitions are dismissed, including *sealing all court records* in certain cases and preventing all *consumer reporting agencies* from making a consumer report containing information about the involuntary filing.

7. Schedules to Be Filed

If an order for relief is entered, the debtor must timely file the required lists, schedules, and statements.

E. SECTION 341 MEETING OF CREDITORS

In a Chapter 7 or Chapter 11 case, within 21 to 40 days after the order for relief, a meeting of creditors is held at the courthouse or at another location within the district, designated by the United States trustee for the convenience of the parties in interest. In a Chapter 12 case, the meeting is held within 21 to 35 days after the order for relief. In a Chapter 13 case, the meeting is held within 21 to 50 days after the order for relief. This meeting is called the *section 341 meeting* of creditors. The debtor must personally attend the meeting, and the United States trustee presides. In North Carolina and Alabama, the bankruptcy administrator is authorized to preside. The United States trustee may also convene a meeting of the debtor's equity security holders, if appropriate.

1. Notice

The clerk of the court provides by mail at least 21 days' notice of the § 341 meeting to the debtor, the trustee, all creditors, and indenture trustees. If notice by mail is impracticable, the court may order that notice be given by publication. In a reorganization case under Chapter 11, equity security holders must be notified of any § 341 meeting of equity security holders. The § 341 notice includes such matters as notice of the order for relief, imposition of the automatic stay, and final dates for filing proofs of claims, complaints to determine dischargeability of certain debts, objections to an individual debtor's discharge, and objections to the debtor's exemptions.

2. Purpose of Section 341 Meeting

The primary function of the § 341 meeting is to provide an opportunity for creditors, the trustee, an examiner, if one has been appointed, any indenture trustee, and the United States trustee or bankruptcy administrator *to examine the debtor under oath* about issues related to the bankruptcy case.

F. CONVERSION

Chapters 7, 11, 12, and 13 provide rules for conversion of a case from one chapter to another when the debtor satisfies the eligibility requirements for the succeeding chapter. A court may order conversion of a Chapter 7 or Chapter 11 case to Chapter 12 or Chapter 13 *only upon the debtor's request.*

1. Effects of Conversion

Conversion operates as an order for relief under the new chapter, but as a general rule does not change the *date* of the filing of the bankruptcy petition, the commencement of the case, or the order for relief. There are a number of exceptions to this rule, in which case the *date of the order for relief* is deemed to be the date that the case was converted. Except for administrative expenses, any claims arising in a Chapter 11, 12, or 13 case after the order for relief but before conversion to another chapter are considered pre-petition claims for all purposes.

2. Conversion from Chapter 13: Property of the Estate

If a case is converted from Chapter 13 to another chapter of the Code, property of the estate in the converted case consists of property of the estate *on the date of the Chapter 13 filing* that remains in the possession or control of the debtor on the date of conversion. If the debtor converts the case in *bad faith,* however, property of the estate in the converted case will consist of the estate property *on the date of conversion* (including property acquired after the date of the Chapter 13 filing).

3. Conversion from Chapter 13: Secured Claims

Valuations of *property* and of *allowed secured claims* in the Chapter 13 case apply in a case converted to Chapters 11 or 12, but not to a case converted to Chapter 7. The allowed secured claims in Chapters 11 or 12 are *reduced by the amount paid* under the *Chapter 13* plan.

G. DISMISSAL

Whether the debtor, a party in interest, the United States trustee, or the court on its own motion may move for the dismissal of a petition, and when the court may or must order a dismissal, are questions that vary according to the chapter of the Code under which the petition was filed. Dismissal usually is *without prejudice.* The effect of a dismissal is *with prejudice,* however, to the extent that the debtor is ineligible to file again within 180 days due to § 109(g), or if the court finds *cause* to dismiss the case with prejudice. If an *individual* in a *voluntary Chapter 7 or Chapter 13 case* fails to file all the information required by § 521(a)(1) *within 45 days* of filing her petition, then her case is *automatically dismissed* on Day 46. While the Code provides for automatic dismissal, it is unclear how that happens, and it is possible, notwithstanding the "automatic dismissal" language that a court order is needed.

IV. OFFICERS OF THE ESTATE

A. TRUSTEE

The trustee is the official representative of the estate and in this capacity can sue or be sued. The trustee has numerous administrative powers and specific duties, which vary according to the chapter under which he is serving.

1. Eligibility

A *disinterested* individual who is competent or a disinterested corporation authorized by its charter or bylaws may serve as trustee. In Chapter 7, 12, or 13 cases, the trustee must *reside or have an office in the judicial district* where the case is pending or in the adjacent district. If necessary, the United States trustee for the district may serve in a Chapter 7, 12, or 13 case, but not in a Chapter 11 case.

a. "Disinterested Person"

The term *excludes* the debtor's (i) creditors, equity security holders, and insiders; (ii) current directors, officers, and employees; (iii) directors, officers, and employees who served during the two years prior to filing for bankruptcy; and (iv) any person with a *materially adverse* interest to the estate or to any class of creditors or equity security holders.

2. Qualification—Bond

Within seven days after appointment or election, and before beginning service, a trustee must file with the court a *bond,* in favor of the United States, in the amount set by the United States trustee. The United States trustee also approves the surety on the bond.

3. Selection of Trustee

a. Chapter 7

All Chapter 7 cases require a trustee chosen from a panel of private trustees maintained by the United States trustee to serve in a particular region. Immediately after entry of the order for relief, the United States trustee appoints a disinterested panel member to serve as the *interim trustee* until the § 341 meeting, at which time the interim trustee will become the permanent trustee unless another person is elected.

b. Chapter 11

In a Chapter 11 case, the debtor generally remains in possession of property of the estate and continues to manage the business, in an effort to reorganize, *without the necessity of a trustee's appointment.* A party in interest or the United States trustee, however, may move at any time after the filing of the bankruptcy petition but before confirmation of a Chapter 11 plan for appointment of a Chapter 11 trustee. The court may order appointment of a Chapter 11 trustee (i) *for cause;* (ii) if appointment is in the *interests of creditors, any equity security holders,* and other interests of the estate; or (iii) grounds exist to *convert or dismiss* the case, but the court determines that appointment of a trustee is in the *best interests of creditors and the estate.*

(i) When U.S. Trustee Must Act

BAPCPA amended the Code to require the United States trustee to move for the appointment of a Chapter 11 trustee if *reasonable grounds* exist to suspect that current members of the debtor's governing body, debtor's chief executive or chief financial officer, or members of the governing body that selected the chief executive or chief financial officer participated in *actual fraud, dishonesty, or criminal conduct* in *managing the debtor* or the *debtor's public financial reporting.*

c. Chapters 13 and 12

In a region where many Chapter 13 cases are filed, the United States trustee ordinarily appoints a qualified individual to serve as a *standing trustee* for all Chapter 13 cases in that region. Otherwise, the United States trustee appoints a disinterested person as the trustee for a particular case, or the United States trustee may serve as the trustee in the case. The same procedure applies in cases under Chapter 12. Usually, however, the Chapter 13 or 12 debtor remains in possession of property of the estate.

4. Duties of Trustee

a. Chapter 7

The *primary* responsibilities of a Chapter 7 trustee are to *collect and reduce to cash* property of the estate, to *make distributions* to claimants in the order prescribed by the Code, and to *close the estate* as expeditiously as is compatible with best interests of parties in interest. A Chapter 7 trustee also has a number of other important statutory duties, including objecting to allowance of improper claims, objecting to the debtor's discharge, if warranted, and timely filing after the § 341 meeting a statement with the court as to whether the filing of an individual debtor's case creates a presumption of abuse.

b. Chapter 11

A trustee who replaces the debtor in possession is usually authorized to *operate the debtor's business* and is charged with certain duties of a Chapter 7 trustee, as well as other duties that relate specifically to a Chapter 11 case, such as the advisability of continuing the debtor's business, and filing a Chapter 11 plan.

c. Chapter 13

A Chapter 13 trustee must perform certain of the duties of a Chapter 7 trustee, but has a number of other important statutory duties, including: (i) providing the required notices related to *domestic support obligations;* (ii) *ensuring that the debtor begins making payments* within 30 days after the plan is filed; (iii) *disbursing payments* to creditors under a confirmed plan; and (iv) if the debtor is engaged in business, *investigating* the debtor's conduct, financial condition, business operations, and the advisability of continuing the business.

d. Chapter 12

A Chapter 12 trustee's duties are similar to those of a Chapter 13 trustee as long as the debtor remains a debtor in possession. If a Chapter 12 debtor is removed from possession, the trustee is charged with many of the duties of a

Chapter 11 trustee, including operation of the debtor's farm or commercial fishing operation.

5. Liability of Trustee

A trustee, as fiduciary of the estate, may be held ***personally liable*** for breach of duties. Courts differ on whether the standard requires intentional, negligent, or gross negligent violation of fiduciary duty.

6. Powers of Trustee

As the representative of the estate, the trustee is granted many administrative powers, including the power to (i) ***file a proof of claim*** on behalf of a creditor; (ii) ***operate the debtor's business*** in a Chapter 11 case and sometimes in Chapter 7 or 12 cases; (iii) ***deposit or invest money;*** (iv) ***employ*** professional persons; (v) ***avoid*** certain transfers and liens; (vi) ***use, sell, or lease property;*** (vii) ***obtain credit;*** (viii) ***assume or reject executory contracts or unexpired leases;*** (ix) demand utility services; (x) abandon property; and (xi) waive a debtor corporation's attorney-client privilege.

7. Removal of Trustee

A trustee, other than the United States trustee, or an examiner may be removed by the court ***for cause.***

B. EXAMINER

1. Role and Capacity

In a Chapter 11 case in which the court has not ordered the appointment of a trustee, the court sometimes will order the appointment of an examiner. The examiner is appointed prior to confirmation of a plan ***to investigate any*** charges of ***fraud, dishonesty, incompetence, or mismanagement*** on the part of the debtor's present or former management. The debtor in possession retains her property and continues to operate the business. A disinterested person other than the United States trustee may serve as examiner.

2. Reasons for Appointment

When a party in interest or the United States trustee requests appointment of an examiner, the court, after notice and a hearing, ***must order*** that an examiner be appointed if the debtor's fixed, liquidated, unsecured debts ***exceed $5 million, excluding*** debts for goods, services, or taxes, and any debts owed to an insider. Also, the court will order the appointment of an examiner if such action is in the ***best interests of creditors, equity security holders, and the estate.***

3. Duties

An examiner's duties include (i) ***investigating*** the debtor's conduct, financial condition, and business operations, as well as the ***advisability of continuing the business;*** (ii) ***filing a report*** of the investigation; and (iii) any other trustee responsibilities that the court directs the debtor in possession not to perform. An ***examiner may not serve as a trustee or professional person*** in the same case in which she has served as examiner.

C. PROFESSIONAL PERSONS

A trustee, a debtor in possession, or creditors' or equity security holders' committees in a Chapter 11 case, with court approval, may hire professional persons, *e.g.*, attorneys or accountants, to perform services with respect to the bankruptcy estate. Professional persons must be ***disinterested persons*** who ***do not have an interest adverse*** to the estate. Creditors, insiders, and equity security holders are *not* disinterested persons. Court approval *must* be obtained *prior to performing services;* otherwise, the professional's application for compensation may be denied by the court.

1. **Special Purpose Attorney**

   The court may authorize a trustee or a debtor in possession to employ a former attorney of the debtor for a *special purpose,* such as continuing legal expertise in an intricate proceeding, provided that the employment is in the *estate's best interest* and the lawyer does not have an adverse interest concerning the specific subject matter of the employment. The purpose may *not* be to represent the trustee in administering the bankruptcy case.

2. **Creditor's Representative**

   In a Chapter 7, 11, or 12 case, a professional person is not disqualified from *employment by a trustee solely* because of her employment by or representation of a creditor, unless another creditor or the United States trustee objects and the court finds an *actual conflict of interest.*

3. **Trustee as Professional Person**

   The court may permit a trustee to also serve as an attorney or accountant for the estate if it is in the estate's best interest.

4. **Creditors' Committee May Hire Professional Persons**

   In a Chapter 11 case, a creditors' committee or an equity security holders' committee may employ attorneys, accountants, or other professionals to perform services for the committee. While representing or in the employ of the committee, the professional person may not represent an entity having an *adverse interest.* Representation of a creditor of the same class as the committee represents, however, does not per se constitute representation of an adverse interest.

D. **OMBUDSMEN**

   BAPCPA amended the Code to provide, under certain circumstances, for the appointment of a *consumer privacy ombudsman* or the appointment of a *patient care ombudsman.*

1. **Consumer Privacy Ombudsman**

   A bankruptcy court cannot approve a sale of *personally identifiable information* that is inconsistent with the debtor's privacy policy unless the court first orders the appointment of a *consumer privacy ombudsman* and subsequently holds a hearing, after notice, on the proposed sale. If the court orders the appointment of a consumer privacy ombudsman, then the United States trustee must appoint *one disinterested person,* other than the United States trustee, to serve as ombudsman *no later than 7 days* before the start of the sale hearing.

2. **Patient Care Ombudsmen**

   If a health care business files for relief under Chapters 7, 9 or 11, then the bankruptcy court must order the appointment, within *30 days* of the start of the case, of a *patient care ombudsman,* unless the court finds that appointment is not necessary for the protection of patients in a specific case. The job of the patient care ombudsman is to *monitor the quality of patient care* and to *represent* the health care business *patients' interests.*

E. COMPENSATION OF OFFICERS

Officers of the estate, including a trustee, an examiner, a Chapter 12 or 13 individual debtor's attorney, a consumer privacy ombudsman, a patient care ombudsman, and any professional person properly employed by a trustee, a debtor in possession, or a creditors' committee may be awarded by the court a ***reasonable fee*** for actual and necessary services, as well as ***reimbursement*** for ***actual and necessary expenses.***

1. Debtor's Attorney

The right of the debtor's attorney to compensation from estate funds varies depending on the chapter of the Code under which the debtor files for relief.

a. Chapter 12 or 13

The Bankruptcy Code expressly provides that the court may award reasonable compensation to the attorney of an individual Chapter 12 or Chapter 13 debtor, based on the ***benefit and necessity of the services*** to the debtor and the criteria outlined below.

b. Chapter 7

The Supreme Court has held that the ***Code does not authorize payment of compensation*** to the Chapter 7 debtor's lawyer ***from the estate,*** unless the lawyer is hired by the trustee and approved by the bankruptcy court. Because the debtor hires the attorney to file her Chapter 7 case, the attorney representing a Chapter 7 debtor must obtain her fee upfront and not rely on compensation from estate funds.

c. Chapter 11

A Chapter 11 debtor may hire an attorney and so long as the bankruptcy court approves the employment, the attorney is entitled to compensation according to the standards set forth in § 330. If the court orders appointment of a Chapter 11 trustee, the debtor's attorney must look to the debtor, not the estate, for compensation for services rendered.

2. Fee Applications

Fee applications must comply with Bankruptcy Rule 2016(a), the procedural guidelines issued by the Executive Office for United States Trustees, and any applicable local rules. The criteria for awarding reasonable compensation include: (i) ***time*** spent; (ii) ***rates*** charged; (iii) ***need*** for the services and ***benefit*** to the administration of the case; (iv) the ***reasonableness of the time*** spent considering the complexity and importance of the work; (v) whether the professional person is ***board certified*** or otherwise has shown ***skill and experience*** in the field of bankruptcy; and (vi) ***fees*** charged by ***comparably skilled attorneys*** in non-bankruptcy cases.

3. Limitations on Professionals' Compensation

a. Modification by Court

The compensation ultimately allowed by the court may vary from the agreed-upon terms if those terms prove to be improvident in light of developments that could not have been anticipated.

b. Denial of Compensation

With certain limited exceptions, if, at any time during employment, a professional person is ***not disinterested*** or ***has an interest adverse to the*** *estate* regarding the subject matter of her employment, the court may deny her compensation for services and reimbursement of expenses.

c. Bifurcation of Trustee's Compensation

If a trustee also serves as an attorney or an accountant for the estate, her fee for professional employment may not include compensation for the performance of her duties as trustee. Compensation for services as trustee must be accounted for separately.

4. Interim Compensation

A trustee, examiner, debtor's attorney, or other professional person may apply for interim compensation or reimbursement of expenses *once every 120 days,* or more frequently, if the court allows, instead of waiting until the conclusion of the bankruptcy case to be paid. Any award of interim compensation will cause a reduction, by that amount, in an award of compensation made under § 330. Interim compensation is generally not an issue in Chapter 12 or 13 cases, because bankruptcy courts have standing orders for such cases that provide an allowed standard fee awarded without application or a hearing, and paid as an administrative claim through the plan.

5. Debtor's Transactions with Attorneys

Even if the debtor's attorney does not apply to the court for compensation, she still must file a statement of any fees paid or any fee agreement made within one year before bankruptcy for legal services related to the case. The statement also must indicate the source of payment. If the court determines that the compensation is unreasonable, it may cancel the fee agreement or order that any excessive portion be returned to the estate or to the entity that made the payment.

6. Sharing of Fees Prohibited

A trustee, examiner, attorney, accountant, or other professional person employed in a bankruptcy case is prohibited from sharing any compensation or reimbursement with another person. There are *two exceptions.* First, compensation or reimbursement may be shared with another member, partner, or associate of the same professional firm. Second, an attorney representing a creditor who files an involuntary petition is permitted to share her fee with any other attorney who contributes to her services or expenses.

F. UNITED STATES TRUSTEE

For each of the 21 regions throughout the nation, the Attorney General appoints one United States trustee for a five-year term. The judicial districts for Alabama and North Carolina are served by bankruptcy administrators appointed by the United States Courts of Appeals for the Fourth and Eleventh Circuits.

1. Administrative Duties

Under supervision of the Attorney General, the United States trustee functions as an administrator of the bankruptcy system in his region and, as such, has various duties, including (i) establishing a *panel of private trustees for Chapter 7* cases; (ii) appointing *interim trustees in Chapter 7* cases; (iii) appointing a trustee or an examiner, if the court orders, in Chapter 11 cases; (iv) appointing a *standing trustee in Chapter 12 and 13* cases; (v) convening and presiding at *§ 341 meetings;* (vi) supervising the *administration of bankruptcy cases* and trustees; (vii) monitoring *applications for employment* of professional persons; and (viii) *reviewing fee applications* of trustees, examiners, attorneys, and other professional persons.

2. Standing

The Code grants a United States trustee standing to appear and be heard as to any issue in a bankruptcy case. However, he cannot file a plan in a Chapter 11 case.

V. THE BANKRUPTCY ESTATE

A. THE BANKRUPTCY ESTATE

The creation of a bankruptcy estate occurs automatically upon the filing of a petition commencing a voluntary, joint, or involuntary bankruptcy case. The estate includes all of the debtor's *legal and equitable interests* in property, real or personal, tangible or intangible, *at the time the petition is filed.* The Code's definition of property of the estate is expansive and includes insurance policies, income tax refunds based on pre-petition earnings, stock options, liquor licenses, patents and copyrights, and business social media accounts. Estate property also includes (i) community property; (ii) interests in property that the trustee recovers or preserves for the benefit of the estate; (iii) certain property that the debtor acquires or becomes entitled to within *six months* after the date of bankruptcy, e.g., by inheritance, life insurance, or property settlement with debtor's spouse; (iv) proceeds, rents, profits, product, or offspring of estate property; and (v) property acquired by the estate after bankruptcy. An *individual Chapter 7 debtor's post-petition earnings are not* included in property of the estate.

1. Ipso Facto or "Bankruptcy" Clauses

Property of the debtor that becomes part of the bankruptcy estate is not affected by a clause in a contract, deed, or nonbankruptcy law that places restrictions or conditions on the debtor's transfer of the property. Likewise, clauses that purport to cause a forfeiture, termination, or modification of the debtor's interest in the property due to (i) the debtor's insolvency, (ii) the debtor's financial condition, (iii) the filing of a bankruptcy case concerning the debtor, or (iv) the appointment of a bankruptcy trustee or a nonbankruptcy custodian or the seizure of property by such persons will not prevent the property from being included in the bankruptcy estate. *Exception:* Debtor's beneficial interest in a traditional spendthrift trust is excluded from the estate if the spendthrift restriction is enforceable under applicable nonbankruptcy law.

2. Property Excluded from Estate

In addition to the post-petition earnings of an individual Chapter 7 debtor and spendthrift trusts enforceable under applicable nonbankruptcy law, the following items are *not included* in property of the estate: (i) a power that may be exercised by the debtor *solely for the benefit of another entity;* (ii) a debtor's interest *as a lessee* of an *expired lease* of nonresidential real property; (iii) certain property of *educational institutions;* (iv) certain interests transferred under a *farmout agreement;* (v) certain *production payments from gas and oil producers;* (vi) certain funds in an *education IRA;* (vii) funds used to buy tuition credits or certificates or contributions to an account that qualifies as a *State tuition program* pursuant to the Internal Revenue Code; (viii) funds withheld by an employer from employee wages or received by an employer from employees for payment as *contributions* to *certain pension and benefit plans;* (ix) *personal property* that the debtor has *pledged or sold* as collateral for a loan or advance from a *licensed pawnbroker;* (x) certain proceeds of money orders; and (xi) certain funds placed into a *qualified ABLE account.*

3. Distinguish Exemptions

An individual debtor is entitled to exempt certain items of estate property. Do not confuse *exclusions* from estate property with *exemptions*. If property is excluded from the estate, it means that the property never comes into the bankruptcy estate. Therefore, there is no need to exempt it.

B. TURNOVER OF PROPERTY TO TRUSTEE

1. Turnover by Entity Other than Custodian

Property that may be used, sold, or leased by the trustee under Bankruptcy Code § 363 or property that may be exempted by the debtor under § 522 must be delivered to the trustee and accounted for *by any entity who is in possession or control* of such property and who is not a custodian. Because an "entity" is defined more broadly than a "person," even a governmental unit or a trust, business or nonbusiness, is subject to the turnover provisions.

2. Turnover of Property Repossessed Before Bankruptcy

A secured creditor who has repossessed collateral before the filing of a Chapter 11 petition but who has not yet sold the collateral to a bona fide purchaser must turn over the collateral to the trustee or the debtor in possession. However, the secured creditor is entitled to adequate protection of its interest.

a. Automatic Stay

There is a split of authority as to whether a creditor that does not turn over property of the estate, but merely continues to hold it, violates the automatic stay provision found in § 362(a)(3), which stays not only "an act to obtain possession of property of the estate," but also an act *"to exercise control over property of the estate."*

3. Payment of Indebtedness to Estate

An entity that owes a matured debt or a debt payable on demand or order that constitutes estate property must pay the trustee the amount of the debt in excess of any setoff permitted the entity under § 553.

4. Exceptions to Turnover

Turnover is not required for property of *inconsequential value or benefit to the estate.* It also is not required if an entity, such as a bank, *in good faith* and without either actual notice or knowledge of the bankruptcy petition transfers property of the estate or pays a debt owing to the debtor, e.g., honors the debtor's check, to an entity other than the trustee. *Note:* The Code does *not protect the payee or transferee,* who are subject to the trustee's avoiding power.

5. Turnover of Property by Custodian

A custodian who has knowledge of the filing of a bankruptcy petition is prohibited from disbursing or administering, other than for preservation, any property of the debtor; any proceeds, rents, profits, products, or offspring of the debtor's property; or any property of the estate in her possession, custody, or control. The custodian must turn over the property to the trustee and file an accounting.

a. "Custodian" Defined

A custodian is: (i) a *receiver or trustee* of the debtor's property appointed in a *nonbankruptcy action;* (ii) an *assignee for the benefit of the debtor's creditors;* or (iii) a *trustee or receiver* designated to take control of the debtor's property to *enforce a lien or to administer the property* for the benefit of creditors.

b. Exceptions to Custodian's Turnover

A custodian's duty to deliver the debtor's property to the trustee *may be excused* in the interests of creditors and, if the debtor is solvent, the interests of equity security holders are better served by allowing a custodian to remain in possession, custody, or control of the property. Unless necessary to prevent fraud or injustice, the bankruptcy court *must excuse* the requirement that a custodian turn over property if the custodian is an assignee for the benefit of creditors who was appointed or took possession of the debtor's property *more than 120 days* before the commencement of the bankruptcy case.

c. Compensation or Surcharge

A bankruptcy court may award a custodian reasonable compensation for her services and actual expenses. A custodian may be liable for wrongful or excessive disbursements.

6. Turnover of Books and Records

The bankruptcy court may order, subject to any valid privilege, an attorney, accountant, or other person to turn over to the trustee any books, records, or other documents concerning the debtor's finances or property. In the case of a *corporate debtor,* the trustee has the power to waive the corporation's attorney-client privilege concerning *pre-bankruptcy communications* made by former officers and directors to the debtor's attorney. The attorney may then be required to testify.

a. No Accountant-Client Privilege

Where access to information relating to the debtor's financial condition is needed for complete and accurate disclosure, an accountant or an accounting firm will be required to turn over documents and work papers in its possession. There is no accountant-client privilege under federal law.

C. CREDITOR'S RIGHT OF SETOFF

A creditor entitled to a right of setoff under state law may set off a debt he owes to the debtor against a claim he holds against the debtor, if *both the debt and the claim are mutual and arose prior to the filing of the bankruptcy case.* The Bankruptcy Code does not create a right of setoff; it merely preserves whatever right otherwise exists.

1. Automatic Stay

Once a bankruptcy petition has been filed, the automatic stay enjoins the post-petition setoff of a pre-petition debt owed to the debtor against a creditor's claim. Therefore, a creditor must obtain *relief from the stay* before a setoff may be exercised. A temporary administrative freeze, pending a judicial determination of the bank's motion to lift the stay, *does not constitute a setoff.*

2. Secured Status of Claim Subject to Setoff

A claim that may be set off *is deemed secured* to the extent of the amount subject to setoff. Therefore, a creditor holding such a claim is entitled to *adequate protection* unless the court lifts the automatic stay and permits the creditor to exercise her right of setoff.

3. **Exceptions to Right of Setoff**

There are several exceptions a creditor's right of setoff. First, there is no right of setoff to the extent that the court has *disallowed the creditor's claim* against the debtor. Second, there is no right of setoff if an entity other than the debtor *transferred the claim to the creditor* after the filing of the bankruptcy petition or *within 90 days* prior to the bankruptcy petition at a time when the *debtor was insolvent.* Finally, there is no right of setoff if the *creditor incurred the debt* owed to the debtor *within 90 days* prior to the bankruptcy petition, at a time when the *debtor was insolvent,* for the *purpose of using that debt as a setoff.*

4. **Creditor's Improved Position Due to Pre-Bankruptcy Setoff**

With certain exceptions, the trustee may avoid and recover for the estate a setoff made by a creditor *within 90 days* prior to the filing of the petition *to the extent* that the creditor (usually a bank) has *improved its position.* The trustee's power to avoid and recover the setoff applies even if the debtor is solvent.

5. **Distinguish Recoupment**

Setoff should be distinguished from the equitable doctrine of recoupment. The *setoff* of mutual debts between two parties involves independent obligations that usually are derived from *separate transactions.* Recoupment, on the other hand, is used by a creditor to reduce its liability to the debtor because of a right that the creditor has arising out of the *same transaction* or occurrence. Recoupment is basically a defense, e.g., overpayment, to the debtor's claim and not a mutual obligation. Neither the automatic stay nor § 553's limitations on setoffs apply to recoupments.

D. **POST-PETITION EFFECT OF SECURITY INTEREST**

An after-acquired property clause in a pre-petition security agreement is *not* effective to create a security interest in property acquired by the debtor or the estate *after* the filing of the bankruptcy petition. *Note:* This provision applies only to *consensual liens* and, thus, does not apply to federal tax liens, which are statutory.

1. **Exception for Certain Post-Petition Proceeds**

If the security interest created by a pre-petition security agreement includes collateral that the debtor *acquired prior to bankruptcy* and also the proceeds, profits, products, or offspring of such collateral, then the security interest is deemed valid and operative as to any *traceable post-petition proceeds, products, offspring, or profits* of the collateral acquired pre-petition.

2. **Exception for Certain Post-Petition Rents and Room Revenues**

If a pre-petition security agreement extends to amounts paid as rent or for charges, fees, accounts, or other payments for hotel, motel, or similar lodgings, then the security interest extends to these post-petition rents, charges, fees, accounts, or other payments.

E. **ABANDONMENT OF ESTATE PROPERTY**

The trustee may abandon property that is *burdensome or of inconsequential value* to the estate. Generally, when abandonment occurs, the property is considered to be abandoned to the debtor; abandonment does not affect the continuing validity of a secured creditor's lien on the property. While abandonment removes the property from the estate, it does not result in a lift of the automatic stay. Any property that the debtor has listed in her schedules that has not been administered before the case is closed is deemed to be abandoned to the debtor.

1. Exception: Violation of Environmental Laws

The trustee is prohibited from abandoning estate property that is in violation of state or federal environmental laws that are "reasonably designed to protect the public health or safety from identified hazards."

VI. THE TRUSTEE'S AVOIDING POWERS

A. TRUSTEE'S AVOIDANCE OF STATUTORY LIENS

The trustee may avoid certain statutory nonconsensual liens.

1. Liens That Arise Automatically Based on the Debtor's Financial Condition

The trustee may avoid a *statutory lien* triggered by events indicating the poor financial condition of the debtor, such as the debtor's *insolvency,* the filing of a *bankruptcy petition,* the appointment of a *custodian,* or the filing of a *nonbankruptcy insolvency proceeding.*

2. Liens Not Perfected Against Bona Fide Purchaser

The trustee also may avoid a statutory lien that is *not perfected or enforceable against a hypothetical bona fide purchaser* at the time that the bankruptcy petition is filed, *unless* the purchaser is one described under § 6323 of the Internal Revenue Code or any similar provision in State or local law. The trustee's avoiding power is *subject to any retroactive perfection* permitted under state law or other nonbankruptcy law.

3. Liens for Rent

Statutory liens for rent or for distress of rent also are avoidable by the trustee.

B. TRUSTEE'S AVOIDING POWERS AS HYPOTHETICAL CREDITOR OR PURCHASER, AND AS SUCCESSOR TO CERTAIN ACTUAL CREDITORS

1. Strong Arm Provision

The Bankruptcy Code grants to the trustee, at the *commencement* of the bankruptcy case, the hypothetical status and the rights and powers of (i) a *judicial lien creditor,* (ii) a creditor with an *unsatisfied execution,* and (iii) a *bona fide purchaser of real property.* Consequently, the trustee is able to avoid any transfer of the debtor's property that any of these entities—*regardless of whether one really exists*—could avoid, "without regard to any knowledge of the trustee or of any creditor." The trustee's avoiding power is *subject to any retroactive perfection* permitted under state law or other nonbankruptcy law.

2. Trustee's Avoiding Power Based on Actual Unsecured Creditors

If there exists at the time of bankruptcy an *actual creditor* who possesses an allowable unsecured claim and who has the right, under applicable nonbankruptcy law, to avoid a transfer of the debtor's property, then the trustee is entitled to avoid the whole transfer *for the benefit of the estate,* even if its value exceeds the amount of the creditor's claim. The trustee's avoiding power does not cover the transfer of a charitable contribution not deemed to be a fraudulent transfer under Code § 548(a)(2).

C. TRUSTEE'S POWER TO AVOID PREFERENCES

The bankruptcy trustee has the power to avoid pre-petition preferential transfers, thereby enlarging the estate for the benefit of creditors. This avoiding power is designed to accomplish an equitable distribution of estate property in the *order established by the Bankruptcy Code* and to prevent the debtor from choosing which creditors to repay.

1. Elements of Preference

The trustee must prove that there was (i) a transfer of the debtor's interest in property, (ii) made to or for the benefit of a creditor, (iii) concerning an antecedent debt, (iv) at a time when the debtor is insolvent, (v) within 90 days prior to filing of the bankruptcy petition or one year if the creditor was an insider, and (vi) that results in the creditor receiving a larger share than the creditor would have received if the estate had been liquidated under Chapter 7 and the transfer had not been made. If any one of the above elements is absent, the trustee may not set aside the transaction as a voidable preference.

a. Presumption of Insolvency

The Bankruptcy Code provides that there is a *rebuttable presumption* that the debtor is insolvent during the *90 days* immediately prior to the date on which the petition commencing the case was filed. Even when the preference period is one year before bankruptcy because the creditor was an insider, the *period during which the presumption of insolvency applies remains the same*—90 days.

b. Secured Creditors

Payments made to a creditor whose allowed claim is *completely secured* do not constitute a preference because such transfers do not result in a greater distribution than a Chapter 7 liquidation would provide.

2. Exceptions to Preference Rule

The trustee may not avoid any of the following transfers:

a. a transfer that is a *substantially contemporaneous exchange* for new value;

b. a transfer for a debt that was *incurred in the ordinary course of business* or financial affairs of the debtor and the transferee, and that was *made either* (i) in the *ordinary course of business* or financial affairs of the debtor and the transferee or (ii) according to *ordinary business terms*;

c. a *purchase-money security interest* securing new value and perfected no later than 30 days after the debtor takes possession of the collateral;

d. an *extension of new unsecured value* by the creditor subsequent to the transfer;

e. a transfer that creates a perfected security interest in the *debtor's inventory, receivables, or proceeds of inventory or receivables* to the extent that the creditor's position has improved, to the prejudice of the estate, during the relevant statutory time period;

f. *statutory liens* that cannot be avoided under § 545;

g. bona fide payment of a *domestic support obligation*;

h. a transfer of property worth less than *$600* by an *individual debtor* with *primarily consumer debts*;

i. a transfer of property worth less than *$6,825* by a debtor whose *debts are not primarily consumer debts*; or

j. a transfer made as part of an *alternative repayment schedule* between the debtor and an approved nonprofit budget and counseling agency.

3. Burden of Proof

The trustee must prove the elements of a voidable preference, but the creditor bears the burden regarding asserted exceptions.

D. Trustee's Power to Avoid Fraudulent Transfers

The trustee has the power to avoid a fraudulent transfer of the debtor's interest in property or the fraudulent incurring of an obligation if the transfer was made or the obligation was incurred by the debtor, voluntarily or involuntarily, *within two years* prior to bankruptcy. The trustee also may avoid certain transfers made by the debtor to a *self-settled trust within ten years* prior to bankruptcy.

1. "Fraudulent" Transfer

a. Actual Intent

A trustee may avoid a transfer if there is *actual intent* to hinder, delay, or defraud a creditor. The law has developed certain "badges of fraud" from which *actual intent may be inferred.*

b. Constructive Fraud

The trustee can prove *constructive fraud* by demonstrating that the debtor did not receive something of *reasonably equivalent value* in exchange for the transfer or obligation *and* the debtor (i) was *insolvent* or rendered insolvent by the transfer or obligation, (ii) was *undercapitalized* after the transfer or incurring the obligation, (iii) intended to incur debts *beyond her ability to repay, or* (iv) made the transfer or incurred the obligation to or for the *benefit of an insider under an employment contract* and not in the ordinary course of business. Certain charitable contributions are not treated as transfers for less than reasonably equivalent value.

2. Good Faith Transferee

A *good faith transferee* or obligee for value is entitled to retain, or to receive a lien on, any property conveyed to her or to enforce an obligation incurred, *to the extent of any value given* by the transferee or obligee to the debtor, *unless* the transfer also is subject to the trustee's avoiding power under §§ 544, 545, or 547.

E. POST-PETITION TRANSACTIONS

The trustee may avoid a transfer of estate property occurring *after the filing* of the bankruptcy petition, unless the transfer falls within one of the exceptions described below or is authorized under the Bankruptcy Code or approved by the court.

1. Transferor Without Notice or Knowledge

A transferor that has *neither actual notice nor knowledge* of the bankruptcy case is protected from liability concerning a good faith post-petition transfer, but the transferee may be subject to the trustee's avoiding power.

2. Exceptions to Trustee's Avoidance

a. Gap Transferee in Involuntary Case

The trustee may avoid a transfer made during the gap period *except to the extent that the transferee gave value, including services, after the start* of the *bankruptcy case* in exchange for the transfer. This exception does not apply to a transaction that involves the satisfaction or securing of a pre-petition debt.

b. Bona Fide Purchaser of Real Property

The trustee cannot avoid a post-petition transfer of real property to a ***good faith purchaser*** who does not know of the bankruptcy case and has paid ***present fair equivalent value*** if notice of the bankruptcy case has not been filed, prior to perfection of the transfer, in the office where real property transactions are recorded for the county in which the land is located.

F. LIMITATIONS ON TRUSTEE'S AVOIDING POWERS

1. Statute of Limitations

Most of the trustee's avoiding powers are subject to a statute of limitations requiring that the trustee ***file an action*** to avoid a transfer before the ***earlier*** of the following time periods:

- the ***later*** of ***two years*** after the entry of the order for relief or ***one year*** after the appointment or election of the first trustee, if the appointment or election occurs before the expiration of the two-year period; or

- ***the time of the closing or dismissal*** of the case.

a. Transfers Affected

This limitations period applies to a trustee's action to avoid: (i) under the strong arm clause; (ii) as successor to certain actual creditors; (iii) a statutory lien; (iv) a preference; (v) a fraudulent transfer; or (vi) a setoff.

b. Distinguish Statute of Limitations for Avoidance of Post-Petition Transactions

To avoid a post-petition transfer, the trustee must file an action before the ***earlier*** of:

- two years after the ***transfer*** was made; or

- the time of the ***closing or dismissal*** of the case.

c. Distinguish Statute of Limitations for Recovery of Avoided Transfer

To the extent that a transfer is avoided, an action to ***recover*** transferred property or, if the court orders, the value of such property must be commenced ***no later than the earlier of:***

- ***one year after avoidance*** of the transfer; or

- the time that the case is ***closed or dismissed.***

2. Retroactive Perfection and Continuation Statements

The trustee's avoiding powers under Code § 544(a) (strong arm clause), § 544(b) (successor to certain actual creditors), § 545 (certain statutory liens), and § 549 (post-petition transactions) are subject to any applicable nonbankruptcy law that permits ***retroactive perfection*** of a security interest, or ***filing of a continuation statement,*** e.g., under the Uniform Commercial Code. The post-petition retroactive perfection and filing of a continuation statement ***are excepted*** from the operation of the ***automatic stay.***

3. Seller's Reclamation of Goods

The trustee's power to avoid (i) a transfer under the strong arm clause, (ii) a statutory lien, (iii) a preference, or (iv) a post-petition transfer is subject to the right of a seller, under certain circumstances, to ***reclaim*** goods that it sold to the debtor.

a. Elements Required for Reclamation

The seller has the right to reclaim **goods** from an **insolvent buyer** if the seller satisfies the following requirements: (i) seller sold the goods in the **ordinary course** of its business; (ii) debtor **received the goods while insolvent;** (iii) debtor received the goods within **45 days of filing** its bankruptcy case; and (iv) seller made a **written reclamation demand** no later than **45 days** after the debtor received the goods *or* **20 days** after the start of the bankruptcy case, if the 45-day period expires after the commencement of the bankruptcy case. The seller's right to reclaim goods is subject to the **prior rights of a creditor with a security interest** in the goods or the proceeds of those goods.

4. Grain Farmers and United States Fishermen

The trustee's power to avoid (i) a transfer under the strong arm clause, (ii) a statutory lien, (iii) a preference, or (iv) a post-petition transfer is subject to any statutory or common law right of a grain farmer or a United States fisherman to **reclaim grain or fish** sold to a grain storage facility or a fish processing facility that is owned or operated by the debtor, if the **debtor received such goods while insolvent.** The grain farmer or U.S. fisherman must make a **written demand for reclamation** no later than **10 days** after the debtor received the grain or fish. If the 10-day period expires after the start of the bankruptcy case, then the demand may be made up to **20 days** after the debtor received the goods.

5. Return of Goods

A Chapter 11 debtor, with the creditor's consent and subject to the prior rights of a creditor with a security interest in the goods or the proceeds of such goods, may return goods shipped by the creditor before bankruptcy, and the creditor may offset the purchase price against any pre-petition claim.

6. Warehouseman's Lien

The trustee may not avoid a warehouseman's lien for **storage, transportation, or costs incidental to the storage and handling of goods,** notwithstanding the Code's provisions on avoidance of statutory liens. Courts are to apply the prohibition against avoidance in a manner consistent with U.C.C. § 7–209 or similar state laws.

G. TRANSFEREE'S LIABILITY TO ESTATE FOR AVOIDED TRANSFER

Any transfer that has been avoided or any lien that is void under Bankruptcy Code § 506(d) is automatically preserved for the estate's benefit. By avoiding a transfer, the trustee is entitled to recover **either the property transferred** or, if ordered by the court, **its value.**

1. From Whom Trustee May Recover

The trustee may seek recovery from (i) the initial transferee, (ii) the entity whom the initial transfer was designed to benefit, or (iii) any future transferee after the first transfer. A trustee who has avoided a transfer is permitted only one satisfaction in the case.

a. Exception for Good Faith Future Transferees

The trustee may not recover from a **future transferee** who (i) did not know that the transfer was voidable, (ii) took the transfer in **good faith,** and (iii) **gave value** in exchange. A future transferee who gives value, takes in good faith, and lacked knowledge of the voidability of the transfer **shelters** all subsequent **good faith transferees.**

2. **Good Faith Transferee's Lien**

If the trustee recovers from a good faith transferee, the transferee receives a *lien on the property recovered,* for the purpose of securing *the lesser* of (i) the cost of any *improvements* transferee made after the transfer, less any profits from the property, *or* (ii) the amount by which such improvements enhanced the property's value.

3. **Statute of Limitations**

To recover property or its value, the trustee must institute an action before the *earlier of* (i) *one year* after the corresponding transfer was avoided *or* (ii) the *time of the closing or dismissal* of the case.

VII. CLAIMS OF CREDITORS

A. FILING PROOFS OF CLAIMS

1. **Claim**

Congress intended to give the word "claim" an expansive definition in the bankruptcy context. The Code defines a claim as a "*right to payment,* whether or not such right is reduced to judgment, liquidated, unliquidated, fixed, contingent, matured, unmatured, disputed, undisputed, legal, equitable, secured, or unsecured." The right to an equitable remedy for breach of performance is considered a claim if the breach gives rise to a *right to payment.*

2. **Claimants**

a. **Who Must File**

Generally, for the claim or interest to be allowed, a *creditor,* whether secured or unsecured, must file a proof of claim and an *equity security holder must* file a proof of interest.

b. **Who May File**

A secured creditor, an unsecured creditor, or an indenture trustee may file a *proof of claim.* An equity security holder may file a *proof of interest.* If a creditor fails to file a proof of claim, a co-debtor, surety, or guarantor, or the debtor or trustee may file a proof of such claim.

3. **Time to File**

The time within which to file a proof of claim or interest depends on the chapter of the Bankruptcy Code governing the particular case.

a. **Chapters 7, 12, and 13**

In a *voluntary case begun in Chapter 7, 12, or 13,* a proof of claim ordinarily must be filed no later than *70 days* after the order for relief. In an *involuntary Chapter 7 case,* a proof of claim is timely filed if it is filed no later than *90 days* after the order for relief.

b. **Converted Cases**

In a case *converted to Chapter 12 or 13,* a proof of claim is timely filed if it is filed no later than *70 days* after the order of conversion. In a case *converted from Chapter 11, 12, or 13 to Chapter 7,* all claims *actually* filed before conversion of the case are considered automatically filed in the Chapter 7 case. Thus, a second filing is not required. However, a claim must be filed if it was only deemed filed in a case converted from Chapter 11.

c. Chapter 11

In a Chapter 11 case, the court fixes and sends notice of a *bar date,* which operates as a deadline for the filing of proofs of claims or interests. Any claim or interest listed in the debtor's schedules is *deemed filed automatically* for the scheduled amount, *unless* the claim or interest is *scheduled as contingent, unliquidated, or disputed.*

d. Exceptions

The following are *exceptions to the general time periods* for filing proofs of claims.

(i) Governmental Unit Claims

A claim by a *governmental unit* in a Chapter 7, 12 or 13 case is timely if it is filed *no later than 180 days* after the order for relief. A claim by a governmental unit resulting from a *tax return filed under § 1308* is timely if it is filed *no later than 180 days* after the order for relief or *60 days* after the filing of the tax return.

(ii) Infants or Incompetent Persons

In a Chapter 7, 11, 12 or 13 case, the court may extend the time period for filing a proof of claim by an *infant, incompetent person, or the representative* of the infant or incompetent person if extending the time period is in *the interest of justice* and will not *unduly delay administration of the case.*

(iii) Entry of Judgment

In a Chapter 7, 11, 12 or 13 case, an *unsecured claim* arising in favor of an entity or that becomes allowable as a result of the entry of a judgment may be filed *within 30 days after the judgment becomes final if* the judgment is for recovery of money or property from the entity, or denial or avoidance of the entity's interest in property.

(iv) Rejection of Executory Contract or Unexpired Lease

In a Chapter 7, 11, 12 or 13 case, the bankruptcy court may set a time for filing of claims arising from the rejection of executory contracts or unexpired leases.

(v) Chapter 7 "No Asset" Cases

If the Chapter 7 trustee notifies the court that unsecured creditors will receive a dividend in the Chapter 7 case, after creditors have received a notice indicating that no dividend would be paid, the bankruptcy clerk must give *at least 90 days' notice* by mail to creditors of the fact that a dividend will be paid and of the date by which creditors must file a proof of claim.

(vi) Creditor Motion to Extend Time Period

In a Chapter 7, 11, 12, or 13 case, the bankruptcy court, upon motion of a creditor, may extend the time period for filing a proof of claim if (1) the court finds that notice was insufficient to give the creditor time to file a proof of claim, because the *debtor failed to timely file the list of creditors' names and addresses or* (2) notice was mailed to a *foreign address* and under *the circumstances was insufficient to give the creditor a reasonable time* to file a proof of claim. The court may extend the time period *no more than 60 days* from the order granting the creditor's motion.

(vii) Secured Creditor on Debtor's Principal Residence

In a Chapter 7, 12 or 13 case, a proof of claim filed by the holder of a claim secured by the *debtor's principal residence* is timely filed if (1) the proof of claim and the documents required by the bankruptcy rules are filed *no later than 70 days* after the order for relief *and* (2) the writing supporting creditor's interest in the property securing the claim, e.g., a copy of the mortgage, and evidence that the creditor's security interest is perfected are filed as supplements to the claim *no later than 120 days* after the order for relief.

4. Claims Deemed Pre-Petition

The following post-petition claims are treated as pre-petition claims for the *purpose of filing*:

a. *a co-debtor's or surety's claim for reimbursement or contribution* that becomes fixed after the bankruptcy petition has been filed;

b. *a claim arising in the ordinary course of the debtor's business* or financial affairs after the filing of an *involuntary petition* but before the earlier of the order for relief or the appointment of a trustee;

c. *a claim arising from the rejection of an executory contract or an unexpired lease* that the trustee or the debtor in possession has not assumed;

d. *a claim arising from the recovery of property* by the trustee or the debtor;

e. *a post-petition tax claim entitled to eighth priority;* and

f. *a claim,* other than one for administrative expenses, *arising after the order for relief* in a Chapter 11, 12, or 13 case, but *before the case is converted to another chapter.*

5. Secured Claims: Chapters 7, 12, and 13

A secured creditor must file a proof of claim "in order to have an allowed claim." *Note:* A secured creditor's lien is not void simply because the creditor fails to file a proof of claim.

6. Secured Claims: Chapter 11

In a Chapter 11 case, a secured creditor need not file a proof of claim if the debtor correctly schedules the creditor's debt and does not list the debt as contingent, unliquidated, or disputed.

7. Fuel Use Tax

Post-BAPCPA, the Code permits the filing of a single fuel use tax claim to cover fuel use taxes that the debtor owes to various state tax authorities, if the requirements of 49 U.S.C. § 31701 are met.

B. ALLOWANCE OF CLAIMS

Unless a party in interest objects, a claim or interest that has been filed will be allowed by the court and will serve as the basis for distribution. Ordinarily, if an objection to a claim is raised, the court, after notice and a hearing, determines the amount of the claim *as of the date of the filing of the bankruptcy petition,* and allows the claim unless it falls within one of the following recognized exceptions.

1. **Exceptions to Allowance**

   The following claims are not allowable:

   a. a claim that is *unenforceable* because the *debtor has a valid defense;*

   b. a claim for *post-petition interest* on an *unsecured claim;*

   c. a claim for *unsecured property tax* in excess of *debtor's equity* in the property;

   d. an unreasonable claim for services of an *insider* or *debtor's attorney;*

   e. a claim for a *nondischargeable domestic support obligation* that is *unmatured* as of the bankruptcy filing date;

   f. a *lessor's excessive claim* for damages for a terminated lease of real property;

   g. an *excessive claim* for an *employee's damages* for termination of an employment contract;

   h. a claim that results from a reduction, due to late payment, in the amount of an otherwise applicable *federal employment tax credit* in connection with *state unemployment insurance taxes;*

   i. a claim by a *possessor of estate property or transferee of an avoidable transfer,* unless the property is returned or its value paid; and

   j. with certain exceptions, a *tardily filed claim.*

2. **Estimation of Claims**

   If a claim is *contingent or unliquidated,* and the fixing or liquidation of it would cause undue delay in the administration of the bankruptcy case, the court must estimate the claim. Similarly, if a *right to an equitable remedy* for breach of performance gives rise to a right to payment, the court must estimate the claim for the purpose of allowance.

3. **Claim for Reimbursement or Contribution**

   The claim of a co-debtor, surety, or guarantor for reimbursement or contribution *will be disallowed* if (i) the claim is *contingent,* i.e., if the surety has not paid the principal creditor, at the time of allowance or disallowance; (ii) the *principal creditor's claim* is disallowed; *or* (iii) the *surety elects subrogation* to the principal creditor's rights instead of reimbursement or contribution.

4. **Claims Deemed Pre-Petition**

   Claims considered pre-petition for the purpose of *allowance or disallowance* are the same as the claims treated as pre-petition for filing purposes.

5. **Reduction of Claim on Unsecured Consumer Debt**

   A debtor may move to *reduce by no more than 20%* the amount of a *claim for an unsecured consumer* debt if the following requirements are satisfied:

   a. the claim is for a *consumer debt* that is *completely unsecured;*

   b. the creditor filing the claim *unreasonably refused to negotiate an alternative repayment schedule* that an approved nonprofit and credit counseling agency proposed on the debtor's behalf;

   c. debtor made the offer *at least 60 days* prior to filing of the petition;

    d.   debtor's offer provided for payment of *at least 60% of the debt* over a period not to exceed the loan's repayment period, or a reasonable extension of that period; and

    e.   no portion of the debt under the alternative repayment schedule is *nondischargeable.*

The debtor must prove by *clear and convincing evidence* that (i) the creditor unreasonably refused to consider the debtor's proposal *and* (ii) the proposal was made before the expiration of the 60-day period referenced above.

C. SECURED CLAIMS

In bankruptcy, a secured claim is one that has been allowed and is either *secured by a lien* on property of the estate or is subject to *setoff.* The Bankruptcy Code treats a claim as secured *only to the extent of the value of the creditor's collateral* or up to the amount subject to setoff.

1. Undersecured Claims: Bifurcation

A claim is *totally secured* if the value of the collateral equals or is greater than the amount of the claim. With certain exceptions, if the amount of the creditor's claim exceeds the value of the collateral, the claim is undersecured and is divided into two separate claims: (i) a *secured claim* equal to the value of the collateral, and (ii) an *unsecured claim* equal to the amount by which the claim exceeds the value of the collateral.

2. Undersecured Claims and Bifurcation: Exceptions

a. Debtor's Principal Residence

In a case filed under Chapter 11 or 13, the plan may not modify the rights of a creditor holding a secured claim secured only by the debtor's principal residence.

b. Hanging Paragraph

In a Chapter 13 case, the debtor may not bifurcate the claim of a creditor holding a *purchase-money security interest* (i) in a *motor vehicle* purchased within *910 days of bankruptcy* and acquired for the *debtor's personal use or* (ii) in *any other thing of value,* if the debt was incurred within *one year of the bankruptcy filing.*

c. Section 1111(b) Election

In a Chapter 11 case, if a creditor elects treatment under § 1111(b), the creditor's claim is treated as a secured claim to the extent that the claim is allowed.

3. Valuation of Collateral

In determining the value of the collateral securing a creditor's claim, the court must take into account both the *purpose of the valuation* and the *intended disposition or use* of the collateral. In *individual Chapter 7 or 13* cases, the value of *personal property* is its *replacement value,* without deduction for the costs of sale or marketing; the valuation time is the *time of the bankruptcy filing.* If the individual Chapter 7 or 13 debtor acquired the collateral for *personal, family, or household purposes,* then *replacement value for personal property* is *retail value,* based on the *age and condition* of the personal property *at the time value is determined.*

4. Oversecured Claims

To the extent that the value of the collateral exceeds the amount of the creditor's claim that it secures, plus any surcharges, the creditor is entitled to the allowance of *post-petition interest,* regardless of whether the creditor's lien is consensual or nonconsensual. Also, any reasonable fees, *e.g.,* attorneys' fees, costs, or other charges *specified in the agreement* or a *state statute under which the claim arose* can be recovered to the extent that the claim is oversecured. Any post-petition interest, and any fees, costs, or charges that are allowed to the holder of an oversecured claim, usually *accrue* until the time of distribution in a Chapter 7 case, or until the effective date of a Chapter 11, 12, or 13 plan. The Code does not require present payments.

5. Surcharge Against Collateral

To the extent that a secured creditor *benefits directly* from the preservation or disposition of the collateral, the trustee or the debtor in possession may be *reimbursed from the collateral* for the necessary and reasonable costs of preserving or disposing of the collateral. This surcharge is *paid ahead of an award of post-petition interest or fees* to an oversecured creditor. In 2005, Congress added the payment of "all ad valorem property taxes with respect to the property" to the expenses that may be charged against a secured creditor's recovery from the collateral.

6. Liens Deemed Void

A valid lien survives bankruptcy even if the secured creditor does not file a proof of claim. In a Chapter 7 case, if the collateral is real property the debtor may not use § 506(d) to strip down the creditor's lien on the real property to the value of the collateral nor may the debtor strip off a junior mortgage if the debt owed on a senior mortgage exceeds the value of the real property.

A lien is *void,* however, to the extent that it secures a claim that is *not an allowed secured claim unless*

a. the claim is *disallowed only* as a *nondischargeable, unmatured domestic support obligation;*

b. the claim is for *reimbursement or contribution* and is *disallowed only under § 502(e);* or

c. the claim is not an allowed secured claim due *only to the failure of the creditor* to *file a proof of claim.*

7. Treatment of Secured Claims

Prior to final distribution to the unsecured creditors in a Chapter 7 case, a secured creditor usually receives cash equal to the total amount of her allowed secured claim or, in the alternative, a return of the property that secures that claim. In Chapters 11, 12, and 13, there are special provisions concerning the treatment of secured claims that must be satisfied for the court to confirm a plan.

8. Adequate Protection

A secured creditor has the right to receive adequate protection of her interest in the collateral, and the failure to provide it constitutes sufficient cause for granting the creditor relief from the automatic stay.

D. ADMINISTRATIVE EXPENSES

1. Priority

After the payment of secured claims from property constituting collateral, entities holding unsecured priority claims are paid. Claims for administrative expenses ordinarily are entitled to the second highest priority, after domestic support obligations, in the distribution of the assets of the estate.

2. Allowable Administrative Expenses

The following items are allowable as administrative expenses, after notice and a hearing:

a. the *actual and necessary post-petition costs of preserving the bankruptcy estate;*

b. obtaining unsecured credit in either the *ordinary or non-ordinary course of the debtor's business;*

c. *retiree benefit payments* that must be made prior to the effective date of a confirmed plan;

d. *wages or salaries* for employees operating the debtor's business in a reorganization case;

e. wages and benefits awarded in an *National Labor Relations Board* proceeding as *back pay* for any post-petition period of time for the debtor's *violation of federal or state law* if payment does not substantially increase the probability of *layoffs, termination,* or *nonpayment of domestic support obligations;*

f. *post-petition taxes* incurred by the estate and *fines or penalties* related to such taxes;

g. compensation and reimbursement to *officers of the estate;*

h. actual and necessary expenses of a creditor who files an *involuntary petition;*

i. actual and necessary expenses of a creditor who, with court approval, *recovers* for the benefit of the *estate property* that the *debtor has either concealed or transferred;*

j. actual and necessary expenses incurred by a creditor in a *criminal prosecution* related to the bankruptcy case or to the debtor's property or business;

k. actual and necessary expenses of a certain parties that makes a *substantial contribution* in a Chapter 11 or Chapter 9 case;

l. actual and necessary expenses, as well as compensation, for the services of a pre-petition custodian who has been superseded under § 543;

m. actual and necessary expenses of an official Chapter 11 creditors' or equity security holders' committee;

n. reasonable compensation for an indenture trustee who has made a *substantial contribution* in a Chapter 11 or Chapter 9 case;

o. witnesses' fees and mileage expenses;

p. monies due a landlord under a *nonresidential real property lease* that was *first assumed* under § 365 and then *later rejected;*

q. actual, necessary costs and expenses incurred in *closing a health care business;*

r. the value of *goods* sold in the *ordinary course of the debtor's business within 20 days* of the start of the debtor's bankruptcy case.

3. Exception: Gap Creditors' Claims

In an *involuntary* case, post-petition claims that arise the *gap period* are *not* treated as administrative expense claims, but rather are given *third priority* in the order of distribution.

4. Exempt Property

As a general rule, administrative expenses are *not payable* out of *property that the debtor exempts.* However, property exempted by the debtor is liable for administrative expenses representing the debtor's fractional share of the cost of avoiding a transfer of such property or the cost of its recovery by the trustee or the debtor.

5. Limitations on KERPS

In BAPCPA, Congress added language to the Code that limits a debtor's ability to claim administrative expense priority for *certain post-petition payments made to insiders.* The purpose of this new provision is to place restrictions on Key Employee Retention Plans ("KERPS"). The Code now provides that a payment made or obligation incurred for the *benefit of an insider* to induce the insider to remain with the debtor's business shall not be allowed or paid unless the court makes certain findings based on evidence in the record.

E. PRIORITY CLAIMS

1. Payment Hierarchy

Priority claims generally are the first *unsecured claims* to be paid in a bankruptcy case following distribution to secured creditors. There are ten tiers of priority claims, which are paid in the following order:

a. first priority is for *domestic support obligations,* but there is a payment hierarchy within the first statutory category;

b. second priority is for *administrative expenses,* including filing and other fees;

c. third priority is for *involuntary case gap claims;*

d. fourth priority is for wages, salaries, or commissions earned by an *individual* (or corporation with only one employee acting as an independent contractor) within *180 days* before either bankruptcy or "the cessation of the debtor's business," whichever is earlier, but limited to *$13,650;*

e. fifth priority is for contributions to an employee benefit plan for services rendered within *180 days* before either bankruptcy or "the cessation of the debtor's business," whichever is earlier, but subject to certain monetary limitations;

f. sixth priority is for allowed unsecured claims of *grain producers* or United States *fishermen* against a debtor who operates or owns a grain storage facility or against a debtor who operates a fish produce storage or processing facility, respectively;

g. seventh priority, also known as the "layaway" priority, is for allowed unsecured claims of individuals, limited to *$3,025,* arising from the pre-petition deposit of money with the debtor for the purchase, lease, or rental of property *or* the purchase of services that were not delivered or provided that were intended for the ***personal, family, or household*** use of the claimant;

h. eighth priority is for pre-petition tax claims, including certain income taxes, property taxes, trust fund taxes, employment taxes, excise taxes, custom duties, and penalties on eighth priority tax claims if for compensation of actual pecuniary loss;

i. ninth priority is for allowed unsecured claims of a ***federal depository institutions regulatory agency*** (such as the FDIC or RTC) for the amount of any deficiency under the debtor's agreement to maintain the capital of an insured depository institution; and

j. tenth priority is for allowed claims for ***death or personal injury*** resulting from the operation of a ***vessel or motor vehicle*** if such operation was unlawful because the debtor was ***intoxicated*** from using alcohol, drugs, or other substances.

2. Exceptions to Equal Treatment of Priority Creditors in a Class

The general rule is that priority creditors ***within a class*** share equally in any distribution. There are several exceptions, however, to this general rule.

a. Domestic Support Obligations

The trustee, if she administers assets to pay a domestic support obligation, is paid first, then a spouse, former spouse, or child of the debtor with a domestic support obligation claim, and finally, a governmental unit with a domestic support obligation assigned to it by a spouse, former spouse, or child of the debtor.

b. Conversion to Chapter 7

If a case is converted from Chapter 11, 12, or 13 to a case under Chapter 7, the administrative expense claims in the Chapter 7 case ***after conversion*** have priority over the administrative expenses incurred prior to conversion.

c. Super-Priority: Inadequately Protected Secured Creditor

If adequate protection is furnished to a creditor whose claim is secured by a lien on the debtor's property, but the adequate protection ultimately proves to be deficient, the creditor will receive an administrative expense claim with ***priority over all other administrative expenses*** allowed against the debtor's estate.

d. Super Super-Priority: Post-Petition Credit

If the trustee or the debtor in possession is unable to obtain unsecured post-petition credit by means of an administrative expense priority, the court may approve new credit or debt with ***priority over all other administrative expense*** claims, ***including any super-priority claims*** arising from the failure of adequate protection.

3. Subrogation

A third party, such as a co-debtor or a surety, who becomes subrogated to the rights of a holder of a claim entitled to a first priority or fourth through ninth priority does ***not*** become subrogated to the holder's right to priority. The subrogated claim is treated as a nonpriority claim. Subrogees to administrative expense claims and gap claims in involuntary cases, however, become subrogated to the respective priorities of such claims.

F. TAX CLAIMS

The bankruptcy court has jurisdiction to determine the amount or legality of any tax, fine, penalty, or addition to tax that has not been contested in and adjudicated by an appropriate judicial or administrative court *prior to bankruptcy.* The court may exercise its power to determine tax liability regardless of whether the tax has been assessed or paid. The court also may determine the *estate's* right to a *tax refund,* but only after the earlier of 120 days after a proper request by the trustee for the refund from the appropriate governmental unit, *or* an actual determination by that governmental unit of the trustee's request. The bankruptcy court *may not* determine the amount or legality of any amount arising in connection with an *ad valorem tax* on the estate's real or personal property if the applicable period for contesting or re-determining that amount under applicable nonbankruptcy law has expired.

1. Tax Liability of Estate

A trustee may request that the appropriate taxing authority determine any unpaid tax liability *of the estate* incurred during the administration of the case. Once the trustee has made the request, the estate, the trustee, and the debtor or a successor to the debtor are discharged from any liability for the tax *upon payment of the tax indicated on the return* if the taxing authority fails to take certain action within the statutory time frames *or upon payment of the tax determined by the taxing authority* or *the court.* There is no discharge if the return is *fraudulent* or contains a *material misrepresentation.*

2. Assessment

After the court makes a determination of a tax liability, the appropriate taxing authority may assess the amount of the tax against the estate, the debtor, or a successor to the debtor, notwithstanding the Code's automatic stay provisions.

3. Interest on Tax Claims

If the Code requires the payment of interest on a *tax claim* or an *administrative tax* claim, or the payment of interest to enable a *tax creditor* to receive the *present value* of its claim, then the interest rate is the applicable *rate under nonbankruptcy law.* In the case of taxes paid pursuant to a confirmed plan under Chapter 11, 12, or 13, the date for determining the interest rate is the calendar month in which the plan is confirmed.

4. Burden of Proof

The Supreme Court has held that "in the absence of modification in the Bankruptcy Code the burden of proof on a tax claim in bankruptcy remains where the substantive tax law puts it."

G. SUBROGATION CLAIMS

A subrogee is an entity that *has paid* a creditor's claim against the debtor because the entity either had secured the claim or was liable with the debtor on the claim as a co-debtor, co-maker, surety, or guarantor. Generally, a subrogee *succeeds to the rights of the creditor* whose claim it paid to the extent of the amount paid, although there are several exceptions to this rule. A co-debtor's claim, either by way of subrogation or for reimbursement or contribution, will be *subordinated to the principal creditor's claim* until that claim is satisfied fully, either through distribution under the Bankruptcy Code or by other means.

H. SUBORDINATION OF CLAIMS

A claim in a bankruptcy case may be subordinated to the payment of other claims by a subordination contract enforceable under applicable nonbankruptcy law.

1. Subordination of Claims for Purchase or Sale of a Security

A claim for damages, rescission, or contribution or reimbursement arising from the purchase or sale of a security of the debtor or its affiliate *must be subordinated* to all claims or interests *senior or equal* to that which the security represents.

a. Exception: Common Stock

If the security is common stock, then the claim will be subordinated to the *same priority as common stock,* not to a lower priority.

2. Equitable Subordination

The court has the equitable power (i) to subordinate all or part of an allowed secured or unsecured claim to another allowed claim, (ii) to subordinate all or part of an allowed interest to another allowed interest, or (iii) to order that any lien securing such a subordinated claim be transferred to the estate. Generally, an *essential element* in the equitable subordination of a claim or interest is showing *inequitable conduct* on the claimant's part. Usually, such misconduct falls into one of the following categories: (i) *fraud, illegality, or breach of fiduciary duties;* (ii) *undercapitalization;* or (iii) the claimant's use of the debtor as a *mere instrumentality or alter ego.*

a. Insiders and Fiduciaries

While a claimant's status as an insider or as a fiduciary generally should not, in the absence of inequitable conduct, result in subordination of his claim, courts usually rigorously examine the dealings of insiders and fiduciaries for *good faith and fairness.*

I. DISTRIBUTION OUTSIDE OF BANKRUPTCY CODE

A creditor of a partnership debtor who receives payment on an allowed claim against the partnership from a general partner who is not a debtor in a Chapter 7 case and who has not secured the creditor's claim with a lien on the general partner's own property is prohibited from receiving any payment on the claim until all of the creditors with whom she would have shared equally have received payment equal to the consideration she received from the general partner.

VIII. DEBTOR'S EXEMPTIONS

A. EXEMPTIONS

1. Fresh Start: Exempt Property

Usually, an individual debtor does not come out of bankruptcy completely dispossessed of all assets, because she is entitled to certain exemptions from property of the estate, either under the Bankruptcy Code or pursuant to applicable state law and nonbankruptcy federal law. These exemptions apply only to individual debtors—not to partnerships or corporations—in cases under Chapters 7, 11, 12, and 13, and exemptions cannot be waived in favor of an unsecured creditor. Thirty-five states have rejected the federal bankruptcy exemption scheme, thereby restricting debtors domiciled there to the exemptions allowable under state law and federal nonbankruptcy law. In states that have not opted out, the debtor is free to choose *either* the federal bankruptcy exemptions or those permitted under applicable state and federal nonbankruptcy law.

2. **Federal Bankruptcy Exemptions**

   a. **Homestead**

   The debtor may exempt up to *$25,150 in real or personal property* used by the debtor or a dependent as a *residence,* or in a *burial plot* for the debtor or a dependent.

   b. **Motor Vehicle**

   There is a maximum exemption of *$4,000* allowed for *one motor vehicle.*

   c. **Household Goods, Crops, Animals**

   There is an exemption of up to *$625* in any item of household furnishings, household goods, clothing, appliances, books, musical instruments, crops, or animals, whose primary purpose is for the *personal, family, or household use* of the debtor or a dependent. *But note*: This exemption *may not exceed $13,400* in total value.

   d. **Jewelry**

   The debtor may exempt up to *$1,700* in jewelry held principally for the personal, family, or household use of the debtor or a dependent.

   e. **Wildcard Exemption**

   There is an exemption of up to *$1,325, plus up to $12,575* of any unused portion of the homestead exemption, *in any property.*

   f. **Tools of the Trade**

   The debtor may exempt up to *$2,525* in her *professional books* or *tools of the trade* or those of a dependent.

   g. **Life Insurance**

   The debtor may exempt any *unmatured* life insurance contract that she owns, except a credit life insurance contract.

   h. **Loan Value or Accrued Interest of Life Insurance**

   There is an exemption of up to *$13,400* in the loan value or in accrued interest or dividends of any unmatured life insurance contract that the debtor owns.

   i. **Health Aids**

   There is an exemption for health aids prescribed by a professional for the debtor or a dependent.

   j. **Government Benefits**

   There is an exemption for the debtor's right to receive social security benefits, veterans' benefits, local public assistance, unemployment benefits or compensation, or disability or illness benefits.

   k. **Alimony, Support, or Maintenance**

   The debtor may exempt payments received for *alimony, support, or maintenance,* to the extent that it is reasonably necessary to support the debtor and any dependent.

l. Pension Plan

With certain exceptions, the debtor may exempt payments under an *eligible pension plan* or similar contract based on length of service, age, illness, disability, or death, to the extent that such payment is reasonably necessary to support the debtor and any dependent.

m. Crime Victim Award

The debtor may exempt property or payments received pursuant to an award under a *crime victim's reparation law.*

n. Wrongful Death Award

There is an exemption for the debtor's right to receive payment arising from the wrongful death of an individual with respect to whom the debtor was a dependent, to the extent that the payment is reasonably necessary to support the debtor and any of her dependents.

o. Life Insurance Proceeds

The debtor may exempt a payment under a life insurance contract that insured the life of an individual if debtor was a dependent of that individual on the date of the individual's death. The debtor may exempt the payment only to the extent that the payment is reasonably necessary to support the debtor and any of her dependents.

p. Personal Injury Award

The debtor may exempt payments, up to a *maximum of $25,150,* arising from *personal bodily injury* of the debtor or an individual with respect to whom the debtor is a dependent. This exemption does not include compensation for pain and suffering or compensation for actual pecuniary loss, such as medical expenses.

q. Loss of Future Earnings

The debtor may exempt compensation for the *loss of future earnings* of either the debtor or an individual with respect to whom the debtor was or is a dependent, to the extent that the payment is reasonably necessary to support the debtor and any of her dependents.

r. Retirement Funds and IRAs

The debtor may exempt retirement funds, so long as the monies are in a fund or account that is exempt from taxation under certain provisions of the Internal Revenue Code. The debtor also may exempt up to *1,362,800* of funds in certain individual retirement accounts. The Supreme Court has held that monies in an inherited IRA do not qualify for the exemption under § 522(b)(3)(C).

3. State Exemptions and Nonbankruptcy Federal Exemptions

If the debtor does not elect the federal bankruptcy exemptions or if the debtor's domiciliary state has opted out, the exemptions available to the debtor are those allowable under applicable state law and nonbankruptcy federal law, subject to the Bankruptcy Code's domiciliary requirement and to new Code restrictions on state homestead exemptions.

a. *Which* State Law Exemptions?

Subject to the Code's domiciliary requirement and to federal restrictions on state homestead exemptions, the exemptions allowable under state law are those in effect: (i) as of the date the bankruptcy petition was filed and (ii) in the state where the debtor has been domiciled for the ***730 days or two years*** prior to filing the bankruptcy petition. If the debtor has not been domiciled in a single state for 730 days, then the exemption law of the place where debtor has been domiciled for the ***180 days immediately preceding the 730-day period*** applies. If the debtor has not been domiciled in a single state for the ***180-day period,*** then the exemption law of the place where debtor has been domiciled for the ***longest portion of the 180-day period*** applies. State law exemptions vary widely from state to state.

b. Federal Limitations on Homestead Exemptions

The Bankruptcy Code now contains three limitations on a debtor's right to fully exempt her homestead under state exemption laws. The limitations apply to ***real or personal property*** that the debtor or a dependent ***uses as a residence*** or ***claims as a homestead,*** a ***cooperative*** that owns property used by the debtor or a dependent as a ***residence,*** or a ***burial plot*** for the debtor or a dependent ("the Property").

(i) The Fraud Limitation

The fraud limitation reduces the amount of the debtor's state exemption to the extent that the debtor, ***with intent to hinder, delay or defraud creditors,*** disposed of ***non-exempt property*** in the ***10-year period*** preceding bankruptcy in order to increase the amount of the state-law exemption taken in the Property described above.

(ii) The 1215-Day Limitation

The Bankruptcy Code places a cap of ***$170,350*** on any interest that the debtor acquires in the Property described above during the ***1215-day period*** preceding the filing of bankruptcy. This restriction does not apply to the ***principal residence of a family farmer.*** It also does not apply if the debtor uses the money received from sale of a residence acquired before the 1215-day period to acquire a new residence in the ***same state*** during the 1215-day period.

(iii) The "Bad Conduct" Limitation

The Bankruptcy Code caps the debtor's exemptible interest at ***$170,350*** on the Property described above in cases involving certain types of bad conduct by the debtor. The cap does not apply to the extent that the amount of the debtor's interest in the property is ***reasonably necessary for the support*** of the debtor and any dependents of the debtor.

c. Nonbankruptcy Federal Law

Federal statutes other than the Bankruptcy Code sometimes provide exemptions that may be claimed under § 522(b)(3)(A), such as Social Security payments, veterans' benefits, civil service retirement benefits, or military pension benefits.

d. Tenancy by the Entirety and Joint Tenancy

A debtor who uses the state exemption alternative also may exempt any interest in property she held, immediately prior to bankruptcy, as a tenant by the entirety or as a joint tenant, to the extent that applicable nonbankruptcy law (usually state property law) exempts such interest from process. It is important to recognize that the treatment of property held by the entirety or in a joint tenancy depends on how state law treats such property.

4. Joint Case

In a joint case, *each debtor* is entitled to a separate claim of any allowable exemptions.

a. Federal Exemptions

Joint debtors who elect the federal exemptions may stack their exemptions. But recall that in a joint case, *both debtors* must choose either the federal exemptions or the state exemptions.

b. State Exemptions

The majority of courts have held that state law controls whether debtors in opt-out states may stack state law exemption values.

5. Effect of Exemptions: Not Liable for Debts

The general rule is that, unless the case is dismissed, property exempted by the debtor is not liable *during or after the case* for any pre-petition debt or any debt deemed to have arisen before bankruptcy. The following kinds of debts, however, may be satisfied from the debtor's exempt property:

a. *nondischargeable taxes;*

b. *domestic support obligations;*

c. *a debt secured by a lien* that is not void under § 506(d) and that has not been avoided under another provision of the Code;

d. *a debt secured by a tax lien* if notice of the lien has been filed properly;

e. *a debt, owed by an institution-affiliated party of an insured financial institution* to a federal depository institutions regulatory agency for fraud or defalcation while acting in a fiduciary capacity, embezzlement, larceny, or willful and malicious injury to another entity or its property; and

f. *a debt in connection with fraud* in obtaining or providing *any financial assistance* for purposes of *financing an education* at an institution of higher learning.

6. Avoidance of Liens That Impair Exemption

Judicial liens, other than a judicial lien securing a debt for a domestic support obligation, and *nonpossessory, nonpurchase-money security interests* in (i) *household goods* and certain other items held *primarily for personal, family, or household use,* (ii) *professional books or tools of the trade,* and (iii) *health aids* may be avoided by the debtor when they *impair an exemption* that the debtor could otherwise claim.

7. Property Recovered by Trustee

The debtor may *exempt* property that the *trustee has recovered* and brought into the estate so long as the debtor, absent the transfer, could have exempted the property under applicable federal or state law, and only if: (i) the debtor *did not voluntarily* transfer the property or conceal it; or (ii) the debtor *could have avoided* the transfer under § 522(f)(1)(B).

8. Avoidance by Debtor

If the trustee can avoid a transfer of property or recover a setoff but does not attempt to pursue it, the debtor may *avoid* the transfer or may *recover* the setoff to the extent that she could have exempted the property under § 522(g)(1) if the trustee had used his avoiding powers.

9. Debtor's Recovery and Exemption

A debtor who avoids a transfer of property or recovers a setoff pursuant to §§ 522(f) or 522(h) may *recover* the property or the setoff in accordance with § 550 and may *exempt* it to the extent permitted under the applicable exemption scheme.

10. Administrative Expenses

Subject to certain exceptions, exempt property usually is not liable for the payment of administrative expenses.

B. REDEMPTION: CHAPTER 7 CASES ONLY

1. Tangible Personal Property

In a Chapter 7 case, an *individual debtor* has the right to redeem *tangible personal property* from a lien that secures a dischargeable consumer debt if the property is held mainly for *personal, family, or household use,* and it either has been *exempted* by the debtor or has been *abandoned* by the trustee. The debtor may retain such collateral by paying the secured party the *amount of the allowed secured claim,* which is determined by the collateral's market value.

a. Lump Sum

To redeem collateral, the debtor must make payment in a lump sum and not by installment payments.

2. Changed Intention

A debtor who has filed a statement of intention to reaffirm a secured consumer debt is not bound irrevocably by the decision and still may redeem the collateral, notwithstanding her original statement of intention.

3. No Waiver

A debtor may exercise her right to redeem collateral even if she has waived the right to redeem.

IX. DISCHARGE OF INDEBTEDNESS

A. EXCEPTIONS TO DISCHARGE

Certain debts of an *individual debtor* are not dischargeable and, therefore, survive the bankruptcy of an individual who has received a discharge under Chapter 7, 11, 12, or 13. A creditor who obtains a judicial determination that a particular debt is nondischargeable is free to pursue the debtor and to attempt to recover that debt subsequent to the debtor's discharge. *Distinguish* a determination of nondischargeability under § 523(a), which excepts *a specific debt* from the debtor's discharge, from the complete denial of a debtor's discharge, which allows *all of the debtor's debts* to survive bankruptcy, and thereafter all claimants to compete for satisfaction of their claims.

1. **Nondischargeable Debts Under § 523(a)**

   a. **Taxes**

   Taxes entitled to *third priority (gap period)* and *eighth priority (various unsecured pre-petition claims)* are not dischargeable. Taxes for which a *return was not filed* or for which a *fraudulent return* was filed also are not dischargeable.

   Note: Discharge rules for third and eighth priority taxes differ for a standard Chapter 13 discharge. Chapter 12 also has special discharge rules for unsecured pre-petition tax claims.

   b. **Fraud**

   Debts for money, property, services, or credit obtained by *false pretenses, a false representation, or actual fraud,* other than a statement about the financial condition of the debtor or an insider, are not dischargeable if the creditor *justifiably* relies on the fraudulent representation. A debt for money, property, services, or credit obtained by the use of a false statement is not dischargeable if (i) the statement was in *writing;* (ii) the statement was *materially* false; (iii) the statement related to the *financial condition* of the *debtor or an insider;* (iv) the creditor owed the debt *reasonably relied upon* the written statement; *and* (v) the debtor made the statement with the *intent to deceive.*

   Note: While this portion of the capsule summary covers exceptions to discharge for individual debtors, keep in mind that confirmation of a Chapter 11 plan does *not discharge a corporate debtor* from a debt owed to a *domestic governmental unit* that was obtained by *false pretenses, false representation, or actual fraud.* Plan confirmation also does *not discharge a corporate debtor* from a debt owed to a *domestic governmental unit* that was obtained by use of a *statement in writing* respecting the debtor's *financial condition.*

   c. **Failure to Schedule Debts in Current Case**

   Debts involving fraud, misrepresentation, or use of a false financial statement; embezzlement, or fraud or defalcation while acting in a fiduciary capacity; or willful and malicious injury are not dischargeable if the debtor's failure to list or schedule the debt in the current case precludes a *creditor without notice or actual knowledge of the bankruptcy case* from timely filing both a proof of claim *and* a complaint to determine the dischargeability of the debt. For any other debt, the debt is not dischargeable if the failure to list or schedule it precludes a creditor who has *no notice or actual knowledge of the bankruptcy case* from timely filing a proof of claim.

   d. **Fiduciary Fraud or Defalcation, and Embezzlement or Larceny**

   Debts for fraud or defalcation *while acting in a fiduciary capacity* are not dischargeable. Debts arising from *embezzlement or larceny* also are not dischargeable, but there is no requirement that the wrongdoing occur in a fiduciary context.

   e. **Domestic Support Obligations**

   Debts owed for *domestic support obligations* are nondischargeable.

f. **Property Settlements and Other Obligations Arising from Separation Agreement or Divorce Decree**

Debts that *do not qualify as domestic support obligations* but that are owed to a *spouse, former spouse, or child of the debtor* and that were incurred in the course of a *divorce or separation* or in connection with a separation agreement, divorce decree, other court order, or a governmental unit's determination based on state or territorial law, are nondischargeable.

Note: Such debts are discharged as part of the standard Chapter 13 discharge.

g. **Willful/Malicious Injury**

Debts for *willful and malicious injury* caused by the debtor to *another entity or its property* are nondischargeable in a *Chapter 7, 11, or 12* case, or in a *Chapter 13* case in which the debtor receives a *hardship discharge.* The standard Chapter 13 discharge excepts from discharge debts for restitution or damages awarded in a *civil action* against the debtor for *willful or malicious injury* resulting in *personal injury or death* of an *individual.*

h. **Fines, Penalties, and Restitution**

In a case under Chapters 7, 11, or 12, or a hardship discharge case under Chapter 13, a *fine, penalty, or forfeiture* payable *to and for the benefit* of a *governmental unit* is not dischargeable to the extent that it is *not compensation for actual pecuniary loss.*

Note: Debts for *restitution or a criminal fine* that are included in the debtor's sentence for *conviction of a crime* are excepted from the standard Chapter 13 discharge.

i. **Restitution for Federal Crimes**

The payment of an order of *restitution* for most *federal* crimes is nondischargeable in a Chapter 7, 11, or 12 case, or a Chapter 13 hardship discharge case. *Fines* ordered in connection with certain *federal* crimes are nondischargeable under *all chapters* of the Code, and liens securing them filed in favor of the United States are *not avoidable* in bankruptcy.

Note: The language governing the standard Chapter 13 discharge for debts for restitution is broader than the language of § 523(a)(13), which is limited to restitution orders issued in federal criminal cases.

j. **Student Loans**

Absent an *undue hardship* on the debtor and her dependents, an educational loan made, insured, or guaranteed by a governmental unit, or extended under a program funded by a governmental unit or a nonprofit institution, or any other educational loan that is a qualified education loan under the Internal Revenue Code is nondischargeable.

k. **Operating a Motor Vehicle, Vessel or Aircraft While Intoxicated**

Any debt for *death or personal injury* resulting from the debtor's use of a motor vehicle, vessel, or aircraft if such operation was unlawful because debtor was *intoxicated* from using alcohol, drugs, or another substance is nondischargeable.

l. **Prior Bankruptcy**

A debt that was or could have been listed in a ***prior case*** in which the debtor ***waived discharge*** or in which the debtor was ***denied discharge*** under § 727(a)(2)–(7) is nondischargeable.

Note: The standard discharge under Chapter 13 does *not* except from discharge such debts from a prior bankruptcy.

m. **Fiduciary Fraud or Defalcation of Officers and Directors of Financial Institutions**

Any debt arising from a final judgment or order, or consent order or decree (i) entered by any federal or state court, (ii) issued by a federal depository institutions regulatory agency, or (iii) contained in a settlement agreement with the debtor, resulting from the debtor's ***fraud or defalcation*** while acting in a ***fiduciary capacity*** with respect to any ***insured depository institution or insured credit union*** is nondischargeable.

Note: Such debts are dischargeable as part of a standard Chapter 13 discharge.

n. **Failure to Maintain Capital of Insured Depository Institutions**

Any debt for ***malicious or reckless*** failure to maintain the capital of an insured depository institution in breach of a commitment to a federal depository institutions regulatory agency is not dischargeable.

Note: Such debts are dischargeable as part of a standard Chapter 13 discharge.

o. **Debts Incurred to Pay Taxes**

Debts incurred to pay taxes that would be nondischargeable under § 523(a)(1), or fines or penalties imposed under federal election law are nondischargeable.

Note: Such debts are dischargeable as part of a standard Chapter 13 discharge.

p. **Condominium Fees**

Fees or assessments for a condominium, a share in a cooperative housing corporation, or a lot in a homeowners' association that become due and payable ***after the order for relief*** are nondischargeable for as long as the debtor or the trustee has a legal, equitable, or possessory ownership interest in the condominium, cooperative housing corporation, or lot.

Note: Such debts are dischargeable as part of a standard Chapter 13 discharge.

q. **Courts Costs**

Fees imposed on a prisoner for filing a case, appeal, complaint, or motion, as well as any other costs assessed in connection with the filing are nondischargeable even if the debtor files *in forma pauperis* or has the status of a prisoner.

Note: Such debts are dischargeable as part of a standard Chapter 13 discharge.

r. Pension Loans

A debt owed for loans from certain *pension, profit-sharing, stock bonus or other plans* is not dischargeable.

Note: Such debts are dischargeable as part of a standard Chapter 13 discharge.

s. Securities Law Violations

A debt owed for violation of *state or federal securities laws,* or for *common law fraud, deceit or misrepresentation* in connection with the *purchase of a security* is nondischargeable if it results from any (i) judgment, order, consent decree or order entered in any federal or state court, or any administrative proceeding, (ii) settlement agreement entered into by the debtor, or (iii) any court or administrative order for damages, fines, penalties, restitution, attorney fees, costs or any other payment owed by the debtor.

Note: Such debts are dischargeable as part of a standard Chapter 13 discharge.

2. Certain Long-Term Debts

Long-term debts, e.g., mortgage, in which the last payment on the debt is due *after* the last payment is due under the debtor's plan, are not part of the Chapter 12 or Chapter 13 discharge, regardless of whether it is a standard or hardship discharge.

3. Proof

The *preponderance-of-the-evidence* standard of proof applies to the exceptions to discharge contained in § 523(a).

4. Prior State Court Judgments

Res judicata does not preclude the bankruptcy court's consideration of evidence of fraud in deciding whether a debt previously reduced to a state court judgment, pursuant to the parties' stipulation, is not dischargeable.

B. EFFECTS OF DISCHARGE

1. Relief from Personal Liability

A debtor is relieved of *personal* liability for all debts that are discharged. Thus, while a valid lien that has not been avoided in the bankruptcy case generally survives *in rem* and ultimately may be enforced against the property securing the debt, no action is permitted against the debtor personally for a deficiency if the debt has been discharged.

2. Co-Debtor or Surety—No Discharge

With limited exceptions, the discharge of a debt of the debtor does *not* affect the liability of any other entity, e.g., a co-debtor, surety, or guarantor, or the property of any other entity for that debt.

3. Voluntary Repayment

The Code expressly permits the debtor to voluntarily repay any debt, but in the absence of an enforceable reaffirmation agreement with a creditor, the debtor has no personal *legal* obligation to repay a debt that has been discharged.

C. REAFFIRMATION AGREEMENTS

A reaffirmation agreement is a voluntary contract between the debtor and the holder of a dischargeable claim whereby the debtor promises to repay all or part of the debt after bankruptcy.

1. Requirements for Enforceability

A reaffirmation agreement is enforceable only if all of the following conditions are satisfied:

a. the agreement is *enforceable under nonbankruptcy law;*

b. the agreement is *executed before* the granting of the *debtor's discharge;*

c. debtor receives the statutorily mandated *disclosures;*

d. the agreement is filed with the court *no later than 60 days* after the first date set for the § 341 meeting;

e. if the debtor was *not represented by an attorney* during negotiation of the agreement, the court must find that the agreement is in the *debtor's best interest* and does not impose an *undue hardship;*

f. debtor does not rescind the agreement before the later of the discharge or *60 days* after the reaffirmation agreement was *filed* with the court; *and*

g. the Code's requirements for a discharge hearing are satisfied.

2. Presumption of Undue Hardship

The Code creates a *presumption of undue hardship* if the scheduled payments on the reaffirmed debt *exceed* the debtor's monthly *income minus expenses.* The presumption applies regardless of whether debtor was represented or not represented by counsel during negotiations for the reaffirmation agreement, but does not apply to reaffirmation agreements in which the creditor is a credit union.

D. PROTECTION AGAINST DISCRIMINATION

In addition to relieving the debtor of personal liability for any debts discharged, the law enhances her fresh start by providing express prohibitions against discriminatory treatment by employers or governmental units. The prohibition applies to discrimination by *governmental units* against a person, i.e., individual, corporation, or partnership, and to discrimination by *private employers* with respect to an *individual's* employment or termination. The prohibition also applies to discrimination by governmental units and lenders engaged in a *guaranteed student loan program.* The Code does not prohibit consideration of an applicant's future financial responsibility or ability if there is no discrimination against bankruptcy debtors.

X. ADMINISTRATIVE POWERS: THE AUTOMATIC STAY

A. THE AUTOMATIC STAY

The automatic stay is a statutory injunction that takes effect *when a bankruptcy petition is filed* and protects the debtor, the property of the estate, and the property of the debtor from certain actions by creditors. It is designed to provide a respite for the debtor and promote an orderly administration of the bankruptcy case. The stay applies to *all entities.*

1. **Acts Enjoined**

   a. **Proceedings Against Debtor**

   The commencement or continuation, including the issuance or service of process, of a *judicial, administrative, or other action* against the debtor is stayed if the action is intended to recover a *pre-petition claim* against the debtor, or if the action was commenced or could have been commenced before the bankruptcy petition was filed.

   b. **Pre-Petition Judgments**

   The automatic stay enjoins enforcement of a *pre-petition judgment* against the debtor or against property of the estate.

   c. **Acts Against Estate Property**

   Any act to *obtain possession* of estate property or property in the possession of the estate, or to *exercise control* over estate property is prohibited, regardless of whether the underlying claim arose before or after the filing of the bankruptcy petition.

   d. **Liens Against Estate Property**

   Any act designed to *create, perfect, or enforce a lien* against *estate property* is enjoined. There is a limited exception to the stay that authorizes post-petition perfection in certain circumstances.

   e. **Liens Against Debtor's Property**

   Any act intended to create, perfect, or enforce a lien against *property of the debtor* is prohibited *to the extent that the lien secures a pre-petition claim.* Property that has been *abandoned* by the trustee under § 554 reverts to the debtor and is protected by the automatic stay from any lien securing a pre-bankruptcy claim. The stay also shields the debtor's *exempt property* and property *acquired post-petition* from a lien securing a pre-petition claim.

   f. **Collection Efforts**

   Any act to *collect, recover, or assess* a claim against the debtor that arose prior to the bankruptcy petition is forbidden.

   g. **Setoffs**

   The automatic stay also enjoins the *post-petition setoff of mutual debts.* Thus, the setoff of a pre-petition debt owing to the debtor against a claim asserted against the debtor is prohibited unless the court grants relief from the stay.

   h. **Tax Court Proceedings**

   The Code stays the *commencement or continuation* of a case in the United States Tax Court concerning the *tax liability* of (i) a corporate debtor for a taxable period that the bankruptcy court may determine or (ii) an individual for a taxable period ending before the order for relief.

2. **Exceptions to the Automatic Stay**

   a. **Criminal Proceedings**

   The commencement or continuation of a criminal action against the debtor is not enjoined by the automatic stay.

b. Family Law Matters

A number of family law actions or proceedings do not violate the automatic stay, including the collection of **domestic support obligations,** and the commencement or continuation of proceedings (i) to establish **paternity** or concerning **child custody or visitation,** (ii) regarding **domestic violence,** or (iii) to **dissolve a marriage.**

c. Certain Acts of Perfection

The automatic stay does not prohibit the perfection of an interest in property to the extent that perfection occurs within the **30-day grace period** allowed by § 547(e)(2)(A), or to the extent that it would prevail over the trustee's avoiding powers pursuant to § 546(b), such as in the case of **retroactive perfection** of a purchase-money security interest under the Uniform Commercial Code. The filing of a **continuation statement** also is excepted from the automatic stay to the same extent.

d. Police or Regulatory Actions

The commencement or continuation of a proceeding by a governmental unit to enforce its police or regulatory power is not stayed. The enforcement of a judgment obtained by a governmental unit in implementing its police or regulatory power is subject to the automatic stay if the judgment is **a money judgment.**

e. Setoffs and Other Contractual Rights: Commodities and Securities Brokers, Repo Participants

The automatic stay does not apply to the rights of certain sophisticated financial parties to liquidate, terminate, or accelerate **a securities contract, a commodities contract, a forward contract, a repurchase agreement, a swap agreement or a master netting agreement.** The exception also applies to **setoff** rights under these agreements.

f. HUD Mortgage Foreclosures

The **commencement** of certain mortgage or deed of trust foreclosure actions by the Secretary of Housing and Urban Development is excepted from the automatic stay.

g. Tax Audits and Assessments

A tax audit, an issuance of a notice of tax deficiency, a demand for tax returns, and an assessment of any tax and issuance of a notice and demand for payment of the assessed tax are excepted from the automatic stay.

h. Recovery of Property by Certain Lessors

The automatic stay also does not prohibit any act by a debtor's lessor to obtain possession of nonresidential real property if the lease has **terminated by the expiration of its stated term** prior to the filing of the bankruptcy petition or during the case.

i. Certain Actions Relating to Negotiable Instruments

The automatic stay does not stay the presentment of a negotiable instrument, sending notice of dishonor, or protesting dishonor of such instrument.

j. Certain Actions Against Educational Institutions

The automatic stay does not apply to any action by an accrediting agency or state licensing body concerning the accreditation status or licensure of the debtor as an educational institution. The stay also does not apply to any action by a guaranty agency or the Secretary of Education concerning the debtor's eligibility to participate in programs under the Higher Education Act of 1965.

k. Repossession of Aircrafts and Vessels

The automatic stay does not apply in a *Chapter 11 case* to certain actions to foreclose on fleet mortgages or security interests in vessels or fishing facilities by the Secretary of Transportation or the Secretary of Commerce if the action is commenced, continued, or concluded *more than 90 days* after filing of the petition. Congress added these exceptions to the Code for *cases filed after August 1, 1986 and before December 31, 1989,* and has not extended this time period.

l. Ad Valorem Property Tax Liens and Special Assessments on Real Property

The automatic stay does not apply to the creation or perfection of a statutory lien for *ad valorem property taxes,* imposed by a governmental unit, that *become due post-petition,* or to *special taxes or special assessments* on real property, regardless of whether ad valorem, imposed by a governmental unit and that *become due post-petition.*

m. Withholding of Income for Pensions

The automatic stay does not apply to the *withholding of income* from a debtor's wages and *collection of those amounts withheld* pursuant to the debtor's agreement authorizing withholding and collection for the benefit of a *pension, profit-sharing, stock bonus or other plan* established under certain sections of the Internal Revenue Code and sponsored by the debtor's employer, or an affiliate, successor, or predecessor of such employer to the extent that the monies withheld and collected are only used to repay certain loans.

n. Prior Bankruptcy Cases

The Code contains two exceptions to the stay for actions against *real property* based on what occurred in the debtor's *prior bankruptcy case.*

(i) Scheme to Delay, Hinder, or Defraud

The bankruptcy court may grant relief from the automatic stay to a creditor whose claim is secured by *real property* if the court finds that the debtor's filing for bankruptcy was part of a *scheme to delay, hinder, or defraud* creditors that involved either (1) *the transfer* of part or all of the real property *without the secured creditor's consent* or (2) *multiple bankruptcy filings* affecting such real property. The court's order remains in effect in any *subsequent bankruptcy case* filed within *two years* after entry of the order, if the order is recorded in compliance with applicable state laws for recording real property liens or notices of interest in real property. In the later bankruptcy case, the debtor may move for relief from such order based on *changed circumstances* or for other *good cause.*

(ii) Ineligible Debtor Based on Prior Bankruptcy Case

The automatic stay does not apply to any act to enforce a lien against or security interest in real property if the debtor is *not eligible to be a debtor* or if the debtor filed the bankruptcy case in *violation of an order in a prior case* prohibiting the debtor from being a debtor in another bankruptcy case.

o. Eviction: Residential Real Property

The Code contains two exceptions to the stay that affect the ability of a lessor to move forward with eviction proceedings, in certain circumstances, without obtaining relief from the automatic stay.

(i) Pre-Petition Judgment for Possession

The automatic stay does not apply to the continuation of any *eviction, unlawful detainer, or similar proceeding* by a lessor of residential real property against a debtor/tenant if the lessor has obtained a *judgment for possession pre-petition.* The exception, however, is subject to § 362(*l*), which keeps the automatic stay in place if the debtor/tenant satisfies certain statutory conditions.

(ii) Property Endangerment or Controlled Substance Use

A lessor of residential real property may commence or continue an eviction action based on *endangerment of the property* or *illegal use of controlled substances on the property* if the lessor files with the court and serves on the debtor a *certification,* under penalty of perjury, that such an *eviction action has been filed* or that the debtor, during the *30 days prior to filing of the certification,* has *endangered* the property or illegally used or allowed the use of a *controlled substance on the property.* The exception, however, is subject to § 362(m), which keeps the automatic stay in place if the debtor/tenant satisfies certain statutory conditions.

p. Non-Avoidable Transfers

The automatic stay does not apply to any transfer that is not avoidable under § 544 and that is not avoidable under § 549.

q. Securities Self-Regulatory Organizations

The automatic stay does not apply to certain conduct by a *securities association* or a *national securities exchange* registered with the Securities Exchange Commission.

r. Setoff Income Tax Refund

The automatic stay does not apply to a governmental unit's setoff, if allowed under nonbankruptcy law, of an *income tax refund for a pre-petition taxable period against a pre-petition tax liability.*

s. Federal Health Care Programs

It is not a violation of the automatic stay for the Secretary of Health and Human Services to exclude the debtor from participating in the Medicare program or any other federal health care program, as defined in the Social Security Act.

t. **Small Business Debtor**

The automatic stay does not apply to a *small business case* if the debtor files a bankruptcy case (subsequent case) *and*:

(i) *is a debtor in a small business case pending* at the time debtor files its subsequent bankruptcy case;

(ii) *was a debtor in a small business case* that was *dismissed for any reason* by an order that became final in the *two-year period* before the date of the order for relief in the subsequent bankruptcy case;

(iii) *was a debtor in a small business case* in which a *plan was confirmed* in the *two-year period* before the date of the order for relief in the second bankruptcy case; *or*

(iv) is an *entity that acquired substantially all of the assets or business of a small business debtor described above in (i)–(iii),* unless such entity establishes by a preponderance of the evidence that it acquired the assets or business in *good faith and not to evade the Code's restrictions.*

3. **Expiration of the Stay**

a. **Individual Chapter 7 Debtors and Personal Property**

In an *individual Chapter 7* case, the automatic stay terminates with respect to *personal property of the estate or of the debtor* that secures a claim or that is subject to a lease, and such property is no longer property of the estate if the debtor fails (i) to *timely file a statement of intention* or to indicate on such statement that it will *surrender or redeem,* the property, *reaffirm the debt* secured by the property, *or assume such unexpired lease;* or (ii) *timely take the action* specified in the statement. The stay does not terminate if the debtor specifies an intention to reaffirm the debt on the original contract terms and the creditor refuses to agree to reaffirmation on those terms.

b. **General Rules**

Unless the court grants relief from the automatic stay, the stay of an *act against estate property* is effective until the property no longer constitutes property of the estate. Unless the court grants relief from the automatic stay, the stay of *any other act* enjoined under § 362(a) continues until a discharge is granted or denied, the case is dismissed, or the case is closed, whichever occurs first.

c. **Serial Filers**

The Code's provisions on serial filers apply only to *individual debtors,* and only if the debtor's prior case was *dismissed,* but not if the debtor's prior case was dismissed because of the means test.

(i) **Prior Pending Case: 30-Day Rule**

If an *individual debtor* files for bankruptcy and there was *pending in the prior year* a Chapter 7, 11, or 13 case that was *dismissed,* the Code provides that the stay in debtor's current bankruptcy case expires after *30 days.* The stay expires, however, only as to a debt, property securing that debt, or a lease *with respect to the debtor.* The majority of courts have held that after 30 days, while the automatic stay expires as to *the debtor and property of the debtor,* it remains in place with regard to *estate property.*

(ii) Two or More Prior Pending Cases

If an individual debtor files for bankruptcy and there were *two or more bankruptcy cases pending in the prior year* that were *dismissed,* the Code provides that the automatic stay in debtor's current bankruptcy case does not go into effect. The rule applies to all prior bankruptcy filings, including those under Chapter 12.

4. Relief from Stay

Upon request, and after notice and a hearing, the court may grant relief from the automatic stay by *terminating, modifying, annulling, or conditioning* the stay.

a. Grounds for Relief

(i) "Cause"

After notice and a hearing, the bankruptcy court must grant relief from the automatic stay to a party in interest if *cause* exists to lift the stay. The Code does not define the term "cause," but cause may include a *lack of adequate protection* of an entity's interest in property or a *debtor's lack of good faith* in filing the bankruptcy petition.

(ii) Acts Against Property

The bankruptcy court will grant relief from the stay of an act against property if (i) the debtor has *no equity* in the property and (ii) the property is *not necessary for an effective reorganization.*

(iii) Single Asset Real Estate

If a creditor's claim is secured by an interest in single asset real estate, the court must grant relief from the automatic stay if the debtor fails either to (i) *file a plan of reorganization* that has a *reasonable possibility of being confirmed* within a *reasonable time;* or (ii) *start to make monthly payments* at the current fair market rate, to each creditor with a claim secured by the real estate, other than creditors with a judgment lien or an unmatured statutory lien.

b. Procedure for Requesting Relief

(i) Acts Against Estate Property: Hearing

When the relief sought is from the stay of an act against *property of the estate,* the stay terminates, by operation of law with respect to the party in interest making the request for stay relief, *30 days* after the motion is filed unless, after notice and a hearing, the court orders that the stay remain operative until a final hearing is concluded.

(ii) Individual Chapter 7, 11, or 13 Case

In an individual debtor's Chapter 7, 11, or 13 case, the automatic stay terminates, by operation of law, *60 days* after a request for relief is made by a party in interest, *unless* (i) the court renders a *final decision during the 60-day period* starting on the date of the request for stay relief; or (ii) the 60-day period is extended by the *agreement of all parties in interest or* by the court for the time that the court finds is required for cause.

(iii) Burden of Proof

In litigation concerning relief from the stay of *any act* enjoined under § 362(a), the *party seeking relief has* the burden of proof *regarding the debtor's equity* in property; the *party opposing relief* must bear the burden of proof *on all other issues.*

(iv) Ex Parte Relief

In the exceptional case in which *irreparable harm* to an entity's interest in property will occur before there is time for notice and a hearing, the court may grant ex parte relief from the stay to prevent the threatened loss.

(v) Appeal

A decision to grant or deny relief from the stay is a final order, which may be appealed.

5. Willful Violation of Stay

An individual who is injured by a *willful* violation of the automatic stay may recover actual damages, costs, attorneys' fees, and, when warranted, punitive damages. If the stay violation is based on an entity's *good faith belief* that the stay has terminated pursuant to § 362(h), then recovery is limited to *actual damages.*

XI.   ADMINISTRATIVE POWERS: §§ 363–366 OF THE CODE

A.   ADEQUATE PROTECTION

1.   Interest in Property

a.   Automatic Stay

If an entity's interest in property is subject to the automatic stay and the entity moves to lift the automatic stay because of a lack of adequate protection, the court must grant relief from the stay or require that the entity's interest in the property be adequately protected.

b.   Property Used, Sold, or Leased

If an entity's interest in property is subject to the automatic stay and the entity moves to lift the automatic stay because of a lack of adequate protection, the court must grant relief from the stay or require that the entity's interest in the property be adequately protected.

c.   Equal or Senior Lien on Property

If an entity's interest in property is subject to the automatic stay and the entity moves to lift the automatic stay because of a lack of adequate protection, the court must grant relief from the stay or require that the entity's interest in the property be adequately protected.

2.   Methods of Providing Adequate Protection

The Code provides three non-exclusive methods for providing adequate protection: (i) *cash or periodic cash payments;* (ii) an *additional or replacement lien;* or (iii) the *indubitable equivalent* of the entity's interest in the property. A substantial *equity cushion* may adequately protect a secured creditor's interest in the property.

3. Valuation of Collateral

In valuing collateral, courts take account of factors such as the *purpose of the valuation* and the *intended use or disposition of the collateral.*

4. Failure of Adequate Protection

If adequate protection is provided to a creditor whose claim is secured by a lien on property of the debtor, but the "adequate protection" eventually is shown to have been deficient, the secured creditor will receive an administrative expense claim with *super-priority,* which means priority over all other administrative expenses allowed in the case.

5. Chapter 12 Cases

The adequate protection provisions of § 361 do not apply to a case under Chapter 12. The Code contains special rules for adequate protection in such cases.

B. USE, SALE, OR LEASE OF PROPERTY

1. Ordinary Course of Business

A trustee or a debtor in possession who is authorized to operate the debtor's business may use, sell, or lease property of the estate in the ordinary course of business *without notice or a hearing,* unless the court orders otherwise. *Exception:* The trustee or the debtor in possession may use, sell, or lease *cash collateral* in the *ordinary course of business only* if she obtains either *court authorization,* after notice and a hearing, or the *consent* of all entities having an interest in the cash collateral.

2. Out of Ordinary Course of Business

After *notice and a hearing,* a trustee or a debtor in possession may use, sell, or lease property of the estate out of the ordinary course of the debtor's business, unless the sale or lease involves *personally identifiable information,* in which case special rules apply. Ordinarily, a secured creditor whose lien secures an allowed claim on property sold *outside the ordinary course of business* may "credit bid" at the sale of such property.

3. Ipso Facto Clauses

The trustee or debtor in possession may use, sell, or lease property in or out of the ordinary course of business, or under the terms of a Chapter 11, 12, or 13 plan, notwithstanding provisions in a contract, lease, or nonbankruptcy law that otherwise would cause a forfeiture, modification, or termination of the debtor's interest in the property because of (i) the debtor's *insolvency or financial condition;* (ii) the debtor's filing of a *bankruptcy case;* (iii) the appointment of a *bankruptcy trustee or a nonbankruptcy custodian;* or (iv) *the seizure of property* by a bankruptcy trustee or nonbankruptcy custodian.

4. Sale Free and Clear

The trustee or the debtor in possession may sell property of the estate, either in or out of the ordinary course of business, free and clear of any interest in the property held by an entity other than the estate *only if one of the following* statutory requirements is satisfied:

a. *applicable state or other nonbankruptcy law allows* a free-and-clear sale of the property;

b. the entity holding the interest *consents to the sale;*

c. *if the interest is a lien,* the *sale price for the property is greater than the total value of all liens* on the property;

d. *there is a bona fide dispute* concerning the entity's interest in the property; *or*

e. *the entity holding the interest could be required to accept a money satisfaction* in a legal or equitable action.

Notwithstanding the conditions for a *free and clear sale,* the trustee or the debtor in possession may sell property free and clear of an entity's *vested or contingent right of dower or curtesy.*

5. **Not Free and Clear: Consumer Credit Transactions**

The sale of any interest in a consumer credit transaction subject to the Truth in Lending Act or any interest in a consumer credit contract is *not free and clear* of any claim or defense related to such consumer credit transaction or consumer credit contract.

6. **Burden of Proof**

In any hearing concerning the use, sale, or lease of property, the trustee or debtor in possession has the burden of proof regarding the question of adequate protection, while the entity claiming an interest in property bears the burden of showing the validity, priority, or extent of that interest.

7. **Appeal: Mootness**

Absent a stay pending appeal, the validity of an authorization to sell or lease property, in or outside the ordinary course of business, is not affected by a reversal or modification on appeal if the purchaser or lessee acted in *good faith,* regardless of the purchaser's or lessee's knowledge of the appeal.

C. OBTAINING CREDIT

1. **In Ordinary Course of Business**

Unless the court orders otherwise, a trustee or debtor in possession authorized to operate the debtor's business may procure *unsecured credit, e.g.,* trade credit, and incur *unsecured debt* in the ordinary course of business without notice or a hearing. Such credit or debt is allowable as an *administrative expense.*

2. **Out of Ordinary Course of Business**

After *notice and a hearing,* the court may approve the request of a trustee or debtor in possession to obtain unsecured credit or to incur unsecured debt *out of the ordinary course of business* as an *allowable expense of administration.*

3. **Priority or Security**

When the trustee or debtor in possession is *unable* to obtain unsecured credit without offering more than an administrative expense, the court, after notice and a hearing, may authorize credit to be acquired or debt to be incurred with (i) *super super-priority status;* (ii) secured by a *lien on unencumbered estate property;* or (iii) secured by a *junior lien on encumbered estate property.*

4. **Priming Lien**

If the trustee or the debtor in possession cannot obtain credit on any basis other than by the grant of a senior or equal lien on property that already is encumbered, the court, after notice and a hearing, may approve new credit or debt to be secured by a lien on estate property that will be *senior or equal* to any lien held by another entity on the same property.

5. **Appeal**

Absent a stay pending appeal, the validity of the court's order authorizing the debtor to obtain credit or to incur debt, or the validity of any lien or priority granted by the court is not affected by a reversal or modification on appeal, so long as the lender acted in *good faith.*

D. EXECUTORY CONTRACTS AND UNEXPIRED LEASES

1. **General Principles**

The debtor in possession or trustee, with the court's approval, may assume or reject an executory contract or an unexpired lease of the debtor.

2. **Assumption of Contracts and Leases in Default**

If there is a pre- or post-petition *default,* the trustee or debtor in possession may assume an executory contract or an unexpired lease *only* if the trustee or debtor in possession (i) *cures* the default or provides *adequate assurance* that the default will be *cured promptly;* (ii) *compensates* or provides *adequate assurance* of prompt compensation for any *monetary loss* caused by the default; and (iii) furnishes *adequate assurance of future performance* of the executory contract or the unexpired lease.

3. **Assignment**

The trustee or debtor in possession may assign an executory contract or an unexpired lease *only after assuming* the contract or lease and *providing adequate assurance* of the assignee's *future performance,* regardless of whether there has been a default.

4. **Agreements Not Assumable or Assignable**

The trustee may not assume or assign certain kinds of executory contracts and unexpired leases, e.g., personal services contracts.

5. **Rejection Constitutes Breach**

The general rule is that a *rejection* by the trustee or debtor in possession *operates as a breach* of the executory contract or the unexpired lease.

6. **Time Limitations for Assumption or Rejection**

   a. **Chapter 7 Cases**

   The trustee, in a case under Chapter 7, has *60 days* after the order for relief within which to assume or reject an *executory contract* or an unexpired lease of *personal property or residential real property.* Otherwise, the contract or the lease is deemed rejected.

   b. **Chapter 11, 12, and 13 Cases**

   Assumption or rejection of an *executory contract* or unexpired lease of *personal property or residential real property* may occur at any time prior to the confirmation of a plan under Chapter 11, 12, or 13.

   c. **Lease of Nonresidential Real Property Under Any Chapter**

   If the debtor is a lessee of nonresidential real property, then a trustee in a case under *any chapter,* or the debtor in possession in Chapter 11, has until the *earlier of* the date of the entry of a *plan confirmation order or 120 days after the order for relief* within which to assume or reject an unexpired lease of the property, or else the lease is deemed rejected and the property must be immediately surrendered to the lessor.

7. **Trustee Obligations Prior to Assumption or Rejection**

   a. **Lease of Nonresidential Real Property**

   The trustee or debtor in possession must timely perform all duties, except those under § 365(b)(2), arising under an unexpired lease of nonresidential real property *after the order for relief* and until assumption or rejection.

   b. **Lease of Commercial Personal Property in Chapter 11**

   In a Chapter 11 case, the trustee or debtor in possession must timely perform all obligations, except those specified under § 365(b)(2), in a lease of *non-consumer personal property* first arising *from 60 days after the order for relief* until the lease is assumed or rejected.

   c. **Executory Contracts and All Other Leases**

   The Code does not contain specific rules about the trustee's or debtor in possession's obligations to perform prior to assumption or rejection of executory contracts, or leases of residential property or consumer personal property.

8. **Ipso Facto Clauses**

   With certain exceptions, an executory contract or unexpired lease may not be terminated or modified *after* the filing of a bankruptcy petition solely on account of an *ipso facto* or other bankruptcy termination clause in the contract or lease.

9. **Debtor as Lessor**

   If the *debtor is the lessor* under an unexpired lease of real property, and the lease has been rejected by the trustee or debtor in possession, the lessee either may consider the lease terminated or, *if the term of the lease has commenced,* retain rights under the lease for the balance of the current term and for any period of renewal or extension enforceable under nonbankruptcy law.

10. **Debtor as Seller**

    If the debtor is the seller under an executory contract to sell real property or a timeshare interest and the trustee or debtor in possession has rejected the executory contract for sale, the buyer, *if in possession,* may treat the contract as terminated or may stay in possession of the real property or timeshare interest.

11. **Intellectual Property**

    If the debtor is the *licensor of a right to intellectual property,* and the trustee or debtor in possession rejects an executory contract under which the license has been granted, the *licensee* may consider the *contract terminated* or *may retain its contractual rights* to the intellectual property, including any right to exclusivity, but excluding any other right to specific performance of the contract, and use the property for the remaining period of the contract and any rightful extension.

E. **UTILITY SERVICE**

A utility may not discontinue, alter, or refuse service to, or discriminate against, the trustee or debtor solely because of the filing of a bankruptcy case or because the debtor failed to timely pay a debt owed for utility services furnished prior to the order for relief. But, a utility may discontinue, alter, or refuse service if, within *20 days* after the order for relief, neither the debtor nor the trustee provides a deposit or other security constituting *adequate assurance of payment* for *post-petition services.* In a *Chapter 11 case,* a utility may alter, refuse, or discontinue service if during the *30-day period* starting with the filing of the petition the debtor or trustee does not provide *adequate assurance of payment* that is *satisfactory to the utility.*

XII. CHAPTER 7: LIQUIDATION

A. INTRODUCTION

1. Eligibility for Relief

Chapter 7 relief is available to *any person* that *resides or has a domicile, a place of business, or property in the United States except* (i) railroads; (ii) domestic savings institutions and insurance companies; (iii) certain small business investment companies; (iv) foreign insurance companies engaged in such business in the United States; and (v) foreign banks, savings and loan associations, and other similar financial institutions that have a branch or agency in the United States. Stockbrokers and commodity brokers may be debtors under special provisions of Chapter 7.

a. Exceptions Based on Financial Situation or Pre-Bankruptcy Conduct

The Code also provides that the following debtors are not eligible for relief under Chapter 7 based on their *current financial situation* or *pre-bankruptcy conduct:*

(i) *an individual or a family farmer* who was a debtor in a case that was *dismissed in the preceding 180 days* because of the debtor's willful failure to obey court orders or to appear before the court, or because of the debtor's request for a voluntary dismissal of the case following a party's request for relief from the automatic stay;

(ii) *above-median income individual debtors with primarily consumer debts* who fail the "means test"; *and*

(iii) with certain limited exceptions, an *individual debtor* who has not obtained *credit counseling* during the *180 days* prior to seeking relief under the Bankruptcy Code.

2. Chapter 7 Trustee

Immediately after the order for relief, the United States trustee appoints a *disinterested member* of the panel of private trustees to serve as the interim trustee in a Chapter 7 case. Then, either a trustee is elected at the § 341 meeting or, as usually occurs, the interim trustee automatically becomes the permanent trustee in the case.

3. Meeting of Creditors

No earlier than 21 and no later than 40 days after the order for relief, the United States trustee convenes and presides at the § 341 meeting.

B. THE MEANS TEST

BAPCPA created a financial eligibility test for *individual Chapter 7 debtors with primarily consumer debts.* The *first step* of this new financial eligibility test is determining whether the individual debtor's income is *above or below the median income* for the debtor's household size in the state in which the debtor resides. The *means test,* which is the second step, only applies to *above-median income debtors.*

1. **The Below-Median Income Debtor**

   The Bankruptcy Code provides that there is no *presumption of abuse* for a *below-median income debtor.* The below median-income debtor's Chapter 7 case still may be dismissed, however, if the court determines that the *petition was filed in bad faith* or *the totality of the debtor's financial situation demonstrates abuse.*

2. **The Above-Median Income Debtor**

   An above-median income debtor must do the *means test* in order to determine whether the debtor's filing for relief under Chapter 7 creates a *presumption of abuse.* If there is no presumption of abuse, then the debtor's case may be dismissed only if it was *filed in bad faith* or if the *totality of the debtor's financial situation demonstrates abuse.*

3. **Above or Below Median?**

   All *individual* debtors must determine their *current monthly income,* because this figure determines the debtor's income status as above or below median. *Current monthly income* is the debtor's *average monthly income from all sources* that the debtor receives during the *six-month period* prior to filing for bankruptcy. The six-month period *ends on the last day of the calendar month immediately preceding* the filing of the bankruptcy case.

4. **Above-Median Income Debtors and the Chapter 7 Means Test**

   To determine whether there is a presumption of abuse, the above-median income debtor subtracts her *monthly expenses* from her *current monthly income.* The debtor then multiplies the *difference by 60* and compares the *product* with the following numbers.

   a. **$8,175:** If the *product is less than $8,175,* then the debtor's filing for relief under Chapter 7 *does not create* a *presumption of abuse.*

   b. **$13,650:** If the *product is greater than $13,650,* then there is a *presumption of abuse.*

   c. **$8,175 ≥ product ≤ $13,650:** If the *product is greater than or equal to $8,175 but also less than or equal to $13,650,* then the debtor must conduct the *secondary abuse test.*

   (i) **Secondary Abuse Test**

   The *secondary abuse test* requires the debtor to compare the product *with* 25% of the debtor's non-priority unsecured claims. If the product *exceeds 25%* of the debtor's non-priority unsecured claims, then the presumption of abuse arises. If the product is *less than 25%* of the debtor's non-priority unsecured claims, then the presumption of abuse does not arise.

5. **Means Test Expenses**

   The means test allows the debtor to deduct from current monthly certain expenses based on *applicable national and local standards,* as well as the *actual amount* that she pays on her *secured debt.* A debtor also may deduct the *actual cost* of *other necessary expenses,* including amounts paid for *federal, state,* and *local taxes, life insurance, alimony, child support,* and *child care.* A debtor's monthly expenses may include *charitable contributions to any qualified religious or charitable entity or organization.*

C. DISTRIBUTION OF PROPERTY OF THE ESTATE

1. Order of Payment

a. Secured Creditors

If the Chapter 7 trustee sells collateral that secures a claim, the secured creditor is paid from the sale proceeds before there is any distribution to priority or general unsecured creditors.

b. Priority Claims

Unsecured claims entitled to priority under § 507 are paid before any distribution to the general unsecured creditors and are paid in the following order of priority provided by the Code:

(i) *administrative expenses of a trustee* to the extent that the trustee administers assets available for payment of *domestic support obligations;*

(ii) *domestic support obligations;*

(iii) *administrative expenses;*

(iv) *involuntary case gap* claims;

(v) *wages, salaries, or commissions;*

(vi) contributions to *employee benefit plans;*

(vii) claims of *grain farmers and United States fishermen;*

(viii) *consumer layaway* claims;

(ix) *unsecured pre-petition taxes;*

(x) *capital requirements of insured depository institution;* and

(xi) claims for *death or personal injury* resulting from *debtor's unlawful operation of a motor vehicle or vessel due to intoxication.*

c. General Unsecured Claims

After satisfying all priority unsecured claims, the Chapter 7 trustee pays allowed unsecured claims that are *timely filed* and *justifiably late-filed* claims.

d. Unexcused Tardy Claims

Allowed claims filed late without justification are paid after all timely filed and justifiably late-filed claims.

e. Penalty Claims

Next in the order of distribution are allowed unsecured or secured claims for *punitive, exemplary, or multiple damages,* or for *fines, penalties, or forfeitures* that do not constitute compensation for actual pecuniary loss.

f. Interest

If there are sufficient funds to pay all of the allowed claims above, then the Chapter 7 trustee will pay interest, at the legal rate, that accrued from the date that the petition was filed on all priority and general unsecured claims pursuant to § 726(a)(1)–(4).

g. Payment to Debtor

If there is any property of the estate left after payment of post-petition interest on the unsecured claims, it is distributed to the debtor.

2. Pro Rata Payment

The general rule is that priority creditors *within a class* share equally in any distribution.

a. Exceptions

(i) Domestic Support Obligations

There is a hierarchy of payment among first priority domestic support obligation claims. The trustee, if she administers assets to pay a domestic support obligation, is paid first, then a spouse, former spouse, or child of the debtor with a domestic support obligation claim, and finally, a governmental unit with a domestic support obligation assigned to it by a spouse, former spouse, or child of the debtor.

(ii) Conversion to Chapter 7

If a case is converted from Chapter 11, 12, or 13 to a case under Chapter 7, the administrative expense claims in the Chapter 7 case *after conversion* have priority over the administrative expenses incurred prior to conversion.

(iii) Super-priority: Inadequately Protected Secured Creditor

If adequate protection is furnished to a creditor whose claim is secured by a lien on the debtor's property, but the adequate protection ultimately proves to be deficient, the creditor will receive an administrative expense claim with *priority over all other administrative expenses* allowed against the debtor's estate.

(iv) Super Super-Priority: Post-Petition Credit

If the trustee or the debtor in possession is unable to obtain unsecured post-petition credit by means of an administrative expense priority, the court may approve new credit or debt with priority over all other administrative expense claims, *including* any super-priority claims arising from the failure of adequate protection.

D. TREATMENT OF CERTAIN LIENS IN A CHAPTER 7 CASE

1. Avoidance of Liens Securing Penalties

The trustee may *avoid a lien* securing the type of claim described in § 726(a)(4) for a fine, penalty, or forfeiture, or for punitive, multiple, or exemplary damages that do not constitute compensation for actual pecuniary loss.

2. Subordination of Tax Liens

The Code provides for the subordination of certain allowed tax claims that are secured by nonavoidable liens, *e.g.*, a perfected tax lien, on estate property. Before subordinating a tax lien on real or personal property, however, the Chapter 7 trustee must first *exhaust* the estate's *unencumbered assets* and recover from the property securing an allowed secured claim the *reasonably and necessary costs and expenses* of disposing of or preserving the property.

Note: With limited exceptions, the subordination rules do not apply to nonavoidable liens for ad valorem taxes on real or personal property.

E. PARTNERSHIP TRUSTEE'S CLAIM AGAINST GENERAL PARTNERS

If the estate of a Chapter 7 partnership debtor lacks sufficient property to fully satisfy all claims against the partnership, the **trustee** is entitled to a claim for the **deficiency** against any general partner who is personally liable, but only to the extent that the general partner is personally liable under applicable nonbankruptcy law.

F. CHAPTER 7 DISCHARGE

The effect of the discharge is to discharge the debtor from all debts that arose prior to the order for relief under Chapter 7, as well as from all debts that are treated under the Code as pre-petition debts. The discharge does not include particular debts that are not dischargeable under § 523. It is important to distinguish between **denial of the entire discharge** under § 727 and a determination under § 523 that a **specific debt is nondischargeable.**

1. Grounds for Denial of Discharge

a. Debtor Not an Individual

Under Chapter 7, only an individual may receive a discharge. Therefore, other persons, e.g., corporations and partnerships, are not granted a discharge.

b. Transfer of Property with Intent to Hinder, Delay, or Defraud Creditors

The debtor will be denied a discharge if with the **intent to hinder, delay, or defraud** a creditor or an officer of the estate entitled to possession of the property, she transferred, removed, concealed, mutilated, or destroyed **property of the debtor,** within **one year** before the filing of the petition, or **property of the estate,** after the petition was filed.

c. Destruction or Concealment of Books or Records

Another ground for denying a discharge to the debtor is her destruction, concealment, mutilation, falsification of, or failure to keep books, records, documents, or other recorded information from which her business transactions or financial state might be determined.

d. Perjury, Bribery, Extortion, and Other Fraudulent Acts

The bankruptcy court will deny a Chapter 7 debtor a discharge if she **knowingly and fraudulently** in or in connection with the bankruptcy case (i) makes a **false oath** or account; (ii) submits or uses a **false claim;** (iii) pays, offers, receives, or obtains money, property, or advantage or a promise of money, property or advantage for acting or forbearing to act, i.e., extortion or bribery, or an attempt at extortion or bribery; or (iv) **withholds any books, records, or other recorded information** concerning the debtor's property or finances from an officer of the estate who is entitled to possession.

e. Failure to Account for Loss of Assets

Another basis for denial of the debtor's discharge is her failure to adequately explain any **loss of assets** or deficiency of assets to meet her liabilities.

f. Violation of Court Order or Refusal to Respond to Material Question

The debtor will be denied a discharge if she (i) **refuses to obey a valid court order,** other than one directing the debtor to testify or to answer a material question; (ii) refuses, for a reason other than the appropriate use of the Fifth Amendment privilege against self-incrimination, to **testify or to answer a material question** that the bankruptcy judge has approved; or (iii) refuses, on the basis of the privilege against self-incrimination, to testify or to answer a judicially approved material question *after she has been granted immunity* regarding the privileged matter.

g. Acts Committed in Insider Case

The bankruptcy court may deny the Chapter 7 debtor a discharge if the debtor commits any act, either during *her bankruptcy case or within one year before the petition* was filed, described in § 727(a)(2)–(6) in connection with a separate *bankruptcy case regarding an insider.*

h. Prior Discharge Obtained Under Chapter 7 or Chapter 11

The bankruptcy court will deny a Chapter 7 debtor a discharge in her *current case* if she previously received a discharge in a Chapter 7 or a Chapter 11 case that was *commenced within eight years* before the date that the petition was filed in the current case.

i. Prior Discharge Obtained Under Chapter 12 or Chapter 13

Similarly, the bankruptcy court will deny a Chapter 7 debtor a discharge if she previously was granted a discharge in a Chapter 12 or a Chapter 13 case that was *commenced within six years* before the date of the filing of the petition in the *current case,* unless (i) all of the allowed unsecured claims in the earlier case were *paid in full; or* (ii) payments under the plan in the earlier case totaled *at least 70%* of the allowed unsecured claims, and the debtor's plan was *proposed in good faith and represented her best effort.*

j. Waiver

If the debtor has executed a court-approved written waiver of discharge after the Chapter 7 order for relief, a discharge will not be granted.

k. Failure to Complete Instructional Course

With limited exceptions, the debtor will be denied a discharge if post-petition she fails to complete an instructional course on personal financial management.

2. Delaying Entry of the Discharge

The bankruptcy court shall not grant a Chapter 7 debtor a discharge if the court finds, after notice and a hearing held *no more than 10 days* before the entry of the discharge, that *reasonable cause* exists to believe either that *§ 522(q)(1) may apply* to the debtor's case *or* that there is a proceeding pending in which the debtor may be found guilty of a *felony listed in § 522(q)(1)(A)* or liable for a *debt described in § 522(q)(1)(B).* While the new provision is situated in the Code's denial-of-discharge section, the section appears to merely *delay, not deny, the debtor's discharge.*

3. Revocation of Discharge

The Chapter 7 debtor's discharge may be revoked for any of the following reasons:

a. *the debtor obtained the discharge fraudulently,* and the party seeking revocation did not discover the fraud until after the discharge was granted;

b. *the debtor acquired or became entitled to acquire property* that would constitute property of the estate, and she *knowingly and fraudulently* failed to disclose this fact or to turn over the property to the trustee;

c. ***the debtor committed one of the acts of impropriety*** described in § 727(a)(6); or

   d. ***the debtor failed to satisfactorily explain*** (i) ***a material misstatement*** in an ***audit*** referred to in 28 U.S.C. § 586(f) *or* (ii) a ***failure to make available for inspection*** accounts, documents, financial records, papers, files and all other papers, things, or property belonging to the debtor that are requested for ***the audit*** referred to in 28 U.S.C. § 586(f).

G. CONVERSION

If a Chapter 7 case has not been converted from Chapter 11, 12, or 13, the debtor has an ***absolute nonwaivable right*** to convert the case from Chapter 7 to any of such other chapters at any time. Unless the debtor requests or consents to conversion, the court may ***not*** convert a Chapter 7 case to one under Chapter 12 or 13.

H. DISMISSAL

1. For Cause

Cause to dismiss a Chapter 7 case includes the following:

   a. the debtor is responsible for an ***unreasonable delay that is prejudicial to creditors;***

   b. the debtor has not paid ***certain fees or charges;*** or

   c. the debtor in a voluntary case has ***not filed a list of creditors and all schedules and statements*** required under § 521(a)(1) within ***15 days,*** or any extension granted by the court, after the petition was filed.

2. Abuse of Chapter 7

a. Means Test

If an ***individual Chapter 7 debtor with primarily consumer debts*** fails the "means test," then a presumption of abuse arises. In such a case, after notice and a hearing, the court, on its own motion or a motion by the Chapter 7 trustee, the United States trustee, the Bankruptcy Administrator in North Carolina or Alabama cases, or any party in interest, may dismiss the debtor's case.

b. Bad Faith or Totality of the Circumstances

In determining whether the filing of a Chapter 7 case ***by an individual debtor with primarily consumer debts*** constitutes abuse, the court must consider (i) whether the debtor ***filed*** the petition in ***bad faith;*** *or* (ii) whether the ***totality of the circumstances of debtor's financial situation*** demonstrates abuse.

3. Crime of Violence

The bankruptcy court may dismiss the case of an individual Chapter 7 debtor who has been convicted of a crime of violence or a drug trafficking crime if the victim of such crime moves for dismissal and the court determines that dismissal is in the best interest of the crime victim.

XIII. CHAPTER 11: REORGANIZATION

A. ELIGIBILITY FOR RELIEF

Relief under Chapter 11 is available to ***any person*** (individual, corporation, or partnership), who ***qualifies to be a debtor under Chapter 7,*** except for a stockbroker or a commodity broker. In addition, ***railroads are eligible*** for relief under special provisions of Chapter 11. An *individual consumer debtor* may file for relief under Chapter 11.

B. ADMINISTRATION OF CHAPTER 11 CASE

1. Creditors' Committees

The Bankruptcy Code provides that shortly after the order for relief, the United States trustee shall appoint a committee of unsecured creditors, usually consisting of those *persons,* willing to serve, that hold the *seven largest unsecured claims* against the debtor. While the Code uses the term "shall," it is not unusual for the United States trustee to be unable to find creditors willing to serve on the unsecured creditors' committee.

a. Creditors' Committee Membership

Membership is not limited to individuals. *Governmental units* generally are excluded from the definition of the term "person," but in certain circumstances *may be eligible* to serve on a Chapter 11 creditors' committee.

b. Additional Committees

The bankruptcy court, upon the request of a party in interest, may order the appointment of additional committees of creditors or equity security holders. The United States trustee appoints the committee.

c. Employment of Attorneys or Accountants

A creditors' committee or an equity security holders' committee may hire *attorneys, accountants, or other professionals* to represent or perform services for the committee. The committee's hiring decision must be made at a scheduled meeting attended by a *majority of the committee members* and *court approval* is required.

2. Debtor in Possession

Unless a trustee is appointed in the case, the *debtor in possession remains in possession* of the property of the estate and has all of the *rights, powers, and duties of a trustee, except* the right to compensation and the duty to investigate the debtor. Unless the court orders otherwise, upon the request of a party in interest and after notice and a hearing, the debtor *continues to operate its business.*

a. Employment of Professionals

Any attorney, accountant, or other professional employed by the debtor in possession must be a *disinterested* person and cannot hold or represent any interest that is *adverse* to the estate.

3. Appointment of Trustee

Normally, the debtor in possession is considered the most appropriate person to operate its business. Nonetheless, after the filing of the petition and prior to confirmation of a plan, a party in interest or the United States trustee may request and the court may order the appointment of a trustee (i) *for cause,* (ii) if the appointment is in the *interests of creditors,* equity security holders, and other interests of the estate, or (iii) if the bankruptcy court determines it is in the *best interests* of the creditors and the estate to appoint a trustee rather than *convert or dismiss* the case.

a. Mandatory Motion by United States Trustee

The United States trustee must move for the appointment of a Chapter 11 trustee if there are ***reasonable grounds to suspect*** that current members of the governing body of the debtor, e.g., the board of directors, the chief executive officer, or the chief financial officer, or members of the governing body who selected the CEO or CFO participated in ***actual fraud, dishonesty, or criminal conduct*** in managing the debtor or the debtor's public financial reporting. While the United States trustee must file a motion for appointment under such circumstances, the bankruptcy court is not required to appoint a Chapter 11 trustee.

b. Choosing a Trustee

If the court orders the appointment of a trustee, generally the United States trustee consults with parties in interest and then ***appoints*** a ***disinterested person,*** other than himself, subject to the court's approval. Alternatively, in cases other than railroad reorganizations, the Code provides for ***election*** of the trustee ***if*** a party in interest requests an election within ***30 days after the court orders appointment*** of a trustee.

4. Appointment of Examiner

In a Chapter 11 case in which the court has not ordered the appointment of a trustee, the court sometimes will order the appointment of an examiner, prior to confirmation of a plan, ***to investigate*** any charges of fraud, dishonesty, incompetence, misconduct, mismanagement, or irregularity on the part of the debtor's present or former management. The appointment is made by the United States trustee, who selects a ***disinterested person*** other than himself. The debtor in possession, however, retains the estate property and continues to operate the business.

5. Right to Be Heard

The ***Securities and Exchange Commission*** may raise, and may appear and be heard on, any issue in a Chapter 11 case. While the SEC may not appeal from any judgment or order, or decree entered in the case, it may join or participate in one brought by a true party in interest.

6. Claims and Interests

a. Proofs of Claims or Interests

In a Chapter 11 case, the court fixes and sends notice of a ***bar date*** that operates as a deadline for filing proofs of claims or interests. A claim or interest that is listed in the schedules filed by the debtor is deemed filed, for the scheduled amount, unless it is scheduled as disputed, contingent, or unliquidated.

b. Secured Claims

In a Chapter 11 case, both recourse and nonrecourse secured claims are treated as recourse claims for the purpose of allowance. A partially secured creditor may elect to have her claim in a Chapter 11 case treated as ***secured to the full extent that the claim is allowed,*** even though under § 506(a) it otherwise would be considered secured only up to the value of the collateral.

7. **Conversion or Dismissal**

   a. **Voluntary Conversion to Chapter 7**

      The debtor may convert a Chapter 11 case to Chapter 7 so long as (i) a Chapter 11 trustee has not been appointed; (ii) the case did not begin with the filing of an involuntary Chapter 11 petition; and (iii) the case was not involuntarily converted to Chapter 11, i.e., debtor did not request the conversion to Chapter 11.

   b. **Mandatory Conversion to Chapter 7 or Dismissal**

      With certain exceptions, the bankruptcy court, upon request of a party in interest, must dismiss a Chapter 11 case or convert it to Chapter 7, whichever is better for creditors and the estate, if the party in interest *establishes "cause"* for dismissal or conversion. The Code has a non-exhaustive list of *16 reasons* that constitute *sufficient cause* for dismissal or conversion, including *substantial or continuing loss to or diminution of the estate* and the absence of a *reasonable likelihood of rehabilitation, gross mismanagement of the estate,* and *failure to comply* with a *court order.*

   c. **Conversion to Chapter 12 or 13**

      The court may convert a Chapter 11 case to a Chapter 12 or 13 case *only if* (i) *the debtor requests the conversion;* (ii) the debtor has *not received a Chapter 11 discharge;* and (iii) if the debtor requests *conversion to Chapter 12,* the court finds that conversion is *equitable.*

C. **REJECTION OF COLLECTIVE BARGAINING AGREEMENTS**

The Code provides detailed rules that the debtor in possession or trustee must satisfy in order to reject a collective bargaining agreement. The rules are those contained at *§ 1113, not § 365,* of the Code. The debtor in possession may not unilaterally terminate or modify any terms of a collective bargaining agreement before compliance with the provisions set forth in § 1113.

D. **RETIREE BENEFITS**

Section 1114 of the Code provides procedural and substantive protections against a Chapter 11 company's *modification of retiree benefits.* The Code's provisions cover both union and non-union employees.

E. **THE DISCLOSURE STATEMENT AND CHAPTER 11 PLAN**

1. **The Disclosure Statement**

   After filing of the petition, the debtor or other plan proponent may not solicit acceptances or rejections of the plan unless they first have provided a plan (or plan summary) and a *written court-approved disclosure statement* to the holders of the claims or interests whose acceptances or rejections are being sought. Because the purpose of the disclosure statement is to provide information to creditors and equity security holders adequate to evaluate the plan, the Code requires that the disclosure statement contain sufficient information, under the circumstances, to enable a *hypothetical reasonable investor* typical of holders of claims or interests of the relevant class to make an *informed decision* to accept or reject the plan. *Note:* The Code contains special rules for small business cases.

2. **Filing a Plan**

   Unless a trustee has been appointed in the case, the *debtor* has the exclusive right to file a plan for the first *120 days after* the order for relief. A small business debtor has the exclusive right to file a plan for the first *180 days after* the order for relief.

3. **Classification of Claims or Interests**

   With the exception of administrative, gap, and tax claims, the Bankruptcy Code requires that a Chapter 11 plan classify the claims and the equity interests in the case.

   a. **"Substantially Similar" Claims or Interests**

      A claim or interest may be placed in a particular class only if it is substantially similar to the other claims or interests included in that class. The Code, however, does *not require* that all substantially similar claims be placed in the same class. While most courts generally allow separate classification of similar claims, there is an important exception: a plan proponent may not separately classify similar claims in an attempt to *gerrymander* the plan confirmation vote.

   b. **Administrative Convenience Claims**

      A plan proponent may create a separate class of *unsecured claims* with a value less than or reduced to an amount that the court approves as reasonable and necessary for *administrative convenience.*

   c. **Secured Claims**

      Usually, if secured creditors' liens are in different property or are entitled to different priorities in the same property, each secured claim should be placed alone in a separate class.

   d. **Priority Claims**

      Administrative expenses, involuntary case gap claims, and unsecured, pre-petition tax claims are *excepted* from the requirement of classification because the standards for confirmation require that the plan provide for such claims on an individual, as opposed to a class, basis. However, *first, fourth, fifth, sixth, seventh, ninth, and tenth priority claims* should be placed in separate classes together with claims of equal priority.

   e. **Interests**

      Equity interests in a sole proprietorship, a partnership, or a corporation must be classified separately from creditors' claims. Furthermore, common stock and preferred stock interests should be placed in different classes.

4. **Contents of Plan: Mandatory Provisions**

   All Chapter 11 plans must do the following:

   a. *classify all claims and interests,* other than priority claims for administrative expenses, involuntary case gap claims, or eighth priority taxes;

   b. specify any class that is *not impaired;*

   c. *describe the treatment* to be accorded *any impaired class;*

   d. *treat every claim or interest within a particular class identically,* unless a holder consents to less favorable treatment;

   e. *establish adequate ways to implement the plan;*

   f. *include, in the charter of a corporate debtor or successor,* or any corporation with which debtor *merged or was consolidated, a provision prohibiting the issuance of nonvoting stock,* and complying with certain other requirements concerning voting powers;

g. *provide for the selection of officers and directors* in a manner consistent with the interests of creditors and equity security holders and that does not violate public policy; and

h. *provide for payment,* in an *individual Chapter 11 case,* of debtor's post-petition earnings or future income *sufficient to execute the plan.*

5. **Contents of Plan: Permissive Provisions**

   In addition to the mandatory items described above, a plan *may:*

   a. *impair or leave unimpaired* any class of claims or interests;

   b. *assume, reject, or assign executory contracts or unexpired leases;*

   c. *settle or adjust any claim or interest* held by the debtor or the estate, or provide for the retention and enforcement of the claim or interest by the debtor, Chapter 11 trustee, or an appointed representative of the estate;

   d. *sell all or substantially all of the estate property,* and distribute the proceeds among claim and interest holders;

   e. *modify the rights of secured creditors or unsecured creditors, unless* the creditor's claim is secured solely by a security interest in real property constituting the *debtor's principal residence*; and

   f. *include any other appropriate measure* that is consistent with the provisions of the Bankruptcy Code.

F. **CONFIRMATION OF PLAN**

1. **Requirements for Confirmation of a Consent Plan**

   a. **Proponent Complies with Code Provisions**

      The proponent of the plan must comply with the applicable provisions of the Code, such as those requiring disclosure of adequate information and solicitation of acceptances.

   b. **Plan in Good Faith**

      The plan must be proposed in good faith and not by any means forbidden by law.

   c. **Payment for Services or Expenses Approved**

      The court must approve as reasonable all payments made by the plan's proponent, the debtor, or a person issuing securities or receiving property under the plan for services or expenses in or in connection with the Chapter 11 case or related to the plan, e.g., attorneys' fees.

   d. **Officers, Directors, Insiders Disclosed**

      The plan must disclose the *names and affiliations* of all individuals who, after plan confirmation, will serve as *officers, directors, or voting trustees* of the debtor, a successor to the debtor, or a debtor affiliate participating in a joint plan with the debtor. The plan proponent must also disclose the *names and proposed compensation of all insiders* who will be employed or retained by the reorganized debtor.

e. Rate Change Approved

If the debtor's rates are regulated by a governmental commission, that commission must approve any rate change proposed by the plan, or the proposed rate change must be expressly conditioned on such approval.

f. "Best Interests of Creditors Test" Met

Each holder of a claim or interest of an *impaired class* either must (i) *accept* the plan *or* (ii) *receive* under the plan property having a *present value,* as of the effective date of the plan, of *not less than the amount* that the holder would receive in a *Chapter 7 liquidation.*

g. All Impaired Classes Accept Plan

Each class of claims or interests must have *accepted* the plan *or be unimpaired* under the plan.

h. Administrative Expenses and Involuntary Gap Claims

The plan must provide for *payment in full in cash* on the effective date of the plan for each claim that is entitled to priority as an administrative expense or as an involuntary case gap claim, unless the holder of the claim consents to different treatment.

i. First, Fourth, Fifth, Sixth, and Seventh Priority Claims

Unless the holder of a particular claim consents to different treatment, the plan must provide the following treatment to *each holder* of a domestic support obligation claim, wage or commission claim, claim for contributions to an employee benefit plan, claim by a grain farmer or United States fisherman, or a claim for a consumer layaway.

(i) *If the class has accepted the plan,* each claimant is entitled to receive deferred cash payments having a present value, as of the effective date of the plan, equal to the allowed amount of her claim.

(ii) *If the class has rejected the plan,* each claimant must receive total payment of her claim, in cash, on the effective date of the plan.

j. Eighth Priority Tax Claims

Unless it consents to different treatment, each tax claimant entitled to eighth priority must receive *regular installment payments in cash:*

(i) having a present value, as of the effective date of the plan, equal to the allowed amount of the claim;

(ii) over a period of time that ends *no later than 5 years from the order for relief;* and

(iii) in a manner *no less favorable* than the plan's treatment—with the exception of a class of creditors under § 1122(b)—of the *most favored non-priority unsecured claim.*

k. Ninth and Tenth Priority Claims

The Code provides no special rules for the treatment of ninth or tenth priority claims.

l.   **At Least One Impaired Class of Claims Accepts Plan**

If the plan *impairs any class of claims,* then the plan must be accepted by *at least one class of claims* that is impaired, excluding any acceptances by insiders of the consenting class.

m.   **Plan Is Feasible**

The plan must be feasible, which means that confirmation of the plan is *not likely* to be followed by the *debtor's liquidation* or the need for *further financial reorganization.*

n.   **Bankruptcy Fees Paid**

All required bankruptcy fees were paid prior to the confirmation hearing, or the plan must provide that they will be paid on the effective date of the plan.

o.   **Retiree Insurance Benefits Protected**

The plan must provide for the continued payment of all retiree benefits at the level originally provided by the debtor unless (i) the debtor or trustee, if one is appointed, and the authorized representative of the recipients agree to a modification or (ii) the court orders the payments to be modified in accordance with § 1114.

p.   **Domestic Support Obligations**

In an individual Chapter 11 case, the debtor must have paid all *post-petition domestic support obligations* required by judicial or administrative order, or by statute. *Distinguish pre-petition domestic support obligations,* which are first-priority claims.

q.   **Disposable Income Requirement: Individual Cases**

If the holder of an *allowed unsecured claim objects* to confirmation of the *individual debtor's* plan, the bankruptcy court cannot confirm the plan unless it provides for either (i) payment of the *present value,* as of the plan's effective date, of such claim; or (ii) payment of the debtor's *projected disposable income* for the *longer* of (a) the five-year period starting when the plan's first payment is due or (b) the period of time during which payments are made under the plan.

r.   **Property Transfers**

Any transfer of property by a non-profit corporation or trust under the plan must be made in accordance with applicable nonbankruptcy law.

2.   **Cramdown**

A plan can be confirmed if all of the above requirements have been satisfied *except* the requirement that every class of claims or interests accept the plan or be unimpaired under the plan if the plan does *not unfairly discriminate* and *is fair and equitable* with respect to any dissenting impaired classes.

a.   **Unfair Discrimination**

The Code does not define "unfair discrimination" and provides no statutory guidance, as it does with the "fair and equitable" requirement. Most courts look at whether the Code provides a justification for the plan's disparate treatment.

b. Fair and Equitable

(i) Secured Claims

A plan satisfies the "fair and equitable" requirement with regard to a secured claim if it provides for (i) the creditor to *retain her lien* on the collateral for the allowed amount of the secured claim, and to receive payment in deferred *cash installments* that total at least the allowed amount of the secured claim and that have a *present value,* as of the effective date of the plan, of at least the value of the collateral; (ii) the creditor to receive the *indubitable equivalent* of her secured claim; *or* (iii) the collateral to be sold free and clear of the creditor's lien, with the *lien attaching to the proceeds* of the sale.

(ii) Unsecured Claims

A plan satisfies the "fair and equitable" requirement with regard to unsecured creditors if it (i) provides that *each creditor* in the class receive property having a *present value,* as of the effective date of the plan, equal to the allowed amount of her unsecured claim; *or* (ii) satisfies the *absolute priority rule,* which requires that no holder of a claim or an interest that is junior to the impaired unsecured class receive or retain any property on account of the junior claim or interest. The Supreme Court has not decided whether there is a *new value exception* to the absolute priority rule. Courts are divided as to whether Congress has repealed the absolute priority rule for cases involving *individual Chapter 11 debtors.*

(iii) Equity Interests

A plan is "fair and equitable" as to interests if (i) the plan provides that each interest holder *receive or retain property* having a *present value,* as of the effective date of the plan, equal to the allowed amount of any fixed liquidation preference or fixed redemption price to which the holder is entitled, or the value of her equity interest, *whichever is the greatest; or* (ii) no interest holder junior to the class receives or retains any property on account of her junior interest.

G. SMALL BUSINESS DEBTORS

1. Definition of a Small Business Debtor

A *small business debtor* is any person *engaged in commercial or business activities,* including any affiliated debtor, whose aggregate *noncontingent unliquidated secured and unsecured debts* are *$2,725,625 or less,* excluding debts owed to *affiliates or insiders,* on the petition filing date. A debtor is *not a small business debtor* if any of the following exclusions apply:

a. the debtor's *primary activity* is the business of *owning or operating real property* or activities incidental to such ownership or operation;

b. the United States trustee has appointed an *official committee of unsecured creditors;*

c. the United States trustee has appointed an *official committee of unsecured creditors* and the court has determined that the committee is *not sufficiently active and representative* to provide effective oversight of the debtor; or

d. the debtor is a member of a *group of affiliated debtors* with *aggregate noncontingent liquidated liabilities greater than $2,725,625,* excluding debts owed to insiders and affiliates.

2. **The Small Business Debtor's Disclosure Statement and Plan**

a. **Disclosure Statement**

If the court determines that a disclosure statement must be filed, then it must be filed *no later than 300 days after* the order for relief. The Bankruptcy Code's disclosure-statement requirements are more flexible for small compared with non-small business cases.

(i) The bankruptcy court may determine that a disclosure statement is not needed because the *plan provides adequate information.*

(ii) The bankruptcy court also may approve a disclosure statement submitted on *standard forms.*

(iii) The bankruptcy court may *conditionally approve* the disclosure statement subject to final approval at a hearing after notice, and the debtor may solicit votes on the plan based on a conditionally approved disclosure statement. The court may combine the final hearing on the disclosure statement with the hearing on plan confirmation.

b. **Plan Deadlines**

Unless the court grants an extension or for cause orders otherwise, the *small business debtor* has the exclusive right to file a plan for the first *180 days after* the order for relief. Unless the court grants an extension, the plan and disclosure statement, if any, must be filed no later than *300 days after* the order for relief. The bankruptcy court must confirm the small business debtor's plan *no later than 45 days after* the plan is filed, unless the time for confirmation is extended

H. **POST-CONFIRMATION MATTERS**

1. **Discharge**

Generally, unless the plan or the confirmation order provides otherwise, confirmation discharges the debtor from *all pre-confirmation debts,* as well as from debts arising from (i) the rejection of executory contracts or unexpired leases not assumed by the trustee or debtor in possession; (ii) the recovery of property by the trustee or the debtor under §§ 522, 550, or 553; and (iii) eighth priority tax claims that occasionally arise post-petition.

a. **Corporate and Artificial Entity Debtors**

A Chapter 11 discharge is not restricted to individual debtors, as in Chapter 7. Confirmation of a plan does not discharge a corporate debtor from any of the following:

(i) debts for *fraud* that are owed to a *domestic governmental unit;*

(ii) debts owed to a person as a result of an action filed against the United States government under 31 U.S.C. § 3721 *et seq.,* or any similar State statute; *or*

(iii) a *tax or customs duty* for which the debtor made a *fraudulent return* or *willfully attempted to evade or defeat.*

b. Individual Debtors

An individual Chapter 11 debtor normally does not receive a discharge upon plan confirmation. Instead, the debtor receives a discharge upon *completion of all payments under the plan.* A Chapter 11 discharge for an individual debtor does not include any debts that are *not dischargeable under § 523.*

2. Revocation of Confirmation Order

Within *180 days* after the entry of the order confirming the Chapter 11 plan, a party in interest may request that the order be revoked, but only on the ground that it was *procured by fraud.*

3. Exemption from Securities Laws

Generally, securities offered or sold by the debtor or its successor under a Chapter 11 plan in exchange for claims against or interests in the debtor or for administrative expense claims are *exempt from the registration requirements* of the 1933 Securities Act and from registration requirements in any state or local securities law.

4. Special Tax Provisions

The issuance, transfer, or exchange of a security *or* the making or delivery of an instrument of transfer under a *confirmed plan* may not be taxed under any law imposing a stamp tax or similar tax. This exemption does not apply to *pre-confirmation transfers.*

I. *MANVILLE*-TYPE TRUST/INJUNCTION

Section 524(g) of the Bankruptcy Code authorizes the bankruptcy court to order the type of trust/injunction used in the *Johns-Manville* case. Section 524(g) applies only to cases in Chapter 11 involving *asbestos-related liabilities* of the debtor when an indeterminable number of substantial future demands for payment necessitate use of the trust in order to deal equitably with claims and future demands.

XIV. CHAPTER 12: FAMILY FARMER OR FAMILY FISHERMAN

A. ELIGIBILITY

Chapter 12 relief is available only to *a family farmer or family fisherman with regular annual income,* and a family farmer or family fisherman with regular annual income is an individual, corporation, or partnership with annual income that is *sufficiently stable and regular* to permit the family farmer or family fisherman to make payments under a Chapter 12 plan. The Code's definition of a family farmer or a family fisherman includes certain *individuals,* or individuals and their spouses, and certain *corporations or partnerships.* The Code establishes debt ceilings for eligibility for Chapter 12; the ceiling for a family farmer is significantly higher than that for an individual Chapter 13 debtor.

1. Voluntary Petition

A case under Chapter 12 may be commenced only by the filing of a voluntary bankruptcy petition.

2. Multiple Petitions

A family farmer is *ineligible* for relief under Chapter 12 if the family farmer was a debtor in a case that was dismissed in the preceding 180 days (i) because of the family farmer's intentional failure to obey court orders or to appear before the court, or (ii) as a result of the family farmer's request for a voluntary dismissal of the case following a party's request for relief from the automatic stay.

B. PROPERTY OF THE ESTATE

Estate property is the same in a Chapter 12 case as in a Chapter 13 case. Ordinarily, a Chapter 12 debtor remains in possession of property of the estate unless otherwise directed by (i) a court order removing the debtor from possession, (ii) a provision in a confirmed plan, or (iii) the confirmation order. Furthermore, the Code expressly provides for a *Chapter 12 debtor in possession to continue to operate the farm or commercial fishing operation.*

C. THE PLAN

1. Filing a Plan

The debtor has the *exclusive right* to file a plan, even if he is not a debtor in possession. A Chapter 12 debtor must file a plan *within 90 days* after the order for relief, unless an extension is granted for cause for which the debtor should not justly be held accountable.

2. Plan Duration

With the exception of payments on certain long-term debts, payments under the *Chapter 12* plan may not extend beyond *three years,* unless the court for cause approves a longer time period. The court, however, may not approve a plan period that is longer than *five years.*

3. Mandatory Plan Provisions

With the following two exceptions, the mandatory provisions of a Chapter 12 plan are essentially the same as those under Chapter 13.

a. In a Chapter 12 case, the holder of a particular claim or interest may consent to less favorable treatment than others of the same class.

b. In a Chapter 12 case, the plan must provide for payment of a *claim owed to a governmental unit* that arises out of the *sale, transfer, exchange, or other disposition* of any farm asset used in the *debtor's farming operation.* The claim must be treated as *unsecured* and is not entitled to *priority.*

4. Permissive Plan Provisions

The provisions that may be included in a plan under Chapter 12 differ from those allowable in a Chapter 13 plan, as follows.

a. Modifying Rights

The power of a Chapter 12 debtor to modify the rights of secured or unsecured creditors is not subject to the exception found in Chapter 13 that prohibits modification of a *claim secured solely by a security interest in real property constituting the principal residence of the debtor.*

b. Sale or Distribution of Property

A Chapter 12 plan may propose to sell all or any part of estate property or distribute all or any part of estate property among entities having an interest in the property.

c. Payment of Secured Claims

A Chapter 12 plan may provide for secured creditors to be paid over a longer period than the three or five years referred to in § 1222(c). However, any such provision must be in conformity with Chapter 12's confirmation requirements.

5. **Confirmation Requirements: Secured Creditors**

The court cannot confirm the debtor's plan unless as to each allowed secured claim:

a. *the secured creditor accepts the plan;*

b. *the debtor surrenders the collateral* to the secured creditor; or

c. *the plan preserves the creditor's lien* on the collateral and provides for the distribution of *cash or other property* having a present value, on the effective date of the plan, of at least the amount of the creditor's allowed secured claim.

6. **Confirmation Requirements: Unsecured Creditors**

a. **Best Interests of Creditors**

As in a Chapter 13 case, the Chapter 12 plan must provide that *each unsecured creditor* holding an allowed claim will receive property having a *present value,* as of the effective date of the plan, that is not less than the amount he would receive for his claim in a case under Chapter 7 if the estate were liquidated on that date, taking into account the exemptions that would be available to the individual Chapter 12 debtor.

b. **Best Efforts**

If an unsecured creditor or the Chapter 12 trustee objects to confirmation of a plan, the bankruptcy court may not confirm the plan unless *one of the following three conditions* is met.

(i) **The plan provides for 100% payment of each unsecured claim.**

(ii) The debtor commits all of his *"projected disposable income"* to plan payments for three years or for any longer plan period approved by the court not exceeding five years.

(iii) The plan proposes to distribute *property whose present value* is equal to or greater than the debtor's *projected disposable income* for the relevant plan period.

D. DISCHARGE

A standard discharge under Chapter 12 differs significantly from a standard Chapter 13 discharge, in that *all debts that are nondischargeable under § 523(a) are not* discharged in a Chapter 12 case in which the debtor is an individual. In Chapter 12, the debts that are nondischargeable under a standard discharge are nondischargeable under a hardship discharge. The court may not grant a discharge to an individual Chapter 12 debtor unless it has found *no reasonable cause to believe* that *§ 522(q)(1) may apply* to the debtor *and* there is proceeding pending in which the debtor may be found guilty of a felony described in *§ 522(q)(1)(A)* or liable for a debt described in *§ 522(q)(1)(B).* While not clear, this provision regarding § 522(q) merely delays the entry of the discharge order.

E. CONVERSION OR DISMISSAL

The debtor has an absolute right to *convert the case to Chapter 7,* and this right cannot be waived. The debtor also has the *non-waivable right to dismiss the case* if it has not been converted earlier from Chapter 7 or Chapter 11. On the request of a party in interest, the court may *dismiss the case for cause.* The Code provides a non-exhaustive list of reasons that constitute "cause," including *gross mismanagement or unreasonable delay by the debtor* that is prejudicial to creditors, failure to *timely file* *a plan, **continuing loss** to or **diminution of** the Chapter 12 estate, and the **absence of a reasonable probability of rehabilitation,** and **material default** under a confirmed plan.*

XV. CHAPTER 13: INDIVIDUAL WITH REGULAR INCOME

A. ELIGIBILITY FOR RELIEF

An individual with regular income is defined as an "individual whose income is sufficiently stable and regular to enable such individual to make payments under a plan under Chapter 13, other than a stockbroker or a commodity broker." A Chapter 13 case may be commenced only by the filing of a voluntary petition.

B. CO-DEBTOR STAY

The filing of a Chapter 13 petition operates not only as a stay of actions against the debtor under § 362, but also as a stay against any civil action or other act by a creditor to collect a **consumer debt from an individual who has guaranteed or secured that debt** or who is otherwise **liable on that consumer debt with the debtor.** The co-debtor stay does not apply if (i) the Chapter 13 case has been **closed, dismissed, or converted to Chapter 7 or 11;** or (ii) the co-debtor's liability was incurred in the **ordinary course** of **his** business.

C. ADMINISTRATION OF CHAPTER 13 CASE

1. Chapter 13 Trustee

In regions where many Chapter 13 cases are filed, the United States trustee ordinarily appoints a qualified individual to serve as a **standing trustee.** Otherwise, the United States trustee appoints a disinterested person as the trustee for a particular case, or the United States trustee may serve as the trustee in the case.

2. Rights and Powers of Debtor

In a Chapter 13 case, the **debtor has the exclusive right** to use, sell, or lease estate property under §§ 363(b), (d), (e), (f), or (*l*). A debtor engaged in business is a **self-employed individual** who incurs trade credit in producing income from her business, which she is **entitled to operate unless the court orders otherwise.** Usually, a Chapter 13 debtor engaged in business also has the exclusive right to use, sell, or lease property in the ordinary course of business and to obtain credit.

3. Post-Petition Claims

Certain kinds of post-petition claims may be filed in a Chapter 13 case: (i) claims for **taxes** that become due during the pendency of the case, and (ii) claims for **consumer debts** incurred by the debtor after the order for relief for property or services that the debtor needs to carry out the plan.

4. Property of Estate

The Chapter 13 estate consists of (i) all property specified in § 541; (ii) all § 541 property acquired by the debtor post-petition, but before the earliest of the closing, dismissal, or conversion of the case; and (iii) all of the debtor's earnings from services performed post-petition, but before the earliest of the closing, dismissal, or conversion of the case. The **debtor retains possession** of all property of the Chapter 13 estate **unless a confirmed plan or confirmation order provides otherwise.**

5. Conversion or Dismissal

The debtor has an absolute right to **convert the case to Chapter 7,** and this right cannot be waived. The debtor also has the nonwaivable right to dismiss the case if it has not been converted earlier from Chapter 7, 11, or 12. Before a Chapter 13 plan is confirmed, the court may convert the case to **Chapter 11 or 12** upon a request by a party in interest (including the debtor) or the United States trustee. If the **debtor is a farmer,** a Chapter 13 case cannot be converted to Chapter 7, 11, or 12 **unless** the debtor requests conversion.

Upon a request by a party in interest or the United States trustee, the court, **for cause,** may **dismiss the case or convert it to Chapter 7,** whichever is better for creditors and the estate. The Code has a non-exhaustive list of what qualifies as "cause," including **unreasonable and prejudicial delay** on the part of the debtor, **failure to timely file a plan, a material default** under a confirmed plan, and **lack of good faith** in filing the Chapter 13 petition.

6. Filing Pre-Petition Tax Returns

If the debtor has not filed **tax returns** for any taxable period ending during the **four years prior to filing of the petition,** the debtor shall file those returns with the appropriate tax authorities no later than the day before the **date first scheduled for the § 341 meeting.**

D. CHAPTER 13 PLAN: CONTENTS AND CONFIRMATION

1. Filing a Plan

Only the **debtor** may file a Chapter 13 plan. She must file the plan with the **petition or within 14 days thereafter** (or within 14 days after conversion to Chapter 13), unless the court grants an extension for cause.

2. Requirements for Plan Confirmation

a. Plan Complies with Code Provisions

The plan must comply with the provisions of Chapter 13, as well as with the other applicable provisions of the Code.

(i) Full Payment of Priority Claims

With the exception of certain domestic support obligations, the plan must provide that all priority claims will be **paid fully in deferred cash payments,** unless a particular creditor consents to different treatment. The plan may provide for less than full payment of **domestic support obligations** that as of the filing of the petition had been assigned to a **governmental unit** or were owed directly to or recoverable by a governmental unit so long as the plan provides that all of the **debtor's projected disposable income** is applied to make plan payments for the **five-year period** starting when the first plan payment is due.

(ii) Plan Length

For a **below-median** income debtor, the Code provides for a **three-year** applicable commitment period. For an **above-median** income debtor, the applicable commitment period is **five years.** But, the Code also states that the plan may not provide for payments over a period that exceeds **five years.**

b. Fees Paid

All fees, charges, or amounts required to be paid prior to confirmation or by the plan must have been paid.

c. Plan Filed in Good Faith

The *plan* must be proposed in *good faith* and not by any means forbidden by law.

d. Best Interests of the Creditors

Each unsecured creditor must receive *property* whose *present value* at least equals what the creditor would receive in a *Chapter 7 liquidation case.*

e. Plan is Feasible

The plan must be *feasible,* which means that the bankruptcy court must find that the plan has a *reasonable chance of success.*

f. Debtor Filed for Bankruptcy in Good Faith

The debtor must have filed the *Chapter 13 petition in good faith. Note:* The debtor's Chapter 13 plan also must be proposed in good faith.

g. Domestic Support Obligations

Debtor must pay all *domestic support obligations* required by judicial or administrative order, or by statute, that came *due after filing* of the petition.

h. Tax Returns

Debtor must have filed all *pre-petition* federal, state, and local *tax returns.*

i. No Material Alteration of Certain Retirement Fund Loans

The Chapter 13 plan may *not materially alter* the terms of a loan taken by the debtor from certain *retirement plan.*

j. Payments to Chapter 7 Trustee in Converted Case

If the debtor's Chapter 7 case was converted to Chapter 13 or dismissed and re-filed under Chapter 13, then the Chapter 13 plan must provide for the payment of *unpaid but allowed compensation to the Chapter 7 trustee.* The Chapter 7 trustee must have been allowed compensation, which remained unpaid, due to the conversion or dismissal of the debtor's Chapter 7 case pursuant to § 707(b).

k. Treatment of Secured Creditors' Claims

The plan must satisfy *one of the following three* requirements for *each allowed secured claim:* (i) the secured creditor *accepted the plan;* (2) the debtor *surrendered the collateral;* or (3) the debtor *complied* with the Code's *cramdown requirements.*

(i) Cramdown

The debtor may *cram down* a non-consenting secured creditor's claim so long as the plan *preserves the creditor's lien* on the collateral and distributes to the creditor *cash or other property* with a *present value,* on the plan's effective date, of at least the *amount of the creditor's allowed secured claim.*

(ii) Cramdown Exception: The Hanging Paragraph

Most courts have held that if the hanging paragraph applies, then the creditor's **secured claim equals the amount that the debtor owes** the secured creditor, regardless of the actual value of the collateral. The hanging paragraph applies if the creditor has a **purchase-money security interest** (1) in a **motor vehicle** that the debtor **acquired for personal use** within **910 days** of filing for bankruptcy; or (2) in **any other thing of value** if the debt was incurred **within one year** of the bankruptcy filing.

(iii) Cramdown Exception: Debtor's Principal Residence

A Chapter 13 debtor cannot **strip down** an undersecured mortgage on the debtor's **principal residence** to the fair market value of the home, if the last payment on the secured creditor's claim is due after the final plan payment.

l. Treatment of Unsecured Creditors' Claims

The debtor's plan must satisfy the **best interests of the creditors** test and, if the trustee or an unsecured creditor objects to plan confirmation, the **projected disposable income** test.

(i) Best Interests of Creditors Test

The plan must provide that **each unsecured creditor** holding an allowed claim will receive property having a **present value,** as of the effective date of the plan, of **not less** than the amount he would **receive** for his claim in a **Chapter 7** case on that date, taking into account the exemptions that would be available to the debtor.

(ii) Projected Disposable Income Test

If the **trustee** or an **unsecured creditor** objects to the plan, then the bankruptcy court cannot confirm the plan unless the plan *either* (a) pays the unsecured creditor the **present value of its claim** *or* (b) provides that the debtor applies all of her **projected disposable income** during the **applicable commitment period** (three or five years), starting on the date of the first plan payment, to making plan payments to her unsecured creditors.

3. Permissive Provisions

a. Classification of Claims

The plan may specify various **classes of unsecured claims,** provided that it does not discriminate unfairly against any particular class.

b. Modification of Creditors' Rights

With the exception of the rights of a creditor whose claim is secured **solely** by a security interest in real property constituting the **debtor's principal residence,** the plan may **modify the rights of secured creditors or unsecured creditors,** e.g., by changing the size and timing of installment payments.

c. Long-Term Debts

If the debtor has a long-term secured or unsecured debt (payment is due after the due date of the final plan payment) in default, the Chapter 13 plan may provide for **curing the default** within a reasonable time and **maintaining payments** while the case is pending.

    d.   **Assumption or Rejection of Executory Contracts or Unexpired Leases**

The plan may provide for any previously unrejected executory contract or unexpired lease to be assumed, rejected, or assigned.

4. Modification of Plan

The debtor has the *exclusive right* to modify a plan *prior to confirmation.*

E. PAYMENTS

Unless the court orders otherwise, the debtor must begin making payments under a proposed plan no later than *30 days* after the earlier of the order for relief or the date that the plan is filed. The debtor must remit *plan payments* to the trustee *except* the debtor (i) *directly pays a lessor* for scheduled post-petition payments on a lease of personal property, and (ii) makes *adequate protection* payments directly to a creditor with a *PMSI in personal property* but only with respect to the post-petition obligation.

1. Administrative Expenses

Prior to or concurrent with each payment to creditors under a Chapter 13 plan, the trustee is required to pay any *unpaid administrative expenses or bankruptcy fees or charges,* as well as the percentage fee set for a standing trustee, if one has been appointed.

F. POST-CONFIRMATION MATTERS

1. Effects of Confirmation

A confirmed plan *binds the debtor and every creditor,* regardless of whether a creditor has accepted or rejected the plan or has objected to confirmation of the plan, or whether the creditor's claim is provided for by the plan.

2. Post-Confirmation Modification

The debtor, the trustee, or an unsecured creditor may request a modification of a plan at any time after it has been confirmed but before all payments have been made. Generally, a request for post-confirmation modification of a plan occurs under circumstances in which the income or expenses of the debtor have *changed materially and unexpectedly.* The modification cannot result in a plan that provides for payments for a period longer than five years.

3. Revocation of Confirmation Order

Within *180 days after an order confirming* a Chapter 13 plan has been entered, a party in interest may request that the order be revoked on the ground that it was *procured by fraud.*

4. Debtor's Failure to Make Payments

If the debtor fails to make all payments under the plan, a party in interest or the United States trustee may move for dismissal of the case or conversion to Chapter 7. Alternatively, the debtor may request a hardship discharge if the circumstances warrant.

G. DISCHARGE

A standard Chapter 13 discharge includes all debts that are provided for by the plan or that have been disallowed by the court. Unless the debtor has executed a court-approved written waiver of discharge subsequent to the order for relief, the debtor will be granted a discharge under Chapter 13 *after* she has made *all payments* under the plan, and *certified* that she has *paid all domestic support obligations* required by *judicial or administrative order, or by statute* and due prior to the date of the certification.

1. Cases to Which Discharge Does Not Apply

a. Instructional Course

With certain limited exceptions, a Chapter 13 debtor will not receive a discharge if she fails to complete the *instructional course on personal financial management* mandated by the Code.

b. Prior Bankruptcy Case

The debtor will not receive a discharge in her current Chapter 13 case if she received a discharge in a case filed under *Chapters 7, 11, or 12* during the *four years prior to the filing* of her current Chapter 13 case. The debtor will not receive a discharge in her current Chapter 13 case if she received a discharge in a case filed under *Chapter 13* during the *two years* prior to the filing of her current Chapter 13 case. The time period runs from the *filing date* of the prior case to the *filing date* of the current Chapter 13 case.

c. Exemption Issue Under § 522(q)

The bankruptcy court may not grant a discharge unless it has determined, after notice and a hearing held *no more than 10 days* before the discharge order that there is *no reasonable cause to believe* that (i) the Code's limitation on state-law exemption rights pursuant to § 522(q)(1) may apply to the debtor, and (ii) there is a pending proceeding in which the debtor may be found guilty of one of the *felonies listed in § 522(q)(1)(A) or* liable for a *debt described in § 522(q)(1)(B).* This provision of the Code should operate to *delay* rather than *permanently deny* the debtor a discharge.

2. Nondischargeable Debts

a. Long-Term Debts

Debts for which the last payment is due after the due date of the final payment required by the Chapter 13 plan are not dischargeable, if the plan provides for curing any default within a reasonable time and maintaining payments while the case is pending.

b. Certain Taxes

The following types of taxes are not dischargeable:

(i) a tax required to be collected or withheld and for which the debtor is liable in any capacity;

(ii) a tax for which a *return, or equivalent report or notice,* if required, was *not filed or given or* was filed or given but *after the date on which it was due and* within the *two year-period prior to filing* of the bankruptcy petition; or

(iii) a tax for which the debtor either made a *fraudulent return or willfully attempted* to *evade or defeat* the tax.

c. Fraud

Debts for money, property, services, or extensions, renewals, or refinancing of credit obtained by *fraud, consumer debts* exceeding *$725* incurred within *90 days* of bankruptcy for *luxury goods,* or *cash advances* exceeding *$1,000* obtained within *70 days* of bankruptcy are not dischargeable.

d. **Unscheduled Debts**

Debts that the debtor did not *list or schedule* in time for the creditor to *timely file a proof of claim* are not dischargeable, unless the creditor had *notice or actual knowledge* in time to make a timely filing.

e. **Section 523(a)(2), (4), and (6)**

Debts that are potentially nondischargeable under *§ 523(a)(2), (4), or (6),* and that the debtor neither *listed nor scheduled* in time for the creditor to *timely file a proof of claim* and *timely request a determination of dischargeability* are not dischargeable, unless the creditor had *notice or actual knowledge* in time to make a timely filing.

f. **Embezzlement**

Debts owed for *embezzlement, larceny,* or *fraud or defalcation in a fiduciary capacity* are not dischargeable.

g. **Domestic Support Obligations**

Domestic support obligations are not dischargeable. *Debts for support* owed under state law to a *state or municipality* that are enforceable under the Social Security Act are not dischargeable.

h. **Student Loans**

Unless excepting the debt from discharge will constitute an *undue hardship* on the debtor and her dependents, *student loan debt* is not dischargeable.

i. **Certain Personal Injury Debts**

Liability for death or personal injury caused by the debtor's operation of a *motor vehicle, vessel, or aircraft* while *intoxicated* from using *alcohol, drugs, or another substance* is not dischargeable.

j. **Restitution**

A debt for *restitution,* or a *criminal fine,* that is included in the debtor's sentence for *conviction of a crime* is not dischargeable. A debt for *restitution* or *damages awarded in a civil action* against the debtor as a result of *willful* or *malicious injury* that caused *death or personal injury* also is nondischargeable.

k. **Certain Consumer Debts**

Post-petition consumer debts for property or services necessary for the debtor to perform the plan are not dischargeable, if the corresponding claims were allowed, and if the trustee's prior approval to incur the debt was practicable but was not obtained.

3. **Hardship Discharge**

Under certain conditions, the debtor may receive a hardship discharge. A Chapter 13 hardship discharge includes the unsecured debts that discharged under a standard Chapter 13 discharge, *except* the following:

(i) debts that are *nondischargeable under § 523(a);*

(ii) *Health Education Assistance Loans ("HEAL")* not meeting the three conditions for discharge under the applicable federal nonbankruptcy statute;

(iii) *long-term debts* provided for under *Chapter 13's cure provision;* and

(iv) *post-petition consumer debts for property or services necessary for the debtor to perform the plan,* if the corresponding claims were allowed, and if the trustee's prior approval to incur the debt was practicable but was not obtained.

4. **Revocation of Discharge**

The court may revoke a Chapter 13 discharge that was *obtained by the debtor's fraud* if the party in interest seeking the revocation *did not discover* the fraud until *after the discharge* was awarded. The party seeking revocation must make its request for revocation no later than *one year* from the *date the discharge was granted.*

Approach to Exams

Your bankruptcy law professor likely will test you on many of the topics summarized below. Take into consideration the following questions and reminders when analyzing and writing your exam answers.

A. Is the debtor *eligible for relief* under a particular chapter of the Bankruptcy Code? [B.C. § 109]

    1. If the debtor is an individual, has the debtor received counseling from an approved nonprofit budget or credit counseling service in the *180 days prior* to filing for bankruptcy? [B.C. § 109(h)]

    2. Make certain that if creditors want to file an *involuntary petition* against the debtor that they file under a chapter that permits involuntary filings and the debtor is a person against whom an involuntary petition may be filed. [B.C. § 303]

B. After the filing of a bankruptcy petition, has any act been committed that violates the *automatic stay?* [B.C. § 362(a)]

    1. Does the act come within one of the *exceptions* to the stay? [B.C. § 362(b)]

    2. Have any secured creditors requested *relief from the automatic stay,* and should such relief be granted?

        a. Has *adequate protection* been provided as required by the Code?

        b. Does the debtor have *equity* in the collateral, and is the property *necessary for an effective reorganization?* [B.C. § 362(d)]

C. If *professional persons,* such as attorneys or accountants, have been employed in the case, has their employment been approved by the court *before* the rendering of professional services? Are they *disinterested persons* who do *not have an interest adverse* to the estate?

D. What *property* comprises the bankruptcy *estate?*

    1. Make sure to consider the different treatment of *post-petition earnings* for individual debtors under the various chapters of the Code. [B.C. §§ 1115, 1207, 1306]

    2. Is there any property in the possession of third parties that is subject to *turnover?*

    3. Are there any transactions that can be *avoided* by the trustee or the debtor in possession, as a result of which additional property can be *recovered* to enlarge the estate for the benefit of creditors?

    4. Is there any property that is burdensome or of inconsequential value to the estate and that may be *abandoned* by the trustee?

E. From the *debtor's* perspective:

    1. Has the debtor filed all *lists, schedules, and statements* that are required?

        a. What is the *connection* between the individual debtor's failure to file or perform her *intention with regard to debts secured by personal property* and lifting of the *automatic stay?* [B.C. §§ 362(h), 521(a)(2), (6)]

2. What *exemptions* are available to an individual debtor under the Code or under applicable nonbankruptcy law? Has the applicable state law *opted out* of the federal exemption scheme?

3. If the debtor takes the *state exemptions*, has the debtor been *domiciled* in the state in which she filed her petition for *730 days* prior to filing for bankruptcy? If not, which state exemptions apply to her case? [B.C. § 522(b)(3)]

4. Do any of the *"mansion loophole" exemption limitations* enacted by BAPCPA apply to debtor's case? [B.C. §§ 522(o), (p), (q)]

5. Does the debtor want to *reaffirm* any debts? [B.C. § 524]

6. Does an individual Chapter 7 debtor want to *redeem* any property? [B.C. § 722]

7. Is the debtor entitled to a *discharge* under the applicable chapter?

8. If the debtor is an individual, are there any *particular debts* that will be *non-dischargeable?* [B.C. §§ 523(a), 1328(a)]

F. What *claims or interests* have been filed in the case? Are they (i) secured claims, (ii) unsecured priority claims, (iii) general unsecured claims, (iv) subordinated claims, or (v) owners' interests?

1. Is there a basis for objecting to the *allowance* of a claim or interest that has been filed?

   a. Does the Code impose limitations on the amount of the claim, e.g., damages for long-term leases? [B.C. § 502(b)(6)]

2. Is a particular claim *fully secured?* If not, remember that an undersecured claim generally is *bifurcated,* resulting in two claims—one that is secured up to the value of the collateral and the other that is unsecured for the amount of the deficiency. [B.C. § 506(a)(1)]

   a. Is the claim secured by *personal property* owned by an *individual* in a *Chapter 7 or 13* case? If so, remember the rules for determining the value of personal property under § 506(a)(2).

3. Is the creditor entitled to *interest* on its claim post-petition and prior to confirmation of a plan in Chapter 11, 12, or 13? [B.C. § 506(b)]

4. How much will each holder of a claim or interest receive on *final distribution* in a Chapter 7 case, or pursuant to a *confirmed plan* in a case under Chapter 11, 12, or 13?

   a. What is the order of payment of priority unsecured claims in a Chapter 7 case? [B.C. § 507(a)]

   b. What treatment does the Code require the debtor provide to priority unsecured creditors under a Chapter 11, 12, or 13 plan? [B.C. §§ 1129(a)(9), 1222(a)(2), 1322(a)(2)]

G. Has *adequate protection* been provided when required by the Code? [B.C. §§ 362(d)(l), 363(e), 364(d)(1)(B)]

1. What is the connection between a *failure of adequate protection* and *priority claim* status? [B.C. § 507(b)]

H. On the *use, sale, or lease* of property:

1. If the property to be used, sold, or leased is *cash collateral*, has the trustee or debtor in possession obtained *consent* of the party with the interest in the cash collateral or *court authorization* after notice and a hearing? [B.C. §§ 363(a), (c)]

2. If the property to be used, sold, or leased is *personally identifiable information about an individual,* has the trustee or debtor in possession satisfied the Code's requirements for such use, sale, or lease? [B.C. § 363(b)]

3. Under what circumstances may a trustee or debtor in possession sell property *free and clear* of the interest of any other entity in the property? [B.C. § 363(f)]

4. What is *credit bidding?* [B.C. § 363(k)]

I. Does the debtor have any unexpired leases or executory contracts?

1. Did the trustee or debtor in possession act within the *Code's time frames* to assume or reject any unexpired lease or executory contract? [B.C. § 365(d)]

2. If the trustee or debtor in possession plans to assume an unexpired lease or executory contract, has the trustee or debtor in possession satisfied the Code's *requirements for assumption,* such as cure of defaults and adequate assurance of future performance? [B.C. § 365(b)]

3. Is the executory contract or unexpired lease one that the trustee or debtor in possession *cannot assign* if assumed? [B.C. § 365(c)]

J. Under *which chapter* of the Code has the case been filed?

1. If it is a **Chapter 7 case:**

   a. Is the debtor an *above- or below-median* income debtor? If an above-median income debtor, does debtor pass the *"means test"?* [B.C. § 707(b)(2)] *Remember:* if debtor fails the means test, she is not eligible for Chapter 7 unless she can rebut the presumption of abuse.

   b. Are there other grounds, besides the means test, for *dismissing* debtor's Chapter 7 case? [B.C. § 707(b)(3)]

   c. Do grounds exist for *converting* the case to another chapter of the Code, if the debtor is eligible for relief under that chapter? [B.C. § 706]

   d. Are there any grounds for *denying the debtor a discharge* under § 727(a)?

2. If it is a **Chapter 11 case:**

   a. Has the debtor in possession sought to obtain *post-petition credit* or DIP financing? Does the lender require certain *controversial provisions,* e.g., cross collateralization or roll-ups, in the loan agreement? [B.C. § 364]

   b. Is there a reason to request the *appointment of a trustee* to replace the debtor in possession? If not, is it appropriate to request the *appointment of an examiner?*

   c. If a trustee has not been appointed, has the debtor filed a plan within the *exclusivity period*? **Remember:** there are different exclusivity periods for non-small business and small business debtors. [B.C. § 1121(b), (e)]

   d. Is the debtor a *small business debtor?* If so, did the debtor propose its plan within *300 days* of filing the petition? [B.C. § 1121(e)]

   e. Is the debtor an *individual?*

      (i) If the plan does not propose to pay unsecured creditors in full and an unsecured creditor objects to confirmation, does the plan satisfy the *projected disposable income* test of § 1129(a)(15)?

      (ii) If the debtor must obtain confirmation of her plan under the unsecured cramdown provisions of the Code, does she live in a jurisdiction that has adopted the *narrow* or the *broad interpretation of the absolute priority rule?* [B.C. § 1129(b)]

    f. Does the debtor's proposed plan include the *mandatory* Chapter 11 plan *provisions?* [B.C. § 1123(a)] Which *permissive provisions* are appropriate to include in the plan? [B.C. § 1123(b)]

    g. How are the claims and interests *classified?*

    h. Which classes are *impaired or unimpaired?* [B.C. § 1124]

    i. Has the court approved the *disclosure statement* concerning the proposed plan? [B.C. § 1125] How do the disclosure statement requirements differ for *small business debtors?* [B.C. § 1125(f)]

    j. Which classes of claims or interests have *accepted or rejected* the plan? [B.C. § 1126]

    k. Can the plan be *confirmed?*

        (i) Are all of the requirements of § 1129(a) satisfied?

        (ii) If all of the requirements of § 1129(a) are met *except* § 1129(a)(8), can the plan be confirmed by *cramdown* under § 1129(b)? Does the plan *not unfairly discriminate* and is the plan *fair and equitable* with respect to any dissenting impaired classes?

3. If it is a Chapter 12 case:

    a. Does the debtor come within the Code's definition of a *family farmer or family fisherman?* [B.C. § 101(18), (19A)]

    b. Is the debtor continuing to operate the farm or fishing operation? Is there a ground for *removal* of the debtor in possession and replacement by the Chapter 12 trustee?

    c. If *adequate protection* is required, does it satisfy § 1205?

    d. Does the debtor's proposed plan include the *mandatory* Chapter 12 plan *provisions?* [B.C. § 1222(a)] Which *permissive provisions* are appropriate to include in the plan? [B.C. § 1222(b)]

    e. Does the plan satisfy the *requirements for confirmation* under § 1225?

        (i) If the plan does not propose to pay unsecured creditors in full and an unsecured creditor objects to confirmation, does the plan satisfy the *projected disposable income* test of § 1225(b)?

4. If it is a Chapter 13 case:

    a. Have any creditors sought relief from the *co-debtor stay,* and should such relief be granted?

    b. Has the debtor begun making *payments within 30 days* after the plan is filed?

    c. Does the debtor's proposed plan include the *mandatory* Chapter 13 *plan provisions?* [B.C. § 1322(a)] Which *permissive provisions* are appropriate to include in the plan? [B.C. § 1322(b)]

    d. Does the plan satisfy the *requirements for plan confirmation* under § 1325?

        (i) If the plan does not propose to pay unsecured creditors in full and an unsecured creditor objects to confirmation, does the plan satisfy the *projected disposable income* test of § 1325(b)?

(ii) Does the **length of debtor's plan** correspond to the debtor's status as an above- or below-median income debtor? [B.C. § 1325(b)(4)]

(iii) Does the debtor have any creditors with **"hanging paragraph"** claims? If so, does the plan pay these creditors the full amount of the debt owed? [B.C. § 1325(a)(9) hanging paragraph]

e. Which debts are **dischargeable** under a standard Chapter 13 discharge? [B.C. § 1328] How does the standard discharge in Chapter 13 differ from that under Chapter 7?

Introduction

Welcome to the study of bankruptcy law. Congress enacted the Bankruptcy Code in 1978 in a major overhaul of U.S. bankruptcy law. In 2005, Congress made significant changes to the Code with the passage of the Bankruptcy Abuse Prevention and Consumer Protection Act. ("BAPCPA")

This study guide follows the basic organizational structure of the Code, as amended by BAPCPA. With the exception of Chapter 12, the Code is divided into odd-numbered chapters. With certain limited exceptions, Chapters 1, 3, and 5 of the Bankruptcy Code apply to all filing chapters of the Code. Chapter 1 contains general provisions, such as definitions. Chapter 3 deals with case administration; its provisions range from those on the compensation of professional persons to those on the automatic stay. Chapter 5 provides rules on matters such as creditor claims, property of the estate, and the avoiding powers.

The filing chapters of the Code are Chapters 7, 9, 11, 12, 13, and 15. Chapter 7 is the liquidation chapter. Chapter 9 is for municipal bankruptcies. Chapter 11 is known as the business reorganization chapter, but individual consumer debtors may file for relief under Chapter 11. Chapter 12 is the reorganization chapter for family farmers and family fishermen. Chapter 13 is limited to individuals and is a reorganization chapter in which debtors pay their creditors over either three or five years. Finally, Chapter 15 is the chapter for cross-border insolvency cases. This study guide does not cover Chapters 9 or 15.

The Code is dense and complex, so there are numerous examples throughout the text to help you to understand the concepts. This study guide also includes more than 130 *yes/no* questions and several short-answer essay questions at the end to test your understanding of the material.

Bankruptcy is an exciting area of law. I hope that this guide makes your study of the Code more enjoyable.

Bankruptcy

Chapter One

Introduction

CONTENTS	PAGE

Chapter Approach

Success on your bankruptcy law examination requires a thorough understanding of the provisions of the Bankruptcy Code in light of the interests that the statute was designed to protect. It is important for you to study the Code language in its bankruptcy context, keeping in mind the definitions in § 101 of the Code as well as certain rules of construction. You must understand the Code's organizational structure, the kinds of relief available under the various chapters, and the manner in which the sections of different chapters interrelate. Finally, you should know the various participants in the bankruptcy case and the different roles that they play, e.g., trustee versus United States trustee, as well as the rules governing bankruptcy petition preparers, who do not participate in the case but prepare documents for filing for a fee.

A. Goals of the Federal Bankruptcy Laws

1. Fresh Start

Bankruptcy is designed to relieve the honest debtor of his debts and to provide him the opportunity for a fresh start financially.

e.g. **Example:** Debtor worked in a manufacturing plant. Recently, he lost his job due to the closing of the factory. Shortly thereafter, he contracted cancer and, after a long bout, recovered. His medical expenses totaled $500,000, he had limited assets and no health insurance, and his only savings account was exhausted. Judgments were obtained against Debtor for $500,000. Debtor then filed a voluntary bankruptcy petition. Were it not for the protection of the bankruptcy laws, Debtor probably would be burdened for the rest of his life by these debts. The Bankruptcy Code, however, allows him to discharge his indebtedness and protects him against harassment by creditors and future actions to collect the amounts owed. While bankruptcy still affords debtors the opportunity for a "fresh start," the Bankruptcy Abuse Prevention and Consumer Protection Act of 2005 ("BAPCPA") made the debtor's decision to file for bankruptcy more complicated than it was prior to BAPCPA's enactment.

2. Forum for Creditors

Creditors also benefit from the establishment of a forum in which there will be either an orderly liquidation of the debtor's estate or a judicially scrutinized plan to partially or fully repay creditors over time. Unsecured creditors are protected from acts such as selective repayment of particular creditors shortly before bankruptcy and fraudulent transfers of the debtor's property. Secured creditors are ensured that their interest in collateral will be adequately protected under certain statutorily defined circumstances.

B. Legislative History

1. Bankruptcy Act

Article 1, Section 8 of the United States Constitution empowers Congress to enact uniform laws on bankruptcy. Under this grant of authority, Congress passed the Bankruptcy Act of 1898 (the "Act"), which the Chandler Act of 1938 substantially amended. [Bankruptcy Act of

1898; Pub. L. No. 75–696 (1938)] Under the Act, the bankruptcy court had *summary jurisdiction,* which meant that it had jurisdiction over the debtor, administration of the estate, and any property in the actual or constructive possession of the court. The Act, however, gave concurrent jurisdiction to the bankruptcy court and state courts for *plenary proceedings,* e.g., disputes about property in the hands of a third party. [H.R. Rep. No. 95–595, at 44 (1977)] Moreover, the bankruptcy court could exercise its jurisdiction over *plenary matters only with consent* of the adverse party. Therefore, the bankruptcy court had no jurisdiction over property in the possession of a third person who had an adverse claim to the property, unless the third party *consented* to the bankruptcy court's jurisdiction. The result was time-consuming litigation about what "constitute[d] adequate possession to give the bankruptcy court jurisdiction and what constitute[d] adequate consent." [H.R. Rep. No. 95–595, at 43 (1977)] The consent requirement also meant that much of the litigation involving property outside of the bankruptcy court's in rem jurisdiction could occur only in the United States district court, under its *plenary jurisdiction,* or in the various state courts. [*See* H.R. Rep. No. 95–595, at 44 (1977) (noting that "a considerable part of a trustee's litigation to recover assets of the estate must be initiated in some court other than the bankruptcy court")] Consequently, the potential number of forums with jurisdiction over issues arising in or related to any single bankruptcy case generally proved to be unduly burdensome and expensive and, as a practical matter, often precluded a trustee's actions to recover property for the benefit of the estate and ultimately for creditors. Moreover, unnecessary and costly litigation regarding which court had proper jurisdiction frequently delayed the efficient administration of bankruptcy cases. [*See* H.R. Rep. No. 95–595, at 45–46 (1977)]

2. Bankruptcy Code

The Bankruptcy Reform Act of 1978 repealed the Bankruptcy Act of 1898, and created the Bankruptcy Code, which became effective on October 1, 1979. [11 U.S.C. §§ 101 *et seq.* (hereafter "B.C.")] The Bankruptcy Code made sweeping substantive changes to the system established under the Bankruptcy Act. The Code substantially expanded the jurisdiction of the bankruptcy court to enable the bankruptcy judge to hear practically all matters arising in or related to the bankruptcy case, thereby eliminating some of the logistical problems of litigation under the Bankruptcy Act. Furthermore, the Code created the United States trustee system to perform the administrative functions previously performed under the Act by bankruptcy judges. Thus, under the Code, bankruptcy judges perform judicial functions while case administration is left to the United States trustees. [*See* H.R. Rep. No. 95–595, at 88–91, 100–102 (1977)] *Note:* The laws concerning jurisdiction are contained in title 28 of the United States Code (Judiciary and Judicial Procedure), not in title 11 (Bankruptcy Code).

3. The *Marathon* Case

In 1982, the United States Supreme Court, in a plurality decision, ruled that the grant of jurisdiction to the bankruptcy courts under the Bankruptcy Reform Act of 1978 was unconstitutional. [**Northern Pipeline Construction Co. v. Marathon Pipe Line Co.,** 458 U.S. 50 (1982) (plurality opinion) (finding that the Bankruptcy Reform Act had vested all the " 'essential attributes' of the judicial power of the United States" in a non-Article III court without the protections of Article III judges, i.e., life-time tenure and a guarantee against diminution of salary); *see id.* (Rehnquist, concurring in the judgment) (limiting conclusion to facts of *Marathon* but concurring in judgment because the grant of authority that violated Article III was not "readily severable from the remaining grant of authority to bankruptcy courts under § 1471")] The plurality and concurring Justices in *Marathon* applied the decision prospectively and stayed the judgment until October 4, 1982. *Marathon* thrust the entire bankruptcy system into a state of turmoil, because Congress did not act for another two years. In the interim, a temporary Emergency Rule was adopted in each federal district to refer bankruptcy cases and proceedings to the bankruptcy courts. Under the Emergency Rule, bankruptcy judges could not enter final orders in a *Marathon*-like proceeding.

4. Bankruptcy Amendments and Federal Judgeship Act of 1984

In 1984, Congress enacted the Bankruptcy Amendments and Federal Judgeship Act. [Pub. L. 98–353 (1984)] The 1984 Act created a system under which the bankruptcy judge's authority to enter final judgments and orders depended on whether Congress had classified the proceeding as *core versus non-core.* The Supreme Court's decision in *Stern v. Marshall* created a fair bit of confusion about the core versus non-core "fix" that Congress created in 1984. [**Stern v. Marshall,** 564 U.S. 462 (2011)] Two post-*Stern* Supreme Court decisions, however, have provided answers on how bankruptcy courts should proceed when dealing with a *Stern* claim. [*See* Chapter Two for a discussion of the case law.]

5. Congress Creates Family Farmer Chapter and U.S. Trustee Program

Congress again made significant changes to the bankruptcy laws in 1986. It added Chapter 12, which now provides relief for family farmers and family fishermen with regular income. It also made permanent the United States trustee system, which prior to 1986 had operated as a pilot program in some judicial districts. The United States trustee program now operates in 88 of the 94 United States judicial districts.

Congress also enacted major amendments to the Bankruptcy Code with the Bankruptcy Reform Act of 1994. [Pub. L. 103–394 (1994)] In 1990 and in 2000, as part of larger legislative enactments, Congress amended certain sections of the Bankruptcy Code and title 28. [Pub. L. 101–508 § 3007 (1990); Pub. L. 106–518 §§ 103–105, 208, 209, 501 (2000)]

6. Bankruptcy Abuse Prevention and Consumer Protection Act ("BAPCPA")

In 2005, Congress passed the Bankruptcy Abuse Prevention and Consumer Protection Act ("BAPCPA"), which made substantial changes to the Bankruptcy Code that affected, among others, both individual consumer and small business debtors. [Pub. L. 109–8 (2005)] Congress created an entry barrier to Chapter 7 with the "means test." Individual consumer debtors who fail the "means test" may not file for relief under Chapter 7. Congress also made the prior "small business election" mandatory, and created new "drop dead" dates for plan proposal and plan confirmation for small business debtors. BAPCPA changed numerous provisions in the Code, which are discussed throughout this outline.

C. Organization of the Bankruptcy Code

1. Chapters 1, 3, and 5

Chapters 1, 3, and 5 of the Bankruptcy Code contain general rules, definitions, and eligibility requirements for bankruptcy relief, as well as provisions about the commencement of a case, the administration of cases, the debtor, the estate and its officers, the trustee's powers to avoid certain transfers and recover property for the estate's benefit, creditors, claims, the automatic stay, adequate protection, and certain administrative powers of a trustee or a debtor in possession. All three chapters apply to cases under Chapters 7, 11, 12, and 13. [B.C. § 103(a)]

2. Chapter 7

The *liquidation* provisions of the Bankruptcy Code are contained in Chapter 7, which contemplates an orderly procedure by which the trustee collects the assets of the debtor's estate, reduces them to cash, and makes distributions to creditors, subject to the debtor's right to retain certain exempt property and the rights of secured parties in their collateral. [B.C. §§ 701 *et seq.*]

3. Chapter 9

Chapter 9 involves adjustments of debts of a municipality and is beyond the scope of this summary.

4. Chapter 11

Chapter 11 is entitled "*reorganization*" and ordinarily concerns a commercial debtor who desires to continue operating a business and to repay creditors concurrently through an acceptable plan of reorganization confirmed by the court. [B.C. §§ 1101 *et seq.*] *Note:* Some Chapter 11 debtors file liquidating, not reorganization, plans. The Bankruptcy Code permits a Chapter 11 plan to provide for the sale of all or substantially all estate property. B.C. § 1123(b)(4). In addition, not all Chapter 11 debtors are commercial entities. The Supreme Court has held that a consumer debtor also may qualify for Chapter 11 relief. [**Toibb v. Radloff,** 501 U.S. 157 (1991)]

5. Chapter 12

Chapter 12 provides relief for debtors who are *family farmers* or *family fishermen* with regular annual income, allowing them to continue to operate their farms or commercial fishing operations. [B.C. §§ 1201 *et seq.*] It allows the family farmer or family fisherman access to the bankruptcy court through a speedier, simpler, and less expensive procedure than under Chapter 11, and with higher debt limitations than those of Chapter 13. [*Compare* B.C. §§ 101(18), (19A) *with* § 109(e)]

6. Chapter 13

Chapter 13 provides a method by which an *individual with regular income* may repay all or a portion of her indebtedness over a period of time, pursuant to a plan proposed by the debtor and confirmed by the court. [B.C. §§ 1301 *et seq.*]

7. Chapter 15

Congress added Chapter 15 to the Code with the passage of BAPCPA. Chapter 15 is for cases of cross-border insolvency, but is beyond the scope of this summary. [B.C. §§ 1501 *et seq.*]

D. Rules of Construction

1. "After Notice and a Hearing"

When the language "after notice and a hearing" appears in the Bankruptcy Code, it means notice and an *opportunity for a hearing* appropriate under the specific circumstances. However, such language authorizes an act without an actual hearing if proper notice is given and (i) no hearing is requested by a party in interest or (ii) there is not enough time for a hearing before the act must be done and the court authorizes the act. [B.C. § 102(1)]

2. "Claim Against the Debtor"

The phrase "claim against the debtor" includes a claim against the debtor's property. [B.C. § 102(2)]

3. "Including"

The words "including" or "includes" are not meant to be limiting, i.e., items need not be listed to fall within the section. [B.C. § 102(3)]

4. "Order for Relief"

The entry of an order for relief in a bankruptcy case occurs automatically by the filing of a *voluntary* petition or a *joint* petition. [B.C. § 301(b)] In other words, the commencement of a voluntary or joint case constitutes the order for relief. In an involuntary case, the court must enter the order for relief; it does not occur automatically upon the filing of a bankruptcy petition. [B.C. § 303(h)] The order for relief is a term that appears throughout the Code as a point of reference in time and means simply that the bankruptcy case may go forward, unless otherwise ordered by the court.

E. Terminology

1. Introduction

There are a number of terms that appear frequently throughout the Code; an understanding of their bankruptcy definitions is helpful.

2. Affiliate

The following categories of *entities or persons* qualify as affiliates:

(a) an *entity* that directly or indirectly owns, controls, or holds *20 percent or more* of the *debtor's* outstanding voting stock;

(b) a *corporation* in which *20 percent or more* of the outstanding voting stock is directly or indirectly owned, controlled, or held *by the debtor or by an entity* that owns, controls, or holds *20 percent or more* of the *debtor's* outstanding voting stock;

(c) a *person* whose *business* the *debtor* operates under a *lease or operating agreement;*

(d) a *person substantially all of whose property the debtor* operates under an *operating agreement;* or

(e) an *entity* that operates the *debtor's business or substantially all of the debtor's property* under a *lease or operating agreement.* [B.C. § 101(2)]

e.g. **Example:** Carla is the sole shareholder of two corporations—Apex, Inc. and Beta Company—that are currently in Chapter 11. Because Carla owns 20 percent or more of both Apex's and Beta's voting stock, Carla is an affiliate of both companies. In addition, Apex is an affiliate of Beta, and Beta is an affiliate of Apex. While Apex does not own 20 percent or more of Beta's stock (and vice versa), Apex is a corporation in which 20 percent or more of its voting stock is owned by an entity, Carla, who owns 20 percent or more of the debtor Beta's stock. Therefore, the corporation Apex is an affiliate of the debtor Beta. Similarly, Beta is a corporation in which 20 percent or more of its stock is owned by an entity, Carla, who owns 20 percent or more of debtor Apex's stock. Thus, the corporation Beta is an affiliate of the debtor Apex.

3. Claim

A claim is a ***right to payment,*** even if it is unliquidated, unmatured, disputed, or contingent. It also includes the "right to an equitable remedy for breach of performance if such breach gives rise to a right to payment." The concept of a claim is significant in determining which debts are discharged and who shares in any distribution from the bankruptcy estate. [B.C. § 101(5)]

e.g. **Example:** Debtor was ordered by a state court to clean up a hazardous waste disposal site. After Debtor failed to comply, the state court appointed a receiver and ordered the receiver to carry out the mandatory injunction while taking possession of Debtor's property, including the disposal site. Debtor then filed a bankruptcy petition. The performance that the receiver sought from Debtor was limited to the payment of money to cover the expense of removal of the wastes. The receiver's ***right to payment of money was a claim,*** and the liability on that claim was a ***debt*** capable of being discharged. [**Ohio v. Kovacs,** 469 U.S. 274 (1985)]

a. Comment

The Supreme Court has emphasized the legislative intent to ascribe the broadest possible definition to "claim." [**Pennsylvania Department of Public Welfare v. Davenport,** 493 U.S. 808 (1990) (noting that Congress had "chose[n] expansive language" in the Code's definitions of "claim" and "debt")]

4. Consumer Debt

A consumer debt is one "incurred by an ***individual*** primarily for a ***personal, family, or household*** purpose." [B.C. § 101(8)]

5. Current Monthly Income

The term ***current monthly income*** is used in the new financial eligibility test that Congress added to the Bankruptcy Code with the passage of BAPCPA. The term also is important for determining a debtor's ***disposable income*** for purposes of payment to the debtor's unsecured creditors in a Chapter 13 case. [B.C. §§ 707(b), 1325(b)] Current monthly income is the ***debtor's average monthly income*** from all sources ***during the six-month period*** that ends on the last day of the calendar month immediately before the debtor's bankruptcy filing. [B.C. § 101(10A)]

6. Debt

"Debt" is defined as a "liability on a claim". [B.C. § 101(12)] Discharge of debts in bankruptcy is the legal means of providing the debtor with a fresh start.

7. Entity

The term "entity" includes persons, trusts, estates, governmental units, and the United States trustee. [B.C. § 101(15)]

8. Insider

An "insider" is largely defined in terms of whether the debtor is an individual, a corporation, a partnership. [B.C. § 101(31)]

a. Individual Debtor

With respect to an individual debtor, the following persons are insiders: relatives, general partners, relatives of general partners, a partnership if the debtor is a general partner, and a corporation if the debtor is an officer, a director, or a person in control. [B.C. §§ 101(31)(A) (insider), 101(9) (corporation), 101(45) (relative)]

b. Corporate Debtor

With respect to a corporate debtor, the following persons are insiders: directors, officers, persons in control of the debtor, general partners of the debtor, relatives of any of the above, and a partnership if the debtor is a general partner. [B.C. § 101(31)(B)]

c. Partnership Debtor

With respect to a partnership debtor, the following persons are insiders: general partners in or of the debtor, persons in control of the debtor, relatives of any of the above, and a partnership if the debtor is a general partner. [B.C. § 101(31)(C)]

d. Affiliates and Managing Directors

The term "insider" also includes the following: (1) an affiliate of the debtor; (2) an insider of an affiliate; or (3) the debtor's managing director. [B.C. §§ 101(31)(E), (F)]

9. Insolvent

With the exception of a partnership, an entity is insolvent if its debts total more than the aggregate value of all of its property, excluding exempt property and property fraudulently transferred. [B.C. § 101(32)(A)] A partnership is insolvent if its debts exceed the total value of (a) all its property, excluding fraudulently transferred property, and (b) the sum of the amounts by which each general partner's personal, non-partnership assets, excluding exempt property and property fraudulently transferred, exceeds each partner's non-partnership debts. [B.C. § 101(32)(B)]

e.g. **Example:** Katya and Levin are general partners of Acme General Partnership. Acme owes $2 million to its creditors. Acme's property is currently valued at $1 million. Katya's non-exempt personal property is valued at $600,000; her personal, non-partnership debts amount to $300,000. Levin's non-exempt property is valued at $500,000; his personal, non-partnership debts equal $200,000. Acme is insolvent because its debts, which are $2 million, exceed $1.6 million, which is the sum of its assets and the net value of its partners' personal, non-partnership assets.

10. Lien

A *lien* is a charge against or an interest in property to secure payment of a debt or the performance of an obligation. [B.C. § 101(36)] A *judicial lien* is a lien obtained by judgment, levy, sequestration, or other legal or equitable proceeding or process. [B.C. § 101(37)] A *security interest* is a lien that is created by agreement. [B.C. § 101(51)]

11. Person

The term person includes *individuals, corporations, and partnerships.* With a limited exception for purposes of creditors' and equity security holders' committees pursuant to § 1102, the term person does not include a governmental unit. [B.C. §§ 101(41), 1102]

12. Transfer

A transfer means any of the following: (a) creation of a *lien;* (b) *retention of title* as a security interest; (c) foreclosure of a *debtor's equity of redemption;* or (d) any *direct or indirect, absolute or conditional, voluntary or involuntary* disposition of or party with property or an interest in property. [B.C. § 101(54)]

F. Participants in the Bankruptcy Case

1. Bankruptcy Administrator

The United States trustee program does not operate in the six judicial districts in Alabama and North Carolina. In those six districts, a **bankruptcy administrator** provides many of the same functions in bankruptcy cases as does the United States trustee. Bankruptcy administrators operate under the jurisdiction of the Administrative Office of the United States Courts.

2. Bankruptcy Judge

For many years, under the Bankruptcy Act, the judicial officer in the case was called the "referee"; however, this terminology is now obsolete. Under the Bankruptcy Code, the judicial officer is referred to as the "bankruptcy judge."

3. Debtor

Under the Bankruptcy Act, the person about whom a bankruptcy case was commenced was called the "bankrupt." Under the Bankruptcy Code, the term is "debtor." [B.C. § 101(13)]

4. Debtor in Possession

In a Chapter 11 case, the debtor is called a "debtor in possession," **unless a trustee has been appointed.** [B.C. § 1101(1)]

5. Trustee

The trustee is the official representative of the estate and, as such, exercises statutory powers principally for the benefit of the **unsecured creditors.** [B.C. § 323(a)]

6. United States Trustee

The United States trustee assumes many of the administrative responsibilities previously performed by the court, including the **appointment and supervision of bankruptcy trustees,** thereby helping to separate the administrative and judicial functions in bankruptcy cases. The United States trustee is appointed for a five-year term by the Attorney General. [28 U.S.C. §§ 581 *et seq.*] The United States trustee's office is a division of the Department of Justice. The program operates in 88 of the 94 judicial districts in the United States. In the remaining six districts in Alabama and North Carolina, bankruptcy administrators oversee the administration of bankruptcy cases.

7. Unsecured Creditor

An unsecured creditor is an entity holding a claim against the debtor that is not secured by collateral.

8. Secured Creditor

A secured creditor is an entity holding a claim against the debtor that is **secured by a lien** on property of the estate or that is **subject to setoff.** [B.C. § 506(a)(1)] Frequently, bankruptcy litigation involves a contest between a secured creditor and the trustee, as the champion of the unsecured creditors, concerning the validity, extent, or priority of an alleged security interest.

9. Creditors' Committee

The Bankruptcy Code provides that in a Chapter 11 case, the United States trustee shall appoint a committee of unsecured creditors. The committee usually consists of those persons willing to serve that hold the *seven largest unsecured claims* against the debtor. The United States trustee may appoint additional committees of creditors or equity security holders. [B.C. §§ 1102(a)(1), (b)(1)] In a *small business case,* after request by a party in interest and a showing of cause, the bankruptcy court may order that an unsecured creditors' committee not be appointed. [B.C. § 1102(a)(3)] In many Chapter 11 cases, not only those involving small business debtors, there is insufficient creditor interest to allow the United States trustee to form a committee of unsecured creditors.

If a creditors' committee is appointed, the committee can be particularly helpful in consulting with the debtor in possession or with a trustee, and also in participating in the formulation of an acceptable plan of reorganization. [B.C. §§ 1102, 1103(c)] In a large Chapter 7 case, the unsecured creditors, at the § 341 meeting, may elect a creditors' committee consisting of between three and eleven unsecured creditors to consult with the trustee about the administration of the estate. [B.C. § 705; *see In re* **Wonder Corporation of America,** 72 B.R. 580 (Bankr. D. Conn. 1987)]

10. Equity Security Holder

An equity security holder is a holder of a share or similar security in a debtor corporation, a holder of a warrant or a right to buy or sell a security in a debtor corporation (but not a right to convert), or a limited partner holding an interest in a limited partnership debtor. [B.C. §§ 101(16), (17)]

In a Chapter 11 case, the United States trustee may appoint a committee of equity security holders. The committee ordinarily consists of those persons willing to serve that hold the *seven largest amounts of the debtor's equity securities.* [B.C. §§ 1102(a)(1), (2), (b)(2)]

11. Professional Persons

Professional persons, e.g., attorneys, accountants, appraisers, and auctioneers, often are hired by a trustee, a debtor in possession, or a creditors' or equity security holders' committee. Their expertise usually plays an important role in a bankruptcy case, and the bankruptcy court must approve their employment and compensation. [B.C. §§ 327–331]

G. Bankruptcy Petition Preparers

1. Background

Bankruptcy petition preparers are not participants *in* the bankruptcy case; for a fee, they prepare petitions and other bankruptcy documents necessary to file a bankruptcy case. In 1994, Congress added a new section to the Code to address concerns about bankruptcy petition preparers taking "unfair advantage of persons who are ignorant of their rights both inside and outside the bankruptcy system." [H.R. Rep. No. 103–385, at 56 (1994)] In 2005, Congress substantially amended the Code's provisions governing bankruptcy petition preparers.

2. Definitions

A *bankruptcy petition preparer* is a person, other than the debtor's attorney or an employee under the direct supervision of the debtor's attorney, who prepares for compensation a document for filing. [B.C. § 110(a)(1)] A *document for filing* is a petition or any other document prepared for filing by a debtor in the bankruptcy court or a district court in connection with a bankruptcy case. [B.C. § 110(a)(2)]

3. Filing Requirements

Before accepting fees or preparing any documents for filing, the bankruptcy petition preparer must provide the debtor with the notice contained in Official Form 119. [B.C. § 110(b)(2)] The bankruptcy petition preparer signs the form under *penalty of perjury.* [*See* Official Form 119, Part 2]

a. Individual Preparer

The bankruptcy petition preparer who prepares a document for filing must *sign* the document and print her *name and address* on the document. After her signature, the preparer must place her *social security number* and the social security number of any individual who assisted her in preparing the document for filing. [B.C. §§ 110(b)(1), (c)]

b. Preparer Not an Individual

If the bankruptcy petition preparer is *not an individual,* then an *officer, principal, responsible person, or partner* of the bankruptcy petition preparer must *sign* and print her *name and address* on the document. [B.C. § 110(b)(1)] The officer, principal, responsible person, or partner of the bankruptcy petition preparer must place her *social security number* after her signature on the document to be filed. [B.C. § 110(c)(2)(B)]

4. Document Copies

For any document that the debtor signs, the bankruptcy petition preparer must provide a copy to the debtor *no later* than the time that the *document is presented to the debtor for her signature.* [B.C. § 110(d)]

5. Prohibited Activities

The Bankruptcy Code prohibits the bankruptcy petition preparer from signing any documents on behalf of the debtor. [B.C. § 110(e)(1)] It *prohibits* a bankruptcy petition preparer from using the word "*legal*" or any similar word in any *advertisements,* and from advertising under any category that includes the word "legal" or any similar term. [B.C. § 110(f)] The Code also provides that the bankruptcy petition preparer cannot receive or collect any payment from the debtor or on behalf of the debtor for *court fees* in association with filing the bankruptcy case. [B.C. § 110(g)] Finally, a bankruptcy petition preparer cannot offer a potential debtor any *legal advice.* [B.C. § 110(e)(2)(A)]

a. What Constitutes Legal Advice?

A bankruptcy petition preparer *cannot advise* a potential debtor

(i) *whether to file* a bankruptcy petition or the *appropriate chapter* of the Code under which to file [B.C. § 110(e)(2)(B)(i)];

(ii) *whether debts will be discharged* in the bankruptcy case [B.C. § 110(e)(2)(B)(ii)];

(iii) whether debtor will be able to *keep her home, car, or other property* after bankruptcy [B.C. § 110(e)(2)(B)(iii)];

(iv) about the *tax consequences* of filing for bankruptcy or the *dischargeability of tax claims* [B.C. § 110(e)(2)(B)(iv)];

(v) whether debtor should promise to repay debts or enter into a *reaffirmation agreement* [B.C. § 110(e)(2)(B)(v)];

(vi) about how to characterize the nature of debtor's interests in property or the debtor's debts [B.C. § 110(e)(2)(B)(vi)]; or

(vii) about *bankruptcy rights and procedures.* [B.C. § 110(e)(2)(B)(vii)]

This is *not an exclusive list* of legal advice; instead, it merely lists some of the types of advice that the Code prevents bankruptcy petition preparers from offering to potential debtors. *Note:* Bankruptcy petition preparers also may run afoul of state rules about the unauthorized practice of law. [*See* B.C. § 110(k)]

6. Fees

While the Supreme Court may promulgate fee rules or the Judicial Conference of the United States may establish guidelines for setting *maximum fees* that bankruptcy petition preparers may charge, neither has done so yet. [B.C. § 110(h)(1); 28 U.S.C. § 2075; 2 Collier ¶ 110.08(1)] The bankruptcy petition preparer must file with the petition a *disclosure under penalty of perjury* of any *fee received* from or on behalf of the debtor in the *12 months prior* to the bankruptcy filing, as well as *any unpaid fee* charged to the debtor. [B.C. § 110(h)(2); Official Form 2800]

a. Excessive Fees

The court must *disallow* and order *immediate turnover* to the bankruptcy trustee of any fee found to be in (i) *excess of the value of services rendered* during the 12 months preceding the filing of the petition; or (ii) *violation of any fee rules or guidelines* established by the Supreme Court or the Judicial Conference of the United States. [B.C. § 110(h)(3); *see In re* **Graham,** 2004 WL 1052963 (Bankr. M.D. Ga. 2004) (holding that $80 was reasonable value of bankruptcy petition preparer services, and disallowing and ordering turnover to Chapter 7 trustee of $119 of $199 fee charged for such services)] The bankruptcy petition preparer has the burden of proving the reasonableness of any fee she collects. [*In re* **Langford,** 2007 WL 3376664 (Bankr. M.D. N.C. 2007)]

(i) Failure to Turn over Fees

If the bankruptcy petition preparer fails to turn over disallowed fees within *30 days of service* of the court's order, the court will impose a *$500 fine* for each failure. [B.C. § 110(h)(5)]

(ii) Exempting Fees

An individual debtor may *exempt* any funds turned over. [B.C. § 110(h)(3)(C)]

(iii) The Motion

The court, on its own initiative, or the debtor, the trustee, a creditor, or the United States trustee or bankruptcy administrator may file a motion for disallowance and turnover of excessive fees. [B.C. § 110(h)(4)]

b. Fee Forfeiture

The bankruptcy court may order that the bankruptcy petition preparer *forfeit all fees in a case* in which the preparer fails to comply with any of § 110's rules governing bankruptcy petition preparers. [B.C. § 110(h)(3)(B)]

e.g. **Example:** Debtor hired Bankruptcy Petition Preparer ("BPP") to prepare various documents, including the petition, schedules, and statements, necessary to file for relief under Chapter 13. BPP failed to put his name or signature on any of the documents, as required by § 110(b)(1). None of the documents contained BPP's social security number, as required by § 110(c)(1). Finally, BPP failed to file the declaration disclosing fees received from the debtor, as required by § 110(h)(2). The bankruptcy court concluded that these violations warranted forfeiture of all fees in the case. [*In re* **Warren,** 2012 WL 8145781 (Bankr. E.D. Cal. 2012)]

7. Damages and Fines

The Code provides for damages payable to the debtor and fines payable to the United States Trustee Fund for violations of the Code's rules governing bankruptcy petition preparers.

a. Damages

The debtor, trustee, or United States trustee or bankruptcy administrator may move for an award of *damages to the debtor* based on the conduct of a bankruptcy petition preparer. After notice and a hearing, the court must award damages to the debtor if a bankruptcy petition preparer violated any of the Code's rules governing bankruptcy petition preparers or the court determines that a bankruptcy petition preparer engaged in any *fraudulent, unfair, or deceptive act.* [B.C. § 110(i)(1)] The award of damages to the debtor shall include the following:

(i)   the debtor's *actual damages* [B.C. § 110(i)(1)(A)];

(ii) the *greater* of either *$2,000* or *twice* the amount that the *debtor paid* for the bankruptcy petition preparer's services [B.C. § 110(i)(1)(B)]; *and*

(iii) reasonable *attorneys' fees and costs* in moving for damages [B.C. § 110(i)(1)(C)]

If the trustee successfully moves for damages on the debtor's behalf, then the bankruptcy petition preparer must pay an *additional $1,000 to the trustee,* as well as reasonable attorneys' fees and costs. [B.C. § 110(i)(2)]

b. Fines

The debtor, trustee, creditor, United States trustee, or bankruptcy administrator may file a motion for an order imposing a fine on a bankruptcy petition preparer. [B.C. § 110(*l*)(3)] For *each failure* to comply with the Code's rules governing the conduct of bankruptcy petition preparers, the bankruptcy court may fine the bankruptcy petition preparer *$500.* [B.C. § 110(*l*)(1)] The bankruptcy court must *triple the fine* in any case in which the court finds that the bankruptcy petition preparer:

(i)   *advised* the debtor to *exclude assets or income* that should have been disclosed on an applicable schedule [B.C. § 110(*l*)(2)(A)];

(ii) *advised* the debtor to use a *false social security number* [B.C. § 110(*l*)(2)(B)];

(iii) *failed* to tell the debtor that the debtor was filing for bankruptcy relief [B.C. § 110(*l*)(2)(C)]; or

(iv) prepared a document for filing that *failed to disclose the identity of the bankruptcy petition prepaper* [B.C. § 110(*l*)(2)(D)]

In districts in which the United States trustees operate, any fine imposed must be paid to the United States trustee, who must deposit it in the *United States Trustee Fund.* [B.C. § 110(*l*)(4)(A)] In one of the six judicial districts in which bankruptcy administrators operate, the fine must be deposited into the special fund of the Treasury available to *offset funds appropriated for operation and maintenance of the courts* of the United States. [B.C. § 110(*l*)(4)(B); 28 U.S.C. § 1931]

Example: Bankruptcy Petition Preparer ("BPP") prepared seven documents for Debtor's Chapter 13 filing. None of the documents contained BPP's name or social security number, as required by the Code. [*See* B.C. §§ 110(b)(1), (c)] While the Code provides that the court may fine a BPP $500 for each failure to comply with the Code's rules, the bankruptcy court determined that $7,000 (7 documents x $500 for failure to provide name and 7 documents x $500 for failure to provide social security number) was excessive, given that court was not aware of any other case in which BPP had failed to comply with § 110's rules. Instead, court concluded that $1,400 was the appropriate fine under § 110(*l*)(1). However, BPP's failure to disclose his identity on the documents prepared for Debtor meant that the $1,400 fine was tripled, pursuant to § 110(*l*)(2)(D). [*In re* **Warren,** *supra*]

8. Injunctions

The bankruptcy court may enjoin a bankruptcy petition preparer from engaging in certain conduct or from acting as a bankruptcy petition preparer. A debtor, trustee, creditor, the United States trustee for the district in which the bankruptcy petition preparer resides or has conducted business, or the United States trustee for the district in which the debtor resides may bring a civil action for such an injunction. [B.C. § 110(j)(1)] The bankruptcy petitioner preparer must pay the *reasonable attorneys' fees and costs* to a debtor, trustee, or creditor that brings a successful action for injunctive relief. [B.C. § 110(j)(4)]

a. Injunction: Particular Acts

If the bankruptcy court determines that the bankruptcy petition preparer has (i) *violated* any of the *Code's rules governing bankruptcy petition preparers* or any other provision of the Bankruptcy Code; (ii) *misrepresented* her *experience or education* as a bankruptcy petition preparer; or (iii) engaged in any *fraudulent, unfair, or deceptive conduct,* then the court may enjoin the bankruptcy petition preparer from engaging in such conduct if injunctive relief is appropriate to prevent a recurrence of the conduct. [B.C. § 110(j)(2)(A)]

b. Injunction: Acting as Bankruptcy Petition Preparer

The bankruptcy court may enjoin a person from acting as a bankruptcy petition preparer if:

(i) she has *continually engaged* in any of the proscribed conduct described above (§ 65) and an *injunction is not sufficient* to prevent her interference with the proper administration of the Code;

(ii) she has *not paid a penalty* imposed; or

(iii) she has *failed to disgorge all fees* ordered by the court.

[B.C. § 110(j)(2)(B)]

c. Injunction: Contempt Power

As part of its contempt power, the bankruptcy court may enjoin a bankruptcy petition preparer who has failed to comply with a prior order of the court under § 110. The court may issue such an injunction on its own motion or on the motion of the trustee, United States trustee, or bankruptcy administrator. [B.C. § 110(j)(3); *see* **Fuller v. United States Trustee,** 2012 WL 4514174 (N.D. W.Va. 2012) (affirming bankruptcy court order under § 110(j)(3) permanently enjoining two bankruptcy petition preparers from acting as bankruptcy petition preparers in district, based on multiple violations of prior bankruptcy court order that defined and limited services preparers could provide, and requiring preparers to turn over excessive fees charged)]

Chapter Two

Jurisdiction and Procedure; Sovereign Immunity

Chapter Approach

An exam question about bankruptcy jurisdiction and procedure will often focus on one or more of the following issues:

1. Is the pending matter a *statutory core* or a *non-core* proceeding? Even if the matter falls within one of the non-exclusive sixteen categories of statutory core proceedings under 28 U.S.C. § 157(b)(2), you still must ask whether it is a *Stern claim.* If the matter is a *Stern* claim, have the parties *consented* to the bankruptcy court entering a final order or judgment? If the parties have not consented, did the bankruptcy court follow the procedure for *non-core proceedings* set forth at 28 U.S.C. § 157(c)? Remember that absent consent of the parties, it is the district court, *not the bankruptcy court,* that must enter final orders and judgment on *Stern* claims and non-core proceedings.

2. Does a particular proceeding involve the trial of a *personal injury tort or wrongful death claim* for the purpose of distribution? If so, the trial must be conducted in the district court.

3. If requested, is there a right to a *jury trial* in a particular bankruptcy proceeding?

4. Should the case or proceeding be *withdrawn* by the district court from the bankruptcy court? Is withdrawal of a particular proceeding mandatory?

5. Is *abstention* from hearing a particular proceeding required or appropriate under the circumstances?

6. Is *venue* of the bankruptcy case or proceeding proper? If a change of venue is requested, what are the criteria for transfer?

7. If an order or judgment is *appealed,* consider the court from which it is appealed, the court to which it is appealed, and whether the order *is final or interlocutory* in the context of bankruptcy.

A. Bankruptcy Courts: Structure and Operation

1. Unit of a District Court

The bankruptcy court in each federal judicial district constitutes a unit of the respective district court, and it receives its authority to hear cases and proceedings by *referral* from the district court. [28 U.S.C. §§ 151, 157(a)] Bankruptcy judges serve as *judicial officers* of the United States district court established under Article III of the Constitution. [28 U.S.C. § 152(a)(1)]

2. Appointment of Bankruptcy Judges

Bankruptcy judges are appointed for a judicial district by the United States court of appeals for the circuit in which the district is located. The judge's *term is for 14 years.* [28 U.S.C. § 152(a)(1)] Only the judicial council for the circuit in which the bankruptcy judge's official duty station is located may remove the judge during the judge's term, but removal is only for incompetence, misconduct, neglect of duty or physical or mental disability. [28 U.S.C. § 152(e)]

3. Chief Bankruptcy Judge

In each district court having more than one bankruptcy judge the district court must designate one judge to serve as *chief bankruptcy judge* of such bankruptcy court. The chief bankruptcy judge must ensure that the bankruptcy court and district court rules are observed and that the business of the bankruptcy court is handled effectively and expeditiously. [28 U.S.C. § 154(b)]

4. Staff of the Bankruptcy Court

Each bankruptcy judge may appoint a secretary and a law clerk, as well as any additional assistants deemed necessary by the Administrative Office of the United States Courts. [28 U.S.C. § 156(a)] If there is a sufficient number of bankruptcy cases and proceedings within a particular jurisdiction, the bankruptcy judges for that district may appoint a clerk of the court. [28 U.S.C. § 156(b)] The bankruptcy court clerk is the official custodian of all bankruptcy court records and dockets, and must pay into the United States Treasury all fees, costs, and other monies that she collects. [28 U.S.C. §§ 156(e), (f)]

5. Bankruptcy Court Records

With certain exceptions, any papers filed in a bankruptcy case and all dockets are *public records* and open to examination by any entity at reasonable times without charge.

a. Exceptions: Trade Secrets and Defamation

The bankruptcy court must, on request of a party in interest, or may, on its own motion, protect:

(i) an entity with regard to a *trade secret or confidential research, development, or commercial information* [B.C. § 107(b)(1)]; or

(ii) a person with regard to *scandalous or defamatory matter* contained in a paper filed in a bankruptcy case [B.C. § 107(b)(2)]

b. Exceptions: Identify Theft

In 2005, Congress added protections to the Code related to concerns about identify theft. The court also may protect an *individual* with regard to the following kinds of information to the extent that the court finds that *disclosure of such information* would create an *undue risk of identity theft* or other *unlawful injury* to the individual or the individual's property:

(i) Any *means of identification,* e.g., social security number, driver's license number, birth date, contained in a paper or to be filed in a bankruptcy case. [B.C. § 107(c)(2)(A); 18 U.S.C. § 1028(d)(7)]

(ii) Any *other information* contained in a paper containing a means of identification that is filed or is to be filed in a bankruptcy case. [B.C. § 107(c)(2)(B)]

Exception: Upon an *ex parte application demonstrating cause,* the court must provide access to the information described above to an entity acting pursuant to the *police or regulatory power* of a domestic governmental unit. [B.C. § 107(c)(1)] Congress added this provision to the Code in 2005.

c. Access to Information

The United States trustee, bankruptcy administrator, trustee or any auditor serving under 28 U.S.C. § 586(f) must have *full access to all information* contained in any paper filed or submitted in a bankruptcy case and *must not disclose* any information specifically protected under § 107 of the Code. [B.C. § 107(c)(3)] Congress added this this provision to the Code in 2005.

B. Bankruptcy Courts: Powers

1. Power of Court

The bankruptcy judge is authorized to implement the provisions of the Bankruptcy Code by issuing *any necessary or appropriate order, judgment, or process.* [B.C. § 105(a); *see* **Marrama v. Citizens Bank,** 549 U.S. 365 (2007) (stating that "broad authority granted to bankruptcy judges" under § 105(a) was "surely adequate" to authorize the bankruptcy court, notwithstanding the language of § 706(a), to deny Chapter 7 debtor's motion to convert to Chapter 13, in order to address abusive litigation practices)] The bankruptcy court, however, may not exercise its power under § 105(a) in such a fashion as to "contravene specific statutory provisions." [**Law v. Siegel,** 571 U.S. 415 (2014) (in unanimous opinion, holding that bankruptcy court erred in surcharging all of debtor's homestead exemption to pay administrative expenses associated with debtor's misconduct, because the surcharge contravened the provisions of § 522 of the Code)] The bankruptcy court does not have the authority to appoint a receiver. [B.C. § 105(b)]

a. Sua Sponte Action by Court

The court is expressly authorized to take any necessary or appropriate action, *on its own motion,* to enforce its orders or to prevent an abuse of process even if the Code provides for such action to be requested by a party in interest, e.g., the dismissal of a Chapter 11 case. [B.C. §§ 105(a), 1112(b); *In re* **Daily Corp.,** 72 B.R. 489 (Bankr. E.D. Pa. 1987)]

b. Status Conferences

The court, on its own motion or on the request of a party in interest, must hold such status conferences as are necessary to further the *expeditious and economical resolution* of the bankruptcy case and issue orders at such conferences, unless inconsistent with the Code or the Federal Rules of Bankruptcy, appropriate to ensure that the case is handled expeditiously and economically. [B.C. § 105(d)(2)] Such orders include:

(i) an order setting a deadline for the trustee to assume or reject an executory contract or unexpired lease [B.C. § 105(d)(2)(A)]; or

(ii) in a Chapter 11 case, an order

    (1) setting a deadline for the debtor or trustee to file a disclosure statement and plan or to solicit acceptances of a plan [B.C. §§ 105(d)(2)(B)(i), (ii)];

    (2) setting a deadline for other parties in interest to file a plan or solicit acceptances of a plan [B.C. §§ 105(d)(2)(B)(iii), (iv)];

    (3) fixing the scope and format of the notice of the hearing on the disclosure statement [B.C. § 105(d)(2)(B)(v)]; or

    (4) combining the disclosure statement hearing with the confirmation hearing. [B.C. § 105(d)(2)(B)(vi)]

c. Contempt

Most courts have held that the bankruptcy court has the authority, either inherently or under § 105, to impose sanctions for civil contempt. [**Price v. Lehtinen (*In re* Lehtinen),** 564 F.3d 1052 (9th Cir. 2009) (stating that bankruptcy courts "generally have the power to sanction attorneys pursuant to (1) their civil contempt authority under 11 U.S.C. § 105(a); and (2) their inherent sanction authority")] It is unclear, however, whether a bankruptcy court may impose criminal contempt sanctions. The circuits are split on the issue. [*See* discussion of cases in *In re* **Hake**, 2006 WL 2846277 (B.A.P. 6th Cir. 2006); *see also* **Kittywalk Systems v. Midnight Pass Inc. (*In re* Midnight Pass Inc.),** 2009 WL 3583957 (Bankr. D. Mass. 2009) (noting circuit split)]

d. Sanctions

The bankruptcy court may impose sanctions on attorneys, law firms, or parties who sign, file, or submit pleadings or other documents, or advocate for positions that (i) are ***not well-grounded in fact or in law,*** allowing for good faith arguments for change of existing law, or (ii) are filed for any ***improper purpose.*** [Bankruptcy Rule 9011(b), (c)] The court may impose sanctions only after notice and a reasonable opportunity to respond. [Bankruptcy Rule 9011(c)] This rule on sanctions does not apply to disclosures and discovery requests, responses, objections, and motions subject to bankruptcy rules governing adversary proceedings. [Bankruptcy Rules 9011(d), 7026–7037]

e. Substantive Consolidation

In appropriate circumstances, the court may order the substantive consolidation of debtors' estates, i.e., the pooling of their assets, debts, and causes of action. The power to substantively consolidate debtors' estates is derived from § 105(a). There is no single test that courts use in making the decision to substantively consolidate. Courts have developed "two distinct types of tests"—"a more traditional, factor based test and a balancing test. Under the traditional test, courts look to several factors in determining whether substantive consolidation is appropriate" while the balancing test "focus[es] on the impact of consolidating the creditors and weighing it against the benefits of consolidation." [*In re* **Introgen Therapeutics,** 429 B.R. 570 (Bankr. W.D. Tex. 2010)]

(i) Distinguish—Procedural Consolidation

Substantive consolidation is rare. ***Procedural consolidation,*** also known as ***joint administration,*** is more common. A court may grant a motion for joint administration for administrative purposes for cases involving two or more related debtors, such as (i) a husband and wife, (ii) a partnership and a general partner, (iii) two or more general partners, or (iv) affiliated corporations. [Bankruptcy Rule 1015(b); *see* B.C. § 101(2) (definition of affiliate)] Joint administration is a "procedural tool permitting use of a single docket for administrative matters, including the listing of filed claims, the combining of notices to creditors of the different estates, and the joint handling of other ministerial matters that may aid in expediting the cases." [**Reider v. FDIC (*In re* Reider),** 31 F.3d 1102 (11th Cir. 1994)]

C. Personal Jurisdiction

1. In General

The Bankruptcy Rules provide for ***nationwide service of process*** by first class prepaid mail, except for subpoenas, in adversary proceedings and contested matters. [Bankruptcy Rules 7004(b), (d), 9014(d)] Personal jurisdiction is established over a defendant in an adversary proceeding or respondent in a contested matter if service of process conforms with Rule 7004 and "the exercise of jurisdiction is consistent with the Constitution and laws of the United States." [Bankruptcy Rule 7004(f)] Courts typically do not use the "minimum contacts" test.

Instead, many conclude that because bankruptcy issues are matters of federal question jurisdiction and the bankruptcy rules provide for nationwide service, a court has personal jurisdiction over any person with *sufficient minimum contacts with the United States,* not with the state in which the bankruptcy case is pending. Not all courts, however, use this *"national contacts" test.* Some courts have held that due process requires consideration of the *Fifth Amendment's reasonableness and fairness* requirements. [*See, e.g., In re* **Correra,** 2018 WL 4027001 (Bankr. N.D. Tex. 2018) (discussing two approaches courts take to analysis of personal jurisdiction); **Gonzales v. Miller (***In re* **Texas Reds, Inc.),** 2010 WL 1711112 (Bankr. D. N.M. 2010)]

2. Service of Process: Insured Depository Institutions

Service of process on an insured depository institution requires certified mail, rather than simply first class mail, unless

a. the institution has appeared by its attorney, in which case the attorney must be served by first class mail [Bankruptcy Rule 7004(h)(1)];

b. the institution has waived in writing its entitlement to certified mail by designating an officer to receive service [Bankruptcy Rule 7004(h)(3)]; or

c. the court orders otherwise after service by certified mail of an application to permit service by first class mail is sent to an officer of the institution that the institution designates. [Bankruptcy Rule 7004(h)(2)]

D. Subject Matter Jurisdiction

1. District Courts

The United States district courts have original jurisdiction over (i) all *cases* under the Bankruptcy Code; (ii) all *civil proceedings* arising under the Code or arising in or related to a case under the Code; (iii) the *debtor's property,* as of the filing of the petition, and (iv) *property of the estate,* wherever located. [28 U.S.C. § 1334]

a. Cases

The jurisdiction of the district courts over *bankruptcy cases* is both *original and exclusive.* Therefore, district court jurisdiction completely preempts any state court's jurisdiction. [28 U.S.C. § 1334(a)]

b. Civil Proceedings

Controversies in the bankruptcy case are called "proceedings." The district court has *original but not exclusive* jurisdiction over them. Such proceedings are designated as either *core* or *non-core.* [28 U.S.C. §§ 1334(b), 157(b)(2)]

c. Debtor's Property

The district courts are vested with *exclusive jurisdiction* over all of the debtor's property, regardless of its location, as of the filing of a bankruptcy petition, as well as all property of the estate. [28 U.S.C. § 1334(e)]

2. Referral to Bankruptcy Courts

Each district has its own rule automatically referring all bankruptcy cases and proceedings to the bankruptcy judges in the district. [28 U.S.C. § 157(a); *see, e.g.,* W.D. Mich. LCivR 83.2(a); L.R. 76.1 (Northern District of New York)]

E. Core Versus Non-Core Proceedings

1. Introduction

There are three categories of proceedings in a bankruptcy case: proceedings that (i) *arise under* title 11; (ii) *arise in* a bankruptcy case; or (3) *are related to* a bankruptcy case. [28 U.S.C. § 157(a)] Whether the bankruptcy court may enter *final judgments and orders* in a proceeding depends on whether the proceeding is a *statutory core or non-core proceeding* and, if the former, *whether it is a Stern claim.* The bankruptcy judge, either on her own motion or on the timely motion of a party, must determine whether a proceeding is core or non-core. The fact that State law may affect the resolution of the proceeding is not solely determinative of the core versus non-core nature of the proceeding. [28 U.S.C. § 157(b)(3)]

a. Core Proceedings

Core proceedings are those that *arise under title 11* or *arise in a bankruptcy case.* [28 U.S.C. § 157(b)(1); **Stern v. Marshall,** 131 S. Ct. 2594 (2011) (stating that "core proceedings are those that arise in a bankruptcy case or under Title 11")] In a *core proceeding,* the bankruptcy court has the *statutory authority* to enter *final judgments and orders,* subject to regular appellate review. [28 U.S.C. §§ 157(b)(1), 158(a)] Congress apparently took the word "core" from Justice Brennan's plurality opinion in *Marathon.* [*See* **Northern Pipeline Construction Co. v. Marathon Pipe Line Company,** 459 U.S. 813 (1982) (noting that "the restructuring of debtor-creditor relations [ ] is at the core of the federal bankruptcy power")]

(i) Statutory Categories

After *Marathon,* Congress passed the Bankruptcy Amendments and Federal Judgeship Act of 1984, which, in part, created a *non-exclusive list* of *16 categories of core proceedings.* The statutory core proceedings include the following:

(1) matters involving *estate administration* [28 U.S.C. § 157(b)(2)(A)];

(2) with the exception of personal injury tort and wrongful death claims, the allowance or disallowance of *claims* against the estate or *exemptions* from estate property, and *estimation of claims and interests* for purposes of confirming a plan [28 U.S.C. § 157(b)(2)(B)];

(3) *counterclaims* by the estate against persons filing claims [28 U.S.C. § 157(b)(2)(C)];

(4) orders to *obtain credit* [28 U.S.C. § 157(b)(2)(D)];

(5) *turnover* orders [28 U.S.C. § 157(b)(2)(E)];

(6) *preference* actions [28 U.S.C. § 157(b)(2)(F)];

(7) motions to terminate, annul, or modify *the automatic stay* [28 U.S.C. § 157(b)(2)(G)];

(8) *fraudulent conveyance* actions [28 U.S.C. § 157(b)(2)(H)];

(9) determinations of *dischargeability* [28 U.S.C. § 157(b)(2)(I)];

(10) *discharge objections* [28 U.S.C. § 157(b)(2)(J)];

(11) determinations of the *validity, extent, or priority of liens* [28 U.S.C. § 157(b)(2)(K)];

(12) *plan confirmations* [28 U.S.C. § 157(b)(2)(L)];

(13) orders approving the *use or lease of property,* including the use of cash collateral [28 U.S.C. § 157(b)(2)(M)];

(14) orders approving the *sale of property,* except property resulting from claims brought by the estate against persons who had not filed claims [28 U.S.C. § 157(b)(2)(N)];

(15) with the exception of personal injury tort or wrongful death claims, *other proceedings* affecting liquidation of estate assets or adjustment of the debtor-creditor or equity security holder relationship [28 U.S.C. § 157(b)(2)(O)]; and

(16) recognition of *foreign proceedings and other matters under Chapter 15* [28 U.S.C. § 157(b)(2)(P)].

(ii) The *Stern* Problem

(1) In *Stern v. Marshall,* the Supreme Court drew into question the framework that Congress had created post-*Marathon.* The Court held that while the bankruptcy court had *the statutory authority under § 157(b)(2)(C)* to enter a final judgment on the debtor's counterclaim for tortious interference, it *did not have the constitutional authority* to do so.

> **e.g.** **Example:** Debtor Vickie filed a state probate court action prior to bankruptcy against Pierce, her husband's son, claiming that Pierce had fraudulently induced Vickie's husband to sign a living trust that did not include her. After her husband died, Vickie filed for bankruptcy, and Pierce filed a complaint in the bankruptcy case claiming that Vickie had defamed him by having her lawyers tell members of the press that Pierce had engaged in fraud to gain control of his father's assets. Pierce filed a proof of claim for the defamation action and sought to have any debt declared non-dischargeable. Vickie filed a counterclaim for tortious interference with the gift that she had expected from her deceased husband. The Supreme Court agreed that Vickie's counterclaim was a statutory core proceeding under § 157(b)(2)(C), but that Article III of the Constitution did not permit the bankruptcy court to enter a final judgment on Vickie's counterclaim. The Court explained that Vickie's counterclaim did not involve public rights, but instead was a claim "under state common law between two private parties." Moreover, the Court concluded that the fact that Pierce had filed a claim in Vickie's case was not relevant, because the issue was the nature of Vickie's counterclaim for tortious interference; it was the "very type of claim" that the Court had held in *Marathon* and *Granfinanciera* had to be decided by an Article III court. The Court also noted "there was never any reason to believe that the process of adjudicating Pierce's proof of claim would necessarily resolve Vickie's counterclaim." Finally, the Court rejected the idea that Pierce had consented to the bankruptcy court's resolution of Vickie's counterclaim, stating that Pierce "had nowhere else to go if he wished to recover from Vickie's estate." [**Stern,** *supra*]

(2) **Remember:** A *Stern* claim is one that falls within the list of core proceedings under § 157(b)(2), but on which the bankruptcy court cannot enter a final judgment or order, because doing so would violate Article III of the Constitution.

(iii) Dealing with *Stern* Claims

The Supreme Court handed down two decisions after *Stern* that explained how bankruptcy courts should handle *Stern* claims.

(1) *Executive Benefits*

In *Executive Benefits,* the Supreme Court, in a unanimous decision, held that the procedure governing non-core proceedings under *§ 157(c) applies to Stern claims.* The Court explained that when faced with a *Stern* claim, the bankruptcy court should enter proposed findings of fact and conclusions of law, which the district court reviews *de novo* before entering a final judgment in the proceeding. [**Executive Benefits Insurance Agency v. Arkison,** 573 U.S. 25 (2015)]

(2) *Wellness*

In *Wellness,* the Supreme Court held that if the parties to a *Stern* claim consent, then the bankruptcy court may enter a final order or judgment on the *Stern* claim. Consent must be *knowing and voluntary,* but *need not be express.* [**Wellness International Network, Ltd. v. Sharif,** 135 S.Ct. 1932 (2015)]

(3) Summary

- If the proceeding falls into one of the statutory categories of core proceedings and is not a *Stern* claim, then the bankruptcy court may enter a final judgment or order.

- If the proceeding falls into one of the statutory categories of core proceedings and is a *Stern* claim, then the bankruptcy court may enter a final judgment or order only with the parties' consent.

- If the proceeding falls into one of the statutory categories of core proceedings and is a *Stern* claim but the parties do not consent to the bankruptcy court entering a final order or judgment, then the bankruptcy court must submit proposed findings of fact and conclusions of law to the district court to review *de novo.*

- If the proceeding is non-core, then the bankruptcy court may enter a final judgment or order with the parties' consent.

- If the proceeding is non-core but the parties do not consent to the bankruptcy court entering a final order or judgment, then the bankruptcy court must submit proposed findings of fact and conclusions of law to the district court to review *de novo.*

b. Non-Core Proceedings

In a *non-core* proceeding, the bankruptcy court must submit *proposed findings of fact and conclusions of law* to the district court, which enters a final judgment or order, after conducting a *de novo review* on all matters on which a party has timely and specifically objected. [28 U.S.C. § 158(c)(1)] If all the parties *consent,* however, the bankruptcy court may enter final judgments and orders, subject to appellate review, in a *non-core* proceeding. [28 U.S.C. § 157(c)(2)]

(i) Personal Injury and Wrongful Death Claims

Proceedings to estimate or liquidate personal injury tort of wrongful death claims for purposes of distribution are not core and must be tried in the district court. [28 U.S.C. § 157(b)(2)(B), (5)]

e.g. **Example:** Prior to bankruptcy, Debtor sold her home to the Deans. The Deans subsequently discovered that the basement of the home was contaminated with mold. The Deans filed suit against Debtor, and the case was submitted to binding arbitration. The arbitrator ruled in favor of the Deans on their property damage claim, and Debtor subsequently filed for relief under Chapter 13. The Deans filed an adversary proceeding in Debtor's Chapter 13 case, objecting to the discharge of a personal injury claim that the automatic stay prevented them from pursuing in state court. (Debtor had scheduled the claim as disputed, contingent, and unliquidated.) The bankruptcy court held that it lacked the "authority to liquidate or estimate the Deans' personal injury claim" and, thus, could not determine whether the claim was nondischargeable. As a result, the court granted the Debtor's motion to dismiss the Deans' adversary proceeding. [**Dean v. Lane (*In re* Lane),** 2018 WL 1027339 (Bankr. W.D. Ky. 2018)]

F. Jury Trials

1. Right to Jury Trial

The United States Supreme Court has held that the Seventh Amendment to the Constitution entitles a party that has *not filed a claim* against the bankruptcy estate to a jury trial of an action by the bankruptcy trustee against that party to recover an allegedly fraudulent conveyance. The Court set out the following framework for analyzing the right to a jury trial.

a. Would the cause of action have been brought *at law* in 18th Century England "prior to the merger of the courts of law and equity"?

b. Is the remedy requested *legal* in nature?

c. Does the action involve a *private as opposed to a public right?*

[**Granfinanciera, S.A. v. Nordberg,** 492 U.S. 33 (1989)]

e.g. **Example—No Claim Filed Against Estate:** Debtor Corporation filed for relief under Chapter 11. The Chapter 11 trustee filed suit against two corporations (Granfinanciera and Medex), seeking $1.7 million in allegedly fraudulent transfers. Neither corporation had filed a claim against Debtor's estate; both requested a jury trial of the trustee's fraudulent conveyance action. The Supreme Court held that Granfinanciera and Medex were entitled under the Seventh Amendment to a jury trial. The Court first concluded that in 18th century England the trustee would have had to bring his fraudulent conveyance action at law, because it involved a "determinate sum of money" and a "court of equity would not have adjudicated it." The Court next explained that the Chapter 11 trustee sought the payment of money, which is the traditional relief at law. Finally, the Court concluded that a fraudulent conveyance action under § 548(a)(2) is "more accurately characterized as a private rather than a public right as [the Court] used those terms in [its] Article III decisions." The fact that Congress had designated fraudulent conveyance actions as "core" did not alter the Court's conclusion. [**Granfinanciera,** *supra; see* **Schoenthal v. Irving Trust Co.,** 287 U.S. 92 (1932) (Bankruptcy Act case, in which bankruptcy trustee sought to recover preferences from recipients who had not filed claims against the bankruptcy estate, holding that bankruptcy trustee had an adequate remedy at law and a suit in equity could not be maintained, and, thus, recipients of alleged preferences had a Seventh Amendment right to jury trial)]

e.g. **Example—Claim Filed Against Estate:** Debtors were uninsured, non-bank institutions that filed for relief under Chapter 11. Creditors held savings certificates issued by Debtors. In the 90 days prior to Debtors' bankruptcy filing, Creditors redeemed some, but not all, of those savings certificates. Creditors filed proofs of claim in Debtors' bankruptcy case. The Chapter 11 trustee filed adversary proceedings in the bankruptcy case to recover the preferential payments. In a per curiam opinion, the Supreme Court held that Creditors were not entitled to a jury trial in the trustee's preference action because they had filed claims in Debtors' bankruptcy case. The Court noted that in *Granfinanciera* it had explained that a creditor triggers the claims allowance process when the creditor files a claim. If the trustee then commences a preference action, that action "becomes part of the claims-allowance process which is triable only in equity." Thus, by filing claims, Creditors brought "themselves with the equitable jurisdiction of the Bankruptcy Court" and were not entitled to a jury trial. [**Langenkamp v. Culp,** 498 U.S. 42 (1990)]

2. Power of Bankruptcy Judges to Hold Jury Trials

In *Granfinanciera,* the Supreme Court did not decide whether bankruptcy courts could conduct jury trials. [**Granfinanciera,** *supra* (stating that it was not deciding whether 28 U.S.C. § 1411 allowed "bankruptcy courts to conduct jury trials in fraudulent conveyance actions")] In 1994, Congress amended title 28 of the United States Code to authorize bankruptcy judges to conduct jury trials, provided that the *district court specially designates the exercise of this jurisdiction* and *all parties expressly consent.* [28 U.S.C. § 157(e)] The reason for the 1994 amendment was to clarify the Supreme Court's *Granfinanciera* decision and resolve a circuit split. [H.R. Rep. 103–385 at 42 (1994) (explaining that "[T]he *Granfinanciera* court had no finding on whether bankruptcy judges could conduct civil trials, and the circuits have reached contrary opinions regarding this issue")] The requirement of express consent in § 157(e) resolves the constitutional question of whether a bankruptcy court—an Article I court—may hold a jury trial. [1 Collier ¶ 3.08(3); *see* **Wellness International v. Sharif,** 135 S. Ct. 1932 (2015) (holding that Article III is not violated if the parties "knowingly and voluntarily consent to adjudication by a bankruptcy judge")]

3. Involuntary Cases

The district court may order that the issues arising in an involuntary bankruptcy case be tried without a jury. [28 U.S.C. § 1441(b)]

4. Personal Injury and Wrongful Death

Nothing in the Bankruptcy Code or in Chapter 87 (district courts) of Title 28 of the United States Code affects an individual's right to a jury trial under applicable nonbankruptcy law with regard to a *personal injury or wrongful death tort claim.* [28 U.S.C. § 1441(a)]

G. Withdrawal of the Reference

1. Permissive Withdrawal

The district court, *for cause,* may withdraw, in whole or in part, a case or proceeding that has been referred to the bankruptcy court either on its own motion or on the timely motion of a party. [28 U.S.C. § 157(d)] The district court judge must hear the motion to withdraw the reference. [Bankruptcy Rule 5011(a)] Courts have articulated various factors that they consider relevant to the permissive withdrawal analysis. [*See, e.g.,* **Shalom Torah Centers v.**

Philadelphia Indemnity Insurance Companies, 2011 WL 1322295 (D. N.J. 2011) (stating that court first should determine whether the proceeding is core or non-core, and then evaluate whether withdrawal would promote uniformity, reduce forum shopping, further the economical use of debtor's and creditors' resources, and expedite the bankruptcy process)] It is important to remember that the statute uses the term "may" not "shall" in the first sentence; therefore, even if the court finds cause, it still may decline to withdraw the reference. [28 U.S.C. § 157(d)]

2. Mandatory Withdrawal

On a timely motion, the district court must withdraw a proceeding from the bankruptcy court if *its resolution* requires consideration of *both* the Bankruptcy Code *and* a *nonbankruptcy federal statute* "regulating organizations or activities affecting interstate commerce." [28 U.S.C. § 157(d)] While the statute says that withdrawal is mandated when resolution requires consideration of *both* the Code and a non-Code federal statute, the vast majority of courts have ignored the express statutory language. Instead, they have interpreted § 157(d) to mandate withdrawal if resolution of the dispute requires "*substantial and material*" consideration of the *non-Code federal statute* and that statute has *more than a de minimis impact* on interstate commerce. [1 Collier ¶ 3.04(2)] Withdrawal is not mandated if the dispute only involves a " 'simple application of well-settled law' "; withdrawal is mandated, however, to resolve "complicated, interpretive issues", in particular issues of first impression. [**Harrelson v. DSSC, Inc.,** 2015 WL 1043338 (M.D. Ala. 2015)] Mandatory withdrawal is not implicated if the dispute requires resolution of a state law, as opposed to a nonbankruptcy federal law. [**Mooring Capital Fund, LLC v. Sullivan,** 2016 WL 4628572 (N.D. W. Va. 2016)]

3. Appeals

A district court order either denying or granting a motion to withdraw the reference is not an appealable final order. [28 U.S.C. § 158(d)(1); *see* **Khan v. Mahia,** 567 Fed. Appx. 53 (2d Cir. 2014) (denial of motion to withdraw the reference of adversary proceeding is not a final order); **Springel v. Prosser (*In re* Prosser),** 2009 WL 798842 (D. V.I. 2009) (stating in footnote that " 'orders granting or denying motions for withdrawal of reference are not final' appealable orders")] As interlocutory orders, § 1292(b) provides the rule for appellate review. [28 U.S.C. § 1292(b)] With the 2005 amendments to § 158(d), however, a party may seek direct review. [1 Collier ¶ 3.04(3)]

H. Abstention

1. Permissive Abstention

The district court may abstain from hearing a *particular* proceeding arising under the Code or arising in or related to a bankruptcy case when *justice, comity with state courts, or respect for state law* favors resolution of the matter in a state forum. [28 U.S.C. § 1334(c)(1)] Courts have used various multi-factor tests to decide whether to permissively abstain. [*See, e.g.,* **Watson v. Zigila,** 2010 WL 3582504 (Bankr. E.D. Mich. 2010) (12-factor test); **McDaniel v. ABN Amro Mortgage Group,** 364 B.R. 644 (S.D. Ohio 2007) (13-factor test)]

Example: McKitrick represented Debtor Corporation in its Chapter 11 case. After the bankruptcy case closed, Debtor sued McKitrick in state court for malpractice. McKitrick removed the case to the federal district court, which referred the case to the bankruptcy court. The bankruptcy court abstained from hearing the malpractice case and remanded it to state court. On appeal, the bankruptcy appellate panel ("BAP") affirmed the bankruptcy court's decision. The BAP noted that the bankruptcy court had reached its conclusion after having found that 8 of the 12 factors that the court had examined weighed in favor of abstention. The court explained that the Debtor's creditors had been paid in full and, thus, any recovery in the malpractice action would not benefit bankruptcy creditors. The issue in the proceeding was governed by state law, i.e., malpractice, and that abstention would return the claim to the court in which it originally was filed. In addition, allowing the malpractice claim to proceed in the bankruptcy court would mean that a state law claim, that otherwise could not be filed in federal court, would proceed in a forum not available to other alleged victims of malpractice. The BAP held that the bankruptcy court had not abused its discretion in abstaining from hearing the malpractice claim against McKitrick. [**Roberts Broadcasting Co. v. DeWoskin (*In re* Roberts Broadcasting Co.),** 568 B.R. 310 (B.A.P. 8th Cir. 2017)]

Remember: There are two statutory grounds for abstention: Code § 305 and 28 U.S.C. § 1334(c). The difference between the two provisions is that under § 305(a), "the court may dismiss a case or suspend *all* proceedings in a bankruptcy case" while § 1334(c) "provides for abstention from *particular* proceedings in a bankruptcy case." [**Efron v. Candelario (*In re* Efron),** 529 B.R. 396 (B.A.P. 1st Cir. 2015)]

2. Mandatory Abstention

On a *timely motion,* the district court must abstain from hearing *a particular* proceeding if all of the following requirements are satisfied:

a.   the proceeding is *related to the bankruptcy case* (non-core), but not arising in the bankruptcy case or under the Code;

b.   the proceeding is based on a *state law claim or cause of action;*

c.   without § 1334(b), the proceeding could not have been brought in a federal court;

d.   the proceeding already has been *filed in an appropriate state court;* and

e.   the proceeding can be *timely adjudicated* in that forum.

[28 U.S.C. § 1334(c)(2)]

(i)   Personal Injury Tort and Wrongful Death

Proceedings based on personal injury tort or wrongful death claims are not subject to mandatory abstention. [28 U.S.C. § 157(b)(2)(B), (b)(4)] The issue is the scope of the statutory exception for personal injury torts. [**Massey Energy Co. v. West Virginia Consumers for Justice,** 351 B.R. 348 (E.D. Va. 2006) ("mandatory abstention is not available for personal injury tort claims")]

3. Distinguish Proceeding from Case

It is important to differentiate between the court's abstaining from hearing a *single proceeding* that is only one component of the bankruptcy case and abstaining from hearing the *whole bankruptcy case.* The court is "limited to abstaining from a particular proceeding" under § 1334(c) while it "may either dismiss the case or, in the alternative, suspend all proceedings within the case" under § 305. [**Graham v. Yoder Machinery Sales (*In re* Weldon F. Stump & Co.),** 373 B.R. 823 (Bankr. N.D. Ohio 2007); *compare* 28 U.S.C. § 1334(c)] *with* B.C. § 305(a)]

The bankruptcy court may, at any time, abstain from hearing *an entire case* by dismissing it or by suspending all proceedings if it finds that abstention would better serve the interests of creditors and the debtor. [B.C. § 305(a)(1)] Abstention also may be proper if a petition for recognition of a *foreign proceeding* has been granted and the court determines that the *purposes of Chapter 15* are best served by dismissal or abstention. [B.C. §§ 305(a)(2), 1515] Notice and a hearing are required, but a separate hearing on the issue of abstention is not necessary if the bankruptcy court has conducted a hearing in which the facts needed for an abstention decision have been gathered. [**Efron v. Candelario (*In re* Efron**), 529 B.R. 396 (B.A.P. 1st Cir. 2015); B.C. § 305(a)] *Note:* This outline does not cover Chapter 15 on ancillary and other cross-border cases.

e.g. **Example:** Debtor obtained a divorce in 2001, and the Commonwealth court in Puerto Rico ("CFI") ordered him to pay $50,000 per month to his former spouse until the marital assets were divided and liquidated. Debtor never voluntarily paid the $50,000 per month, and he and his ex-wife fought in the CFI for a decade before the CFI awarded the ex-wife approximately $3.3 million in past-due payments and interest. Several weeks later, Debtor filed for relief under Chapter 11. The bankruptcy court dismissed the case on two grounds, one of which was abstention under § 305(a)(1). The bankruptcy court found that Debtor's case served no bankruptcy purpose because it basically was a two-party dispute between Debtor and his ex-wife. The court explained that the CFI was the appropriate forum for resolving issues of local family and inheritance law, given that court's expertise in those areas of law. The bankruptcy court also noted that because Debtor had refused to pay the monthly sum owed to his ex-wife, which the court had determined was a domestic support obligation, Debtor could not confirm a Chapter 11 plan. The court also found that dismissal would not prejudice Debtor's other unsecured creditors, whom he proposed to pay in full. Finally, the bankruptcy court explained that dismissal would save the administrative costs associated with bankruptcy; money spent on estate professionals was money not used to pay Debtor's creditors. The BAP affirmed the bankruptcy court's decision. The BAP noted that courts examine a "wide variety" of factors in making an abstention decision pursuant to § 305(a). "A significant factor in favor of dismissing a case pursuant to § 305(a)(1) is the absence of a true bankruptcy purpose, particularly where the bankruptcy case constitutes a two-party dispute between the debtor and a single creditor." The BAP rejected Debtor's arguments that his bankruptcy case was not simply a two-party dispute, and concluded that "the bankruptcy court's findings amply support[ed] its decision that the interests of all creditors and the debtor [were] better served by dismissing the case pursuant to § 305(a)." [**Efron,** *supra*]

4. Appeals of Abstention Orders

With one exception, a bankruptcy court's order in favor of or against abstention, whether permissive or mandatory, from hearing a particular proceeding may be appealed to the district court or bankruptcy appellate panel. An abstention decision by the district court or bankruptcy appellate panel, however, may not be appealed to the court of appeals or the Supreme Court. [28 U.S.C. § 1334(d)] There is one statutory exception: a decision to abstain under mandatory abstention may be appealed not only to the district court or bankruptcy appellate panel, but also the court of appeals and the Supreme Court. [28 U.S.C. § 1334(d)]

Note: Some authority, which is in conflict with the language of § 1334(d), has allowed appellate review of a decision *to abstain,* for example, to ensure that the statutory requirements for mandatory abstention are satisfied. [1 Collier ¶ 3.05(6)(a)]

I. Removal

1. Civil Actions

A party may remove any claim or cause of action in a civil proceeding from a nonbankruptcy court to the federal district court for the district where the civil action is pending, if there is proper jurisdiction under 28 U.S.C. § 1334. [28 U.S.C. § 1452(a); *but see* **Rivet v. Regions Bank of Louisiana,** 522 U.S. 470 (1998) (holding improper removal of a state court mortgage action, explaining that a prior federal bankruptcy court judgment had not transformed the state-law claims into federal claims but instead had extinguished them, and holding that there is no "preclusion exception to the rule . . . that a defendant cannot remove on the basis of a federal defense")] Upon removal to the district court, the action then is automatically referred to the bankruptcy court. [28 U.S.C. § 157(a)] The notice of removal is filed in the bankruptcy court. [Bankruptcy Rules 9027(a)(1), 9001(3)]

a. Exceptions

Proceedings in the United States Tax Court or civil actions by governmental units to enforce their police or regulatory powers are not subject to removal. [28 U.S.C. § 1452(a)]

2. Remand

The court to which a claim or cause of action has been removed has the power, based on the equities, to remand the action to the forum where it was pending. [28 U.S.C. § 1452(b)]

a. Appeal

A bankruptcy court's order to remand or not to remand a removed proceeding is reviewable by the district court, but a remand decision by the district court is not reviewable by the court of appeals or the Supreme Court. [28 U.S.C. § 1452(b); **Things Remembered, Inc. v. Petrarca,** 516 U.S. 124 (1995) (district court order remanding on jurisdictional, as opposed to equitable, basis held not reviewable by court of appeals)]

J. Venue

1. Bankruptcy Case

The appropriate venue for the *filing of a bankruptcy petition* is in the federal district where the debtor has maintained her *residence, domicile, principal place of business* in the United States, or *principal assets* in the United States during, or for the longest portion of, the 180-day period immediately before commencement of the case. [28 U.S.C. § 1408(1)] The statute is written in the disjunctive; thus, a person or entity may file for relief under the Bankruptcy Code in any district that satisfies one of the four alternatives for venue: (i) the debtor's *domicile,* (ii) the debtor's *residence,* (iii) the location of the debtor's *principal place of business* in the United States, *or* (iv) the location of the debtor's *principal assets* in the United States. [*In re* **First Fruits Holdings, LLC,** 2018 WL 2759384 (Bankr. E.D. N.C. 2018)] Venue is also proper in a district where a bankruptcy case concerning a general partner, partnership, or affiliate of the debtor is pending. [28 U.S.C. § 1408(2); B.C. § 101(2) (definition of affiliate)]

e.g. **Example:** Debtor filed for bankruptcy in the Western District of Missouri. Debtor's residence and domicile were in Colorado, but Debtor's principal place of business—his law office—was located in the Western District of Missouri. Creditor filed a motion to dismiss the bankruptcy case for improper venue. The bankruptcy court granted the motion, concluding that Debtor was a resident of Colorado and that the majority of his assets were located in Colorado. On appeal, the court reversed and remanded. The Bankruptcy Appellate Panel ("BAP") explained that because the § 1408 provides "four alternative bases for venue, the statute allows many possible locations where an entity or individual may file for bankruptcy protection." The Debtor did not contest that his residence, domicile, and the location of his principal assets were in Colorado. Debtor argued, however, that his principal place of business was in Missouri, thereby making venue proper. The BAP reversed the bankruptcy court's decision, concluding that the bankruptcy court had erred in finding that the residence and principal place of business of a sole proprietor necessarily must be the same. The BAP remanded for a determination by the bankruptcy court of the Debtor's principal place of business. [**Broady v. Harvey (*In re* Broady**), 247 B.R. 470 (B.A.P. 8th Cir. 2000)]

Note: Remember that the state law exemptions applicable to debtor's case may *not* be the exemptions for the state in which debtor files for bankruptcy and in which venue is proper. [B.C. § 522(b)(3)]

2. Bankruptcy Proceedings

The general rule for a *proceeding* arising under the Code, or arising in or related to a bankruptcy case, is that venue lies in the ***district in which the case is pending.*** [28 U.S.C. § 1409(a)] *Note:* The venue rules under 28 U.S.C. § 1408 apply to filing of the bankruptcy case itself, i.e., where you file the bankruptcy petition. The venue rules under 28 U.S.C. § 1409 apply to *proceedings* arising under the Code, or in or related to the bankruptcy case.

a. Exception—Proceedings for Recovery of Small Debts

With the exception of certain post-petition claims, a bankruptcy trustee must file a proceeding *arising in or related to* the bankruptcy case in the district where the defendant resides if the proceeding is to recover:

(i) *money or property* worth less than *$1,375;*

(ii) *a consumer debt* of less than *$20,450;* or

(iii) *a non-consumer debt against a non-insider* of less than *$13,650.*

[28 U.S.C. § 1409(b)] The reason for this "small debt" exception is to "prevent[ ] unfairness to distant debtors of the estate, when the cost of defending would be greater than the cost of paying the debt owed." [H.R. Rep. No. 95–595, at 446 (1977) (discussion of 28 U.S.C. § 1475(b), which has been superseded and replaced by § 1409(b); *see* 1 Collier ¶ 1409(2))]

Note: The language of §§ 1409(a) and (b) differ. Section 1409(a) covers proceedings arising under the Bankruptcy Code, or arising in or related to a bankruptcy case. Section 1409(b) covers proceedings arising in or related to a bankruptcy case. [**Creditors' Trust v. Crown Packaging Corp. (*In re* Nukote**), 457 B.R. 668 (Bankr. M.D. Tenn. 2011) (noting that "there is no reference to proceedings 'arising under title 11' in § 1409(b)")] The legislative history does not explain the difference in wording. [*See* **Creditors' Trust**, *supra* (after exhaustive review of legislative history, concluding that "no discussion of the inclusion or exclusion of the phrase 'arising under title 11' in either subsection (a) or (b) ha[d] been discovered")]

b. Exception to the Small Debt Exception—Certain Post-Petition Claims of Trustee

The trustee may bring a proceeding ***arising under the Code, or arising in or related to*** a bankruptcy case based on a claim that arises ***post-petition from the operation of the debtor's business*** only in the district where the action could have been filed under applicable nonbankruptcy venue law. [28 U.S.C. § 1409(d)] This rule applies even if the trustee's claim is for a small amount that, otherwise, would qualify for the exception contained in 28 U.S.C. § 1409(b).

c. Post-Petition Claims Against Estate

A proceeding ***against the trustee*** based on a cause of action that arises post-petition from the operation of the debtor's business may be brought either in the district where the case is pending *or* in the district where the action could have been commenced under applicable nonbankruptcy venue law. [28 U.S.C. § 1409(e); B.C. §§ 323(a), 1107]

d. Trustee as Statutory Successor

A seldom-used *permissive* venue provision provides the trustee, as the statutory successor to the debtor or to creditors under Code §§ 541 or 544(b), the *option* of commencing a proceeding arising in or related to the bankruptcy case in the district where the case is pending *or* in the district where it could have been brought by the debtor or such creditors under applicable nonbankruptcy venue law if the bankruptcy case had not been filed. [28 U.S.C. § 1409(c)] This provision, however, is subject to the small debt exception explained above. [28 U.S.C. § 1409(b)]

3. Change of Venue

A case may be transferred by one district court to another "in the interest of justice or for the convenience of the parties." [28 U.S.C. § 1412; Bankruptcy Rule 1014(a)(1)] The bankruptcy court can order a transfer, since motions to change venue generally are treated as core proceedings. [*See, e.g.,* **Terry Manufacturing Co. v. Steel Law Firm, P.C. (*In re* Terry Manufacturing Co.),** 323 B.R. 507 (Bankr. M.D. Ala. 2005)]

a. When Venue of the Case Is Proper

The decision to transfer venue lies within the bankruptcy court's sound discretion, and the moving party bears the burden of proof. [**Gentry Steel Fabrication, Inc. v. Howard S. Wright Construction Co. (*In re* Gentry Steel Fabrication, Inc.),** 325 B.R. 311 (Bankr. M.D. Ala. 2005)] If the bankruptcy case was filed in a proper district, the court examines various factors in ruling on a request to change the venue to another district. The tests used by the courts vary. Some courts use different multi-factor tests, depending on whether the court is analyzing the transfer motion under the "interest of justice" or the "convenience of the parties" prong of § 1412. [*See, e.g.,* **Terry Manufacturing,** *supra* (using 7-factor test for evaluating the "interest of justice" and 5-factor test for evaluating "convenience of the parties"); **Gentry Steel,** *supra* (same)] Other courts employ a single, multi-factor test in ruling on a motion to transfer venue of a bankruptcy case. [*See, e.g.,* ***In re* Rehoboth Hospitality, LP,** 2011 WL 5024267 (Bankr. D. Del. 2011) (using 8-factor test] The factors used in these various tests, however, often are similar. Some common factors include (i) the economics of estate administration; (ii) the proximity of needed witnesses to the court; and (iii) the proximity of the debtor and creditors to the court.

b. When Venue of the Case Is Improper

If a case was filed in the wrong district, i.e., venue is improper, the bankruptcy court, upon motion of a party in interest or *sua sponte,* may transfer the case to another district if transfer is in *the interest of justice* or for the *convenience of the parties.* Notice and a hearing are required. [Bankruptcy Rule 1014(a)(2)]

(i) May the Bankruptcy Court Dismiss the Case?

What is unclear is whether the court may *dismiss the case.* While Bankruptcy Rule 1014 provides that the court "may dismiss the case or transfer" it, 28 U.S.C. § 1412 is silent on dismissal, stating only that the court "may transfer" the case. [28 U.S.C. § 1412; Bankruptcy Rule 1014(a)(2)] The difference in language has led to confusion, but a noted commentator concludes that dismissal should not be an option for the *bankruptcy court*, in part, due to the fact that 28 U.S.C. § 1406 provides that if venue is improper in the *district court*, the court may dismiss or transfer the case. [1 Collier ¶ 4.05(4)(a); *compare* 28 U.S.C. § 1406(a) *with* 28 U.S.C. § 1412]

(ii) Must Transfer Be to a Proper Venue?

Unlike § 1406, § 1412 does not provide that the transfer be to a district in which the case "could have been brought." [*Compare* 28 U.S.C. § 1406(a) *with* 28 U.S.C. § 1412] Bankruptcy Rule 1014 also does not require transfer to a proper venue. [Bankruptcy Rule 1014(a)(2); *see* 1 Collier ¶ 4.05]

(iii) Retain the Case

May the bankruptcy court simply *not* transfer the case and instead retain it? The answer to that question is not clear. [1 Collier ¶ 4.05(4)(a)]

K. Appeals

1. Appeal from Bankruptcy Court

An appeal may be taken from the bankruptcy court to the federal district court or to a bankruptcy appellate panel, if the jurisdiction has such a panel. [28 U.S.C. § 158] Under certain limited circumstances, a party may appeal directly to the court of appeals. [28 U.S.C. § 158(d)(2)]

a. District Court

The appellate jurisdiction of the district court and the bankruptcy appellate panel includes appeals from final orders, judgments, and decrees of the bankruptcy court, and from interlocutory orders extending or shortening the debtor's exclusivity period for filing a plan. [28 U.S.C. § 158(a); B.C. § 1121(d)] Appellate jurisdiction over interlocutory orders is by leave of the district court or the bankruptcy appellate panel. [28 U.S.C. § 158(a)(3); Bankruptcy Rule 8004]

(i) Distinguish—Recommendations from Bankruptcy Court

Proposed *findings of fact and conclusions of law* submitted by the bankruptcy court to the district court in a *non-core matter* or a *Stern claim* are *not issues on appeal,* but merely recommendations to the district court for: (i) its consideration; (ii) *de novo* review of matters objected to; and (iii) entry of final order or judgment. [28 U.S.C. § 157(c)(1)]

b. Bankruptcy Appellate Panels: Overview

The judicial council of each circuit must establish a bankruptcy appellate panel, comprised of bankruptcy judges from that circuit, to hear appeals *unless* (i) there are *insufficient judicial resources* or (ii) the procedure would cause *undue delay or increased cost* to parties in bankruptcy cases. [28 U.S.C. § 158(b)(1)] Each appeal is to be heard by three members of the bankruptcy appellate panel who are not from the district where the appeal arises. [28 U.S.C. § 158(b)(5), (c)(1)]

Unless the appellant elects at the time of the appeal or any other party elects, no later than *30 days* after service of the appeal notice, to have the district court hear the appeal, the bankruptcy appellate panel will hear the appeal. [28 U.S.C. § 158(c)(1); *see* Bankruptcy Rule 8005]

Note: Currently, the First, Sixth, Eighth, Ninth, and Tenth Circuits have established Bankruptcy Appellate Panels.

c. Bankruptcy Appellate Panel Decisions: Precedential Value

Decisions of the bankruptcy appellate panel bind the parties to the dispute before the court. But, whether the panel's decisions are binding on bankruptcy courts within the circuit is unclear. Some courts hold that decisions of the bankruptcy appellate panel are binding on all bankruptcy courts within the circuit. Other courts conclude that the decisions are not binding on any bankruptcy court within the circuit. Still other courts hold that the decisions are binding only on the bankruptcy courts in the district from which the appeal arose. [*See* **Rhiel v. Ohio-Health Corp. (*In re* Hunter),** 380 B.R. 753 (Bankr. S.D. Ohio 2008) (discussing various approaches taken by the courts)]

d. Direct Appeal to Circuit Court

In 2005, Congress added a new subsection to § 158(d) to provide, under certain circumstances, for a direct appeal to the circuit court. The legislative history shows that Congress added the subsection because it wanted to " 'establish a dependable body of case law' " and was concerned about "the paucity of settled bankruptcy-law precedent." [**Weber v. United States Trustee,** 484 F.3d 154 (2d Cir. 2007)]

(i) File Notice of Appeal

The orders from which a direct appeal may be taken are those described in § 158(a)—final orders, judgments, and decrees; interlocutory orders expanding or shortening the exclusivity period under § 1121; and other interlocutory orders and decrees. [28 U.S.C. §§ 158(a), (d)(2)(A)] The process for securing a direct appeal involves several steps.

The party seeking a direct appeal must file a *timely notice of appeal.* [Bankruptcy Rule 8006(a)(2) (stating certification is effective when, among other things, a "timely appeal has been taken" under Bankruptcy Rules 8003 or 8004)]

(ii) Certification

There must be the requisite statutory certification made either by (a) the *bankruptcy court, district court, or bankruptcy appellate panel* involved or (b) *all the appellants and appellees,* if any. The court may act on its own motion or on the request of a party in interest. [28 U.S.C. § 158(d)(2)(A)] The request for certification must be made *no later than 60 days* after entry of the judgment, order, or decree. [28 U.S.C. § 158(d)(2)(E)]

(1) Circumstances Justifying Direct Appeal

The statute provides three alternative sets of circumstances that would justify a direct appeal. Thus, the certification must state that:

(a) the judgment, order or decree involves a legal question on which there is *no controlling decision* from the Supreme Court or the court of appeals for the circuit *or* involves a matter of *public importance* [28 U.S.C. § 158(d)(2)(A)(i)];

(b) the judgment, order, or decree involves a legal question requiring *resolution of conflicting decisions* [28 U.S.C. § 158(d)(2)(A)(ii); *see* **In re MPF Holding US LLC,** 444 B.R. 719 (Bankr. S.D. Tex. 2011) (certifying direct appeal, because bankruptcy court's interpretation of

Fifth Circuit precedent conflicted with interpretation of other bankruptcy courts, including two other judges in Northern District of Texas)]; *or*

(c) an immediate appeal from the judgment, order, or decree may *materially advance the progress* of the case or proceeding [28 U.S.C. § 158(d)(2)(A)(iii)].

Note: Section 158(d)(2) is drafted in the disjunctive, so only *one of the three conditions* must be satisfied.

(2) When the Court Must Certify

If the bankruptcy court, district court, or bankruptcy appellate panel, either on it its own motion or on request of a party in interest, determines that one of the three reasons outlined above for certification exists, then the court must make the certification. [28 U.S.C. § 158(d)(2)(B)(i)] The court also must make the certification if it receives a request from a *majority of appellants and a majority of appellees,* if any, to make the certification. [28 U.S.C. § 158(d)(2)(B)(ii)] There is a drafting issue in § 158(d)(2)(B)(ii); unlike § 158(d)(2)(B)(i), it fails to specifically state that one of the three circumstances must exist before the court must make the certification. As a result, it is unclear whether a certification by a majority of appellants and appellees, without more, suffices. [1 Collier ¶ 5.06(1)]

(iii) Authorization by Court of Appeals

The Court of Appeals must authorize the direct appeal. [28 U.S.C. § 158(d)(2)(A)] Thus, even if there is a certification that complies with the statutory requirements, the Court of Appeals may decide not to accept the direct appeal. [**Weber,** *supra* (declining to exercise jurisdiction to hear appeal); *see* **In re City of Detroit,** 504 B.R. 191 (Bankr. E.D. Mich. 2013) (certifying that appeals of its order involved matter of public importance but recommending that Court of Appeals decline to authorize the direct appeals)]

e. "Clearly Erroneous" Standard

On appeal, the reviewing court must use the "clearly erroneous" standard with regard to the bankruptcy court's findings of fact. [Bankruptcy Rules 7052 (adversary proceedings), 9014(c) (contested matters)] The bankruptcy court's conclusions of law, however, are subject to *de novo* review. [**Fannie Mae v. Village Green I, GP,** 483 B.R. 807 (W.D. Tenn. 2012)]

f. Interlocutory Orders

The district court or bankruptcy appellate panel may grant leave to appeal an interlocutory order of the bankruptcy court. A party seeking leave to appeal must file a notice of appeal with the bankruptcy court clerk within *14 days* of the bankruptcy court's order. [28 U.S.C. § 158(a)(3); Bankruptcy Rules 8004(a), 8002(a)(1)] Neither the Code nor the Bankruptcy Rules provides a standard for determining whether to grant leave to appeal. Most courts, however, apply the "analogous standard for certifying an interlocutory appeal set forth in 28 U.S.C. § 1292(b)." [**Law Debenture Trust Co. v. Calpine Corp. (In re Calpine Corp.),** 356 B.R. 585 (S.D. N.Y. 2007); *see also* **Cadles of Grassy Meadows II, LLC v. St. Clair (In re St. Clair),** 2014 WL 279850 (E.D. N.Y. 2014) (stating that "majority of courts in [Second Circuit] and elsewhere" have held that the appropriate standard is set forth in § 1292(b))] Section 1292(b) provides for review of an interlocutory order if (i) there is a controlling question of law as to which there is substantial ground for difference of opinion, and (ii) an immediate appeal may materially advance the ultimate termination of the litigation. [28 U.S.C. § 1292(b)] In other words, leave to appeal an interlocutory order is justified only under *exceptional circumstances.* [**Law Debenture,** *supra*]

g. Time for Appeal

With certain limited exceptions, a party must file a notice of appeal *14 days* after entry of the bankruptcy judge's order, judgment, or decree being appealed. The notice of appeal must be filed with the clerk of the *bankruptcy court.* [28 U.S.C. § 158(c)(2); Bankruptcy Rules 8002(a)(1)] The district court or bankruptcy appellate panel lacks jurisdiction to hear a case in which a timely notice of appeal is not filed. [*In re* **Dorsey,** 870 F.3d 359 (5th Cir. 2017) (stating that failure to timely file a notice of appeal is jurisdictional); *see* Bankruptcy Rule 8003(a)(1)]

2. Appeal from District Court or Bankruptcy Appellate Panel

An appeal may be taken to the circuit court from a *final decision, order, or judgment* of: (i) the district court, in its *appellate capacity* or (ii) the bankruptcy appellate panel. [28 U.S.C. § 158(d)(1)] The Supreme Court has held that appeals from *interlocutory orders* of the district court sitting in its appellate capacity are governed by the general standard for review of interlocutory orders. [**Connecticut National Bank v. Germain,** 503 U.S. 249 (1992)]

a. Remands

What if the district court or appellate panel, in reviewing a bankruptcy court final order, remands the case to the bankruptcy court? Is the district court's or appellate panel's decision final or interlocutory? The majority of circuits hold that a district court or BAP order remanding a case to the bankruptcy court for "significant further proceedings" is not final and appealable. If the remand order is for a "purely ministerial function," then it is final and appealable under § 158(d)(1). [*See, e.g.,* **Gordon v. Bank of America (***In re* **Gordon),** 743 F.3d 720 (10th Cir. 2014) (holding that district court order reversing bankruptcy court order confirming debtors' Chapter 13 plan and remanding to the bankruptcy court for entry of plan confirmation and related orders was not final and appealable order); *In re* **Swegan,** 555 F.3d. 510 (6th Cir. 2009) (holding that bankruptcy appellate court order reversing bankruptcy court order granting summary judgment to debtor on his motion to discharge debt and remanding the adversary proceeding for trial was not final and appealable); **Settembre v. Fidelity & Guaranty Life Insurance Co.,** 552 F.3d 438 (6th Cir. 2009) (holding that district court order reversing bankruptcy court order granting summary judgment to creditor on its denial of discharge complaint and remanding case for trial was not final and appealable order)]

b. What Constitutes a Final Order?

Deciding whether a particular order is final is not an easy task, but it is an important one because § 158 provides that the courts of appeals have jurisdiction of *final* orders, judgments, and decrees. [28 U.S.C. § 158(d)(1)] The reason for the finality requirement is to "prevent piecemeal reviews and obstructing or impeding ongoing judicial proceedings" and to promote "judicial efficiency and hasten[ ] the ultimate termination of litigation." [*In re* **City of Detroit,** 504 B.R. 191 (Bankr. E.D. Mich. 2013); *see* **Eisen v. Carlisle & Jacquelin,** 417 U.S. 156 (1974) (not a bankruptcy case)]

Unlike ordinary civil litigation, bankruptcy cases involve an "aggregation of individual controversies." [1 Collier ¶ 5.08(1)(b)] As a result, in the bankruptcy context, courts have taken a pragmatic approach and apply what some courts call "flexible finality," which recognizes that the "breadth of bankruptcy cases necessitates an approach that allows for the efficient resolution of certain discrete disputes that may arise in a given bankruptcy." [*In re* **McKinney,** 610 F.3d 399 (7th Cir. 2010); *but see* **Ritzen Group, Inc. v. Jackson Masonry, LLC (*In re* Jackson Masonry, LLC),** 2018 WL 4997779 (6th Cir. 2018) (noting that "courts have taken the loose finality in bankruptcy as a license for judicial invention" which has resulted in "a series of vague tests that are impossible to apply consistently")] Courts have developed a liberal definition of finality in the context of bankruptcy by viewing *a proceeding* as the "relevant judicial unit for purposes of finality." Thus, an order that "conclusively determines a separable dispute over a creditor's claim or priority" is final. [*In re* **Saco Local Development Corp.,** 711 F.2d 441 (1st Cir. 1983)]

e.g. **Example—Final Order:** An order holding that Insurance Company's claim for Debtor's "employee group life, health, and disability insurance premiums" was entitled to priority status under § 507(a)(4) constituted a final appealable order, because it "effectively settle[d] the amount due the creditor." [*In re* **Saco Local Development Corp.,** *supra*]

e.g. **Example—Not Final:** Debtor filed for relief under Chapter 13. Debtor owned property on which Bank held the mortgage. Debtor proposed a Chapter 13 plan; Bank objected to its treatment under the plan. The bankruptcy court denied confirmation and ordered Debtor to propose a new plan within 30 days. In a unanimous decision, the Supreme Court held that an order denying confirmation of a plan is not a final order that a debtor can immediately appeal. The Court explained that the "relevant proceeding is the process of attempting to arrive at an approved plan that would allow the bankruptcy to move forward." The bankruptcy court's order denying confirmation did not terminate that proceeding, because Debtor was free to propose another plan. [**Bullard v. Blue Hills Bank,** 135 S.Ct. 1686 (2015)]

3. District Court as Court of Original Jurisdiction

If the district court functions as a court of original jurisdiction, rather than as an appellate court, e.g., in **non-core or Stern-claim** proceedings in which the parties do not consent or in proceedings that have been **withdrawn,** the general standard for an appeal to the circuit court of the district court's final decision governs. [28 U.S.C. § 1291]

4. Orders Concerning Automatic Stay

The circuits that have addressed the issue all have held that a bankruptcy court order lifting the automatic stay is a final order. The vast majority of courts also have ruled that a bankruptcy court order refusing to lift the automatic stay is a final order. [1 Collier ¶ 5.09]

L. Sovereign Immunity

1. Waiver

Bankruptcy Code § 106 waives the sovereign immunity of governmental units with respect to a number of bankruptcy issues. [*See* B.C. § 106(a)(1) (listing sections for which sovereign immunity is abrogated)] This waiver is intended to apply to monetary recoveries, other than punitive damages awards, as well as to declaratory or injunctive relief. [B.C. §§ 106(a)(1), (3)]

a. Illustrations of Waiver

A governmental unit's sovereign immunity is waived with respect to the trustee's avoidance powers, because §§ 542, 543, 544, 545, 547, 548, and 549, respectively, are included in the list in § 106(a)(1).

b. Distinguish § 541 Property Provision

It is significant that § 541 on property of the estate is excluded from the sections specified in § 106(a)(1), the effect of which is that the trustee has no greater rights than the debtor concerning causes of action under § 541. Therefore, if property of the estate includes a debtor's cause of action against a governmental unit that is barred by sovereign immunity, the trustee cannot pursue the action.

e.g. **Example:** Debtor is a farmer who entered into a ten-year lease with Tribe for more than a million acres of farmland. The leased property is held in trust for the Tribe by the United States. The Bureau of Indian Affairs ("BIA") approved the lease. Several years into the lease, the BIA informed Debtor that a bridge connecting the north and south portions of the property was dangerous and would be removed. Debtor was unsuccessful in working out an arrangement with the BIA or a reduction in rent from the Tribe, and was unable to use the north end of the property as a result of the bridge's removal. Debtor defaulted on the lease and subsequently filed for relief under Chapter 11. Debtor files an inverse condemnation action against the BIA in bankruptcy court and asks for $2 million in damages. Debtor's action may not proceed against the BIA in bankruptcy court. The cause of action belongs to the bankruptcy estate and any recovery becomes property of the estate, but § 106 of the Bankruptcy Code does not waive the government's sovereign immunity as to Debtor's takings clause cause of action. Instead, the Tucker Act waives the government's sovereign immunity, but only for suits filed in the United States Court of Federal Claims. Because the bankruptcy court lacks jurisdiction to hear Tucker Act claims, the cause of action is transferred to the Federal Court of Claims. [**McGuire v. United States,** 550 F.3d 903 (9th Cir. 2008)]

2. Offset Against Governmental Claims Permitted

If property of the estate includes a claim against a governmental unit that would be barred by sovereign immunity, the trustee can offset that claim against a claim of the governmental unit, e.g., an unrelated tax claim, but only up to the amount of the government's claim, *regardless of whether a claim of the governmental unit has been filed or allowed.* [B.C. § 106(c)]

3. Compulsory Counterclaims: Sovereign Immunity Waived

If a governmental unit has filed a proof of claim in the bankruptcy case, then it is deemed to have waived sovereign immunity with regard to a compulsory counterclaim to its claim that arose out of the same transaction or occurrence. [B.C. § 106(b)]

4. State Sovereign Immunity and § 106

The Supreme Court has concluded that the States, by giving Congress the power to make uniform laws on bankruptcy, agreed "not to assert any sovereign immunity defense they might have had in proceedings" created by Congress under the Bankruptcy Clause. In a case involving a preference avoidance action brought by the liquidating supervisor in a Chapter 11 case against a State entity, the Court explained that the issue was not whether Congress had abrogated the State's sovereign immunity under § 106(a). Rather, the question was whether Congress' decision to make States amenable to preference actions fell within the scope of its powers under the Bankruptcy Clause. The Court concluded that it was "beyond peradventure" that Congress had such power, which "arises from the Bankruptcy Clause itself." [**Central Virginia Community College v. Katz,** 546 U.S. 356 (2006)] The Supreme Court's opinion in a nonbankruptcy case decided prior to *Katz* raised serious questions about the validity of § 106's waiver of the states' Eleventh Amendment sovereign immunity. [*See* **Seminole Tribe of Florida v. Florida,** 517 U.S. 44 (1996)] In *Katz,* the majority acknowledged that statements made in *Seminole Tribe* "reflected an assumption that the holding in that case would apply to the Bankruptcy Clause." But, after "careful study and reflection," the Court concluded "that that assumption was erroneous." [**Central Virginia Community College v. Katz,** *supra*] Thus, the Court's decision in *Katz* appears to have settled the question of § 106(a)'s constitutionality. [2 Collier ¶ 106.02]

Chapter Three

Commencement and Administration of the Case

Chapter Approach

In answering an examination question concerning the commencement of a bankruptcy case, be certain to consider all of the items on the following checklist:

1. *Is the debtor a person* as defined in the Bankruptcy Code—i.e., an individual, a partnership, or a corporation?

2. *Does the debtor have a residence, domicile, place of business,* or *property* in the United States?

3. *What kind of relief* is most suitable under the debtor's financial circumstances? Of course, the debtor's future expected income will be an important factor in determining whether repayment to creditors under a Chapter 11, 12, or 13 plan is feasible or whether liquidation under Chapter 7 is more appropriate.

4. *Is the debtor eligible* under the desired chapter?

5. *If the debtor is married,* is it advisable to file a *joint* petition?

6. *Is the filing of an involuntary case* against the debtor being considered by creditors?

   a. Will the case be filed under *Chapter 7 or Chapter 11?* (Remember that an involuntary petition cannot be filed under Chapter 12 or Chapter 13.)

   b. Is the debtor *generally not paying debts as they come due?*

   c. If the debtor has *12 or more creditors* holding noncontingent, undisputed claims, are there *at least three* such creditors who are willing to file an involuntary petition, and does the aggregate of their *unsecured,* noncontingent, undisputed claims total at least *$16,750?*

   d. If the debtor has *fewer than 12* creditors holding noncontingent, undisputed claims, is there *one* (or more) such creditor(s) willing to file an involuntary petition and does the aggregate of that creditor's (creditors') *unsecured,* noncontingent, undisputed claim(s) total at least *$16,750?*

7. *Is there a ground for dismissal* of the bankruptcy petition? Has the petition been filed in *good faith?*

8. *Do circumstances indicate that conversion* to another chapter would be more appropriate than the chapter under which the case was filed? Is the debtor eligible for relief under the other chapter?

A. Eligibility Requirements: All Chapters

1. Only Persons May File

Only a *person* (individual, partnership, or corporation) that *resides* or has a *domicile, a place of business, or property in the United States* is eligible to be a debtor under the Bankruptcy Code. (*Note:* A municipality also may be eligible under Chapter 9, but that is a topic that is beyond the scope of this book.) [B.C. § 109(a)]

a. **Insolvency Not Required**

A person need not be insolvent to be eligible to be a debtor under the Code. [B.C. § 109]

b. **Corporation Is a Person**

The bankruptcy definition of the term "corporation" is expansive and includes business trusts and most companies or associations with corporate attributes. [B.C. § 101(9)(A)] A limited partnership is not a corporation for purposes of the Bankruptcy Code. [B.C. § 101(9)(B)] Determining whether an entity qualifies as a corporation for purposes of the Bankruptcy Code is a federal question, so the fact that an entity is a corporation for state law purposes is not dispositive. Nonetheless, if an entity is a corporation under state law, then it "enjoys a presumption of being a corporation for purposes of § 101(9)" and the party claiming that the entity is not a corporation under § 101(9) bears the burden of proof on that issue. [*In re* **Charles St. African Methodist Episcopal Church,** 478 B.R. 73 (Bankr. D. Mass. 2012)]

e.g. **Example—Labor Union:** A labor union is eligible for relief under the Bankruptcy Code. The Code defines the term "corporation" to include an "unincorporated company or association." [B.C. § 101(9)(A)(iv)] The legislative history shows that the term "unincorporated association" was "intended specifically to include a labor union." [H.R. Rep. 95–595, at 309 (1977); *see* **In re Lane County Sheriff's Officers Association, Inc.,** 16 B.R. 190 (Bankr. D. Or. 1981)]

e.g. **Example—Business Trust:** Debtor Catholic School Employees Pension Trust ("Pension Trust") filed for relief under Chapter 11. Numerous creditors filed motions to dismiss, claiming that the Pension Trust was not eligible to file a bankruptcy petition because it was not a business trust and, hence, not a corporation for purposes of the Bankruptcy Code. The bankruptcy court dismissed the petition. The court explained that the Pension Trust was established to preserve the trust *res,* not to generate income or profit. In addition, the Pension Trust did not engage in business activities other than activities incidental to protecting and preserving the trust corpus. Thus, the court held that Pension Trust was not a business trust and, thus, not eligible to file for relief under the Bankruptcy Code. [*In re* **Catholic School Employees Pension Trust,** 584 B.R. 82 (Bankr. D. P.R. 2018); B.C. § 101(9)(A)(v)]

2. When a Debtor May Not File for Bankruptcy Relief

In 2005, Congress added a pre-bankruptcy credit counseling requirement for individual debtors. With limited exceptions, an individual may not file for bankruptcy until she has satisfied this credit counseling requirement. The Code also prevents certain individual debtors from re-filing for bankruptcy after dismissal of their earlier bankruptcy case.

a. **Individual Credit Counseling Requirement**

An ***individual debtor*** may not file for relief under any chapter of the Bankruptcy Code for which she is otherwise eligible unless ***prior to filing*** she first obtained ***credit counseling*** from an ***approved nonprofit budget and credit counseling agency*** during the ***180 days*** before filing her bankruptcy petition. Credit counseling may be in the form of ***individual or group briefings*** conducted in person, over the ***phone or on the Internet.*** [B.C. § 109(h)(1)]

b. **Exceptions to Credit Counseling Requirement**

In the following situations, an individual debtor need not satisfy the Code's credit counseling requirement before filing for bankruptcy.

(i) No Agencies in District

The credit-counseling requirement does not apply to a debtor who resides in a district for which the United States trustee or the Bankruptcy Administrator has determined that the credit counseling agencies in the district are not *reasonably able* to provide such services.

(ii) Temporary Exigent Circumstances Certification

A debtor who, due to *exigent circumstances,* was unable to obtain credit-counseling services *during the 5 days* starting on the date on which she requested such services may obtain a *temporary waiver* of the requirement that she obtain credit counseling *prior* to filing for relief under the Bankruptcy Code. To obtain a waiver of the pre-filing credit-counseling requirement, the debtor must submit to the bankruptcy court a *certification* that

(a) describes the *exigent circumstances;*

(b) states the debtor's efforts to obtain counseling during the *5-day period;* and

(c) is *satisfactory to the court.* [B.C. § 109(h)(3)(A)]

Note: This exception is only a *temporary,* pre-filing waiver of the credit counseling requirement. The debtor who uses this exception must obtain credit counseling services *no later than 30 days after filing the petition,* unless the bankruptcy court, on a showing of *cause, extends* the 30 days an additional *15 days.* [B.C. § 109(h)(3)(B)]

(iii) Disabled, Incapacitated, or Active Military Duty

The credit counseling requirement does not apply to a debtor whom the court, *after notice and a hearing,* determines is unable to meet the requirement due to *incapacity, disability, or active military duty in a military combat zone.* [B.C. § 109(h)(4)]

c. Nonprofit Budget and Credit Counseling Agencies

The bankruptcy court clerk must maintain a *publicly available list* of nonprofit budget and credit counseling services that the United States trustee or bankruptcy administrator has approved. [B.C. § 111(a)(1)] To qualify, an agency must demonstrate that it will provide *qualified counselors,* maintain adequate provision for *safekeeping and payment* of *client funds,* provide *adequate counseling* for client credit problems, and deal responsibly and effectively with other matters related to the *quality, effectiveness, and financial security of its services.* [B.C. § 111(c)(1)] If the agency charges a fee, the *fee must be reasonable,* and services must be provided without regard to ability to pay. [B.C. § 111(c)(2)(B)] The agency *cannot pay commissions or bonuses* to its trained counselors that are based on the outcome of the agency's counseling services. [B.C. § 111(c)(2)(F)] No agency may provide to a *credit reporting agency* information about whether a debtor has received or sought instruction on personal financial management from the agency. [B.C. § 111(g)(1)]

(i) Damages

If a nonprofit budget and credit counseling agency *willfully or negligently* fails to comply with any Code requirement with respect to the debtor, it will be liable for *actual damages* that the debtor incurred as a result of the violation and any *court costs or reasonable attorneys' fees* incurred in an action to recover such damages. [B.C. § 111(g)(2)]

d. Multiple Petitions

An *individual* or a *family farmer* is not eligible to file a petition under any chapter of the Bankruptcy Code if she has been a debtor in a case that was *dismissed in the preceding 180 days,* either because of the debtor's willful failure to obey court orders or "to appear before the court in proper prosecution of the case," *or* because she requested a voluntary dismissal of the case following a party's request for relief from the automatic stay. [B.C. § 109(g)] *Rationale:* This provision is intended to curtail abusive and repetitive filings, particularly in consumer bankruptcy cases. Another Code provision that addresses Congress' concern with abusive and repetitive filings is § 362(c), which Congress amended with the passage of BAPCPA in 2005.

e.g. **Example—Failure to obey court orders or prosecute case:** Husband and Wife filed for relief under Chapter 7. The bankruptcy court dismissed their petition for "cause," citing debtors' failure (i) to attend at least two § 341 meetings, (ii) to produce business records, and (iii) to truthfully and fully disclose their assets and business enterprises. Thirty-six days after dismissal, Husband filed again for relief under Chapter 7 and Creditor filed a motion to dismiss the petition pursuant to § 109(g). The bankruptcy court granted Creditor's motion to dismiss. First, the court held that Husband's failure to attend multiple § 341 meetings constituted willful failure to abide by court orders. The court noted that most courts have found that "attendance at section 341 meetings is mandated by court order, as that term is used in section 109(g)(1)." Second, the court held that Husband's petition merited dismissal under the second prong of § 109(g)(1)— willful failure to properly prosecute the bankruptcy case. The bankruptcy court explained that proper prosecution is not limited to physical appearance before the court; it applies to the debtor's compliance with his statutory duties. Because Husband had failed in his prior Chapter 7 case to attend § 341 meetings and accurately disclose assets and liabilities on both his schedules and to the Chapter 7 trustee, Husband had failed to perform his statutory duties. This conduct constituted willful failure to appear before the court in proper prosecution of the case. [*In re* **Wen Hua Xu,** 386 B.R. 451 (Bankr. S.D. N.Y. 2008)]

e.g. **Example—Debtor's voluntary dismissal following creditor's request for relief from stay:** Husband and Wife filed for relief under Chapter 13 in April of 2015. (Prior to April 2015, Wife had filed four petitions for relief under Chapter 13 dating back to September of 2011, and Husband had filed two petitions for Chapter 13 relief in 2013 and 2014.) In their joint April 2015 Chapter 13 case, Creditor moved for relief from the automatic stay as to debtors' homestead; later that same day, debtors sought voluntary dismissal of their case. The bankruptcy court granted the debtors' motion to dismiss at the end of July of 2015. About two and half months later, in October of 2015, Husband and Wife filed again for relief under the Bankruptcy Code, although this time they filed a Chapter 11 case. The bankruptcy court dismissed debtors' Chapter 11 case, because debtors were ineligible for bankruptcy relief under § 109(g)(2). [*In re* **Gibas,** 543 B.R. 570 (Bankr. E.D. Wis. 2016)]

B. Chapter-Specific Eligibility Requirements

1. Chapter 7: "Liquidation"

With certain exceptions, Chapter 7 relief is available to *any person* that resides or has a domicile, a place of business, or property in the United States. [B.C. §§ 109(a), (b), 101(41)] *Stockbrokers, commodity brokers, and clearing banks* may be debtors under special provisions of Chapter 7, which are beyond the scope of this summary. [B.C. §§ 741 *et seq.* (stockbrokers), 761 *et seq.* (commodity brokers), 781 *et seq.* (clearing banks)]

a. Exception: Individual Debtors Who Fail "Means" Test

Individual debtors with primarily consumer debts who fail the "means test" are not eligible to file for relief under Chapter 7. [B.C. § 707(b)]

b. Exception: Railroads

Railroads are not eligible for Chapter 7 relief. [B.C. § 109(b)(1)]

c. Exception: Domestic Savings Institutions and Insurance Companies

Domestic banks, insurance companies, credit unions, savings and loan associations, building and loan associations, homestead associations, cooperative banks, and other similar domestic institutions are not eligible for relief under Chapter 7. However, some banking institutions may file for relief under Chapter 7 if a petition is filed at the direction of the Board of Governors of the Federal Reserve System. [B.C. § 109(b)(2)]

(i) Rationale

These kinds of financial institutions are regulated directly by the banking and insurance industries, and "alternate provision is made for their liquidation under various regulatory laws." [H.R. Rep. No. 95–595, at 318 (1977)]

d. Exception: Small Business Investment Companies

Small business investment companies licensed by the Small Business Administration under the Small Business Investment Act of 1958 are not eligible for Chapter 7 relief. [B.C. § 109(b)(2); 15 U.S.C. § 681] The reason for the exclusion is to protect the interests of the Small Business Administration from being subordinated to those of other creditors. [2 Collier ¶ 109.03(3)(a)]

e. Exception: Foreign Savings Institutions and Insurance Companies

A foreign insurance company that is *engaged in such business in the United States* is not eligible for relief under Chapter 7. [B.C. § 109(b)(3)(A)] Foreign banks, savings and loan associations, and other similar financial institutions that have a *branch or agency in the United States* are not eligible for Chapter 7 relief. [B.C. § 109(b)(3)(B); 12 U.S.C. § 3101(b)]

2. Chapter 11: "Reorganization"

Generally, only an individual, partnership, or corporation that is eligible for relief under Chapter 7 may be a debtor under Chapter 11. [B.C. § 109(d)] There are several differences, however, between eligibility under Chapter 7 and eligibility under Chapter 11.

a. **Difference #1: Individual Debtors with Primarily Consumer Debts**

An individual debtor with primarily consumer debts who fails the "means test" may not file for relief under Chapter 7. Chapter 11 does not have a "means test." Chapter 11 is designed principally for business reorganizations, but the Supreme Court has held that a consumer debtor, i.e., an individual not engaged in business, also may qualify for relief under this chapter. [**Toibb v. Radloff,** 501 U.S. 157 (1991)] The vast majority of individual consumer debtors do *not* file for relief under Chapter 11. For example, in calendar year 2016, only one-tenth of one percent of petitions filed by individuals with primarily consumer debt were filed under Chapter 11. [BAPCPA Report—2016]

b. **Difference #2: Stockbrokers and Commodity Brokers**

Stockbrokers and commodity brokers *cannot* be debtors under Chapter 11. [B.C. § 109(d)]

c. **Difference #3: Railroads**

Railroads *are eligible* for relief under special provisions of Chapter 11. [*Compare* B.C. § 109(b)(1) *with* B.C. §§ 109(d), 1161 *et seq.*]

3. Chapter 12: "Family Farmer or Family Fisherman with Regular Annual Income"

A *family farmer or family fisherman* whose *yearly income* is sufficiently *stable and regular* to fund a Chapter 12 plan may file a petition under that chapter. [B.C. §§ 109(f), 101(19), 101(19B)] Certain individuals, individuals and their spouses, corporations, or partnerships may qualify as a family farmer or a family fisherman. [B.C. §§ 101(18), 101(19B)] A Chapter 12 case may be commenced only by the filing of a *voluntary* bankruptcy petition; it can never be commenced by an involuntary petition. [B.C. § 303(a)]

4. Chapter 13: "Adjustment of Debts of Individual with Regular Income"

Chapter 13 relief is available *only to an individual who has regular income,* whose *unsecured debts* total less than *$419,275,* and whose *secured debts* total less than *$1,257,850.* The indebtedness used for these calculations must be noncontingent and liquidated liabilities, determined as of the date of the filing of the petition. [B.C. § 109(e)]

a. **"Individual with Regular Income"**

An individual with regular income is defined as an "individual whose income is sufficiently stable and regular to enable such individual to make payments under a plan under Chapter 13." [B.C. § 101(30)]

(i) Sources of Regular Income

A Chapter 13 debtor's regular income usually is generated from wages or salary, but it may be derived from almost any legitimate source, e.g., interest income, rental income, a pension, a business, a trust, social security, or even Aid to Families with Dependent Children. The key issue is whether it is sufficiently stable and capable of funding the debtor's repayment plan.

Note on Social Security Income: Courts are divided on whether Social Security benefits may be considered in determining a debtor's regular income for purposes of eligibility for relief under Chapter 13. [*See* **Santiago-Monteverde v. Pereira (*In** *re* **Santiago-Monteverde),** 512 B.R. 432 (S.D. N.Y. 2014) (noting split in authority and holding that "Social Security income may not be considered in a Chapter 13 eligibility determination")]

b. Voluntary Petition

A Chapter 13 case must be commenced by the debtor's voluntary petition; it can never be commenced by an involuntary petition. [B.C. § 303(a)]

c. Joint Case

An individual with regular income and his spouse may file a joint petition under Chapter 13, provided that their *aggregate unsecured* indebtedness is less than *$419,275* and that their *aggregate secured* indebtedness is less than *$1,257,850.* [B.C. §§ 302(a), 109(e)]

d. Exception: Stockbrokers and Commodity Brokers

Stockbrokers and commodity brokers do *not* qualify for relief under Chapter 13. [B.C. § 109(e)]

PERSONS *NOT* ELIGIBLE FOR RELIEF UNDER PARTICULAR CHAPTERS—A SUMMARY

Chapter 7	Chapter 11	Chapter 12	Chapter 13
Individual who has not satisfied credit counseling requirement or an exception to requirement § 109(h)	Individual who has not satisfied credit counseling requirement or an exception to requirement § 109(h)	Individual who has not satisfied credit counseling requirement or an exception to requirement § 109(h)	Individual who has not satisfied credit counseling requirement or an exception to requirement § 109(h)
Individual or family farmer with multiple petitions § 109(g)	Individual or family farmer with multiple petitions § 109(g)	Individual or family farmer with multiple petitions § 109(g)	Individual or family farmer with multiple petitions § 109(g)
Individual with primarily consumer debts who fails "means test" § 707(b)	Domestic banks, savings institutions, credit unions, insurance companies, and the like §§ 109(b), (d)	Persons who do not qualify as family farmers or family fishermen with regular annual income § 109(f)	Persons who are not individuals, such as corporations and partnerships § 109(e)
Railroads § 109(b)(1)	Small business investment companies § 109(b)(2)		Individuals who do not have sufficiently stable and regular income to fund a plan § 109(e)
Domestic banks, savings institutions, credit unions,	Foreign insurance companies engaged in business in the United States		Individuals whose unsecured debts are ≥ $419,275 § 109(e)

insurance companies, and the like § 109(b)(2)	§§ 109(b)(3)(A), (d)		
Small business investment companies § 109(b)(2)	Foreign savings institutions and the like with branch or agency in United States §§ 109(b)(3)(B), (d)		Individuals whose secured debts are ≥ $1,257,850 § 109(e)
Foreign insurance companies engaged in business in the United States § 109(b)(3)(A)	Stock brokers § 109(d)		Stock brokers § 109(e)
Foreign savings institutions and the like with branch or agency in United States § 109(b)(3)(B)	Commodity brokers § 109(d)		Commodity brokers § 109(e)

C. Voluntary Case

1. Filing the Petition

A voluntary case is *commenced* when an eligible debtor files a petition under Chapter 7, 11, 12, or 13. At that time, the appropriate filing fee should be paid, except under special circumstances when the court approves an individual's application to pay the fee in installments. [Bankruptcy Rule 1006; 28 U.S.C. § 1930] The filing of a voluntary petition statutorily constitutes an *order for relief* under a particular chapter. [B.C. § 301(b)]

a. Consumer Debtor

Before the start of the bankruptcy case, the clerk of the court must provide a debtor who is an *individual with primarily consumer debts* written notice that contains the following information:

(1) a brief description of chapters 7, 11, 12, and 13, and the *purposes, benefits, and costs of proceeding under each chapter* [B.C. § 342(b)(1)(A)];

(2) available *services* from *credit counseling agencies* [B.C. § 342(b)(1)(B)];

(3) a statement notifying the debtor that she may be *fined, imprisoned,* or both for knowingly and fraudulently *concealing assets or* making *false oaths or statements* under penalty of perjury [B.C. § 342(b)(2)(A)]; and

(4) a statement that all information that the debtor provides in the case is *subject to examination by the Attorney General.* [B.C. § 342(b)(2)(B)]

Official Form 2010 contains the information required to be disclosed by § 342(b) of the Bankruptcy Code.

b. Notice

The Code requires notice of the order for relief. [B.C. § 342(a)] This notice is sent to **all parties in interest,** including the debtor, all creditors, equity security holders in a Chapter 11 case, indenture trustees, the United States trustee, the appropriate taxing authorities, and state and federal governmental agencies if the debtor is subject to regulation. [Bankruptcy Rule 2002(d), (f), (k)] Holders of community claims also should receive notice to avoid issues arising under § 524(a)(3). [3 Collier § 342.02(2)] A debt is not dischargeable if the creditor did not receive notice in time to file a proof of claim and, for certain debts, in time to request a nondischargeability determination. [B.C. § 523(a)(3)] The notice generally is included in the same document as the notice of the § 341 meeting of creditors. [*See* Official Forms 309A–I]

c. Joint Case of Husband and Wife

An individual debtor who desires to file a single petition together with his spouse may commence a joint case. [B.C. § 302(a)] Debtors electing to file jointly pay only one filing fee. The filing of a joint petition operates automatically as an order for relief in the case. [B.C. § 302(a)]

(i) Legally Married

The debtors must be legally married; a joint petition may not be filed if they merely cohabitate. [***In re Lucero,*** 408 B.R. 348 (Bankr. C.D. Cal. 2009)] After the Supreme Court's decision in **Obergefell v. Hodges,** same-sex couples may legally marry; thus, they are eligible to file a joint bankruptcy petition. [B.C. § 302; *see also* **Obergefell v. Hodges,** 576 U.S. ___ (2015)] Bankruptcy courts have reached different conclusions on whether same-sex individuals who are not married but are partners in a state-recognized civil union or domestic partnership qualify to file a joint petition under § 302 of the Bankruptcy Code. [*Compare **In re* Villaverde,** 540 B.R. 431 (Bankr. C.D. Cal. 2015) (holding that a same-sex couple registered in California as domestic partners is not eligible to file a joint Chapter 13 petition, because they are not spouses for bankruptcy purposes) *with **In re* Simmons,** 2018 WL 2271000 (Bankr. N.D. Ill. 2018) (same-sex individuals holding a certificate of civil union under Illinois law have a status that is "substantively identical" to that of a couple married under Illinois law and, therefore, are considered spouses for purposes of the Bankruptcy Code and may file a joint petition)]

(ii) Only in a Voluntary Case

The option to file a joint petition is available only in a voluntary case. [B.C. § 302(a)]

(iii) Consolidation

In a joint case, the court *may* consolidate the debtors' estates by pooling their assets and liabilities, especially if their property and debts are held jointly. [B.C. § 302(b)] Filing a joint petition does not automatically consolidate the joint debtors' respective estates. Consolidation "merges the debtors' estates, thereby subjecting all assets held by either debtor to the claim of all creditors," regardless of whether the claims were incurred by one or both debtors. [***In re* Eichhorn,** 338 B.R. 793 (Bankr. S.D. Ill. 2006)]

(1) Distinguish Joint Administration

Consolidation of the debtors' estates should be distinguished from *joint administration.* Under certain circumstances, e.g., when there is a joint petition, two or more separate petitions concerning a husband and wife in the same court, a debtor and an affiliate, the judge may expedite the cases by ordering joint administration regarding matters such as notices to creditors, listing of claims, other similar functions, and the appointment of a single trustee. [Bankruptcy Rule 1015(b)]

d. Corporation

State law determines who has authority to file a voluntary bankruptcy petition on behalf of a corporation or a limited liability company. [*See* **Price v. Gurney,** 324 U.S. 100 (1945) (holding that under Chapter X of the Bankruptcy Act that the court must dismiss a petition filed by an entity without the authority to do so under local law); **DB Capital Holdings, LLC v. Aspen HH Ventures, LLC (*In re* DB Capital Holdings, LLC),** 2010 WL 4025811 (B.A.P. 10th Cir. 2010) (citing *Price* for proposition that state law determines who has authority to file a bankruptcy case on behalf of a limited liability company organized under state law)] If the person or entity filing the petition lacks authority to do so under state law, then the bankruptcy court must dismiss the petition. [**Franchise Servs. of N. Am. v. United States Trustee (*In re* Franchise Servs. of N. Am.),** 2018 WL 2325909 (5th Cir. 2018)]

e. Partnership

A petition filed by fewer than all the general partners in a partnership is treated as an involuntary petition. [B.C. § 303(b)(3)(A)]

2. Schedules, Statements, Documents and Debtor Duties in General

Congress created a number of new filing obligations and other duties for individual debtors with the passage of BAPCPA. A debtor's failure to file certain forms or paper work, or to perform certain statutory duties may result in dismissal of the case or lifting of the automatic stay.

a. Schedules, Statements and Documents with the Petition

With the exception of a municipal debtor under Chapter 9, *all debtors* must file the following schedules, statements, and documents *with the petition:*

(i) a *list of creditors* with addresses [B.C. § 521(a)(1)(A); Bankruptcy Rule 1007(a)(1)];

(ii) for *an individual debtor with primarily consumer debts,* a certificate by the debtor's attorney or if the debtor is not represented by an attorney a statement by the debtor that the attorney delivered or that the debtor read the notice required by *§ 342(b),* which explains the various chapters available to the debtor and the costs and benefits of each chapter [B.C. § 521(a)(1)(B)(iii)];

(iii) for *an individual debtor,* a statement showing compliance with the *credit counseling* requirement and a copy of any *debt repayment plan* [B.C. §§ 109(h), 521(b); Bankruptcy Rule 1007(b)(3) & (c)];

(iv) for *an individual debtor* who *rents* her residence and *wishes to stay in the rented residence after filing for bankruptcy* even though the *landlord has obtained an eviction judgment* against her, the *Initial Statement About an Eviction Judgment Against You* and deposit with the bankruptcy court clerk of the *amount of rent due during the 30 days after filing for bankruptcy* [Official Form 101A];

(v) for *an individual debtor,* a statement of the debtor's *social security number* [Bankruptcy Rule 1007(f)]; and

(vi) for a *corporate debtor,* other than a governmental unit, a *corporate ownership statement* that discloses any corporation owning 10% or more of the debtor's stock. [Bankruptcy Rule 1007(a)(1), 7007.1(a)]

b. Schedules, Statements and Documents Within 14 Days

All debtors, except a municipal debtor, must file the following schedules, statements, or documents either *with the petition* or *14 days* thereafter [Bankruptcy Rule 1007(c)]:

(i) a *schedule of assets and liabilities* along with a *summary table* of those assets and liabilities [B.C. § 521(a)(1)(B)(i); Bankruptcy Rule 1007(b)(1)(A)];

(ii) for *an individual debtor,* a schedule of *current income and expenditures* [B.C. § 521(a)(1)(B)(ii); Bankruptcy Rule 1007(b)(1)(B)];

(iii) a schedule of *executory contracts and unexpired leases* [Bankruptcy Rule 1007(b)(1)(C);

(iv) a *statement of financial affairs* [B.C. § 521(a)(1)(B)(iii); Bankruptcy Rule 1007(b)(1)(D)];

(v) copies of all *pay stubs* that the debtor received from her employer within *60 days* of the bankruptcy filing [B.C. § 521(a)(1)(B)(iv); Bankruptcy Rule 1007(b)(1)(E)];

(vi) a record, if applicable, of any interest that the debtor has in an *education individual retirement account* [B.C. § 521(c); Bankruptcy Rule 1007(b)(1)(F)];

(vii) for *individual debtors,* an itemized statement of *current monthly income* [B.C. § 521(a)(1)(B)(v); Bankruptcy Rule 1007(b)(4)–(6), (c); Official Forms 122A-1, 122B, 122C-1]; and

(viii) a statement disclosing any reasonably anticipated *increase in income or expenditures* for the *12-month period* following the filing of the petition. [B.C. § 521(a)(1)(B)(vi); *see* **CFCU Federal Credit Union v. Frisbie,** 2009 WL 3153247 (W.D. N.Y. 2009) (holding that "the duty to disclose only exists if the debtor reasonably anticipates her income or expenses may increase")]

c. Other Debtor Duties

Debtors also have the following additional duties.

(i) If a trustee has been appointed in the case, to cooperate with the trustee in the administration of the estate. [B.C. § 521(a)(3); Bankruptcy Rule 4002(a)(4)]

(ii) To surrender to the trustee all property of the estate and any relevant books, records, and documents (even if immunity has not been granted). [B.C. § 521(a)(4)] *Note:* In a Chapter 12 or Chapter 13 case, the debtor usually may remain in possession of estate property. [B.C. §§ 1207(b), 1306(b)]

(iii) For an *individual debtor,* to attend the discharge hearing if one is held by the court. [B.C. §§ 521(a)(5), 524(d); *see also* Bankruptcy Rule 4002(a)(2)]

(iv) To file a statement of any change of address. [Bankruptcy Rule 4002(a)(5)]

3. Chapter-Specific Schedules, Statements, Documents and Duties

In addition to the schedules, statements, documents and duties required of all debtors, the Code imposes additional filing requirements and obligations based on the nature of the debtor and filing chapter.

a. Chapter 7: Individual Debtor

An *individual* debtor filing for relief under *Chapter 7* must file the following additional paperwork and perform the following additional duties.

(i) Either *with the petition or no later than 14 days* thereafter, file the *Chapter 7 Means Test Calculation* form but only if the debtor has *primarily consumer debts* and her income *exceeds the median income* for her state and household size. [B.C. § 707(b)(2); Bankruptcy Rule 1007(b)(4); Official Form 122A-2]

(ii) Within the *earlier of 30 days from the petition* or on or before the *§ 341 meeting,* with regard to property subject to a security interest *state her intention* to (1) *surrender* the property; (2) *redeem* the property; or (3) *reaffirm the debt* that the property secures. [B.C. § 521(a)(2)(A); Official Form 108]

(iii) *Within 30 days* of the date set for the *§ 341 meeting, perform her intention* with regard to the property as to which she filed her statement of intention. [B.C. § 521(a)(2)(B)]

(iv) *No later than 7 days before the § 341 meeting,* provide a copy of the federal income tax return filed for the year immediately before the filing of the bankruptcy petition to the *trustee* and any *creditor* that makes *a timely request* for a copy. [B.C. § 521(e)(2)]

(v) No later than *60 days* from the date first set for the *§ 341 meeting,* file a statement that she has completed an *approved instructional course on personal financial management.* [B.C. § 727(a)(11); Bankruptcy Rule 1007(b)(7), (c)]

b. Chapter 11: Small Business Debtor

With the passage of BAPCPA in 2005, Congress amended the Bankruptcy Code to add a new § 308, which lists reporting duties for *small business debtors.* A small business debtor must file *periodic financial and other reports* that contain information as to the following:

(i) the debtor's *profitability* [B.C. § 308(b)(1)];

(ii) *reasonable approximations* of debtor's *projected cash receipts and disbursements* over a reasonable time frame [B.C. § 308(b)(2)];

(iii) *comparisons* of *actual* cash receipts and disbursements with *earlier projections* [B.C. § 308(b)(3)];

(iv) debtor's *compliance* with *reporting requirements* under the Code and the Bankruptcy Rules [B.C. § 308(b)(4)(A)];

(v) debtor's *timely filing of tax returns* and other required *government filings,* and *payment of taxes* and *administrative expenses* when due [B.C. § 308(b)(4)(A)]; and

(vi) other matters that are in the *best interests of the debtor and creditors,* and in the public interest in *fair and efficient bankruptcy procedures.* [B.C. § 308(b)(6)]

If the small business debtor is not in compliance with its reporting obligations under the Code, is not filing tax returns or other government filings on time, or is not paying taxes and administrative expenses when due, then the debtor must explain what obligations it is not performing, the cost of such failures, and when the debtor intends to remedy such failures. [B.C. § 308(b)(5)]

c. Chapter 11: Individual Debtor

If the debtor claims a *state exemption* in *excess of $170,350* in a *burial plot,* property used by the debtor or a dependent as a *residence,* or property claimed by a debtor or dependent as a *homestead,* the debtor must file a statement as to whether a *proceeding is pending* in which the debtor may be found *guilty of certain felonies.* The debtor must file the statement *no earlier* than the *last plan payment* or the filing of a *motion for discharge.* [B.C. § 522(q); Bankruptcy Rule 1007(b)(8), (c)]

d. Chapter 11: Corporate Debtor

A corporate debtor must file with the petition a separate list disclosing the names and addresses of the *creditors holding the 20 largest unsecured claims* (excluding insiders) and the amounts of their claims. [Bankruptcy Rule 1007(d)] The debtor also must file a detailed list of its equity security holders no later than *14 days* after filing its voluntary petition. [Bankruptcy Rule 1007(a)(3)]

e. Chapter 12

(i) A Chapter 12 debtor must file a *proposed plan* of repayment *with the petition* or *within 90 days* after the order for relief. [B.C. § 1221; Bankruptcy Rule 3015(a)]

(ii) If an individual Chapter 12 debtor claims a *state exemption* in *excess of $170,350* in a *burial plot,* property used by the debtor or a dependent as a *residence,* or property claimed by a debtor or dependent as a *homestead,* the debtor must file a statement as to whether a *proceeding is pending* in which the debtor may be found *guilty of certain felonies.* The debtor must file the statement *no earlier* than the *last plan payment* or the filing of a *motion for discharge.* [B.C. § 522(q); Bankruptcy Rule 1007(b)(8), (c)]

f. Chapter 13

A Chapter 13 debtor must file or provide the following additional statements and documents.

(i) The debtor must file a *proposed plan* of repayment *with the petition* or *within 14* days thereafter. [B.C. § 1321; Bankruptcy Rule 3015(b)]

(ii) No later than *60 days* from the date first set for the *§ 341 meeting,* the debtor must file a statement that she has completed an *approved instructional course on personal financial management.* [B.C. § 1328(g)(1); Bankruptcy Rule 1007(b)(7), (c)]

(iii) *No later than 7 days before the § 341 meeting,* provide a copy of the federal income tax return filed for the year immediately before the filing of the bankruptcy petition to the *trustee* and any *creditor* that makes *a timely request* for a copy. [B.C. § 521(e)(2)]

(iv) If the debtor claims a *state exemption* in *excess of $170,350* in a *burial plot,* property used by the debtor or a dependent as a *residence,* or property claimed by a debtor or dependent as a *homestead,* the debtor must file a *statement* as to whether a *proceeding is pending* in which the debtor may be found *guilty of certain felonies.* The debtor must file the statement *no earlier* than the *last plan payment* or the filing of a *motion for discharge.* [B.C. § 522(q); Bankruptcy Rule 1007(b)(8), (c)]

4. Automatic Stay

When a ***bankruptcy petition is filed,*** commencing a voluntary or an involuntary case, the automatic stay becomes effective against ***all entities,*** including a governmental unit, to protect the debtor, her property, and the property of the bankruptcy estate from creditors, while the debtor is granted a respite. The stay is a statutory injunction and helps to ensure an orderly administration of the case and an evenhanded treatment of creditors so that the creditors' shares in the ultimate distribution will not depend on a race to the courthouse. [B.C. § 362(a)]

D. Involuntary Case

1. Eligibility

An involuntary petition may be filed only under ***Chapter 7 or Chapter 11*** (not under Chapter 12 or Chapter 13) against a person who qualifies as a debtor under the applicable chapter. [B.C. § 303(a)]

a. Exceptions

Even if filed under Chapter 7 or Chapter 11, an involuntary petition may *not* be filed against (i) a farmer, (ii) a family farmer, or (iii) a nonprofit or charitable corporation. [B.C. § 303(a)]

2. Filing the Petition

a. Petitioning Entities

An involuntary case may be commenced against a debtor by the filing of a petition by the following entities. [B.C. § 303(b)]

(i) Three or More Creditors

If there are ***at least 12 creditors*** (excluding the debtor's insiders and employees, and transferees of voidable transfers) holding claims against the debtor that are neither contingent as to liability nor the subject of a bona fide dispute as to liability or amount, ***three or more of these entities*** may file an involuntary petition provided that at least ***$16,750*** of their claims, in the aggregate, are ***unsecured, noncontingent, and undisputed.*** [B.C. § 303(b)(1)] BAPCPA added "and amount" to the language modifying "bona fide dispute" in § 303(b). As a result, a dispute a about any part of a claim, even if the debtor does not dispute the entire dollar amount, means that the entire claim is subject to bona fide dispute and cannot count for purposes of § 303(b). [***In re*** Vicor Techs., 2013 WL 1397460 (Bankr. S.D. Fla. 2013)]

(ii) One or More Creditors

If there are ***fewer than 12 creditors,*** excluding the debtor's insiders and employees, and transferees of voidable transfers, holding noncontingent, undisputed claims against the debtor, one or more of these entities may file an involuntary petition provided that at least ***$16,750*** of the claims, in the ***aggregate, are unsecured, noncontingent, and undisputed.*** [B.C. § 303(b)(2)]

(1) Joining Additional Petitioning Creditors

After an involuntary petition has been filed but before the court either has entered an order for relief or has dismissed the case, additional unsecured creditors with noncontingent claims may be joined as petitioning creditors to cure a defective filing by a single creditor who, *in good faith,* erroneously believed that the debtor had fewer than 12 creditors. [B.C. § 303(c)] However, if the creditor knows that the debtor has at least 12 creditors, but files an involuntary petition for the purpose of resolving a contract dispute, additional petitioning creditors may not be joined, and the involuntary petition should be dismissed for bad faith. [**Bock Transp., Inc. v. Paul (*In re* Bock Transp., Inc.),** 327 B.R. 378 (B.A.P. 8th Cir. 2005)]

(iii) General Partner

An involuntary case against a partnership debtor may be filed by fewer than all of the general partners. [B.C. § 303(b)(3)(A)] If relief has been ordered concerning all of the general partners, an involuntary petition against the partnership may be filed by (i) a general partner, (ii) the trustee of a general partner, or (iii) a creditor holding a claim against the partnership. [B.C. § 303(b)(3)(B)]

b. Indemnity Bond

The petitioning entities may be ordered by the court to file a bond to indemnify the debtor for any damages that might be awarded if the involuntary petition subsequently is dismissed. Notice and a hearing are required, and *cause* must be shown for the filing of the bond. [B.C. § 303(e)]

3. Answer

Only the debtor, or in the case of a partnership debtor a non-petitioning general partner, may file an answer to the involuntary petition. In the answer, the debtor tries to controvert the allegations made in the petition. [B.C. § 303(d)]

4. Entry of an Order for Relief

The court will enter an order for relief against the debtor under the appropriate chapter for any of the following reasons.

a. Untimely Answer

If the involuntary petition is *not answered within 21 days* after it is served, generally an order for relief will be entered. The court may extend the time to respond if service is made by publication outside the state in which the court is located. [B.C. § 303(h); Bankruptcy Rules 1011(b), 1013(b)]

b. Debtor's General Nonpayment of Debts as They Mature

If after a trial, the court finds that the debtor is *generally not paying her undisputed debts as they become due,* an order for relief will be entered. [B.C. § 303(h)(1)] To determine whether a debtor is generally not paying her debts as they become due, the court considers " 'the number of unpaid claims, the amount of the claims, the materiality of nonpayment and the overall conduct of the debtor's financial affairs.' " [*In re* **Vicor Techs.,** 2013 WL 1397460 (Bankr. S.D. Fla. 2013)]

c. Appointment of a Custodian

The court also will enter an order for relief if, after a trial, it finds that within *120 days* before the petition was filed, a *custodian was appointed or took charge* of the debtor's property, other than for the purpose of enforcing a lien against less than substantially all of such property. [B.C. §§ 303(h)(2), 101(11)]

5. Gap Period

During the interim between the *filing of an involuntary petition and the entry of an order for relief* (the gap period), the debtor may remain in possession of her property, continue to operate her business, and use, acquire, or dispose of assets, unless the court denies these privileges or appoints an interim trustee. [B.C. § 303(f)]

a. Transfers During Gap Period

If the debtor makes a transfer during the gap period, the transfer is not subject to the trustee's avoiding powers *to the extent of post-petition value given in exchange for the transfer* by the transferee. "Value" includes services, such as those of the debtor's attorney. To be free of the trustee's avoiding power, the purpose of the transfer must not be to satisfy or secure a pre-petition debt. [B.C. § 549(b)]

b. Priority for Gap Creditors

Any creditors whose claims arise in the ordinary course of the debtor's business or financial affairs before the *earlier of* the appointment of a trustee or entry of the order for relief are entitled to *second priority status* in the order of distribution to claimants. [B.C. §§ 502(f), 507(a)(2)]

c. Interim Trustee

During the gap period in a Chapter 7 case, on request by a party in interest and after notice to the debtor and a hearing, the court may direct the United States trustee to appoint an interim trustee if the court finds that such an appointment is needed to *preserve property of the estate* or to *avoid loss.* If an interim trustee is appointed, she takes possession of property of the estate and, if applicable, operates the debtor's business. [B.C. § 303(g)]

(i) Note

The court may permit the debtor, prior to an order for relief, to retake possession of property from a Chapter 7 interim trustee upon the filing of a bond in an amount set by the court. [B.C. § 303(g)]

6. Dismissal of Involuntary Petition

a. Damages Possible

If the court dismisses an involuntary petition other than on the consent of all the petitioning entities *and the debtor,* and if the debtor has not waived her right to damages, then the court may award a judgment to the debtor and against the petitioners for costs and/or reasonable attorneys' fees. [B.C. § 303(i)(1)] *Rationale:* This provision is designed to prevent the indiscriminate filing of an involuntary petition by creditors.

(i) Punitive Damages for Bad Faith

When the court dismisses an involuntary petition, and finds that a petitioning entity filed the petition in *bad faith,* the court may award the debtor damages proximately caused by the involuntary petition and/or punitive damages. [B.C. § 303(i)(2)] The debtor may recover for actual damages, costs and attorneys' fees, and punitive damages. [2 Collier ¶ 303.33(3) (stating that a "debtor can recover under both paragraphs (1) and (2) of section 303(i)")]

b. Protection for Individuals

BAPCPA added certain protections for an *individual debtor* whose involuntary bankruptcy petition is dismissed by the court.

(i) If the petition was *false* or contained *materially false, fictitious, or fraudulent statements,* the court, upon the debtor's motion, must *seal all court records* related to the petition and all references to such petition. [B.C. § 303(k)(1)]

(ii) If the court dismisses an involuntary petition against an *individual,* the court also may issue an order *preventing all consumer reporting agencies* from making a consumer report containing information about the petition or the involuntary bankruptcy case. [B.C. § 303(k)(2)]

(iii) The court may, upon motion of the debtor and for *good cause, expunge* any records related to an involuntary bankruptcy petition involving *bankruptcy crimes.* [B.C. § 303(k)(3); 18 U.S.C. §§ 152, 157] For example, filing a fraudulent involuntary petition is bankruptcy fraud punishable by five years' imprisonment, a fine, or both. [18 U.S.C. § 157(1)] The court, however, may not expunge the records related to such an involuntary petition until the relevant statute of limitations, which is five years, has expired. [B.C. § 303(k)(3); 18 U.S.C. § 3282(a)]

c. Notice and Hearing

The court may dismiss an involuntary petition on the motion of a petitioning creditor, on the consent of all petitioning creditors and the debtor, or for lack of prosecution only after *notice* and an opportunity for a *hearing* is given to *all creditors.* [B.C. § 303(j)]

7. Schedules to Be Filed

If an order for relief is entered in an involuntary case, the debtor must file the required lists, schedules, and statements within the time limits fixed by Bankruptcy Rule 1007.

E. Section 341 Meeting of Creditors

1. Time and Place

In a Chapter 7 or Chapter 11 case, within 21 to 40 days after the order for relief, a meeting of creditors is held at the courthouse or at another location within the district, designated by the United States trustee for the convenience of the parties in interest. In a Chapter 12 case, the meeting is held within 21 to 35 days after the order for relief. In a Chapter 13 case, the meeting is held within 21 to 50 days after the order for relief.) This meeting is called the *section 341 meeting* of creditors. [B.C. § 341(a); Bankruptcy Rule 2003(a)]

a. Meeting of Equity Security Holders

When appropriate, a meeting of the debtor's equity security holders also may be convened by the United States trustee. [B.C. § 341(b)] If the United States trustee convenes a meeting of equity security holders, the United States trustee sets the date for the meeting and presides at it. [Bankruptcy Rule 2003(b)(2)]

2. No § 341 Meeting

On request of a party interest, the bankruptcy court, for *cause,* may order the United States trustee not to convene a meeting of creditors or equity security holders if the debtor has filed a plan on which it solicited pre-petition acceptances. Notice and a hearing are required. [B.C. § 341(e)]

3. Notice

The clerk of the court provides by mail at least 21 days' notice of the § 341 meeting to the debtor, the trustee, all creditors, and indenture trustees. If notice by mail is impracticable, the court may order that notice be given by publication. [Bankruptcy Rule 2002(a)(1), (*l*)] In a reorganization case under Chapter 11, equity security holders must be notified of any § 341 meeting of equity security holders. [Bankruptcy Rule 2002(d)]

a. Contents of Notice

The notice of the § 341 meeting of creditors also includes notice of the following:

(i) order for relief [B.C. § 342(a); Official Forms 309A–309I];

(ii) the imposition of the automatic stay [B.C. § 362(a); Official Forms 309A–309I];

(iii) the deadline for filing proofs of claims, if one is set at the time of notice [B.C. § 501(a); Official Forms 309B, 309D, 309E–309I];

(iv) the deadline for filing complaints to determine the dischargeability of certain debts [B.C. §§ 523(c); Official Forms 309A–309B, 309E–309I];

(v) in an individual Chapter 7, 11 or 13 case, the deadline for filing objections to the debtor's entire discharge [B.C. §§ 727(a), 1141(d)(3), 1328(f); Official Forms 309A–309B, 309E, 309I];

(vi) in an individual case, the deadline for filing objections to the debtor's claim of exempt property [B.C. § 522; Official Forms 309A–309B, 309E, 309G, 309I];

(vii) in a Chapter 7 case, the right to file a motion to dismiss if the presumption of abuse arises [B.C. § 707(b); Official Forms 309A–309B]; and

(viii) in a Chapter 12 or 13 case, whether the debtor had filed plan at the time of notice and whether a confirmation hearing date has been set. [Official Forms 309G-I]

4. United States Trustee Presides

The § 341 meeting is not a judicial hearing; thus, the United States trustee, or an assistant United States trustee, convenes and presides at the meeting. This procedure is designed to separate the administrative functions from the judicial functions of the court. Moreover, the judge is prohibited from attending the § 341 meeting, because facts and circumstances concerning issues to be adjudicated by the court in subsequent proceedings in the bankruptcy case are likely to be discussed. [B.C. § 341; Bankruptcy Rule 2003(b)]

Note: The judicial districts of Alabama and North Carolina are not within the United States trustee system; instead, they have bankruptcy administrators who are authorized to preside at the meetings of creditors and examine the debtor. [11 U.S.C. § 341 Notes]

5. Debtor Must Attend

The debtor must personally attend the § 341 meeting. The courts are divided about whether a bankruptcy court has the discretion under § 343 to waive the debtor's attendance at the § 341 meeting. [*In re* **Palmer,** 2015 WL 534503 (Bankr. W.D. La. 2015); B.C. § 343] A majority of courts, however, waive physical attendance at the § 341 meeting for good cause. [*In re* **Alleca,** 582 B.R. 530 (Bankr. M.D. Ala. 2018)]

Example: Debtor filed a petition for relief under Chapter 13. Debtor was 83 years old, had suffered a stroke, was bedridden, partially paralyzed, and unable to hold a conversation for more than five minutes because she was in a "confused state." Debtor appointed her granddaughter as power of attorney to appear on her behalf in the bankruptcy proceeding. The court concluded that "Congress did not intend to remove bankruptcy courts' discretion to waive debtor's appearance at § 341 meetings," in particular in cases in which the debtor's appearance was impossible. The court went on to explain that it would be the rare case, however, in which the debtor could not attend in person or telephonically; in those rare cases, a representative of the debtor with full knowledge of the debtor's financial affairs must appear. [*In re* **Palmer,** *supra*]

Example: Debtor, incarcerated in federal prison for his role in a Ponzi scheme, filed for relief under Chapter 7. Debtor moved the court to excuse his attendance at the § 341 meeting and instead have the trustee examine him through the use of interrogatories. The bankruptcy court denied Debtor's motion and found that Debtor had not met his burden of showing an alternative method existed that was equivalent to his attendance at a § 341 meeting. First, Debtor failed to comply with the local bankruptcy rule's requirement to provide copies of both his judgment and conviction. Second, the bankruptcy court found that the use of interrogatories, given the complexity of Debtor's bankruptcy case and the Ponzi scheme that led to his imprisonment, would create "insurmountable difficult[ies] [for the trustee] in fulfilling her duties." [*In re* **Alleca,** *supra*]

6. Purpose of Section 341 Meeting

The primary function of the § 341 meeting is to provide an opportunity for creditors, the trustee, an examiner, if one has been appointed, any indenture trustee, and the United States trustee or bankruptcy administrator *to examine the debtor under oath* about issues related to the bankruptcy case. [B.C. § 343] Typical questions concern the location and condition of a secured creditor's collateral, the exemptions claimed by the debtor, the facts relating to an allegedly non-dischargeable debt, the disappearance of assets, the operation of the debtor's business, the reasons for filing, goals for reorganization, and in a Chapter 7 case whether debtor's filing is an abuse under § 707(b). [3–341 Collier ¶ 341.02(5)(d)] In a Chapter 7 or Chapter 13 case, a creditor holding a consumer debt may attend and participate in the § 341 meeting even if she is not represented by an attorney. [B.C. § 341(c)]

a. Distinguish Examination Under Bankruptcy Rule 2004

Frequently, there are many parties interested in examining the debtor at the § 341 meeting, and the time allotted to each is limited. Therefore, any party in interest may file a motion for examination of the debtor under Bankruptcy Rule 2004 ("2004 Exam"). [Bankruptcy Rule 2004(a)] For cause shown, the bankruptcy court may order that the 2004 Exam be held at any time or place that the court designates, even a location outside the district in which the bankruptcy court sits. [Bankruptcy Rule 2004(d)]

b. Examination by Trustee in Chapter 7

In a Chapter 7 case, before the conclusion of the meeting of creditors or equity security holders, the trustee must orally examine the Chapter 7 debtor to ensure her awareness of the following:

(i) the potential effects of seeking a bankruptcy discharge, including the effects on the debtor's credit history [B.C. § 341(d)(1)];

(ii) the debtor's ability to file a petition under a different chapter of the Code [B.C. § 341(d)(2)];

(iii) the effect of receiving a discharge [B.C. § 341(d)(3)]; and

(iv) the effect of reaffirming a debt, including the debtor's understanding that a reaffirmation is not required under the Code or under state law, and that the debtor would be personally liable for a subsequent default. [B.C. § 341(d)(4); § 524(d)]

c. Other Business in Chapter 7 Case

If a sufficient number of unsecured creditors make the request, unsecured creditors eligible to vote may vote to elect the Chapter 7 trustee at the § 341 meeting. [B.C. § 702(b)] Unsecured creditors eligible to vote on a Chapter 7 trustee under § 702 also may elect a committee of unsecured creditors that would consult with the trustee and United States trustee on administration of the debtor's Chapter 7 case. [B.C. § 705] Unsecured creditors' committees in Chapter 7 are rare.

d. Debtor's Immunity from Prosecution

If an individual debtor validly asserts the constitutional privilege against self-incrimination, she may be granted immunity from prosecution *by the district court judge.* She then may be required to provide information at the § 341 meeting or at a hearing in the case despite the privilege. [B.C. § 344; 18 U.S.C. § 6003; *see* **Kastigar v. United States,** 406 U.S. 441 (1972)]

F. Conversion

1. Authorization

Chapters 7, 11, 12, and 13 provide rules for conversion of a case from one chapter to another when the debtor satisfies the eligibility requirements for the succeeding chapter. A court may order conversion of a Chapter 7 or Chapter 11 case to Chapter 12 or Chapter 13 *only upon the debtor's request.* [B.C. §§ 706(c), 1112(d)] If a case is converted to Chapter 13, the debtor must file a plan within 14 days thereafter. [Bankruptcy Rule 3015(b)]

2. Effects of Conversion

The conversion of a case to another chapter operates as an order for relief under the new chapter but, as a general rule, does not alter the *date* of the filing of the bankruptcy petition, the commencement of the case, or the order for relief. [B.C. § 348(a)]

a. Exceptions

There are a number of exceptions to this rule, in which case the *date of the order for relief* is deemed to be the date that the case was converted. [B.C. § 348(b)] For example, § 701 provides that the United States trustee, promptly after the order for relief, shall appoint an interim trustee to serve as the Chapter 7 trustee until the election or designation of a trustee under § 702. [B.C. §§ 701(a), 702] Therefore, in a case converted to Chapter 7, the time for the United States trustee to act starts with the date of conversion, not with the date of the filing of the original petition.

In addition to these exceptions, there are two instances in which date of the *order of conversion* is considered to be the date of the *order for relief* [B.C. § 348(c)]:

(i) the required notice of the order for relief [B.C. § 342(a)]; and

(ii) the time allowed under § 365(d) for the trustee to assume or reject an executory contract or an unexpired lease of the debtor.

3. Pre-Conversion Claims

Except for administrative expenses, any claims arising in a Chapter 11, 12, or 13 case after the order for relief but before conversion to another chapter are considered pre-petition claims for all purposes. [B.C. § 348(d)]

4. Trustee or Examiner

The service of a trustee or an examiner in a case that is converted from Chapter 7, 11, 12, or 13 is terminated by the conversion to another chapter. [B.C. § 348(e)]

5. Conversion from Chapter 13

a. Property of the Estate

If a case is converted from Chapter 13 to another chapter of the Code, property of the estate in the converted case consists of property of the estate *on the date of the Chapter 13 filing* that remains in the possession or control of the debtor on the date of conversion. [B.C. § 348(f)(1)(A)] If the debtor converts the case in *bad faith,* however, property of the estate in the converted case will consist of the estate property *on the date of conversion* (including property acquired after the date of the Chapter 13 filing). [B.C. § 348(f)(2)]

b. Secured Claims

Valuations of *property* and of *allowed secured claims* in the Chapter 13 case apply in a case converted to Chapters 11 or 12, but not to a case converted to Chapter 7. The allowed secured claims in Chapters 11 or 12 are *reduced by the amount paid* under the *Chapter 13* plan. [B.C. § 348(f)(1)(B)] Unless a secured claim was paid in full as of the date of conversion from Chapter 13, the claim is still secured, notwithstanding any valuation or determination of the amount of the secured claim in the Chapter 13 case prior to conversion. [B.C. § 348(f)(1)(C)(i)] Finally, unless a *pre-bankruptcy default* has been cured under the plan as of the date of conversion, the default has the effect given under nonbankruptcy law. [B.C. § 348(f)(1)(C)(ii)]

G. Dismissal

1. Different Rules for Chapters 7, 11, 12, and 13

Whether the debtor, a party in interest, the United States trustee, or the court on its own motion may move for the dismissal of a petition, and when the court may or must order a dismissal, are questions that vary according to the chapter of the Code under which the petition was filed. [*See* B.C. §§ 707, 1112, 1208, 1307] These rules will be discussed more specifically in connection with each chapter.

2. Effect of Dismissal

Generally, the dismissal of a case is *without prejudice* to the debtor's right to file a subsequent petition and obtain a discharge of debts that could have been discharged in the case dismissed. [B.C. § 349(a)]

a. Exceptions

The effect of a dismissal is *with prejudice*, however, to the extent that the debtor is ineligible to file again within 180 days due to § 109(g), or if the court finds *cause* to dismiss the case with prejudice. [B.C. § 349(a)]

3. Automatic Dismissal

If an *individual* in a *voluntary Chapter 7 or Chapter 13 case* fails to file all the information required by § 521(a)(1) *within 45 days* of filing her petition, then her case is *automatically dismissed* on Day 46. [B.C. § 521(i)(1)] While the Code provides for automatic dismissal, it is unclear how that happens, and it is possible, notwithstanding the "automatic dismissal" language that a court order is needed. [3 Collier ¶ 349.01(3)(h); § 521(i)(1), (2)]

Chapter Four

Case Administration: Officers of the Estate

CONTENTS	PAGE

Chapter Approach

This chapter discusses the roles and duties of a bankruptcy trustee, an examiner, professional persons, and the United States trustee. The relevant provisions of the Bankruptcy Code are contained in §§ 321 through 333.

Regarding bankruptcy trustees, remember that the nature of relief available varies according to the chapters of the Bankruptcy Code. Thus, appointment of a *bankruptcy trustee* is necessary in a Chapter 7 case to collect and liquidate the assets of the estate and to distribute the proceeds to creditors. Under Chapter 11 (reorganization), however, appointment of a trustee is the exception, and a *debtor in possession* is preferred. In Chapter 13 (individual repayment) cases and in Chapter 12 (family farmer and family fisherman) cases, a trustee's service also is required, although the debtor usually remains in possession of property of the estate. In Chapters 12 and 13, there often is a standing trustee for all such cases in the jurisdiction.

In a Chapter 11 case, sometimes an *examiner* will be appointed, in which case the debtor remains in possession of her property and her business. The examiner will investigate the debtor's conduct and business operations, help determine the advisability of continuing the debtor's business, and report to the court.

In answering an examination question about the employment and compensation of a *professional person,* e.g., an attorney, always make certain that *court approval* has been obtained *before* the professional services are performed; otherwise, the professional may be denied compensation. Furthermore, make sure that a professional hired by a trustee or a debtor in possession is a *disinterested person* and that she does not have an interest adverse to the estate.

The main thing to know about the *United States trustee* is that the trustee assumes many of the administrative responsibilities previously performed by the bankruptcy court, including the appointment and supervision of bankruptcy trustees, as well as the review of fee applications of attorneys and other professional persons, thereby helping to separate the administrative and judicial functions in bankruptcy cases. Remember that the United States trustee system does not operate in the six judicial districts in Alabama and North Carolina; instead, bankruptcy administrators perform many of the functions performed by the United States trustee.

A. Trustee

1. Role and Capacity

The trustee is the official representative of the estate. The trustee's duties are set by statute. Besides various administrative powers, the trustee has authority to initiate and defend lawsuits. [B.C. § 323]

2. Eligibility

An individual or corporation is eligible to serve as a trustee. The trustee does not have to be a lawyer. An individual must be competent to perform the required responsibilities, and a corporation must be authorized by its charter or bylaws to serve as a trustee. In a Chapter 7, 12, or 13 case, the trustee also must reside, or have an office, in the judicial district where the bankruptcy case is pending or in the adjacent district. [B.C. § 321(a)] The Code's general eligibility requirements to serve as a trustee do not include disinterestedness. [B.C. § 321] Nonetheless, courts have held that a trustee must be disinterested in order to avoid not only actual conflicts of interest but also the appearance of conflicts that may undermine the integrity of the bankruptcy system. [*In re* **Barkany,** 542 B.R. 699 (Bankr. E.D. N.Y. 2015)]

a. "Disinterested Person"

The bankruptcy definition of a disinterested person *excludes* the following entities:

(i) *creditors, equity security holders, and insiders* [B.C. § 101(14)(A)];

(ii) current *directors, officers, and employees* of the debtor, and those who have been directors, officers, of employees of the debtor within two years prior to the commencement of the case [B.C. § 101(14)(B)]; and

(iii) *any person with a materially adverse interest* to the estate or to any class of creditors or equity security holders. [B.C. § 101(14)(C)]

b. Examiner Precluded

Any person who has served as an examiner is prohibited from becoming a trustee in the same case. [B.C. § 321(b)]

c. United States Trustee

If necessary, the United States trustee for the respective judicial district may serve as the trustee in a Chapter 7, 12, or 13 case, but not in a Chapter 11 case. [B.C. §§ 321(c), 1104(d)]

3. Qualification of Trustee—Bond

Within seven days after appointment or election, and before beginning service, a trustee must file with the court a *bond,* in favor of the United States, in the amount set by the United States trustee. The United States trustee also approves the surety on the bond. [B.C. § 322]

4. Selection of Trustee

The chapter of the Bankruptcy Code governing the particular case determines whether a trustee is required, and if so, how the trustee is to be chosen.

a. Chapter 7

All Chapter 7 cases require the services of a trustee. Each United States trustee establishes and maintains a panel of private trustees to serve in the Chapter 7 cases for the particular region. There are 21 regions. [28 U.S.C. §§ 586(a)(1), 581(a)] In the six judicial districts in Alabama and North Carolina that are not part of the U.S. trustee system, the bankruptcy administrator maintains the panel of private trustees.

(i) Interim Trustee

Immediately after the entry of the order for relief in a Chapter 7 case, the United States trustee appoints a disinterested member of the private panel to serve as the interim trustee until the § 341 meeting. At the § 341 meeting, the interim trustee will become the permanent trustee unless another person is elected by creditors. In most cases, no election is held and the interim trustee serves as the permanent trustee in the case. [B.C. §§ 701(a), 702(b), (d)]

(ii) Election of Trustee

If an election is requested by creditors who hold at least 20% in amount of the claims entitled to vote for a trustee, an election is conducted at the § 341 meeting. [B.C. § 702(b)]

(1) Who May Vote

A creditor is eligible to vote for a trustee only if the creditor: (i) holds an allowable, *unsecured, nonpriority,* undisputed, fixed, and liquidated claim; (ii) does not have an interest that is materially adverse to other creditors holding such claims; and (iii) is not an insider. [B.C. § 702(a)] A creditor is entitled to vote if, at or before the § 341 meeting, the creditor has filed a *proof of claim* or a writing setting forth facts evidencing a right to vote *unless* an objection is made that the claim or proof of claim is insufficient on its face. [Bankruptcy Rule 2003(b)(3)]

(2) Votes Needed to Be Elected

Election of a candidate as the permanent trustee requires (i) that creditors holding at least *20% in amount* of the eligible voting claims *actually vote,* and (ii) that the candidate receive votes representing a majority *in amount* of the claims that have been voted. [B.C. § 702(c)]

e.g. **Example:** There are $100,000 in allowable, undisputed, fixed, and liquidated unsecured claims in Debtor's Chapter 7 case. Creditors holding $15,000 in claims vote, and all votes are cast in favor of electing Person A as trustee. Person A does not have sufficient votes to be elected. Even though Person A received the votes representing a majority in amount of claims actually voted, 20% in amount of all eligible claims ($20,000) did not vote in the election.

b. Chapter 11

In a Chapter 11 case, the debtor generally remains in possession of property of the estate and continues to manage the business, in an effort to reorganize, *without the necessity of a trustee's appointment.* The rationale is that the debtor's current management ordinarily is better acquainted with and more experienced in the particular business operations than an outside trustee. A party in interest or the United States trustee, however, may move at any time after the filing of the bankruptcy petition but before confirmation of a Chapter 11 plan for appointment of a Chapter 11 trustee. [B.C. § 1104(a)]

Reasons for appointment of a trustee are:

(i) *cause,* which includes *fraud, dishonesty, incompetence, or gross mismanagement* by current management either before or after the start of the bankruptcy case [B.C. § 1104(a)(1)];

(ii) appointment is in the *interests of creditors, any equity security holders,* and other interests of the estate [B.C. § 1104(a)(2)]; or

(iii) grounds exist to *convert or dismiss* the case, but the bankruptcy court determines that appointment of a trustee is in the *best interests of creditors and the estate.* [B.C. § 1104(a)(3)]

(1) When the United States Trustee Must Act

BAPCPA added a new subsection to § 1104 that requires the United States trustee to move for the appointment of a Chapter 11 trustee if *reasonable grounds* exist to suspect that current members of the debtor's governing body, debtor's chief executive or chief financial officer, or members of the governing body that selected the chief executive or chief financial officer participated in *actual fraud, dishonesty, or criminal conduct* in *managing the debtor* or the *debtor's public financial reporting.* [B.C. § 1104(e)]

(2) Appointment of Trustee

Once the bankruptcy court orders the appointment of a trustee, the United States trustee consults with parties in interest and then appoints a disinterested person, subject to the court's approval. The United States trustee may not serve as the trustee in the case. [B.C. § 1104(d)]

(3) Election of Trustee

If appointment of a trustee is ordered, in cases other than railroad reorganizations, the Code authorizes *election* of the trustee, *rather than appointment,* if a party in interest requests an election within *30 days* after the court orders the appointment. The election is held at a meeting of the creditors convened by the United States trustee and is conducted in the same manner as the election of a trustee under Chapter 7. The trustee must be a disinterested person. [B.C. §§ 1104(b)] If a Chapter 11 trustee is elected, then the United States trustee must file a report certifying the election. Upon filing of the report, the services of any trustee already appointed by the United States trustee under § 1104(d) are terminated. [B.C. § 1104(b)(2)]

c. Chapters 13 and 12

In a region where many Chapter 13 cases are filed, the United States trustee ordinarily appoints a qualified individual to serve as a *standing trustee* for all Chapter 13 cases in that region. Otherwise, the United States trustee appoints a disinterested person as the trustee for a particular case, or the United States trustee may serve as the trustee in the case. [B.C. § 1302(a); 28 U.S.C. § 586(b)] The same procedure applies in cases under Chapter 12. [B.C. § 1202(a); 28 U.S.C. § 586(b)] Usually, however, the Chapter 13 or 12 debtor remains in possession of property of the estate. [B.C. §§ 1306(b), 1207(b)]

5. Duties of Trustee

The duties of a trustee vary according to the chapter under which the trustee is serving, although some of the basic functions overlap. [B.C. §§ 704, 1106(a), 1202(b), 1302(b)]

a. Chapter 7: Primary Responsibilities

The primary responsibilities of a Chapter 7 trustee are to *collect and reduce to cash* property of the estate, to *make distributions* to claimants in the order prescribed by the Code, and to *close the estate* as expeditiously as is compatible with best interests of parties in interest. [B.C. §§ 704(a)(1), 725, 726]

b. Chapter 7: Additional Responsibilities

A Chapter 7 trustee has the following additional duties:

(i)   to *account* for all property received [B.C. § 704(a)(2)];

(ii)   to *ensure* an individual debtor's performance of her intentions regarding collateral securing debts [B.C. §§ 704(a)(3), 521(a)(2)(B)];

(iii)   to *investigate* the debtor's financial affairs [B.C. § 704(a)(4)];

(iv)   to *examine proofs of claims* and to object to the allowance of any improper claims [B.C. § 704(a)(5)];

(v)   to *object to the debtor's discharge,* if circumstances warrant [B.C. § 704(a)(6)];

(vi) to *provide information* requested by parties in interest about the estate and the administration of the estate [B.C. § 704(a)(7)];

(vii) to *file periodic financial reports,* including a statement of receipts and disbursements with the court, the United States trustee, and the appropriate taxing authorities, if the trustee is operating the debtor's business [B.C. § 704(a)(8)];

(viii) to *prepare and file* with the court and the United States trustee a *final report and account* concerning the case [B.C. § 704(a)(9)];

(ix) to *continue to perform* the duties of an *administrator of an employee benefit plan,* if, at the commencement of the case, the debtor served as such an administrator [B.C. § 704(a)(11)];

(x) to *use reasonable and best efforts,* in a case involving a *health care business* that is closing, to *transfer patients* to a facility that is in the *vicinity* of the business that is closing and that also provides *services substantially similar* to the health care business that is closing [B.C. § 704(a)(12)];

(xi) to *file,* no later than *10 days after* the date of the first *§ 341 meeting,* a statement with the court as to whether the filing of an individual debtor's Chapter 7 bankruptcy case creates a presumption of abuse [B.C. §§ 704(b)(1)(A), 707(b)];

(xii) to *file,* no later than *30 days after* the statement that filing of the debtor's Chapter 7 case creates a *presumption of abuse,* a *motion to dismiss or convert* the debtor's case or a statement explaining why such a motion is not appropriate [B.C. §§ 704(b)(2), 707(b)];

(xiii) to *provide written notice* to the holder of a *domestic support obligation claim,* if there is such a claim in the debtor's case, of the right to assistance from a state child support enforcement agency in collecting child support both during and after the case, and of the claim holder's right to payment in a Chapter 7 case [B.C. §§ 704(a)(10), (c)(1)(A)];

(xiv) to *provide written notice* to the applicable state child support enforcement agency of the existence of a *domestic support obligation,* if there is such a claim in the debtor's case [B.C. §§ 704(a)(10), (c)(1)(B)]; and

(xv) to *provide written notice* both to the holder of a *domestic support obligation claim* and the applicable state child support enforcement agency, in a case involving a domestic support obligation, of the *granting of a discharge* to the debtor. [B.C. §§ 704(a)(10), (c)(1)(C)]

c. Chapter 11

A Chapter 11 trustee, appointed to replace a debtor in possession, ordinarily is authorized to *operate the debtor's business* [B.C. § 1108] and is charged with the following responsibilities:

(i) *to account* for all property received, to *examine proofs of claims* and object to improper ones, to *provide information* to parties in interest about the estate or its administration, to *file periodic financial reports* with the court, the United States trustee, and taxing authorities, to *prepare and file a final report and account,* to *continue,* in the appropriate case, to perform the duties of an *administrator of an employee benefit plan,* and to use *reasonable and best efforts* to transfer patients of a *health care business* that is closing to a facility with *substantially similar services.* [B.C. §§ 1106(a)(1), 704(a)(2), (5), (7), (8), (9), (11), (12)];

(ii)   to file any documents required under section 521(a)(1), e.g., schedules, statements, pay stubs, that the debtor has not filed [B.C. §§ 1106(a)(2), 521(a)(1)];

(iii)   to *investigate* the debtor's conduct, financial condition, and business operations, as well as the *advisability of continuing the debtor's business* [B.C. § 1106(a)(3)];

(iv)   to *file a report of the investigation* relating any facts evidencing fraud, dishonesty, incompetence, misconduct, or mismanagement, or pertaining to a cause of action that the estate holds, and to send a copy of the findings to any creditors' committee, equity security holders' committee, indenture trustee, or any entity that the court designates [B.C. § 1106(a)(4)];

(v)   to *file a Chapter 11 plan* as soon as feasible, or recommend conversion of the case to another chapter or dismissal [B.C. § 1106(a)(5)];

(vi)   to *provide information,* if available, to the taxing authorities concerning any year for which the debtor failed to file a return [B.C. § 1106(a)(6)];

(vii) *after a plan has been confirmed,* to *file* any required reports [B.C. § 1106(a)(7)];

(viii) to *provide written notice* to the holder of a *domestic support obligation claim,* if there is such a claim in the debtor's case, of the right to assistance from a state child support enforcement agency in collecting child support both during and after the case, and of the claim holder's right to payment in a Chapter 7 case [B.C. §§ 1106(a)(8), (c)(1)(A); *see also* §§ 1106(a)(1), 704(a)(10)];

(ix)   to *provide written notice* to the applicable state child support enforcement agency of the existence of a *domestic support obligation,* if there is such a claim in the debtor's case [B.C. §§ 1106(a)(8), (c)(1)(B); *see also* §§ 1106(a)(1), 704(a)(10)]; and

(x)   to *provide written notice* both to the holder of a *domestic support obligation claim* and the applicable state child support enforcement agency, in a case involving a domestic support obligation, of the *granting of a discharge* to the debtor. [B.C. §§ 1106(a)(8), (c)(1)(C); *see also* §§ 1106(a)(1), 704(a)(10)]

d.   Chapter 13

A Chapter 13 trustee has the following duties:

(i)   *to account* for all property received, to *ensure* debtor performs her intentions regarding collateral securing debts, to *investigate* debtor's financial affairs, to *examine proofs of claims* and object to improper ones, to *object* to debtor's discharge, if circumstances warrant, to *provide information* to the parties in interest about the estate and its administration, and to *prepare and file a final report and account* of the estate's administration. [B.C. §§ 1302(b)(1), 704(a)(2), (3), (4), (5), (6), (7), (9)];

(ii)   *to testify* at any hearing regarding (i) valuation of property on which there is a lien, (ii) confirmation of a Chapter 13 plan, or (iii) post-confirmation modification of a plan [B.C. § 1302(b)(2)];

(iii) *to furnish nonlegal advice* to the debtor, and to assist the debtor in implementing the plan [B.C. § 1302(b)(4)];

(iv)   *to ensure that the debtor begins making the payments* proposed by the plan no later than 30 days after the filing of the plan or the order for relief, whichever is earlier [B.C. §§ 1302(b)(5), 1326(a)(1)];

(v)   to *provide written notice* to the holder of a *domestic support obligation claim,* if there is such a claim in the debtor's case, of the right to assistance from a state child support enforcement agency in collecting child support both during and after the case, and of the claim holder's right to payment in a Chapter 7 case [B.C. §§ 1302(b)(6), (d)(1)(A)];

(vi) to *provide written notice* to the applicable state child support enforcement agency of the existence of a *domestic support obligation,* if there is such a claim in the debtor's case [B.C. §§ 1302(b)(6), (d)(1)(B)];

(vii) to *provide written notice* both to the holder of a *domestic support obligation claim* and the applicable state child support enforcement agency, in a case involving a domestic support obligation, of the *granting of a discharge* to the debtor [B.C. §§ 1302(b)(6), (d)(1)(C)];

(viii) if the debtor is engaged in business, to *investigate* the debtor's conduct, financial condition, and business operations, as well as the *advisability of continuing the debtor's business* [B.C. §§ 1302(c), 1106(a)(3)];

(ix) if the debtor is engaged in business, to *file a report of the investigation* relating any facts evidencing *fraud, dishonesty, incompetence, misconduct, or mismanagement,* or pertaining to a cause of action that the estate holds, and to send a copy of the findings to any entity that the court designates [B.C. §§ 1302(c), 1106(a)(4)]; and

(x) *ordinarily, to disburse the payments* to creditors under a confirmed plan. [B.C. § 1326(c)]

e. Chapter 12

The duties of a Chapter 12 trustee are similar to those of a Chapter 13 trustee as long as the debtor continues to be a debtor in possession. The Code, however, *does not require* the Chapter 12 trustee, unlike the Chapter 13 trustee, to *investigate* the debtor's financial affairs. [B.C. §§ 1202(b)(1), 1302(b)(1), 704(a)(4)] In addition, the Chapter 12 trustee's obligation to *investigate and file a report* on the debtor's business operations, and *investigate the advisability of continuing the debtor's business* are triggered by a request for *cause* by a party in interest, the trustee, or the United States trustee. [B.C. § 1202(b)(2)] By comparison, the Chapter 13 trustee must carry out these duties if the debtor is engaged in business operations. [B.C. § 1302(c)] If a Chapter 12 debtor is removed from possession, however, the trustee is charged with many of the duties of a Chapter 11 trustee, including operation of the debtor's farm or commercial fishing operation. [B.C. §§ 1202(b)(5), 1204]

TRUSTEES—A SUMMARY OF IMPORTANT POINTS		**GILBERT**
CHAPTER	**APPOINTMENT & ESTATE PROPERTY**	**PRIMARY DUTIES**
CHAPTER 7	Immediately after entry of the order for relief, the United States trustee appoints an interim trustee, who usually becomes the permanent trustee unless, at the meeting of creditors, an election is requested by creditors holding at least 20% in amount of the claims entitled to vote for a trustee. Debtor must relinquish to the trustee all property of the estate. Any entity in possession of property that the trustee can use, sell, or lease *or* that the debtor can exempt	The trustee: • Collects and reduces to money property of the bankruptcy estate; • Makes distributions to creditors in the order prescribed by the Code; and • Closes the estate as expeditiously as is compatible with the best interests of parties in interest.

	must turn the property over to the trustee (with a few exceptions).	
CHAPTER 11	Generally, a trustee is *not* appointed, and the debtor remains in possession of the estate property and continues to operate the business. However, the court may order appointment of a trustee *for cause* (e.g., fraud, dishonesty, incompetence, or gross mismanagement by *current management*), if appointment is in the *interests of creditors,* or if grounds exist to *convert or dismiss* but the court decides that appointing a trustee is in the *best interests of creditors and the estate.* If the court orders appointment, then: • The United States trustee will appoint a trustee—after consulting with creditors, equity security holders, and any other parties in interest—who will serve, subject to court approval. The United States trustee may not serve as the trustee. • Alternatively (except in railroad reorganizations), within 30 days after the court orders the appointment, a party in interest can request election of a trustee.	If a trustee is appointed, the trustee: • Replaces the debtor in possession; • Takes possession of the property; • Is authorized to operate debtor's business unless the court orders otherwise; • Investigates the debtor's conduct and financial condition, as well as the advisability of continuing the business, and files a report of the investigation; and • Files a Chapter 11 plan as soon as feasible (or recommends dismissal or conversion of the case to another chapter).
CHAPTER 13	In regions where there are many such cases, the United States trustee ordinarily appoints a standing trustee to serve in all such cases in the region. Otherwise, the United States trustee serves or appoints a trustee for each particular case. Usually, the debtor retains possession of all property of the estate, unless a confirmed plan or an order provides otherwise.	The trustee is primarily a disbursing agent who: • Ensures that the debtor begins to make payments within the *earlier of* (i) *30 days* after the plan is filed or (ii) the order for relief; • Disburses payments to creditors under a confirmed plan; and • Testifies at hearings about confirmation (or post-confirmation modification) of a plan or valuation of property subject to a lien.
CHAPTER 12	Same as Chapter 13.	The trustee's duties are very similar to those in Chapter 13 as long as the debtor continues to be a debtor in possession. If a Chapter 12 debtor is removed from possession, the trustee is charged with several of the duties of a Chapter 11 trustee and also with operation of the debtor's farm or commercial fishing operation.

6. Liability of Trustee

As a fiduciary of the estate, a trustee may be held *personally liable* for breach of duties. [**Mosser v. Darrow,** 341 U.S. 267 (1951)] There is a split of authority among the circuits "as to the extent of a trustee's liability based upon the nature of the breach." [***In re* Cutright,** 2012 WL 1945703 (Bankr. E.D. Va. 2012)] Some jurisdictions hold trustees personally liable for *either* intentional or negligent violations of their fiduciary duties. [**LeBlanc v. Salem (*In re* Mailman Steam Carpet Cleaning Service),** 196 F.3d 1 (1st Cir. 1999)] Other jurisdictions impose personal liability only for intentional violations of the trustee's duties. [**Yadkin Valley Bank & Trust Co. v. McGee,** 819 F.2d 74 (4th Cir. 1987)] The Fifth Circuit has taken an intermediate position and has held that the "proper standard is gross negligence." [**Dodson v. Huff (*In re* Smyth),** 207 F.3d 758 (5th Cir. 2000)]

7. Powers of Trustee

The bankruptcy trustee, as the representative of the estate, is entrusted with a variety of administrative powers that he may use when appropriate. Included among them are the powers to:

a. *file a proof of claim on behalf of a creditor* who has not timely filed his claim [B.C. § 501(c)];

b. *operate the debtor's business* (i) in a Chapter 11 case, unless ordered otherwise; (ii) sometimes in a Chapter 7 case, for a short period prior to liquidation, if the court permits; or (iii) in a Chapter 12 case in which the court has removed the debtor in possession [B.C. §§ 1108, 721, 1202(b)(5), 1203];

c. *deposit or invest money* of the estate [B.C. § 345];

d. *employ professional persons,* such as attorneys, accountants, auctioneers, or appraisers [B.C. § 327(a)];

e. *avoid certain transfers and liens,* and thereby enlarge the estate for the benefit of creditors [B.C. §§ 544–551, 553];

f. *use, sell, or lease property* of the estate [B.C. § 363];

g. *obtain credit* [B.C. § 364];

h. *assume or reject executory contracts or unexpired leases* [B.C. § 365];

i. *demand utility services* for the estate [B.C. § 366];

j. *abandon property* of the estate [B.C. § 554]; and

k. *waive a debtor corporation's attorney-client privilege* concerning communications made by former officers and directors to the debtor's attorney before the bankruptcy petition was filed. [**Commodity Futures Trading Commission v. Weintraub,** 471 U.S. 343 (1985)]

EXAM TIP　　　　　　　　　　　　　　　　　　　　　　　　　　**GILBERT**

If the debtor is a corporation whose officers or directors are suspected of pre-petition fraud, the trustee's power to *waive the attorney-client privilege* can be a valuable tool, enabling the trustee to question the debtor's pre-petition attorney and obtain information relating to the fraud.

---

8. Removal of Trustee

A trustee, other than the United States trustee, or an examiner may be removed by the court *for cause.* The Bankruptcy Code does not define "cause," but most courts require actual fraud or injury for removal of a trustee. [3 Collier ¶ 324.02(2)] Notice and a hearing are required. [B.C. § 324(a)] If the court removes a trustee or examiner for cause in a particular case, the trustee or examiner is *removed in all other cases* in which the trustee or examiner is serving, unless the court orders otherwise. [B.C. § 324(b)]

B. Examiner

1. Role and Capacity

In a Chapter 11 case in which the court has not ordered the appointment of a trustee, the court sometimes will order the appointment of an examiner. The examiner is appointed prior to confirmation of a plan *to investigate any* charges of *fraud, dishonesty, incompetence, or mismanagement* on the part of the debtor's present or former management. The debtor in possession retains her property and continues to operate the business. [B.C. § 1104(c)]

2. Eligibility

The United States trustee selects a disinterested person other than herself to act as examiner. [B.C. § 1104(d)]

3. Reasons for Appointment

When a party in interest or the United States trustee requests appointment of an examiner, the court, after notice and a hearing, *must order* that an examiner be appointed if the debtor's fixed, liquidated, unsecured debts *exceed $5 million, excluding* debts for goods, services, or taxes, and any debts owed to an insider. [B.C. § 1104(c)(2)] The existence of *large debenture debt* is a good example of such a circumstance. Also, the court will order the appointment of an examiner if such action is in the *best interests of creditors, equity security holders, and the estate.* [B.C. § 1104(c)(1)] The appointment is then made by the United States trustee, after consulting with the parties in interest, and is subject to approval by the court. [B.C. § 1104(d)]

4. Duties of Examiner

An examiner's duties include the following:

a. *to investigate the debtor's conduct, financial condition, and business operations,* as well as the *advisability of continuing* the debtor's business [B.C. §§ 1106(b), (a)(3)];

b. *to file a report of the investigation* relating any facts evidencing *fraud, dishonesty, incompetence, misconduct, or mismanagement,* and to send a copy of the findings to any creditors' committee, equity security holders' committee, any indenture trustee or any other entity that the court designates [B.C. §§ 1106(b), (a)(4)]; and

c. *any other responsibilities of a trustee* that the judge directs the debtor in possession not to perform. [B.C. § 1106(b)]

5. Examiner May Not Serve as Trustee or Professional Person

An examiner in a Chapter 11 case may not serve as the trustee, if one is appointed, or be employed as a professional person by the trustee *in the same case.* [B.C. §§ 321(b), 327(f)]

C. Professional Persons

1. Role and Capacity

A trustee, a debtor in possession, or creditors' or equity security holders' committees in a Chapter 11 case, with court approval, may hire professional persons, e.g., attorneys or accountants, to perform services with respect to the bankruptcy estate. [B.C. §§ 327(a), 1102, 1107(a), 1203]

2. Eligibility

Professional persons must be *disinterested persons* who *do not have an interest adverse* to the estate. [B.C. §§ 101(14), 327(a)] Court approval *must* be obtained *prior to performing services;* otherwise, the professional's application for compensation may be denied by the court.

a. Who Is a Professional Person?

The Bankruptcy Code includes *attorneys, accountants, auctioneers, and appraisers* as professional persons. [B.C. § 327(a)] The Bankruptcy Code defines attorney as an "attorney, professional law association, corporation, or partnership, authorized under applicable law to practice law." [B.C. § 101(4)] The Code defines "accountant" as an "accountant authorized under applicable law to practice public accounting, and includes [a] professional accounting association, corporation, or partnership, if so authorized." [B.C. § 101(1)] The Code contains no definitions for auctioneers or appraisers, but no officer or employee of the judicial branch or of the Department of Justice may serve as an auctioneer or appraiser. [Bankruptcy Rule 6005] The courts have held a wide range of persons to be professional persons, including "personal property brokerage firms, management consultants, employment agencies, pension plan administrators, secretaries for the statutory creditors' committee, mediators, and public relations firms." [3 Collier ¶ 327.02(6)(a)]

b. Approval Before Hiring

It is important to obtain judicial approval to hire a professional before she begins to perform services, because many courts will not grant approval retroactively. Therefore, the failure to apply for approval first may result in denial of any compensation to the professional, even if her services have benefited the estate. [*See, e.g., In re* **Land,** 943 F.2d 1265 (10th Cir. 1991) (affirming bankruptcy court decision that ordered return of attorney's fees to debtor's brother, who had financed state court litigation that was primary asset in debtor's bankruptcy case, because attorney had not sought bankruptcy court approval prior to employment)]

(i) Various standards for Granting Retroactive Relief

There are several tests that the courts have adopted for determining when to grant retroactive relief. [*In re* **Kearney,** 581 B.R. 644 (Bankr. D. N.M. 2018)] Most courts require *extraordinary or exceptional circumstances.* Courts differ, however, as to whether inattention or inadvertence precludes a finding of extraordinary or exceptional circumstances.

e.g. **Example:** Debtors filed for relief under Chapter 11. They hired SRR to appraise two pieces of real property for Debtors, but failed to obtain bankruptcy court approval prior to SRR's hiring. Ten months later, Debtors filed an application to employ SRR. No party disputed that SRR's work had provided some benefit to the bankruptcy court. Nonetheless, the bankruptcy court concluded that exceptional circumstances did not exist and denied the application. The court noted that SRR was a sophisticated party and the facts showed nothing more than inattention and inadvertence. The bankruptcy court concluded that if such behavior constituted "exceptional circumstances," then the exception would swallow the rule requiring approval prior to employment. [*In re* **Greektown Holding, LLC,** 2010 WL 7343848 (Bankr. E.D. Mich. 2010)]

Example: Debtor filed for relief under Chapter 7. Debtor owned two parcels of real property with his brother that the Chapter 7 trustee concluded had value for the estate. The trustee hired the law firm of Danning Gill to pursue the estate's interest in the properties. Danning Gill began its work for the trustee in late January, but did not file an employment application. Danning Gill and Debtor's attorney negotiated a settlement and sale of the properties to the Debtor. The bankruptcy court approved the settlement. Approximately 11 months after hiring Danning Gill, the Chapter 7 trustee filed an application to employ the firm. The bankruptcy court approved the application, and the Ninth Circuit's B.A.P. affirmed. The B.A.P. explained that to establish exceptional circumstances the applicant had to (i) provide a satisfactory explanation for not obtaining approval prior to employment and (ii) show that its services provided a significant benefit to the estate. There was no dispute that Danning Gill's work was of significant benefit to the estate. Even though Danning Gill acknowledged that its failure to file a timely application for employment resulted from "inadvertence or oversight," the B.A.P. affirmed the bankruptcy court's determination that Danning Gill had provided a satisfactory explanation for not timely filing an application for employment. [**Watson v. Gill (*In re* Watson),** 2015 WL 3939781 (B.A.P. 9th Cir. 2015)]

Some courts have adopted the ***excusable neglect*** standard. [***In re* Singson,** 41 F.3d 316 (7th Cir. 1994) (rejecting the "extraordinary circumstances" test but also explaining that "excusable neglect" is a higher standard than "simple neglect"); **Blocksom v. Brown (*In re* Brown),** 555 B.R. 854 (Bankr. S.D. Ga. 2016) (applying excusable neglect standard and explaining that "the mere presence of neglect is not fatal if it is excusable")] Some other courts use ***multi-factor tests,*** the most common being the nine-factor test adopted in *Twinton Properties,* which requires that the applicant demonstrate each factor by clear and convincing evidence. [***In re* Twinton Properties Partnership,** 27 B.R. 817 (Bankr. M.D. Tenn. 1983)]

c. "Disinterested"

Creditors, insiders, and equity security holders are ***not*** disinterested persons. [B.C. § 101(14)]

(i) Officers, Directors, and Employees

A professional person, such as an attorney or an accountant, who is or has been an officer, a director, or an employee of the debtor within two years prior to bankruptcy is not considered to be disinterested and, therefore, generally may not be employed as a professional person by the trustee or the debtor in possession. [B.C. §§ 101(14)(B), 327(a)] Also, it would appear that any other attorney or accountant in the same law or accounting firm is not disinterested.

(1) Exceptions

A trustee who is permitted to operate the debtor's business; may retain ***essential*** salaried professionals, such as attorneys and accountants, who have been regularly employed by the debtor. [B.C. § 327(b); *see also* B.C. §§ 721, 1108, 1202] Also, in a Chapter 11 case, a professional person is not disqualified from employment by a debtor in possession ***solely*** because she was employed by the debtor, or represented the debtor, prior to bankruptcy. [B.C. § 1107(b)]

(ii) Debtor's Pre-Petition Attorney

An attorney who is owed a pre-petition debt by the debtor for legal fees might not be considered disinterested and so would be ineligible for employment. Thus, the court could deny compensation for the attorney's fees and costs in connection with her employment. [B.C. § 328(c)] *Note:* Bankruptcy Rule 2014 requires that a verified statement of the professional accompany the application for employment, and it is critical that this statement *fully disclose the claim.* Some courts hold that an attorney holding a pre-petition claim against the debtor is *per se* ineligible for employment. Other courts engage in a fact-intensive inquiry to determine whether the attorney's pre-petition claim creates a materially adverse interest.

d. Special Purpose Attorney

The court may authorize a trustee or a debtor in possession to employ a former attorney of the debtor for a *special purpose,* such as continuing legal expertise in an intricate proceeding, provided that the employment is in the *estate's best interest* and the lawyer does not have an adverse interest concerning the specific subject matter of the employment. The purpose may *not* be to represent the trustee in administering the bankruptcy case. [B.C. § 327(e)]

e. Creditor's Representative

In a Chapter 7, 11, or 12 case, a professional person is not disqualified from *employment by a trustee solely* because of her employment by or representation of a creditor, unless another creditor or the United States trustee objects and the court finds an *actual conflict of interest.* [B.C. § 327(c)]

f. Trustee as a Professional Person

The court may permit the trustee also to serve as an attorney or an accountant for the estate if that employment is in the estate's best interest. [B.C. § 327(d)]

3. Creditors' Committee May Hire Professional Persons

In a Chapter 11 case, a creditors' committee or an equity security holders' committee may employ attorneys, accountants, or other professionals to perform services for the committee. [B.C. § 1103(a)] While representing or in the employ of the committee, the professional person may not represent an entity having an *adverse interest.* Representation of a creditor of the same class as the committee represents, however, does not per se constitute representation of an adverse interest. [B.C. § 1103(b)] Thus, an attorney representing the official unsecured creditors' committee in a Chapter 11 case also may represent an unsecured creditor in the case; representation of the unsecured creditor does not per se constitute representation of an adverse interest.

D. Ombudsmen

1. BAPCPA's Changes

BAPCPA added two new sections to Chapter 3 of the Bankruptcy Code, both of which set forth the rules for appointment of ombudsmen. Section 332 provides for the appointment of a *consumer privacy ombudsman* while § 333 provides for the appointment of a *patient care ombudsman.*

a. Consumer Privacy Ombudsman

A bankruptcy court cannot approve a sale of *personally identifiable information* that is inconsistent with the debtor's privacy policy unless the court first orders the appointment of a *consumer privacy ombudsman* and subsequently holds a hearing, after notice, on the proposed sale. [B.C. § 363(b)(1)(B)] If the court orders the appointment of a consumer privacy ombudsman, then the United States trustee must appoint *one disinterested person,* other than the United States trustee, to serve as ombudsman *no later than 7 days* before the start of the sale hearing. [B.C. § 332(a)]

(i) Sale Hearing

The consumer privacy ombudsman may appear and be heard at the sale hearing and must provide information to the court to assist with the court's consideration of the facts, circumstances, and conditions of the proposed sale. The information may include the following:

(1) the *debtor's privacy policy;*

(2) the possible *losses or gains of privacy* to consumers if the court approves the sale;

(3) the potential *costs and benefits* to consumers if the court approves the sale; and

(4) any *alternatives* that would mitigate potential losses of privacy or potential costs to consumers.

[B.C. § 332(b)]

(ii) Confidentiality

The consumer privacy ombudsman cannot disclose any personally identifiable information she obtains. [B.C. § 332(c)]

b. Patient Care Ombudsman

If a health care business files for relief under Chapters 7, 9 or 11, then the bankruptcy court must order the appointment, within *30 days* of the start of the case, of a *patient care ombudsman,* unless the court finds that appointment is not necessary for the protection of patients in a specific case. The job of the patient care ombudsman is to *monitor the quality of patient care* and to *represent* the health care business *patients' interests.* [B.C. § 333(a)(1)]

(i) Health Care Business

A *health care business* is any public or private entity, whether for profit or not for profit, that is primarily engaged in offering to the general public *facilities and services* for the *diagnosis or treatment of injury, deformity or disease* and *surgical, drug treatment, psychiatric, or obstetric care.* [B.C. § 101(27A)] A health care business includes any general or specialized hospital, ancillary ambulatory, emergency, or surgical treatment center, hospice, home health agency, or any similar health care entity. [B.C. § 101(27B)] Most courts use the following four-part test for determining whether a debtor is a "health care business" under § 101(27A):

(1) debtor is a *public or private* entity;

(2) debtor is primarily engaged in offering facilities and services to the *general public;*

(3) the facilities and services are offered to the public for *diagnosis and treatment* of injury, deformity, or disease; and

(4) the facilities and services are offered to the public for *surgical care, drug treatment, psychiatric care, or obstetric care.*

[*In re* **Medical Associates of Pinellas, LLC,** 360 B.R. 356 (Bankr. M.D. Fla. 2007)]

(ii) Long-Term Care Facility

A long-term care facility is a *health care business.* A long-term care facility includes a skilled nursing facility, intermediate care facility, assisted living facility, home for the aged, or domiciliary care facility. It also includes any specialized hospital, ancillary ambulatory, emergency, or surgical treatment center, hospice, home health agency, or any similar health care entity that is primarily engaged in offering room, board, laundry, or personal assistance with activities of daily living. [B.C. § 101(27A)(B)]

(iii) Determining Nature of Debtor

If a debtor checks the "Health Care Business" box on the voluntary petition, then the case proceeds as one involving a health care business. [Bankruptcy Rule 1021(a); Official Form 201] If the debtor is a health care business but does not check the petition box, then the United States trustee or any party in interest may file a motion to determine whether the debtor is a health care business. [Bankruptcy Rule 1021(b)]

(iv) Appointment

The United States trustee appoints *one disinterested person,* other than the United States trustee, to serve as the patient care ombudsman for the health care business. [B.C. § 333(a)(2)(A)] If the debtor is a *long-term care facility,* the United States trustee may appoint the State Long-Term Care Ombudsman under the Older Americans Act of 1965 for the state in which the bankruptcy case is pending. [B.C. § 333(a)(2)(B)] If the United States trustee does not appoint the State Long-Term Care Ombudsman, then the United States trustee must provide notice to the State Long-Term Care Ombudsman of the name and address of the person appointed as the patient care ombudsman. [B.C. § 333(a)(2)(C)]

(v) Protection of Patients

A debtor may be a health care business, but the court still may decide not to appoint an ombudsman based on the specific facts of the debtor's case. In deciding whether appointment is necessary for the *protection of patients,* many courts examine a non-exclusive list of the following nine factors:

(1) *cause of the bankruptcy;*

(2) whether there are *licensing or supervising authorities overseeing* the debtor;

(3) debtor's *history* of patient care;

(4) patients' ability to *protect their rights;*

(5) level of *dependency of patients* on the debtor's facility;

(6) likelihood there will be *tension* between the *interests of patients and those of debtor;*

(7) *potential harm* to patients if the debtor drastically reduces its level of patient care;

(8) presence and sufficiency of *internal safeguards* for appropriate care; and

(9) effect that appointment of an ombudsman will have on the *cost of reorganization.*

[*In re* **Alternate Family Care,** 377 B.R. 754 (Bankr. S.D. Fla. 2007)]

(vi) Duties

The patient care ombudsman has the following statutory duties:

(1) to *monitor the quality of patient care,* to the extent necessary, including interviewing patients and doctors [B.C. § 333(b)(1)];

(2) to *report,* at a hearing or in writing, on the *quality of care* no later than *60 days after appointment* and at least every 60 days thereafter [B.C. § 333(b)(2)];

(3) to *file a motion or written report,* with notice to the parties in interest, if the ombudsman determines that the quality of care is *declining significantly* or is being *materially compromised* [B.C. § 333(b)(3)];

(4) to *maintain as confidential* any information related to patients, including patient records [B.C. § 333(c)(1)]; and

(5) to *obtain prior court approval* for any review of *confidential patient records* and to abide by any restrictions that the bankruptcy court imposes in order to protect confidentiality. [B.C. § 333(c)(1)]

E. Compensation of Officers

1. In General

Officers of the estate, including a trustee, an examiner, a Chapter 12 or 13 individual debtor's attorney, a consumer privacy ombudsman, a patient care ombudsman, and any professional person properly employed by a trustee, a debtor in possession, or a creditors' committee may be awarded by the court a *reasonable fee* for actual and necessary services, as well as *reimbursement* for *actual and necessary expenses.* [B.C. § 330(a)(1), (a)(4)(B)]

2. Debtor's Attorney

The right of the debtor's attorney to compensation from estate funds varies depending on the chapter of the Code under which the debtor files for relief.

a. Chapter 12 or 13

The Bankruptcy Code expressly provides that the court may award reasonable compensation to the attorney of an individual Chapter 12 or Chapter 13 debtor, based on the benefit and necessity of the services to the debtor and the statutory criteria listed below. [B.C. § 330(a)(4)(B)]

b. Chapter 7

The Supreme Court has held that § 330(a)(1) does not authorize payment of compensation to the Chapter 7 debtor's lawyer from the estate, unless the lawyer was employed pursuant to § 327. Section 327, however, speaks in terms of the *trustee's* employment of professional persons, including attorneys. Thus, a Chapter 7 attorney is only entitled to compensation under § 330(a)(1) if she is hired by the trustee and approved by the bankruptcy court. [**Lamie v. United States Trustee,** 540 U.S. 526 (2004)] Because the debtor hires the attorney to file her Chapter 7 case, the attorney representing a Chapter

7 debtor must obtain her fee upfront and not rely on compensation from estate funds under § 330(a)(1).

c. Chapter 11

A Chapter 11 debtor normally is a debtor in possession and, as such, has the rights, other than the right to compensation, of a trustee. Thus, the Chapter 11 debtor may hire an attorney and so long as the bankruptcy court approves the employment, the attorney is entitled to compensation according to the standards set forth in § 330. [B.C. §§ 1107(a), 327] Once the bankruptcy court orders appointment of a Chapter 11 trustee, however, the debtor is no longer a debtor in possession and does not have the rights and powers of a trustee under § 1107(a). Therefore, after the appointment of a Chapter 11 trustee, the debtor's attorney must look to the debtor, not the estate, for compensation for services rendered. [*See* **Morrison v. United States Trustee,** 2010 WL 2653394 (E.D. N.Y. 2010) (noting that the language interpreted in *Lamie* "is not limited to Chapter 7, and there is no basis in law to presume that a different result would follow where a Chapter 11 trustee has been appointed"); *see also* ***In re* Miles,** 2011 WL 1124183 (Bankr. N.D. Ga. 2011)]

3. Fee Application

An application for compensation for services or reimbursement of necessary expenses must include a ***detailed*** statement of (i) the services performed, (ii) the time spent, (iii) the expenses incurred, and (iv) the amounts requested. It also must include disclosures concerning (i) payments that have been made or promised, (ii) the source of such payments, (iii) the sharing of, or any agreement to share, compensation previously received or to be received, and (iv) the details concerning any sharing of, or agreement to share, compensation, unless the sharing is with other members of the same firm of attorneys or accountants. A copy of the fee application must be sent to the United States trustee. [Bankruptcy Rule 2016(a)] The application must contain all information required by the ***procedural guidelines issued by the Executive Office for United States Trustees.*** [28 C.F.R. Part 58, Appendix A, B] Also, local bankruptcy rules may require additional information and always should be consulted.

Note: The Supreme Court has held that § 330(a)(1) does not authorize bankruptcy courts to award compensation to attorneys for work defending their fee applications. [**Baker Botts LLP v. ASARCO LLC,** 135 S.Ct. 2158 (2015)]

4. Criteria for Determining Reasonable Compensation

In determining a reasonable fee, the court must consider the nature, extent, and value of the services, taking into account all relevant factors, including the following:

a. the ***time*** spent [B.C. § 330(a)(3)(A)];

b. the ***rates*** charged [B.C. § 330(a)(3)(B)];

c. whether the ***services were necessary or beneficial*** for the administration or completion of the case when the services were rendered [B.C. § 330(a)(3)(C)];

d. whether the services were performed within a ***reasonable time,*** considering the nature, complexity, and importance of work [B.C. § 330(a)(3)(D)];

e. whether the professional person is ***board certified*** or has otherwise shown ***skill and experience*** in the field of bankruptcy [B.C. § 330(a)(3)(E)]; and

f. whether the ***compensation is reasonable*** based on the ***customary fees*** charged by comparably skilled practitioners in nonbankruptcy cases. [B.C. § 330(a)(3)(F)]

The court cannot allow compensation for services that are (i) unnecessarily duplicative, (ii) not reasonably likely to benefit the estate, or (iii) not necessary to the administration of the case. [B.C. § 330(a)(4)(A)]

5. Limitations on Professionals' Compensation

An award of compensation to a professional person is subject to several statutory limitations. [B.C. § 328]

a. Modification By Court

A professional person may be hired by a trustee, a debtor in possession, or a creditors' or equity security holders' committee on any reasonable basis, including a retainer, an hourly standard, or a contingent fee. However, the compensation ultimately allowed by the court may vary from the agreed-upon terms if those terms prove to be improvident in light of developments that could not have been anticipated. [B.C. § 328(a)]

b. Denial of Compensation

If, at any time during employment, a professional person is *not disinterested* or *has an interest adverse to the estate* regarding the subject matter of her employment, the court may deny her compensation for services and reimbursement of expenses. [B.C. § 328(c)]

(i) Exceptions

This rule is subject to three possible exceptions for (i) a creditor's representative [B.C. § 327(c)], (ii) a "special purpose" attorney [B.C. § 327(e)], and (iii) a professional hired by the debtor before the bankruptcy case. [B.C. § 1107(b)]

EXAM TIP   🔲GILBERT

If an exam question raises an issue regarding a professional's compensation in connection with a bankruptcy proceeding, be sure to mention that the professional must have been approved by the court *before* performing the services and that the professional must be a *disinterested person* who does *not have an adverse interest* throughout the proceeding. Failure to disclose "interestedness" or any adverse interest may result in denial of fees and possibly sanctions. Also, remember to note that compensation must be *reasonable* and is subject to modification by the court.

---

c. Bifurcation of Trustee's Compensation

If a trustee also serves as an attorney or an accountant for the estate, her fee for professional employment may not include compensation for the performance of her duties as trustee. Compensation for services as trustee must be accounted for separately. [B.C. § 328(b)]

6. No-Asset Cases

In a case filed under Chapter 7, the trustee is entitled to receive a minimum compensation of $60 (out of the filing fee) if the estate has no property from which to make disbursements to creditors. [B.C. § 330(b)]

7. Trustee's Maximum Compensation

The maximum compensation that may be awarded for a *trustee's services,* other than reimbursement for necessary expenses, varies according to the chapter under which the case is filed. [B.C. § 326]

a. Chapters 7 and 11

In a Chapter 7 or Chapter 11 case, a trustee's compensation may not be greater than 25% of the first $5,000 disbursed by the trustee to parties in interest, 10% of the next $45,000, 5% of any amount disbursed in excess of $50,000, but not more than $1 million, and reasonable compensation not to exceed 3% of amounts more than $1 million. [B.C. § 326(a)]

(i) Exclusion of Disbursements to Debtor

Any disbursements by the trustee to the debtor, such as exempt property, are excluded from the computation. [B.C. § 326(a)]

(ii) Inclusion of Disbursements to Secured Creditors

On the other hand, generally the calculation of the trustee's total disbursements includes payments made to holders of secured claims. [B.C. § 326(a)] Courts, however, have held that a credit bid under § 363(k) is not included in the trustee's total disbursements for purposes of calculating the trustee's compensation. [*See, e.g.,* **Tamn v. United States Trustee (*In re* Hokulani),** 776 F.3d 1083 (9th Cir. 2015) (holding that § 326(a) does not allow the trustee to collect fees on a credit bid transaction, because the statute says "moneys disbursed" and a credit bid involves the trustee turning property over to a secured creditor in exchange for a reduction in the amount that the estate owes to the secured creditor); *compare* **In re WM Six Forks, LLC,** 502 B.R. 88 (Bankr. E.D. N.C. 2013) (finding that the amount of a credit bid is included in calculating the quarterly fee due the United States trustee under § 1930(a)(6) and comparing the language of § 326—moneys disbursed—with that of § 1930(a)(6)—disbursements)]

b. Chapter 12 and Chapter 13

The maximum compensation that a standing Chapter 12 or Chapter 13 trustee may receive is the lesser of 5% of all payments made under the plans that she administered, or the highest yearly basic salary rate for a United States employee at level V of the Executive Schedule plus the cash value of certain employment benefits. [28 U.S.C. § 586(e)]

For a non-standing trustee appointed in a particular case under Chapter 12 or Chapter 13, the maximum compensation is 5% of all payments made under the plan. [B.C. § 326(b)]

8. Interim Compensation

A trustee, examiner, debtor's attorney, or other professional person may apply for interim compensation or reimbursement of expenses once every 120 days, or more frequently, if the court allows, instead of waiting until the conclusion of the bankruptcy case to be paid. [B.C. § 331] After notice and a hearing, the court may approve the application. Any award of interim compensation will cause a reduction, by that amount, in an award of compensation made under § 330. [B.C. § 330(a)(5)] Interim compensation is generally not an issue in Chapter 12 or 13 cases. Bankruptcy courts have standing orders for such cases that provide an allowed standard fee awarded without application or a hearing and paid as an administrative claim through the plan. [3 Collier ¶ 331.07]

9. Debtor's Transactions with Attorneys

Even if the debtor's attorney does not apply to the court for compensation, she still must file a statement of any fees paid or any fee agreement made within one year before bankruptcy for legal services related to the case. The statement also must indicate the source of payment. [B.C. § 329(a); Bankruptcy Rule 2016(b)] If the court determines that the compensation is unreasonable, it may cancel the fee agreement or order that any excessive portion be returned to the estate or to the entity that made the payment. [B.C. § 329(b); Bankruptcy Rule 2017] While the debtor's attorney must report any fees paid within the year prior to filing for bankruptcy, there is no limitations period for disgorgement of excessive fees. [B.C. § 329(b); Bankruptcy Rule 2017(a); **Arnes v. Bouhgton (*In re* Prudhomme),** 43 F.3d 1000 (5th Cir. 1995) (ordering disgorgement of excessive fees paid more than one year before bankruptcy as a sanction for nondisclosure)]

10. Sharing of Fees Prohibited

A trustee, examiner, attorney, accountant, or other professional person employed in a bankruptcy case is prohibited from sharing any compensation or reimbursement with another person. [B.C. § 504(a)] This rule is subject to two exceptions.

a. Exception—Members of Same Firm

Compensation or reimbursement may be shared with another member, partner, or associate of the same professional firm. [B.C. § 504(b)(1)]

b. Exception—Involuntary Case

An attorney representing a creditor who files an involuntary petition is permitted to share her fee with any other attorney who contributes to her services or expenses. [B.C. § 504(b)(2)]

F. United States Trustee

1. Appointment and Term

For each of the 21 regions throughout the nation, the Attorney General appoints one United States trustee for a five-year term. If necessary, the Attorney General also may appoint assistant United States trustees. [28 U.S.C. §§ 581, 582]

a. Exceptions

The judicial districts for Alabama and North Carolina are served by bankruptcy administrators appointed by the United States Courts of Appeals for the Fourth and Eleventh Circuits.

2. Administrative Duties

The United States trustee performs numerous administrative functions under the supervision of the Attorney General. Some of these duties are as follows:

a. *to establish and supervise a panel of private trustees* to serve in Chapter 7 cases [28 U.S.C. § 586(a)(1)];

b. *to appoint an interim trustee* from the private panel in a Chapter 7 case [B.C. § 701(a)(1)];

c. *to appoint a trustee or an examiner* in a Chapter 11 case when the court orders such appointment to be made, or *to convene a meeting of creditors to elect a trustee* when the court orders a trustee's appointment and a party in interest timely requests an election, instead [B.C. §§ 1104(b), (d)];

d. *to appoint a standing trustee* for Chapter 12 or Chapter 13 cases, or, instead, *to appoint a trustee* for a particular case under Chapter 12 or Chapter 13 [28 U.S.C. § 586(b); B.C. §§ 1202(a), 1302(a)];

e. in a Chapter 11 case, *to appoint and monitor creditors' committees and equity security holders' committees* [B.C. § 1102(a); 28 U.S.C. § 586(a)(3)(E)];

f. *to convene and preside at the § 341 meeting* of creditors and, if appropriate, *to examine the debtor* at that meeting [B.C. §§ 341, 343];

g. *if necessary, to serve as the trustee* in a case under Chapter 7, 12, or 13, but not in a Chapter 11 case [28 U.S.C. § 586(a)(2); B.C. § 1104(d)];

h. *to supervise the administration of bankruptcy cases and trustees* [28 U.S.C. § 586(a)(3)];

i. *to monitor applications for the employment of professional persons* and, if appropriate, file comments with the court regarding their approval [28 U.S.C. § 586(a)(3)(I)];

j. *to review fee applications* of trustees, examiners, attorneys, and other professional persons (generally based on uniform application of procedural guidelines adopted by its Executive Office), file comments with the court concerning the applications, and, if appropriate, file objections [28 U.S.C. § 586(a)(3)(A)];

k. *to monitor plans* filed in cases under Chapter 11, 12, and 13, and, if appropriate, to file with the court comments regarding such plans [28 U.S.C. §§ 586(a)(3)(B), (C)];

l. *to monitor Chapter 11 disclosure statements* and, if appropriate, file comments with the court [28 U.S.C. § 586(a)(3)(B)];

n. *to monitor the progress of bankruptcy cases* and take actions that are necessary to avoid undue delay [28 U.S.C. § 586(a)(3)(G)];

o. to take appropriate action *to ensure that the debtor timely files all necessary reports,* schedules, and fees [28 U.S.C. § 586(a)(3)(D)];

p. *to inform the United States Attorney about crimes* that may have been committed under federal law [28 U.S.C. § 586(a)(3)(F)];

q. *to deposit or invest under § 345 money* received as the trustee in bankruptcy cases [28 U.S.C. § 586(a)(4)];

r. *to make any reports* that the Attorney General directs, including the debtor audits required by BAPCPA [28 U.S.C. § 586(a)(5)];

s. *to perform other duties* prescribed by the Attorney General [28 U.S.C. § 586(a)(6)];

t. *to perform an initial debtor interview in a small business case* as soon as possible after the order for relief but before the first § 341 meeting [28 U.S.C. § 586(a)(7)(A)];

u. if appropriate, *to visit the business premises of a small business debtor,* ascertain the state of the *books and records,* and *verify* that the small business debtor has *filed its tax returns* [28 U.S.C. § 586(a)(7)(B)];

v. *to review and monitor* the small business debtor's activities to determine whether the debtor will be unable to confirm a plan [28 U.S.C. § 586(a)(7)(C)]; and

w. ***to promptly file a motion to convert or dismiss*** a Chapter 11 case after finding ***material grounds*** for such relief [28 U.S.C. § 586(a)(8); B.C. § 1112]

3. Right to Raise Issues

The Bankruptcy Code grants the United States trustee the right to raise, appear and be heard with respect to any issue in a bankruptcy case. The United States trustee may not file a plan in a case under Chapter 11. [B.C. § 307]

Chapter Five

The Bankruptcy Estate

CONTENTS	PAGE

Chapter Approach

The bankruptcy estate contains all property described in Bankruptcy Code § 541. "Section 541 property" includes all of the debtor's legal and equitable interests in property at the time the bankruptcy petition is filed, certain kinds of property acquired by the debtor within 180 days after the date of bankruptcy, **and** property that the trustee brings into the estate by exercising her **avoiding powers.** (Chapter 6 of this outline covers the trustee's avoiding powers.) As a general rule, any entity that has possession or custody of estate property must **turn over** such property to the trustee. The trustee may **abandon** property that is either burdensome or of inconsequential value to the estate. The trustee, however, may not abandon property in violation of state or federal environmental laws if the result threatens the health or safety of the public with "imminent and identifiable harm."

A. The Bankruptcy Estate

1. Property Included in Bankruptcy Estate

The creation of a bankruptcy estate occurs automatically upon the filing of a petition commencing a voluntary, joint, or involuntary bankruptcy case. The estate consists of a comprehensive range of rights and interests in property, regardless of the property's location or the entity in possession, as well as various causes of action and claims held by the debtor. [B.C. § 541(a)] The Supreme Court has held that Congress generally has left to state law "the determination of property rights in the assets of a bankrupt's estate . . . unless some federal interest requires a different result." [**Butner v. United States,** 440 U.S. 48 (1979) (decided under Bankruptcy Act); *see also* **Travelers Casualty & Surety Co. v. Pacific Gas and Electric Co.,** 549 U.S. 443 (2007) (citing *Butner* for proposition that " 'state law governs the substance of claims' " and holding that the Bankruptcy Code does not disallow a contract-based claim for attorney's fees simply because the fees were incurred litigating issues of bankruptcy law")]

a. All Legal and Equitable Interests of Debtor

The estate includes all of the debtor's legal and equitable interests in property, real or personal, tangible or intangible, **at the time the petition is filed.** [B.C. § 541(a)(1)] The Bankruptcy Code's definition of property of the estate is expansive, as evidenced by the following examples of legal and equitable interests in property that may be included in the estate:

(i) **bank deposits** [5 Collier ¶ 541.08];

(ii) **stocks and stock options** [**Doucet v. Drydock Coal Com (*In re Oakley*),** 2009 WL 1687775 (B.A.P. 6th Cir. 2009) (debtor's shares in his family firm)];

(iii) **insurance policies and payments under those policies** [**Stinnett v. LaPlante (*In re* Stinnett),** 465 F.3d 309 (7th Cir. 2006) (noting that "[a]s a general matter, insurance contracts in which the debtor has an interest" when bankruptcy is filed are estate property and concluding that disability payments under a disability insurance contract are proceeds of that policy); *In re* **Sunland,** 2014 WL 7011747 (Bankr. D. N.M. 2014) (citing cases, including those involving product liability insurance)];

(iv) **compensation** received post-petition for **pre-petition** employment services;

(v)   *executory contracts;*

(vi)   *pre-petition personal injury claims* by the debtor [**Wischan v. Adler (*In re* Wischan),** 77 F.3d 875 (5th Cir. 1996)];

(vii)   *causes of action for damage to property* [4 Norton § 61:7];

(viii) *other rights of action,* including actions against corporate officers and directors for breach of their fiduciary duties [**Torch Liquidating Trust v. Stockstill,** 561 F.3d 377 (5th Cir. 2009) (citing cases); 4 Norton § 61:7];

(ix)   *income tax refunds* based on *pre-petition* earnings or losses [**Kokoszka v. Belford,** 417 U.S. 642 (1974) (decided under Bankruptcy Act); **Garcia Matos v. Oliveras Rivera (*In re* Garcia Matos),** 478 B.R. 506 (B.A.P. 1st Cir. 2012) (citing cases)];

(x)   *net operating loss carryovers* [*In re* **Prudential Lines, Inc.,** 928 F.2d 565 (2d Cir. 1991)];

(xi)   *earned income credit,* prorated to the date of the bankruptcy petition [**Wood v. Jones (*In re* Montgomery),** 224 F.3d 1193 (10th Cir. 2000); **Johnston v. Hazlett (*In re* Johnston),** 209 F.3d 611 (6th Cir. 2000) (citing cases)];

(xii)   *licenses, copyrights, and patents*;

(xiii) *a remainder interest in real property* [*In re* **Saunders,** 2011 WL 671765 (Bankr. M.D. Ga. 2011) (stating that "[i]t is [ ] well-known that a vested remainder interest in real property is property of the estate")];

(xiv)   *a right to possession of property* under an unexpired lease [*In re* **Tel-A-Communications Consultants, Inc.,** 50 B.R. 250 (Bankr. D. Conn. 1985); *but compare* B.C. § 541(b)(2)];

(xv)   *a liquor license* [*In re* **The Ground Round, Inc.,** 482 F.3d 15 (1st Cir. 2011)];

(xvi)   *business social media accounts* [*In re* **CTLI, LLC,** 528 B.R. 359 (Bankr. S.D. Tex. 2015)];

(xvii) *a debtor's right to redeem pawned property* under state law [**Schnitzel, Inc. v. Sorensen (*In re* Sorensen),** 586 B.R. 327 (B.A.P. 9th Cir. 2018)]; and

(xviii) *a debtor's right of redemption under state law arising at a post-petition foreclosure sale of real property* in which the estate had not abandoned its interest. [**Schlarman v. Nageleisen (*In re* Nageleisen),** 527 B.R. 258 (Bankr. E.D. Ky. 2015)]

b. Limitation

The estate's interest in property is no greater than the debtor's interest when the bankruptcy petition is filed. [**Witko v. Menotte (*In re* Witko),** 374 F.3d 1040 (11th Cir. 2004) ("Congress expressly cautioned that the Bankruptcy Code 'is not intended to expand the debtor's rights against others more than they exist at the commencement of the case. . . .[The trustee] could take no greater rights than the debtor himself had' ") (quoting from legislative history)]

c. Other Kinds of Estate Property

In addition to the debtor's legal and equitable interests in property as of the date of bankruptcy, estate property also includes the following:

(i) Community Property

All of the debtor and debtor's spouse's community property, as defined under applicable state law, at the time of the filing of the bankruptcy petition becomes property of the estate if the property is under the debtor's sole or joint control or is liable for a claim against the debtor or for a joint claim against the debtor and debtor's spouse. [B.C. § 541(a)(2)]

(ii) Property Recovered by Trustee

Any interests in property that the trustee recovers or preserves for the benefit of the estate, e.g., if the trustee has avoided a preferential or fraudulent transfer of the debtor's interest in property, are included in property of the estate. [B.C. § 541(a)(3), (4)]

(iii) Certain Property Acquired Post-Petition

Property that the debtor obtains or becomes entitled to within *180 days after the date of bankruptcy* is included in the estate if two conditions are satisfied:

(1) the property would have been estate property had the debtor had an interest in the property on the date of the bankruptcy filing; and

(2) the property is from a bequest, devise, inheritance, property settlement with the debtor's spouse, divorce decree, or beneficial interest in a life insurance policy or death benefit plan is considered to be property of the estate. [B.C. § 541(a)(5)]

e.g. **Example:** Debtor filed for relief under Chapter 7. Within 180 days after filing for bankruptcy, Debtor received a distribution from an inter vivos spendthrift trust after the trust's settlor, a distant relative of the Debtor's, passed away. The Chapter 7 trustee claimed that the distribution constituted property of the estate under § 541(a)(5), but the bankruptcy court disagreed. The court found that the Debtor had not acquired or become entitled to the distribution by "bequest, devise, or inheritance", under § 541(a)(5)(A) and, thus, the distribution was not estate property. (Neither § 541(a)(5)(B) or (C) applied to the facts of the case.) The court explained that an inter vivos trust, unlike a testamentary trust, is not created by a will. Thus, Debtor did not receive the distribution by bequest or devise. The court noted that there was no evidence that the relative had died intestate and, thus, Debtor did not receive the distribution as an inheritance under the laws of intestacy. Therefore, the distribution was not estate property under § 541(a)(5)(A). [*In re* **Dayton,** 2018 WL 576748 (Bankr. W.D. Mo. 2018)]

EXAM TIP   🔖GILBERT

On your exam, if you have to determine what property should be included in the bankruptcy estate, it is easy to forget that some property acquired post-petition should be included. Remember to include the following property if the property would have been estate property had debtor had an interest in the property at the time of bankruptcy filing *and* debtor acquired or became entitled to acquire the property within *180 days* after the bankruptcy petition was filed:

- Property acquired by *bequest or inheritance;*
- Property acquired through a *property settlement or divorce decree;* and

---

- Property acquired through a beneficial interest in a *life insurance policy or a death benefit plan.*

(iv) Proceeds of Estate Property

Proceeds, rents, profits, products, or offspring emanating from estate property also become property of the estate. [B.C. § 541(a)(6)]

e.g. **Example:** Debtor filed for relief under Chapter 13, but her case was dismissed. After dismissal, Bank obtained a default judgment against Debtor that ordered a sale of real property that the Debtor and her non-filing spouse owned. Before the property was sold, Debtor filed for relief under Chapter 7. After the bankruptcy court ordered a lift of stay without abandonment, a foreclosure sale took place. The amount obtained at the foreclosure sale was so small that it triggered Debtor's right of redemption under applicable nonbankruptcy law. The bankruptcy court held that Debtor's right of redemption was estate property because under § 541(a)(6) it was a proceed of the foreclosure sale. [**Schlarman v. Nageleisen (*In re* Nageleisen),** 527 B.R. 258 (Bankr. E.D. Ky. 2015)]

e.g. **Example:** Husband and Wife filed a joint petition for relief under Chapter 7. Prior to bankruptcy, Husband took a job with D&G, a holding company for a number of car dealerships. Husband also purchased a 33% interest in D&G. Husband's compensation with D&G included a base salary of $10,000 per month and a 5% monthly bonus based on the net profit of the D&G companies. If the companies did not make a profit in a particular month, then Husband did not earn a bonus that month. Husband and Wife argued that Husband's post-petition bonuses constituted earnings from service performed after the commencement of the case. The bankruptcy court rejected that argument and found that the bonuses were actually dividends from D&G's earnings. The court concluded that because the "bonuses" were "proceeds" or "profits" from Debtor's ownership interest in D&G, they constituted property of the estate under § 541(a)(6). [***In re* Cook,** 454 B.R. 204 (Bankr. N.D. Fla. 2011)]

(1) Exception: Individual Debtor's Post-Petition Earnings

In a Chapter 7 case, an *individual debtor's earnings* for services rendered *after* the filing of the petition are *not* included in property of the estate. [B.C. § 541(a)(6)] In Chapters 11, 12, and 13, however, an individual debtor's earnings from services rendered after the filing of the petition but before the earlier of the closing, dismissal, or conversion of the case are included in property of the estate. [B.C. §§ 1115(a)(2), 1207(a)(2), 1306(a)(2)]

(v) Property Acquired by Estate After Bankruptcy

Any property that the *estate* acquires after the filing of the petition becomes property of the estate. [B.C. § 541(a)(7)] Be careful to distinguish between property that the *debtor* acquires from property that the *estate* acquires after filing of the petition. This subsection of the Code applies only to property acquired by the *estate,* not by the *debtor.*

e.g. **Example:** In August of 2013, Debtor's spouse filed a divorce action in state court. The following summer, in July of 2014, Debtor filed for relief under Chapter 7. In March of 2015, Debtor's spouse filed a motion for relief of stay to allow the divorce proceeding to continue. The bankruptcy court granted the spouse's motion, and in June of 2015, the state court entered a consent judgment of divorce.

That judgment awarded Debtor a 50% interest in certain inventory and required Debtor's spouse to pay Debtor $2,700 within 30 days of entry of the consent judgment. The Debtor claimed that the inventory and $2,700 were not property of the estate, because he acquired them pursuant to the consent judgment of divorce, which was entered more than 180 days after filing of his Chapter 7 case and, thus, § 541(a)(5)(B) did not apply. The bankruptcy court held that the inventory and $2,700 were estate property under §§ 541(a)(1) and (a)(7). The court explained that in Michigan the filing of an action for divorce creates a marital estate. When Debtor filed for bankruptcy, his interest in the marital estate became property of the estate under § 541(a)(1), even though Debtor's interest in the marital property was contingent at the time. Debtor's contingent interest vested, however, upon entry of the consent judgment of divorce; at that time, the Debtor's right to the inventory and $2,700 became estate property under § 541(a)(7). Therefore, the court concluded that it was "immaterial" that the state court had entered the consent judgment of divorce more than 180 days after Debtor had filed for bankruptcy. [*In re* **Kooi,** 547 B.R. 244 (Bankr. W.D. Mich. 2016)]

2. Invalid Clauses: Ipso Facto or "Bankruptcy" Clauses

Property of the debtor that becomes part of the bankruptcy estate is not affected by a clause in a contract, deed, or nonbankruptcy law that places restrictions or conditions on the debtor's transfer of the property. Likewise, clauses that purport to cause a forfeiture, termination, or modification of the debtor's interest in the property due to (i) the debtor's insolvency, (ii) the debtor's financial condition, (iii) the filing of a bankruptcy case concerning the debtor, or (iv) the appointment of a bankruptcy trustee or a nonbankruptcy custodian or the seizure of property by such persons will not prevent the property from being included in the bankruptcy estate. Such clauses are *unenforceable* under Bankruptcy Code § 541(c)(1).

a. Exception for Certain Trusts

An exception to this principle provides for the enforceability of a restriction on the transfer of the debtor's beneficial interest in a trust, if that restriction is enforceable under *applicable nonbankruptcy law.* [B.C. § 541(c)(2)] Courts consistently have applied this exception to traditional spendthrift trusts, and the Supreme Court has held that it also covers ERISA-qualified pension plans. [**Patterson v. Shumate,** 504 U.S. 753 (1992)] The effect of the exception is to exclude the debtor's interest in the trust of the ERISA plan from property of the bankruptcy estate.

Note: BAPCPA added § 541(b)(7), which is a new exclusion from estate property for a variety of pension plans that might not qualify as ERISA-qualified. This new exclusion has eliminated in many cases the need to litigate the question of whether § 541(c)(2) excludes the debtor's pension benefits from her estate.

(i) Distinguish Payment of Trust Income to Debtor

The income from a testamentary spendthrift trust that is *paid or owing* to a debtor-beneficiary within 180 days after the filing of the bankruptcy petition is included in the estate even though the corpus of the trust is excluded and beyond the trustee's reach. [B.C. § 541(a)(5); *In re* **Dayton,** 2018 WL 576748 (Bankr. W.D. Mo. 2018) (explaining the difference between inter vivos and testamentary trusts in context of § 541(a)(5))]

3. Property Excluded from Estate

In addition to the post-petition earnings of an individual Chapter 7 and spendthrift trusts enforceable under applicable nonbankruptcy law, the following items are ***not included*** in property of the estate.

a. Certain Powers

A power that may be exercised by the debtor ***solely for the benefit of another entity*** is not part of the estate. If the debtor can exercise the power for her own benefit, this exclusion does not apply. [B.C. § 541(b)(1)]

e.g. **Example:** Debtor filed for relief under Chapter 13. Debtor used the Tennessee state exemptions and on Schedule C exempted the full fair market value of about $30,000 in child support arrearages. The Chapter 13 trustee objected to Debtor's plan, claiming, in part, that the plan was not proposed in good faith because Debtor had claimed inappropriate exemptions in the child support arrearages. The bankruptcy court overruled the trustee's objection. The court explained that under Tennessee law a custodial parent holds child support payments in a constructive trust for the minor child as beneficiary. The debtor holds these monies "for the benefit of an entity other than the debtor" and, therefore, they are excluded from the bankruptcy estate under § 541(b)(1). [***In re* Turner,** 2014 Bankr. LEXIS 5417 (Bankr. W.D. Tenn. 2014)]

b. Expired Commercial Lease of Real Property

A debtor's interest ***as a lessee*** of nonresidential real property is excluded from property of the estate if that interest has terminated due to the expiration of the lease's stated term *prior* to the filing of the petition. Property of the estate ceases to include any interest of the debtor as a lessee if the lease expires *during* the bankruptcy case. [B.C. § 541(b)(2)]

c. Certain Property of Educational Institutions

The debtor's eligibility to participate in programs under the Higher Education Act of 1965 and the debtor's accreditation status or state licensure as an educational institution are excluded from estate property. [B.C. § 541(b)(3)]

d. Farmout Agreements

Certain interests of the debtor (in liquid or gaseous hydrocarbons) transferred under a farmout agreement are also excluded from the estate. [B.C. §§ 541(b)(4)(A), 101(21A)]

e. Production Payments

Certain production payments from oil or gas producers are excluded from property of the estate, too. [B.C. § 541(b)(4)(B); 101(42A), (56A)] "A production payment is an interest in the product of an oil or gas producer that lasts for a limited period of time and that is not affected by production costs. The owner has no other interest in the property or business of the producer other than the interest in the product that is produced." [H.R. Rep. No. 103–835, at 46 (1994)] For example, when a debtor owns oil or gas wells and finances the drilling by promising to pay, in cash or in kind, a percentage as production occurs, these payments are not included in the property of the estate. [B.C. § 541(b)(4)(B)]

f. Education IRA

BAPCPA created an exclusion from estate property for certain funds placed into an education individual retirement account *no later than one year* before filing for bankruptcy. The exclusion applies *only if* all the following conditions are satisfied:

(i) the designated *beneficiary* is the debtor's *child, stepchild, grandchild, or stepgrandchild* for the taxable year in which the funds were placed in the account [B.C. § 541(b)(5)(A)];

(ii) the funds are not pledged or promised in connection with a credit extension [B.C. § 541(b)(5)(B)(i)]; and

(iii) the funds are *not excess contributions,* as defined by § 4973(e) of the Internal Revenue Code [B.C. § 541(b)(5)(B)(ii)].

There is a limitation, however, on the amount of funds excluded from the estate in the case of funds placed into such accounts between *720 and 365 days preceding bankruptcy.* In such a case, the debtor may exclude no more than a total of *$6,825* in all accounts for each designated beneficiary. [B.C. § 541(b)(5)(C)]

g. State Tuition Programs

BAPCPA added an exclusion from estate property for funds used to buy tuition credits or certificates or contributed to an account that qualifies as a *State tuition program* pursuant to *§ 529(b)(1)* of the Internal Revenue Code *no later than one year prior* to the bankruptcy filing. [B.C. § 541(b)(6)] The funds are excluded from the bankruptcy estate only if all the following conditions are satisfied:

(i) the designated *beneficiary* is the debtor's *child, stepchild, grandchild, or stepgrandchild* for the taxable year in which the funds were paid or contributed [B.C. § 541(b)(6)(A)];

(ii) the *aggregate* amount paid or contributed for *each beneficiary* does not exceed total contributions allowed under *§ 529(b)(6)* of the Internal Revenue Code, as adjusted for inflation as of the date of the bankruptcy filing. [B.C. § 541(b)(6)(B)]

As with education IRAs, there is a limitation on the amount of funds excluded from the estate in the case of funds paid or contributed to such § 529 plans between *720 and 365 days preceding bankruptcy.* In such a case, the debtor may exclude no more than a total of *$6,825* in all accounts for each designated beneficiary. [B.C. § 541(b)(6)(C)]

h. Pension Plan, Deferred Compensation, and Tax-Deferred Annuity Monies

BAPCPA added an exclusion from estate property for funds withheld by an employer from employee wages or received by an employer from employees for payment as *contributions* to any of the following *four types of plans*:

(i) *employee benefit plans* under Title I of ERISA or a governmental employee benefit plans under § 414(d) of the Internal Revenue Code [B.C. §§ 541(b)(7)(A)(i)(I), (B)(i)(I)];

(ii) *deferred compensation plans* under § 457 of the Internal Revenue Code, which includes certain pension plans for state and local government employees, and charities [B.C. §§ 541(b)(7)(A)(i)(II), (B)(i)(II); 5 Collier ¶ 541.23(1)];

(iii) *tax deferred annuities* under § 403(b) of the Internal Revenue Code, which includes retirement plans for certain public school employees and ministers [B.C. §§ 541(b)(7)(A)(i)(III), (B)(i)(III); 5 Collier ¶ 541.23(1)]; and

(iv) *health insurance plans* regulated by State law [B.C. §§ 541(b)(7)(A)(ii), (B)(ii)].

Courts have held that *any* amounts in a retirement, deferred compensation plan, or health insurance plan are excluded from the bankruptcy estate, not simply monies that the employer holds at the commencement of the bankruptcy case.

Example: Husband and Wife filed for relief under Chapter 7. At the time of the bankruptcy filing, Wife had approximately $120,000 in a 403(b) retirement plan. Debtors exempted about one third of the monies using Vermont's exemptions, and argued that the remainder of the funds were not part of the bankruptcy estate under § 541(b)(7). The trustee argued that the exclusion under § 541(b)(7) only applied to the "gap period" between withholding and remittance of the monies to the plan. Thus, the trustee claimed that Debtors could not exclude the remaining $78,000 in Wife's 403(b) account. The bankruptcy court rejected the trustee's argument. The court noted that while there were no cases dealing specifically with 403(b) plans, the cases on 401(k) and ERISA-qualified savings plan spoke "with one voice in concluding that [such plans] are not property of the bankruptcy estate." The court noted that the same logic that applied to other type of plans under § 541(b)(7) applied to 403(b) plans. Thus, the court held that the $78,000 in Wife's 403(b) that Debtors had not exempted was not an issue, because those funds "were never part of the bankruptcy estate in the first instance." [*In re* **Leahy,** 370 B.R. 620 (Bankr. D. Vt. 2007)]

i.   **Pawnbrokers**

BAPCPA added an exclusion from estate property for *personal property* that the debtor has *pledged or sold* as collateral for a loan or advance from a *person licensed* to make such loans or advances. [B.C. § 541(b)(8)] For the exclusion to apply, all the following conditions must be met:

(i)   the *pledgee or transferee* must be in *possession* of the personal property [B.C. § 541(b)(8)(A)];

(ii) the debtor is not required to repay the loan or advance or redeem the property or buy it back at a specific price [B.C. § 541(b)(8)(B)]; and

(iii) neither the debtor nor the trustee has exercised any right under the contract or State law to *redeem* the property in the time period provided by State law or § 108(b) of the Code. [B.C. § 541(b)(8)(C)]

Finally, § 541(b)(8) provides that it is subject to §§ 541 through 562 of the Code. As a result, the trustee may seek to avoid a pledge or sale of personal property that otherwise is covered by this subsection. [5 Collier ¶ 541.24]

Example: Debtor pledged jewelry to R&J, a licensed pawnbroker, as collateral for pawn loans. Before the loans' termination date, Debtor filed for relief under Chapter 13. R&J sent Debtor a notice of the loans' termination date, which provided for the ten-day right to redeem under California law. Debtor did not redeem the jewelry, and instead proposed a plan under which she would make monthly payments on the pawn loans. Debtor filed an adversary proceeding against R&J, asking the court to enjoin R&J from disposing of the jewelry. R&J responded that the jewelry was not property of the bankruptcy estate under § 541(a)(8), because Debtor had not redeemed the jewelry within the time frame provided by § 541(a)(8)(C). The Ninth Circuit's Bankruptcy Appellate Panel found that the time period for redemption had *not* lapsed. The court explained that the time period under state law applied, as it was later than the 60-day period provided by § 108(b)(2). The court then found that R&J's notice was void *ab initio* because R&J had sent the notice during the bankruptcy case without first moving to lift the automatic stay. As a result, the ten-day redemption period never began to run and Debtor's right to redeem was not extinguished. Thus, the jewelry was not removed from the bankruptcy estate under § 541(b)(8). The court distinguished its decision from those cases in which state law provides that pawned property *automatically* vests in the pawnbroker following the expiration of the redemption period. By comparison, California and a minority of other states require the pawnbroker to give notice before the pawned property vests in the pawnbroker. Because R&J did not move to lift the automatic stay, its notice was void and Debtor's redemption right did not terminate. [**Schnitzel, Inc. v. Sorensen (*In re Sorensen*),** 586 B.R. 327 (B.A.P. 9th Cir. 2018)]

j. Proceeds of Money Orders

Proceeds of money orders sold within 14 days of bankruptcy, if there was an agreement between the debtor and the money order issuer not to commingle proceeds with property of the debtor, and the money order issuer took action to require the debtor's compliance with the prohibition before bankruptcy. Because the proceeds should have been segregated, they are excluded from the bankruptcy estate. [B.C. § 541(b)(9)]

k. ABLE Funds

As part of the Tax Increase Prevention Act of 2014, Congress added § 541(b)(10) to the Code, which excludes from estate property funds placed in a *qualified ABLE account,* as defined by § 529A(b) of the Internal Revenue Code, no later than *one year prior to the bankruptcy* filing. [B.C. § 541(b)(10); 5 Collier ¶ 541.25A] A State may create an ABLE program that allows contributions to ABLE accounts to cover certain disability expenses for disabled state residents. [5 Collier ¶ 541.25A] The exclusion applies if all the following conditions are satisfied:

(i) the designated *beneficiary* is the debtor's *child, stepchild, grandchild, or stepgrandchild* for the taxable year in which the funds were placed in the account [B.C. § 541(b)(10)(A)];

(ii) the funds are *not pledged or promised* in connection with a *credit extension* [B.C. § 541(b)(10)(B)(i)]; and

(iii) the funds are *not excess contributions,* as defined by § 4973(h) of the Internal Revenue Code [B.C. § 541(b)(10)(B)(ii)].

There is a limitation on the amount of funds excluded from the estate in the case of funds placed into such accounts between *720 and 365 days preceding bankruptcy.* In such a case, the debtor may exclude no more than a total of *$6,825* in all accounts for each designated beneficiary. [B.C. § 541(b)(10)(C)]

4. Distinguish Exemptions

An individual debtor is entitled to exempt certain items of estate property. Do not confuse *exclusions* from estate property with *exemptions.* If property is excluded from the estate under § 541(b), it means that the property never comes into the bankruptcy estate. Therefore, there is no need to exempt it. [*See* **Traina v. Sewell (*In re* Sewell),** 180 F.3d 707 (5th Cir. 1999) (stating that "[e]xemptions come into play only when property is included in the bankruptcy estate . . . ; by definition, *excluded* property never forms part of the bankruptcy estate and thus need not be tested for exempt status")] By comparison, exemptions apply to estate property. In doing an analysis, first ask whether the property is excluded from the bankruptcy estate. If it is, then do *not* look for exemptions. If the property comes into the bankruptcy estate, the debtor may exempt it, thereby removing the possibility, if the full value is exempted, of the trustee selling the property to distribute the proceeds to unsecured creditors. [B.C. § 522(b)]

B. Turnover of Property to Trustee

1. Turnover by Entity Other than Custodian

Property that may be used, sold, or leased by the trustee under Bankruptcy Code § 363 or property that may be exempted by the debtor under § 522 must be delivered to the trustee and accounted for *by any entity who is in possession or control* of such property and who is not a custodian. [B.C. § 542(a)]

a. "Entity"

Because an "entity" is defined more broadly than a "person," even a governmental unit or a trust, business or nonbusiness, is subject to the turnover provisions. [B.C. § 101(15)]

b. Turnover of Property Repossessed Before Bankruptcy

A secured creditor who has repossessed collateral before the filing of a Chapter 11 petition but who has not yet sold the collateral to a bona fide purchaser must turn over the collateral to the trustee or the debtor in possession, since ownership is not transferred until a sale occurs. [**United States v. Whiting Pools, Inc.,** 462 U.S. 198 (1983)] However, the secured creditor is entitled to adequate protection of its interest. [B.C. §§ 363(e), 361; **United States v. Whiting Pools, Inc.,** *supra*]

(i) Note

In *Whiting Pools,* the Supreme Court made clear that it expressed no view on whether § 542(a) applied as broadly in Chapter 7 and 13, as it did in Chapter 11. Nonetheless, many courts have extended the reasoning of *Whiting Pools* to cases involving a pre-petition repossession by a secured creditor in a Chapter 13 case. [*See, e.g.,* **Weber v. SEFCU (*In re* Weber),** 719 F.3d 72 (2d Cir. 2013) (noting that debtor had equitable interest in property because repossession did not transfer ownership and that under *Whiting Pools* this equitable interest gave the estate a possessory interest in the secured property); **Transouth Financial Corp. v. Sharon (*In re* Sharon),** 234 B.R. 676 (B.A.P. 6th Cir. 1999) (applying *Whiting Pools* and concluding that possession of the vehicle "was part of the bundle of rights" that became estate property upon filing of the petition); *but see* **In re Kalter,** 292 F.3d 1350 (11th Cir. 2002) (not discussing *Whiting Pools* and holding that under Florida law, debtor lost ownership of vehicle on pre-petition repossession; thus, vehicle was not property of the estate and was not subject to turnover)] The *Whiting Pools* reasoning also has been extended to pledged property in the possession of a secured creditor in a Chapter 7 liquidation case. [*In re* **Gerwer,** 898 F.2d 730 (9th Cir. 1990)]

(ii) Automatic Stay

There is a split of authority as to whether a creditor that does not turn over property of the estate, but merely continues to hold it, violates the automatic stay provision found in § 362(a)(3), which stays not only "an act to obtain possession of property of the estate," but also an act *"to exercise control over property of the estate."* More specifically, the issue is whether the obligation to turn over property is "self-effectuating" upon the bankruptcy filing and, thus, failure to do so is a violation of the automatic stay, or whether a creditor only violates the stay if it fails to comply with a court order, after notice and a hearing, that compels turnover. [*See, e.g.,* ***In re Hundley***, 2007 U.S. Dist. LEXIS 26206 (D. Kan. 2007) (affirming bankruptcy court's "finding that the automatic stay and Section 542(a) required the Bank to turn over the vehicle to the debtors even without a hearing and an order from the court")] Most courts that have addressed the issue have determined that failure to turn over property to the trustee, even absent a court order, violates the automatic stay. [*See, e.g.,* **Weber v. SEFCU (*In re* Weber)**, 719 F.3d 72 (2d Cir. 2013) (failure to promptly deliver vehicle to trustee after notice of Chapter 13 filing was stay violation); **Unified People's Federal Credit Union v. Yates (*In re* Yates)**, 332 B.R. 1 (B.A.P. 10th Cir. 2005) (credit union violated automatic stay when it refused to turn over vehicle after Chapter 13 debtors had filed for bankruptcy); **Transouth Fin. Corp. v. Sharon (*In re* Sharon)**, 234 B.R. 676 (B.A.P. 6th Cir. 1999) (stay violation in Chapter 13 case for failing to turn over vehicle after demand); *but see* **Barringer v. EAB Leasing (*In re* Barringer)**, 244 B.R. 402 (Bankr. E.D. Mich. 1999) (right of possession to property legally repossessed pre-petition does not become estate property upon bankruptcy filing and remains non-estate property until court orders turnover; thus, creditor does not violate the stay prior to such court order)]

2. Payment of Indebtedness to Estate

An entity that owes a matured debt or a debt payable on demand or order that constitutes estate property must pay the trustee (or a payee of a check drawn by the trustee) the amount of the debt in excess of any setoff permitted the entity under § 553. [B.C. § 542(b)] An example is a bank's obligation to pay to the trustee money in debtor's checking account.

a. Bank's Freeze of Debtor's Account

The United States Supreme Court has held that § 542(b)'s setoff exception coupled with the general rule on setoff in § 553(a) justify a bank's ***temporary hold*** on a debtor's checking account up to the amount allegedly subject to setoff while the bank seeks relief from the automatic stay and the court's determination of its right to a setoff. Such an administrative freeze pending the court's ruling keeps the debtor from spending the funds in the account and thereby making the bank's setoff rights useless. [**Citizens Bank of Maryland v. Strumpf**, 516 U.S. 16 (1995)]

3. Exceptions to Turnover

In the following situations, an entity is not obligated to turn over property to the trustee.

a. Property of Inconsequential Value

If the property in the possession or under the control of a noncustodian "is of inconsequential value or benefit to the estate," turnover is not required. [B.C. § 542(a)]

b. Transfer Without Actual Notice or Knowledge of Bankruptcy Case

Turnover is not required if an entity, such as a bank, ***in good faith*** and without either actual notice or knowledge of the bankruptcy petition transfers property of the estate or pays a debt owing to the debtor, e.g., honors the debtor's check, to an entity other than the trustee. [B.C. § 542(c)]

e.g. **Example:** On August 1, Debtor, who has a checking account with funds on deposit in Bank, draws a check payable to the order of Payee. On August 2, Debtor files a voluntary bankruptcy petition. On August 3, Bank, with neither actual notice nor knowledge of the commencement of the bankruptcy case, pays the amount of the check to Payee in good faith. Bank, as payor, is not liable for turnover. [B.C. § 542(c)]

(i) Transferee Not Protected

Note that § 542(c) does *not* apply to the payee or transferee in such a transaction. The payee or transferee may be subject to the trustee's avoiding power under § 549 and to liability under § 550. [5 Collier ¶ 542.04]

(ii) Post-Petition Setoff Not Excepted

Even if a bank lacks actual notice or knowledge of the bankruptcy petition, it may not set off a pre-petition debt without obtaining judicial relief from the automatic stay. [B.C. §§ 542(c), 362(a)(7)]

4. Turnover of Property by Custodian

A custodian who has knowledge of the filing of a bankruptcy petition is prohibited from disbursing or administering, other than for preservation, any property of the debtor; any proceeds, rents, profits, products, or offspring of the debtor's property; or any property of the estate in her possession, custody, or control. The custodian must turn over the property to the trustee and file an accounting. [B.C. §§ 543(a), (b)]

a. "Custodian" Defined

A custodian is: (i) a receiver or trustee of the debtor's property appointed in a nonbankruptcy action; (ii) an assignee for the benefit of the debtor's creditors; or (iii) a trustee or receiver designated to take control of the debtor's property to enforce a lien or to administer the property for the benefit of creditors. [B.C. § 101(11)]

e.g. **Example:** Debtors, fifty-seven financially distressed cash currency exchanges, filed for relief under Chapter 11. Prior to bankruptcy, thirty-three of the exchanges were placed under state administrative receiverships pursuant to Illinois law. A receiver for the Director of Financial Institutions ("Director"), which regulates currency exchanges, was appointed. The receiver took title to all of Debtors assets, and state liquidation proceedings were commenced against Debtors. The Seventh Circuit rejected the Director's argument that the term "custodian" included only court-appointed receivers and not administrative receivers. The court concluded that the state administrative receiver was a custodian under federal bankruptcy law, and affirmed the bankruptcy court's order directing the Director to turn over debtor's property to the bankruptcy trustee. [*In re* **Cash Currency Exchange, Inc.,** 762 F.2d 542 (7th Cir. 1985)]

b. Exceptions to Custodian's Turnover

A custodian's duty to deliver the debtor's property to the trustee *may be excused* in the interests of creditors and, if the debtor is solvent, the interests of equity security holders are better served by allowing a custodian to remain in possession, custody or control of the property. Unless necessary to prevent fraud or injustice, the bankruptcy court *must excuse* the requirement that a custodian turn over property if the custodian is an assignee for the benefit of creditors who was appointed or took possession of the debtor's property *more than 120 days* before the commencement of the bankruptcy case. [B.C. § 543(d)]

c. Compensation or Surcharge

A bankruptcy court, after notice and a hearing, may award a custodian reasonable compensation for her services and actual expenses. [B.C. § 543(c)(2)] On the other hand, with the exception of an assignee for the benefit of creditors who was appointed or took possession more than 120 days before bankruptcy, a custodian may be liable for wrongful or excessive disbursements. [B.C. § 543(c)(3)]

5. Turnover of Books and Records

The bankruptcy court, after notice and a hearing, may order, subject to any valid privilege, an attorney, accountant, or other person to turn over to the trustee any books, records, or other documents concerning the debtor's finances or property. [B.C. § 542(e)]

a. Waiver of Corporate Attorney-Client Privilege

In the case of a **corporate debtor,** the trustee has the power to waive the corporation's attorney-client privilege concerning **pre-bankruptcy communications** made by former officers and directors to the debtor's attorney. The attorney may then be required to testify. [**Commodity Futures Trading Commission v. Weintraub,** 471 U.S. 343 (1985)]

(i) Rationale

Upon appointment, the bankruptcy trustee effectively becomes the corporate debtor's new management, and she is expected to investigate the conduct of the corporation's prior officers and directors. Thus, the corporate attorney-client privilege also must pass from former management to the trustee in order to facilitate the trustee's search for any misappropriated corporate assets or insider fraud. [**Commodity Futures Trading Commission v. Weintraub,** *supra*]

(ii) Note

The Supreme Court in *Weintraub* specifically noted that its holding had "no bearing on the problem of individual bankruptcy, which [it had] no reason to address." The lower courts since *Weintraub* have adopted several approaches to the issue with the most common being a case-specific analysis that weighs the harm to the individual against the duty of the trustee to maximize the estate. [***In re* Tarkington,** 2010 WL 1416813 (Bankr. E.D. N.C. 2010)] Courts have held, however, that the attorney-client privilege does not apply to information that the debtor discloses in preparing her petition and schedules. [*See, e.g.,* **United States v. White,** 950 F.2d 426 (7th Cir. 1991); **Tarkington,** *supra; but see **In re* Stickle,** 2016 WL 417047 (Bankr. S.D. Fla, 2016) (disagreeing with those cases like *White* and *Tarkington* in which the court "applied a bright-line rule" that information disclosed in preparing schedules and the petition was not protected by the attorney-client privilege)]

b. No Accountant-Client Privilege

Where access to information relating to the debtor's financial condition is needed for complete and accurate disclosure, an accountant or an accounting firm will be required to turn over documents and work papers in its possession. There is no accountant-client privilege under federal law. [*See* **Couch v. United States,** 409 U.S. 322 (1973) (noting in a criminal case that no such privilege existed under federal law).] Courts also have refused to recognize state evidentiary accountant-client privileges in proceedings involving traditional questions of federal bankruptcy law. [***In re* International Horizons, Inc.,** 689 F.2d 996 (11th Cir. 1982)]

C. Creditor's Right of Setoff

1. Right of Setoff

A creditor entitled to a right of setoff under state law may set off a debt he owes to the debtor against a claim he holds against the debtor, if **both the debt and the claim are mutual and** *arose prior to the filing of the bankruptcy case.* [B.C. § 553(a)] The Bankruptcy Code does not create a right of setoff; it merely preserves whatever right otherwise exists. [*See* **Citizens Bank v. Strumpf,** 516 U.S. 16 (1995)] The Bankruptcy Code does not define "mutual debt." The courts, however, apply a three-prong test for mutuality. The debts must be between the *same parties* who stand in the *same capacity,* and the debts must be in the *same right.* [*See, e.g.,* **Faasoa v. Army & Air Force Exchange Serv. (In re Faasoa),** 576 B.R. 631 (Bankr. S.D. Cal. 2017)]

a. Same Parties

(i) The same party requirement means that *triangular setoffs* generally are not allowed.

> **e.g.** **Example:** Debtor Steel Corporation owes $100,000 to Outland, Inc. for steel that Steel had purchased from Outland prior to Steel's filing for relief under Chapter 11. Also prior to bankruptcy, Steel had sold $115,000 of finished product to Riley Company, a wholly owned subsidiary of Steel. Outland may not set off Riley's $115,000 debt to Steel against Outland's $100,000 claim against the debtor Steel. Outland and Riley are separate corporate entities. Thus, Steel's debt to Outland and Riley's debt to Steel are not mutual. [B.C. § 553(a); *see* **In re Berger Steel Co.,** 327 F.2d 401 (7th Cir. 1964) (decided under Bankruptcy Act of 1898)]

(ii) The federal government is considered a *unitary creditor.* As a result, one federal agency may offset a debt that it owes to the debtor against a debt that the debtor owes to another federal agency. Some courts have applied this *unitary creditor* theory not only to the federal government but also to state governments. [*See, e.g.,* **Cottle v. Arizona Corp. Comm'n (In re Cottle),** 2016 WL 6081030 (B.A.P. 9th Cir. 2016) (holding that the bankruptcy court had not erred in treating Arizona Corporation Commission and State of Arizona as a unitary creditor for purposes of setoff under § 553)]

b. Same Capacity

The *same capacity* requirement often arises in the context of *fiduciary relationships.* Money received by a trustee in trust or by a person acting in a fiduciary capacity may not be used to set off an obligation owed by the debtor to the trustee or fiduciary in her *individual* capacity.

> **e.g.** **Example:** David owes Fiona $500 in his individual capacity. Fiona, as trustee for a trust, owes David $100. Fiona may not setoff the $100 against the debt Dennis owes to her. The debts are not mutual, because Fiona's obligation arises in her capacity as trustee, while David's obligation arises in his individual capacity. [5 Collier ¶ 553.03(3)(c)(i)]

Note: While exceptions do exist, the general rule is that a bank and a person holding a general deposit account at the bank stand in the position of debtor and creditor. [**Libby v. Hopkins,** 104 U.S. 303 (1881)] Thus, the bank and depositor stand in the same capacity, and setoff is possible.

c. Same Right

Setoff is not allowed if the debt is not in the *same right.* The issue arises in cases involving joint debts.

> **e.g.** **Example:** Amy and Ben are jointly liable on a $1,200 debt to Delilah, who has filed for relief under Chapter 7. Delilah owes an unrelated debt of $1,200 to Ben and his sister Clara. Ben may not setoff his debt to Delilah in her Chapter 7 case against

his and his sister's joint claim against Delilah. The debts are not mutual. [*See, e.g.,* **Gray v. Rollo,** 85 U.S. 629 (1873)]

2. Automatic Stay

Once a bankruptcy petition has been filed, the automatic stay enjoins the post-petition setoff of a pre-petition debt owed to the debtor against a creditor's claim. [B.C. § 362(a)(7)] Therefore, a creditor must obtain *relief from the stay* before a setoff may be exercised. Furthermore, the right of setoff may be subject to the trustee's use, sale, or lease of property under § 363, although adequate protection must be provided to the creditor. [B.C. §§ 553(a), 363(e)]

a. Post-Petition Administrative Freeze of Debtor's Bank Account

The United States Supreme Court has held that a bank's *temporary hold* on a debtor's deposit account up to the amount allegedly subject to setoff, while the bank seeks relief from the automatic stay and the court's determination of its right to a setoff, does not violate the automatic stay. A temporary administrative freeze, pending a judicial determination of the bank's motion to lift the stay *does not constitute a setoff.* [**Citizens Bank v. Strumpf,** *supra*] It is a permissible response to the bank's dilemma of protecting its right of setoff, if one exists, from the debtor's dissipation of the cash in his deposit account.

Note: Based on the facts in *Strumpf,* it appears that the creditor should *promptly request relief from the automatic stay* and a determination of its right of setoff.

3. Secured Status of Claim Subject to Setoff

A claim that may be set off *is deemed secured* to the extent of the amount subject to setoff. Therefore, a creditor holding such a claim is entitled to *adequate protection* unless the court lifts the automatic stay and permits the creditor to exercise her right of setoff. [B.C. §§ 506(a), 362(d)(1)]

4. Exceptions to Right of Setoff

A creditor's right of setoff is subject to the following exceptions under the Code.

a. Disallowed Claim

There is no right of setoff to the extent that the court has disallowed the creditor's claim against the debtor. [B.C. § 553(a)(1)]

b. Claim Transferred by Non-Debtor Party

There is no right of setoff if an entity other than the debtor transferred the claim to the creditor after the filing of the bankruptcy petition or within 90 days prior to the bankruptcy petition at a time when the debtor was insolvent. [B.C. § 553(a)(2)] *Note:* For purposes of § 553, there is a *statutory presumption* that the debtor was insolvent during the 90 days immediately preceding bankruptcy. [B.C. § 553(c)]

e.g. **Example:** Digby, Inc. recently filed for relief under Chapter 11. Digby operates a small business that has been in financial trouble for the past six months. At the time of bankruptcy filing, Local Bank held $30,000 of Digby's funds in a general account. Prior to bankruptcy, Tito Company sold goods worth $30,000 to Digby on unsecured credit. When Tito was unable to collect from Digby, Tito sold its $30,000 claim to Local Bank for $25,000 in the month prior to Digby's bankruptcy filing. Local Bank cannot setoff its $30,000 debt against the $25,000 claim against Digby, because Tito transferred the claim to Local Bank during the 90 days prior to the bankruptcy filing while Digby was presumed to be insolvent.

c.   Exceptions to the Exception

With the enactment of BAPCPA, Congress carved out a number of exceptions to the rule that claims transferred by a non-debtor party within 90 days of the bankruptcy filing cannot serve as the basis for setoff. These exceptions involve sophisticated financial arrangements, such as swaps, master netting agreements, repo agreements, and commodities and forward contracts. [B.C. §§ 553(a)(2), 362(b)(6), 362(b)(7), 362(b)(17), 362(b)(27), 555, 556, 559, 560, & 561] A transaction falling into one of these enumerated exceptions *does not run afoul* of the prohibition against setoff for traded claims.

d.   Debt Created for Purpose of Setoff

There is no right of setoff if the creditor incurred the debt owed to the debtor within 90 days prior to the bankruptcy petition, at a time when the debtor was insolvent, for the purpose of using that debt as a setoff. [B.C. § 553(a)(3)]

Example: Bank loaned Debtor, a small business, $200,000 on an unsecured basis. Debtor keeps its corporate account at Bank. Bank realizes that Debtor is in financial difficulty. One month before Debtor files for bankruptcy, Bank requires Debtor to keep at least 10% of its outstanding loan balance in its corporate account at the Bank. Debtor files for relief under Chapter 11. At that time, Debtor has $50,000 in its corporate account. Bank may set off only $30,000 of the $50,000 in Debtor's account. Bank's requirement that Debtor maintain at least a $20,000 balance (10% of $200,000 loan) runs afoul of § 553(a)(3), because Bank required the balance within 90 days of bankruptcy while Debtor was insolvent for the purpose of creating a right of setoff. *Note:* Congress carved out the same exceptions under § 553(a)(3) that exist for traded claims under § 553(a)(2).

e.   Creditor's Improved Position Due to Pre-Bankruptcy Setoff

With certain exceptions, the trustee may avoid and recover for the estate a setoff made by a creditor within 90 days prior to the filing of the petition *to the extent that* the creditor (usually a bank) has improved its position. [B.C. § 553(b)(1)]

(i)   Rationale

This exception is designed to deter lenders from executing pre-petition setoffs, especially since the need for available cash ordinarily is critical during the months immediately before the commencement of a bankruptcy case.

(ii)   Amount Recoverable

The trustee may recover the amount by which any insufficiency on the date of the setoff is less than the insufficiency present on the *later of* the 90th day before bankruptcy *or on the first date within the 90-day pre-petition period on which an insufficiency existed.* [B.C. § 553(b)(1)]

(1)   "Insufficiency" Defined

An insufficiency is computed by subtracting the amount that the creditor owes to the debtor (e.g., the balance in the debtor's deposit account, where the creditor is a bank) from the amount of the creditor's claim against the debtor. [B.C. § 553(b)(2)]

Example: Debtor owed Bank $100,000 on an unsecured loan. On the 90th day before the filing of Debtor's bankruptcy petition, Debtor's checking account with Bank had a balance of $100,000. This balance remained unchanged until the 60th day before bankruptcy, when the account held $60,000. This was the first date on which an insufficiency existed. On the 50th day before bankruptcy, the account balance was $50,000, but on the 40th day before bankruptcy it was $70,000, at which time Bank set off $70,000 against the unpaid loan. The amount recoverable by the trustee is $10,000, since the insufficiency on the date of setoff ($30,000) constitutes a $10,000 improvement in Bank's position relative to the insufficiency ($40,000) on the first date that one existed during the 90-day period. [B.C. § 553(b)(1); *see* 5 Collier ¶ 553.09(2)(b)]

(iii) Debtor May Be Solvent

Section 553(b)(1) may apply even if the debtor is solvent.

(iv) Exceptions

The trustee's avoidance and recovery powers under § 553(b) *do not apply* to setoff rights arising from:

(1) certain *sophisticated financial transactions,* e.g., swaps, repo agreements [B.C. §§ 362(b)(6), (7), (17) & (27); 555, 556, 559 & 560];

(2) the *rejection of unexpired leases of real property* in which the *debtor is the lessor* [B.C. §§ 365(h) & (i)]; or

(3) the *return of goods* that a creditor had *shipped pre-petition* to the debtor in a Chapter 11 case. [B.C. § 546(h)]

f. Creditor's Bad Faith Conduct

Setoffs are permissive, not mandatory, and lie within the court's equitable discretion. [**Faasoa v. Army & Air Force Exchange Service (*In re* Faasoa),** 576 B.R. 631 (Bankr. S.D. Cal. 2017)] Therefore, a court may deny setoff if the creditor's conduct is inequitable or in bad faith. [**Regal Financial Bank v. Heaton (*In re* Heaton),** 2011 WL 1980936 (Bankr. N.D. Cal. 2011) (disallowing Bank to set off attorney fees owed to debtors, resulting from loss in adversary proceeding, against debtors' pre-petition debt not only because of lack of mutuality but also because setoff would be inequitable)]

5. Distinguish Recoupment

Setoff should be distinguished from the equitable doctrine of recoupment, which sometimes is used to prevent unjust enrichment. The *setoff* of mutual debts between two parties involves independent obligations that usually are derived from *separate transactions.* Recoupment, on the other hand, is used by a creditor to reduce its liability to the debtor because of a right that the creditor has arising out of the *same transaction* or occurrence. Recoupment is basically a defense, e.g., overpayment, to the debtor's claim and not a mutual obligation. Neither the automatic stay nor § 553's limitations on setoffs apply to recoupments. [**Malinowski v. New York State DOL (*In re* Malinowski),** 156 F.3d 131 (2d Cir. 1998) (explaining that recoupment "comes into bankruptcy law through the common law, rather than statute . . . and is not subject to the limitations of section 553 or the automatic stay); *see also* **United States v. Johnson (*In re* Johnson),** 586 B.R. 449 (N.D. Ill. 2018) (noting that a "significant body of authority holds that recoupment does not violate the automatic stay")]

The distinction between setoff and recoupment is important to remember. While a creditor may not set off a pre-petition claim against a post-petition debt, a creditor might be able to recover, for example, an overpayment under the doctrine of recoupment. Remember that the distinction between these two rights is that a setoff involves independent obligations, usually derived from **separate transactions,** whereas recoupment arises out of the **same transaction.** Also remember that setoff is subject to the **automatic stay,** but recoupment is not.

D. Post-Petition Effect of Security Interest

1. General Rule for After-Acquired Property Clauses

An after-acquired property clause in a pre-petition security agreement is **not** effective to create a security interest in property acquired by the debtor or the estate **after** the filing of the bankruptcy petition. [B.C. § 552(a)] **Note:** This provision applies only to **consensual liens** and, thus, does not apply to federal tax liens, which are statutory. [B.C. §§ 101(50), (51); **In re Wampler,** 345 B.R. 730 (Bankr. D. Kan. 2006)]

2. Exception for Certain Post-Petition Proceeds

If the security interest created by a pre-petition security agreement includes collateral that the debtor **acquired prior to bankruptcy** and also the proceeds, profits, products, or offspring of such collateral, then the security interest is deemed valid and operative as to any **traceable post-petition proceeds, products, offspring, or profits** of the collateral acquired pre-petition. [B.C. § 552(b)(1)] **Note:** The exception does **not** apply to proceeds, products, offspring, or profits of collateral acquired post-petition.

e.g. **Example:** Debtor is a small business. Two years ago, Debtor obtained a working capital loan from Bank. Debtor granted Bank a security interest in Debtor's inventory and accounts receivable, whether "now owned or hereafter acquired." Bank properly perfected its interest. Debtor recently filed for relief under Chapter 11. After filing for bankruptcy, Debtor bought new inventory using cash from its corporate account. The cash is traceable to sales of inventory acquired pre-petition. Therefore, Bank's security interest attaches to the new inventory, because the post-petition inventory is proceeds of cash, which, in turn, were proceeds of pre-petition collateral on which the Bank has a valid security interest. [B.C. § 552(b)(1); U.C.C. § 9–315]

a. Note: Judicial Discretion Allowed

The court has authority not to apply this exception, depending on the equities of the case. Notice and a hearing are required. [B.C. § 552(b)(1)]

e.g. **Example:** Secured Creditor has a security interest in raw materials valued at $1 million. Debtor invests $100,000 and turns those raw materials into product that Debtor sells for $1.5 million. Secured Creditor claims that it has a security interest in those sale proceeds under § 552(b). The bankruptcy court, however, may decide that to add the sale proceeds to the secured creditor's collateral would be inequitable because "the general creditors were in effect responsible for much or all of the increase in the value of the proceeds over the original collateral." [*See* **J. Catton Farms v. First**

National Bank of Chicago, 779 F.2d 1242 (7th Cir. 1985) (example is drawn from court's opinion)]

3. Exception for Certain Post-Petition Rents and Room Revenues

If a pre-petition security agreement extends to amounts paid as rent or for charges, fees, accounts, or other payments for hotel, motel, or similar lodgings, then the security interest extends to these post-petition rents, charges, fees, accounts or other payments. As with the exception for proceeds, products, offspring, and profits, the court, after notice and a hearing, may decide not to apply this exception based on the equities of the case. [B.C. § 552(b)(2)]

E. Abandonment of Estate Property

1. Inconsequential or Burdensome Property

The trustee may abandon property that is *burdensome or of inconsequential value* to the estate. Notice and the opportunity for a hearing are required; however, the court is not likely to conduct a hearing unless an objection to the abandonment is filed. [B.C. § 554(a); Bankruptcy Rule 6007] Generally, when abandonment occurs, the property is considered to be abandoned to the debtor, although abandonment does not affect the continuing validity of a secured creditor's lien on the property. While abandonment removes the property from the estate, it does not result in a lift of the automatic stay so as to permit a secured creditor to recover the abandoned property in order to collect on a pre-petition claim against the debtor. [5 Collier ¶ 552.02(4)]

a. Exception: Violation of Environmental Laws

The trustee is prohibited from abandoning estate property that is in violation of state or federal environmental laws that are "reasonably designed to protect the public health or safety from identified hazards." The Court explained that its exception to the abandonment power was a "narrow one" and that the abandonment power "is not to be fettered by law or regulations not reasonably calculated to protect the public health or safety from imminent or identifiable harm." [**Midlantic National Bank v. New Jersey Department of Environmental Protection,** 474 U.S. 494 (1986)]

e.g. **Example:** Debtor operates a waste oil processing facility. Debtor violates a state environmental law by accepting oil contaminated with certain prohibited toxic chemicals, which are extremely dangerous both to the natural environment and to the public. Debtor files a voluntary Chapter 11 petition and subsequently is ordered by the state environmental protection agency to clean up the site. There is no equity in the property, and the expected cost of cleanup is $2.5 million. The case is converted to Chapter 7, and the trustee seeks to abandon the property as burdensome to the estate. Abandonment is not permitted because it would violate the state environmental law and would constitute an imminent threat to the health and safety of the community. [**Midlantic National Bank v. New Jersey Department of Environmental Protection,** *supra*]

(i) Automatic Stay

An environmental protection agency's cleanup order does not violate the automatic stay, because one of the exceptions to the stay permits a state or federal regulatory unit to initiate or continue an action to enforce its regulatory power even after a bankruptcy petition has been filed. [B.C. § 362(b)(4)]

2. Request to Abandon Burdensome Property

A party in interest may make a motion for abandonment, and the court, after notice and the opportunity for a hearing, may order the trustee to abandon property that is burdensome or of inconsequential value to the estate. [B.C. § 554(b)]

3. Unadministered Property

Any property that the debtor has listed in her schedules that has not been administered before the case is closed is deemed to be abandoned to the debtor, unless the court rules differently. [B.C. §§ 554(c), 521(a)(1)]

Chapter Six

The Bankruptcy Estate: The Trustee's Avoiding Powers

Chapter Approach

As mentioned in the introduction to Chapter 5 of this summary, the bankruptcy estate includes property that the trustee brings into the estate by exercising her *avoiding powers.* One of the most important bankruptcy topics for exam purposes concerns the trustee's avoiding powers. You will undoubtedly see a question that asks you to discuss these powers. Recall that under appropriate circumstances, the trustee may avoid certain *setoffs* [B.C. § 553], *statutory liens* [B.C. § 545], *preferences* [B.C. § 547], *fraudulent transfers* [B.C. § 548], *post-petition transactions* [B.C. § 549], as well as other transfers that can be defeated because of the *different statuses* conferred upon the trustee by the *strong arm clause* of the Bankruptcy Code. [B.C. § 544(a)] Remember that, as of the commencement of the bankruptcy case, the trustee has the rights and powers of a *hypothetical* (i) judicial lien creditor, (ii) creditor with an unsatisfied execution, and (iii) bona fide purchaser who has perfected the transfer of real property from the debtor. Also, if there is an *actual* unsecured creditor who has the right to avoid a transfer of the debtor's property under nonbankruptcy law, the trustee can step into that creditor's shoes to avoid the transfer for the benefit of the estate. [B.C. § 544(b)]

With respect to the time periods for the trustee to exercise her avoiding powers, keep in mind that for voidable preferences, the *90 days* prior to the filing of the bankruptcy petition constitutes the preference period, unless the creditor was an insider, in which case, the preference period extends to *one year* before bankruptcy. If a question concerns a fraudulent transfer, remember that, under § 548, the trustee can avoid such a transfer made within *two years* before bankruptcy. Also, sometimes state fraudulent transfer laws may be applied under § 544(b) to avoid transfers that occurred more than two years before bankruptcy.

Finally, you should be aware that in a Chapter 11 case, the trustee's avoiding powers ordinarily may be exercised by the debtor in possession if a trustee has not been appointed.

A. Trustee's Avoidance of Statutory Liens

1. In General

The trustee has several avoiding powers that may be used to enlarge the bankruptcy estate for the benefit of creditors. One is the trustee's power to avoid certain types of statutory liens on the debtor's property. These liens, e.g., mechanics' liens, are expressly created by statute and are *not consensual.* [B.C. §§ 545, 101(53)]

2. Avoidable Statutory Liens

The trustee may avoid the following kinds of statutory liens.

a. Liens Arising Automatically Due to Debtor's Financial Condition

The trustee may avoid a *statutory lien* triggered by any of the following events, usually indicating the poor financial condition of the debtor:

(i) *the filing of a petition* concerning the debtor *under the Bankruptcy Code* [B.C. § 545(1)(A)];

(ii) *the filing of an insolvency proceeding* concerning the debtor *outside* of the Bankruptcy Code [B.C. § 545(1)(B)];

(iii) *the appointment of a custodian* [B.C. § 545(1)(C)];

(iv) *the debtor's insolvency* [B.C. § 545(1)(D)];

(v) *the failure of the debtor's financial condition to satisfy a specified standard* [B.C. § 545(1)(E)]; or

(vi) *an execution against the debtor's property by an entity other than the holder of a statutory lien* of this type [B.C. § 545(1)(F)].

b. **Liens Not Perfected Against Bona Fide Purchaser**

The trustee also may avoid a statutory lien that is not perfected or enforceable against a hypothetical bona fide purchaser at the time that the bankruptcy petition is filed, *unless* the purchaser is one described under § 6323 of the Internal Revenue Code or any similar provision in State or local law. [B.C. § 545(2)] To resolve a pre-BAPCPA split of authority as to the trustee's authority under § 545(2) to avoid filed federal tax liens, Congress added the language excepting certain purchasers from the trustee's avoiding power under § 545(2). For example, the Internal Revenue Code protects certain purchasers from the operation of the tax lien *even if* notice of the lien has been filed. Thus, the purpose of the exception is to make clear that while the trustee is a *hypothetical bona fide purchaser* at the time of bankruptcy filing, she is not a purchaser as defined in § 6323(h) of the Internal Revenue Code. As a result, if the exception in § 545(2) applies, the trustee cannot avoid the tax lien. [5 Collier ¶ 545.03(4)]

e.g. **Example:** Mainline Equipment did not pay personal property taxes assessed by Los Angeles County (the "County"). The County then recorded certificates of tax liens that resulted in broad liens on all of Mainline's personal property located within the County. Mainline subsequently filed for relief under Chapter 11. As debtor in possession, Mainline had the same rights as a trustee in bankruptcy and, thus, sought to avoid, pursuant to § 545(2), the County's tax liens. Mainline argued that the liens were not perfected as against it, a bona fide purchaser. The Bankruptcy Appellate Panel for the Ninth Circuit agreed. California's revenue and tax code provided that tax liens were not valid against a subsequent purchaser in good faith for value. Mainline, as DIP, enjoyed the status of a bona fide purchaser and, thus, could avoid the tax liens. The exception in § 545(2) apparently did not apply, because California law made tax liens subject to the rights of a bona fide purchaser and, thus, was not a State law provision "similar" to § 6323 of the Internal Revenue Code. [**Los Angeles County Treasurer & Tax Collector vs. Mainline Equipment, Inc.,** 539 B.R. 165 (B.A.P. 9th Cir. 2015)]

(i) **Retroactive Perfection**

The trustee's avoiding power under Code section 545(2) is subject to any retroactive perfection permitted under state law or other nonbankruptcy law. [B.C. § 546(b)]

c. **Liens for Rent**

Statutory liens for rent or for distress of rent also are avoidable by the trustee. [B.C. §§ 545(3), (4)]

B. Trustee's Avoiding Powers as Hypothetical Creditor or Purchaser, and as Successor to Certain Actual Creditors

1. Strong Arm Provision

The Bankruptcy Code grants to the trustee, at the commencement of the bankruptcy case, the hypothetical status and the rights and powers of (i) a *judicial lien creditor*, (ii) a creditor with an *unsatisfied execution*, and (iii) a *bona fide purchaser of real property*. Consequently, the trustee is able to avoid any transfer of the debtor's property that any of these entities—*regardless of whether one really exists*—could avoid, "without regard to any knowledge of the trustee or of any creditor." [B.C. § 544(a)]

a. Judicial Lien Creditor

The trustee is accorded the rights and powers of a *hypothetical* creditor who furnishes credit to the debtor at the time that the bankruptcy case is commenced, and who simultaneously acquires a *judicial lien* on as much of the debtor's property as is permitted under applicable state or other nonbankruptcy law. [B.C. § 544(a)(1)]

e.g. **Example:** On June 1, Debtor borrows $5,000 from Finance Company, granting a security interest in a famous painting recently inherited by Debtor. On December 1, Debtor files a voluntary bankruptcy petition. At this time, Finance Company has not perfected its security interest in the painting. Because, under the Uniform Commercial Code ("U.C.C."), a judicial lien has priority over an unperfected security interest [U.C.C. § 9–317(a)], the trustee's hypothetical judicial lien as of the time the case was commenced will prevail over Finance Company's unperfected security interest in the painting. Hence, the trustee will be able to avoid the security interest and thereby increase the amount available for distribution to the unsecured creditors. [B.C. § 544(a)(1)]

(i) Exception: State Law Allows Retroactive Perfection

The rights and powers of the trustee under § 544 are subject to any retroactive perfection allowable under applicable nonbankruptcy law. [B.C. § 546(b)]

e.g. **Example:** Bank loans Debtor $10,000 and obtains a *purchase-money security interest* in the new office furniture that Debtor purchases with the loan proceeds on June 1 and takes into her possession on the same day. On June 8, Debtor files a voluntary bankruptcy petition. On June 9, Bank perfects its security interest by filing a U.C.C. financing statement. The trustee, as a hypothetical judicial lien creditor as of the commencement of the case, will be *unable* to avoid Bank's security interest in the furniture, because the trustee's powers under § 544 are subject to retroactive perfection allowable under applicable nonbankruptcy law. [B.C. § 546(b)] Here, such law is the U.C.C.'s 20-day grace period (following Debtor's taking possession of the furniture) for Bank to perfect a purchase-money security interest that will have priority over an intervening judicial lien creditor. [U.C.C. § 9–317(e)] Moreover, Bank's filing of a U.C.C. financing statement after the start of the bankruptcy case does not violate the automatic stay. Section 362(b)(3) of the

Code provides an exception for acts to perfect an interest in property to the extent that the trustee's rights and powers are subject to such perfection under § 546(b). [§§ 362(b)(3), 546(b)]

e.g. **Example:**

#1	#2	#3	Chapter 7 filing	#4
June 1	*July 5*	*August 29*	*September 2*	*September 6*

#1: On June 1, Creditor loaned Debtor $50,000, and took a security interest in Debtor's existing office equipment. Creditor filed a UCC-1 in the proper state office on August 5. The Chapter 7 trustee cannot avoid Creditor's security interest because Creditor perfected on August 5, about a month before the Chapter 7 trustee became a lien creditor by virtue of Debtor's Chapter 7 filing. [B.C. § 544(a)(1); UCC § 9–317(a)(2)]

#2: On July 5, Creditor loaned Debtor $100,000. Creditor and Debtor signed a security agreement that granted Creditor a security interest in a valuable painting that Debtor owned. Creditor did not file a UCC-1. The Chapter 7 trustee can avoid Creditor's security interest, because the Chapter 7 trustee became a lien creditor *before* Creditor *either* (i) perfected its interest *or* (ii) satisfied the requirements of UCC § 9–203(b)(3), e.g., signing a security agreement, *and* filed a UCC-1. While Creditor has a valid security agreement, it failed to file a UCC-1. Therefore, the Chapter 7 trustee prevails.

#3 & #4: On August 29, Debtor received office computers that it had purchased with a $75,000 loan that it had received from Creditor. The parties signed a security agreement that granted Creditor a security interest in Debtor's office computers. Section 9–317(e) of the UCC provides that a creditor with a purchase-money security interest will have priority over the rights of a lien creditor that arise between attachment and the UCC-1 filing. Creditor filed its UCC-1 on September 6, which is within 20 days of August 29, when Debtor received the collateral. In addition, Creditor's filing of a UCC-1 does not violate the automatic stay. [*See* B.C. §§ 362(b)(3), 546(b)]

b. Creditor with Unsatisfied Execution

The trustee also is granted the rights and powers of a *hypothetical* creditor who extends credit to the debtor at the time that the bankruptcy case is filed, and who acquires, at that time, an *unsatisfied execution* concerning the indebtedness. [B.C. § 544(a)(2)]

c. Bona Fide Purchaser of Real Property

In addition, the trustee is given the rights and powers of a *hypothetical* bona fide purchaser *who has perfected the transfer of real property* (exclusive of fixtures) from the debtor at the time of bankruptcy. Thus, the trustee may avoid any transfer voidable by such a bona fide purchaser. [B.C. § 544(a)(3)]

(i) Exception: Constructive Notice

A trustee may not avoid an unrecorded transfer of real property if, under state law, she is charged with constructive notice of the rights of another entity. It is not the trustee's personal knowledge that is important (her own knowledge is disregarded in her capacity as a hypothetical bona fide purchaser); it is the existence of constructive notice under nonbankruptcy law sufficient to defeat the priority of a bona fide purchaser that will nullify the avoiding power of the trustee. [B.C.

§ 544(a)(3); **Ball v. Loyd (*In re* Dailey),** 2009 WL 2431254 (B.A.P. 10th Cir. 2009)]

e.g. **Example:** Creditor Bank held a recorded mortgage on debtors' home. While the mortgage correctly stated the street address and parcel identification number, it incorrectly stated the lot number of the property. Under Kansas law, however, recorded documents in the debtors' chain of title would have put a purchaser on constructive notice of the Bank's interest in the debtors' property or on constructive notice of facts requiring investigation that would have led to discovery of the Bank's mortgage. [**Hamilton v. Washington Mutual Bank,** 563 F.3d 1171 (10th Cir. 2009)]

2. Trustee's Avoiding Power Based on Actual Unsecured Creditors

If there exists at the time of bankruptcy an *actual creditor* who possesses an allowable unsecured claim and who has the right, under applicable nonbankruptcy law, to avoid a transfer of the debtor's property, then the trustee is entitled to avoid the whole transfer *for the benefit of the estate,* even if its value exceeds the amount of the creditor's claim. [B.C. § 544(b)(1)] Unlike § 544(a), § 544(b) requires the existence of an *actual creditor* at the time of the bankruptcy filing who could avoid the transaction in question. The trustee's recovery is for the benefit of all creditors, even those that extended credit *after* the transaction sought to be avoided. [**Moore v. Bay,** 284 U.S. 4 (1931)] Nonbankruptcy law determines the extent of the trustee's right to avoid under § 544(b). The Uniform Fraudulent Transfer Act and the 2014 Voidable Transactions Act are the nonbankruptcy laws most commonly used by trustees under § 544(b). [5 Collier ¶ 544.06(2)]

e.g. **Example:** On March 1, 2015, Bank made a $10,000 unsecured loan to Debtor. On January 2, 2016, Debtor transferred real property, valued at $50,000, to Best Friend for no consideration and with the undisputed intention of defrauding Debtor's creditors. On April 1, 2018, Debtor, who still owed $10,000 to Bank, filed a voluntary bankruptcy petition. All of the events took place in Pennsylvania, which has a four-year "lookback" period under its Uniform Fraudulent Transfer Act. The trustee cannot avoid Debtor's fraudulent transfer of the property under Bankruptcy Code § 548(a) because it occurred more than two years prior to bankruptcy. Bank is an *actual unsecured creditor* that (i) extended credit before January 2, 2016, (ii) may avoid the transfer under Pennsylvania law, and (iii) holds an allowable claim as of April 1, 2018. Thus, under Bankruptcy Code § 544(b)(1), the trustee may use the Pennsylvania Uniform Fraudulent Transfer Act to avoid the transfer and thereby bring the real property or its total value into the estate *for the benefit of all the unsecured creditors,* including Bank, which then will share *pro rata* with the other unsecured creditors.

a. Exception for Certain Charitable Contributions

The trustee's avoiding power under § 544(b)(1) does not cover the transfer of a charitable contribution not deemed to be a fraudulent transfer under Code § 548(a)(2). The commencement of the bankruptcy case preempts any person's claim to recover such a transferred contribution under federal or state law. [B.C. § 544(b)(2)]

C. Trustee's Power to Avoid Preferences

1. In General

The bankruptcy trustee has the power to avoid pre-petition preferential transfers. Use of this power constitutes another method by which, in appropriate circumstances, the bankruptcy estate may be enlarged for the benefit of creditors. [B.C. § 547]

a. Purpose

This avoiding power is designed to accomplish an equitable distribution of estate property in the *order established by the Bankruptcy Code* and to prevent the debtor from choosing which creditors to repay.

e.g. **Example:** Debtor owes $5,000 to Bank and $5,000 to Credit Union. Both creditors are unsecured, and neither is entitled to priority under the Code. On May 1, Debtor, who is insolvent, uses all of her remaining cash to repay Credit Union in full, while paying nothing to Bank. On June 1, Debtor files a voluntary Chapter 7 petition, and there are no assets available for distribution. The trustee may avoid the preferential transfer to Credit Union and recover the $5,000 payment for the benefit of the estate. After full payment of all priority claims in the case, including administrative expenses, Credit Union and Bank will share *pro rata* with any other general unsecured creditors. [B.C. § 547(b)]

2. Elements of Preference

In order to avoid a preferential transfer, the trustee must prove all of the following elements:

a. a *transfer* of the *debtor's interest in property* [B.C. § 547(b)];

b. made *to or for the benefit of a creditor* [B.C. § 547(b)(1)];

c. concerning an *antecedent debt* [B.C. § 547(b)(2)];

d. made at a time *when the debtor is insolvent* [B.C. § 547(b)(3)];

e. *within 90 days* prior to filing of the bankruptcy petition or one year if the creditor was an insider [B.C. § 547(b)(4)]; and

f. that *results in the creditor receiving a larger share* than the creditor would have received under the Bankruptcy Code if the estate had been liquidated under Chapter 7 and the transfer had not been made. [B.C. § 547(b)(5)]

If *any* of the above elements is absent, the trustee may not set aside the transaction as a voidable preference.

a. Transfer of the Debtor's Interest In Property

(i) Transfer

A transfer is any *voluntary or involuntary* disposition of property or an interest in property. "Transfer" includes, for example, the debtor's conveyance of a security interest or a mortgage, the fixing of a lien on property of the debtor by judicial process, or even a foreclosure sale of collateral securing a debt. [B.C. § 101(54)]

(ii) Debtor's Interest in Property

The subject matter of the transfer must be a ***property interest of the debtor.*** [B.C. § 547(b)] The ***earmarking doctrine*** is a "judicially created exception to the statutory power of the bankruptcy trustee under § 547 to avoid or set aside an otherwise preferential transfer of assets." [**Campbell v. Hanover Ins. Co.,** 709 F.3d 388 (4th Cir. 2013)] The earmarking doctrine exception applies in cases in which there is no diminution in the value of the debtor's estate, because another entity's property is used to repay a creditor. A majority of courts place the burden of proof of the earmarking defense on the defendant in the preference action. [**Campbell,** *supra*]

e.g. **Example:** Darien is in significant financial distress. He owes his unsecured creditors $50,000. One of those creditors is Carl, who is owed $5,000. Lulu, Darien's sister, pays Carl $5,000. A few days later, Darien files for relief under Chapter 7. There are insufficient funds to pay anything to Darien's general unsecured creditors. Carl received a preference because he obtained full payment pre-petition while Darien's other unsecured creditors received nothing in the Chapter 7 case. But, the payment to Carl did not affect Darien's bankruptcy estate; the estate's assets were no less than before Lulu's transfer to Carl. The transfer merely substituted Lulu for Carl with respect to the debt owed by Darien.

(1) Trust-Fund Taxes

The Supreme Court has held that a debtor's payments to the I.R.S. of trust-fund taxes, e.g., withheld federal income and Federal Insurance Contribution Act taxes, from its general operating accounts are not voidable preferences because they are not transfers of the debtor's property. [**Begier v. I.R.S.,** 496 U.S. 53 (1990)]

b. To or for Benefit of a Creditor

The recipient or beneficiary of the transfer must be the ***debtor's creditor.*** The fact that the creditor is a creditor of another entity closely connected to the debtor, e.g., a corporate debtor's president, is not sufficient to make a transfer preferential. [B.C. §§ 547(b)(1), 101(10); *see* **Griffin v. US Foods, Inc. (*In re* Bilbo),** 2014 WL 689097 (Bankr. N.D. Ga. 2014)]

(i) Transfer *Benefits* a Creditor

A transfer may be preferential as to a creditor even if another entity actually received the property transferred. The key is whether the transfer ***benefits the creditor.***

e.g. **Example:** Anne and Ben are the sole shareholders and directors of *AB, Inc.,* a debtor in bankruptcy. Pre-petition, Bank loaned *AB* funds for its operations, and Anne and Ben guaranteed the loan. Anne and Ben, as sole shareholders and directors of the firm, are insiders of *AB* and, thus, the preference period extends to one year before the bankruptcy filing. [B.C. §§ 101(31), 547(b)(4)(B)] Anne and Ben also are creditors of *AB,* because they hold claims against the debtor due to their contingent right to payment if *AB* defaults on its obligation to Bank. [B.C. § 101(5)(A)] Pre-petition payments to Bank on the loan are preferences as to Anne and Ben. The payments are transfers of debtor property (money from *AB)* for the benefit of creditors Anne and Ben, because payment to Bank reduces the amount that Anne and Ben would have to pay if *AB* defaults on its obligation to Bank. [*See* **Levit v. Ingersoll Rand Fin. Corp. (*In re* Deprizio),** 847 F.2d 1186 (7th Cir. 1989)]

c. On Account of an Antecedent Debt

The transfer must concern a debt that was incurred by the debtor *before the transfer was executed.* [B.C. § 547(b)(2)] The Bankruptcy Code defines "debt" as "liability on a claim." [B.C. § 101(12)]

e.g. **Example:** Two months prior to filing for bankruptcy, Debtor purchased a used lawn mower from his neighbor for $200. Neighbor showed Debtor the lawn mower and they negotiated a $200 price; Debtor paid Neighbor $200 in cash on the spot and took the lawn mower to his house. Debtor subsequently filed for relief under Chapter 7. There is no preference, because there is no transfer on account of an antecedent debt. The debt and the transfer happened at the same time. Had Neighbor agreed to sell and transfer the mower to Debtor with Debtor coming back in a few days with the cash for the mower, then the $200 would be a transfer for an antecedent debt. In this second scenario, the debt arose when the parties made the contract for the mower. Payment (the transfer) followed several days later, so the debt was incurred before the transfer happened. Even if the $200 payment satisfied the elements of a preference, however, the *de minimis* exception at § 547(b)(8) would prevent the trustee from pursuing Neighbor for the $200.

d. Debtor's Insolvency

The transfer must have occurred when the debtor was insolvent, which generally means that his debts were greater than the aggregate value of his assets, excluding exempt property or property that has been transferred fraudulently. [B.C. §§ 547(b)(3), 101(32)] The Bankruptcy Code provides that there is a *rebuttable presumption* that the debtor is insolvent during the *90 days* immediately prior to the date on which the petition commencing the case was filed. [B.C. § 547(f)] This presumption is rebuttable. Thus, the transferee or the beneficiary of a transfer that the trustee seeks to avoid may present evidence to rebut the presumption of the debtor's insolvency at the time of the transfer. The trustee then must prove insolvency to avoid the transfer.

e. Preference Period: Within Ninety Days Before Filing

To constitute a preference, the transfer must have been made *within 90 days prior to the filing of the bankruptcy petition* unless the creditor was an insider at the time of the transfer, in which case the preference period extends to one year before bankruptcy. [B.C. §§ 547(b)(4), 101(31)] The rules set forth in § 547(e) determine *when* a transfer is deemed to have been made for purposes of § 547.

(i) Presumption of Insolvency is Limited to Ninety Days

Even when the preference period is one year before bankruptcy because the creditor was an insider, the *period during which the presumption of insolvency applies remains the same*—90 days. [**Lanik v. Smith (*In re* Cox Motor Express of Greensboro, Inc.),** 2016 WL 4259801 (Bankr. M.D. N.C. 2016) (insolvency presumption applies only for 90 days prior to filing of petition and "trustee must prove the debtor's insolvency during the remainder of the insider preference period")]

f. Creditor Receives Greater Share in Distribution

A transfer is preferential only if it enables the creditor to obtain a larger distribution than the creditor would have received in a Chapter 7 case if the transfer had not occurred. [B.C. § 547(b)(5)] This computation is based on a hypothetical liquidation of the estate as of the date of the filing of the bankruptcy petition. Therefore, unless unsecured creditors would recover 100% of their claims in a Chapter 7 case, any payment to a general unsecured creditor during the 90-day period may constitute a preference. [**Moser v. Bank of Tyler (*In re* Loggins),** 513 B.R. 682 (Bankr. E.D. Tex. 2014)]

Example: Dionysus has filed for relief under the Bankruptcy Code. He owes his general unsecured creditors $50,000, and it is expected that such creditors would receive a 20% dividend in a Chapter 7 liquidation case. Frank is a friend of Dionysus, and loaned him $5,000 about a year ago. Dionysus paid Frank $1,000 on the eve of bankruptcy. Unless one of the exceptions under § 547(c) applies, the payment to Frank is a preference. Frank is a creditor who received a transfer of property from the debtor within 90 days of the bankruptcy filing when the debtor is presumed insolvent. Frank also received more than he would have received in a Chapter 7 case. With the pre-petition payment, Frank receives $1,000, which was paid on the eve of bankruptcy, plus $800, which is 20% of the remaining $4,000 debt. If there were no pre-petition payment, then Frank would receive $1,000, which is 20% of the $5,000 debt owed to him. Therefore, with the pre-petition payment, Frank's recovery is 36% ($1,800/$5,000) while without the pre-petition payment it is 20% ($1,000/$5,000). (*Note:* the numbers are approximate, because recovery of the preferential payment will increase the *pro rata* distribution to general unsecured creditors.)

(i) Secured Creditors

Payments made to a creditor whose allowed claim is completely secured do not constitute a preference because such transfers do not result in a greater distribution than a Chapter 7 liquidation would provide.

Example: Two years ago, Bank loaned Debtor $50,000 and took a security interest in a valuable painting that Debtor owned. Debtor made the regular monthly payments on the Bank loan, but in the 90 days prior to filing for bankruptcy Debtor paid an additional $5,000 to Bank towards the loan's principal. The $5,000 payment was not made in the ordinary course. When Debtor filed for relief under the Bankruptcy Code, the painting was valued at $75,000, and the loan balance was $40,000 ($45,000 − $5,000 paid in the 90-day period). The $5,000 payment to Bank is not a preference. In a Chapter 7 case, if the painting were sold to pay the Bank's loan, the Bank would recover $40,000 along with the $5,000 paid pre-petition on the loan. Had the $5,000 payment not been made pre-petition, the Bank would receive $45,000 from the sale of the painting. In other words, the Bank would receive $45,000 regardless of whether the payment was made pre-petition.

Example: Two years ago, Bank loaned Debtor $50,000 and took a security interest in a valuable painting that Debtor owned. Debtor made the regular monthly payments on the Bank loan, but in the 90 days prior to filing for bankruptcy Debtor paid an additional $5,000 to Bank towards the loan's principal. The $5,000 payments were not made in the ordinary course. When Debtor filed for relief under the Bankruptcy Code, the painting was valued at $30,000, and the loan balance was $40,000 ($45,000 − $5,000 paid in the 90-day period). In this case, the $5,000 payment *is* a preference. Courts generally apply the pre-petition preferential payment first to the unsecured portion of the creditor's claim. Bank would receive $30,000 on its secured claim (the value of the painting). If the general unsecured creditors received a 10% dividend, then Bank would get $1,000 on its unsecured claim of $10,000 ($40,000 − $30,000 collateral value). With the $5,000 pre-petition payment, Bank would receive $36,000 − $30,000 + $1,000 + $5,000. Without the $5,000 pre-petition payment, however, Bank would receive only $31,500. (*Note:*

the numbers are approximate, because recovery of the preferential payment will increase the *pro rata* distribution to general unsecured creditors.)

3. Exceptions to Preference Rule

The following transfers are not avoidable by the trustee. [B.C. § 547(c)]

a. Substantially Contemporaneous Exchange for New Value

To the extent that a transfer is a substantially contemporaneous exchange for new value, it is not avoidable. This exception requires two elements: (i) that the debtor and the creditor **intended** the transfer to constitute a contemporaneous exchange **for new value** furnished to the debtor, and (ii) that the transfer **actually was** a substantially contemporaneous exchange. [B.C. § 547(c)(1)]

(i) Parties' Intent

The debtor and creditor must intend that the transfer be a **contemporaneous exchange** for **new value.** [**Hechinger Inv. Co. of Delaware v. Universal Forest Prods. (*In re* Hechninger Inv. Co. of Delaware), 489 F.3d 568 (3d Cir. 2007)** ("Whether the parties intended a contemporaneous exchange is a question of fact to be decided in the first instance by the factfinder")]

Example: At 10 a.m. on June 1, Bank loaned Debtor $10,000 on an **unsecured** basis. At 2 p.m. on the same day, Bank discovered that Debtor was experiencing unusual monetary problems, and it demanded collateral to secure the debt. Debtor immediately complied by delivering certain securities to Bank as collateral. Two hours later, an involuntary bankruptcy petition was filed against Debtor. The transfer of the securities does not come within this exception because it was **not intended** by Debtor and Bank to be a contemporaneous exchange for new value. Thus, the trustee may avoid it as a preference if all the elements of § 547(b) are present. [**National City Bank of New York v. Hotchkiss,** 231 U.S. 50 (1913)]

(1) "New Value" Defined

The Code defines new value as "money or money's worth in goods, services, or new credit, or release by a transferee of property previously transferred to such transferee in a transaction that is neither void nor voidable by the debtor or the trustee under any applicable law. . . ." New value does not include "an obligation substituted for an existing obligation." [B.C. § 547(a)(2); **Manchester v. First Bank & Trust Co. (*In re* Moses),** 265 B.R. 641 (B.A.P. 10th Cir. 2000) (paying on an existing bank loan is satisfaction of an antecedent debt and, hence, is not new value)]

(a) Proof

Appellate courts have held that proof of the **specific dollar amount** of new value given to the debtor (i.e., not merely "some" new value) is required to satisfy this exception. [**In re Spada,** 903 F.2d 971 (3d Cir. 1990)] Moreover, the party raising the defense under § 547(c)(1) has the burden of proof. [B.C. § 547(g); **Gold v. Myers Controlled Power, LLC (*In re* Truland Group),** 2018 WL 333865 (Bankr. E.D. Va. 2018)]

(ii) In Fact Substantially Contemporaneous

The transfer also must **in fact** be substantially contemporaneous. [**Gold v. Myers Controlled Power,** *supra* (citing cases on time periods courts consider to be and not to be substantially contemporaneous, and concluding that "a gap of 44 days, and a gap of 23 days, are simply too long to be considered truly 'contemporaneous" under Section 547(c)(1)")] A majority of the Courts of Appeals that have addressed the issue have "rejected a bright-line rule" for determining what constitutes a substantially contemporaneous exchange. Instead, courts look at the totality of the circumstances in each case. [**Burtch v. Connecticut Community Bank (*In re* J. Silver Clothing, Inc.),** 453 B.R. 518 (Bankr. D. Del. 2011); **Reynolds v. Quality Timber Products (*In re* Git-N-Go, Inc.),** 2007 WL 3232195 (Bankr. N.D. Okla. 2007)]

b. Transfer in Ordinary Course of Business

To satisfy the ordinary course of business exception, the creditor must demonstrate two things. First, the ***debt was incurred*** in the ***ordinary course of business*** or ***financial affairs*** of the debtor and the transferee. Second, the ***transfer was made*** either (i) in the ***ordinary course of business*** or ***financial affairs*** of the debtor and the transferee *or* (ii) according to ***ordinary business terms.*** [B.C. § 547(c)(2)]

(i) Ordinary Course Transfer

(1) Ordinary Course of Business or Financial Affairs

This is the subjective prong of the test, because it looks at whether the transfer is consistent with past business or financial practices of the debtor and creditor. In order to apply the test, courts first must determine the baseline period against which to compare the transfer. The baseline should be a period during which the debtor was financially healthy. Factors that courts consider " 'include the amount transferred, the timing of the payment, the historic course of dealings between the debtor and the transferee, and the circumstances under which the transfer was effected.' " [**Wiscovitch-Rentas v. Villa Blanca VB Plaza LLC (*In re* PMC Mktg. Corp.),** 543 B.R. 345 (B.A.P. 1st Cir. 2016)] Several Courts of Appeals have ruled that a first-time transaction may qualify for the ordinary course exception, because the Bankruptcy Code directs the court to examine the ordinary course of business of the debtor and creditor/transferee, not the ordinary course of business *between* the debtor and creditor/transferee. [**Jubber v. SMC Elec. Prods. (*In re* CW Mining Co.),** 798 F.3d 983 (10th Cir. 2015)]

(2) Ordinary Business Terms

Determining whether the transfer was made *"according to ordinary business terms"* is an objective test. [**Wiscovitch-Rentas v. Villa Blanca VB Plaza LLC (*In re* PMC Mktg. Corp.),** 543 B.R. 345 (B.A.P. 1st Cir. 2016); **Stahl v. Whelan Elec., Inc. (*In re* Modtech Holdings, Inc.),** 503 B.R. 737 (Bankr. C.D. Cal. 2013)] The test requires the court to compare the challenged transfer with the norms in the relevant industry. A transfer made according to ordinary business terms is a transaction that is not so unusual or out of line with relevant industry practice that it is an aberration or a flagrant deviation from relevant industry norms. [**Sass v. Vector Consulting, Inc. (*In re* Am. Home Mortg. Holdings, Inc.),** 476 B.R. 124 (Bankr. D. Del. 2012) (summarizing tests from various Courts of Appeal)]

(ii) Late Payments

Late payments, by themselves, do not defeat a creditor's claim that transfers were made in the ordinary course of the creditor's and debtor's business. Instead, courts look to whether the debtor paid late outside the preference period and, if so, compare the lateness of preference period payments against non-preference period payments. [**Wiscovitch-Rentas v. Villa Blanca VB Plaza LLC (*In re* PMC Mktg. Corp.),** 543 B.R. 345 (B.A.P. 1st Cir. 2016)]

(iii) Long-Term Debt

The Supreme Court has held that payments on long-term debt, as well as payments on short-term debt, may qualify for the "ordinary course of business" exception. [**Union Bank v. Wolas,** 502 U.S. 151 (1991)]

c. Purchase-Money Security Interest Securing New Value

A *security interest* securing *new value* extended to the debtor for the purpose of acquiring certain property described in the security agreement and actually purchased by the debtor with the funds furnished by the creditor is protected from avoidance by the trustee. [B.C. § 547(c)(3)]

(i) Tracing Necessary

For this exception to apply, the debtor actually must use the new value received from the creditor to purchase the collateral. In other words, the creditor must prove that the security interest is a purchase-money security interest. [B.C. § 547(g)] If the creditor's funds are commingled with funds in a general debtor account, then it may prove difficult for the creditor to satisfy the exception's requirement that the debtor used *creditor's funds* to purchase the collateral. If the creditor is unable to trace its funds, then it cannot prove it has a purchase-money security interest and § 547(c)(4)'s exception does not apply. [B.C. § 547(c)(3)(A)(iv); 5 Collier ¶ 547.04(3)]

(ii) Perfection Within Thirty Days After Possession

The secured party must perfect his purchase-money security interest no later than *30 days* after the debtor takes possession of the collateral; failure to perfect within that time renders the transfer voidable. [B.C. § 547(c)(3)(B)]

e.g. **Example:** On December 15, Diane Debtor purchased and took possession of a new car using funds from Creditor Financial Services to do so. Thirty-two days later, on January 16, Creditor Financial Services took the steps necessary under state law to perfect its security interest. State law provides creditors with 40 days to perfect their liens on motor vehicles. Federal, not state, law governs the relation-back or grace period for perfection. Thus, Creditor does not satisfy the requirements of § 547(c)(3) and the trustee may avoid Creditor Financial's security interest in the vehicle as a preference. [*See* **Fidelity Financial Services, Inc. v. Fink,** 522 U.S. 211 (1998) (holding 20-day rule, then in effect under § 547(c)(3)(B), controlling even though applicable state law provided for a longer grace period)]

d. Subsequent Advance of New Value

A transfer is not avoidable to the extent that, *subsequent to the transfer,* the creditor extended *new* pre-petition value that is "not secured by an otherwise unavoidable security interest" and that has not been repaid by "an otherwise unavoidable transfer." [B.C. § 547(c)(4)] This exception is designed to induce creditors to continue extending credit and doing business with debtors in financial straits. [*See* **IRFM, Inc. v. Ever-Fresh Food Co.,** 52 F.2d 228 (9th Cir. 1995)] While the exception protects the creditor that has received a preferential payment, it is "not unfair" to the debtor's other creditors because the new value replenishes the estate. [*See* **Laker v. Vallette (*In re* Toyota of Jefferson),** 14 F.3d 1088 (5th Cir. 1994)] There are several points to keep in mind in applying this exception.

(i) The exception only applies to new value extended *after* the preferential transfer.

(ii) The exception does *not* apply if the creditor extending the new value has a security interest that is "valid and enforceable at the time of the bankruptcy." [*See* **IRFM, Inc. v. Ever-Fresh Food Co.,** 52 F.2d 228 (9th Cir. 1995); **Intercontinental Polymers, Inc. v. Equistar Chems., LP (*In re* Intercontinental Polymers, Inc.),** 359 B.R. 868 (Bankr. E.D. Tenn. 2005)]

(iii) The ***majority rule*** is that the new value may be applied to offset any preferential transfer that precedes the new value and not simply the preferential transfer *immediately* preceding the provision of new value.

 Example: *Epicerie,* the debtor, is a high-end grocery market that filed for bankruptcy on August 3. *Laitier* is one of *Epicerie's* suppliers of cheese and dairy products. While the parties' terms of payment required *Epicerie* to pay for goods upon delivery, *Epicerie* paid *Laitier* a week or more after delivery during the 90 days prior to the bankruptcy filing. *Epicerie's* payments also did not comport with industry standards. During the 90 days prior to *Epicerie's* bankruptcy filing, the following transactions occurred:

June 18: $20,000 payment to *Laitier*

June 30: $28,000 of goods shipped to *Epicerie*

July 10: $15,000 payment to *Laitier*

July 5: $10,000 of goods shipped to *Epicerie*

July 23: $20,000 payment to *Laitier*

The June 30 shipment of goods is new value, which means that the trustee may not recover the $20,000 payment made to *Laitier* on June 18. The trustee may recover $5,000 of the July 10 payment and the entire $20,000 payment made on July 23, however. The $8,000 by which the June 30 new value exceeds the June 18 preferential payment *may not* be used to protect the July 10 $15,000 payment to *Laitier.* **Remember**: the new value exception requires that the creditor extend new value *after* the preferential transfer. The June 30 new value *precedes* the July 10 preferential payment of $15,000. The July 5 new value is only $10,000, so $5,000 of the July 10 payment to *Laitier* is avoidable by the trustee. In addition, there is no new value extended after the July 23 payment; hence the entire $20,000 payment is avoidable. ***Note:*** None of the payments qualify for the ordinary business transaction exception because the facts state that the payments were not made according to either industry standards or the parties' typical payment terms.

 Example: Same facts as in the above example, except the payments and deliveries during the 90 days prior to bankruptcy were as follows:

June 18: $20,000 payment to *Laitier*

June 30: $15,000 of goods shipped to *Epicerie*

July 10: $15,000 payment to *Laitier*

July 5: $20,000 of goods shipped to *Epicerie*

The trustee cannot avoid the June 18 $20,000 payment or the July 10 $15,000 payment. The $15,000 new value on June 30 protects $15,000 of the June 18 preferential transfer. The July 5 new value of $20,000 protects both the July 10

$15,000 preferential payment *and* the remaining $5,000 of the June 18 preferential payment. The majority of courts do not require that the new value apply *only* to the immediately preceding preferential transfer.

(1) Comment

Some courts have held that a creditor that receives critical vendor payments or administrative priority payments pursuant to § 503(b)(9) for the new value provided to the debtor cannot use the new value exception under § 547(c)(4) as a defense to a preference action. [5 Collier ¶ 547.04(4)(e)]

e. Security Interest in Inventory and Receivables

A transfer that creates a perfected security interest in the debtor's *inventory, receivables, or proceeds of inventory or receivables* is voidable only *to the extent that the creditor's position has improved,* to the prejudice of the estate, during the period beginning on the later of the 90th day (or one year, if the secured party was an insider at the time of the transfer) before bankruptcy *or* the first date on which the creditor gave new value pursuant to the security agreement, and ending on the date that the petition was filed. [B.C. § 547(c)(5); B.C. §§ 547(a)(1) (definition of inventory) & (a)(3) (definition of receivable)]

(i) Why Is an Exception Needed?

Floating liens create a preference problem for secured creditors. The transfer of a security interest does not occur until the debtor has rights in the collateral. [B.C. § 547(e)(3)] If a secured creditor takes a security interest in a debtor's inventory, whether now owned or hereafter acquired, the security interest attaches to after-acquired inventory when the debtor acquires rights in the collateral, e.g., makes a contract for a delivery of inventory, not when the creditor originally perfected its security interest in the inventory. That means that the security interest attaching to the after-acquired inventory creates a transfer on account of an antecedent debt, which is one of the elements of a preference. [B.C. § 547(b)(2)] If the after-acquired inventory is purchased by the debtor during the 90-day window preceding the debtor's bankruptcy filing, then there is a transfer (security interest) to a creditor on account of an antecedent debt during the 90 days preceding bankruptcy when the debtor is presumed insolvent and the creditor is secured, as opposed to unsecured, in that inventory, which seems to improve the secured creditor's position. [B.C. §§ 547(b), (f)]

(ii) Improvement in Position Test

This exception protects a creditor with a "floating lien" so long as the creditor's position does not improve during the time period described in § 547(c)(5). [5 Collier ¶ 547.04(5)] The key is whether there is "prejudice [to] other creditors holding unsecured claims." [B.C. § 547(c)(5)] In other words, if the position of the creditor with the "floating lien" on the date of bankruptcy filing has not improved relative to its position 90 days prior to the bankruptcy filing, then there is no improvement in position and no preference to avoid. In determining how much, if any, a creditor has improved her position, the court examines the amount of any insufficiency, i.e., the difference between the outstanding balance of the debt owed and the value of the collateral, existing at *two specific times*:

- the 90th day before bankruptcy (or the first date on which new value was extended) and

- the date that the bankruptcy petition was filed.

Thus, regardless of any fluctuations during the preference period, the transfer will be voidable only to the extent that the insufficiency has been reduced between these two dates.

e.g. **Example:** Two years ago, Financier extended Acme a revolving line of credit to use for Acme's purchase of inventory. The parties signed a valid security agreement giving Financier a security interest in all Acme's inventory whether now owned or hereafter acquired. On October 2, Acme filed for relief under Chapter 11. Acme's inventory normally turns over completely every 30–40 days; therefore, all inventory on the date of bankruptcy filing was acquired within 90 days of the filing. On the date of bankruptcy, Acme owed Financier $1 million and Acme's inventory was valued at $1.1 million. (Acme made no payments to Financier between July 3 and October 2.) On July 3, 90 days prior to Acme's filing, Acme owed Financier $1 million, and Acme had inventory valued at $1 million. While the inventory increased from $1 million to $1.1 million during the 90-day period prior to filing for bankruptcy, Financier's position did not improve. Financier was fully secured on July 3 and fully secured on October 2. In other words, if the inventory were sold on July 3 Financier would receive $1 million. If the inventory were sold on October 2, Financier would receive $1 million. Therefore, there is nothing for the trustee to avoid.

e.g. **Example:** Two years ago, Financier extended Acme a revolving line of credit to use for Acme's purchase of inventory. The parties signed a valid security agreement giving Financier a security interest in all Acme's inventory whether now owned or hereafter acquired. On October 2, Acme filed for relief under Chapter 11. Acme's inventory normally turns over completely every 30–40 days; therefore, all inventory on the date of bankruptcy was acquired within 90 days of the bankruptcy filing. On the date of bankruptcy, Acme owed Financier $1 million and Acme's inventory was valued at $900,000. (Acme made no payments to Financier between July 3 and October 2.) On July 3, 90 days prior to Acme's filing, Acme owed Financier $1 million, and Acme had inventory valued at $800,000. The trustee may avoid $100,000 of Acme's security interest, because Acme's position improved by that amount from July 3 to October 2. On July 3, Acme was unsecured in the amount of $200,000 [$1 million loan − $800,000 in collateral]. On October 2, Acme was unsecured in the amount of only $100,000 [$1 million loan − $900,000 in collateral].

Note: The transfer is not voidable if the creditor's improvement in position did not harm the unsecured creditors, such as a case in which the insufficiency's reduction was caused *solely* by a seasonal appreciation in the value of collateral consisting of an inventory of swimwear held in storage in New York for 90 days from January until the filing of the petition in April. [*See* 5 Collier ¶ 547.04(5)]

(iii) "Receivable"

For purposes of a preference, a receivable is defined as a "right to payment, whether or not such right has been earned by performance." [B.C. § 547(a)(3)]

f. Statutory Lien

The sixth exception makes the fixing of a statutory lien, such as a tax lien, a mechanic's lien, or an artisan's lien, not avoidable as a preference *if the lien cannot be avoided under Bankruptcy Code § 545,* even if it was perfected within 90 days before bankruptcy. [B.C. § 547(c)(6); 5 Collier ¶ 547.04(6)]

Example: On September 1, Sam's Service Station perfects an artisan's lien against Debtor's automobile for unpaid repairs to the engine. On November 1, Debtor files a Chapter 7 bankruptcy petition. Sam's has remained continuously in possession of the automobile, and under the relevant state statute the lien is enforceable against a bona fide purchaser. Since the lien is not avoidable under § 545, it also is not subject to the trustee's power to avoid preferential transfers.

g. Domestic Support Obligation

Bona fide payment of a ***domestic support obligation*** is not avoidable by the trustee. [B.C. §§ 547(c)(7), 101(14A)]

h. Consumer Payments Under $600

A transfer of property worth less than $600 by an individual debtor with primarily consumer debts is not avoidable by the trustee. [B.C. § 547(c)(8)] The majority of courts ***aggregate all transfers*** made in the 90-day period to a single creditor rather than consider each transfer individually when determining whether the $600 exception applies. Most courts also allow the trustee to ***avoid the entire amount*** of money transferred and not simply the amount exceeding $599.

Example: Debtor filed for relief under Chapter 7. In the 90 days prior to the bankruptcy filing, $857 of Debtor's wages had been garnished pursuant to a state court judgment obtained by Creditor. None of the six garnishment payments exceeded $151. Creditor claimed that *each* garnishment payment was less than $600 and, thus, each payment was protected by § 547(c)(8). The bankruptcy court disagreed and concluded that the aggregated transfers totaling $857 were not protected from avoidance pursuant to § 547(c)(8). [**Rainsdon v. Action Collection Servs. (*In re* Robles),** 2007 WL 1792320 (Bankr. D. Id. 2007)]

Example: Debtor filed for relief under Chapter 7. In the 90 days prior to the bankruptcy filing, $1,108 of Debtor's wages had been garnished pursuant to a state court judgment obtained by Creditor. The largest of the individual garnishment payments was $116.10. Creditor claimed that *each* garnishment payment was less than $600 and, thus, each payment was protected by § 547(c)(8). The bankruptcy court disagreed and concluded that the aggregated transfers totaling $1,108 were not protected from avoidance pursuant to § 547(c)(8). Creditor also argued that only the amount over $599 was subject to avoidance. The bankruptcy court disagreed and held that the *entire* $1,108 was subject to avoidance. [**Maus v. Joint Twp. Dist. Mem. Hosp. (*In re* Maus),** 282 B.R. 836 (Bankr. N.D. Ohio 2002)]

i. Non-Consumer Payments Less than $6,825

A transfer of property worth less than $6,825 by a debtor whose debts are ***not primarily consumer debts*** is not avoidable by the trustee. [B.C. § 547(c)(9)] The current $6,825 figure will increase on April 1, 2022. [B.C. § 104(a)] The issues of aggregation and the amount to avoid under § 547(c)(8) also are issues under § 547(c)(9). There is little case law on these issues under § 547(c)(9). The Ninth Circuit's B.A.P., however, turned to the case law under § 547(c)(8), noting the similarity of the language in subsections (c)(8) and (c)(9). [**Western States Glass Corp. v. Barris (*In re* Bay Area Glass),** 454 B.R. 486 (B.A.P. 9th Cir. 2011) ("Where Congress employs the same language in sequential subsections of a statute, we may infer that it intended the same meaning for the language in both subsections.")]

j. Alternative Repayment Schedules

The trustee may not avoid a transfer if the transfer was made as part of an *alternative repayment schedule* between the debtor and an approved nonprofit budget and counseling agency. [B.C. §§ 547(h), 111]

CHECKLIST OF EXCEPTIONS TO THE PREFERENCE RULE ▪GILBERT

THE FOLLOWING TRANSFERS ARE EXCEPTED FROM THE VOIDABLE PREFERENCE RULE:

☑ Transfers that the debtor and creditor intended to be and that actually were *substantially contemporaneous exchanges* for new value

☑ Transfers made *in the ordinary course of business* of the debtor and creditor *or* according to *ordinary business terms,* for the purpose of repaying a *debt that was incurred* in the *debtor's and creditor's ordinary course of business*

☑ *Purchase-money security interests* securing new value given to the debtor to acquire certain property (actually purchased with the new value) if the creditor perfects within 30 days of the debtor's possession of the collateral

☑ An *extension of new value* made subsequent to the transfer

☑ Perfected *security interests in inventory or receivables* (or proceeds of either) to the extent that they did not improve the creditor's position to the prejudice of the estate during the pre-petition period stated in Code § 547(c)(5)

☑ The fixing of a *statutory lien* (such as a tax lien, mechanic's lien, or artisan's lien) that *cannot be avoided under Bankruptcy Code § 545*

☑ Payments of *domestic support obligations*

☑ Transfers to the same creditor by an individual debtor with *primarily consumer debts* of *property with an aggregate value less than $600*

☑ Transfers to the same creditor by a debtor whose debts are *not primarily consumer debts* of *property whose aggregate value is less than $6,825*

☑ Transfers pursuant to an *alternative repayment schedule* with an approved nonprofit budget and counseling agency

---

4. Special Rules for Preferences

For the purpose of preference determination, the Code specifies when certain transfers *are deemed to have been perfected* and when certain transfers are *considered to have been made.* [B.C. § 547(e)]

a. When Perfection Occurs

A transfer of *real property* is deemed perfected when, under state law (i.e., recording statutes), a *subsequent bona fide purchaser* of the property cannot acquire an interest superior to that of the transferee. A transfer of *fixtures or personal property* is deemed perfected when, under state law (i.e., U.C.C. Article 9), a creditor on a simple contract cannot acquire a *judicial lien* that is superior to the transferee's interest. [B.C. § 547(e)(1)]

b. When Transfer Is Made

For the purpose of preference analysis, the time a transfer is considered to have been made depends on when the transfer was perfected [B.C. § 547(e)(2)], provided that the debtor had acquired rights in the property at the time of the transfer. [B.C. § 547(e)(3)]

(i) Perfection Within Thirty Days

A transfer is considered to have been made on the date it became effective between the parties if perfection occurs within the next thirty days. [B.C. § 547(e)(2)(A)]

(ii) Perfection After Thirty Days

A transfer is deemed to have been made on the date that it is perfected if perfection occurs *more than 30 days* after the transfer originally became effective between the parties. [B.C. § 547(e)(2)(B)]

e.g. **Example:** On December 5, 2017, Dylan purchased a new car from Cathay Luxury Motors ("CLM"). He signed a promissory note for the $48,000 purchase price and granted CLM a security interest in the vehicle. CLM, however, did not perfect the security interest until April 5, 2018. Dylan filed for relief under Chapter 7 on May 10, 2018. The trustee can avoid CLM's security interest in the vehicle. The granting of the security interest was a transfer to the creditor of the debtor's interest in property. [B.C. § 547(b)(1)] Because perfection did not occur within 30 days of December 5, the transfer of the security interest is deemed to have occurred on April 5, when CLM perfected. [B.C. § 547(e)(2)(B)] As a result, the transfer is on account of an antecedent debt, because the debt arose on December 5 and the transfer occurred four months later. [B.C. § 547(b)(2)] April 5 is within 90 days of the bankruptcy filing when the debtor is presumed to be insolvent. [B.C. §§ 547(b)(3) & (4), 547(f)] Finally, the transfer of the security interest makes CLM a secured creditor but had the transfer not occurred CLM would be a general unsecured creditor in the Chapter 7 case; therefore, the transfer allows CLM to receive more than it would had the transfer not taken place. [B.C. § 547(b)(5); *see* **Howell v. Brown (*In re* Pritchett)**, 515 B.R. 656 (Bankr. N.D. Ga. 2014)]

(iii) No Perfection Before Bankruptcy

A transfer is deemed to have been made immediately prior to bankruptcy if perfection has not occurred by the time the petition is filed or within 30 days after the transfer became effective between the parties, whichever is later. [B.C. § 547(e)(2)(C)]

e.g. **Example:** In 2003, Bank loaned Debtor $196,000, and Debtor granted Bank a mortgage on his home. Bank failed to record the mortgage. Debtor subsequently filed for relief under Chapter 7. Bank's failure to record the mortgage means that the transfer of the mortgage occurred immediately prior to Debtor's filing for bankruptcy, which creates a preference problem for the Bank. [B.C. § 547(e)(2)(C); *see* **Wells Fargo Home Mortgage, Inc. v. Lundquist,** 592 F.3d 838 (8th Cir. 2010)]

(iv) Debtor's Rights in Property

With respect to preferences, a transfer is not deemed to have been made until the debtor has obtained rights in the property transferred. [B.C. § 547(e)(3)]

(1) Inventory and Receivables

In exchange for a line of credit from a bank to finance its purchases of inventory, a debtor often will grant the bank a security interest in debtor's inventory, whether "now owned or hereafter acquired." The reason for doing so is that inventory turns over quickly. If the security interest did not "float" to cover new purchases of inventory, the bank quickly could end up an unsecured creditor. Section 547(e)(3) provides that a transfer does not occur until the debtor has rights in the collateral. If a debtor buys inventory in the 90 days prior to filing for bankruptcy, there is a preference issue. The bank's security interest floats and attaches to the inventory, but not until the debtor acquires rights in the inventory. That means that the debtor has transferred an interest in property—the lien on the inventory—to a creditor, within 90 days of bankruptcy when the debtor is presumed insolvent, on account of an antecedent debt (line of credit), and the transfer of the security interest to the new inventory improves the bank's position. The Code's solution to this problem is the improvement-in-position test for inventory and receivables at § 547(c)(5). [B.C. § 547(c)(5)]

(2) Rights in Garnished Wages

Although there is a split of authority, the vast majority of cases hold that, even if a garnishment lien has been executed more than 90 days before bankruptcy, the amounts of the debtor's wages garnished during the preference period are voidable transfers because the debtor does not acquire rights in wages until she has earned them. [***In re* Morehead,** 249 F.3d 445 (6th Cir. 2001); **Tower Credit, Inc. v. Schott,** 550 B.R. 299 (M.D. La. 2016)] If during the 90 days prior to bankruptcy, the aggregate value of the garnishments against an individual debtor with primarily consumer debts is less than $600, then the exception at § 547(c)(8) applies and the trustee may not avoid the transfer of the garnished wages.

c. When Transfer Occurs if Debtor Pays by Check

If the debtor pays a creditor by check, the transfer is deemed to have occurred, for purposes of the § 547(b) preference period, *at the time the bank honors the check.* [**Barnhill v. Johnson,** 503 U.S. 393 (1992)] In *Barnhill,* the Supreme Court noted that the Courts of Appeals that had considered the question had unanimously used the date of delivery for purposes of the preference exceptions under § 547(c). But the question of whether the date of delivery versus the date of honor applied to the preference *exceptions* was not before the Court; thus, it expressed no view on the issue. When deciding whether a preference exception under § 547(c) applies, most courts hold that the transfer occurs on the date that the *check is delivered, not honored. [See, e.g.,* **Littleton v. Hinton (***In re* **Triple H Auto & Truck Sales, Inc.),** 2009 WL 348858 (Bankr. S.D. Ala. 2009) (stating that for purposes of § 547(c)(1), the transfer occurs on the date that the check is delivered so long as the check is presented within a reasonable time and honored by the bank); **Rifken v. Entec Distribution, LLC (***In re* **Felt Mfg. Co.),** 2009 WL 3348300 (Bankr. D. N.H. 2009) (stating that "[c]ourts consistently hold that for new value purposes under § 547(c)(4), the transfer involving a payment by check occurs when the check is received by the creditor"); **Savage & Associates v. Mandl (***In re* **Teligent Inc.),** 380 B.R. 324 (Bankr. S.D. N.Y. 2008) (stating that for purposes of § 547(c)(2) the transfer happens when the check is delivered, so long as the check is honored within 30 days of delivery)]

(i) Note

This issue can take on great importance when the debtor's check is delivered to the creditor more than 90 days before bankruptcy but is honored by the bank within the preference period.

5. Burden of Proof

The trustee has the burden of proof concerning the existence of a voidable preference, but the creditor bears the burden of proof concerning any exception that might be asserted. [B.C. § 547(g)]

D. Trustee's Power to Avoid Fraudulent Transfers

1. In General

The trustee has the power to avoid a fraudulent transfer of the debtor's interest in property or the fraudulent incurring of an obligation if the transfer was made or the obligation was incurred by the debtor, voluntarily or involuntarily, *within two years* prior to bankruptcy. [B.C. § 548(a)] The trustee also may avoid certain transfers made by the debtor to a *self-settled trust within ten years* prior to bankruptcy. [B.C. § 548(e)]

2. "Transfer"

A transfer is a *voluntary or involuntary* disposition of property or an interest in property. A transfer includes, for example, the debtor's conveyance of a security interest or mortgage, the fixing of a lien on the debtor's property by judicial process, or even a foreclosure sale of collateral securing a debt. [B.C. § 101(54)]

a. When Transfer Occurs

For purposes of Bankruptcy Code § 548, a transfer is deemed to have been made when it is sufficiently perfected to preclude a subsequent bona fide purchaser from acquiring a superior interest in the property. However, if such perfection has not occurred prior to the filing of the petition, the transfer is deemed to be made immediately prior to bankruptcy. [B.C. § 548(d)(1)]

3. "Fraudulent" Transfer

A trustee may avoid a transfer if there is *actual intent* to hinder, delay, or defraud a creditor. [B.C. § 548(a)(1)(A)] The trustee also may avoid a transfer that is *constructively fraudulent.* [B.C. § 548(a)(1)(B)]

a. Actual Intent to Hinder, Delay, or Defraud

A transfer of the debtor's property is fraudulent if it was made with *actual intent* to hinder, delay, or defraud a creditor. [B.C. § 548(a)(1)(A)]

e.g. **Example:** On March 1, Debtor, who was hopelessly in debt, transferred all of his assets into his wife's name for no consideration and for the express purpose of placing them out of the reach of his creditors. On March 3, Debtor filed a voluntary bankruptcy petition. The trustee may avoid the conveyance of Debtor's assets as a fraudulent transfer and may recover them for the benefit of the estate. [B.C. §§ 548(a)(1)(A), 550(a)]

(i) Badges of Fraud

The debtor's actual intent to hinder, delay, or defraud creditors usually is not as obvious as in the example above. Thus, the law has developed certain "badges of fraud" from which *actual intent may be inferred.* Both the Uniform Fraudulent Transfer Act and the Uniform Voidable Transactions Act provide the following non-exhaustive list of badges of fraud, which many courts use:

(1) *inadequate or no consideration* is received for the transfer made or obligation incurred;

(2) the *transferee is an insider,* **e.g.,** *a relative,* of the debtor;

(3) the *debtor keeps possession or control of the transferred property;*

(4) the *transfer occurs or the obligation is incurred at a time after creditors have filed suit or threatened to file suit against the debtor;*

(5) the debtor is *insolvent or becomes insolvent* shortly after the transfer was made or obligation incurred;

(6) the transfer or obligation is *concealed;*

(7) the transfer is of *substantially all the debtor's assets;*

(8) the debtor *absconds;*

(9) the transfer occurs shortly before or shortly after a *substantial debt* is incurred; and

(10) the debtor transferred her *essential business assets* to a lienor who then transfers the assets to an insider of the debtor.

[Uniform Fraudulent Transfer Act § 4(b); Uniform Voidable Transactions Act § 4(b)] It is not necessary to prove all the badges of fraud. The presence or absence of any particular badge of fraud is not dispositive. The inquiry is fact intensive, and courts look to all the circumstances surrounding the transfer made or obligation incurred. [**Osherow v. Texas Silica Logistics J.V. (*In re* FWLL, Inc.),** 2018 WL 1684308 (Bankr. W.D. Tex. 2018)]

(ii) Insolvency Not Required

If actual intent can be proved, the transfer is voidable regardless of whether the debtor was insolvent at the time of the transfer. [B.C. § 548(a)(1)(A)]

(iii) Ten-Year Reach Back Period

BAPCPA added a provision to § 548 that extends the reach back period to *ten years* for certain cases of *actual fraud* involving transfers to *self-settled trusts.* [B.C. § 548(e)] The trustee may avoid the transfer if:

(1) the debtor made the transfer [§ 548(e)(1)(B)];

(2) the transfer was to a *self-settled trust* [§ 548(e)(1)(A)];

(3) the debtor is the *beneficiary* of that trust [§ 548(e)(1)(C)]; and

(4) the debtor made the transfer with *actual intent to hinder, delay, or defraud* current creditors or entities that become creditors after the date of the transfer. [B.C. § 548(e)(1)(D)]

The Code defines a *transfer,* for purposes of § 548(e), to include a transfer the debtor made in anticipation of a money judgment, settlement, civil penalty, equitable order or criminal fine incurred or that the debtor believe would be incurred for (i) violations of *state or federal securities laws,* (ii) violations of *regulations or orders* issued under state or federal securities laws, or for (iii) *fraud, deceit or manipulation in a fiduciary capacity* under §§ 12 or 15(d) of the Securities Exchange Act of 1934 or under § 6 of the Securities Act of 1933. [B.C. § 548(e)(2)] Section 548(e)(2) uses the word "include" to define transfer; therefore, § 548(e) is not limited to the specific types of transfers listed. [B.C. § 102(3)]

b. Constructive Fraud

The Code provides that the trustee may prove *constructive fraud* by demonstrating that the debtor did not receive something of *reasonably equivalent value* in exchange for the transfer or obligation *and* the debtor (i) was *insolvent* or rendered insolvent by the transfer or obligation, (ii) was *undercapitalized* after the transfer or incurring the obligation, (iii) intended to incur debts *beyond her ability to repay, or* (iv) made the transfer or incurred the obligation to or for the *benefit of an insider under an employment contract* and not in the ordinary course of business. [B.C. §§ 548(a)(1)(B)(i), (ii)(I)–(IV)]

(i) What is Reasonably Equivalent Value?

The *first step* in determining reasonably equivalent value is determining whether the debtor received *any* value for the transfer. This part of the analysis is simple, because the Code defines value. For purposes of § 548, value includes not only property, but also the "satisfaction or securing of a present or antecedent debt of the debtor." [B.C. § 548(d)(2)(A)] If the debtor receives value, then the *second step* is deciding whether the value received is reasonably equivalent to the value transferred. This inquiry is fact intensive.

The Supreme Court has held that the sale price received at a *non-collusive* foreclosure sale conclusively constitutes reasonably equivalent value, if "all the requirements of the State's foreclosure law have been complied with." Any fraud, collusion, or other defect in the sale that would invalidate it under state law "will deprive the sale price of its conclusive force" and subject the sale to possible avoidance under § 548. [**BFP v. Resolution Trust Corp.,** 511 U.S. 531 (1994)]

(ii) Receipt of Less than Reasonably Equivalent Value and Debtor's Insolvency

A transaction is considered to be fraudulent if the debtor received *less than reasonably equivalent value* for the transfer or obligation and was *insolvent* on the date the conveyance occurred or *became insolvent* as a consequence of it. [B.C. §§ 548(a)(1)(B)(i), (ii)(I)]

Example: Debtor filed for relief under Chapter 7. For two years prior to filing for bankruptcy, Debtor paid about $5,500 to University to cover some of her son's tuition and educational expenses. The Chapter 7 trustee filed an adversary proceeding to avoid and recover the money paid to University under § 548(a)(1)(b)(i), (ii)(I). The Debtor was insolvent at the time she paid University or was rendered insolvent by virtue of the transfers made to University. Thus, the only issue before the court was whether Debtor received reasonably equivalent value in exchange for the tuition payments made to University. The bankruptcy court held that Debtor received no "legally cognizable value" and, thus, could not have received reasonably equivalent value for the transfers. The court explained that the Code's definition of value is "limited to economic benefits" and does not take account of "moral or familial obligations." [*See* **Boscrino v. Board of Trustees of**

Connecticut State Univ. System (*In re* Knight), 2017 WL 4410455 (Bankr. D. Conn. 2017)]

e.g. **Example:** On May 1, 2001, Debtor's auction bid of $1 billion to purchase 14 radio spectrum licenses at their current market value was accepted by the F.C.C. as the high bid, and Debtor made a down payment of $100 million. On June 1, 2001, Debtor filed license application forms. On December 1, 2001, the F.C.C. approved the applications and granted Debtor the licenses, which had declined significantly in value to $200 million, rendering Debtor insolvent. Also on December 1, 2001, Debtor executed promissory notes totaling $900 million to the F.C.C. for the balance of the purchase price. On July 1, 2002, Debtor filed a Chapter 11 bankruptcy petition and also sought to avoid the transaction as a constructive fraudulent transfer under Code § 548(a)(1)(B)(i), (ii)(I). If *the date of the transfer* is deemed to be May 1—the date the auction closed—then Debtor loses because the value of the licenses was "by definition" the fair market value. [*See* **FCC v. NextWave Personal Communications, Inc. (*In re* NextWave Personal Communications, Inc.),** 200 F.3d 43 (2d Cir. 1999) (holding that Debtor's obligation to pay for spectrum licenses was not a fraudulent transfer, because the licenses' fair market value was equivalent to the bids that the F.C.C. had accepted at the close of the auction)] However, if the date of the transfer is deemed to be December 1—the date the licenses were approved and the promissory notes signed—then Debtor wins because Debtor did not receive reasonably equivalent value. [*See* **United States v. GWI PCS 1, Inc. (*In re* GWI PCS 1 Inc.),** 230 F.3d 788 (5th Cir. 2000) (holding that Debtor's obligation to pay for spectrum licenses was a fraudulent transfer, because that obligation did not arise at the close of the auction but only later after the F.C.C. had approved Debtor's application and Debtor had executed the notes for the balance of the purchase price)]

(iii) Receipt of Less than Reasonably Equivalent Value and Debtor's Undercapitalization

A transaction also is deemed fraudulent if the debtor received *less than reasonably equivalent value* for the transfer or obligation and was left with *unreasonably small capital* for the operation of the debtor's business. [B.C. §§ 548(a)(1)(B)(i), (ii)(II)]

(1) Leveraged Buyout

The purchase of a target corporation sometimes is accomplished by means of a leveraged buyout (also called "asset-based lending"), in which the purchasing company uses the assets of the target corporation as collateral for a bank loan obtained to finance the purchase price. The acquiring company borrows money to buy the stock of the target corporation. The shareholders of the target are cashed out using the borrowed funds. The acquiring company uses the assets of the target company as collateral for the loan. The target company increases its debt burden; the risk of default is borne by the target's general unsecured creditors. Thus, the target company receives no *direct* benefit from the LBO. If the transaction results in the undercapitalization or insolvency of the company acquired, the transfer might constitute a fraudulent conveyance in the event of the target corporation's bankruptcy, because the target does not receive reasonably equivalent value in exchange for the grant of a security interest in *its own assets.* [**United States v. Tabor Court Realty Corp.,** 803 F.2d 1288 (3d Cir. 1986) (case under Pennsylvania Uniform Fraudulent Conveyances Act holding that fraudulent conveyance law applied to LBOs, and upholding district court's determination that LBO transaction had rendered target insolvent and target did not receive fair consideration); *but see* **Mellon Bank, N.A. v. Metro Communications, Inc.,** 945 F.2d 635 (3d Cir. 1991) (court may take into account indirect benefits, e.g., debtor's ability to borrow money and creation of strong synergy by new affiliation, in deciding the question of reasonably equivalent value)]

(iv) Receipt of Less than Reasonably Equivalent Value and Debtor's Intentional Over-Extension

Another kind of transaction that is deemed to be fraudulent is one in which the debtor receives *less than reasonably equivalent value* for the transfer or obligation, and intends to incur or believes she will incur debts that she will be *unable to repay* as they mature. [B.C. §§ 548(a)(1)(B)(i), (ii)(III)]

(v) Receipt of Less than Reasonably Equivalent Value and Transfer to Insider

BAPCPA added a type of avoidable transaction that specifically involves insiders. This new subsection in § 548(a)(1)(B) applies if the debtor made a transfer or incurred an obligation (1) for less than reasonably equivalent value, (2) to or for the benefit of an insider, (3) under an employment contract, and (4) not in the ordinary course of business. [B.C. §§ 548(a)(1)(B)(i), (ii)(IV)]

c. Exception for Certain Charitable Contributions

Certain charitable contributions are not treated as transfers for less than reasonably equivalent value under § 548(a)(1)(B). A transfer of cash or a financial instrument, e.g., stocks or bonds, by a *natural person* to a qualified charitable or religious entity or organization (as defined by the Internal Revenue Code) will not be deemed fraudulent if the contribution: (i) does not exceed 15% of the debtor's gross annual income for the year of the contribution *or* (ii) is consistent with the debtor's normal practices concerning charitable contributions. [B.C. §§ 548(a)(2), (d)(3), (4)]

d. Distinguish Third-Party Transactions with Indirect Benefit to Debtor

Courts generally find that there is no reasonably equivalent value if a transfer or obligation benefits a third party and not the debtor. Some courts, however, have recognized an exception, known as the "indirect benefit rule," to this general principle. Thus, if the transfer does not adversely affect the debtor's net worth, because there is an indirect benefit to the debtor, then a court may find reasonably equivalent value. Courts require that this indirect benefit be quantifiable. [5 Collier ¶ 548.05(2)(b); **Rubin v. Manufacturers Hanover Trust Co.,** 661 F.2d 979 (2d Cir. 1981)]

e.g. **Example:** Debtor was in the business of selling general merchandise to grocery stores. Debtor tried to obtain a $150,000 working capital loan from Bank, but Bank refused to make the loan due to Debtor's financial performance. Bank, however, agreed to loan the necessary capital to Debtor's three individual shareholders ("Shareholders"). While Shareholders were responsible for the loan, the loan proceeds were deposited directly into Debtor's corporate checking account. Debtor then granted Bank a security interest in its inventory, equipment, and accounts. Less than a year later, Debtor stopped doing business, and Debtor's creditors filed an involuntary petition under Chapter 7 against Debtor. The Chapter 7 trustee sought to avoid the security interest granted to Bank and claimed that the $150,000 loan that Shareholders contributed to Debtor was a capital contribution. Thus, the trustee argued that Debtor's grant of a security interest to Bank diminished the estate by $150,000. The bankruptcy court and the B.A.P. agreed with the trustee, but the Ninth Circuit reversed. The court explained that while Debtor was not a party to the $150,000 loan, it clearly benefited from that loan. In fact, Bank deposited the loan proceeds directly into Debtor's corporate account. Debtor benefited from the loan in the amount of $150,000, and Bank received a security interest in Debtor's collateral equivalent to Shareholders' $150,000 debt to Bank. The court concluded that there was no "net loss to Debtor's estate nor the funds available to the unsecured creditors." As a result, Debtor received reasonably equivalent value for the security interest granted to Bank. [**Frontier Bank v. Brown (*In re* Northern Merchandise, Inc.),** 371 F.3d 1056 (9th Cir. 2004)]

4. Good Faith Transferee

A *good faith transferee* or obligee for value is entitled to retain, or to receive a lien on, any property conveyed to her or to enforce an obligation incurred, *to the extent of any value given* by the transferee or obligee to the debtor. [B.C. § 548(c)] This provision applies to transfers voidable under § 548, unless the transfer also is subject to the trustee's avoiding power under §§ 544, 545, or 547.

a. Good Faith

In determining good faith, courts use an *objective, not a subjective, test.* They look to whether a transferee has information that puts it on inquiry notice about the fraudulent nature of the transaction or the debtor's insolvency. Failure to diligently inquire may result in a finding that the transferee is not a good faith transferee for purposes of § 548(c). [**Christian Brothers High School Endowment v. Bayou No Leverage Fund, LLC (*In re* Bayou Group, LLC),** 439 B.R. 284 (S.D. N.Y. 2010)]

b. Value

The Code defines value as "property, or satisfaction or securing of a present or antecedent debt of the debtor." An unperformed promise to provide the debtor or a relative of the debtor with support does not constitute value. [B.C. § 548(d)(2)(A)]

5. Partnership Debtor

Any transfer by a partnership debtor *to a general partner* within *two years* prior to bankruptcy is voidable if it was made at a time when the debtor was *insolvent* or if it caused the debtor to become insolvent. [B.C. § 548(b)]

EXAM TIP   ◭GILBERT

Remember that there could be a longer reach back period than the two years allowed under § 548 if the trustee can find an *actual creditor* who, at the time of bankruptcy, has an allowable *unsecured claim* and has the right under *applicable nonbankruptcy law* to avoid a transfer of the debtor's property. [B.C. § 544(b)]

E. Post-Petition Transactions

1. General Rule

The trustee may avoid a transfer of estate property occurring after the filing of the bankruptcy petition, unless the transfer falls within one of the exceptions described below or is authorized under the Bankruptcy Code or approved by the court. [B.C. § 549(a)]

Example: Lewis, the chief financial officer for Cresta Corporation, issued a check to Castello, the attorney Cresta had hired to represent the firm in bankruptcy. Castello declined the check and asked for payment by cashier's check instead. Lewis delivered a cashier's check to Castello drawn on Lewis's personal bank account. The next day, Cresta issued a check to reimburse Lewis, and Cresta filed for relief under Chapter 7 that same day. Four days after Cresta filed for bankruptcy, its reimbursement check to Lewis cleared the bank. The transfer of the check to Lewis is a post-petition transfer that the Chapter 7 trustee may avoid. The transfer occurred post-petition on the date that the bank honored the check, and was not authorized by either the Code or the bankruptcy court. [**Lewis v. Kaelin (*In re* Cresta Technology Corp.),** 583 B.R. 224 (B.A.P. 9th Cir. 2018)]

Compare: Debtor, a widget manufacturer, files a voluntary Chapter 11 petition. A trustee is not appointed, and Debtor continues to operate the business as a debtor in possession, making numerous sales of widgets in the ordinary course of business. Because the Bankruptcy Code permits these types of transactions without court approval, they are valid post-petition transfers and are not subject to avoidance. [B.C. § 363(c)(1)]

2. Transferor Without Notice or Knowledge

A transferor that has neither actual notice nor knowledge of the bankruptcy case is protected from liability concerning a good faith post-petition transfer. [B.C. §§ 549(a)(2)(A), 542(c)] For example, if a bank honors the debtor's check after the commencement of the case, the bank is not liable for honoring the check, if it had neither actual notice nor knowledge of the bankruptcy case. The transferee/payee on the check, however, may be subject to the trustee's avoiding power under § 549(a)(2)(A).

Example: Prior to filing for bankruptcy, Debtor took out a loan from Payday Loans ("PL"). Debtor gave PL a postdated check that covered the loan's principal and interest. About a week later, Debtor filed for relief under Chapter 13. After the commencement of Debtor's bankruptcy case, PL presented Debtor's check to Bank for payment. Bank, without notice or knowledge of the bankruptcy case, honored the check and paid PL. Section 542(c) authorized the transfer that took place when Bank honored Debtor's check. But, § 542(c) only protects the drawee bank, not the transferee PL. Thus, under § 549(a)(2), the trustee may avoid the post-petition transfer to PL of funds from Debtor's checking account. [B.C. § 549(a)(2)(A); *see* **Buckeye Check Cashing, Inc. v. Meadows (*In re* Meadows),** 396 B.R. 485 (B.A.P. 6th Cir. 2008)]

3. Exceptions to Trustee's Avoidance

The trustee's power to avoid post-petition transfers is subject to the following exceptions and limitations:

a. Gap Transferee in Involuntary Case

The debtor may continue to operate its business and dispose of property during the gap period—the time between the filing of an involuntary petition and the entry of an order for relief. [B.C. § 303(f)] The trustee, however, may avoid a transfer made during the gap period *except to the extent that the transferee gave value, including services, after the start* of the *bankruptcy case* in exchange for the transfer. This exception does not apply to a transaction that involves the satisfaction or securing of a pre-petition debt. [B.C. § 549(a)(2)(A), (b)] The reason for this exception is to allow a business to continue its normal business operations during the gap period. If creditors feared having the trustee pursue them to recover post-petition transfers for goods or services rendered to the debtor, then filing of an involuntary petition could cause substantial harm to the debtor.

Example: Debtor operated Mastro Properties, a sole proprietorship in the real estate and investment business. MKM is Debtor's son and the sole member of MKM LLC, which was formed to hold life insurance policies on Debtor. MKM LLC's transactions were run through Mastro's accounting system and MKM had no independent financial existence until June, when MKM LCC opened a bank account with $900,000 in insurance proceeds provided by Mastro. On July 10, three of Debtor's secured creditors filed an involuntary Chapter 7 petition against Debtor. Between July 10 and August 21, when the court entered an order for relief, Mastro issued six checks totaling $366,000 to MKM LLC. The Chapter 7 trustee sought to avoid these transfers. MKM LLC claimed that the checks were compensation for services that MKM had provided to Debtor, and that the net effect of various transfers between Mastro and MKM LLC had benefited, not harmed, Debtor. The court rejected both claims. First, the court noted that MKM offered no evidence of the services provided to Debtor during the gap period. Second, the court explained that MKM LLC offered no evidence that the cash payments it had received were used to fund Mastro's operations during the gap period. The fact that MKM LLC never had been a supplier of cash to the Debtor, did not have cash of its own and relied on Debtor's assets for the cash in its bank account, and had no independent financial existence until shortly before the filing of the involuntary petition led the court to agree with the trustee that the gap period transfers to MKM LLC did not merit the exception at § 549(a)(2)(A). [**Mastro v. Rigby (*In re* Mastro)**, 2011 WL 3300370 (B.A.P. 9th Cir. 2011)]

(i) Notice or Knowledge Irrelevant

This exception applies regardless of whether the gap transferee has notice or knowledge of the bankruptcy case. [B.C. § 549(b)]

b. Bona Fide Purchaser of Real Property

The trustee cannot avoid a post-petition transfer of real property to a *good faith purchaser* who does not know of the bankruptcy case and has paid *present fair equivalent value* if notice of the bankruptcy case has not been filed, prior to perfection of the transfer, in the office where real property transactions are recorded for the county in which the land is located. [B.C. § 549(c)]

(i) Less than Present Fair Equivalent Value

If notice of the bankruptcy petition has not been filed in the proper office for recording before perfection of the transfer, and a good faith purchaser without knowledge of the case has given less than present fair equivalent value, she is entitled to a lien on the property, but only to the extent of the *present value furnished.* [B.C. § 549(c)]

F. Limitations on Trustee's Avoiding Powers

1. Statute of Limitations

Most of the trustee's avoiding powers are subject to a statute of limitations requiring that the trustee *file an action* to avoid a transfer before the *earlier* of the following time periods:

- the *later* of *two years* after the entry of the order for relief or *one year* after the appointment or election of the first trustee, if the appointment or election occurs before the expiration of the two-year period; or

- *the time of the closing or dismissal* of the case. [B.C. § 546(a)]

a. Transfers Affected

This period of limitations applies to a trustee's action to avoid:

(i) a transfer avoidable under the strong arm clause [B.C. § 544(a)];

(ii) a transfer avoidable by the trustee as successor to certain actual creditors [B.C. § 544(b)];

(iii) a statutory lien [B.C. § 545];

(iv) a preference [B.C. § 547];

(v) a fraudulent transfer [B.C. § 548]; or

(vi) a setoff [B.C. § 553].

b. Distinguish Statute of Limitations for Avoidance of Post-Petition Transactions

To avoid a post-petition transfer, the trustee must file an action before the *earlier* of:

- two years after the *transfer* was made; or

- the time of the *closing or dismissal* of the case. [B.C. § 549(d)]

c. Distinguish Statute of Limitations for Recovery of Avoided Transfer

To the extent that a transfer is avoided, an action to *recover* transferred property or, if the court orders, the value of such property must be commenced *no later than the earlier of:*

- *one year after avoidance* of the transfer; or

- the time that the case is *closed or dismissed.* [B.C. § 550(f)]

d. Equitable Tolling

Case law has consistently held that limitations periods may be equitably tolled because of fraud or misrepresentation that the trustee did not discover notwithstanding due diligence on her part, or extraordinary circumstances beyond the trustee's control that make it impossible for her to file an action on time. [5 Collier ¶ 546.02(3)] Courts use equitable tolling sparingly. [*See, e.g.,* **Montoya v. Sasso (*In re* Sasso),** 550 B.R. 550 (Bankr. D. N.M. 2016) (stating that "[e]quitable tolling should be applied sparingly"); **Gugino v. Turner (*In re* Clark),** 2015 WL 5545258 (Bankr. D. Idaho 2015) (stating that in the Ninth Circuit equitable tolling is " 'rarely applied and disfavored' " and "should be applied 'only sparingly' ")]

2. Retroactive Perfection

The trustee's avoiding powers under Code §§ 544(a) (strong arm clause), 544(b) (successor to certain actual creditors), 545 (certain statutory liens), and 549 (post-petition transactions) are subject to any applicable nonbankruptcy law that permits retroactive perfection of a security interest. Such laws usually are state statutes, such as U.C.C. § 9–317(e) which provides a *20-day grace period* in which to perfect a purchase-money security interest that will have priority over an intervening lien creditor. Thus, when such a statute applies, the Bankruptcy Code allows a creditor to perfect its security interest *post-petition* with retroactive effect, provided that perfection occurs within the time permitted under the applicable nonbankruptcy law. [B.C. § 546(b)(1)(A)]

e.g. **Example:** Debtor borrows $10,000 from Bank and grants Bank a purchase-money security interest in a new business computer. With the loan proceeds, Debtor purchases and receives delivery of the computer on April 1. On April 5, Debtor files a voluntary bankruptcy petition, and on April 6, Bank files a U.C.C. financing statement to perfect its security interest in the computer. Applicable state law provides a 20-day grace period, after the debtor receives delivery of the collateral, within which the secured party may perfect a purchase-money security interest and still have priority over an intervening lien creditor. Therefore, the trustee, having the rights of a hypothetical judicial lien creditor on the date of bankruptcy, is subject to Bank's retroactive perfection, and will be unable to avoid Bank's purchase-money security interest. [B.C. §§ 546(b), 544(a)(1); U.C.C. § 9–317(e)]

EXAM TIP 🔖 GILBERT

Retroactive perfection issues are somewhat common, so you need to keep this possibility in mind. If a creditor perfects a security interest after a bankruptcy petition is filed, the creditor might be able to trump the trustee's avoiding power if a *nonbankruptcy law* permits retroactive perfection of the creditor's security interest. The most common such law is U.C.C. § 9–317(e), under which post-petition perfection of a *purchase-money security interest* may relate back to a pre-petition date if the creditor files a financing statement within 20 days after the debtor receives delivery of the collateral.

---

    a. Note

Section 546(b)(1)(A) is not only limited to statutes allowing retroactive perfection. It covers "any law that permits perfection of an interest in property to be effective against an entity that acquires rights in such property before the date of perfection." For example, it has been used to allow the post-petition perfection of an environmental superlien which, under state law, "trumps all other encumbrances, no matter when filed." [*In re* **229 Main Street Ltd. Partnership,** 262 F.3d 1 (1st Cir. 2001)]

    b. Continuation Statements

The trustee's rights and avoiding powers under sections 544(a) (strong arm clause), 544(b) (successor to certain actual creditors), 545 (certain statutory liens), and 549 (post-petition transfers) also are subject to any applicable law permitting secured creditors to maintain or continue perfection of an interest in property, such as by filing a continuation statement under U.C.C. § 9–515(e). [B.C. § 546(b)(1)(B)]

    c. Exception to Automatic Stay

The post-petition retroactive perfection and filing of a continuation statement described above *are excepted* from the operation of the automatic stay. [B.C. § 362(b)(3)]

3. Seller's Reclamation of Goods

The trustee's power to avoid (i) a transfer under the strong arm clause [B.C. § 544(a)], (ii) a statutory lien [B.C. § 545], (iii) a preference [B.C. § 547], or (iv) a post-petition transfer [B.C. § 549] is subject to the right of a seller, under certain circumstances, to *reclaim* goods that it sold to the debtor. [*See* B.C. § 546(c)]

a. Elements Required for Reclamation

Congress substantially changed § 546(c) with the passage of BAPCPA in 2005. The following elements must be present for a **seller to reclaim goods** sold to the debtor. [B.C. § 546(c)]

(i) Goods

The property sought to be reclaimed must be goods. Courts usually use the U.C.C.'s definition to determine what constitutes "goods." [U.C.C. § 2–105; 5 Collier ¶ 546.04(2)(b)(i)]

(ii) Sale in Ordinary Course of Seller's Business

For the seller to reclaim the goods, the seller must have sold the goods to the debtor in the ordinary course of the seller's business. [B.C. § 546(c)]

(iii) Debtor Insolvent

The debtor must have received the goods while insolvent under the Bankruptcy Code's "balance sheet" definition of insolvency. [B.C. § 101(32)]

(1) "Receipt"

Courts usually use the U.C.C.'s definition of "receipt" to determine when the debtor received the goods subject to a seller's claim for reclamation. [U.C.C. § 2–103(1)(c); 5 Collier ¶ 546.04(2)(b)(v)] Therefore, the debtor is deemed to have received the goods when it has taken **physical possession** of them.

(iv) Received Within 45 Days

The seller's right to reclaim goods sold to the seller is limited to goods that the debtor **received within 45 days** of the start of debtor's bankruptcy case. [B.C. § 546(c)] The debtor receives goods when it takes physical possession of them.

(v) Written Demand for Reclamation

The seller must make a written demand for reclamation no later than:

(1) **45 days** after the debtor received the goods; or

(2) **20 days** after the start of the bankruptcy case, if the 45-day period expires after the commencement of the bankruptcy case. [B.C. § 546(c)(1)]

(a) Computing the Time Period

The seller's right to reclamation only applies to goods received by the debtor within 45 days of the bankruptcy case. Thus, it appears that the language in § 546(c) referencing a 45-day period for making a written demand for reclamation is superfluous. Except in a case in which Day 45 lands on the date of bankruptcy filing, the 45-day period will *always* expire after the filing of the bankruptcy case. Therefore, the seller always will have 20 days after the bankruptcy case has begun to make a written demand for reclamation. [5 Collier ¶ 546.04(2)(b)(iv)]

Example: Debtor receives goods from Seller on April 1. Debtor files for relief under Chapter 7 on May 15. The Federal Rules of Bankruptcy Procedure provide that in counting days, the day triggering the event is not included. [Bankruptcy Rule 9006(a)(1)] April 1—the day that Debtor received the goods—is not included when counting the 45 days;

thus, Day 45 is May 16. Because the 45-day period expires after the start of the bankruptcy case, Seller has 20 days to make a written demand for reclamation. [5 Collier ¶ 546.04(2)(b)(iv)]

b.   Subject to Secured Creditor Interest

The seller's right to reclaim goods is subject to the prior rights of a creditor with a security interest in the goods or the proceeds of those goods. [B.C. § 546(c)(1)]

c.   Seller Fails to Give Notice

If the seller of goods fails to provide the debtor with the required notice for reclamation, the seller still may qualify for an administrative expense claim under § 503(b)(9). [B.C. §§ 546(c)(2), 503(b)(9)]

d.   Grain Farmers and United States Fishermen

The trustee's power to avoid (i) a transfer under the strong arm clause [B.C. § 544(a)], (ii) a statutory lien [B.C. § 545], (iii) a preference [B.C. § 547], or (iv) a post-petition transfer [B.C. § 549] is subject to any statutory or common law right of a grain farmer or a United States fisherman to reclaim grain or fish sold to a grain storage facility or a fish processing facility that is owned or operated by the debtor, if the debtor received such goods while insolvent. [B.C. § 546(d)]

(i)   Written Demand

The grain farmer or U.S. fisherman must make a written demand for reclamation no later than *10 days* after the debtor received the grain or fish. If the 10-day period expires after the start of the bankruptcy case, then the demand may be made up to *20 days* after the debtor received the goods. [B.C. § 546(d)(1)]

(ii)   Grant of Lien

The bankruptcy court may deny reclamation to a grain farmer or U.S. fisherman that has made a proper demand for reclamation only if the court grants the seller a lien securing her claim. [B.C. § 546(d)(2)]

4. Return of Goods

A Chapter 11 debtor, with the creditor's consent and subject to the prior rights of a creditor with a security interest in the goods or the proceeds of such goods, may return goods shipped by the creditor before bankruptcy, and the creditor may offset the purchase price against any pre-petition claim. This action requires a motion by the trustee within *120 days* after the order for relief, notice and a hearing, and a determination by the court that a return is in the estate's best interests. [B.C. § 546(h)]

5. Warehouseman's Lien

BAPCPA added protection for certain liens by warehousemen. The trustee may not avoid a warehouseman's lien for *storage, transportation, or costs incidental to the storage and handling of goods,* notwithstanding the Code's provisions on avoidance of statutory liens under § 545(2) and (3). [B.C. §§ 546(i)(1), 545(2), (3)] Courts are to apply the prohibition against avoidance in a manner consistent with U.C.C. § 7–209 or similar state laws. [B.C. § 546(i)(2)] The Code does not define what constitutes storage, transportation, or costs incidental to storage and handling of goods. U.C.C. § 7–209, however, provides that the warehouseman's lien covers such storage and transportation costs as insurance and labor, and the Official Comments provide that the "lien is limited to the usual charges arising out of a storage transaction." [U.C.C. § 7–209(a), Official Comment 1; *see also* 5 Collier ¶ 546.10]

G. Transferee's Liability to Estate for Avoided Transfer

1. Automatic Preservation for Benefit of Estate

Any transfer that has been avoided or any lien that is void under Bankruptcy Code § 506(d) is automatically preserved for the estate's benefit. [B.C. § 551]

2. What Trustee May Recover

By avoiding a transfer, the trustee is entitled to recover *either the property transferred* or, if ordered by the court, *its value.* [B.C. § 550(a)]

3. From Whom Trustee May Recover

The trustee may seek recovery from any of the following parties:

- the initial transferee;
- the entity whom the initial transfer was designed to benefit; or
- any future transferee after the first transfer. [B.C. § 550(a)]

a. Initial Transferee

Unlike a secondary or other subsequent transferee, the initial person to whom the debtor makes a transfer cannot defend against the trustee's recovery action by claiming good faith or lack of knowledge of the voidability of the transaction. Thus, whether an entity is an initial transferee is important to determining the party from whom the trustee may recover the property transferred in the avoided transaction.

(i) Conduit Test

An entity that receives a transfer directly from the debtor is an *initial transferee.* Courts, however, have carved out an exception for initial transferees "who are 'mere conduits' with no real control" over the transferred funds. Under the *"control" or "conduit" test,* an entity is an initial transferee "only if [it] exercise[s] legal control over the assets received, such that [it] [has] the right to use the assets for [its] own purposes, and not if [it] merely served as a conduit for assets that were under the actual control of the debtor-transferor or the real initial transferee." [**Andreini & Co. v. Pony Express Delivery Services,** 440 F.3d 1296 (11th Cir. 2006); *see also* **Martinez v. Hutton (*In re* Harwell),** 628 F.3d 1313 (11th Cir. 2010) (in addition to showing transferee's lack of control over the assets received also requiring good faith on the part of that transferee in a fraudulent conveyance case)] For example, banks and insurance brokers are fiduciaries or agents for the debtor and, thus, may have limited control over the funds transferred to them. [*See* **Andreini & Co.,** *supra*]

e.g. **Example:** Insurance Broker ("Broker") arranges insurance coverage for its clients and bills those clients for the premiums due under the relevant insurance policies. Under state law, premium payments must be deposited into a client trust account with Broker. When Broker receives premiums, it sends those payments on to the insurance company. Debtor wrote a check to Broker's client trust account to cover premiums due for Debtor's workers' compensation insurance. Broker then transferred the premium payments to the insurance company, because those premiums either were overdue or shortly due. Unbeknownst to Broker, Debtor was in serious financial trouble, and its premium check bounced. About three weeks later, Debtor directly wired the amount due on the bounced check to Broker's client trust account. Two days later, Debtor filed for relief under Chapter 11. Both the bankruptcy and district courts concluded that Broker was an initial transferee from whom the trustee could recover the funds wired by Debtor into Broker's client trust account. The Eleventh Circuit, however, reversed after concluding that Broker was *not* an initial transferee. The court provided several reasons for its conclusion. First, Broker never intended to become a creditor of Debtor; instead, it was simply Broker's practice to immediately forward premium payments received in the client trust account. Second, Broker did not know of Debtor's financial problems and Debtor had never before sent Broker an insufficient funds check. Third, Debtor's check to make good on the earlier bounced check was transferred directly into Broker's client trust account. Under state law, Broker had limited control over the account. Broker was a fiduciary of the trust account monies, which could be used only to pay clients' insurance premiums. Debtor's transfer to Broker's client trust account was a preference and avoidable; however, the trustee could not recover the money from Broker as an initial transferee under § 550(a)(1). [**Andreini & Co.,** *supra*]

b. Exception for Good Faith Future Transferees

The trustee may not recover from a ***future transferee*** who (i) did not know that the transfer was voidable, (ii) took the transfer in ***good faith,*** and (iii) ***gave value*** in exchange. A future transferee who gives value, takes in good faith, and lacked knowledge of the voidability of the transfer ***shelters*** all subsequent ***good faith transferees.*** [B.C. § 550(b)]

(i) Value

For purposes of this exception, value includes the "satisfaction or securing of a present or antecedent debt." [B.C. § 550(b)(1)]

 Example: Debtor transfers a painting to Allen, the initial transferee. Allen, in turn, sells the painting to Barbara, who pays value, in good faith, and without knowing that the transfer to Allen was voidable. Barbara, in turn, gives the painting to Carl as a gift. Carl takes the painting in good faith. Carl has not paid value, but because Barbara "shelters" Carl, the trustee may not recover the painting or its value from Carl.

c. Insiders and Non-Insiders

With the Bankruptcy Reform Act of 1994, Congress provided protection from trustee recovery actions to non-insiders in preference cases involving insiders. Thus, if a trustee avoids a preference made between 90 days and one year prior to bankruptcy for the benefit of a creditor that is an insider, the trustee may not *recover* the preferential transfer from a transferee that is not an insider. [B.C. § 550(c)] With BAPCPA, Congress expanded the protection for non-insiders in preference actions involving insiders. The Code now provides that if the trustee avoids a preferential transfer made to a non-insider between 90 days and one year prior to bankruptcy for the benefit of a creditor that is an insider, the transfer is *avoided only* as to the insider, not the non-insider. [B.C. § 547(i)]

 Example: On January 1, Debtor Corporation, while insolvent, paid $100,000 to Bank in full satisfaction of an unsecured antecedent loan, which Officer of

Debtor Corporation had guaranteed. Still insolvent on June 1, Debtor Corporation filed a voluntary bankruptcy petition. The trustee can *avoid* the January 1 transfer as a preference, and the transfer is considered avoided only as to Officer. [B.C. § 547(i)] Even though the transfer occurred more than 90 days before bankruptcy, it benefited Officer, an insider-guarantor, and was made within one year before the bankruptcy petition was filed. [B.C. § 547(b)(4)(B)] The trustee cannot *recover* the $100,000 from Bank, a non-insider; any recovery must come from Officer, the insider-guarantor. [B.C. § 550(c)]

4. Single Satisfaction

A trustee who has avoided a transfer is permitted only one satisfaction in the case. [B.C. § 550(d)]

5. Good Faith Transferee's Lien

If the trustee recovers from a good faith transferee under § 550(a), the transferee receives a *lien on the property recovered,* for the purpose of securing the cost of *the lesser* of:

- the cost of any *improvements* she made after the transfer, less any profits from the property; or

- the amount by which such improvements enhanced the property's value. [B.C. § 550(e)(1)]

a. What Is an Improvement?

Improvements include any of the following:

(i) *physical additions* or changes to the property;

(ii) property *repairs;*

(iii) *payment of taxes* on the property;

(iv) *payment of any debt secured by a lien that is superior or equal* to the rights of the trustee; and

(v) *preservation of the property.* [B.C. § 550(e)(2)]

e.g. **Example:** Dan and Ben are long-time friends. A year ago, Ben loaned Dan, who was in financial trouble, $25,000. Dan recently filed for relief under Chapter 7. About two months prior to filing for bankruptcy, Dan gave Ben an old camper worth about $20,000 as repayment for the loan. Ben has spent about $5,000 refurbishing the camper and has had offers to buy it for $30,000. The trustee will be able to avoid the transfer of the camper to Ben as a preference under § 547(b). In addition, the trustee can recover the property from Ben, who is an initial transferee. So long as Ben is a good faith transferee, however, he will have a lien on the camper in the amount of $5,000, which is the lesser of the cost of improvements and the $10,000 increase in value of the camper due to Ben's improvements.

6. Statute of Limitations

To recover property or its value under section 550, the trustee must institute an action before the earlier of (i) *one year* after the corresponding transfer was avoided, or (ii) the *time of the closing or dismissal* of the case. [B.C. § 550(f)]

Chapter Seven
Claims of Creditors

Chapter Approach

This chapter discusses (i) who the various claimants are in a bankruptcy case; (ii) how they may qualify to participate in the distribution of the assets of the estate; and (iii) which kinds of claims are paid ahead of others. You must understand the following issues to answer exam questions on these topics. Use the following general approach.

1. Ordinarily, the *filing of a proof of claim* by a creditor or a *proof of interest* by an equity security holder is the first step taken by an entity seeking payment in the case, although it is not required in all instances. Remember that if a creditor does not file a proof of claim, the debtor, trustee, or a co-debtor or surety may file one on the creditor's behalf.

2. Next ascertain *whether a claim is allowable* under Bankruptcy Code § 502. Allowance is the basis for the distribution of assets of the estate, whether in a Chapter 7 liquidation case or pursuant to a repayment plan under Chapter 11, 12, or 13. If a claim is not allowed, the creditor will not receive a distributive share of the estate.

3. If an exam question requires you to evaluate a *secured claim,* be sure to determine the value of the property that secures it, because the claim is deemed secured only *up to the value of the collateral.* Therefore, if the claim is undersecured, it will be necessary to bifurcate the claim into two claims: one secured and the other unsecured.

4. When considering *unsecured claims,* determine whether a particular claim fits into any of the *ten priority categories,* which are paid ahead of the rest of the general unsecured claims. The first priority claims are domestic support obligations, followed, in order, by administrative expenses, involuntary case gap claims, wages and commissions, employee benefit contributions, claims of grain farmers or United States fishermen, consumer "layaway" claims, taxes, claims of certain federal regulators for the debtor's failure to maintain the capital requirements of an insured depository institution, and claims for death or personal injury resulting from operation of a motor vehicle or vessel while intoxicated.

5. Check the facts of the question for a *claim of a co-debtor or surety* who has paid the principal creditor. Note that the co-debtor or surety must elect between a claim for reimbursement or contribution, on one hand, or a claim for subrogation to the rights of the principal creditor, on the other.

6. Finally, keep in mind that, sometimes, certain claims or interests are *subordinated* in bankruptcy, such as a claim governed by an enforceable subordination agreement, a claim for rescission or damages arising from the purchase or sale of a security of the debtor, or a claim involving some misconduct on the part of the claimant that triggers the doctrine of equitable subordination.

A. Filing Proofs of Claims

1. Claim

The Code defines a claim as a "*right to payment,* whether or not such right is reduced to judgment, liquidated, unliquidated, fixed, contingent, matured, unmatured, disputed, undisputed, legal, equitable, secured, or unsecured." [B.C. § 101(5)(A)]

Example: Husband and Wife were in divorce proceedings when Husband filed for relief under Chapter 7. Wife timely filed a proof of claim for approximately $578,000 against Husband's estate based on an estimate of her expected share of the marital assets.

Husband argued that Wife's interest in equitably dividing the marital property in Husband's bankruptcy estate was not a "claim," because the state court had not entered a final divorce decree and under state law a spouse's right to share in marital property through equitable distribution arises upon entry of the divorce judgment. The court found that even though there was no final divorce judgment when Husband filed for bankruptcy, Wife's interest, though "unliquidated and contingent on a final decree apportioning marital property, perhaps unmatured, and likely disputed" constituted a claim under § 101(5). Noting the "expansive definition" of "claim" in the Bankruptcy Code, the court distinguished between when a claim *accrues* and when a claim *exists*. While Wife's right to payment was contingent on entry of a final divorce decree, that right to payment *existed* at the time of bankruptcy filing; therefore, she had a claim in Husband's bankruptcy case. [*In re* **Ruitenberg**, 745 F.3d 647 (3d Cir. 2014)]

a. Equitable Remedy

The right to an equitable remedy for breach of performance is considered a claim if the breach gives rise to a *right to payment.* [B.C. § 101(5)(B)]

(i) Environmental Cleanup Order

A state's right to the payment of a money judgment to enforce a state court's environmental cleanup order against the debtor is a claim. [**Ohio v. Kovacs,** 469 U.S. 274 (1985)]

(1) Trend

"Courts have disagreed about whether injunctions requiring a debtor to clean up contaminated property constitute 'claims.' So long as a monetary payment is not being sought, or monetary payment is viewed as a 'suboptimal' remedy for the creditor, a growing number of courts will not classify a request for injunctive relief as a claim." [2 Collier ¶ 101.05(5)]

(ii) Covenant not to Compete

While the courts are split on whether an equitable remedy for breach of a covenant not to compete constitutes a claim, the majority of courts have held that the right to equitable relief for breach of such covenants is not a claim for purposes of § 101(5). Some courts have relied on the Supreme Court's reasoning in *Kovacs* that complying with an injunction does not require the expenditure of money. Other courts have concluded that because injunctive relief is granted when the remedy at law is inadequate no alternative right to payment exists, as required by § 101(5)(B). [*In re* **Lafemina,** 2017 WL 4404254 (Bankr. E.D. N.Y. 2017) (discussing approaches)] If neither state law nor the parties' agreement provides for a right to payment as an alternative to injunctive relief, then a creditor's right to equitable relief for breach of a covenant not to compete does not constitute a claim and, therefore, is not dischargeable in bankruptcy. [*See In re* **Hurvitz,** 554 B.R. 35 (Bankr. D. Mass. 2016)]

b. Claims Against Property

A claim against property of the debtor is also considered to be a claim against the debtor. [B.C. § 102(2)]

c. Broad Interpretation of "Claim"

As the Supreme Court has made clear in several decisions, "Congress intended . . . to adopt the broadest available definition of 'claim.' " [**Johnson v. Home State Bank,** 501 U.S. 78 (1991); *see* **Pennsylvania Dep't of Public Welfare v. Davenport,** 495 U.S. 552 (1990) ("Congress chose expansive language" when defining the term "claim"); **Ohio v. Kovacs,** 469 U.S. 274 (1984) ("Congress desired a broad definition of 'claim' ")] Recognizing this intent to give "claim" an expansive definition in the bankruptcy context, a majority of courts have held that pre-petition claims may include causes of action arising from pre-bankruptcy conduct and pre-petition legal relationships, even if the cause of action under state or other applicable nonbankruptcy law did not accrue until after the petition was filed. [*In re* **Johns-Manville Corp.,** 57 B.R. 680 (Bankr. S.D. N.Y. 1986)]

e.g. **Example:** Victim was a user of an intrauterine device ("IUD") manufactured and sold by Debtor Corporation. The device caused serious bodily harm to Victim before Debtor Corporation filed a Chapter 11 petition, although Victim did not discover the cause of her injury until shortly after the bankruptcy case was filed. Victim has a pre-petition claim that arose "when the acts giving rise to the alleged liability were performed." [*In re* **A.H. Robins Co.,** 63 B.R. 986 (Bankr. E.D. Va. 1986), *aff'd,* 839 F.2d 198 (4th Cir. 1988)]

e.g. **Example:** Debtors, who operated a joint dental practice, filed for relief under Chapter 7. Patient received dental treatment from both Debtors prior to bankruptcy. After the bankruptcy filing, Patient experienced serious problems with the dental work and filed suit in state court against Debtors alleging negligent treatment. Debtors moved for sanctions for violation of the automatic stay, so Patient filed an adversary proceeding in the bankruptcy court seeking a declaration that her claim arose post-petition upon discovery of her injuries. The bankruptcy court held that Patient's claim arose at the time of Debtors' pre-petition conduct. Thus, the automatic stay prohibited her state court action against Debtors. [*In re* **Edge,** 60 B.R. 690 (Bankr. M.D. Tenn. 1986)]

d. Future Tort Claims

Courts have grappled with how to deal with future tort claimants in mass tort cases. The problem is the same regardless of the nature of the product involved—asbestos, silicone gel implants, or IUDs. The debtor files for relief under Chapter 11 and there are an unknown number of people who have used or been affected by the debtor's product, but have not yet manifested an injury. The problem is best illustrated by the asbestos tort claims of victims who have been exposed to asbestos but *whose injuries have not yet become apparent.* For example, mesothelioma, which results from exposure to asbestos, does not occur until decades after exposure. These circumstances possibly are covered by the broad definition of "claim." Significantly, courts have held that these potential tort claimants are parties in interest and are entitled to the appointment of a legal representative. [B.C. § 1109(b); *In re* **Johns-Manville Corp.,** 36 B.R. 743 (Bankr. S.D. N.Y. 1984), *aff'd* 52 B.R. 940 (S.D. N.Y. 1985) (finding that future tort claimants "are parties in interest under Code Section 1109(b) in need of a legal representative to act independently and impartially where appropriate in the case")] The bankruptcy court in the *Johns-Manville* case confirmed a plan that provided for an Asbestos Health Trust to satisfy the claims of present and future asbestos victims. Funding for the trust included monies from settlements with the firm's insurers and a percentage of future firm profits. But all claimants, both present and future, were subject to an "injunction channeling all asbestos-related personal injury claims to the Trust," thereby precluding any suit against the reorganized company and limiting claimants to recovery from the Trust. [*See* **Kane v. Johns-Manville Corp.,** 843 F.2d 636 (2d Cir. 1988) (describing the Trust)] The Bankruptcy Code now provides for the type of trust/injunction used in the *Johns-Manville* case in Chapter 11 cases involving *asbestos-related liabilities.* [B.C. § 524(g)]

2. Claimants

a. Who Must File

Generally, for the claim or interest to be allowed, a *creditor,* whether secured or unsecured, must file a proof of claim and an *equity security holder must* file a proof of interest. [Bankruptcy Rule 3002]

b. Who May File

A secured creditor, an unsecured creditor, or an indenture trustee may file a *proof of claim.* An equity security holder may file a *proof of interest.* [B.C. § 501(a)] If a creditor fails to file a proof of claim, a co-debtor, surety, or guarantor, or the debtor or trustee may file a proof of such claim. [B.C. § 501(b), (c)]

(i) Creditor

The Bankruptcy Code defines a creditor to include an entity

(1) holding a *claim against the debtor* that arose or is deemed to have arisen *at or prior to the order for relief* [B.C. § 101(10)(A)];

(2) possessing a community claim [B.C. § 101(10)(C)]; or

(3) that has a claim *against the estate* for any of the following:

    (a) in an *involuntary case,* a claim arising in the *ordinary course* of debtor's business during *the gap period* between the start of the case and the order for relief [B.C. §§ 101(10)(B), 502(f)];

    (b) a claim arising from the *rejection* of an *executory contract or unexpired lease* [B.C. §§ 101(10)(B), 502(g)];

    (c) a claim arising from the *recovery of property* under §§ 522, 550, or 553 [B.C. §§ 101(10)(B), 502(h)];

    (d) a claim that arises *post-petition* for a *tax entitled to priority* under § 507(a)(8) [B.C. §§ 101(10)(B), 502(i)]; or

    (e) a claim that arises *post-petition but prior to conversion* in a case converted from chapter 11, 12 or 13, except a claim for administrative expenses. [B.C. §§ 101(10)(B), 348(d)]

(ii) Indenture Trustee

An indenture trustee is a trustee under a mortgage, deed of trust, or indenture contract relating to an outstanding security that constitutes a *claim* against the debtor, a *claim secured by a lien* against any of the debtor's property, or an *equity security* of the debtor. For example, if the debtor issues $10 million of debentures, the indenture is the bond contract, and the indenture trustee is the representative of the bondholders. [B.C. §§ 101(28), (29)]

(iii) Equity Security Holder

An equity security holder is one in possession of a share in a corporation, an interest of a limited partner in a limited partnership, or a warrant or right (other than a right to convert) to buy or sell an equity security interest. [B.C. §§ 101(16), (17)]

(iv) Co-Debtor, Surety, or Guarantor

A co-debtor, surety, or guarantor of the debtor may file a proof of claim *for a creditor* if the creditor has not timely filed a proof of claim. [B.C. § 501(b)] The purpose of this filing is to decrease the surety's ultimate liability to the extent of a distribution to the principal creditor from the estate. [Bankruptcy Rule 3005(a)]

(v) Debtor or Trustee

If a creditor does not timely file a proof of claim, the debtor or the trustee may file a proof of claim *in the creditor's name* within 30 days after the expiration of the time provided for filing claims. [B.C. § 501(c); Bankruptcy Rule 3004] The debtor may wish to file a proof of claim if the debt owed to the creditor is nondischargeable, because any distribution in the bankruptcy case would reduce the debtor's post-bankruptcy liability for a debt that is not discharged. [*See* B.C. § 501(c) Historical and Statutory Notes ("[t]he purpose of [§ 501(c)] is mainly to protect the debtor if the creditor's claim is nondischargeable"); Bankruptcy Rule 3004, 2005 Advisory Committee Notes (giving the debtor the chance "to file a claim ensures that the claim will participate in any distribution . . . [which] is particularly important for claims that are nondischargeable.")]

3. Time to File

The time within which to file a proof of claim or interest depends on the chapter of the Bankruptcy Code governing the particular case.

a. Chapters 7, 12, and 13

In a *voluntary case begun in Chapter 7, 12, or 13,* a proof of claim ordinarily must be filed no later than *70 days* after the order for relief. In an *involuntary Chapter 7 case,* a proof of claim is timely filed if it is filed no later than *90 days* after the order for relief.

b. Converted Cases

In a case *converted to Chapter 12 or 13,* a proof of claim is timely filed if it is filed no later than *70 days* after the order of conversion. [Bankruptcy Rule 3002(c); 2017 Advisory Committee Notes] In a case converted from Chapter 11, 12, or 13 to Chapter 7, all claims *actually* filed before conversion of the case are considered automatically filed in the Chapter 7 case. Thus, a second filing is not required. [Bankruptcy Rule 1019(3)] However, a claim must be filed if it was only deemed filed in a case converted from Chapter 11.

c. Chapter 11

In a Chapter 11 case, the court fixes and sends notice of a *bar date,* which operates as a deadline for the filing of proofs of claims or interests. [Bankruptcy Rules 3003(c)(3), 2002(a)(7)] Any claim or interest listed in the debtor's schedules is *deemed filed automatically* for the scheduled amount, unless the claim or interest is scheduled as contingent, unliquidated, or disputed. [B.C. § 1111(a); Bankruptcy Rule 3003(b)] Thus, if the debtor schedules a creditor's claim and does not indicate that the claim is contingent, unliquidated, or disputed, the creditor need not file a proof of claim.

d. Exceptions

The following are *exceptions to the general time periods* for filing proofs of claims.

(i) Governmental Unit Claims

With the exception of a claim resulting from a tax return filed under § 1308, a claim by a *governmental unit* in a Chapter 7, 12 or 13 case is timely if it is filed *no later than 180 days* after the order for relief. A claim by a governmental unit resulting from a *tax return filed under § 1308* is timely if it is filed *no later than 180 days* after the order for relief or *60 days* after the filing of the tax return. [Bankruptcy Rule 3002(c)(1)]

(ii) Infants or Incompetent Persons

In a Chapter 7, 11, 12 or 13 case, the court may extend the time period for filing a proof of claim by an *infant, incompetent person, or the representative* of the infant or incompetent person if extending the time period is in *the interest of justice* and will not *unduly delay administration of the case.* [Bankruptcy Rules 3002(c)(2), 3003(c)(3)]

(iii) Entry of Judgment

In a Chapter 7, 11, 12 or 13 case, an *unsecured claim* arising in favor of an entity or that becomes allowable as a result of the entry of a judgment may be filed *within 30 days after the judgment becomes final if* the judgment is for recovery of money or property from the entity, or denial or avoidance of the entity's interest in property. [Bankruptcy Rules 3002(c)(3), 3003(c)(3)]

(iv) Rejection of Executory Contract or Unexpired Lease

In a Chapter 7, 11, 12 or 13 case, the bankruptcy court may set a time for filing of claims arising from the rejection of executory contracts or unexpired leases. [Bankruptcy Rules 3002(c)(4), 3003(c)(3)]

(v) Chapter 7 "No Asset" Cases

If the Chapter 7 trustee notifies the court that unsecured creditors will receive a dividend in the Chapter 7 case, after creditors have received a notice indicating that no dividend would be paid, the bankruptcy clerk must give *at least 90 days' notice* by mail to creditors of the fact that a dividend will be paid and of the date by which creditors must file a proof of claim. [Bankruptcy Rules 3002(c)(5), 2002(e)]

(vi) Creditor Motion to Extend Time Period

In a Chapter 7, 11, 12, or 13 case, a creditor may file a motion to extend the time within which to file a proof of claim. The creditor may file such a motion either before or after the time period for filing proofs of claim has expired. The bankruptcy court may extend the time period if the court finds either of the following:

(1) notice was insufficient to give the creditor time to file a proof of claim, because the *debtor failed to timely file the list of creditors' names and addresses* required by Bankruptcy Rule 1007(a); or

(2) notice was mailed to a *foreign address* and under *the circumstances was insufficient to give the creditor a reasonable time* to file a proof of claim.

The court may extend the time period *no more than 60 days* from the order granting the creditor's motion. [Bankruptcy Rules 3002(c)(6), 3003(c)(3)]

(vii) Secured Creditor on Debtor's Principal Residence

In a Chapter 7, 12 or 13 case, a proof of claim filed by the holder of a claim secured by the *debtor's principal residence* is timely filed if:

(1) the proof of claim and the documents required by Bankruptcy Rule 3001(c)(2) are filed *no later than 70 days* after the order for relief [Bankruptcy Rules 3002(c)(7)(A), 3001(c)(2); Official Form 410A]; and

(2) the writing supporting creditor's interest in the property securing the claim, e.g., a copy of the mortgage, and evidence that the creditor's security interest is perfected are filed as supplements to the claim *no later than 120 days* after the order for relief. [Bankruptcy Rules 3002(c)(7)(B), 3001(c)(1), (d)]

e. Late Filing

(i) Filing by Debtor

In a Chapter 7, 11, 12 or 13 case, if a creditor fails to timely file a proof of claim, the debtor or trustee may file a proof of claim within *30 days after the claims filing period* provided by the relevant bankruptcy rule. [Bankruptcy Rules 3004, 3002(c), 3003(c)]

(ii) Excusable Neglect

In a Chapter 11 case, filing a proof of claim after the bar date is permitted based on excusable neglect. [Bankruptcy Rule 9006(b)(1)] Bankruptcy Rule 9006(b) provides that the bankruptcy court may enlarge the time for filing a proof of claim in a Chapter 7, 12 or 13 case only according to the terms provided in Bankruptcy Rule 3002(c); in other words, the excusable neglect standard of Rule 9006(b) does not apply in Chapters 7, 12, or 13. [Bankruptcy Rule 9006(b)(3); *see, e.g.,* **In re Sunland, Inc.,** 536 B.R. 920 (Bankr. D. N.M. 2015) (explaining that Bankruptcy Rule 3002(c) governs claim filing deadlines in Chapter 7 and finding that "Rule 3002(c) has no 'excusable neglect' provision"); **In re Jackson, 482 B.R. 659** (Bankr. S.D. Fla. 2012) (creditor failing to timely file a proof of claim may not rely on "excusable neglect" in Chapter 7, 12 or 13 cases); **Gold v. Gold (*In re* Gold),** 375 B.R. 316 (Bankr. N.D. Tex. 2007) (in Chapter 13, "Rule 9006(b)(3) does not permit extending the Rule 3002(c) deadline for 'excusable neglect' ")]

(1) Factors to Consider

In determining whether there is excusable neglect sufficient to allow a late filing in a Chapter 11 case, the Supreme Court has held that all relevant circumstances should be considered, including:

(a) any *prejudice to the debtor,*

(b) the *length of the delay* and its effect on judicial proceedings,

(c) the *reason for the delay* and whether it was within the reasonable control of the party and her attorney, and

(d) whether the party and counsel acted in *good faith.*

The Court ruled that the issue is whether the *neglect of the party and the attorney* is excusable and held that clients will "be held accountable for the acts and omissions of their chosen counsel." [**Pioneer Investment Services Co. v. Brunswick Associates Limited Partnership,** 507 U.S. 380 (1993) (holding that neglect was excusable because of unusual and inconspicuous placement of bar date notice, and the absence of any evidence of bad faith or prejudice to debtor or the administration of justice)] The decision in *Pioneer,* according to the author of a leading treatise, created a "concept of excusable neglect governed, not by an easily ascertainable standard, but by one that leads to unpredictable results, dependent upon the equities of each case." [10 Collier ¶ 9006.06(3)]

(2) Untimely Amendments to Timely Filed Claim

With the exception of certain late-filed claims in Chapter 7, an untimely filed claim is not allowed. [B.C. § 502(b)(9)] If a creditor files a timely claim, however, and later files an untimely amendment, is the amendment allowed? In making this determination, a bankruptcy court must determine whether the amendment relates back to the timely filed claim or is nothing more than a new claim disguised as an amendment. Generally, a bankruptcy court will allow an untimely amendment that: (i) cures a defect in the original claim, (ii) describes the claim with greater particularity, or (iii) pleads a new theory of recovery on the facts stated in the original claim. [*In re* **Peak Web LLC,** 2017 WL 5197117 (Bankr. D. Ore. 2017)]

4. Claims Deemed Pre-Petition

The following post-petition claims are treated as pre-petition claims for the ***purpose of filing*** [B.C. § 501(d)]:

a. ***a co-debtor's or surety's claim for reimbursement or contribution*** that becomes fixed after the bankruptcy petition has been filed [B.C. § 502(e)(2)];

b. ***a claim arising in the ordinary course of the debtor's business*** or financial affairs after the filing of an ***involuntary petition*** but before the earlier of the order for relief or the appointment of a trustee [B.C. § 502(f)];

c. ***a claim arising from the rejection of an executory contract or an unexpired lease*** that the trustee or the debtor in possession has not assumed [B.C. § 502(g)];

d. ***a claim arising from the recovery of property*** by the trustee or the debtor [B.C. § 502(h)];

e. ***a post-petition tax claim entitled to eighth priority*** [B.C. §§ 502(i), 507(a)(8)] (because eighth priority tax claims usually are pre-petition, § 502(i) covers the occasional situation where a tax claim arises post-petition as a result of pre-petition activities of the debtor); and

f. ***a claim,*** other than one for administrative expenses, ***arising after the order for relief*** in a Chapter 11, 12, or 13 case, but ***before the case is converted to another chapter.*** [B.C. § 348(d)]

5. Secured Claims: Chapters 7, 12, and 13

Prior to December 1, 2017, the bankruptcy rules required an unsecured creditor to file a proof of claim and an equity security holder to file a proof of interest. A secured creditor did not have to file a proof of claim unless a party in interest "requested a determination and allowance or disallowance under § 502." [Bankruptcy Rule 3002, Notes of Advisory Committee] Rule 3002(a) was amended, however, and now a secured creditor must file a proof of claim "in order to have an allowed claim." [Bankruptcy Rule 3002, Notes of Advisory Committee on 2017 Amendments]

Note: A secured creditor's lien is not void simply because the creditor fails to file a proof of claim. [B.C. § 506(d)(2); Bankruptcy Rule 3002(a)]

6. Secured Claims: Chapter 11

In a Chapter 11 case, a secured creditor need not file a proof of claim if the debtor correctly schedules the creditor's debt and does not list the debt as contingent, unliquidated, or disputed. [Bankruptcy Rule 3003(c)(2)]

7. Fuel Use Tax

In 2005, with the passage of BAPCPA, Congress added a provision to the Code permitting the filing of a single fuel use tax claim to cover fuel use taxes that the debtor owes to various state tax authorities. [4 Collier ¶ 501.06] This new subsection applies if the requirements of 49 U.S.C. § 31701 are met. [B.C. § 501(e)]

B. Allowance of Claims

1. General Rule: Allowance

Unless a party in interest objects, a claim or interest that has been filed will be allowed by the court and will serve as the basis for distribution. [B.C. § 502(a)] The Supreme Court has stated that " 'state law governs the substance of claims' " and that "claims enforceable under applicable state law will be allowed in bankruptcy unless they are expressly disallowed. See 11 U.S.C. § 502(b)." [**Travelers Casualty & Surety Co. v. PG&E,** 549 U.S. 443 (2007)]

a. Partnership Debtor

If the debtor is a partnership in a Chapter 7 case, a creditor of any of the general partners of the partnership is deemed to be a party in interest for the purpose of objecting to allowance of a claim. [B.C. § 502(a)]

b. Objection

Ordinarily, if an objection to a claim is raised, the court, after notice and a hearing, determines the amount of the claim *as of the date of the filing of the bankruptcy petition,* and allows the claim unless it falls within one of the following recognized exceptions. [B.C. § 502(b)]

2. Exceptions to Allowance

A claim for any of the following items is not allowable in a bankruptcy case. [B.C. § 502(b)]

a. Claim Unenforceable Due to Valid Defense

A claim that is unenforceable against the debtor and her property because the debtor has a *valid defense* under any applicable law or agreement, e.g., the statute of limitations or failure of consideration, is not allowable. Thus, the trustee may assert any defense that is available to the debtor with regard to a creditor's claim. [B.C. § 558] Section 502(b)(1)'s exception does not include a claim that is unenforceable solely because it is unmatured or contingent. [B.C. § 502(b)(1)]

Note: If state law does not extinguish a debt on which the statute of limitations has run, a creditor may file a claim for such a debt, because the debtor's liability for the debt still constitutes a claim under § 101(5)(A). [**Midland Funding, LLC v. Johnson,** 137 S. Ct. 1407 (2017) (specific issue arose under Fair Debt Collection Practices Act)] The trustee, of course, may object to the claim on the basis that the statute of limitations on the debt has expired, and the bankruptcy court may disallow the claim.

b. Claim for Post-Petition Interest

Unmatured interest on an ***unsecured claim*** is generally not allowable. Unmatured interest is interest that is not yet due and payable at the time of the bankruptcy filing. [B.C. § 502(b)(2); *see **In re** Energy Future Holdings Corp.*, 540 B.R. 109 (Bankr. D. Del. 2015) (sustaining debtor's objection to payment of post-petition interest and holding that creditor's allowed unsecured claim was limited to principal, accrued fees, and interest due as of the petition filing date)]

Note: In the rare case in which the bankruptcy estate is ***solvent,*** unsecured creditors are entitled to post-petition interest. [4 Collier ¶ 502.03(3)(c)] For example, in a Chapter 7 case, unsecured creditors will receive post-petition interest *if* all allowed (i) priority claims, (ii) timely filed unsecured claims, (iii) untimely filed unsecured claims, and (iv) claims for fines, penalties, or punitive damages that are not compensation for pecuniary loss are paid first and in full. [B.C. § 726(a)(5)]

c. Claim for Unsecured Property Tax in Excess of Debtor's Equity

An unsecured property tax claim is allowable, but only up to the debtor's equity in the property. Amounts owed in excess of the debtor's equity in the property are not allowed. The rationale for this limitation is to ensure that the estate is not depleted by paying taxes on property with no value to the estate. [B.C. § 502(b)(3); 4 Collier ¶ 502.03(4)(a)]

e.g. **Example:** Debtor, LLC, which owns a vacant hotel property, filed for relief under Chapter 11. At the time that Debtor filed for bankruptcy, it owed County $3,786,980, of which $1,916,782 was for taxes and $1,870,198 was for water and sewage charges. The hotel, however, was worth only $690,000. County filed a claim in Debtor's bankruptcy case for $3,786,980. The court held that § 502(b)(3) only applies to the tax portion of the County's claim, not to the charges for water and sewage. The tax portion of County's claim exceeded the value of the bankruptcy estate's interest in the hotel by $1,226,782 (tax portion of claim of $1,916,782 − $690,000 value of hotel); therefore, the court disallowed $1,226,782 of County's claim under § 502(b)(3). County has an allowed claim for $2,560,198 − $690,000 (taxes) + $1,870,198 (water and sewage). [***In re** Shefa, LLC,* 524 B.R. 717 (Bankr. E.D. Mich. 2015)]

Note: A tax claim disallowed under § 502(b)(3) is not entitled to priority under § 507(a)(8) and is not entitled to any distribution in the bankruptcy case. [*See **In re** Shefa, supra*]

d. Unreasonable Claim for Insider's or Attorney's Services

The services of an insider or an attorney of the debtor are allowable, but only up to a reasonable value. Amounts claimed above a reasonable value are not allowed. [B.C. § 502(b)(4)]

e. Unmatured Claim for Domestic Support Obligation

A claim for a nondischargeable domestic support obligation that is unmatured as of the date of bankruptcy is not allowable. [B.C. §§ 502(b)(5), 523(a)(5)]

e.g. **Example:** Husband and Wife divorced prior to Husband's filing for relief under Chapter 11. Under the terms of the parties' divorce agreement, Husband was to pay Wife $33,333.34 each month for a period of ten years. At the time of his bankruptcy filing, Husband was current on these monthly payments. Wife filed a claim in Husband's bankruptcy case for $2.33 million in *future* spousal support payments. Wife asserted that the future spousal support payments were not "unmatured" because the divorce judgment no longer could be modified or reviewed and, therefore, the spousal support payments had vested. The bankruptcy court disagreed and held that the mere fact that Husband could not modify or seek review of the divorce agreement did not transform the future spousal support payments into a matured obligation. The court found that the payments were not yet due and owing and, thus, were unmatured and subject to the limitation provided by § 502(b)(4). The court disallowed Wife's claim for $2.33 million in spousal support payments due from Husband in the future. But, the court explained that while the Wife's domestic support obligation was not an allowed claim it still was nondischargeable. [*In re* **Meier**, 2014 WL 6686541 (Bankr. N.D. Ill. 2014)]

f.   Excessive Claim for Damages for Terminated Lease of Real Property

A *lessor's damages* for termination of a *lease of real property* are allowable, but only up to the *greater* of the rent due under the lease, without acceleration, for one year *or* 15% of the remaining term of the lease, not to exceed three years, after the earlier of the date of bankruptcy or the date the property was repossessed or relinquished. Claims for damages above that amount are not allowed. [B.C. § 502(b)(6)(A)] The landlord's claim also is allowable for any unpaid rent due, without acceleration, as of the earlier of these two dates. Section 502(b)(6)'s cap does *not* apply to rent due and owing on the petition date. [B.C. § 502(b)(6)(B); 4 Collier ¶ 502.03(7)(e)]

e.g. **Example #1:** Debtor and Landlord sign a lease for ten years at a monthly rent of $10,000. Debtor repudiates the lease and immediately files for bankruptcy. Debtor is current on the rent at the time of bankruptcy filing, and at that time, there are seven years left on the lease. Landlord is quickly able to re-let the premises, but for only $7,500 per month, not $10,000 per month. Landlord files a claim in Debtor's bankruptcy case for $210,000 for the $2,500 difference in rent for the seven years (84 months) left on Debtor's lease. One year's rent is $120,000. Fifteen percent of the remaining term of the lease is 1.05 years (7 years x .15), which does not exceed three years, and amounts to $126,000 in rent (1.05 years x $120,000 yearly rent). Section 502(b)(6) provides for the *greater* of one year's rent ($120,000) or the rent for 15% of the remaining term, not to exceed three years ($126,000). Landlord's claim is not allowed for any amount in excess of $126,000. Therefore, Landlord may not recover for $84,000 ($210,000 − $126,000) in damages incurred by virtue of Debtor's breach of the lease.

e.g. **Example #2:** Same facts as in Example #1, except there are six years remaining on the lease at the time Debtor breaches and files for bankruptcy. Landlord's damages now are $180,000 (6 years at $30,000 [$2,500 per year difference x 12 months]). Landlord's claim, however, is allowable for only one year's rent of $120,000; the remaining $60,000 is disallowed under § 502(b)(6). The reason is that the remaining lease term now is less than 80 months. The calculation is as follows: 15% of the remaining six-year lease term is .9, which is less than three years, and translates into $108,000 (.9 x $120,000 yearly rent). Because one year's rent is greater than $108,000, Landlord's claim is disallowed for $60,000 ($180,000 damages − $120,000).

Shortcut: This section's language is complicated. A shortcut for determining which time period applies is as follows:

(i)   Remaining time on the lease is less than 80 months: the time period is one year (*see* Example #2 above).

(ii) Remaining time on the lease exceeds 240 months: the time period is three years, because 240 months equals 20 years, and 15% of 20 years is three years, which is the maximum allowed under the statute.

(iii) Remaining time on the lease is between 80 and 240 months: the time period is 15% of the remaining term of the lease (*see* Example #1 above).

[4 Collier ¶ 502.03(7)(c)]

g. Excessive Claim for Employer's Termination of Contract

An employee's damages for termination of an employment contract are allowable, but only up to *one year's compensation under the contract,* after the earlier of the date of the bankruptcy petition or the date the employee's performance was terminated. Claims for damages above that amount are not allowed. [B.C. § 502(b)(7)(A)] The employee's claim also is allowable for any unpaid wages on the earlier of the two dates. Section 502(b)(7)'s cap on the employee's claim does *not* apply to compensation due and owing on the petition date. [B.C. § 502(b)(7)(B)]

h. Claim for Employment Tax Credit

A claim that results from a reduction, due to late payment, in the amount of an otherwise applicable federal employment tax credit in connection with state unemployment insurance taxes is not allowable. [B.C. § 502(b)(8)]

i. Claim by Possessor of Estate Property or Transferee of Avoidable Transfer

Any claim of an entity that is in possession of property recoverable by the estate or that is a transferee of an avoidable transfer is not allowable *unless* the entity has returned the property or paid its value. [B.C. § 502(d)]

j. Tardy Claim

A tardily filed claim will be disallowed unless and to the extent permitted by the Federal Rules of Bankruptcy Procedure or unless one of the following exceptions applies. [B.C. § 502(b)(9); Bankruptcy Rule 3002(c)]

(i) The court may allow a late *nonpriority* unsecured claim if (1) the creditor did not have notice or actual knowledge of the bankruptcy case to be able to file his claim timely, but the claim was filed in time for distribution, or (2) there is money left in the estate after paying all claims beyond those specified in §§ 726(a)(1) and (a)(2). [B.C. §§ 502(b)(9), 726(a)(2)(C), (a)(3)]

(ii) The court may allow late *priority* claims, if filing was made before the *earlier* of (1) 10 days after mailing of the trustee's final report; and (2) the start of the trustee's distribution under § 726. [B.C. §§ 502(b)(9), 726(a)(1)]

Note: For late *administrative expense* claims, the bankruptcy court also must approve the tardy filing *for cause.* [B.C. § 503(a)]

(iii) *Governmental claims, other than for taxes under § 1308*, are timely filed if filed up to 180 days after the order for relief, unless the Federal Rules of Bankruptcy Procedure provide for a longer time. [B.C. § 502(b)(9); Bankruptcy Rule 3002(c)(1)] *Governmental claims for taxes under § 1308* are timely filed if filed no later than *180 days after the order for relief* or *60 days* after the date on which the return was filed. [B.C. §§ 502(b)(9), 1308; Bankruptcy Rule 3002(c)(1)]

THE FOLLOWING CLAIMS ARE NOT ALLOWABLE IN A BANKRUPTCY CASE IF THERE IS AN OBJECTION:

☑ Claims that *are unenforceable due to a valid defense,* other than claims that are unenforceable solely because they are unmatured or contingent

☑ *Post-petition or unmatured interest on unsecured claims* unless the estate is solvent

☑ Claims for an *unsecured property tax* in excess of the debtor's equity in the property

☑ Claims *above a reasonable value for the services of an insider or attorney of the debtor*

☑ Claims for *nondischargeable domestic support obligations* that are unmatured as of the date of the bankruptcy

☑ Claims for *damages for a terminated lease of real property in excess of* the amount allowable under the formula in Code § 502(b)(6)

☑ Claims for *damages for an employer's termination of an employment contract in excess of* one year's compensation *plus the wages owed* on the earlier of the date of bankruptcy or the employee's termination

☑ Claims for *disallowance of a federal employment tax credit* due to late payment of state unemployment insurance taxes

☑ Claims of *possessors of property recoverable by the estate,* and claims of *transferees of avoidable transfers,* unless the possessor or transferee has returned the property or paid its value

☑ Claims that are *filed tardily,* with certain exceptions

3. Estimation of Claims

If a claim is *contingent or unliquidated,* and the fixing or liquidation of it would cause undue delay in the administration of the bankruptcy case, the court must estimate the claim. This estimate is *for the purpose of allowance* and, in general, once allowed, the claim stands "on equal footing" with other allowed claims under § 502. [B.C. § 502(c)(1); 4 Collier ¶ 502.04(3)]

e.g. **Example:** Debtor Corporation, a manufacturer of asbestos-containing products that had seriously harmed the health of thousands of individuals, filed a Chapter 11 petition. Victim filed a motion to withdraw a proceeding to the district court for immediate trial of his personal injury claim in order to determine the amount of his damages and, thus, his claim against Debtor Corporation. The district court ruled against Victim and concluded that the motion to withdraw was premature. The court noted that Debtor Corporation had not yet developed a plan, and that the time and expense of thousands of individual trials to determine damages could "deplete the estate and leave other creditors with empty judgments." To avoid undue delay in the administration of the case, the bankruptcy judge could estimate the tort claim for the purpose of allowing the claim, and not for the purpose of distribution, since any trial of the latter issue had to occur in the district court. [*See In re* **Johns-Manville Corp.,** 45 B.R. 823 (S.D.N.Y. 1984)]

a. Equitable Remedy

Similarly, if a right to an equitable remedy for breach of performance gives rise to a right to payment, the court must estimate the claim for the purpose of allowance. [B.C. § 502(c)(2)]

4. Claim for Reimbursement or Contribution

The claim of a co-debtor, surety, or guarantor for reimbursement or contribution *will be disallowed* if (i) the claim is *contingent,* i.e., if the surety has not paid the principal creditor, at the time of allowance or disallowance; (ii) the *principal creditor's claim* is disallowed; *or* (iii) the *surety elects subrogation,* under § 509, to the principal creditor's rights instead of reimbursement or contribution. [B.C. § 502(e)(1)]

a. Payment by Co-Debtor, Surety, or Guarantor

If the co-debtor, surety, or guarantor pays the principal creditor after the petition has been filed, her claim for reimbursement or contribution then becomes fixed and will be allowed or disallowed as a *pre-petition claim.* [B.C. § 502(e)(2)]

5. Claims Deemed Pre-Petition

The following types of claims are considered pre-petition claims for the purpose of allowance or disallowance:

a. *claims arising in the ordinary course of the debtor's business or financial affairs* after the commencement of an *involuntary* case but before the earlier of the appointment of a trustee or the order for relief [B.C. § 502(f)];

b. *claims arising from the trustee's* or debtor in possession's *rejection of executory contracts or unexpired leases* that have not been assumed [B.C. § 502(g)];

c. *claims arising from the recovery of property* by the trustee or the debtor [B.C. §§ 502(h), 522(i), 550, 553];

d. *post-petition tax claims entitled to eighth priority* [B.C. §§ 502(i), 507(a)(8)] (while eighth priority tax claims generally are pre-petition claims, § 502(i) covers the situation in which a priority tax claim arises post-petition as a result of pre-petition activities of the debtor); and

e. *claims,* other than for administrative expenses, arising after the order for relief in a Chapter 11, 12, or 13 case but *prior to conversion to another chapter.* [B.C. § 348(d)]

6. Reduction of Claim on Unsecured Consumer Debt

With the passage of BAPCPA, Congress added a provision to § 502(b) that allows a debtor to move to *reduce by no more than 20%* the amount of a *claim for an unsecured consumer* debt. The section only applies if the following requirements are satisfied:

(a) the claim is for a *consumer debt* that is *completely unsecured* [B.C. § 502(k)(1)(A)];

(b) the creditor filing the claim *unreasonably refused to negotiate an alternative repayment schedule* that an approved nonprofit and credit counseling agency under § 111 proposed on the debtor's behalf [B.C. § 502(k)(1)(A)];

(c) the debtor's offer was made *at least 60 days* prior to filing of the petition [B.C. § 502(k)(1)(B)(i)];

(d) the debtor's offer provided for payment of *at least 60% of the debt* over a period not to exceed the loan's repayment period, or a reasonable extension of that period [B.C. § 502(k)(1)(B)(ii)]; and

(e) no portion of the debt under the alternative repayment schedule is *nondischargeable.* [B.C. § 502(k)(1)(C)]

The debtor must prove by *clear and convincing evidence* that (i) the creditor unreasonably refused to consider the debtor's proposal *and* (ii) the proposal was made before the expiration of the 60-day period referenced above. [B.C. § 502(k)(2)] The standards that Congress created make the prospect of a debtor succeeding under § 502(k) "more illusory than practical and realistic." [*In re* **Hayes,** 385 B.R. 644 (Bankr. N.D. Ohio 2007)]

C. Secured Claims

1. Definition

In bankruptcy, a secured claim is one that has been allowed and is either *secured by a lien* on property of the estate or is subject to *setoff.* [B.C. § 506(a)] The Bankruptcy Code treats a claim as secured *only to the extent of the value of the creditor's collateral* or up to the amount subject to setoff.

2. Undersecured Claims: Bifurcation

A claim is totally secured if the value of the collateral equals or is greater than the amount of the claim. With certain exceptions, if the amount of the creditor's claim exceeds the value of the collateral, the claim is undersecured and is divided into two separate claims: (i) a *secured claim* equal to the value of the collateral, and (ii) an *unsecured claim* equal to the amount by which the claim exceeds the value of the collateral. [B.C. § 506(a)]

e.g. **Example:** Bank has an allowed claim against Debtor in the amount of $200,000 arising from a loan agreement secured by a first mortgage on Debtor's vacation condo, which is not Debtor's principal residence. If the value of Debtor's condo is $200,000 or more, Bank's claim is fully secured. However, if Debtor's condo is valued at $160,000, Bank is considered to be undersecured, and its $200,000 claim will be bifurcated into a secured claim for $160,000 and an unsecured claim for $40,000.

EXAM TIP   **GILBERT**

Bifurcation of undersecured claims is an extremely important concept in bankruptcy, and it is likely that you will be asked to apply it on an exam. Remember, if a creditor is *undersecured,* she is treated as if she has *two claims:* a secured claim equal to the value of the collateral and an unsecured claim for the rest of the debt.

---

3. Undersecured Claims and Bifurcation: Exceptions

The Bankruptcy Code contains certain notable exceptions to the general rule that an undersecured creditor's debt is divided into a secured and an unsecured claim.

a. Debtor's Principal Residence

In a case filed under Chapter 11 or 13, the plan may not modify the rights of a creditor holding a secured claim secured only by the debtor's principal residence. [B.C. §§ 1123(b)(5), 1322(b)(2)]

b. Hanging Paragraph

In a Chapter 13 case, the debtor may not bifurcate the claim of a creditor holding a *purchase-money security interest* (i) in a *motor vehicle* purchased within *910 days of bankruptcy* and acquired for the ***debtor's personal use*** *or* (ii) in ***any other thing of value*** if the debt was incurred within ***one year of the bankruptcy filing.*** [B.C. § 1326(a)(9) hanging paragraph]

c. Section 1111(b) Election

In a Chapter 11 case, if a creditor elects treatment under § 1111(b), the creditor's claim is treated as a secured claim to the extent that the claim is allowed. [B.C. § 1111(b)(2)]

4. Valuation of Collateral

The value of the collateral securing a creditor's claim is a question of fact under the particular circumstances. The court's determination must take into account both the ***purpose of the valuation*** and the ***intended disposition or use*** of the collateral. [B.C. § 506(a)]

a. Purpose of the Valuation

There are various occasions when a bankruptcy judge is required to value property securing a creditor's claim. For example, a judge may value property for any of the following purposes [4 Collier ¶ 506.03(4)(a)(iv)]:

(i) determining a creditor's entitlement to adequate protection [B.C. § 361];

(ii) deciding whether a creditor is entitled to relief from the automatic stay for a lack of adequate protection [B.C. § 362(d)];

(iii) determining whether debtor has any equity in property for purposes of a creditor's motion to lift the stay [B.C. § 362(d)(2)];

(iv) determining whether a debtor is ineligible for Chapter 13 because her secured debts exceed the statutory secured debt ceiling [B.C. § 109(e)]; or

(v) deciding whether debtor's plan under Chapter 11, 12, or 13 proposes to pay secured creditors the present value of their secured claims. [B.C. §§ 1129(b)(2)(A), 1225(a)(5), 1325(a)(5)]

b. Proposed Use or Disposition

Collateral may have a different value depending on its use or disposition. For example, liquidation value may be appropriate if the secured party is permitted to foreclose on the collateral. While the Supreme Court and Congress have provided *some* guidance, many questions remain about both the appropriate valuation standard to use in some cases and the time for determining valuation.

(i) The Supreme Court's Decision in *Rash*

The Supreme Court has held that in a Chapter 13 case in which the debtor desires to keep and use a secured creditor's collateral over the creditor's objection ("cramdown"), the collateral's value is its ***replacement value,*** which the Court described as the "cost the debtor would incur to obtain a like asset for the same 'proposed . . . use.'" The Court declined to elaborate on whether replacement value was retail or wholesale value, or some other value. It did explain, however, that replacement value does not include items, such as warranties, that the debtor does not receive when the debtor keeps a vehicle. [**Associates Commercial Corp. v. Rash,** 520 U.S. 953 (1997)]

(ii) BAPCPA Amendment to § 506(a)

Congress added subsection (2) to § 506(a) with the passage of BAPCPA in 2005. Section 506(a)(2) only applies to ***personal property*** and ***individuals in Chapter 7 or***

13. The first sentence of § 506(a)(2) provides that in individual Chapter 7 or 13 cases, the value of *personal property* is its *replacement value,* without deduction for the costs of sale or marketing; the valuation time is the *time of the bankruptcy filing.* The second sentence of § 506(a)(2) then provides that *replacement value for personal property* in individual Chapter 7 or 13 cases is *retail value,* if the debtor acquired the collateral for *personal, family, or household purposes.* Retail value, however, is based on the *age and condition* of the personal property *at the time value is determined.* [B.C. § 506(a)(2)]

e.g. **Example:** Debtor files for relief under Chapter 13, and plans to retain her car, which she purchased three years ago from Creditor. Debtor financed the purchase through Creditor; she acquired the vehicle for personal, family, or household purposes. Debtor owes $10,000 on the car. Given its age and condition, the vehicle's retail value is $7,000. Creditor has a secured claim for $7,000 and an unsecured claim for $3,000 in Debtor's Chapter 13 case.

Remember: Section 506(a)(2) does not apply to Chapter 11 or 12 cases. It also does not apply to valuation of real property in Chapter 7 or 13 cases.

c. Time of Valuation

In an individual Chapter 7 or 13 case in which the collateral is personal property acquired for *business use,* i.e., not for personal, family, or household purposes, valuation of the collateral is on the "date of the filing of the petition." In an individual Chapter 7 or 13 case involving valuation of personal property acquired for *personal, family, or business use,* valuation is based on the "age and condition of the property at the time value is determined." Thus, it is unclear in cases involving personal property acquired for personal, family, or household purposes which collateral value controls: the value on the petition date or the value when valuation is determined, e.g., plan confirmation in a Chapter 13 case. [*See, e.g.,* **In re Cook,** 415 B.R. 529 (Bankr. D. Kan. 2009) (holding that vehicle valuation is date of valuation hearing in Chapter 13 case)] For Chapter 11 and 12 cases, which are not governed by the language of § 506(a)(2), courts disagree as to the date to use for valuing collateral. [4 Collier ¶ 506.03(10)]

5. Oversecured Claims

To the extent that the value of the collateral exceeds the amount of the creditor's claim that it secures, plus any surcharges under Code section 506(c), the creditor is entitled to the allowance of *post-petition interest,* regardless of whether the creditor's lien is consensual, e.g., a mortgage or a U.C.C. security interest, or nonconsensual, e.g., a tax lien. [**United States v. Ron Pair Enterprises, Inc.,** 489 U.S. 235 (1989) (holding that a nonconsensual oversecured claim entitles the creditor holding that claim to post-petition interest under § 506(b)] Also, any reasonable fees, e.g., attorneys' fees, costs, or other charges *specified in the agreement* or a *state statute under which the claim arose* can be recovered to the extent that the claim is oversecured. [B.C. § 506(b)] *Remember:* unsecured and undersecured creditors are not entitled to post-petition interest under § 506(b). [*See* **United Savings Association of Texas v. Timbers of Inwood Forest Associates,** 484 U.S. 365 (1988)]

a. Distinguish Time Periods

It is important to distinguish a secured creditor's entitlement to interest across three time periods in Chapter 11, 12, and 13 cases.

(i) Pre-petition Interest

Any creditor, including an unsecured creditor, may add pre-petition interest to its claim if the creditor's agreement with the debtor provides for the payment of interest on tardily-paid debts. Depending on the amount of interest and the value of any collateral, the interest claimed may end up as part of a creditor's unsecured claim.

e.g. **Example:** Creditor's and Debtor's agreement provides for the payment of interest at the contract rate of 10% on payments received more than 10 days after the payment due date. Creditor has a security interest in a piece of collateral owned by the Debtor. The collateral value is $10,000, while Debtor owes Creditor $11,000. At the time of bankruptcy filing, Debtor also owes Creditor $100 in interest for late payment. Creditor has a secured claim in Debtor's bankruptcy case for $10,000; Creditor's unsecured claim of $1,100 includes the pre-petition interest of $100.

(ii) Post-Petition, Pre-Confirmation Interest

Section 506(b) entitles oversecured creditors to the payment of interest up to the value of the creditor's oversecurity. Unsecured creditors or undersecured creditors are not entitled to post-petition, pre-confirmation interest on their claims.

e.g. **Example:** Debtor files for relief under Chapter 11. Creditor has a security interest in a piece of collateral owned by Debtor. The collateral is valued at $100,000; Creditor's claim is $98,000. Creditor is oversecured by $2,000, and is entitled to interest on its $98,000 claim during the period between filing of the petition and confirmation of the Chapter 11 plan. Creditor is limited, however, to $2,000 in interest. If post-petition, pre-confirmation interest is $3,000, Creditor is entitled to $2,000; a claim for the remaining $1,000 will be disallowed as unmatured interest under § 502(b)(2).

(iii) Post-Petition, Post-Confirmation Interest

A plan under Chapters 11, 12, or 13 must pay interest on a creditor's secured claim in order to satisfy the requirement that secured creditors receive the ***present value*** of their secured claim. [B.C. §§ 1129(b)(2)(A)(i)(II), 1225(a)(5)(B)(ii), 1325(a)(5)(B)(ii)] An undersecured creditor will receive post-confirmation interest on the secured portion of its claim, but is not entitled to post-petition, pre-confirmation interest under § 506(b) because it is not oversecured.

e.g. **Example:** Creditor loaned Debtor $30,000, and perfected a security interest in a piece of collateral owned by Debtor. Debtor subsequently filed for relief under Chapter 13. The balance on the loan is $28,000, but the collateral is worth only $25,000. Creditor has a secured claim for $25,000 and an unsecured claim for $3,000. Creditor is not entitled to post-petition, pre-confirmation interest on its $28,000 claim, because Creditor is undersecured. Debtor's plan, however, must pay interest on Creditor's $25,000 secured claim in order to provide Creditor with the present value of its secured claim, which will be paid out over time under Debtor's Chapter 13 plan.

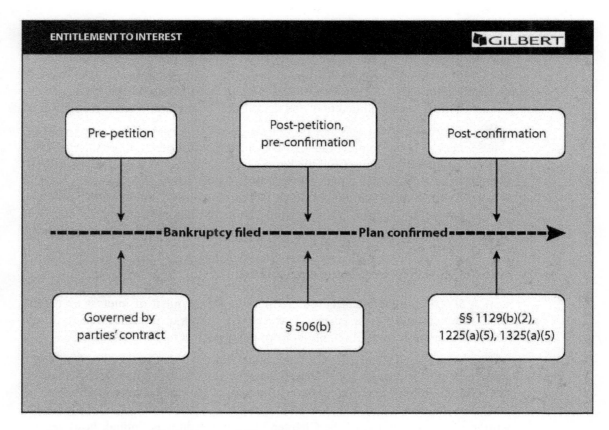

b. Payment of Interest and Fees

Any post-petition interest, and any fees, costs, or charges that are allowed to the holder of an oversecured claim, usually *accrue* until the time of distribution in a Chapter 7 case, or until the effective date of a Chapter 11, 12, or 13 plan. Present payments are not required by the statute. [B.C. § 506(b); 4 Collier ¶ 506.04(4)]

c. Interest Rate

In the case of an oversecured consensual lien, most courts use the interest rate in the parties' contract. [*In re* **Smith,** 463 B.R. 756 (Bankr. E.D. Pa. 2012)] Whether a contractual post-default interest rate will be applied depends on the facts and equities of the particular case, with a rebuttable presumption in favor of the default rate. [**Prudential Insurance Co. v. City of Boston (***In re* **SW Boston Hotel Venture, LLC),** 479 B.R. 210 (B.A.P. 1st Cir. 2012)]

6. Surcharge Against Collateral

To the extent that a secured creditor *benefits directly* from the preservation or disposition of the collateral, the trustee or the debtor in possession may be *reimbursed* from the collateral for the necessary and reasonable costs of preserving or disposing of the collateral. This surcharge is paid ahead of an award of post-petition interest or fees to an oversecured creditor. In 2005, Congress added the payment of "all ad valorem property taxes with respect to the property" to the expenses that may be charged against a secured creditor's recovery from the collateral. [B.C. § 506(c)]

a. Note

The Supreme Court has ruled that an administrative claimant does not have an independent right, i.e., standing, to recover its claim from a secured party's collateral under § 506(c). [**Hartford Underwriters Insurance Co. v. Union Planters Bank, N.A.,** 530 U.S. 1 (2000)] In *Hartford,* Debtor filed for relief under Chapter 11. Debtor owed Bank more than $4 million, and Bank held a security interest in essentially all of Debtor's real and personal property. During Debtor's Chapter 11 case, Insurer provided workers' compensation coverage to Debtor. Debtor, however, failed to pay the premiums and at the time that Debtor's case converted to Chapter 11, Debtor owed Insurer more than $50,000. Insurer had been unaware of the bankruptcy case until conversion, at which time it applied to the bankruptcy court for allowance of an administrative expense to be charged against the collateral securing Bank's claim under § 506(c). In a unanimous opinion, the Court held that the plain language of § 506(c) empowers only the *trustee* to recover costs from collateral securing an allowed secured claim. The Court, however, expressly declined to address the question of derivative standing: can third parties act in the "trustee's stead" under § 506(c) if the trustee or debtor in possession refuses to bring an action? The issue remains unresolved.

7. Liens Deemed Void

a. Section 506(d)

A lien is *void* to the extent that it secures a claim that is *not an allowed secured claim unless*

(i) the claim is *disallowed only* under § 523(a)(5) as a *nondischargeable, unmatured domestic support obligation* [B.C. § 502(d)(1)];

(ii) the claim is for *reimbursement or contribution* and is *disallowed only under § 502(e)* [B.C. § 502(d)(1)]; or

(iii) the claim is not an allowed secured claim due *only to the failure of the creditor* to *file a proof of claim* under § 501. [B.C. § 502(d)(2)]

b. Real Property: *Dewsnup* and *Caulkett*

In a Chapter 7 case, if the collateral is real property worth less than the amount of the claim it secures, the debtor may not use Code § 506(d) to strip down the creditor's lien on the real property to the value of the collateral. [**Dewsnup v. Timm,** 502 U.S. 410 (1992)] In a later Chapter 7 case, the Supreme Court applied the rule from *Dewsnup* to preclude a debtor from stripping off a junior mortgage on real property when the debt owed on a senior mortgage exceeded the value of the real property. [**Bank of America v. Caulkett,** 135 S.Ct. 1995 (2015)]

Example: Debtor owns a home subject to Bank's properly recorded mortgage of $80,000. When Debtor files a voluntary Chapter 7 petition, the present market value of the home is $50,000. Debtor seeks to avoid Bank's lien on his residence to the extent of $30,000. Debtor may not strip down Bank's lien to the value of the collateral.

Example: Debtor filed for relief under Chapter 7. Debtor's home is valued at $100,000. First Bank holds the senior mortgage on Debtor's home, and Debtor owes First Bank $105,000. Second Bank holds the junior mortgage on Debtor's home; Debtor owes Second Bank $50,000. Debtor moves to strip off Second Bank's mortgage, because Second Bank's lien is completely underwater; if Debtor sold his home today, Second Bank would receive nothing from the sale. Debtor may not void Second Bank's junior lien under § 506(d). The reasoning of *Dewsnup* also applies to a junior mortgage that is wholly underwater because the debt owed on the senior mortgage exceeds the value of the property.

8. Treatment of Secured Claims

Prior to final distribution to the unsecured creditors in a Chapter 7 case, a secured creditor usually receives cash equal to the total amount of her allowed secured claim or, in the alternative, a return of the property that secures that claim. [B.C. § 725] For example, the trustee may sell collateral that has equity and use the net proceeds to pay the corresponding secured claim, with any excess being remitted to the estate. In Chapters 11, 12, and 13, there are special provisions concerning the treatment of secured claims that must be satisfied for the court to confirm a plan.

9. Adequate Protection

A secured creditor has the right to receive adequate protection of her interest in the collateral [B.C. § 361], and the failure to provide it constitutes sufficient cause for granting the creditor relief from the automatic stay. [B.C. § 362(d)(1)] Also, the secured creditor is entitled to adequate protection if her collateral is used, sold, or leased by the trustee or the debtor in possession [B.C. § 363(e)], or if the creditor's lien on the collateral is primed by a senior or equal lien authorized by the court for the purpose of enabling the trustee or the debtor in possession to obtain credit. [B.C. § 364(d)(1)(B)]

D. Administrative Expenses

1. Priority

After the payment of secured claims from property constituting collateral, entities holding unsecured priority claims are paid. Claims for administrative expenses ordinarily are entitled to the second highest priority, after domestic support obligations, in the distribution of the assets of the estate. [B.C. §§ 503, 507(a)(1)]

2. Filing a Request

Generally, a request for administrative expenses must be *timely filed.* The court may approve, for cause, the late filing of such a claim. [B.C. § 503(a)] Not all creditors, however, must file a request in order to have their administrative expense claim paid. A creditor with a claim for *post-petition trade debt* incurred in the *ordinary course of the debtor's business* normally is paid without the creditor having to file a request for payment as an administrative expense. [4 Collier ¶ 503.02] In addition, in 2005, Congress added a subsection to § 503(b) that provides that a *governmental unit* is not required to file a request for payment of *certain taxes and related penalties and fines* that are allowable as administrative expenses. [B.C. §§ 503(b)(1)(B)–(D)]

3. Allowable Administrative Expenses

The following items are allowable as administrative expenses, after notice and a hearing. [*See* B.C. § 503(b)]

a. Post-Petition Costs of Preserving Estate

The *actual and necessary post-petition costs of preserving the bankruptcy estate* are administrative expenses.

(i) Environmental Claims

Reasonable costs incurred by an environmental agency to clean up hazardous wastes that violate environmental laws, and civil fines and penalties imposed for post-petition violations of environmental laws are entitled to administrative expense priority. [B.C. § 503(b)(1)(A); *see* **Munce's Superior Petroleum**

Prods. v. New Hampshire Department of Environmental Services (*In re Munce's Superior Petroleum Prods.*), 736 F.3d 567 (1st Cir. 2013) (holding that post-petition fine for contempt for debtor's failure to comply with earlier post-petition state court order requiring debtor to bring facilities into compliance with state environmental law was entitled to administrative expense priority)]

(ii)   Obtaining Unsecured Credit

A trustee authorized to run the debtor's business may obtain or incur unsecured credit in the ***ordinary course of the debtor's business*** that is allowable as an administrative expense. [B.C. § 364(a)] After notice and a hearing, the bankruptcy court may authorize the trustee to obtain or incur ***unsecured credit other than in the ordinary course of the debtor's business*** that is allowable as an administrative expense. [B.C. § 364(b)]

(iii)   Pre-Confirmation Retiree Benefits

In a Chapter 11 case, retiree benefit payments that must be made prior to the effective date of a confirmed plan are allowable as administrative expenses. [B.C. § 1114(e)(2)]

(iv)   Wages, Salaries, and Commissions

Wages or salaries for employees operating the debtor's business in a reorganization case, for example, are allowable as administrative expense claims. It is important to distinguish claims for post-petition wages and salaries, which may have administrative expense status and, thus, second priority of payment from pre-petition wages and salaries, which may qualify for fourth-priority of payment. [B.C. §§ 503(b)(1), 507(a)(2), 507(a)(4)]

(v)   NLRB Proceeding and Back Pay

Wages and benefits awarded in an ***National Labor Relations Board*** proceeding as ***back pay*** for any post-petition period of time for the debtor's ***violation of federal or state law*** are allowable as administrative expenses if the bankruptcy court determines that paying such wages and benefits ***will not substantially increase*** the ***probability of layoffs or termination*** of current employees or the ***nonpayment of domestic support obligations.*** [B.C. § 503(b)(1)(A)(ii)] Congress added this new provision when it enacted BAPCPA. The back pay award must result from a violation of state or federal law, not a breach of a collective bargaining agreement. [*See In re* **Philadelphia Newspapers, LLC,** 433 B.R. 164 (Bankr. E.D. Penn. 2010)]

(vi)   Post-Petition Taxes and Penalties

Post-petition taxes incurred by the estate, e.g., taxes arising from the management of the debtor's business by the debtor in possession or a trustee in a Chapter 11 case, are administrative expenses. [B.C. § 503(b)(1)(B)(i)] A ***fine or penalty*** relating to such a post-petition tax of the estate also is allowable as an administrative expense. [B.C. § 503(b)(1)(C)] The great weight of appellate authority holds that ***interest*** on post-petition taxes is an administrative expense. [*See, e.g.,* **United States v. Yellin (*In re* Weinstein),** 272 F.3d 39 (1st Cir. 2001)]

Note: Make sure that you distinguish post-petition taxes accorded second priority status as administrative expenses from taxes accorded eighty priority status.

Section 503(b) specifically excepts from administrative expense priority "a tax of a kind specified in section 507(a)(8)." [B.C. § 503(b)(1)(B)(i)]

(vii) Compensation and Reimbursement

Compensation and reimbursement awarded to a trustee, an examiner, a consumer privacy ombudsman, a patient care ombudsman, a Chapter 12 or 13 individual debtor's attorney, or a professional person employed by a trustee, Chapter 11 debtor in possession, or creditors' committee, are administrative expenses. [B.C. §§ 503(b)(2), 330(a), 332, 333]

(viii) Expenses of Filing an Involuntary Petition

The actual and necessary expenses of a creditor who files an involuntary petition against the debtor are administrative expenses. [B.C. § 503(b)(3)(A)] Administrative expenses include *reasonable compensation* for services, as well as *reimbursement* of actual and necessary expenses, of an *attorney or an accountant* of a creditor who files an involuntary petition. [B.C. § 503(b)(4)] The creditor itself, however, is not entitled to compensation or reimbursement.

(ix) Expenses of Recovery of Concealed or Transferred Property

The actual and necessary expenses of a creditor who, with court approval, *recovers* for the benefit of the *estate property* that the *debtor has either concealed or transferred* are administrative expenses. [B.C. § 503(b)(3)(B)] Administrative expenses include *reasonable compensation* for services, as well as *reimbursement* of actual and necessary expenses, of *an attorney or an accountant* of such a creditor. [B.C. § 503(b)(4)]

(x) Expenses of Criminal Prosecution

The actual and necessary expenses incurred by a creditor in a *criminal prosecution* related to the bankruptcy case or to the debtor's property or business are administrative expenses. [B.C. § 503(b)(3)(C)] Administrative expenses include *reasonable compensation* for services, as well as *reimbursement* of actual and necessary expenses, of an *attorney or an accountant* of such a creditor. [B.C. § 503(b)(4)]

(xi) Expenses of Substantial Contributor

The actual and necessary expenses of a creditor, an indenture trustee, an equity security holder, or an *unofficial* creditors' or equity security holders' committee, i.e., one not appointed by the United States trustee under § 1102, that makes a *substantial contribution* in a Chapter 11 or Chapter 9 case are administrative expenses. [B.C. § 503(b)(3)(D)] Administrative expenses include *reasonable compensation* for services, as well as *reimbursement* of actual and necessary expenses, of an *attorney or an accountant* of such creditor, indenture trustee, equity security holder, or unofficial creditors' or equity security holders' committee. [B.C. § 503(b)(4)]

(xii) Expenses and Compensation of Pre-Petition Custodian

The actual and necessary expenses, as well as compensation, for the services of a pre-petition custodian who has been superseded under Bankruptcy Code § 543 are administrative expenses. [B.C. § 503(b)(3)(E)]

(xiii) Expenses of Official Chapter 11 Creditors' Committee

The actual and necessary expenses incurred by the members of an official Chapter 11 creditors' or equity security holders' committee—one appointed under § 1102—in performing the duties of the committee are treated as administrative expenses. [B.C. § 503(b)(3)(F)] Such expenses would include, for example, travel and lodging, but not compensation for services rendered.

(xiv) Compensation of Indenture Trustee

Reasonable compensation for the services of an indenture trustee who has made a *substantial contribution* in a Chapter 11 or Chapter 9 case is an administrative expense. [B.C. §§ 503(b)(5), 101(29)]

(xv) Witnesses' Fees

Witnesses' fees and mileage expenses are administrative expenses. [B.C. § 503(b)(6); 28 U.S.C. § 1821]

(xvi) Nonresidential Real Property Leases

A landlord may have an allowable administrative expense claim for monies due under a *nonresidential real property lease* that was *first assumed* under § 365 and then *later rejected.* The landlord's claim is for *all monetary obligations* due for the *two-year period* following the later of the rejection date or the date that the trustee turned the premises over to the landlord. Monetary obligations *do not* include *penalty provisions* under the lease or damages resulting from the *trustee's failure to operate the premises.* The landlord's claim is subject to setoff or reduction *only* for monies received from an entity other than the debtor. If the landlord's damages exceed the cap provided in this section, only the amount under the cap is entitled to administrative expense priority. The rest of the landlord's claim is an unsecured claim subject to any relevant limitation placed on damages under § 502(b)(6). [B.C. § 503(b)(7)] This is a new provision that Congress enacted as part of BAPCPA.

(xvii) Closing Health Care Business

The actual, necessary costs and expenses that a trustee or a federal or state department or agency incurs in *closing a health care business* are allowable administrative expenses. [B.C. § 503(b)(8)] Such costs and expenses include *disposing of patient records* and *transferring patients* from the health care facility that is closing to another health care business. [B.C. §§ 503(b)(8)(A), (B)] This is a new provision that Congress enacted as part of BAPCPA.

(xviii) Certain Pre-Petition Sales of Goods

A creditor that sold *goods* in the *ordinary course of the debtor's business* has an allowable administrative expense claim for the value of goods sold *within 20 days* of the start of the debtor's bankruptcy case. [B.C. § 503(b)(9)] This is a new provision that Congress enacted as part of BAPCPA. The Bankruptcy Code does not define "goods," but a number of courts have turned for guidance to the Uniform Commercial Code's definition at § 2–105. [*In re* **Pilgrim's Pride Corp.,** 421 B.R. 231 (Bankr. N.D. Tex. 2009)]

Note: A pre-petition seller of goods to the debtor also may have a right to reclaim goods sold within 45 days of the start of the debtor's bankruptcy case. [B.C. § 546(c)]

4. Exception: Gap Creditors' Claims

In an ***involuntary*** case, post-petition claims that arise "in the ordinary course of the debtor's business or financial affairs . . . before the earlier of the appointment of a trustee [or] the order for relief" are ***not*** treated as administrative expense claims, but rather are given ***third priority*** in the order of distribution. [B.C. §§ 503(b), 507(a)(3), 502(f)]

Note: Make sure you distinguish between the creditor filing the involuntary petition and the creditor that provides goods and services in the gap period. The former has an administrative expense claim, while the latter does not. The gap creditor's claim does have priority, however.

5. Exempt Property

As a general rule, administrative expenses are not payable out of property that the debtor exempts. [B.C. § 522(k)] However, property exempted by the debtor is liable for administrative expenses representing the debtor's fractional share of the cost of avoiding a transfer of such property or the cost of its recovery by the trustee or the debtor. [B.C. § 522(k)(1), (2)]

6. Limitations on KERPS

In BAPCPA, Congress added language to the Code that limits a debtor's ability to claim administrative expense priority for ***certain post-petition payments made to insiders.*** The purpose of this new provision is to place restrictions on Key Employee Retention Plans ("KERPS"). The Code now provides that a payment made or obligation incurred for the ***benefit of an insider*** to induce the insider to remain with the debtor's business shall not be allowed or paid unless the court makes the following findings based on evidence in the record:

(i) the transfer or obligation is essential to retain the insider because she has a ***bona fide offer*** from another business at the ***same or greater compensation.*** [B.C. §§ 503(c)(1)(A), 101(31)]; *and*

(ii) the insider's services are ***essential to the business' survival*** [B.C. §§ 503(c)(1)(A), 101(31)]; *and*

(iii) the court finds *either of the following:*

    (1) the transfer or payment does not exceed an amount equal to ***10 times the average*** transfer or payment of a similar kind made to ***non-management employees*** during the calendar year in which the insider transfer or obligation was made [B.C. §§ 503(c)(1)(C)(i), 101(31)]; *or*

    (2) if the debtor made no transfers to non-management employees during the relevant calendar year, then the transfer or obligation for the insider's benefit does not exceed an amount that is ***25% of the amount of any similar transfer or obligation*** made to ***the insider*** in the ***calendar year prior*** to the calendar year in which the contested transfer or obligation takes place. [B.C. §§ 503(c)(1)(C)(ii), 101(31)]

A ***severance payment*** made to an insider also "shall neither be allowed nor paid" unless the payment is part of a ***program applicable to all full-time employees*** and the severance payment amount does not ***exceed 10 times the average severance*** paid to ***non-management employees*** during the same calendar year. [B.C. §§ 503(c)(2), 101(31)] Finally, any transfers made or obligations incurred ***outside the ordinary course of business,*** including those for the benefit of officers, managers, or consultants hired after filing of the bankruptcy petition, "shall neither be allowed nor paid" unless *justified* by the *facts and circumstances of the case.* [B.C. § 503(c)(3)]

D. Priority Claims

1. In General

Priority claims generally are the first *unsecured claims* to be paid in a bankruptcy case following distribution to secured creditors. There are ten tiers of priority claims [B.C. § 507(a)] which, in a Chapter 7 case, are entitled to payment in the order of their priority ranking. Thus, all of the claims in a priority level must be paid in full before moving down to the next priority level. The general (nonpriority) unsecured creditors receive payment only after all priority unsecured creditors are paid. [B.C. § 726(a)(1)]

Example: Debtor files for relief under Chapter 7. Debtor has $12,000 in unencumbered, non-exempt assets. Administrative expenses are $2,000, and Debtor has $20,000 in priority tax claims. Unsecured claims total $60,000. The administrative expenses will be paid in full, because they are second priority. The remaining $10,000 does not cover the $20,000 in priority tax claims; the tax claimants share *pro rata,* which means that each claimant receives 50% ($10,000 available/$20,000 claims) of its claim. The unsecured creditors receive nothing.

2. Order of Priority

BAPCPA made several changes to the Code's priority scheme. Among those changes was the addition of a tenth priority for personal injury claims resulting from intoxicated operation of a vehicle or vessel. Congress also moved alimony and child support obligations—now termed domestic support obligations—from seventh to first priority.

Priority claims that have been *allowed* are paid in the following order. [B.C. § 507(a)]

a. First Priority: Domestic Support Obligations

The first priority under § 507(a) is for *domestic support obligations,* but within that priority scheme is a payment hierarchy. First paid are certain *administrative expenses of a trustee* elected or appointed in Chapter 7, 11, 12, or 13, to the extent that the trustee *administers assets* that are *used to pay the domestic support obligation.* [B.C. § 507(a)(1)(C)] The Code allows first payment *only* for the trustee's expenses for the actual, necessary costs of preserving the estate, the trustee's compensation, and fees and mileage. [B.C. §§ 503(b)(1)(A), (2), (6), 330] Second paid are allowed unsecured claims for domestic support obligations *owed to or recoverable by* a spouse, former spouse, or child of the debtor, or the child's parent, legal guardian, or legal representative. The claim may be filed by the person owed the obligation or a governmental unit on behalf of such person. [B.C. §§ 507(a)(1)(A), 101(14A)] Third paid are domestic support obligations that a spouse, former spouse, or child of the debtor, or that child's parent, legal guardian, or legal representative have *assigned to a governmental unit.* A voluntary assignment of a domestic support obligation to a governmental unit for purposes of collecting the obligation, however, falls within the category of second-paid, not third-paid, claims under § 507(a)(1). Also included in this third category under § 507(a)(1) are domestic support obligations that *are owed directly to or recoverable by a governmental unit* under applicable nonbankruptcy law. [B.C. § 507(a)(1)(B)]

Example: Debtor files for relief under Chapter 7; at the time he files for bankruptcy, Debtor owes his former spouse ("Spouse") $10,000 in alimony and child support payments. Debtor has $20,000 in non-exempt assets. The Chapter 7 trustee incurs $4,000 in administrative expenses, of which $1,000 was spent administering assets to pay Spouse's domestic support obligation. The Chapter 7 trustee is paid $1,000 first; Spouse then is paid $10,000. The trustee's other $3,000 in administrative expenses are accorded second priority status under § 507(a)(2). The $6,000 remaining of the $20,000 in non-exempt assets is paid to other priority claimants, in the order provided by the Code, and then to timely filed general unsecured creditors.

b. Second Priority: Administrative Expenses

The second priority includes administrative expenses, the filing fee for the particular case, certain quarterly fees required in Chapter 11 cases, and unsecured claims of any Federal reserve bank related to loans made through programs or facilities authorized under § 13(3) of the Federal Reserve Act. [B.C. § 507(a)(2); 28 U.S.C. § 1930; 12 U.S.C. § 343]

c. Third Priority: Involuntary Case Gap Claims

The third priority includes those allowed unsecured claims in an involuntary case that arise in the *ordinary course* of the debtor's business or financial affairs in the *gap period,* which is the time between *filing of the involuntary petition* and the *earlier* of the *order for relief* and the *appointment of a trustee.* [B.C. §§ 507(a)(3), 502(f)]

Distinguish: Third priority allowed claims of a creditor that provides goods or services to the debtor during the gap period from the second priority administrative expenses of a creditor that files the involuntary petition against the debtor. [B.C. §§ 507(a)(3), 503(b)(3)(A)]

d. Fourth Priority: Wages and Commissions

The fourth priority includes wages, salaries, or commissions earned by an *individual* within *180 days* before either bankruptcy or "the cessation of the debtor's business," whichever is earlier. This provision applies regardless of the individual's position of employment and includes vacation pay, severance pay, and sick leave pay. [B.C. § 507(a)(3)(A)] The fourth priority also includes commissions earned by an *individual or a corporation with only one employee,* acting as an *independent contractor* in the sale of goods or services for the debtor in the *ordinary course* of the debtor's business; the *180-day time limit* applies to these commissions, as well. In order to qualify for fourth-priority status, at least *75%* of the individual's or corporation's *earnings* from acting as an independent contractor during the *12 months prior to bankruptcy* must have been earned from the debtor. [B.C. § 507(a)(3)(B)]

(i) Limitation

Each fourth priority claim is limited to $13,650. [B.C. § 507(a)(4)]

e.g. **Example:** Patty Parker is the president of Debtor Corporation. Debtor Corporation filed for relief under Chapter 7 on June 1 and stopped doing business on the same day. From February 1 until June 1, Parker earned, in the employ of Debtor Corporation, $20,000 in salary, which remained unpaid as of June 1. Because any individual employee is entitled to a priority for wages or salaries earned within the 180-day period before either bankruptcy or cessation of Debtor Corporation's business, whichever is earlier, Parker will receive fourth priority treatment of $13,650 of the $20,000 she is owed in past-due salary. Parker will have a general unsecured claim for the remaining $6,350. If funds remain after all priority creditors are paid, then Parker will share *pro rata* with other unsecured creditors in those funds. [B.C. § 507(a)(4)(A)]

(ii) "Cessation of Business"

The courts have construed the language "cessation of the debtor's business" to mean the date on which the debtor stops doing business altogether. There is no cessation of the debtor's business simply because the debtor closes some stores, outlets, or divisions, but continues to operate—albeit on a reduced scale. [B.C. § 507(a)(4)]

e.g. **Example:** Debtor Corporation owns and operates several seafood restaurants. In 2007, it closed one restaurant but continued to operate several others. Employees sued and, in 2008, ultimately settled with Debtor for $400,000. Debtor Corporation paid on the settlement until it filed for relief under Chapter 11 in 2010. Employees filed a claim for the remainder of the settlement and argued that the claim was entitled to fourth-priority status. The bankruptcy court held that Employees did not have a fourth priority claim. Employees' earnings were for a period in 2007, which was more than 180 days prior to Debtor's 2010 Chapter 11 filing. The court rejected Employees' argument that the closing of the restaurant at which they had worked constituted a "cessation of the debtor's business." The court noted that Debtor operated several other restaurants and that the closing of one of those restaurants did not constitute a cessation of Debtor's business. [*In re* **McGrath's Publick Fish House, Inc.,** 2011 WL 66026 (Bankr. D. Ore. 2011)]

e. Fifth Priority: Employee Benefit Plans

The fifth priority is for contributions to an employee benefit plan for services rendered within *180 days* before either bankruptcy or "the cessation of the debtor's business," whichever is earlier. [B.C. § 507(a)(5)]

(i) Limitation

This priority is limited to the number of employees covered by the plan multiplied by $13,650 *minus*: (i) the total amount paid to such employees as fourth priority wage claims *plus* (ii) the total amount paid by the bankruptcy estate to any other benefit plan for such employees. [B.C. § 507(a)(5)(B)] Employee pension plans, life insurance plans, and health insurance plans are the most common examples of fifth priority claims. The Supreme Court has held that unpaid premiums on a workers' compensation policy purchased by debtor for its employees do not enjoy fifth-priority status under the Bankruptcy Code. [**Howard Delivery Service v. Zurich American Insurance Co.,** 547 U.S. 651 (2006)]

Distinguish: The $13,650 limit for wages, salaries, and commissions under § 507(a)(4) is per employee. Note the language "for each individual" in § 507(a)(4). No such language appears in the employee benefit plans' provision. Thus, § 507(a)(5) "provides an aggregate limit on recovery" under that provision; not an individualized recovery per employee." [**Consolidated Freightways Corp. v. Aetna, Inc. (*In re* Consolidated Freightways Corp.),** 564 F.3d 1161 (9th Cir. 2009)]

f. Sixth Priority: Grain Farmers and United States Fishermen

The sixth priority is for allowed unsecured claims of grain producers or United States fishermen against a debtor who operates or owns a grain storage facility or against a debtor who operates a fish produce storage or processing facility, respectively. [B.C. § 507(a)(6)]

(i) Limitation

Each farmer or fisherman is limited to $6,725 for a sixth priority claim. [B.C. § 507(a)(6)]

g. Seventh Priority: Consumer Claims

The seventh priority, which also is known as the "layaway" priority, is for allowed unsecured claims of individuals arising from the pre-petition deposit of money with the debtor for the purchase, lease, or rental of property *or* the purchase of services that were not delivered or provided. The property or services must have been intended for the ***personal, family, or household*** use of the claimant. [B.C. § 507(a)(7)]

(i) Limitation

Each individual is limited to $3,025 for a seventh priority claim. [B.C. § 507(a)(7)]

h. Eighth Priority: Taxes

The eighth priority includes the following unsecured pre-petition tax claims of governmental units. [B.C. § 507(a)(8)]

(i) Income Tax

Income taxes for a ***taxable year ending on or before the filing of the bankruptcy petition*** are eighth priority claims.

(1) Return Last Due

An income tax for which a ***return was last due,*** including extensions, ***within three years*** prior to the date of the bankruptcy petition is an eighth priority claim. [B.C. § 507(a)(8)(A)(i)]

e.g. **Example:** Debtor filed for relief under Chapter 7 on March 5, 2018. Debtor has not paid his income taxes for 2014 or 2015. The income taxes for both years are entitled to priority under § 507(a)(8)(A). March 5, 2015 is three years prior to Debtor's filing of the Chapter 7 petition. Debtor's 2015 income taxes were last due on April 15, 2015, and his 2015 taxes were last due on April 15, 2016. Both dates fall *after* March 5, 2015; thus, both years' taxes are entitled to priority.

(2) Assessed Within 240 Days

An income tax that has been ***assessed within 240 days*** before the date of the petition is an eighth priority claim. [B.C. § 507(a)(8)(A)(ii)] There are two situations in which the Code extends the 240-day period. First, the time period during which an offer in compromise was pending or in effect *plus* 30 days is not counted in calculating the 240-day period. [B.C. § 507(a)(8)(A)(ii)(I)] Second, the period during which the automatic stay was in effect in a prior bankruptcy case *plus* 90 days is not counted in calculating the 240-day period. BAPCPA added this latter time extension. [B.C. § 507(a)(8)(A)(ii)(II)]

(3) Assessable Post-Petition

An income tax that was not assessed pre-petition but which is ***assessable post-petition, other than*** a tax that is nondischargeable because a return was not filed, a return was filed late within two years prior to bankruptcy, or the debtor filed a fraudulent return or intentionally tried to evade the tax. [B.C. §§ 507(a)(8)(A)(iii); 523(a)(1)(B), (C)]

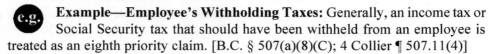 **Example:** Debtor filed for relief under Chapter 11 in March 2017. At the time of his bankruptcy filing, the IRS was auditing his liability for federal income taxes for the years 2010, 2011, and 2012. In November 2017, the IRS issued a notice of deficiency to Debtor for tax years 2010 through 2012. The taxes are entitled to eighth priority under § 507(a)(8)(A)(iii), because they were not assessed pre-petition but were assessable post-petition. *Note:* The taxes are outside the three-year reach back period under § 507(a)(8)(A)(i). [*See, e.g.,* **Fein v. United States (*In re* Fein),** 22 F.3d 631 (5th Cir. 1994)]

(ii) Property Tax

A property tax incurred prior to bankruptcy that was last payable without a penalty *within one year* before the date of the petition is an eighth priority claim. [B.C. § 507(a)(8)(B)]

Distinguish: Post-petition property taxes, which are allowable as an administrative expense claim and, thus, second priority from pre-petition property taxes, which are eighth priority.

(iii) Trust Fund Tax

Any trust fund tax that the debtor was *obligated to collect or withhold* from a third party and for which the debtor is liable in any capacity is an eighth priority claim. [B.C. § 507(a)(8)(C)] Under this provision, the debtor could be either an employer or a responsible person or officer liable for the trust fund tax under the Internal Revenue Code's 100% penalty. [26 U.S.C. § 6672(a); *see* 4 Collier ¶ 507.11(4)(a)]

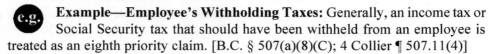 **Example—Employee's Withholding Taxes:** Generally, an income tax or Social Security tax that should have been withheld from an employee is treated as an eighth priority claim. [B.C. § 507(a)(8)(C); 4 Collier ¶ 507.11(4)]

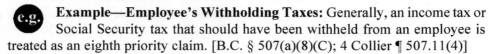 **Example—Sales Taxes:** Sales taxes that a debtor is required under state law to collect from its retail customers are trust fund taxes and entitled to eighth priority. [*See In re* **Calabrese,** 689 F.3d 312 (3d Cir. 2012)]

(1) No Time Limit

A claim for a trust fund tax qualifies as an eighth priority item regardless of the age of the tax liability. [4 Collier ¶ 507.11(4)]

(iv) Employment Tax

An employment tax concerning wages, salaries, or commissions earned from the debtor before bankruptcy and for which a return was last due *within three years* before the date of the petition is an eighth priority claim. [B.C. § 507(a)(8)(D)] For example, the employer must withhold 7.65% of an employee's gross wages for Social Security and Medicare taxes. The employer also must pay its portion of Social Security and Medicare taxes on those wages, which is 7.65% of each employee's gross wages. The employer's 7.65% is a priority tax employment claim under § 507(a)(8)(D); the amount that an employer has withheld from its employees' wages is an eighth priority claim under § 507(a)(8)(C).

(v) Excise Tax

An excise tax concerning a transaction that occurred *or* for which a return was last due *within three years* before bankruptcy is an eighth priority claim. [B.C. § 507(a)(8)(E)]

(vi) Customs Duties

Certain customs duties relating to the *importation of merchandise* entered for *consumption within one or four years,* depending on the circumstances, before bankruptcy are eighth priority claims. [B.C. § 507(a)(8)(F)]

(vii) Penalty on Eighth Priority Tax Claim

A penalty attributable to an eighth priority tax claim is also an eighth priority claim, but only if the penalty constitutes *compensation for actual pecuniary loss.* [B.C. § 507(a)(8)(G)]

(viii) Additional Issues Related to Priority Tax Claims

(1) *Pro Rata* Distribution

In a Chapter 7 case, if there are insufficient funds to pay all eighth priority tax claims, those tax claims share on a *pro rata* basis any monies remaining for distribution. There is no payment hierarchy among the eighth priority tax claims, unlike the payment hierarchy that exists for first priority domestic support obligations. [B.C. §§ 507(a)(1), (8)]

e.g. **Example:** Debtor files for relief under Chapter 7. After paying all administrative expenses, the trustee has $10,000 left to distribute. Debtor owes $15,000 in federal income taxes, $5,000 in state income taxes, and $5,000 in property taxes. All taxes are entitled to eighth priority status. Each tax creditor receives 40% of its claim ($10,000 assets/$25,000 tax claims). Thus, the IRS receives $6,000, and the state and property taxing authorities each receive $2,000.

(2) Suspension of Time Periods

BAPCPA added language in a hanging paragraph at the end of § 507(a)(8). The new language provides that any applicable time limit under § 507(a)(8), e.g., one year for property taxes, *does not run for the period during* which:

(i) *applicable nonbankruptcy law prevented* a governmental unit from collecting a tax because the debtor had requested a hearing and an appeal of collection action taken or proposed against the debtor, *plus 90 days;* or

(ii) the *automatic stay* was in effect in a prior bankruptcy case or collection was precluded because of one or more confirmed plans, *plus 90 days.*

(3) Erroneous Refund

A claim for an erroneous refund or credit of a tax is entitled to the *same priority* as the tax to which it pertains. [B.C. § 507(c)]

(4) Pre-Petition Interest

Almost all courts view pre-petition interest as part of an eighth priority tax claim, and thus an equivalent priority status is given to any interest accrued on the tax before bankruptcy. [*In re* **Colonial BancGroup, Inc.,** 2012 Bankr. LEXIS 3004 (Bankr. M.D. Ala. 2012) (stating that "[i]t is well established that interest has the same priority as the underlying tax provided that the interest accrued pre-petition")]

i. **Ninth Priority: Failure to Maintain Capital Requirements of an Insured Depository Institution**

The ninth priority is for allowed unsecured claims of a federal depository institutions regulatory agency (such as the FDIC or RTC) for the amount of any deficiency under the debtor's agreement to maintain the capital of an insured depository institution. [B.C. §§ 507(a)(9), 101(21B), 101(35)]

j. **Tenth Priority: Operation of a Vehicle or Vessel While Intoxicated**

BAPCPA added a tenth priority to § 507(a). This priority applies to allowed claims for *death or personal injury* resulting from the operation of a *vessel or motor vehicle* if such operation was unlawful because the debtor was *intoxicated* from using alcohol, drugs, or other substances. [B.C. § 507(a)(10)]

3. Exceptions to Equal Treatment of Priority Creditors in a Class

The general rule is that priority creditors *within a class* share equally in any distribution. Thus, within a priority class, there is no payment hierarchy. There are several exceptions, however, to this general rule.

a. **Domestic Support Obligations**

There is a hierarchy of payment among first priority domestic support obligation claims. The trustee, if she administers assets to pay a domestic support obligation, is paid first, then a spouse, former spouse, or child of the debtor with a domestic support obligation claim, and finally, a governmental unit with a domestic support obligation assigned to it by a spouse, former spouse, or child of the debtor. [B.C. § 507(a)(1)(A)–(C)]

b. **Conversion to Chapter 7**

If a case is converted from Chapter 11, 12, or 13 to a case under Chapter 7, the administrative expense claims in the Chapter 7 case *after conversion* have priority over the administrative expenses incurred prior to conversion. [B.C. § 726(b)]

c. **Super-Priority: Inadequately Protected Secured Creditor**

If adequate protection is furnished under §§ 362, 363, or 364 to a creditor whose claim is secured by a lien on the debtor's property, but the adequate protection ultimately proves to be deficient, the creditor will receive an administrative expense claim with *priority over all other administrative expenses* allowed against the debtor's estate. [B.C. § 507(b)]

e.g. **Example:** Debtor filed for relief under Chapter 11. Debtor owed Creditor $2.7 million, which was secured by a properly perfected security interest in Debtor's accounts receivable. Debtor sought an order to use cash collateral, and at the cash collateral hearing the accounts receivable were valued at $836,616. The bankruptcy court entered an order authorizing Debtor to use cash collateral and granting adequate protection to Creditor in the form of a replacement lien on Debtor's post-petition accounts receivable and inventory, up to $836,616. Debtor's reorganization effort failed, and there was a shortfall of more than $427,000 in Creditor's adequate protection. As a result, the bankruptcy court held that Creditor had a super-priority claim under § 507(b) for $427,766, which was the amount that Creditor was not adequately protected. There were not enough assets in the estate, however, to pay Creditor's claim. Because the Code provides that a super-priority administrative claim must be paid prior to any other administrative claim, the bankruptcy court ordered the disgorgement of interim fees paid to other professionals in the case—Debtor's attorneys and the lawyer for the unsecured creditors' committee. [*In re* **Wilson-Seafresh, Inc.,** 263 B.R. 624 (Bankr. N.D. Fla. 2001]

d. Super Super-Priority: Post-Petition Credit

If the trustee or the debtor in possession is unable to obtain unsecured post-petition credit by means of an administrative expense priority, the court may approve new credit or debt with *priority over all other administrative expense* claims, *including any super-priority claims* arising from the failure of adequate protection. [B.C. § 364(c)(1)]

4. Subrogation

A third party, such as a co-debtor or a surety, who becomes subrogated to the rights of a holder of a claim entitled to a first priority or fourth through ninth priority does *not* become subrogated to the holder's right to priority. Therefore, the subrogated claim is treated as a nonpriority claim. [B.C. § 507(d)]

a. Distinguish Assignment

It is important to distinguish subrogation from assignment. Section 507(d) does not apply to assignments and, thus, an assignee of a priority claim should have the same right to priority as the assignor. A subrogee acquires a claim because it paid a debt on which it was legally or contractually obligated. With an assignment, however, the assignee pays a claim even though it has no legal or contractual obligation to pay. [4 Collier ¶ 507.16; *see* **Nova Information Systems v. Premier Operations, Ltd. (***In re* **Premier Operations),** 294 B.R. 213 (S.D. N.Y. 2003) (addressing creditor's argument that it had a priority claim under § 507(a)(6) because it was an assignee, not a subrogee, of customers' claims, and noting the distinction between a creditor that voluntarily pays on claims in a negotiated transaction with consideration and a creditor that pays on a claim "unwillingly by operation of other contractual or legal obligations")]

b. Administrative Expenses and Involuntary Case Gap Claims

Subrogees to administrative expense claims and gap claims in involuntary cases become subrogated to the respective priorities of such claims. [4 Collier ¶ 507.16; §§ 507(d), 507(a)(2), (3)]

E. Tax Claims

1. Determination of Tax Liability

The bankruptcy court has jurisdiction to determine the amount or legality of any tax, fine, penalty, or addition to tax that has not been contested in and adjudicated by an appropriate judicial or administrative court *prior to bankruptcy.* The court may exercise its power to determine tax liability regardless of whether the tax has been assessed or paid. [B.C. §§ 505(a)(1), (2)(A)] In BAPCPA, Congress created a limitation on the bankruptcy court's powers with regard to ad valorem taxes. Thus, the bankruptcy court *may not* determine the amount or legality of any amount arising in connection with an *ad valorem tax* on the estate's real or personal property if the applicable period for contesting or re-determining that amount under applicable nonbankruptcy law has expired. [B.C. § 505(a)(2)(C)]

e.g. **Example:** Debtor filed for relief under Chapter 11. Tax Collector filed a proof of claim in Debtor's bankruptcy case for unpaid ad valorem taxes, based on the appraised value of 20 investment properties that Debtor owned. Prior to bankruptcy, Appraiser had certified the tax rolls to Tax Collector for collection of taxes. Under state law, Debtor had 60 days from certification to file suit to challenge Appraiser's valuation for tax purposes. Debtor did not do so. Instead, after the 60-day period had expired, Debtor objected to Tax Collector's proof of claim and argued that the assessed value of the 20 properties exceeded their actual value. The bankruptcy court held that Debtor's objection was timely under § 108 of the Code, even though the time to contest the Appraiser's value had run under state law. The district court affirmed the bankruptcy court's decision. The Court of Appeals, however, reversed the district court's decision and held that Congress intended with § 505(a)(2)(C) "to create an exception to the general time limits for contesting a tax assessment set forth in § 108(a)." The court noted that § 505(a)(2)(C) speaks in terms of the expiration of a time period under applicable *nonbankruptcy* law and that § 108 is a bankruptcy law, not a nonbankruptcy law. Thus, the court found that because the time period for contesting the appraisal had run under state law, Debtor's objection to Tax Collector's claim was untimely. [**Dubov v. Read (*In re* Read),** 692 F.3d 1185 (11th Cir. 2012)]

2. Tax Refund

The bankruptcy court also may determine the *estate's* right to a tax refund, but only after the earlier of 120 days after a proper request by the trustee for the refund from the appropriate governmental unit, *or* an actual determination by that governmental unit of the trustee's request. [B.C. § 505(a)(2)(B)]

3. Tax Liability of Estate

A trustee may request that the appropriate taxing authority determine any unpaid tax liability *of the estate* incurred during the administration of the case. The trustee does this by tendering to the governmental unit a tax return accompanied by a request for a determination of the tax to the address provided by the governmental unit for making such requests. [B.C. § 505(b)]

a. Discharge upon Payment

Once the trustee has requested a determination of the estate's liability for taxes incurred during the case, the estate, the trustee, and the debtor or a successor to the debtor are discharged from any liability for the tax:

(i) *upon payment of the tax indicated on the return* if the taxing authority either (1) fails to notify the trustee within 60 days that the return has been chosen for audit, or (2) fails to complete an audit and notify the trustee of any tax owing within 180 days (or such additional time allowed by the court for cause) after the trustee's request for determination [B.C. § 505(b)(2)(A)];

(ii) *upon payment of the tax determined by the taxing authority* [B.C. § 505(b)(2)(C)]; or

(iii) *upon payment of the tax determined by the court,* after notice and a hearing, after the taxing authority has finished its audit. [B.C. § 505(b)(2)(B)]

b. Exception for Fraud

The estate, trustee, and the debtor or any successor to the debtor are not discharged from tax liability incurred by the estate during the case if the return tendered by the trustee to the taxing authority is *fraudulent* or contains a *material misrepresentation.* [B.C. § 505(b)(2)]

4. Assessment

After the court makes a determination of a tax liability under § 505, the appropriate taxing authority may assess the amount of the tax against the estate, the debtor, or a successor to the debtor, notwithstanding the Code's automatic stay provisions. [B.C. §§ 505(c), 362]

5. Interest on Tax Claims

BAPCPA added a new section to the Code that spells out the rate at which interest is to be paid on tax claims. If the Code requires the payment of interest on a *tax claim* or an *administrative tax* claim, or the payment of interest to enable a *tax creditor* to receive the *present value* of its claim, then the interest rate is the applicable *rate under nonbankruptcy law.* [B.C. § 511(a)] In the case of taxes paid pursuant to a confirmed plan under Chapter 11, 12, or 13, the date for determining the interest rate is the calendar month in which the plan is confirmed. [B.C. § 511(b)]

6. Proof

The Supreme Court, in a unanimous decision, has held that "in the absence of modification in the Bankruptcy Code the burden of proof on a tax claim in bankruptcy remains where the substantive tax law puts it." [**Raleigh v. Illinois Department of Revenue,** 530 U.S. 15 (2000)]

7. Address for § 505 Requests

The bankruptcy clerk must maintain a list under which federal, state, and local taxing authorities may *designate an address for service of requests under § 505* and describe where to obtain more information for filing such requests. If the taxing authority does not provide the bankruptcy clerk with an address for service of § 505 requests, then these requests may be served at the address for filing of a tax return or protest with the relevant taxing authority. [B.C. § 505(b)(1)] Congress added this subsection in BAPCPA.

F. Subrogation Claims

1. Subrogee

A subrogee is an entity that *has paid* a creditor's claim against the debtor because the entity either had secured the claim or was liable with the debtor on the claim as a co-debtor, co-maker, surety, or guarantor. [B.C. § 509(a)]

2. Subrogee Receives Creditor's Rights

Generally, a subrogee succeeds to the rights of the creditor whose claim it paid to the extent of the amount paid. [B.C. § 509(a)] But remember that the subrogee of a first or fourth through ninth priority claim does not become subrogated to the holder's right to priority. [B.C. § 507(d)]

3. Exceptions

Subrogation to the rights of a creditor is not allowed in the following situations. [B.C. § 509(b)]

a. Reimbursement or Contribution Claim Allowed

To the extent that a corresponding claim of the co-debtor for reimbursement or contribution has been allowed under Bankruptcy Code § 502, subrogation is not allowed. [B.C. § 509(b)(1)(A)]

(i) Rationale

A co-debtor who has paid the principal creditor's claim is entitled to only one satisfaction of its debt. Thus, she must choose between filing a claim for reimbursement or contribution, on the one hand, and subrogation to the principal creditor's claim, on the other. [B.C. §§ 502(e)(2), 509(a)]

b. Reimbursement or Contribution Claim Disallowed

Subrogation is not allowed to the extent that a corresponding claim of the co-debtor for reimbursement or contribution has been disallowed, for example for one of the reasons specified in § 502(b). This provision does *not* apply if the claim was disallowed on the basis of § 502(e). [B.C. § 509(b)(1)(B)]

c. Reimbursement or Contribution Claim Subordinated

To the extent that a corresponding claim of the co-debtor for reimbursement or contribution has been subordinated under § 510, subrogation is not allowed. [B.C. § 509(b)(1)(C)]

d. Co-Debtor Received Consideration

To the extent that the co-debtor, rather than the debtor, received the consideration for the claim held by the principal creditor, subrogation is not allowed. [B.C. § 509(b)(2)]

4. Subordination to Principal Creditor's Claim

A co-debtor's claim, either by way of subrogation or for reimbursement or contribution, will be subordinated to the principal creditor's claim until that claim is satisfied fully, either through distribution under the Bankruptcy Code or by other means. [B.C. § 509(c)]

G. Subordination of Claims

1. Subordination Agreement

A claim in a bankruptcy case may be subordinated to the payment of other claims by a subordination contract enforceable under applicable nonbankruptcy law. [B.C. § 510(a)]

2. Subordination of Claims for Purchase or Sale of a Security

A claim for damages, rescission, or contribution or reimbursement arising from the purchase or sale of a security of the debtor or its affiliate *must be subordinated* to all claims or interests *senior or equal* to that which the security represents. [B.C. § 510(b)] One reason for the subordination rule is that Congress determined that the "risk of illegality in securities issuance should be borne by those investing in securities and not by general creditors." Another is that creditors rely on the equity cushion that shareholder investment provides. [*In re* **Lehman Bros., Inc.**, 519 B.R. 434 (S.D. N.Y. 2014)]

a. Exception: Common Stock

If the security is common stock, then the claim will be subordinated to the *same priority as common stock,* not to a lower priority. [B.C. § 510(b)]

e.g. **Example:** Debtor Corporation files a voluntary Chapter 7 petition, and Security Holder files a claim for rescission of certain purchases of *preferred stock,* based on alleged violations by Debtor Corporation of § 10(b) of the Securities Exchange Act of 1934. [15 U.S.C. § 78j(b)] A claim for rescission means that Security Holder wants to *undo* the transaction. She no longer wants to hold an equity position in Debtor Corporation; she wants damages from Debtor Corporation based on a theory of restitution. Under § 510, however, a claim for rescission results in the Security Holder being subordinated to the interest (preferred shareholder) that she held prior to rescission. Thus, Security Holder does not share in any distribution as part of the class of general unsecured creditors based on undoing the sale of preferred stock to her. Nor does she share in any distribution made to the preferred shareholders, Instead, Security Holder's claim for rescission is be paid *after* preferred shareholders are paid. In other words, her claim for rescission is subordinated to a position *below* the interests of the preferred shareholders but *above* the interests of the common shareholders.

e.g. **Example:** Assume the same facts as above, except that Security Holder's claim is for rescission of certain purchases of Debtor Corporation's *debentures.* Because debentures are unsecured debt, Security Holder, before rescission, has a general unsecured claim. Under § 510, however, the claim for rescission results in Security Holder being subordinated below the position that she held prior to rescission. Therefore, Security Holder's claim will be subordinated to a level below the claims of the general unsecured creditors but above the interests of the preferred shareholders.

e.g. **Example:** Assume that one of the claimants in Debtor Corporation's bankruptcy case is Accountant, who has been held liable, in federal district court, to certain common shareholders for damages arising from the sale of Debtor Corporation's securities in violation of the federal securities laws. Accountant has paid the judgment and now seeks reimbursement or contribution from Debtor Corporation. Accountant's claim will be subordinated to the claims of general unsecured creditors and will share in any distribution with the holders of common stock.

3. Equitable Subordination

The court, after notice and a hearing, also has the equitable power (i) to subordinate all or part of an allowed secured or unsecured claim to another allowed claim, (ii) to subordinate all or part of an allowed interest to another allowed interest, or (iii) to order that any lien securing such a subordinated claim be transferred to the estate. [B.C. § 510(c)]

a. Test

The Fifth Circuit in the pre-Code case of *In re Mobile Steel* established what has become the standard test for equitable subordination. [**United States v. Noland,** 517 U.S. 535 (1996) (noting that district courts and courts of appeals had "generally followed the *Mobile Steel* formulation"); **Sender v. Bronze Group, Ltd. (***In re* **Hedged-Investment Assocs.,** 380 F.3d 1292 (10th Cir. 2004) (stating that *Mobile Steel* has become "the standard formulation of the common law of equitable subordination")] The *Mobile Steel* test requires proof of the following elements:

(i) *inequitable conduct* on the part of the claimant to be subordinated;

(ii) *injury to the creditors* of the debtor, or an *unfair advantage* to the claimant, due to the misconduct; and

(iii) equitable subordination of the claim is *not inconsistent with the provisions of the Bankruptcy Code.*

[**Benjamin v. Diamond (*In re* Mobile Steel Co.**), 563 F.2d 692 (5th Cir. 1977)]

b. Inequitable Conduct

Generally, an essential element in the equitable subordination of a claim or interest is showing inequitable conduct on the claimant's part. Usually, such misconduct falls into one of the following categories: (i) fraud, illegality, or breach of fiduciary duties; (ii) undercapitalization; or (iii) the claimant's use of the debtor as a mere instrumentality or alter ego. [**Official Committee of Unsecured Creditors of HH Liquidation, LLC v. Comvest Group Holdings, LLC (*In re* HH Liquidation, LLC**), 590 B.R. 211 (Bankr. D. Del. 2018)] While citing favorably to the *Mobile Steel* test, the Supreme Court left open the question of whether "a bankruptcy court must always find creditor misconduct before a claim may be equitable subordinated." [**United States v. Noland**, 517 U.S. 535 (1996)]

c. Causation

When equitable subordination is used, the claim or interest is subordinated only to the extent necessary to offset the harm caused to the debtor and his creditors by the claimant's conduct.

d. Insiders and Fiduciaries

While a claimant's status as an insider or as a fiduciary generally should not, in the absence of inequitable conduct, result in subordination of his claim, courts usually rigorously examine the dealings of insiders and fiduciaries for *good faith and fairness.* [**Pepper v. Litton**, 308 U.S. 295 (1939)] In a case involving an insider, the trustee has the burden of presenting material evidence of the insider's unfair conduct. The insider then must rebut that evidence by demonstrating that her transactions with the debtor were fair. If the case involves a non-insider, however, there must be evidence of more egregious behavior, such as "fraud, spoliation or overreaching." [**Schubert v. Lucent Technologies, Inc. (*In re* Winstar Communications, Inc.**), 554 F.3d 382 (3d Cir. 2009)] The burden-shifting framework used in equitable subordination cases involving insiders does not apply to cases involving non-insiders. The trustee always has the burden of proof. [***In re* NJ Affordable Homes Corp.**, 2013 WL 6048836 (Bankr. D. N.J. 2013)]

H. Distribution Outside of Bankruptcy Code

1. Creditors of Partnership

A creditor of a partnership debtor who receives payment on an allowed claim against the partnership from a general partner who is not a debtor in a Chapter 7 case and who has not secured the creditor's claim with a lien on the general partner's own property is prohibited from receiving any payment on the claim until all of the creditors with whom she would have shared equally have received payment equal to the consideration she received from the general partner. [B.C. § 508]

IN A CHAPTER 7 CASE, CLAIMS GENERALLY ARE SATISFIED IN THE FOLLOWING ORDER:

☑ *Secured claims,* out of the collateral securing them (cash or the collateral itself)

☑ *Unsecured priority claims:* All claims in each category are paid before any claims in a lower category are paid

First — *Domestic support obligations and administrative expenses* of trustee to the extent the trustee administers assets to pay the domestic support obligation claim

Second — *Administrative expenses,* such as the actual and necessary costs of preserving the estate (e.g., normal operating expenses of a Chapter 11 business), post-petition taxes incurred by the estate, trustee and examiner fees, certain attorney and accountant fees and bankruptcy filing fees and certain Chapter 11 quarterly fees. A secured creditor may have a super-priority claim for adequate protection deficiencies. With court approval, a creditor that extends post-petition credit or debt to the debtor will have a super super-priority administrative expense that has priority over all other administrative expenses, including those with super-priority

Third — *Involuntary case gap claims* that arise in the ordinary course of the debtor's business or financial affairs between the time an involuntary petition is filed and the earlier of the appointment of a trustee or the order for relief

Fourth — *Claims for wages or commissions* earned up to 180 days before the earlier of the filing of the bankruptcy petition or the cessation of the debtor's business; limited to $13,650 per claim

Fifth — *Employee benefit plan contributions* for services rendered within 180 days before the earlier of the filing of the bankruptcy petition or the cessation of the debtor's business; limited to the number of employees covered by the plan times $13,650, minus (a) the total amount paid to such employees under the fourth priority plus (b) the total amount paid by the estate to any other benefit plan for such employees

Sixth — *Claims of grain farmers and U.S. fishermen* against debtors who run grain or fish processing or storage facilities; limited to $6,725 per claim

Seventh — *Claims of individuals for return of pre-petition deposits on consumer goods or services* that were not delivered or performed; limited to $3,025 per claim

Eighth — *Certain tax claims,* such as an income tax for which a return was due within three years before the bankruptcy petition was filed

Ninth — *Claims of a federal depository institutions regulatory agency* for the amount of any deficiency under the debtor's agreement to maintain the capital of an insured depository institution

Tenth — *Death or personal injury claims* arising from debtor's operation of a motor vehicle or vessel while intoxicated

☑ *General unsecured claims*

IN A CASE UNDER CHAPTER 11, 12, OR 13, PAYMENT MUST COMPLY WITH THE REQUIREMENTS FOR CONFIRMATION UNDER THE RESPECTIVE CHAPTER, AND PAYMENT MAY BE ALTERED PURSUANT TO A PLAN.

Chapter Eight
Debtor's Exemptions

CONTENTS

Chapter Approach

This is the first of two chapters covering the areas of bankruptcy law that give the debtor a "fresh start." This chapter covers exemptions and redemption; both topics deal with the debtor's ability to exit bankruptcy with property sufficient to embark on a fresh financial start. The next chapter covers discharge and the Code's provisions protecting debtors against discrimination post-bankruptcy. An individual debtor is entitled to *exempt* certain *property* from the bankruptcy estate. *See* Chapter 5. By allowing the debtor to exempt property, the Code ensures that bankruptcy does not leave the debtor destitute and without the basic necessities of life. The debtor may elect either the exemptions provided for by the Bankruptcy Code, if the debtor's domiciliary state has not opted out, or those permitted under applicable state exemption law. Exemption law after the Bankruptcy Abuse Prevention and Consumer Protection Act ("BAPCPA") now contains federal limitations on exemptions even for debtors using the exemptions provided by state law. Congress enacted these limitations to curtail debtors from forum shopping in an effort to obtain the benefit of more favorable exemptions.

Your professor may test you on the debtor's ability to avoid certain liens and security interests in order to take full advantage of available exemptions. You need to understand how to apply the Code's rules that allow a debtor to avoid judicial liens and certain nonpossessory nonpurchase-money security interests to the extent that they *impair an exemption* of the debtor.

Finally, an individual debtor may choose to *redeem* tangible personal property from a lien by paying the secured party the market value of the collateral. Redemption, however, is available only in a Chapter 7 case and only for dischargeable consumer debts.

A. Exemptions

1. Fresh Start: Exempt Property

Usually, an individual debtor does not come out of bankruptcy completely dispossessed of all assets, because she is entitled to certain exemptions from property of the estate, either under the Bankruptcy Code or pursuant to applicable state law and nonbankruptcy federal law. These exemptions apply only to individual debtors—not to partnerships or corporations—in cases under Chapters 7, 11, 12, and 13, and exemptions cannot be waived in favor of an unsecured creditor. [B.C. §§ 103(a), 522(e)]

a. States Opting out

Thirty-five states have rejected the federal bankruptcy exemption scheme, thereby restricting debtors domiciled there to the exemptions allowable under state law and federal nonbankruptcy law. These states are: Alabama, Arizona, California, Colorado, Delaware, Florida, Georgia, Idaho, Illinois, Indiana, Iowa, Kansas, Kentucky, Louisiana, Maine, Maryland, Mississippi, Missouri, Montana, Nebraska, Nevada, New Hampshire, New York, North Carolina, North Dakota, Ohio, Oklahoma, Oregon, South Carolina, South Dakota, Tennessee, Utah, Virginia, West Virginia, and Wyoming. Section 522(b)(2) authorizes the states to opt out.

b. States Not Opting out

In states that have not opted out, the debtor is free to choose *either* the federal bankruptcy exemptions or those permitted under applicable state and federal nonbankruptcy law. [B.C. §§ 522(b)(1), (2)]

(i) Joint Case

In a case filed or administered jointly, both spouses must elect the same exemption plan, either state or federal. If the debtors are not able to agree, they will be deemed to have chosen the federal bankruptcy exemptions. [B.C. § 522(b)]

2. Federal Bankruptcy Exemptions

In states that have not opted out, the debtor may elect the federal exemptions. The maximum amount of the exemptions increases every three years. [B.C. § 104(a)] The next increase will occur on *April 1, 2022.* Currently, the maximum exemptions of a debtor's interests in property permitted under the Code are as follows. [B.C. § 522(d)]

a. Homestead

The debtor may exempt up to $25,150 in real or personal property used by the debtor or a dependent as a *residence,* or in a *burial plot* for the debtor or a dependent. [B.C. § 522(d)(1)]

b. Motor Vehicle

There is a maximum exemption of $4,000 allowed for *one* motor vehicle. [B.C. § 522(d)(2)]

c. Household Goods, Crops, Animals

There is an exemption of up to $625 in any item of household furnishings, household goods, clothing, appliances, books, musical instruments, crops, or animals, whose primary purpose is for the *personal, family, or household use* of the debtor or a dependent. *But note*: This exemption may not exceed $13,400 in total value. [B.C. § 522(d)(3)]

d. Jewelry

There is an exemption of up to $1,700 in jewelry held principally for the personal, family, or household use of the debtor or a dependent. [B.C. § 522(d)(4)]

e. Wildcard Exemption

There is an exemption of up to $1,325, plus up to $12,575 of any unused portion of the homestead exemption, *in any property.* [B.C. § 522(d)(1), (5)] This exemption, with a current ceiling of $13,900, is designed primarily for the benefit of non-homeowner debtors.

e.g. **Example:** Doris rents an apartment. Several years ago, her grandmother passed away and left her a necklace and earring set valued at approximately $15,000. Doris may use the jewelry exemption to exempt $1,700 of the set's value, and because she rents she may apply the entire wild card exemption of $13,900 to the remaining value of the necklace and earring set.

e.g. **Example:** Doris has $25,150 in equity in her home. Several years ago, her grandmother passed away and left her a necklace and earring set valued at approximately $14,000. Doris uses the homestead exemption to exempt $25,150 of the equity in her home. That leaves her only $1,325of the wild card exemption to apply to the jewelry set. While Doris also may use the jewelry exemption, the combined wild card and jewelry exemptions permit Doris to exempt only $3,025 of the jewelry set's $14,000 value.

f. Tools of the Trade

The debtor may exempt up to $2,525 in her professional books or tools of the trade or those of a dependent. [B.C. § 522(d)(6)]

g. Life Insurance

The debtor may exempt any *unmatured* life insurance contract that she owns, except a credit life insurance contract. [B.C. § 522(d)(7)]

h. Loan Value or Accrued Interest of Life Insurance

There is an exemption of up to $13,400 in the loan value or in accrued interest or dividends of any unmatured life insurance contract that the debtor owns. [B.C. § 522(d)(8)]

(i) Insured

For purposes of this exemption, the insured must be either the debtor or an individual with respect to whom the debtor is a dependent. [B.C. § 522(d)(8)] For purposes of § 522, a dependent includes, but is not limited to, a spouse, regardless of whether the spouse is, in fact, dependent. [B.C. § 522(a)(1)]

i. Health Aids

There is an exemption for health aids prescribed by a professional for the debtor or a dependent. [B.C. § 522(d)(9)]

j. Government Benefits

There is an exemption for the debtor's right to receive social security benefits, veterans' benefits, local public assistance, unemployment benefits or compensation, or disability or illness benefits. [B.C. §§ 522(d)(10)(A)–(C)]

k. Alimony, Support, or Maintenance

The debtor may exempt payments received for alimony, support, or maintenance, to the extent that it is reasonably necessary to support the debtor and any dependent. [B.C. § 522(d)(10)(D)]

l. Pension Plan

The debtor may exempt payments under an eligible pension plan or similar contract based on length of service, age, illness, disability, or death, to the extent that such payment is reasonably necessary to support the debtor and any dependent, is exempted. [B.C. § 522(d)(10)(E)]

(i) Exception

This exemption does not apply **(1)** to payments under a plan or contract that was established by or under the auspices of an insider that employed the debtor at the time that the debtor's rights arose; **(2)** such payments are on account of age or length of service; and **(3)** the plan or contract does not qualify under § 401(a), 403(a), 403(b), or 408 of the Internal Revenue Code. [B.C. §§ 522(d)(10)(E)(i)–(iii)]

m. Crime Victim Award

The debtor may exempt property or payments received pursuant to an award under a crime victim's reparation law. [B.C. § 522(d)(11)(A)]

n. Wrongful Death Award

There is an exemption for the debtor's right to receive payment arising from the wrongful death of an individual with respect to whom the debtor was a dependent, to the extent that the payment is reasonably necessary to support the debtor and any of her dependents. [B.C. § 522(d)(11)(B)]

o. Life Insurance Proceeds

The debtor may exempt a payment under a life insurance contract that insured the life of an individual if debtor was a dependent of that individual on the date of the individual's death. The debtor may exempt the payment only to the extent that the payment is reasonably necessary to support the debtor and any of her dependents. [B.C. § 522(d)(11)(C)]

p. Personal Injury Award

The debtor may exempt payments, up to a maximum of $25,150, arising from personal bodily injury of the debtor or an individual with respect to whom the debtor is a dependent, is exempted. This exemption does not include compensation for pain and suffering or compensation for actual pecuniary loss, such as medical expenses. [B.C. § 522(d)(11)(D)]

q. Loss of Future Earnings

The debtor may exempt compensation for the loss of future earnings of either the debtor or an individual with respect to whom the debtor was or is a dependent, to the extent that the payment is reasonably necessary to support the debtor and any of her dependents. [B.C. § 522(d)(11)(E)]

r. Retirement Funds

Congress added an exemption in BAPCPA for the debtor's retirements funds, so long as the monies are in a fund or account that is exempt from taxation under certain provisions of the Internal Revenue Code. [B.C. § 522(d)(12); 26 U.S.C. §§ 401, 403, 408, 408A, 414, 457, 501(a)] At the same time, Congress created a limit on the aggregate value of assets in certain IRAs that an individual debtor may exempt. [B.C. § 522(n); 26 U.S.C. §§ 408, 408A] The *limitation* now stands at *$1,362,800.* The limitation does not apply to certain simplified employee pensions or simple retirement accounts. [B.C. § 522(n); 26 U.S.C. §§ 408(k), (p)] The aggregate value limitation also does not apply to certain rollover contributions and earnings on those contributions. [B.C. § 522(n); 26 U.S.C. §§ 402(c), (e)(6); 403(a)(4), (5); 403(b)(8)] Finally, a court may increase the monetary cap in the interests of justice. [B.C. § 522(n)]

3. State Exemptions and Nonbankruptcy Federal Exemptions

a. Introduction

If the debtor does not elect the federal bankruptcy exemptions or if the debtor's domiciliary state has opted out, the exemptions available to the debtor are those allowable under applicable state law and nonbankruptcy federal law, subject to the Bankruptcy Code's domiciliary requirement and to new Code restrictions on state homestead exemptions. [B.C. §§ 522(b)(3), (o), (p), (q)]

b. *Which State Law Exemptions?*

BAPCPA made the determination of which state law exemptions apply to the debtor more difficult. Subject to the Code's domiciliary requirement and to federal restrictions on state homestead exemptions, the exemptions allowable under state law are those in effect: (i) as of the date the bankruptcy petition was filed and (ii) in the state where the debtor has been domiciled for the *730 days or two years* prior to filing the bankruptcy petition. If the debtor has not been domiciled in a single state for 730 days, then the exemption law of the place where debtor has been domiciled for the *180 days immediately preceding the 730-day period* applies. If the debtor has not been domiciled in a single state for the *180-day period,* then the exemption law of the place where debtor has been domiciled for the *longest portion of the 180-day period* applies. State law exemptions vary widely from state to state. [B.C. § 522(b)(2)(A)]

Example: Darren files for relief under Chapter 7 on March 5, 2018, in the Western District of Michigan. Darren grew up in Chicago, Illinois, but changed his domicile to Grand Rapids, Michigan on July 5, 2017. As a result, Darren has lived in Michigan for only eight months, which is less than the 730 days required by the Bankruptcy Code. Two years or 730 days prior to March 5, 2018 is March 5, 2016. For the six months prior to March 5, 2016, Darren was domiciled in Chicago, Illinois. Therefore, the Illinois exemptions apply to Darren's case, even though he lives in Michigan at the time of his bankruptcy filing.

c. Problems with the Domiciliary Requirement

(i) The "Hanging Paragraph"

If the 730-day/180-day domiciliary requirement results in the debtor being ineligible for any exemption, then the debtor may elect the federal exemptions. This new "hanging paragraph" applies regardless of whether debtor's domicile is in an opt-out state. [B.C. § 522(b)(3)]

Example: On April 19, 2006, Debtor filed for relief under Chapter 7 in the bankruptcy court for the Middle District of Florida. At the time that he filed for bankruptcy, Debtor had lived in Florida for less than a year. Prior to the Florida move, Debtor's domicile was Indiana. In his bankruptcy case, Debtor claimed the federal exemptions, even though Florida is an opt-out state. The trustee objected, claiming that Debtor was limited to Indiana's exemptions. Indiana, however, limited its exemptions to debtors domiciled in the state on the date of the bankruptcy filing. The bankruptcy court held that Debtor could claim the federal exemptions based on the "hanging paragraph" at the end of § 522(b)(3). The court explained that Debtor could not claim the Florida exemptions, because he was not domiciled in Florida at the time of bankruptcy, and also could not claim the Indiana exemptions, which were limited to debtors domiciled in Indiana at the time of bankruptcy filing. Because the operation of the domiciliary requirement rendered Debtor ineligible for any exemption, the court concluded that Debtor could claim the federal exemptions. [*In re* **West,** 352 B.R. 905 (Bankr. M.D. Fla. 2006)]

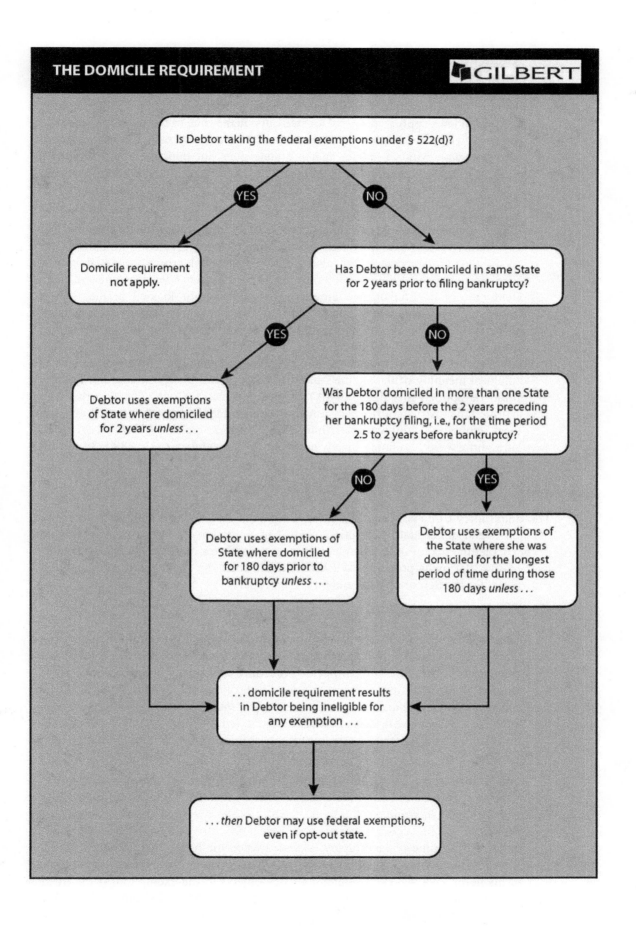

(ii) Application of a State's Exemptions to Property Located Outside the State

Another issue under the Code's new domiciliary requirement is whether a state's exemption laws apply to property located outside the state of bankruptcy filing when state exemption law is silent on that question. The *majority rule* is the *state-specific interpretation,* which provides that if a state does not limit the application of its exemption laws to property located inside the state then the bankruptcy court may apply a state's exemption laws to the debtor's property wherever it may be located.

e.g. **Example:** Married Debtors filed for relief under Chapter 7 in the Northern District of West Virginia approximately four months after moving from Louisiana. Debtors exempted real and personal property located in Louisiana using the Louisiana exemptions, but also exempted personal property located in West Virginia using the Louisiana exemptions. The Chapter 7 trustee objected to the Debtors' use of Louisiana exemptions to property not located in the State of Louisiana. The bankruptcy court held that Debtors could exempt their personal property in West Virginia using Louisiana's exemptions. On appeal, the district court affirmed the bankruptcy court's decision and adopted the state-specific interpretation. The district court held that the state-specific interpretation was the "plainest meaning of the statute" and the "most liberal interpretation that feasibly" could be applied to § 522(b)(3)(A) of the Bankruptcy Code. The Fourth Circuit affirmed the district court's decision and explained that "the state-specific approach 'best embodies congressional intent,' in that it treats § 522(b)(3)(A) as a 'straightforward . . . choice-of-law provision.' " [**Sheehan v. Ash,** 889 F.3d 171 (4th Cir. 2018)]

d. Federal Limitations on Homestead Exemptions

The Bankruptcy Code now contains three limitations on a debtor's right to fully exempt her homestead under state exemption laws. The limitations apply to *real or personal property* that the debtor or a dependent *uses as a residence* or *claims as a homestead,* a *cooperative* that owns property used by the debtor or a dependent as a *residence,* or a *burial plot* for the debtor or a dependent ("the Property").

(i) The Fraud Limitation

The fraud limitation reduces the amount of the debtor's state exemption to the extent that the debtor, *with intent to hinder, delay or defraud creditors,* disposed of *non-exempt property* in the *10-year period* preceding bankruptcy in order to increase the amount of the state-law exemption taken in the Property described above. Courts apply the same standard for *intent to hinder, delay or defraud creditors* under § 522(o) that they use under § 548. [B.C. §§ 522(o), 548(a)(1)(A)] If the debtor files for relief under Chapter 7, the trustee also may object to the debtor's discharge under § 727(a)(2).

e.g. **Example:** Debtor files for relief under Chapter 7. He owns a home valued, at the time of bankruptcy, at $400,000. A month prior to bankruptcy, Debtor had $100,000 in equity in his home. Debtor withdrew large sums of non-exempt cash from several accounts and applied these sums to pay down the mortgage on his home. At the time of bankruptcy, Debtor owned the home free and clear. Debtor lives in a state with a generous homestead exemption, so he exempts all $400,000 of his home's value. The Chapter 7 trustee objects to the exemption. If the trustee can show that Debtor acted with intent to hinder, delay, or defraud creditors, then Debtor may only exempt $100,000 of his home's value.

(ii) The 1215-Day Limitation

The Bankruptcy Code places a cap of *$170,350* on any interest that the debtor acquires in the Property described above during the *1215-day period* preceding the filing of bankruptcy. [B.C. § 522(p)(1)] This restriction does not apply to the *principal residence of a family farmer.* [B.C. § 522(p)(2)(A)] It also does not apply if the debtor uses the money received from sale of a residence acquired before the 1215-day period to acquire a new residence in the *same state* during the 1215-day period. [B.C. § 522(p)(2)(B)]

(iii) The "Bad Conduct" Limitation

The Bankruptcy Code caps the debtor's exemptible interest at *$170,350* on the Property described above in cases involving certain types of bad conduct by the debtor. The cap does not apply to the extent that the amount of the debtor's interest in the property is *reasonably necessary for the support* of the debtor and any dependents of the debtor. [B.C. §§ 522(q)(1), (2)] The cap applies to the debtor who:

(1) is a *felon* and the court determines that filing for bankruptcy is an *abuse* of the Bankruptcy Code [B.C. § 522(q)(1)(A)];

(2) owes a debt arising from *violations of the federal or state securities laws,* or regulations or orders issued pursuant to federal or state securities laws [B.C. § 522(q)(1)(B)(i)];

(3) owes a debt arising from *fraud, deceit, or manipulation in a fiduciary capacity* or in connection with the *purchase or sale of securities registered under the federal securities laws* [B.C. § 522(q)(1)(B)(ii)];

(4) owes a debt arising from any *civil remedy under 18 U.S.C. § 1964* [B.C. § 522(q)(1)(B)(iii)]; or

(5) owes a debt arising from any *criminal act, intentional tort, or willful or reckless misconduct* that caused *physical injury or death* to another person in the *five years* prior to filing for bankruptcy. [B.C. § 522(q)(1)(B)(iv)]

(iv) "Electing" State Exemptions

The Bankruptcy Code provides that the restrictions on exemptions in §§ 552(p) and (q) apply "as a result of [the debtor's] electing" the state law exemptions. Courts have grappled with whether Congress intended this language to apply only to debtors in states that have not opted out of the federal exemptions. In opt-out states, debtors must select the state exemptions and, therefore, do not elect them. The issue is limited to §§ 522(p) and (q), because § 522(o) does not contain the "as a result of electing" language. The *majority rule* is that *§§ 522(p) and (q) apply in both opt-out and non-opt-out states,* because Congress intended, when drafting those sections, to close the so-called mansion loophole.

e.g. **Example:** Debtors filed for relief under Chapter 7. They listed a home worth $318,000 and noted that the home was subject to a mortgage of $158,000. The debtors used Nevada's exemptions to exempt the remaining $160,000 in equity in their home. The Chapter 7 trustee objected to the debtors' exemption, claiming that the debtors had not owned their home for at least 1215 days before the bankruptcy filing. The debtors argued that § 522(p) did not apply to them, because they filed for bankruptcy in an opt-out state and, thus, had not elected the state law exemptions. The bankruptcy court rejected the debtors' argument and concluded that the "electing" language in § 522(p) was a scrivener's error. The bankruptcy court held that "Congress intended to close the mansion loophole in opt-in states as well as opt-out states." [*In re* **Kane,** 336 B.R. 477 (Bankr. D. Nev. 2006)]

e. Nonbankruptcy Federal Law

Federal statutes other than the Bankruptcy Code sometimes provide exemptions that may be claimed under § 522(b)(3)(A), such as Social Security payments [42 U.S.C. § 407], veterans' benefits [38 U.S.C. § 5301], civil service retirement benefits [5 U.S.C. § 8346(a)], or military pension benefits. [38 U.S.C. § 5301] For a list of other benefits that the debtor may exempt, *see* 4 Collier ¶ 522.02(3).

f. Tenancy by the Entirety and Joint Tenancy

A debtor who uses the state exemption alternative also may exempt any interest in property she held, immediately prior to bankruptcy, as a tenant by the entirety or as a joint tenant, to the extent that applicable nonbankruptcy law (usually state property law) exempts such interest from process. [B.C. § 522(b)(3)(B)] It is important to recognize that the treatment of property held by the entirety or in a joint tenancy depends on how state law treats such property.

(i) Which State Law Governs?

The location of the property determines the applicable state law. The 730-day/180-day domiciliary timelines are located in § 522(b)(3)(A), while the entireties property and joint tenancy provision is located in § 522(b)(3)(B). Therefore, the phrase "applicable nonbankruptcy law" in § 522(b)(3)(B) is the law of the state where such property is located. [4 Collier ¶ 522.06]

(ii) Tenancy by the Entirety

If only one of the tenants is a debtor in the case, her entitlement to exempt property under section 522(b)(3)(B) may depend not only on any protection from process afforded by applicable nonbankruptcy law, but also on the absence of any joint creditors. When a bankruptcy petition is filed by one spouse holding property as a tenant by the entirety with her non-filing husband, the property is exempt in most jurisdictions if there are *no joint* creditors. [B.C. § 522(b)(2)(B)] However, the First, Third, Fourth, Sixth and Eighth Circuits, interpreting various state exemption laws, have ruled that property held by the entirety is not exempt to the extent of any claims in the case by creditors to whom the debtor and her spouse are *indebted jointly.* [**Edmonston v. Murphy** *(In re* **Edmonston),** 107 F.3d 74 (1st Cir. 1997) (holding that debtor was not entitled to exemption for his residence, which was entireties property, because Massachusetts law allowed joint creditors to reach entireties property); *In re* **Garner,** 952 F.2d 232 (8th Cir. 1991) (holding that under Missouri law joint creditors may reach entireties property); **Sumy v. Schlossberg,** 777 F.2d 921 (4th Cir. 1985) ("reaffirming the guiding principle of all of [the Circuit's] relevant cases that joint creditors are entitled . . . to reach entireties property to satisfy their claims"); *In re* **Grosslight,** 757 F.2d 773 (6th Cir. 1985) (joint creditor may reach a "spouse's individual undivided interest in entireties property"); and **Napotnik v. Equibank & Parkvale Sav. Assoc.,** 679 F.2d 316 (3d Cir. 1982) (debtor could not avoid joint creditor's judicial lien on entireties property and could exempt only the equity in excess of that joint creditor's lien)]

The Seventh Circuit reached a different conclusion when interpreting Indiana's exemption laws. The court concluded that Indiana law "create[d] a blanket exemption for entirety property in the bankruptcy context." Thus, a debtor who owns entireties property with her non-debtor spouse may exempt the entireties property in her bankruptcy case and protect it from the claims of joint creditors. [*In re* **Paeplow**, 972 F.2d 730 (7th Cir. 1992)]

(iii) Joint Tenancy

When a joint tenant files for relief under the Bankruptcy Code, her proportionate interest in the joint tenancy becomes property of the estate. If the debtor owns property as a joint tenant with two other non-debtors, the debtor's one-third interest in the property becomes estate property. The issue, then, is the extent of the debtor's exemption in the property. The Eighth Circuit held that under Missouri law the debtor, one of three joint tenants, could take the entire state law homestead exemption, because there was no evidence that her non-debtor co-tenants had claimed an exemption in the property. [**Abernathy v. LaBarge (*In re* Abernathy**), 259 B.R. 330 (8th Cir. 2001)]

The courts are split as to whether filing for bankruptcy severs the joint tenancy, thereby destroying the right of survivorship. The issue arises when one joint tenant dies during the pendency of the bankruptcy case. Does the trustee become a tenant in common with the surviving prior joint tenants?

e.g. **Example:** Debtor and her father were joint tenants of three certificates of deposit ("CDs"). Debtor filed for bankruptcy but died during the pendency of the bankruptcy case. The trustee claimed that one-half of the CD funds belonged to the bankruptcy estate, because filing for bankruptcy had severed the joint tenancy with the non-debtor father and, thus, destroyed the father's right of survivorship to the CDs. The trustee claimed that he and Debtor's father held the CDs as tenants in common. The bankruptcy court rejected the trustee's argument. The court held that § 522(b)(2)(B) "treats tenants by the entireties and joint tenants identically" and, thus, if filing for bankruptcy "does not sever the estate of [a] tenant by the entirety, then such filing does not sever joint tenants." The bankruptcy court also found that bankruptcy filing did not sever a joint tenancy under West Virginia law. Thus, the CD funds passed to Debtor's father by his right of survivorship. [*In re* **DeMarco**, 114 B.R. 121 (Bankr. W.D. W.Va. 1990)]

cf. **Compare:** A married couple filed a joint petition for relief under the Bankruptcy Code. During the pendency of the case, the husband died. The couple owned real property as joint tenants. The bankruptcy court held that the bankruptcy filing severed the joint tenancy, thereby terminating the wife's right to survivorship and making her and the trustee tenants in common. The court ruled that the deceased husband's bankruptcy estate held a one-half interest in the real property. [*In re* **Tyson**, 48 B.R. 412 (Bankr. C.D. Ill. 1985)]

(iv) Sale of Property

The trustee may *sell* both the *estate's interest* and the *interest of any co-owner* in property in which the debtor, as of the commencement of the case, had an undivided interest as a *tenant in common, joint tenant, or tenant by the entirety*. The trustee must satisfy the conditions set forth in Bankruptcy Code § 363(h).

g. Retirement Funds

(i) Introduction

With BAPCPA, Congress expanded the right of debtors to exempt retirement funds. It added a new subsection to § 522(d) allowing debtors who elect the federal exemptions to exempt certain retirement funds. [B.C. § 522(d)(12); 26 U.S.C. §§ 401, 403, 408, 408A, 414, 457, 501(a)] At the same time, Congress gave debtors claiming state exemptions the same right to exempt retirement funds as provided to debtors claiming the federal exemptions. [B.C. § 522(b)(3)(C)]

(ii) Monetary Cap

The Bankruptcy Code places a cap of *$1,362,800* on the amount of retirement assets that a debtor may exempt in an *individual retirement account* under *§ 408 or § 408A (Roth IRA)* of the Internal Revenue Code. A *simplified employee pension plan* under *§ 408(k)* and a *simple retirement account* under *§ 408(p)* of the Internal Revenue Code are *not included* under the rule. The dollar limitation *does not apply* to amounts in the individual retirement account that are attributable to *rollover contributions* under §§ 402(c), 402(e)(6), 403(a)(4), 403(a)(5), and 403(b)(8) of the Internal Revenue Code or to *earnings on such rollover contributions.* [B.C. § 522(n)]

(iii) Type of Funds Covered

The debtor may exempt retirement funds, using either § 522(d)(12) (federal exemptions) or § 522(b)(3)(C) (state exemptions), in the following situations:

(1) the *retirement fund* has received a *favorable determination* under the relevant section of the Internal Revenue Code of 1986 and that determination is *in effect on the petition filing date* [B.C. § 522(b)(4)(A); 26 U.S.C. § 7805];

(2) the *retirement fund* has *not* received a *favorable determination* under the relevant section of the Internal Revenue Code of 1986 *but the debtor demonstrates* that:

    (a) there is no *prior determination to the contrary* by a court or the IRS; and

    (b) the retirement fund *substantially complies* with applicable requirements of the Internal Revenue Code *or* the *debtor is not materially responsible* for the fund's failure to *substantially comply* [B.C. § 522(b)(4)(B)];

(3) a *direct transfer from a tax-exempt fund* [B.C. § 522(b)(4)(B); 26 U.S.C. §§ 401, 401(a)(31), 403, 408, 408A, 414, 457, 501(a)];

(4) an eligible *rollover distribution* under the Internal Revenue Code [B.C. § 522(b)(4)(D)(i); 26 U.S.C. § 402(c)]; or

(5) a *distribution from a tax-exempt fund or account* that, to the extent allowed by law, is *deposited into a tax-exempt fund or account* no later than *60 days* after the distribution. [B.C. § 522(b)(4)(D)(ii); 26 U.S.C. §§ 401, 403, 408, 408A, 414, 457, 501(a)]

(iv) Inherited IRA

An inherited IRA is a traditional or a Roth IRA that is inherited after the death of the IRA's owner. The Supreme Court, in a unanimous opinion, has held that monies in an inherited IRA do not qualify for exemption under § 522(b)(3)(C) because the monies do not constitute retirement funds. The Court explained that several characteristics of an inherited IRA, including the Tax Code's requirement that the heir withdraw all the funds within five years of the owner's death or take minimum annual distributions, differentiated it from traditional and Roth IRAs used for retirement planning. If a surviving spouse inherits the IRA, she may treat it as an inherited IRA *or* roll it over into her own IRA. If she rolls it over, then she can exempt it under § 522(b)(3)(C). The Internal Revenue Code, however, provides the roll over option only to a surviving spouse. [**Clark v. Rameker,** 573 U.S. 122 (2014); *see* **Lerbakken v. Sieloff and Associates (*In re* Lerbakken),** 590 B.R. 895 (B.A.P. 8th Cir. 2018) (holding that debtor could not exempt retirement monies that he received in divorce settlement, because the Supreme Court in *Clark v. Rameker* had "clearly suggest[ed] that the exemption is limited to individuals who create and contribute funds into the retirement account [and that] [r]etirement funds obtained or received by any other means do not meet this definition")]

4. Joint Case

In a joint case, ***each debtor*** is entitled to a separate claim of any allowable exemptions. [B.C. § 522(m)]

a. Federal Exemptions

The law is clear that joint debtors who elect the federal exemptions may stack their exemptions. Thus, a married couple may exempt up to $50,300 in their homestead and up to $26,800 in certain items intended for the personal, family, or household use of the debtors. [B.C. § 522(m)] *Note:* Married debtors cannot double the $625 per item limit for household goods, however. The purpose of § 522(m) is not to give married couples the right to exempt better, i.e., more expensive, items of household goods than their single debtor counterparts.

(i) But Recall

In a joint case, ***both debtors*** must choose either the federal exemptions or the state exemptions, because the Code prohibits the stacking of federal and state exemptions. Thus, one spouse may not elect the federal exemptions while the other spouse elects the state exemptions. [B.C. § 522(b)(1)]

b. State Exemptions

In opt-out states, where debtors cannot elect the federal exemptions, the question has arisen as to whether married debtors may use § 522(m) to double the value of their states' exemption value. The majority of courts have held that state law controls whether debtors in opt-out states may stack state law exemption values. Thus, § 522(m) creates no "right to exemption doubling under state law where it does not otherwise exist." [***In re* Pace,** 521 B.R. 124 (Bankr. N.D. Miss. 2014)]

e.g. **Example:** Husband and Wife filed a joint petition for relief under Chapter 7 in the bankruptcy court for the Northern District of Mississippi. Mississippi law, at the time, provided for a $75,000 homestead. Debtors doubled the homestead exemption value and exempted the full $130,000 value of their home. The Chapter 7 trustee objected to the exemption, and the bankruptcy court ruled in favor of the trustee. The court held that the Mississippi "statute [did] not provide for more than one homestead exemption to be applied to a single residence, regardless of how many individuals reside[d] therein." As a result, debtors only could exempt $75,000 of the $130,000 equity in their home. [***In re* Pace,** 521 B.R. 124 (Bankr. N.D. Miss. 2014)]

Note: The analysis differs, however, in cases involving § 522(p). Section 522(m) provides that "*this* section shall apply separately with respect to each debtor in a joint case." [B.C. § 522(m)] Section 522(p) is a subsection of § 522 and, thus, included within § 522(m)'s "this section" language. As a result, some courts have held that married debtors may double the homestead value limitation in § 522(p). [***In re* Rasmussen,** 349 B.R. 747 (Bankr. M.D. Fla. 2006)]

Example: Husband and Wife filed a joint petition for relief under Chapter 7 in the Middle District of Florida. The couple exempted equity worth $175,000 in their home. Because the debtors had not owned their home for at least 1215 days prior to filing for bankruptcy, the Chapter 7 trustee objected to the exemption under § 522(p). The bankruptcy court allowed the debtors to exempt the full $175,000 in equity by stacking, pursuant to § 522(m), the then-$125,000 exemption limitation for a homestead acquired within 1215 days of bankruptcy filing. [*In re* **Rasmussen,** *supra*]

5. List of Exemptions

The debtor must file a list of the property that she claims as exempt. If the debtor fails to file a list of exemptions, a dependent of the debtor may file the list. [B.C. § 522(*l*); Bankruptcy Rule 4003(a); Official Form 106C]

a. Amendments

The debtor may amend her list of exemptions as a matter of course at any time before the close of the case. [Bankruptcy Rule 1009(a)] A bankruptcy court, however, has the discretion to deny an amendment if the debtor proposes the amendment in bad faith or the amendment would prejudice creditors. [**Grueneich v. Doeling (*In re* Grueneich),** 400 B.R. 680 (B.A.P. 8th Cir. 2009)]

b. Objections

(i) In General

Any party in interest may object to the debtor's claim of exemptions. With limited exceptions, the objection must be filed within *30 days after the later* of: (i) the conclusion of the § 341 meeting or (ii) the filing of an amendment to the list or supplemental schedules, unless *for cause* the court grants an extension. A request for an extension must be filed within the 30-day period to object. [Bankruptcy Rule 4003(b)(1)] Objections must be served on the trustee, the debtor and the debtor's attorney, and any person who filed the list and that person's attorney. [Bankruptcy Rule 4003(b)(4)]

(ii) By Trustee for Fraud

The *trustee* may file an objection to the debtor's claimed exemptions at any time *before one year after the closing* of the case if the debtor *fraudulently asserted* the claimed exemptions. The trustee must deliver or mail its objection to the debtor, the debtor's attorney, and to any person filing the list of exempt property as well as that person's attorney. [Bankruptcy Rule 4003(b)(2)]

(iii) Homestead Exemption Limitation

Any party in interest may object to the debtor's claim of exemption under § 522(q). The objection must be filed *before the case closes.* If the debtor first claims the exemption in a reopened case, then the objection must be filed before the reopened case closes. [Bankruptcy Rule 4003(b)(3); B.C. § 522(q)]

(iv) Failure to Object

If no objection is filed by a party in interest, the property described on the debtor's list of exemptions is deemed as exempt. [B.C. § 522(*l*)] In two cases, the Supreme Court has weighed in on the consequences of a failure to object within the 30-day time frame established by Bankruptcy Rule 4003(b)(1).

Example: Debtor exempted a potential award from a pending employment discrimination lawsuit and listed the value of the exemption as "unknown." The trustee did not object. After the period for objection had expired, the lawsuit settled for $110,000, and the trustee sought the proceeds, claiming that the debtor could legitimately exempt only a small portion of the $110,000 award. The Supreme Court held that a late objection will not be allowed even if the debtor has no colorable basis for claiming the exemption. [**Taylor v. Freeland & Kronz,** 503 U.S. 638 (1992)]

Example: Debtor listed $10,718 worth of business equipment and using the federal exemptions then in effect exempted the full value of that equipment. An appraisal of the equipment showed a value in excess of the $10,718 assigned by the debtor and the trustee moved to auction the equipment in order to capture the excess value for the benefit of the estate's creditors. The debtor objected, claiming that by equating the exemption amount with the value provided for the equipment she intended to exempt the full value of that equipment, regardless of whether it exceeded the value exempted or allowed under the exemption. The Supreme Court held that the trustee was not obligated to object within the time frame established by the Bankruptcy Rules in order to preserve the estate's right to value in excess of the debtor's claimed exemption. The Court distinguished *Taylor,* resting its decision on notice to the trustee and other possible objecting parties. If the trustee or objecting party knows or cannot determine that the exemption amount claimed, e.g., debtor puts "unknown" on Schedule C, exceeds the exemption's monetary limit, then the exemption stands if there is no timely objection. Where the exemption amount claimed, however, does not exceed the exemption's monetary limit, then there is no duty to object. [**Schwab v. Reilly,** 560 U.S. 770 (2010)]

Note: The current version of Schedule C (exemptions) now contains a box for the debtor to check that says "100% of fair market value, up to any applicable statutory limit." [Official Form 106C] Bankruptcy Rule 4003(b) also has been amended to allow the trustee additional time to object in cases of alleged fraud.

6. Effect of Exemptions: Not Liable for Debts

The general rule is that, unless the case is dismissed, property exempted by the debtor is not liable *during or after the case* for any pre-petition debt or any debt deemed to have arisen before bankruptcy. [B.C. § 522(c)]

a. Exceptions

There are certain kinds of debts which may be satisfied from the debtor's exempt property. They are the following:

(i) *nondischargeable taxes* [B.C. §§ 522(c)(1), 523(a)(1)];

(ii) *domestic support obligations* [B.C. §§ 522(c)(1), 523(a)(5)];

(iii) *a debt secured by a lien* that is not void under § 506(d) *and* that has not been avoided under another provision of the Code [B.C. § 522(c)(2)(A)];

(iv) *a debt secured by a tax lien* if notice of the lien has been filed properly [B.C. § 522(c)(2)(B)];

(v) *a debt, owed by an institution-affiliated party of an insured financial institution* to a federal depository institutions regulatory agency for fraud or defalcation while acting in a fiduciary capacity, embezzlement, larceny, *or* willful and malicious injury to another entity or its property [B.C. §§ 522(c)(3), 523(a)(4), (6)]; and

(vi) *a debt in connection with fraud* in obtaining or providing *any financial assistance* for purposes of *financing an education* at an institution of higher learning. [B.C. § 522(c)(4); 20 U.S.C. § 1001]

7. Avoidance of Liens That Impair Exemption

Most judicial liens and certain nonpossessory, nonpurchase-money security interests may be avoided by the debtor when they *impair an exemption* that the debtor could otherwise claim. [B.C. § 522(f)(1)] To avoid such a lien, the debtor must have had an interest in the property *before* the lien attached, because technically it is the *fixing of the lien* that may be avoided. [**Farrey v. Sanderfoot**, 500 U.S. 291 (1991)] The debtor may bring a proceeding to avoid such a lien by filing a motion or by serving a Chapter 12 or Chapter 13 plan on the affected creditors. [Bankruptcy Rule 4003(d)]

a. "Impair an Exemption"

The phrase "impair an exemption" is defined in terms of the following statutorily prescribed mathematical computation. [B.C. § 522(f)(2)(A)]

Judicial lien or nonpossessory non-purchase-money security interest

+ All other liens

+ Amount of the exemption available in the absence of any lien

Sum X

- The value of the debtor's interest in the property *without* any liens

Amount that lien impairs the exemption

If the value of the property is less than the total of the liens and the exemption, the exemption is impaired to the extent of the difference. If the property is subject to more than one lien, the calculation should not include a lien that has been avoided. [B.C. § 522(f)(2)(B)] Note, however, that this formula does not apply to a mortgage foreclosure judgment. [B.C. § 522(f)(2)(C)]

e.g. **Example:** Debtor owns property worth $50,000. There is a judicial lien on the property of $20,000. The state homestead exemption is $30,000. The lien does not impair the debtor's exemption, because the difference between the value of the property and the judicial lien is $30,000; thus, Debtor has $30,000 in equity, all of which she may exempt using the state's $30,000 homestead exemption. The formula produces the same result. $20,000 (judicial lien) + $0 (all other liens) + $30,000 (amount of exemption if no liens) = $50,000 (Sum X in formula above). Conclusion: $50,000 (Sum X) − $50,000 (value of property without any liens) = $0, which means that the exemption is not impaired and the lien cannot be avoided at all.

e.g. **Example:** Same facts as in the prior example except the judicial lien is in the amount of $40,000. Sum X from the statutory calculation above is $70,000: $40,000 (judicial lien) + $0 (all other liens) + $30,000 (exemption *if* no liens at all). Subtracting $50,000, which is the value of the property without any liens, from $70,000 leaves $20,000 or the extent of the impairment. Thus, the lien can be avoided in the amount of $20,000.

b. Judicial Lien

A judicial lien is avoidable to the extent that it impairs an exemption of the debtor. [B.C. § 522(f)(1)(A)] Under the Code, a judicial lien is a "lien obtained by judgment, levy, sequestration, or other legal or equitable process or proceeding." [B.C. § 101(36)] While a mortgage is a lien, it is a consensual, not a judicial, lien. [*Compare* B.C. § 101(36) *with* § 101(37)] Thus, a debtor may not invoke § 522(f) to avoid a mortgage on her home.

Example: Several years ago, Debtor took out a mortgage with Bank Three to purchase her home. Debtor recently filed for relief under Chapter 7. Her home is valued at $100,000, and the mortgage balance is $90,000. The state's homestead exemption is $30,000. Debtor may exempt the $10,000 in equity that she has in the home, but the mortgage is not a judicial lien. Therefore, the Debtor may not avoid it in order to take the full $30,000 state homestead exemption.

Example: Creditor obtains and records a judgment. Under state law, the judgment constitutes a lien on the debtor's home. Such a lien is called a judicial lien, and it can be avoided to the extent that it impairs an exemption.

(i) Exception: Domestic Support Obligations

A judicial lien securing a debt for a domestic support obligation is ***not avoidable.*** [B.C. § 522(f)(1)(A)]

c. Security Interest

The debtor may avoid a ***nonpossessory, nonpurchase-money*** security interest in any of the following items, to the extent that it "impairs an exemption to which the debtor would have been entitled:" [B.C. § 522(f)(1)(B)]

- ***household goods*** or furnishings, clothing, jewelry, appliances, books, musical instruments, crops, or animals that are held primarily for the debtor's (or a dependent's) ***personal, family, or household use*** [B.C. § 522(f)(1)(B)(i)];

- ***professional books or tools of the trade,*** e.g., a dentist's tools, of the debtor or a dependent [B.C. § 522(f)(1)(B)(ii)]; or

- ***health aids,*** e.g., a wheelchair, prescribed by a professional for the debtor or a dependent [B.C. § 522(f)(1)(B)(iii)].

(i) What is a Nonpossessory, Nonpurchase-Money Security Interest?

(1) Nonpossessory

The security interest is avoidable by the debtor only if it is nonpossessory. [B.C. § 522(f)(1)(B)] Thus, the security interest is not avoidable if the creditor has perfected by taking possession of the collateral, such as in the case of a pledge.

(2) Nonpurchase-Money

The security interest is avoidable by the debtor only if it is ***not*** purchase-money in nature. [B.C. § 522(f)(1)(B)] A purchase-money security interest arises if a creditor advances to enable the debtor to purchase the collateral, and the debtor uses that money or credit to do so. [*See* U.C.C. § 9–103]

Example: On February 1, Debtors purchased from Seller on credit a 42-foot utility flatbed trailer and granted to Seller a security interest in the trailer and, in lieu of a down payment, a security interest in a certain old cab-tractor owned by Debtors. Both the utility trailer and the cab-tractor were used in Debtors' trucking business. After experiencing financial difficulties, Debtors filed a Chapter 7 petition on November 1, electing the federal exemptions and seeking to avoid, under § 522(f)(1)(B), the liens on both the utility trailer and the cab-tractor. The bankruptcy court held that the debtors could not avoid the lien on the utility trailer because was a purchase-money security interest. However, the lien on the cab-tractor was a nonpossessory, *nonpurchase-money* security interest in a tool of the trade of Debtors and, thus, was avoidable to the extent that it impaired an exemption to which Debtors were entitled. [B.C. § 522(f)(1)(B)(ii); *In re* **Dillon,** 18 B.R. 252 (Bankr. E.D. Cal. 1982)]

(a) Refinancing

There is a split of authority concerning whether the refinancing of a debt secured by a purchase-money security interest extinguishes the purchase-money quality of the security interest. There are two basic rules—the transformation rule and the dual status rule—that courts apply not only to cases involving lien avoidance under § 522(f) but also to cases involving the hanging paragraph under § 1325(a)(9). Under the *transformation rule,* refinancing destroys the purchase-money status of the original loan, because the money provided through refinancing is not used to buy the collateral. [*See In re* **Huddle,** 2007 WL 2332390 (Bankr. E.D. Va. 2007) (hanging paragraph case); *see also* **United States v. Juan Madriz Haro,** 2009 U.S. Dist. LEXIS 73253 (C.D. Cal. 2009) (explaining rule but in context of real property mortgage)] Under the *dual status rule,* a security interest may be both purchase-money and non-purchase-money; it is purchase-money to the extent that the debtor used loan proceeds to purchase the collateral securing the interest and non-purchase-money with regard to any obligations unrelated to the purchase of the collateral. [*See In re* **McCauley,** 398 B.R. 41 (Bankr. D. Colo. 2008) (hanging paragraph case); *see also* U.C.C. § 9–103 Official Comment 7]

(3) U.C.C. Article 9

Article 9 leaves to the courts the choice of rule in consumer goods transactions. [U.C.C. § 9–103(h)] For nonconsumer goods transactions, it adopts the dual status rule, but this rule is not binding on the bankruptcy courts. [U.C.C. § 9–103(f), Official Comments 7 & 8]

(ii) What Are Household Goods?

With BAPCPA, Congress codified the definition of "household goods," using a modified version of the Federal Trade Commission's definition. The term "household goods" means:

(1) *clothing, furniture, appliances, linens, china, crockery, and kitchenware* [B.C. § 522(f)(4)(A)(i)–(iii), (vii)–(x)];

(2) one *radio* [B.C. § 522(f)(4)(A)(iv)];

(3) one *television* [B.C. § 522(f)(4)(A)(v)];

(4) one *personal computer* and related equipment [B.C. § 522(f)(4)(A)(xv)];

(5) *educational materials and equipment* for primary use by the debtor's minor dependent children [B.C. § 522(f)(4)(A)(ix)];

(6) *medical equipment and supplies* [B.C. § 522(f)(4)(A)(xii)];

(7) *furniture* used *exclusively* for *minor children* or *elderly or disabled* dependents of the debtor [B.C. § 522(f)(4)(A)(xiii)]; and

(8) *personal effects* of the debtor and her dependents, including *wedding rings* and *toys and hobby equipment* of minor dependent children [B.C. § 522(f)(4)(A)(xiv)].

(iii) Not Household Goods

The term "household goods" does not include:

(1) *works of art,* unless the works of art were done by the debtor or a relative, or are of the debtor or a relative [§ 522(f)(4)(B)(i)];

(2) *electronic equipment* (excluding one television, radio, and VCR) with a fair market value *in excess of $725* [B.C. § 522(f)(4)(B)(ii)];

(3) *antiques* with fair market value *in excess of $725* [B.C. § 522(f)(4)(B)(iii)];

(4) *jewelry* (excluding wedding rings) with fair market value *in excess of $725* [B.C. § 522(f)(4)(B)(iv)]; and

(5) *a computer* (excluding the personal computer provided in § 522(f)(4)(A)(xv)), *motor vehicles,* including a tractor or lawn mower, *boats, or motorized recreational devices,* including *watercraft* and *aircraft.* [B.C. § 522(f)(4)(B)(v)]

(iv) What Are Tools of the Trade?

Courts differ about what constitutes tools or implements of the trade, in part, because the language of states' tools of the trade exemptions varies. [*See, e.g.,* **Larson v. Sharp (*In re* Sharp),** 508 B.R. 457 (B.A.P. 10th Cir. 2014) (requiring the court to interpret what constitutes "gainful occupation" under Colorado's tools of the trade exemption)] The ability to avoid a lien using § 522(f)(1)(B)(ii)'s tools of the trade provision also depends on whether the debtor uses the federal § 522(d)(6) tools of the trade exemption or a state law tools of the trade exemption. [*In re* **Nickeas,** 503 B.R. 453 (Bankr. W.D. Wis. 2013)] Thus, the Seventh Circuit held that debtors could use § 522(f)(1)(B)(ii) to avoid a lien on farm equipment because debtors had used Wisconsin's tools of the trade exemption. [*In re* **Thompson,** 867 F.2d 416 (7th Cir. 1989)] But, the Seventh Circuit also has held that because the federal exemptions were much narrower a debtor using the § 522(d)(6) tools of the trade exemption could not avoid a lien under § 522(f)(1)(B)(ii) on farm equipment similar to that in *Thompson.* [*In re* **Patterson,** 825 F.2d 1140 (7th Cir. 1987); *see In re* **Nickeas,** 503 B.R. 453 (Bankr. W.D. Wis. 2013) for an explanation of the difference between the two Seventh Circuit cases] The tools for which the debtor claims the exemption must not be for a hobby or pastime. [**Larson v. Sharp (*In re* Sharp),** 508 B.R. 457 (B.A.P. 10th Cir. 2014)]

(1) Vehicles

While a car may qualify as a tool of the trade, the vehicle must be used for more than mere transportation to and from work. A car used only for commuting to and from work does not qualify as a tool of the trade. [*In re* **King,** 451 B.R. 884 (Bankr. N.D. Iowa 2011)] Thus, a debtor who worked as a law clerk and tutor could not avoid a lien on her car using § 522(f)(1)(B)(ii), because traveling was "merely incidental" to her work. [**Mitchell v. First Franklin Corp. (*In re* Mitchell),** 2018 WL 1442256 (Bankr. N.D. Ga. 2018)]

(v) Cap on Amount Avoided

A debtor *may not* avoid a *nonpossessory, non-purchase-money security interest* on *implements, professional books, or tools of the trade* to the extent that the property's value *exceeds $6,825.* [B.C. § 522(f)(3)] The monetary limitation on lien avoidance, however, *only applies* if the following conditions are satisfied:

(1) a *state has opted out* of the federal exemptions or the *debtor has waived* the right to claim the federal exemptions [§ 522(f)(3)(A)]; and

(2) applicable state law allows the *debtor unlimited exemptions except* to the extent that the property is subject to a *consensual lien,* or *prohibits the avoidance of a consensual lien* on property that otherwise would be *exempt.* [B.C. § 522(f)(3)(B)]

(vi) Problems with Interpreting § 522(f)(3)(A)

The language of both § 522(f)(3)(A) and (B) is problematic. First, § 522(e) of the Code makes exemption waivers unenforceable, so what does "State law . . . prohibits a debtor from claiming [federal] exemptions" (opt-out) in § 522(f)(3)(A) mean? Some courts have concluded that the language does not mean what it literally says. Instead, § 522(f)(3)(A) applies not only to debtors who live in opt-out states but also to debtors who live in non-opt-out states but elect the state, not the federal, exemptions. [*In re* **Ehlen,** 202 B.R. 742 (Bankr. W.D. Wis. 1996)]

Second, it is unclear how often § 522(f)(3)'s cap would apply to debtors seeking to avoid a lien on tools of the trade. The problem is that in most states neither of § 522(f)(3)(B)'s alternatives apply. Section 522(f)(3)(B) is satisfied if state law allows the debtor to claim unlimited exemptions. The provision does *not* say that state law permits an unlimited exemption for tools of the trade. Yet no state provides debtors with unlimited exemptions for *all* categories of collateral. [4 Collier ¶ 522.11(6)(c)] A second way to satisfy § 522(f)(3)(B) is if state law prohibits the avoidance of consensual liens. [4 Collier ¶ 522.11(6)(c)] Not many states do so, however. Thus, there is no monetary cap on lien avoidance for tools of the trade if neither of the two alternatives at § 522(f)(3)(B) applies.

e.g. **Example:** Married debtors filed for relief under Chapter 7, and moved to avoid liens on farm equipment and machinery in the amount of $26,000, pursuant to § 522(f)(1)(B)(ii). Minnesota allowed a $13,000 exemption for farm equipment and machinery, and each debtor claimed the full exemption. Lienholders objected, in part, on the ground of § 522(f)(3)'s monetary limitation, which then stood at $5,000. The bankruptcy court concluded that Minnesota did not have unlimited exemptions and that Minnesota law did not "speak to lien avoidance." Therefore, the court held that § 522(f)(3)'s then-$5,000 cap did not apply and debtors could avoid the liens in the amount of $26,000. [*In re* **Zimmel,** 185 B.R. 786 (Bankr. D. Minn. 1995)]

(vii) Federal Wildcard Exemption

Remember that a nonpossessory, nonpurchase-money security interest in tools of the trade is avoidable only to the extent that it impairs an exemption to which the debtor would have been entitled. Although the maximum federal exemption for tools of the trade is $2,525, the exemption may be supplemented by an amount equal to $1,325 plus up to $12,575 of any unused part of the debtor's homestead exemption, or, in a joint case, $2,650 plus up to $25,150 of any unused part of the homestead exemptions. [B.C. §§ 522(d)(5), (6)]

8. Property Recovered by Trustee

The debtor may *exempt* property that the *trustee has recovered* and brought into the estate so long as the debtor, absent the transfer, could have exempted the property under applicable federal or state law, and only if:

(a) the debtor *did not voluntarily* transfer the property or conceal it [B.C. § 522(g)(1)]; or

(b) the debtor *could have avoided* the transfer under § 522(f)(1)(B). [B.C. § 522(g)(2)]

 Example: Husband and Wife ("Debtors") filed for relief under Chapter 7. Prior to bankruptcy, Husband's brother loaned Debtors $80,000 and took a security interest in Debtors' Corvette. When Debtors realized that Brother had failed to properly perfect his security interest, they listed the Corvette as exempt. The Chapter 7 trustee moved to compel turnover of the Corvette to the bankruptcy estate, and Debtors responded that the Corvette was exempt. The 9th Circuit B.A.P. affirmed the bankruptcy court's determination that Debtors could not exempt the Corvette under § 522(g)(1)(A), because Debtors had voluntarily transferred a security interest in the Corvette to Brother. [**Wharton v. Schwartzer (*In re* Wharton),** 563 B.R. 289 (B.A.P. 9th Cir. 2017)]

 Example: Husband and Wife filed for relief under Chapter 7. Prior to bankruptcy, Judgment Creditor obtained a $10,000 judgment in state court against Husband. Judgment Creditor later obtained an order authorizing a sheriff or court officer to seize personal property of the Husband to satisfy the state court judgment. Court Officer showed up at Husband's home about two weeks later to seize property in satisfaction of the judgment. Court Officer informed Husband that he would accept $4,000 in cash instead of seizing property in the Debtors' garage. Husband's father then wrote a check payable to Husband; Husband and Court Officer went to the bank where Husband cashed the check and gave Court Officer $4,000 in cash. After deducting statutory fees and expenses, Judgment Creditor received $3548.80 in partial satisfaction of the state court judgment. After Debtors filed their Chapter 7 petition, Judgment Creditor remitted $3548.80 to the Chapter 7 trustee in response to the trustee's demand for return of the funds as a preferential transfer. Husband then amended his schedules to exempt the recovered funds pursuant to the federal wild card exemption. The Chapter 7 trustee argued that Husband had voluntarily transferred the money pre-petition and, thus, § 522(g)(1)(A) precluded him from exempting the funds. The bankruptcy court held that because the transfer of funds "occurred by operation of law . . .[it] was involuntary for purposes of 522(g)." Thus, Husband was entitled to exempt the funds using § 522(d)(5). [***In re* Hill,** 566 B.R. 891 (Bankr. W.D. Mich. 2017)]

(i) Limitation

This provision may be used to exempt property only to the extent that the debtor has not already claimed the maximum amount allowable for the relevant category of exemption. [B.C. § 522(j)]

9. Avoidance by Debtor

If the trustee can avoid a transfer of property or recover a setoff but does not attempt to pursue it, the debtor may *avoid* the transfer or may *recover* the setoff to the extent that she could have exempted the property under § 522(g)(1) if the trustee had used his avoiding powers. [B.C. § 522(h)] Section 522(h) protects the debtor's exemption rights. The trustee may have little incentive to pursue an avoidance action in cases in which the recovery is not distributed to estate creditors but rather is claimed by the debtor as exempt.

 Example: Debtor inherited her mother's home upon her mother's death in 2007. In 2014, the City of Milwaukee ("City") foreclosed on the property because real estate taxes had not been paid. Only after the foreclosure did Debtor take the steps necessary to record her interest in the property. Approximately a month after the foreclosure, Debtor filed for relief under Chapter 13. Debtor initiated an adversary proceeding against the City to set aside as a fraudulent conveyance the transfer of Debtor's home pursuant to the tax foreclosure judgment. The City moved to dismiss the adversary complaint and argued that Debtor had no standing to bring the proceeding under §§ 522(h) and 548(a)(1)(B)(i), (ii)(I), because she was not the record owner and, thus, there was no transfer of the debtor's interest in property. The bankruptcy court disagreed. The court held that under Wisconsin law Debtor acquired her interest in the home when her mother died and, thus, Debtor had an interest in the property at the time of the tax foreclosure sale. Because the Chapter 13 trustee had not sought to avoid the transfer, Debtor could use § 522(h) to do so. The transfer pursuant to the tax foreclosure sale was involuntary, the Debtor had not concealed the property, and if Debtor were successful in avoiding the transfer under § 548, then she would be able to exempt the full value of the home under Wisconsin law, thereby satisfying the requirements of § 522(g) and (h). [**Martin v. City of Milwaukee (*In re* Martin),** 2014 WL 7011042 (Bankr. E.D. Wis. 2014)]

10. Debtor's Recovery and Exemption

A debtor who avoids a transfer of property or recovers a setoff pursuant to §§ 522(f) or 522(h) may *recover* the property or the setoff in accordance with § 550 and may *exempt* it to the extent permitted under the applicable exemption scheme. [B.C. § 522(i), (b)]

a. Limitation

Section 522(i) may be used to exempt property only to the extent that the debtor already has not claimed the maximum amount allowable for the relevant category of exemption. [B.C. § 522(j)]

11. Administrative Expenses

Subject to certain exceptions, exempt property usually is not liable for the payment of administrative expenses. [B.C. § 522(k)]

B. Redemption: Chapter 7 Cases Only

1. Tangible Personal Property

In a Chapter 7 case, an *individual debtor* has the right to redeem *tangible personal property* from a lien that secures a dischargeable consumer debt if the property is held mainly for *personal, family, or household use,* and it either has been *exempted* by the debtor or has been *abandoned* by the trustee. The debtor may retain such collateral by paying the secured party the *amount of the allowed secured claim,* which is determined by the collateral's market value. [B.C. §§ 722, 506(a)]

> **e.g.** **Example:** Debtor, an individual, files a Chapter 7 petition and lists among her assets the family car, which currently is valued at $7,000, is subject to a purchase-money security interest in favor of Bank, and is used solely for personal driving. The outstanding balance on the car loan is $10,000. Debtor may redeem the automobile by paying a lump sum of $7,000 to Bank.

a. Lump Sum

To redeem collateral, the debtor must make payment in a lump sum and not by installment payments. In 2005, Congress added "in full at the time of redemption" to the end of § 722 to make clear the requirement of lump sum, not installment, payment.

2. Changed Intention

A debtor who has filed a statement of intention to reaffirm a secured consumer debt is not bound irrevocably by the decision and still may redeem the collateral, notwithstanding her original statement of intention. [*See* savings clause following B.C. § 521(a)(2)(B)] BAPCPA, however, created a more complex set of rules regarding the debtor's statement of intention.

3. No Waiver

A debtor may exercise her right to redeem collateral even if she has waived the right to redeem. [B.C. § 722]

Chapter Nine
Discharge of Indebtedness

CONTENTS	PAGE

Chapter Approach

This chapter is the second of two chapters addressing the areas of bankruptcy law that give the debtor a "fresh start." The chapter covers the effects of the debtor's discharge, the ever-growing list of nondischargeable debts, and the Code's provisions protecting the debtor from discrimination post-bankruptcy.

First, the main source of the debtor's fresh start is the *discharge* of indebtedness. The key things to remember are that a discharge *relieves the debtor of personal liability* on all debts that are discharged and also *permanently enjoins* creditors from attempting to collect or recover such claims from the debtor personally. A discharge, however, does not necessarily wipe the slate totally clean. For example, a Chapter 7 discharge granted to an individual debtor (a standard Chapter 13 discharge has different criteria for nondischargeability of particular debts) does not include *nineteen categories* of *nondischargeable debts* described in Bankruptcy Code § 523(a).

Second, in some cases in which the debt is secured by a nonavoidable lien on collateral that the debtor wishes to retain, the debtor may desire to enter into a *reaffirmation agreement.* Keep in mind that a reaffirmation agreement is enforceable only if it complies with the Code's requirements. Prior to BAPCPA's enactment, some courts allowed the debtor to continue paying on secured debt for her automobile, for example, and "ride through" bankruptcy without entering into a reaffirmation agreement. With BAPCPA, Congress enacted a number of changes to the Code, including to the automatic stay, in order to close off the "ride through" as an option in bankruptcy. These changes, however, did not eliminate the ability of debtors to "ride through" in all cases.

Finally, remember that the law *prohibits discrimination* by a governmental unit, by a private employer, or by a lender engaged in a guaranteed student loan program against a person who has been a debtor in a bankruptcy case.

A. Nondischargeable Debts

1. Exceptions to Discharge

Certain debts of an *individual debtor* are not dischargeable and, therefore, survive the bankruptcy of an individual who has received a discharge under Chapter 7, 11, 12, or 13. [B.C. §§ 523(a), 1141(d)(2), 1228(a), 1328(a)]

a. Effect of Nondischargeability

Unlike the creditors whose claims against the debtor are expunged by the discharge and who, thus, are enjoined permanently from attempting to collect or recover such debts personally from the debtor, a creditor who obtains a judicial determination that a particular debt is nondischargeable is free to pursue the debtor and to attempt to recover that debt subsequent to the debtor's discharge. [*Compare* B.C. § 524(a)(2) *with* § 523(a)]

b. Distinguish: Denial of Debtor's Discharge

A determination of nondischargeability under § 523(a) excepts *a specific debt* from the debtor's discharge. On the other hand, the complete denial of a debtor's discharge allows *all of the debtor's debts* to survive bankruptcy, and thereafter all claimants may compete for satisfaction of their claims. The court may deny an individual Chapter 7 debtor a discharge based on certain misconduct. [*See, e.g.,* B.C. §§ 727(a)(1)–(7)] The Code also provides for denial of discharge in a Chapter 7 or Chapter 13 case if a debtor files for bankruptcy too closely on the heels of a prior bankruptcy case in which she received a discharge, regardless of whether the prior case was filed under Chapter 7, 11, 12, or 13. [*See, e.g.,* B.C. §§ 727(a)(8), (a)(9), 1328(f)] The permissible time between filings depends on the chapter(s) under which the successive cases were filed.

2. Nondischargeable Debts Under § 523(a)

Section 523(a) lists the debts that are not dischargeable in an individual *Chapter 7 or Chapter 11* case, or pursuant to a *hardship discharge in Chapter 13.* [B.C. §§ 523(a), 1141(d)(2), 1328(b)] In a *Chapter 13 non-hardship or standard discharge* case, some, but not all, of the debts listed in § 523(a) are not discharged. [B.C. § 1328(a)(2)] With the exception of unsecured debts for certain taxes, § 523(a) lists the debts that are not dischargeable in an individual *Chapter 12* case. [B.C. § 1228(a)] In both Chapters 12 and 13, the Code also excepts from discharge other debts.

Remember: § 523 only applies to *individual debtors.* The following is the list of nondischargeable debts under § 523(a). **Note the "Exception"** section for each category of debt, which indicates whether the debt is nondischargeable in a Chapter 12 or Chapter 13 case.

a. Taxes

The following taxes are nondischargeable. [B.C. § 523(a)(1)]

(i) Gap Period Taxes

Third priority claims are those that arise during the *gap period* in an involuntary case in the ordinary course of the debtor's business. [B.C. §§ 507(a)(3), 502(f)] The Code provides that in an individual case a tax claim that is a third priority claim, i.e., it arises during the gap period, is not dischargeable. [B.C. § 523(a)(1)(A)]

Exception in Chapter 13: Gap period tax claims are discharged in a Chapter 13 case if the debtor obtains a standard discharge. [B.C. §§ 1328(a)(2), 523(a)(1)(A); *see In re* Ladona, 2017 WL 2437233 (Bankr. D. N.H. 2017) (stating that "based on their exclusion from 11 U.S.C. § 1328(a)(2), priority tax debts under 11 U.S.C. § 523(a)(1)(A) are dischargeable in Chapter 13 cases")]

(ii) Income, Property, and Other Taxes

Eighth priority taxes include various unsecured pre-petition tax claims, e.g., an income tax for which a return was due within three years prior to bankruptcy. [B.C. § 523(a)(1)(A)]

Note: In a unanimous opinion, the Supreme Court has held that the "three-year lookback period" of Code § 507(a)(8)(A)(i) is tolled during the pendency of a prior bankruptcy case. Thus, the time during which a debtor's prior bankruptcy case is pending does not count toward the three-year lookback period. [**Young v. United States,** 535 U.S. 43 (2002) (married debtors' taxes were nondischargeable because "the IRS was disabled from protecting its claim during the pendency of the [debtors' prior] Chapter 13 petition, and this period of disability tolled the three-year lookback period when the [debtors] filed their Chapter 7 petition")]

Exception in Chapter 12: Debts for unsecured taxes that arise pre-petition and debts for unsecured taxes that arise post-petition but prior to discharge are *dischargeable in a Chapter 12* case if those taxes result from the sale, transfer, exchange or other disposition of property used in the *debtor's farming operation.* [B.C. § 1232(a)(4)] These taxes are treated as pre-petition claims that are not entitled to priority under § 507. [B.C. §§ 1232(a)(1), (2)] The debtor must provide for them in the Chapter 12 plan. [B.C. § 1232(a)(3)]

Exception in Chapter 13: With the *exception of trust fund taxes* under § 507(a)(8)(C), eighth priority tax claims are dischargeable in a Chapter 13 case in which the debtor obtains a standard discharge. [B.C. § 1328(a)(2)]

(iii) Return not Filed

Taxes for which a *return or equivalent report or notice either has not been filed or given,* or was filed or given *late and within two years* of bankruptcy are not dischargeable. [B.C. § 523(a)(1)(B)]

(iv) Fraudulent Return

Taxes for which the *debtor filed a fraudulent return or "willfully attempted in any manner to evade or defeat"* the tax are not dischargeable. [B.C. § 523(a)(1)(C)]

(1) Definition of Return

BAPCPA added a hanging paragraph to the end of § 523(a) to define the word "return." [*See* **Wogoman v. IRS (*In re* Wogoman),** 475 B.R. 239 (B.A.P. 10th Cir. 2012)] The Code now defines "return" to mean a *return* that satisfies the *requirements of applicable nonbankruptcy law.* It includes a return prepared pursuant to § 6020(a) of the Internal Revenue Code or a similar State or local law, or a written stipulation to a judgment or final order entered by a nonbankruptcy tribunal. A return does *not* include a return made pursuant to § 6020(b) of the Internal Revenue Code or similar State or local law. [B.C. § 523(a)(19) hanging paragraph]

Note: This portion of the summary covers exceptions to discharge for *individual debtors.* In 2005, however, Congress added an exception to § 1141 of the Code that mirrors the above exception to discharge but that applies to *corporate debtors.* The Code now provides that confirmation of a Chapter 11 plan does not discharge a *corporation* from any debt for a *tax or customs duty* for which the debtor made a *fraudulent return* or *willfully attempted* in any manner to *evade or defeat the tax or customs duty.* [B.C. § 1141(d)(6)(B)]

(v) Post-Petition Interest on Nondischargeable Tax Debt

In a case under the Bankruptcy Act, the Supreme Court, in a unanimous opinion, held that post-petition interest on a nondischargeable tax debt also is not dischargeable. [**Bruning v. United States,** 376 U.S. 358 (1964)] The vast majority of courts have held that *Bruning* applies to cases under the Code. [*See In re* **Tuttle,** 291 F.3d 1238 (10th Cir. 2002) (noting "the great weight of authority")] Thus, *post-petition interest* on a nondischargeable tax is also nondischargeable. Courts also have consistently held that *pre-petition interest* on a nondischargeable tax is nondischargeable. [3 Norton 3d § 57:8]

b. Fraud

(i) False Pretenses or Representation, or Actual Fraud

Debts for money, property, services, or credit obtained by *false pretenses or representation or actual fraud,* other than a statement about the financial condition of the debtor or an insider, are not dischargeable if the creditor *justifiably* relies on the fraudulent representation. [B.C. § 523(a)(2)(A); **Field v. Mans,** 516 U.S. 59

(1995)] The Supreme Court has held that the words "actual fraud" in § 523(a)(2)(A) include "forms of fraud, like fraudulent conveyance schemes, that can be effected without a false representation."[**Husky International Electronics, Inc. v. Ritz,** 136 S.Ct. 1581 (2016)]

Note: This portion of the summary covers exceptions to discharge for *individual debtors.* In 2005, however, Congress added an exception to § 1141 of the Code that provides that confirmation of a Chapter 11 plan does *not discharge a corporate debtor* from a debt owed to a *domestic governmental unit* that was obtained by *false pretenses, false representation, or actual fraud.* [B.C. §§ 1141(d)(6)(A), 523(a)(2)(A)]

(1) Credit Cards: Implied Representation Theory

An issue with applying § 523(a)(2)(A) to credit cards is that the retailer taking the card receives payment from the credit card company. When the consumer/debtor presents her credit card to the retailer, the retailer does not expect payment from the debtor. It waits for approval from the credit card company, which makes payment to the retailer. In other words, there is no false representation by the consumer/debtor to the retailer. But without a false representation, where is the fraud? To deal with this problem, a number of courts have held that *each time* the debtor uses a credit card, she *impliedly represents* to the card issuer that she *intends to repay the debt.* [*See, e.g.,* **Citibank v. Spradley (***In re* **Spradley),** 313 B.R. 119 (Bankr. E.D. N.Y. 2004) (citing cases)]

(2) Did Debtor Know?

The creditor must demonstrate that at the time that the debt was incurred the debtor *knew that the representation* of her intent to repay was *false.* Courts use various factors to determine whether the debtor *subjectively* knew her representation was false:

(a)   the *time* between debtor using the card and filing for bankruptcy;

(b)   whether *debtor consulted with an attorney* about filing for bankruptcy before using her card;

(c)   the *number of charges;*

(d)   the *amount* of the charges;

(e)   the debtor's *financial condition* when she used her card;

(f)   whether the charges *exceeded the card's limit;*

(g)   whether debtor made *multiple charges* on the same day;

(h)   whether the debtor was *employed;*

(i)   debtor's *employment prospects;*

(j)   debtor's *financial sophistication;*

(k)   whether Debtor's *buying habits* changed suddenly; and

(l)   whether the charges at issue were for *luxuries or for necessities.*

[**Citibank v. Spradley (***In re* **Spradley),** 313 B.R. 119 (Bankr. E.D. N.Y. 2004)]

(3) Statutory Presumptions

Consumer debts totaling more than *$725* for *luxury goods or services* owed to a single creditor and incurred by an individual debtor within *90 days* before the order for relief are presumed to be nondischargeable. Similarly, *cash advances* totaling more than *$1,000* that are extensions of consumer credit pursuant to an open-end credit plan received by an individual debtor within *70 days* before the order for relief are presumed to be nondischargeable. [B.C. § 523(a)(2)(C)]

(a) "Consumer"

The definition of the terms "consumer", "credit," and "open end credit plan" are the same as those in § 103 of the Truth in Lending Act. [B.C. § 523(a)(2)(C)(ii)(I)]

(b) "Luxury Goods or Services"

Goods or services that a debtor or a dependent reasonably needs for maintenance or support are not considered to be luxury items. [B.C. § 523(a)(2)(C)(ii)(II)]

(4) Punitive Damages

The Supreme Court, in a unanimous opinion, has ruled that any liability arising from fraud under § 523(a)(2)(A), such as punitive damages or attorneys' fees, is nondischargeable. [**Cohen v. De La Cruz**, 523 U.S. 213 (1998)]

(ii) False Financial Statements

A debt for money, property, services, or credit obtained by the use of a false statement is nondischargeable *only* if the following elements are present:

(1) the statement was in *writing* [B.C. § 523(a)(2)(B)];

(2) the statement was *materially* false [B.C. § 523(a)(2)(B)(i)];

(3) the statement related to the *financial condition* of the *debtor or an insider* [B.C. § 523(a)(2)(B)(ii)];

(4) the creditor owed the debt *reasonably relied upon* the written statement [B.C. § 523(a)(2)(B)(iii)]; *and*

(5) the debtor made the statement with the *intent to deceive.* [B.C. § 523(a)(2)(B)(iv)]

e.g. **Example:** Appling hired the law firm of Lamar, Archer & Cofrin ("Lamar") to represent him in business litigation. By March of 2005, Appling owed the firm $60,000 in legal fees. Lamar told Appling that unless the past-due amount was paid, the firm would withdraw from the representation and put a lien on its work product. In March, Appling told his attorneys that he expected a $100,000 tax refund, which would have covered his outstanding legal fees. In reliance on Appling's statement, Lamar continued to represent Appling and did not start collection activities for the past-due bills. In October of 2005, Appling and his wife received a refund of only $59,851, which they put into their business. The next month, Appling met with his lawyers and told them that he had not yet received his tax refund. In reliance on that statement, Lamar completed the pending litigation on Appling's behalf and delayed collection activities on the past-due bills. Appling never paid his attorneys, so Lamar sued and obtained a judgment for more than $100,000 in outstanding legal fees. Appling and his wife then filed for relief under Chapter 7.

The Supreme Court, in a unanimous opinion, held that "a statement about a single asset, [i.e., income tax refund], can be a 'statement respecting the debtor's financial condition' under § 523(a)(2) of the Bankruptcy Code." The Court explained that a "statement is 'respecting' a debtor's financial condition if it has a direct relation to or impact on the debtor's overall financial status. A single asset has a direct relation to and impact on aggregate financial condition." Statements about a single asset convey information about the debtor's solvency and ability to repay a debt. Appling's statements about his income tax refund were statements respecting his financial condition, because they indicated that he could pay his past-due attorney fees. Those statements, however, were oral, not written, as required by § 523(a)(2)(B). Therefore, the debt to his attorneys was dischargeable. [**Lamar, Archer & Cofrin, LLP v. Appling,** 138 S.Ct. 1752 (2018)]

Note: This portion of the summary covers exceptions to discharge for *individual debtors.* In 2005, however, Congress added an exception to § 1141 of the Code that provides that confirmation of a Chapter 11 plan does *not discharge a corporate debtor* from a debt owed to a *domestic governmental unit* that was obtained by use of a *statement in writing* respecting the debtor's *financial condition.* [B.C. §§ 1141(d)(6)(A), 523(a)(2)(B)]

(iii) Costs and Attorneys' Fees

A creditor who unsuccessfully brings a proceeding to have a *consumer debt* declared nondischargeable under § 523(a)(2) is liable to the debtor for costs and reasonable attorneys' fees if the court finds that the creditor's complaint was not substantially justified. [B.C. § 523(d)] The court will not impose costs and attorneys' fees on the creditor if an award would be *unjust* due to special circumstances. [B.C. § 523(d)]

c. Failure to Schedule Debts in Current Case

A debt that the debtor fails to list or schedule in her current case as the Code requires is nondischargeable under the following circumstances.

(i) Sections 523(a)(2), (a)(4), or (a)(6) Debts

For debts involving fraud, misrepresentation, or use of a false financial statement [§ 523(a)(2)], larceny, embezzlement, or fraud or defalcation while acting in a fiduciary capacity [§ 523(a)(4)], or willful and malicious injury [§ 523(a)(6)], the debt is not dischargeable if the failure to list or schedule the debt precludes a *creditor without notice or actual knowledge of the bankruptcy case* from timely filing both a proof of claim *and* a complaint to determine the dischargeability of the debt. [B.C. §§ 523(a)(3)(B), (c)]

(ii) Other Debts

For any debt other than those described in §§ 523(a)(2), (a)(4), or (a)(6), the debt is not dischargeable if the failure to list or schedule it precludes a creditor who has *no notice or actual knowledge of the bankruptcy case* from timely filing a proof of claim. [B.C. § 523(a)(3)(A)]

d. Fiduciary Fraud or Defalcation, and Embezzlement or Larceny

Debts for fraud or defalcation *while acting in a fiduciary capacity* are nondischargeable. Debts arising from *embezzlement or larceny* also are nondischargeable, but there is no requirement that the wrongdoing occur in a fiduciary context. [B.C. § 523(a)(4)]

(i) Fraud in a Fiduciary Capacity

Courts consistently have held that fraud, for purposes of § 523(a)(4), requires intentional deceit or wrongdoing. Implied or constructive fraud does not suffice. [**Bannon v. Tyson (*In re* Tyson),** 450 B.R. 514 (Bankr. E.D. Pa. 2011); **Marshall v. Youngblood (*In re* Youngblood),** 2009 WL 1232103 (Bankr. S.D. Tex. 2009); **Wood v. Borland (*In re* Borland),** 2009 WL 9084773 (Bankr. E.D. Cal. 2009)]

Note: For purposes of § 523(a)(4), any institution-affiliated party of an insured depository institution is deemed to be acting in a fiduciary capacity. [B.C. §§ 523(e), 101(33), (35)]

(ii) Defalcation in a Fiduciary Capacity

The Supreme Court has held that the term "defalcation" under § 523(a)(4) "includes a culpable state of mind requirement . . . involving knowledge of, or gross recklessness in respect to, the improper nature of the relevant fiduciary behavior." [**Bullock v. BankChampaign,** 560 U.S. 267 (2013)] Defalcation requires intentional wrongdoing when the conduct does not involve "bad faith, moral turpitude, or other immoral conduct." The Court explained that the requisite intentional wrongdoing includes "not only conduct that the fiduciary knows is improper but also reckless conduct of the kind that the criminal law often treats as equivalent." Thus, in a case in which there is no *actual knowledge* of wrongdoing, there may be defalcation if the "fiduciary 'consciously disregards' (or is willfully blind to) 'a substantial and justifiable risk' that his conduct will turn out to violate a fiduciary duty."

e. Domestic Support Obligations

Debts owed for *domestic support obligations* are nondischargeable. [B.C. §§ 523(a)(5), 101(14A)]

f. Property Settlements and Other Obligations Arising from Separation Agreement or Divorce Decree

Debts that *do not qualify as domestic support obligations* but that are owed to a *spouse, former spouse, or child of the debtor* and that were incurred in the course of a *divorce or separation* or in connection with a separation agreement, divorce decree, other court order, or a governmental unit's determination based on state or territorial law, are nondischargeable. [B.C. § 523(a)(15)]

Exception—Chapter 13: Such debts are dischargeable for the debtor who receives a standard Chapter 13 discharge, but not the Chapter 13 debtor who receives a hardship discharge. [B.C. §§ 1328(a)(2), 1328(b), (c)(2), 523(a)(15)]

(i) Rationale

In a divorce, the custodial parent sometimes accepts a low amount of child support in exchange for the other parent's assuming the couple's marital debts. If the noncustodial parent could be discharged from these debts by declaring bankruptcy, the marital debts would unfairly fall on the custodial parent.

g. Willful/Malicious Injury

The Code has different tests for nondischargeability of debts for willful/malicious injury, depending on whether the case is filed under Chapter 7, 11, or 12 as opposed to under Chapter 13.

(i) Willful *and* Malicious Injury

Debts for *willful and malicious injury* caused by the debtor to *another entity or its property* are nondischargeable in a *Chapter 7, 11, or 12* case, or in a *Chapter 13* case in which the debtor receives a *hardship discharge.* [B.C. § 523(a)(6)]

e.g. **Example:** Debtor is a physician who treated Patient/Creditor for a foot injury. Debtor admitted Patient/Creditor to the hospital for treatment and prescribed oral penicillin, rather than intravenous penicillin, which would have been more effective. Debtor did so because he believed that Patient/Creditor was concerned with the cost of treatment. When Debtor left on a business trip, other doctors took over Patient's/Creditor's care and decided to transfer her case to an infectious disease specialist. When Debtor returned, he canceled the transfer and stopped all antibiotics, because he thought the infection had subsided. Instead, Patient/Creditor had to have her leg amputated below the knee. Debtor had no malpractice insurance. Patient/Creditor sued and obtained a $350,000 judgment against Debtor, who filed for relief under Chapter 7. The bankruptcy court found that the $350,000 judgment was nondischargeable under § 523(a)(6). But, in a unanimous decision, the Supreme Court held that the judgment did not qualify as a nondischargeable debt under § 523(a)(6). The Court explained that § 523(a)(6) required a "deliberate or intentional *injury,* not merely a deliberate or intentional *act* that [led] to injury." The Court explained that injuries caused by reckless or negligent conduct do not satisfy the requirements of § 523(a)(6). [**Kawaauhau v. Geiger,** 523 U.S. 57 (1998)]

(1) "Willful"

The Supreme Court has held that because the word "willful" modifies the word "injury", "nondischargeability [under § 523(a)(6)] takes a deliberate or intentional *injury,* not merely a deliberate or intentional *act* that leads to injury." [**Kawaauhau v. Geiger,** *supra*] The issue left unanswered by the Supreme Court in *Geiger* was the state of mind needed to satisfy § 523(a)(6)'s requirement of a willful injury. Of the courts addressing the issue, most have adopted a *subjective* standard such that the willful injury requirement is satisfied "only when the debtor has a subjective motive to inflict injury or when the debtor believes that injury is substantially certain to result from his own conduct." [**Carillo v. Su (*In re* Su),** 290 F.3d 1140 (9th Cir. 2002); 4 Collier ¶ 523.12 (2)]

(2) "Malicious"

The predominant view is that the debtor's malice may be inferred from her deliberate conduct under the circumstances. [**Viener v. Jacobs (*In re* Jacobs),** 381 B.R. 128 (Bankr. E.D. Penn. 2008)] There are variations on the courts' basic formulation of the malice standard, but generally, malice means that the debtor intentionally engaged in a wrongful act or consciously disregarded a duty without just cause or excuse. [*See, e.g., **In re** Arvanitis,* 523 B.R. 633 (Bankr. N.D. Ill. 2015) ("Maliciousness requires proof of conscious disregard of a duty without just cause or excuse"); *In re* **O'Donnell,** 523 B.R. 308 (Bankr. D. Mass. 2014) (proof of malice requires an injury that was "objectively wrongful or lacking in just cause or excuse" and the debtor "inflicted the injury in 'conscious disregard' of her duties"); *In re* **Osborne,** 520 B.R. 861 (Bankr. D. N.M. 2014) ("The 'malicious' element requires proof of 'an intentional, wrongful act, done without justification or excuse' "] Personal animus or ill will are not required. [*In re* **Bayer,** 521 B.R. 491 (Bankr. N.D. Penn. 2014)]

e.g. **Example:** Husband and Wife ("Debtors") operated a small dairy farm. In order to keep the farm operating when dairy prices fell precipitously, Debtors took out three loans from the U.S. Farm Service Agency ("FSA"). As collateral for the loans, Debtors executed two mortgages on real property in FSA's favor and granted FSA a security interest in Debtors' farm equipment, machinery, crops, and cattle. FSA properly perfected its security interest. The loan documents contained very specific language requiring Debtors to obtain FSA's consent before disposing of any of the collateral securing the loans. Without obtaining FSA's consent, Husband sold, both under his own name and another person's name, more than one hundred head of cattle. The sales netted more than $84,000 in proceeds, of which FSA received nothing. When FSA discovered the sales, it demanded compensation for or replacement of the collateral. Debtors filed for relief under Chapter 7, and FSA filed an adversary proceeding to have the debt declared nondischargeable as a conversion that was willful and malicious under § 523(a)(6). The bankruptcy court found that Husband's conduct was willful and malicious, and held that his debt to FSA was not discharged. On the question of malice, the court first noted that it could infer, given the specific language in the loan documents, that Husband's "injurious acts were done in 'knowing disregard' of FSA's rights." Second, the court explained that while Husband did not use the sale proceeds for personal gain, he elevated the rights of certain creditors over those of FSA. Because there was no testimony from Husband, the court could not find just cause or excuse for Husband's conduct, e.g., Husband acted to keep the farm afloat or in the reasonable belief, based on past dealings, that he was allowed to dispose of FSA's collateral. [*In re* **Shelmidine,** 519 B.R. 385 (Bankr. N.D. N.Y. 2014)]

(ii) Willful *or* Malicious

The standard Chapter 13 discharge excepts from discharge debts for restitution or damages awarded in a *civil action* against the debtor for *willful or malicious injury* resulting in *personal injury or death* of an *individual.* [B.C. § 1328(a)(4)] The Chapter 13 exception from discharge differs from § 523(a)(6)'s exception from discharge in the following ways:

(1) A creditor need only prove *willful or malicious injury* under § 1328(a)(4). By comparison, § 523(a)(6) requires proof of both *willfulness and maliciousness.*

(2) Section 1328(a)(4) applies *only* to individuals. Section 523(a)(6) applies to "entities," which includes individuals and corporations. [B.C. §§ 101(15), (41)]

(3) Section 1328(a)(4) only excepts from discharge willful or malicious injury that results in *personal injury or death.* Section 523(a)(6) includes not only personal injury or death, but *also harm to property.*

(4) Section 1328(a)(4) says "awarded in a civil action." Section 523(a)(6) contains no such language. There is little case law on the issue, but there is a question as to whether the phrase "awarded in a civil action" requires the creditor to have obtained a judgment pre-petition against the debtor in order to have the debt declared nondischargeable. [*See* **Waag v. Perman (*In re* Waag),** 418 B.R. 373 (B.A.P. 9th Cir. 2009) (affirming bankruptcy court decision that § 1328(a)(4) did not require a pre-petition judgment for nondischargeability); **Morrison v. Harrsch (*In re* Harrsch),** 432 B.R. 169 (Bankr. E.D. Pa. 2010) (concerned about the "vagaries of timing" and holding that the "award" for damages could be entered after the start of debtor's bankruptcy case); *but see* **Parsons v. Byrd (*In re* Byrd)**, 388 B.R. 875 (Bankr. C.D. Ill. 2007) (in the first published case on the issue post-BAPCPA, bankruptcy court held that the word "awarded" was past tense, which meant that a pre-petition award was a "prerequisite to a finding of nondischargeability under § 1328(a)(4)")]

h. Fines, Penalties, and Restitution

(i) Fines, Penalties, or Forfeitures

In a case under Chapters 7, 11, or 12, or a hardship discharge case under Chapter 13, a *fine, penalty, or forfeiture* payable *to and for the benefit* of a *governmental unit* is nondischargeable to the extent that it is *not compensation for actual pecuniary loss.* [B.C. §§ 523(a)(7), 1328(b)] The exception applies to both *criminal and civil penalties, fines and forfeitures.* [**Disciplinary Bd. v. Feingold (*In re* Feingold)**, 730 F.3d 1268 (11th Cir. 2013)]

e.g. **Example:** The Commonwealth of Pennsylvania disbarred Debtor from the practice of law. The Disciplinary Board subsequently filed a complaint in state court to enjoin Debtor from the practice of law and to appoint a conservator to protect Debtor's clients and take possession of Debtor's client files. The state court, at the conclusion of its proceedings, assessed approximately $45,000 in costs and expenses associated with the conservatorship and disciplinary proceedings against the Debtor. Debtor then filed for relief under Chapter 7. The Eleventh Circuit held that the $45,000 debt was not dischargeable. The court held that the costs assessed in the attorney disciplinary proceedings were punitive and not compensatory in nature. Noting that the attorney disciplinary system served the dual functions of deterrence and protection of the public, the court concluded that the costs assessed against Debtor constituted a " 'fine, penalty, or forfeiture' within the meaning of § 523(a)(7)." The court also explained that the costs assessed were not for actual pecuniary loss, because the Disciplinary Board had to "perform its public function whether it could recoup the costs associated with it or not." [**Disciplinary Bd. v. Feingold (*In re* Feingold)**, *supra*]

cf. **Compare:** Client hired Debtor as his attorney to assist with modification of his home mortgage loan. Client paid Debtor $5,500 in advance of any modification; taking fees in advance of a residential home modification violated California law. Client fired Debtor and sought refund of the $5,500 under California's mandatory attorney fee arbitration program. The arbitrator ruled against Debtor and found that she owed Client a full refund of the $5,500. Debtor made a few payments on the arbitration award, but then claimed that she had insufficient funds to continue to pay. The arbitrator then filed an action in the state bar court, which found that Debtor could afford to pay and suspended Debtor's license to practice law until she refunded the remainder of the $5,500 to Client. Debtor then filed for relief under Chapter 7. The court held that the debt was dischargeable, because it was the amount that Debtor owed to Client; thus, it was compensation for actual pecuniary loss and not a fine or penalty. [**Scheer v. State Bar (*In re* Scheer)**, 819 F.3d 1206 (9th Cir. 2016)]

(1) Tax Penalties

Section 523(a)(7) carves out *two exceptions* to nondischargeability for tax penalties. If a tax penalty fits within either exception, it is *dischargeable.*

(a) **Dischargeable tax:** A tax penalty that relates to a tax that does *not* qualify as nondischargeable under § 523(a)(1) is dischargeable. [B.C. § 523(a)(7)(A)]

(b) **More than Three Years Before Bankruptcy:** A tax penalty that relates to a tax imposed with regard to a transaction or event that occurred *more than three years* prior to the bankruptcy filing is dischargeable. [B.C. § 523(a)(7)(B)]

(2) State Criminal Restitution

Court-ordered state criminal restitution payments imposed as part of a defendant's sentence and as a condition for probation are penal in nature and, thus, nondischargeable. [B.C. § 523(a)(7); **Kelly v. Robinson,** 479 U.S. 36 (1986)] The Supreme Court in *Kelly* stated: "Because criminal proceedings focus on the State's interest in rehabilitation and punishment, rather than the victim's desire for compensation, we conclude that restitution orders imposed in such proceedings operate 'for the benefit of' the State . . . [and] are not assessed 'for . . . compensation' of the victim."

(3) Civil Restitution

Courts are split on the question whether § 523(a)(7) excepts from discharge civil restitution awards. [*In re* **Styer,** 477 B.R. 584 (Bankr. E.D. Pa. 2012)]

Example: HUD obtained a judgment against Debtors making them jointly and severally liable for $8.65 million related to Debtors' violations of the Interstate Land Sales Full Disclosure Act, including sales of lots at over three times their assessed value. The Fourth Circuit held that the judgment was not dischargeable under § 523(a)(7). The court acknowledged that HUD intended to use all or some of the funds to reimburse the victims of Debtors' misconduct, but also noted that HUD had no obligation to remit funds to anyone. The court narrowly interpreted the phrase "not compensation for actual pecuniary loss" and focused on the nature of the government's interest. "So long as the government's interest in enforcing a debt is *penal,* it makes no difference that injured persons may thereby receive compensation for pecuniary loss. In other words, the 'not compensation for actual pecuniary loss' phrase in § 523(a)(7) refers to *the government's* pecuniary loss." [**Department of Housing & Urban Development v. Cost Control Marketing & Sales Management of Virginia, Inc.,** 64 F.3d 920 (4th Cir. 1995)]

Compare: The State of Illinois sued Debtor for violating the Illinois Consumer Fraud and Deceptive Business Practices Act. The state court found that Debtor had defrauded his customers and, among other things, ordered him to pay restitution in the amount of $210,000. The order provided for payment of restitution to the Illinois Attorney General, but for the victims of Debtor's fraudulent conduct. The Seventh Circuit held that the $210,000 civil restitution award was dischargeable because it was not paid "for the benefit of a government unit." While the money was paid *to* the State of Illinois, the funds were to be distributed to the victims of Debtor's fraudulent activity. Thus, the requirements of § 523(a)(7) were not satisfied. The civil restitution award was for the benefit of the victims, not for the benefit of the governmental unit—the State of Illinois. [*In re* **Towers,** 162 F.3d 952 (7th Cir. 1998)]

(ii) Restitution or Fines in Criminal Sentence in Chapter 13

Debts for *restitution or a criminal fine* that are included in the debtor's sentence for *conviction of a crime* are excepted from the standard Chapter 13 discharge. [B.C. § 1328(a)(3)] Section 1328(a)(3) differs from § 523(a)(7) in the following ways.

(1) Section 523(a)(7) applies to all fines owed to a governmental unit, while § 1328(a)(3) only excepts criminal fines from discharge if they are *included in the sentence for conviction* of a crime.

(2) Section 523(a)(7) specifically states that the fine or penalty must not be compensation for actual pecuniary loss. Section 1328(a)(3) contains no such limitation.

i. Restitution for Federal Crimes

The payment of an order of *restitution* under title 18 of the United States Code, for most *federal* crimes, is nondischargeable in a Chapter 7, 11, or 12 case, or a Chapter 13 hardship discharge case. [B.C. § 523(a)(13)] *Fines* ordered in connection with certain *federal* crimes are nondischargeable under *all chapters* of the Code, and liens securing them filed in favor of the United States are *not avoidable* in bankruptcy. [18 U.S.C. § 3613(e)]

Note: Section 1328(a)(3) governs the dischargeability of debts for restitution in a Chapter 13 case. Section 1328(a)(3) is broader than § 523(a)(13), which is limited to restitution orders issued in federal criminal cases.

j. Student Loans

Pre-BAPCPA, only educational loans funded by a governmental unit or nonprofit institution were nondischargeable. BAPCPA expanded the categories of educational loans subject to the Code's nondischargeability provision. Thus, absent an *undue hardship* on the debtor and her dependents, an educational loan made, insured, or guaranteed by a governmental unit, or extended under a program funded by a governmental unit or a nonprofit institution, or any other educational loan that is a qualified education loan under the Internal Revenue Code is nondischargeable. [B.C. § 523(a)(8)] The exception to discharge for student loans applies to Chapters 7, 11, 12, and all Chapter 13 cases, regardless of whether the debtor obtains a standard or hardship discharge. [B.C. §§ 523(a), 1141(d)(2), 1228(a)(2), 1328(a)(2)]

(i) Undue Hardship

A debtor will receive a discharge of her student loans if she can prove "undue hardship." Most courts use the *Brunner* test for undue hardship, which requires proof of the following elements:

(1) *the debtor and her dependents cannot maintain a "minimal standard of living,"* based on current income and expenses, if repayment is required;

(2) *the debtor's current situation,* e.g., finances, ability to get a job, medical condition, is likely to *persist for a significant portion of the repayment period;* and

(3) *the debtor has made good faith efforts to repay the student loan.*

[*In re* **Brunner,** 46 B.R. 752 (S.D.N.Y. 1985), *aff'd,* 831 F.2d 395 (2d Cir. 1987); B.C. § 523(a)(8)]

(ii) HEAL Loans

A Health Education Assistance Loan ("HEAL") is a loan extended for educational purposes to a health professional, e.g., a medical student, by a private lender, such as a bank. The United States Department of Health and Human Services guarantees the loan. A HEAL loan is not dischargeable unless three statutory conditions are satisfied, one of which is a finding by the court that the *failure to discharge* the debt would be *unconscionable.* [42 U.S.C. § 292f(g)]; **Woody v. DOJ (*In re* Woody),** 494 F.3d 939 (10th Cir. 2007)]

(1) Unconscionability

The unconscionability standard under 42 U.S.C. § 292f(g) is far more difficult to satisfy than the "undue hardship" test of § 523(a)(8). The bankruptcy court must determine whether "nondischarge would be shockingly unfair, harsh, or unjust, or otherwise unconscionable." The test is fact-intensive, and requires courts to examine the totality of the debtor's circumstances, including her income and earning ability, her health, the debtor's standard of living and expenses, the ability of dependents to provide financial support, the debtor's good faith attempts to pay her HEAL loans, the amount of debt owed and the interest rate on the loans, and whether the debtor has tried to maximize her income. These factors are not exclusive, and bankruptcy courts must consider any additional factors that bear on the unconscionability analysis. [**Woody v. DOJ (*In re* Woody),** *supra*]

(2) Other Elements

In addition to unconscionability, the discharge of a HEAL loan requires proof (i) that *seven years* have expired from the date that repayment was required to begin, and (ii) that with regard to a HEAL borrower who is carrying on her profession but not repaid her HEAL loans, the Secretary of Health and Human Services *has not waived statutory rights to reduce payments* owed to the HEAL borrower for health services provided under federal law up to an amount equal to the balance due on her HEAL loans. [42 U.S.C. § 292f(g), (f)]

k. Operating a Motor Vehicle, Vessel or Aircraft While Intoxicated

Any debt for *death or personal injury* resulting from the debtor's use of a motor vehicle, vessel, or aircraft if such operation was unlawful because debtor was *intoxicated* from using alcohol, drugs, or another substance is nondischargeable. [B.C. § 523(a)(9)]

l. Prior Bankruptcy

A debt that was or could have been listed in a *prior case* in which the debtor *waived discharge* or in which the debtor was *denied discharge* under § 727(a)(2)–(7) is nondischargeable. [B.C. § 523(a)(10)] The denial-of-discharge language is tied to § 727, and only to specific subsections of § 727.

Exception: The standard discharge under Chapter 13 does *not* except from discharge such debts from a prior bankruptcy.

Distinguish: It is important to distinguish § 523(a)(10), which excepts *particular debts,* from a *complete denial of discharge* in a bankruptcy case filed within certain time periods after the debtor received a discharge in a prior bankruptcy case. [*Compare* B.C. § 523(a)(10) *with* B.C. §§ 727(a)(8), 1328(f)]

e.g. **Example:** In May of 2014, Debtor filed for relief under Chapter 7 but was denied a discharge under § 727(a)(2), because she had made a fraudulent conveyance of her property within a year of her Chapter 7 filing. Debtor subsequently files for relief under Chapter 13. Debtor will not be denied a discharge of the debts from her prior Chapter 7 case, because Chapter 13 does not except from discharge debts under § 523(a)(10). But, the date of Debtor's subsequent Chapter 13 filing affects her right to a standard discharge in the later Chapter 13 case. If Debtor filed her later Chapter 13 case in August of 2018, she will receive a standard discharge upon completing her plan payments. But, if Debtor filed her later Chapter 13 case in February of 2018, she will not receive a discharge, even if she completes her plan payments, because she filed her later Chapter 13 case *less than 4 years* after having filed for relief under Chapter 7. [B.C. § 1328(f)(1)]

e.g. **Example:** Debtor filed for relief under Chapter 7 in February of 2010. Debtor was denied a discharge in that case under § 727(a)(11), because she failed to complete the instructional course on personal financial management that is required by Bankruptcy Code § 111. Debtor files for relief under Chapter 7 in August of 2018. Section 523(a)(10) only applies to a denial of discharge under §§ 727(a)(2) through (7). As a result, the prior denial of discharge pursuant to § 727(a)(11) does not affect Debtor's ability to receive a discharge in her current Chapter 7 case.

m. Fiduciary Fraud or Defalcation of Officers and Directors of Financial Institutions

Any debt arising from a final judgment or order, or consent order or decree (i) entered by any federal or state court, (ii) issued by a federal depository institutions regulatory agency, or (iii) contained in a settlement agreement with the debtor, resulting from the debtor's *fraud or defalcation* while acting in a *fiduciary capacity* with respect to any *insured depository institution or insured credit union* is nondischargeable. [B.C. §§ 523(a)(11), 101(21B), (34), (35)]

Exception: Such debts are dischargeable as part of a standard Chapter 13 discharge. [B.C. § 1328(a)]

Note: For purposes of § 523(a)(11), any institution-affiliated party of an insured depository institution is deemed to be acting in a fiduciary capacity. [B.C. §§ 523(e), 101(33), (35)]

n. Failure to Maintain Capital of Insured Depository Institutions

Any debt for *malicious or reckless* failure to maintain the capital of an insured depository institution in breach of a commitment to a federal depository institutions regulatory agency is nondischargeable. [B.C. § 523(a)(12)]

Exception: Such debts are dischargeable as part of a standard Chapter 13 discharge. [B.C. § 1328(a)]

o. Debts Incurred to Pay Taxes

Debts incurred to pay taxes that would be nondischargeable under § 523(a)(1), or fines or penalties imposed under federal election law are nondischargeable. [B.C. §§ 523(a)(14), (14A), (14B)] This provision should facilitate the use of credit cards to pay taxes. Prior to BAPCPA's passage, § 523(a)(14) only applied to federal taxes that would be dischargeable under § 523(a)(1). It now applies to *all* taxes that would be dischargeable under § 523(a)(1), as well as to fines or penalties for federal election law violations.

Exception: Such debts are dischargeable as part of a standard Chapter 13 discharge. [B.C. § 1328(a)]

p. Condominium Fees

Fees or assessments for a condominium, a share in a cooperative housing corporation, or a lot in a homeowners' association that become due and payable *after the order for relief* are nondischargeable for as long as the debtor or the trustee has a legal, equitable, or possessory ownership interest in the condominium, cooperative housing corporation, or lot. [B.C. § 523(a)(16)]

Exception: Such debts are dischargeable as part of a standard Chapter 13 discharge. [B.C. § 1328(a)]

q. Court Costs

Fees imposed on a prisoner for filing a case, appeal, complaint, or motion, as well as any other costs assessed in connection with the filing are nondischargeable even if the debtor files *in forma pauperis* or has the status of a prisoner. [B.C. § 523(a)(17)]

Exception: Such debts are dischargeable as part of a standard Chapter 13 discharge. [B.C. § 1328(a)]

r. Pension Loans

A debt owed to a *pension, profit-sharing, stock bonus or other plan* established under the Internal Revenue Code for certain loans permitted by ERISA (29 U.S.C. § 1108(b)(1)), or subject to the Internal Revenue Code's rules on loans as distributions (26 U.S.C. § 72(p)), or loans from a thrift savings plan permitted under the federal employees retirement system (5 U.S.C. § 8433(g) are not dischargeable. [B.C. § 523(a)(18)] BAPCPA added this exception to discharge.

Exception: Such debts are dischargeable as part of a standard Chapter 13 discharge. [B.C. § 1328(a)]

s. Securities Law Violations

A debt owed for violation of *state or federal securities laws,* or for *common law fraud, deceit or misrepresentation* in connection with the *purchase of a security* is nondischargeable if it results from any (i) judgment, order, consent decree or order entered in any federal or state court, or any administrative proceeding, (ii) settlement agreement entered into by the debtor, or (iii) any court or administrative order for damages, fines, penalties, restitution, attorney fees, costs or any other payment owed by the debtor. The debt is nondischargeable regardless of when the liability determination is made: before, on, or after the petition filing date. [B.C. § 523(a)(19)] Congress added § 523(a)(19) to the Bankruptcy Code in 2002 as part of the Corporate and Criminal Fraud Accountability Act, which is Title VIII of the Sarbanes-Oxley Act of 2002. [**McKinny v. Allison,** 2013 U.S. Dist. LEXIS 155245 (E.D. N.C. 2013)] In 2005, Congress closed a loophole that allowed debtors to argue that the exception applied only to judgments entered prior to the bankruptcy filing. [4 Collier ¶ 523.27]

Exception: Such debts are dischargeable as part of a standard Chapter 13 discharge. [B.C. § 1328(a)]

3. Certain Long-Term Debts

A debtor may have certain long-term debts, e.g., mortgage, in which the last payment on the debt is due *after* the last payment is due under the debtor's plan. These long-term debts are not part of the Chapter 12 or Chapter 13 discharge, regardless of whether it is a standard or hardship discharge. [B.C. §§ 1228(a)(1), 1228(b), (c)(1), 1222(b)(5), (9); 1328(a)(1), 1328(b), (c)(1), 1322(b)(5)]

NONDISCHARGEABLE DEBTS

A "Y" in the Chapter column indicates that the debt in Column A is *not* dischargeable. Variations on the nondischargeability of a debt are indicated in Columns B through F.

(A) Category of Debt	(B) Ch. 7	(C) Ch. 11	(D) Ch. 12	(E) Ch. 13— standard	(F) Ch. 13— hardship
Third and eighth priority taxes § 523(a)(1)(A)	Y	Y	Y, *except* taxes on disposition of property used in debtor's farming operation	N. Only trust fund taxes under § 507(a)(8)(C) are not dischargeable.	Y
No return or late return § 523(a)(1)(B)	Y	Y	Y	Y	Y
Fraudulent return § 523(a)(1)(C)	Y	Y	Y	Y	Y
Fraud, false pretenses, false financial statements § 523(a)(2)	Y	Y	Y	Y	Y
Failure to schedule debt in current case § 523(a)(3)	Y	Y	Y	Y	Y
Fraud or defalcation in fiduciary capacity, and embezzlement or larceny § 523(a)(4)	Y	Y	Y	Y	Y
Domestic support obligations § 523(a)(5)	Y	Y	Y	Y	Y
Settlements & Obligations from separation or divorce § 523(a)(15)	Y	Y	Y	N	Y
Willful and malicious injury to person or property § 523(a)(6)	Y	Y	Y	§ 1328(a)(4) requires willful *or* malicious injury and limited to harm to persons	Y
Fines, penalties, forfeitures, restitution, except certain tax penalties § 523(a)(7)	Y	Y	Y	§ 1328(a)(3) excepts from discharge debts for restitution or criminal fines included in debtor's sentence—state or federal	Y
Restitution: some federal crimes § 523(a)(13)	Y	Y	Y	§ 523(a)(13) not apply, *but see* § 1328(a)(3)	Y
Fines: certain federal crimes; liens not avoidable 18 U.S.C. § 3613(e)	Y	Y	Y	Y	Y
Student loans unless "undue hardship" § 523(a)(8)	Y	Y	Y	Y	Y

(A) Category of Debt	(B) Ch. 7	(C) Ch. 11	(D) Ch. 12	(E) Ch. 13— standard	(F) Ch. 13— hardship
HEAL loans 42 U.S.C. § 292f(g)	Y	Y	Y	Y	Y
Death, personal injury from operating motor vehicle, vessel or aircraft while intoxicated § 523(a)(9)	Y	Y	Y	Y	Y
Waiver of discharge or denial of discharge in prior case § 523(a)(10)	Y	Y	Y	N	Y
Fiduciary fraud, defalcation financial institutions § 523(a)(11)	Y	Y	Y	N	Y
Failure to maintain capital insured depository institution § 523(a)(12)	Y	Y	Y	N	Y
Debts nondischargeable taxes, election law fines/penalties § 523(a)(14)	Y	Y	Y	N	Y
Condominium fees § 523(a)(16)	Y	Y	Y	N	Y
Court costs: prisoners § 523(a)(17)	Y	Y	Y	N	Y
Pension loans § 523(a)(18)	Y	Y	Y	N	Y
Securities law violations § 523(a)(11)	Y	Y	Y	N	Y
Certain long-term debts	N	N	Y §§ 1228(a)(1), 1222(b)(5), (9)	Y §§ 1328(a)(1), 1322(b)(5)	Y §§ 1222(c)(1), 1322(c)(1)

4. Proof

In a unanimous decision, the Supreme Court has held that the ***preponderance-of-the-evidence*** standard of proof applies to the exceptions to discharge contained in § 523(a). [**Grogan v. Garner,** 498 U.S. 279 (1991)]

5. Prior State Court Judgments

In a Bankruptcy Act case, the Supreme Court, in a unanimous opinion, held that *res judicata* did not preclude the bankruptcy court's consideration of evidence of fraud in deciding whether a debt previously reduced to a state court judgment, pursuant to the parties' stipulation, was nondischargeable. [**Brown v. Felsen,** 442 U.S. 127 (1979)]

e.g. **Example:** Debtor owned a car dealership, and Creditor guaranteed Bank's loan that financed the purchase of vehicles for the dealership. When Bank sued to collect on the loan, Creditor alleged that Debtor had fraudulently induced Creditor to sign the guarantee for the loan. The parties entered into a stipulation that provided that Bank could recover against both Creditor and Debtor, but that Creditor had a right to judgment against Debtor. Both the stipulation and resulting judgment were silent on the basis for Debtor's liability to Creditor. Debtor subsequently filed for relief under the Bankruptcy Act. Creditor argued that the debt owed to him was nondischargeable, under § 17 of the Bankruptcy Act, because of Debtor's fraud. Debtor claimed that the prior state court action had not resulted in a finding of fraud and, thus, res judicata prevented Creditor from re-litigating the nature of the debt before the bankruptcy court. The bankruptcy court ruled in favor of Debtor and concluded that nothing in the state court record provided a basis for a finding of fraud. The district court and the Court of Appeals affirmed. The Supreme Court reversed. The Court held that "neither the interests served by res judicata . . . nor the policies of the Bankruptcy Act would be well served by foreclosing [Creditor] from submitting additional evidence to prove his case." The Court explained that when the issues related to nondischargeability of a debt for fraud are not the same as those underlying a state court collection proceeding, the parties do not have an incentive to litigate the discharge question in state court. A contrary rule, according to the Court, would force a creditor to litigate a fraud/nondischargeability issue simply to protect himself against the possibility of a future bankruptcy proceeding. The Supreme Court also noted that in 1970 Congress had amended the Bankruptcy Act to give exclusive jurisdiction over certain nondischargeability claims, including the fraud claim at issue, to the bankruptcy courts. The Court explained that "it would be inconsistent with the philosophy of the 1970 amendments to adopt a policy of res judicata which takes these § 17 questions away from bankruptcy courts and forces them back into state courts." [**Brown v. Felsen,** *supra*]

Example: Creditors purchased Company from Debtors for $610,000. Several months later, Creditors sued Debtors for fraud in connection with the sale of Company. The parties settled the lawsuit; the settlement agreement provided that Debtors would pay Creditors $300,000 and that Creditors would execute releases of all claims arising from the litigation. Debtors failed to pay $100,000 of the monies owed under the settlement agreement, and Creditors filed suit to collect in state court. Debtors then filed for relief under Chapter 7. Creditors argued that the $100,000 debt owed to them was nondischargeable based on fraud. The bankruptcy court ruled against Creditors, and both the district court and Court of Appeals affirmed. The Supreme Court reversed and held that the decision in *Brown v. Felsen* governed the outcome. The Court explained that the fact that the "relevant debt here is embodied in a settlement, not in a stipulation and consent judgment," as in *Brown,* was not dispositive. The Court concluded that, as in *Brown,* what had not been established was that the parties had intended to resolve the question of fraud for purposes of a nondischargeability action in bankruptcy. Thus, the settlement agreement did not bar Creditors from showing that the debt owed to them arose from fraud and, therefore, was not dischargeable under § 523(a)(2)(A). [**Archer v. Warner,** 538 U.S. 314 (2003)]

a. Collateral Estoppel

The Supreme Court has ruled that the doctrine of collateral estoppel *applies* in discharge exception proceedings under § 523(a) to preclude the retrial of issues of fact that have been "actually litigated and determined" in an earlier action in a nonbankruptcy court. [**Grogan v. Garner,** *supra*]

(i) Elements

Courts have articulated the elements necessary for collateral estoppel in similar, but not identical, ways. One common articulation requires the following elements:

(1) the issue in the prior action is *identical* to the one involved in the current proceeding action;

(2) the issue was *actually litigated* in the prior action;

(3) the resolution of the issue in the prior action was a *necessary part* of the *judgment* in that prior action; and

(4) the parties in the prior action are the same as those in the current proceeding.

[**P.B. Surf, Ltd. v. Savage (*In re* Savage),** 2015 WL 4498910 (Bankr. N.D. Ala. 2015)]

(ii) Consent Judgment

If the parties settled the prior state court action by a consent judgment, collateral estoppel may not apply because the *actually litigated* requirement may not be satisfied. [*See, e.g.,* **Giannetti Construction Corp. v. Fodale (*In re* Fodale)**, 2012 WL 718904 (Bankr. E.D. Mich. 2012) (noting that under Michigan law "consent judgments are not generally given collateral estoppel effect" because the actual litigation element of collateral estoppel is missing)] The bankruptcy court must find that the parties understood that the agreement would conclusively determine the issue of dischargeability in the event of bankruptcy. [*See, e.g.,* **McKinny v. Allison**, 2013 U.S. Dist. LEXIS 155425 (E.D. N.C. 2013) (finding that bankruptcy court would need to conduct further proceedings to determine that the parties intended to foreclose litigation of the issue of liability under § 523(a)(19) when settlement agreement contained express statement that parties admitted no liability)] The consent judgment should include specific findings of fact supporting liability and nondischargeability. [*See, e.g.,* **P.B. Surf, Ltd. v. Savage (*In re* Savage),** *supra* (holding that consent judgment contained no findings of fact to support an admission by debtors that the elements of §§ 523(a)(2)(A), (4) or (6) had been established, even though debtors had stipulated that debt would not be dischargeable in bankruptcy]

6. Special Rules

a. Debts Under Bankruptcy Code §§ 523(a)(1), (a)(3), and (a)(8)

Debts for *taxes, unscheduled liabilities, educational loans,* or *HEAL* loans that were held to be nondischargeable in a prior bankruptcy case concerning the debtor are dischargeable in a subsequent bankruptcy case, unless these debts are *independently* nondischargeable by the terms of § 523(a) or, for HEAL loans, under 42 U.S.C. § 292f(g), in the later bankruptcy case. [B.C. § 523(b)]

b. Debts Under Bankruptcy Code §§ 523(a)(2), (a)(4), and (a)(6)

The bankruptcy court has exclusive jurisdiction to determine the dischargeability of the following types of debts [B.C. § 523(c)(1)]:

(i) *debts for fraudulently obtaining money, property, services, or credit* [B.C. § 523(a)(2)];

(ii) *debts for fraud or defalcation by a fiduciary,* for embezzlement, or for larceny [B.C. § 523(a)(4)]; and

(iii) *debts for willful and malicious injury to persons or property.* [B.C. § 523(a)(6)]

In individual Chapter 7, 11, and 12 cases, debts under §§ 523(a)(2), (4), and (6) are excepted from discharge. Recall that the standard discharge in Chapter 13 excepts from discharge debts under §§ 523(a)(2) and (a)(4), but not § 523(a)(6). Instead, in Chapter 13, the exception for debts for certain *willful or malicious injuries* is found at § 1328(a)(4). In a Chapter 7, 11 or 12 case, a *complaint* requesting determination of the dischargeability of debts under §§ 523(a)(2), (a)(4), (a)(6) *must be filed by the creditor within 60 days after the first date set* for the § 341 meeting, unless the deadline is extended by the court for cause. In a Chapter 13 case, the rule is the same: a *complaint* requesting determination of the dischargeability of debts under §§ 523(a)(2) or (a)(4) *must be filed by the creditor within 60 days after the first date set* for the § 341 meeting, unless the deadline is extended by the court for cause. [Bankruptcy Rule 4007(c)] Otherwise, the debts are discharged. This deadline applies even if the meeting is continued and held at a later date. [Bankruptcy Rule 4007(c)]

Because debts under § 523(a)(6) are excepted from the *hardship discharge* under Chapter 13, when a Chapter 13 debtor moves for such a discharge, the bankruptcy court must enter an order fixing the time within which to file a complaint to determine dischargeability of a debt under § 523(a)(6). [Bankruptcy Rule 4007(d)]

c. Other Dischargeability Proceedings

A complaint requesting a determination of the dischargeability of a debt, *other than* one under §§ 523(a)(2), (a)(4), or (a)(6) may be filed at any time, even if it requires reopening the case. [Bankruptcy Rule 4007(b)]

B. Effects of Discharge

1. Relief from Personal Liability

A debtor is relieved of *personal* liability for all debts that are discharged. [B.C. § 524(a)(1), (2)] Thus, while a valid lien that has not been avoided in the bankruptcy case generally survives *in rem* and ultimately may be enforced against the property securing the debt, no action is permitted against the debtor personally for a deficiency if the debt has been discharged.

EXAM TIP   🔖GILBERT

The main goal of bankruptcy is to give the honest debtor a fresh start. This is accomplished by relieving the debtor from *personal liability* for all debts that are discharged.

---

a. "Debt" Defined

The Bankruptcy Code defines "debt" as "liability on a claim." [B.C. § 101(12)]

b. Judgments

A discharge automatically *voids any judgment* against the debtor for *personal liability* on a debt that is included in the discharge. [B.C. § 524(a)(1)]

c. Injunction

A discharge also constitutes a permanent statutory injunction prohibiting creditors from taking any action, or filing or continuing a law suit, designed to recover or collect a discharged debt from the debtor personally. [B.C. § 524(a)(2)]

e.g. **Example:** Debtor breached her lease with Landlord. Landlord filed state court actions for damages resulting from the nonpayment of rent and for possession of the premises. The state court granted judgment in favor of Landlord, but before Landlord could evict Debtor, she filed for relief under Chapter 7. The Chapter 7 trustee did not assume Debtor's lease and, thus, it was deemed rejected. Debtor received a discharge in her Chapter 7 case. Subsequently, Landlord filed a complaint in state court against Debtor for breach of the lease. The commencement of the post-bankruptcy state court action is a violation of the discharge injunction because it is an effort to collect on a pre-petition claim. [**Baxter v. Summerfield Investment Group, LLC (*In re* Baxter),** 2015 WL 6122158 (Bankr. D. Md. 2015)]

e.g. **Example:** Debtor enrolled in a master's program at University. Debtor stopped paying tuition, but University allowed her to sit for exams and to sign up for classes. Debtor completed her program and received her master's degree. When Debtor asked for a transcript, University refused to provide one to her until she paid her back tuition, which amounted to more than $6,000. Debtor then filed for bankruptcy and received a discharge. Debtor, once again, requested a transcript from University and agreed to pay the transcript fee. University, once again, refused to provide a transcript because Debtor had failed to pay the tuition she owed University. Debtor has a state law right to a certified copy of her transcript. Thus, University's failure to provide Debtor with a transcript violates the discharge injunction because it is an effort to collect on a pre-petition debt. (Debtor's past-due tuition was not a nondischargeable student loan.) [*In re* **Kuehn,** 563 F.3d 829 (7th Cir. 2009)]

Note: The Bankruptcy Code provides specific and detailed rules for so-called "channeling injunctions" in Chapter 11 asbestos cases. [B.C. §§ 524(g)]

d. Community Property

With two exceptions, in community property states, a discharge also enjoins any act by a creditor to collect or recover an allowable community claim from community property acquired by the debtor *after* the filing of the bankruptcy case. [B.C. § 524(a)(3)]

e.g. **Example:** Husband files for relief under Chapter 7, and has *no* nondischargeable debts. Wife does not file for bankruptcy but had she done so on the same day as Husband, she also would have had *no* nondischargeable debts. Creditors of Husband or Wife that hold community claims on the date of Husband's bankruptcy filing may not bring claims against community property that Husband and Wife acquire after Husband's bankruptcy. [*See* 4 Collier ¶ 524.02(3)(a)]

There are two exceptions to this rule.

(i) Nondischargeable Debts

If the community claim is *nondischargeable* under § 523(a), or under §§ 1228(a)(1) or 1328(a)(1) in the debtor's case *or* *would be nondischargeable* in the case of debtor's spouse had debtor's spouse filed a petition on the same day as debtor filed her petition, then the discharge injunction does not prohibit a creditor with an allowable community claim from taking action to recover on that claim from community property acquired after the filing of the bankruptcy petition. [B.C. § 524(a)(3)]

(ii) Discharge Denial

If the *debtor's spouse has been denied a discharge* in a case filed within six years of the debtor's petition or *would be denied a discharge in a Chapter 7 case* had she filed bankruptcy on the date of the debtor's petition, then the discharge injunction does not prohibit a creditor with an allowable community claim from taking action to recover on that claim from community property acquired after the filing of the bankruptcy petition. [B.C. §§ 524(b)(1), (2); *see* 4 Collier ¶ 524.02(3)(b) ("Sections 524(b)(1)(A) and (B) apply if *both* spouses are debtors, and sections 524(b)(2)(A) and (B) apply if only one spouse is a debtor.")]

2. Co-Debtor or Surety—No Discharge

With limited exceptions, the discharge of a debt of the debtor does *not* affect the liability of any other entity, e.g., a co-debtor, surety, or guarantor, or the property of any other entity for that debt. [B.C. § 524(e)]

Exception: Under certain circumstances, the creditor of a non-debtor spouse may not collect against community property acquired post-petition. [B.C. § 524(a)(3)]

Exception: The Code allows a ***channeling injunction*** issued in a Chapter 11 asbestos case to bar actions against non-debtor third parties so long as certain statutory requirements are satisfied. [B.C. § 524(g)(4)(A)]

Exception: The courts are split as to whether the bankruptcy court may confirm a reorganization plan that includes a provision releasing certain non-debtors of liability or permanently enjoining suits against them. [4 Collier ¶ 524.05]

3. Voluntary Repayment

The Code expressly permits the debtor to voluntarily repay any debt. [B.C. § 524(f)] However, in the absence of an enforceable reaffirmation agreement with a creditor, the debtor has no personal *legal* obligation to repay a debt that has been discharged.

C. Reaffirmation Agreements

1. Definition

A reaffirmation agreement is a voluntary contract between the debtor and the holder of a dischargeable claim whereby the debtor promises to repay all or part of the debt after bankruptcy. [B.C. § 524(c)] The debtor may not unilaterally reaffirm a debt. [*In re* **Turner,** 156 F.3d 713 (7th Cir. 1998)]

2. Requirements for Enforceability

A reaffirmation agreement is enforceable only if all of the following conditions are satisfied. [B.C. § 524(c)]

a. Enforceable Contract

The reaffirmation agreement must be enforceable under nonbankruptcy law.

b. Made Before Discharge

The agreement must have been executed prior to the granting of the debtor's discharge. [B.C. § 524(c)(1)]

c. Disclosures

At or before the time that the debtor signs the reaffirmation agreement, the debtor must receive a detailed set of ***disclosures*** that Congress added to the Code in 2005 with the passage of BAPCPA. [B.C. §§ 524(c)(2), (k)] If the disclosures are provided in ***good faith,*** then this requirement for an enforceable reaffirmation agreement is satisfied. [B.C. § 524(*l*)(3)]

The debtor must receive a ***disclosure statement*** that includes, among other things, the amount of the debt reaffirmed, the amount of any costs and fees, the annual percentage rate on the reaffirmed debt, a repayment schedule, and statements explaining the debtor's rights and obligations with regard to a reaffirmed debt. [B.C. § 524(k)(3)] The debtor also must receive the following:

(i) the ***reaffirmation agreement*** itself, the basic form of which is provided for in the Code [B.C. §§ 524(k)(1), (4)];

(ii) the ***declaration,*** which is a ***certification by the debtor's attorney, if any,*** that the attorney informed the debtor of the ***legal effect and consequences*** of entering into the reaffirmation agreement, that debtor made a ***voluntary and informed choice*** in making the agreement, and that the agreement does *not impose an undue hardship* on the debtor [B.C. §§ 524(k)(1), (5)];

(iii) the *debtor's statement in support of the reaffirmation agreement,* the language of which is provided in the Code [B.C. §§ 524(k)(1), (6)];

(iv) the *motion for court approval* of the reaffirmation agreement in cases in which the debtor is *not represented* by counsel or a *presumption of undue hardship* exists [B.C. §§ 524(k)(1), (7), (m)]; and

(v) the form of *court order* approving the reaffirmation agreement in cases in which court approval is needed. [B.C. §§ 524(k)(1), (8)]

d. Filing with Court and Attorney's Declaration

The agreement, accompanied by a cover sheet prepared as prescribed by Official Form 427, must be filed with the court *no later than 60 days* after the first date set for the § 341 meeting. [B.C. § 524(c)(3); Bankruptcy Rule 4004(a); Official Form 427] If the debtor was *represented by counsel,* the declaration by the debtor's attorney also must be filed. [B.C. § 524(c)(3)] If an individual debtor was *not represented by counsel* when she negotiated a reaffirmation agreement and the debtor wants to reaffirm a *consumer debt not secured by the debtor's real property,* the bankruptcy court must find that the agreement is in the *debtor's best interest* and that it does *not impose an undue hardship* on the debtor or a dependent. [B.C. §§ 524(d)(2), (c)(6)(A)]

e.g. **Example:** Married Debtors filed for relief under Chapter 7. Debtors' attorney negotiated several reaffirmation agreements between Debtors and Bank for debts secured by real property that Debtors operated as residential rental properties. Debtors' attorney declined to sign the declaration in support of the reaffirmation agreements. (The debt was not consumer debt.) Because Debtors' attorney did not file the required certification, the bankruptcy court treated Debtors' case as if they had not been represented by counsel during the negotiation of the reaffirmation agreements. Thus, the court had to make the "best interests" and "undue hardship" determinations required by the Code for unrepresented debtors. [*In re* **Martin,** 2011 WL 10818345 (Bankr. S.D. Ohio 2011); *see* § 524(a)(6)(A)]

e. No Rescission

The debtor must not have rescinded the reaffirmation agreement at any time before the *later* of the *discharge* or *60 days after* the reaffirmation agreement was *filed* with the court. [B.C. § 524(c)(4)]

f. Discharge Hearing

The requirements concerning a discharge hearing must have been fulfilled. [B.C. §§ 524(c)(5), (d)] A discharge hearing is a judicial hearing at which the court informs an *individual debtor* whether her discharge has been granted or denied under Chapter 7, 11, 12, or 13. [B.C. § 524(d)]

(i) Permissive

If the debtor either does not reaffirm any debts, or does reaffirm and was *represented by an attorney* when the agreement was negotiated, a discharge hearing is discretionary with the court. However, if the judge schedules a hearing, the debtor must attend. [B.C. §§ 524(d), 521(a)(5)]

(ii) Mandatory: Unrepresented Debtor

If an individual debtor who receives a discharge desires to enter into one or more reaffirmation agreements negotiated *without attorney representation,* the court must hold a discharge hearing and the debtor must attend in person. [B.C. §§ 524(d), 521(5)] At that time, the court must advise the debtor that a *reaffirmation agreement* is completely voluntary and is *not required* either by the Bankruptcy Code or by state law. The judge also must inform the debtor that the legal effect of the agreement is to bind the debtor contractually to repay a debt that could have been discharged and, thus, expose the debtor to personal liability should the debtor default on the agreement in the future. [B.C. § 524(d)(1)] Finally, an agreement reaffirming a *consumer debt not secured by the debtor's real property* is enforceable *only if* the court finds that the agreement is in the *debtor's best interest* and that it does *not impose an undue hardship* on the debtor or a dependent. [B.C. § 524(d)(2), (c)(6)(A)]

(1) Best Interests of the Debtor

The Bankruptcy Code does not define what constitutes "best interests of the debtor." A bankruptcy court must determine whether the reaffirmation agreement benefits the debtor financially or economically. Courts examine a variety of factors in making a "best interests" finding. Those factors include the following:

- whether debtor's decision to reaffirm was *voluntary and informed*;
- the *nature of the debt*—secured or unsecured;
- the *amount of equity* debtor has in the collateral;
- the *likelihood* that the *creditor will repossess* the collateral if there is no reaffirmation agreement;
- the extent to which the *debtor needs the collateral*, e.g., car for work;
- the debtor's *payment history*; and
- the *alternatives to reaffirmation* that are available to the debtor.

[*In re* **Martin,** *supra*; *see* **BankBoston v. Claflin (***In re* **Claflin), 249 B.R. 840 (B.A.P. 1st Cir. 2000)** (listing similar factors to determine "best interests" and "undue hardship" in a case decided prior to BAPCPA's creation of undue hardship presumption)]

e.g. **Example:** Debtor filed for relief under Chapter 7. Prior to bankruptcy, Debtor had purchased a vehicle and financed the purchase through Bank. Debtor entered into a reaffirmation agreement with Bank, in which Debtor agreed to pay Bank a total of $23,400 on the vehicle valued at $22,500. Debtor did not have the assistance of counsel when negotiating her agreement with Bank. Debtor entered into the reaffirmation agreement out of concern that post-bankruptcy Bank would repossess her vehicle based on an *ipso facto* clause in her contract with Bank. (The parties' contract provided that a default occurs if the Debtor files for bankruptcy.) State law, however, provides that a default is enforceable only to the extent that payment is not made as required by the parties' contract. State law does not allow Bank to repossess Debtor's vehicle post-bankruptcy so long as Debtor remains current on her car payments. Thus, reaffirmation does not make sense as a way to avoid the threat of repossession. Debtor avoids repossession by making her monthly car payments on time, not by signing a reaffirmation agreement. In addition, reaffirmation excludes the unsecured portion of Bank's debt from discharge. Therefore, the reaffirmation agreement is not in Debtor's best interest, because all reaffirmation does is increase the amount that Debtor must pay to Bank if she defaults by not paying on the vehicle after her discharge in bankruptcy. [*See In re* **Henderson,** 492 B.R. 537 (Bankr. D. Nev. 2013)]

g. Presumption of Undue Hardship

BAPCPA added a section to the Code that creates a ***presumption of undue hardship*** if the scheduled payments on the reaffirmed debt ***exceed*** the debtor's monthly ***income minus expenses.*** The presumption applies regardless of whether debtor was represented or not represented by counsel during negotiations for the reaffirmation agreement. [B.C. § 524(m)(1)] The presumption does not apply to reaffirmation agreements in which the creditor is a credit union. [B.C. § 524(m)(2)] The bankruptcy court must review the presumption, which is in effect for ***60 days after*** the reaffirmation agreement is filed with the court. The ***debtor may rebut the presumption*** with a written statement identifying other sources of funds for paying the reaffirmed debt. If the presumption is not rebutted, the bankruptcy court ***may disapprove*** the reaffirmation agreement. The Code does ***not require*** the court to disapprove the agreement; it only requires "review" of the presumption. The bankruptcy court, however, may not disapprove an agreement without first conducting ***a hearing, upon notice, prior to the entry of debtor's discharge.*** [B.C. § 524(m)(1)]

Note: While the Code does not require the court to disapprove a reaffirmation agreement if the presumption of undue hardship is not rebutted, keep in mind that the bankruptcy court must make a finding of no undue hardship before approving a reaffirmation agreement if the Debtor did not have counsel during negotiation of that agreement. [B.C. § 524(c)(6)(A)(i)] Therefore, in cases in which the Debtor did not have legal representation during negotiation of the reaffirmation agreement, the court should not approve that agreement if the presumption of undue hardship is not rebutted.

3. Creditor Pressure Forbidden

The automatic stay prohibits creditors from attempting to coerce the debtor to reaffirm any pre-petition indebtedness. [B.C. § 362(a)(6)]

4. Permissible Creditor Actions

Notwithstanding the Code's requirements for reaffirmation agreements, a creditor may accept payments from the debtor before and after the filing of a reaffirmation agreement. [B.C. § 524(*l*)(1)] A creditor also may accept payments from the debtor under a reaffirmation agreement if the creditor ***believes in good faith*** that the agreement is effective. [B.C. § 524(*l*)(2)] Finally, the requirement to make certain disclosures to the debtor is satisfied if the required ***disclosures are given in good faith.*** [B.C. § 524(*l*)(3)] BAPCPA added these provisions to the Code's reaffirmation rules.

5. The "Ride Through"

Prior to BAPCPA's passage, several circuits permitted a debtor to "ride through" bankruptcy and retain collateral securing a debt so long as she continued to make regular loan payments to the secured creditor. For example, in a circuit that allowed the "ride through," a debtor who owned a car and was current on her car payments pre-bankruptcy could simply continue to pay the bank or secured lender that held the security interest in her vehicle; the debtor did not have to reaffirm the debt (or redeem the car) in order to keep the car. Congress, however, made a number of changes to the Code that affect the "ride through." Those changes are discussed more fully in Chapter Ten, because under some circumstances the debtor's failure to file or perform her intention, as required by § 521, triggers termination of the automatic stay.

🔲 GILBERT

CHECKLIST OF REQUIREMENTS FOR ENFORCEABILITY OF A REAFFIRMATION AGREEMENT

ALL OF THE FOLLOWING ELEMENTS ARE REQUIRED FOR A REAFFIRMATION AGREEMENT TO BE ENFORCEABLE:

- ☑ The agreement is *enforceable under nonbankruptcy law.*

- ☑ The agreement must be *executed before the debtor's discharge is granted.*

- ☑ The debtor must receive the *disclosures set forth at § 524(k).*

- ☑ The agreement must be *filed with the court.*

- ☑ If the debtor is *represented by an attorney* during negotiation of the reaffirmation agreement, the attorney must file an *affidavit or declaration* stating that: (i) the debtor was *fully informed* and entered into the agreement voluntarily, (ii) the agreement will *not impose undue hardship* on the debtor or the debtor's dependents, and (iii) the attorney has fully advised the debtor of the *legal effect and consequences* of the reaffirmation and any subsequent default.

- ☑ If the debtor is an individual *not represented by an attorney* during the negotiation of the reaffirmation agreement, the court must hold a *discharge hearing and the debtor must attend.* The court must explain that the debtor is *not required to reaffirm* the debt, and the *legal effect and consequences* of the reaffirmation agreement and of default under such agreement. If the debt is a *consumer debt not secured by real property* of the debtor, the court must approve the agreement based on a finding that it is in the debtor's *best interest* and does not cause an *undue hardship* for the debtor or a dependent.

- ☑ The debtor must *not rescind* the reaffirmation agreement at any time before the *later* of the *discharge* or *60 days after* the reaffirmation agreement is *filed* with the court.

- ☑ If a *presumption of undue hardship* arises because the scheduled payments on the reaffirmed debt *exceed* the debtor's monthly *income minus expenses,* the bankruptcy court must review the presumption, which is in effect for *60 days after* the reaffirmation agreement is filed with the court. If the presumption is not rebutted, the bankruptcy court *may disapprove* the reaffirmation agreement. The bankruptcy court, however, may not disapprove an agreement without first conducting a hearing, upon notice, prior to the entry of debtor's discharge.

D. Protection Against Discrimination

1. Introduction

In addition to relieving the debtor of personal liability for any debts discharged, the law enhances her fresh start by providing express prohibitions against discriminatory treatment by employers or governmental units. [B.C. § 525]

2. Governmental Discrimination

A governmental unit may not discriminate against a *person solely* because that person (i) is or was a debtor in a bankruptcy case, (ii) was insolvent before or during such a case, or (iii) has not paid a debt that was discharged or is dischargeable in the case. The government also may not discriminate against any person with whom the debtor has been associated. This prohibition prevents a governmental unit from (i) terminating an employee; (ii) denying employment; (iii) discriminating with respect to employment; or (iv) denying, revoking, suspending, or declining to renew a license, franchise, or similar privilege for any of these reasons. [B.C. § 525(a); **FCC v. NextWave Personal Communications, Inc.,** 537 U.S. 293 (2003); **Perez v. Campbell,** 402 U.S. 637 (1971) (decided under Bankruptcy Act)]

a. Distinguish—Post-Bankruptcy Credit

Section 525 "does not prohibit consideration of other factors, such as future financial responsibility or ability . . . if applied nondiscriminatorily." [H.R. Rep. No. 95–595, at 367 (1977)]

3. Private Employer

A private employer may not discriminate with respect to employment against an *individual* who has been a debtor in a bankruptcy case or terminate the individual's employment, if such treatment is based solely upon any of the three reasons described above in connection with the statutory ban on governmental discrimination. A private employer also may not discriminate against any person with whom the debtor has been associated. [B.C. § 525(b)]

Example: Debtor filed for relief under Chapter 13 in 2006. The next year, she applied for a job with Employer who made her an offer of employment contingent on passing a drug test and a background check. When the background check revealed Debtor's Chapter 13 filing, Employer rescinded its offer. Debtor claimed that Employer had violated the anti-discrimination prohibition contained at § 525(b). The bankruptcy court and district court ruled against Debtor. The Fifth Circuit affirmed. The court compared the language of § 525(b) on private employers with that of § 525(a) on governmental units. Section 525(a) prohibits a governmental unit from *denying,* terminating, or discriminating with respect to employment of a debtor. By comparison, § 525(b) only prohibits terminating or discriminating with respect to debtor's employment. Thus, the court held that this difference in statutory language meant that "Congress did not prohibit employers from denying employment to persons based on their bankruptcy status." [**Burnett v. Stewart Title, Inc. (*In re* Burnett),** 635 F.3d 169 (5th Cir. 2011); *see also* **Myers v. TooJay's Management Corp.,** 640 F.3d 1278 (11th Cir. 2011)]

4. Student Loans

Any *governmental unit* operating a student grant or loan program or *lender* engaged in the business of *making loans guaranteed under a student loan program* is prohibited from discriminating against a student loan or grant applicant because the applicant (i) is or was a debtor in a bankruptcy case, (ii) was insolvent before or during such a case, or (iii) failed to pay a debt that was discharged or is dischargeable in the case. [B.C. § 525(c)(1)] A student loan program means any program under Title IV of the Higher Education Act of 1965 or a similar program operated under State or local law. [B.C. § 525(c)(2)]

Chapter Ten

Administrative Powers: The Automatic Stay

CONTENTS	PAGE

Chapter Approach

Chapter 3 of the Bankruptcy Code includes a subchapter on various administrative powers. This chapter, which covers the automatic stay, is the first of two chapters on those administrative powers. The next chapter of this summary covers the remaining powers—(1) adequate protection, (2) the use, sale, or lease of property, (3) obtaining credit, (4) executory contracts and unexpired leases, and (5) utility service.

Your bankruptcy exam likely will include questions requiring you to know the actions to which the stay applies, as well as the ever-growing number of exceptions that Congress has created to operation of the automatic stay. The following questions should help you to focus on the important points for discussion of the topics.

Does a particular act come within any of the types of conduct *prohibited* by the automatic stay provisions of § 362(a)? Remember that filing a bankruptcy petition operates as a stay of various actions against the *debtor, the debtor's property,* and *property of the estate.* There are numerous exceptions to the stay, so be sure to check whether the act is *excepted from the stay* under § 362(b). In addition, with the passage of BAPCPA, Congress added § 362(n), which details the circumstances under which the automatic stay does not apply in the case of a *small business debtor.*

Also, ask yourself whether the debtor's bankruptcy case is one in which the automatic stay *terminates* based on the happening of certain events? With BAPCPA, Congress added new subsections to the Code, i.e., §§ 362(c)(3), (h), that *terminate the automatic stay* in cases involving *serial filers* and *individual Chapter 7 debtors* who fail to timely satisfy the requirements of § 521(a)(2). Pay attention to these provisions, which contain detailed and complicated rules. Understanding how the Code's various sections and subsections relate to each other is critical to your ability to correctly analyze exam questions and problems.

Finally, if the act is subject to the automatic stay, is there a basis for granting *relief from the stay?*

A. Automatic Stay

1. Introduction

The automatic stay is a statutory injunction that takes effect *when a bankruptcy petition is filed* and protects the debtor, the property of the estate, and the property of the debtor from certain actions by creditors. It is designed to provide a respite for the debtor and promote an orderly administration of the bankruptcy case. The stay applies to *all entities.* [B.C. § 362, 101(15)]

EXAM TIP

You need to remember that the automatic stay starts when the *bankruptcy petition* is filed. This rule applies in both voluntary and involuntary cases. Do not confuse it with the entry of an order for relief, which in an involuntary case, happens later.

---

2. Acts Enjoined

Once the bankruptcy petition has been filed, the automatic stay prohibits the following acts. [B.C. § 362(a)]

a. Proceedings Against Debtor

The commencement or continuation, including the issuance or service of process, of a *judicial, administrative, or other action* against the debtor is stayed if the action is intended to recover a *pre-petition claim* against the debtor, or if the action was commenced or could have been commenced before the bankruptcy petition was filed. [B.C. § 362(a)(1)]

(i) Claim

Congress intended that the courts give an expansive definition to the word "claim" in the Code. [*See* **Johnson v. Home State Bank,** 501 U.S. 78 (1991) ("Congress intended . . . to adopt the broadest available definition of 'claim' "); **Pennsylvania Dep't of Public Welfare v. Davenport,** 495 U.S. 552 (1990) ("Congress chose expansive language" when defining the term "claim"); **Ohio v. Kovacs,** 469 U.S. 274 (1984) ("Congress desired a broad definition of 'claim' ")] Recognizing this intent to give "claim" an expansive definition in the bankruptcy context, a majority of courts have held that pre-petition claims may include causes of action arising from pre-bankruptcy conduct and pre-petition legal relationships, even if the cause of action under state or other applicable nonbankruptcy law did not accrue until after the petition was filed. [*In re* **Johns-Manville Corp.,** 57 B.R. 680 (Bankr. S.D. N.Y. 1986)]

(1) Distinguish Post-Petition Claims

Causes of action *against the debtor* that are purely post-petition in nature, such as fraud committed by the debtor after the filing of the bankruptcy petition, are not barred by the automatic stay. [*In re* **Vacuum Cleaner Corp. of America,** 58 B.R. 101 (Bankr. E.D. Pa. 1986)]

b. Pre-Petition Judgments

The automatic stay enjoins enforcement of a pre-petition judgment against the debtor or against property of the estate. [B.C. § 362(a)(2)]

c. Acts Against Estate Property

Any act to obtain possession of estate property or property in the possession of the estate, or to exercise control over estate property is prohibited, regardless of whether the underlying claim arose before or after the filing of the bankruptcy petition. [B.C. § 362(a)(3)]

e.g. **Example:** Insurance Company issued a "prepaid excess officers and directors liability" policy to Debtor, which shortly thereafter filed a voluntary Chapter 11 bankruptcy petition. Insurance Company then canceled the policy and sent notice to Debtor. Cancellation of the policy violated the automatic stay because the insurance policy constituted property of the estate. [B.C. § 362(a)(3); *In re* **Minoco Group of Companies, Ltd.,** 799 F.2d 517 (9th Cir. 1986)]

d. Liens Against Estate Property

Any act designed to create, perfect, or enforce a lien against *estate property* is enjoined. [B.C. § 362(a)(4)]

e.g. **Example:** Debtor LLC owned property on which it had not paid property taxes for more than five years. As a result, County scheduled the property for sale at an internet auction. After Debtor's right of redemption expired and the internet auction started but before it concluded, Debtor filed for relief under Chapter 7. The auction continued, notwithstanding the bankruptcy filing, and the property sold the next day. Debtor's right of redemption expired the evening before the internet auction was to take place. The bankruptcy court held that sale of the property was "an action [by County] to enforce its tax lien post-petition to collect its pre-petition claim against the Debtor." Thus, the court concluded that County had violated § 362(a)(4) (as well as §§ 362(a)(3) and (a)(6)). [*In re* **Meridian LLC,** 553 B.R. 807 (Bankr. S.D. Cal. 2016)]

e.g. **Example:** Bank extends a loan to Debtor Corporation, and Debtor grants Bank a security interest in its equipment. (The loan is not used to purchase equipment.) Debtor subsequently files for relief under Chapter 11. Bank then files a financing statement, under Article 9 of the Uniform Commercial Code, in an effort to perfect its security interest in the equipment. Bank has violated the automatic stay, because the equipment is property of the estate and Bank tried post-petition to perfect its lien against estate property. [B.C. § 362(a)(4)]

(i) Limited Exception

There is a limited exception to the stay that authorizes post-petition perfection in certain circumstances. [B.C. § 362(b)(3)]

e. Liens Against Debtor's Property

Any act intended to create, perfect, or enforce a lien against ***property of the debtor*** is prohibited ***to the extent that the lien secures a pre-petition claim.*** [B.C. § 362(a)(5)] Property that has been ***abandoned*** by the trustee under § 554 reverts to the debtor and is protected by the automatic stay from any lien securing a pre-bankruptcy claim. The stay also shields the debtor's ***exempt property*** and property ***acquired post-petition*** from a lien securing a pre-petition claim. [B.C. § 362(a)(5)] The purpose of this provision is to avoid "certain creditors [receiving] preferential treatment . . . [and] circumvent[ion] [of] the debtors' discharge." [H.R. Rep. No. 95–595, at 341 (1977)]

EXAM TIP   ♦GILBERT

If your exam question involves property that the trustee has abandoned, remember that a creditor whose claim is secured by that property must obtain the ***court's relief from the automatic stay*** before proceeding against the property under nonbankruptcy law. Even if the debtor agrees to relinquish the collateral to the creditor, it is essential to first obtain a court order granting relief from the stay.

---

f. Collection Efforts

Any act to collect, recover, or assess a claim against the debtor that arose prior to the bankruptcy petition is forbidden. Thus, creditors may not bother or intimidate the debtor about repayment of pre-petition obligations. [B.C. § 362(a)(6)]

e.g. **Example:** On March 1, Debtor, owing $2,000 to Credit Union, filed a Chapter 7 petition, and notice of the case was sent to Credit Union. Between March 2 and April 1, Credit Union's agent telephoned Debtor on 10 different occasions, demanding repayment of its claim. These acts violate the automatic stay and may subject Credit Union to actual damages, including costs and attorneys' fees, and potentially punitive damages, as well. [B.C. §§ 362(a)(6), (k)(1)]

e.g. **Example:** Debtor enrolled in a master degree program. Debtor stopped paying tuition during her first year, but University allowed her to take exams and sign up for new classes. She completed her course work and received a degree. At graduation, Debtor owed more than $6,000 to University. Debtor filed for relief under Chapter 7 and during her bankruptcy case requested a transcript from University. While Debtor offered to pay the transcript fee, University refused to provide a transcript. The University's refusal to give Debtor a copy of her transcript was "an act to collect a debt and thereby violated the automatic stay." [*In re* **Kuehn,** 563 F.3d 289 (7th Cir. 2009)]

g. Setoffs

The automatic stay also enjoins the post-petition setoff of mutual debts. Thus, the setoff of a pre-petition debt owing to the debtor against a claim asserted against the debtor is prohibited unless the court grants relief from the stay. [B.C. §§ 362(a)(7), 553]

(i) Distinguish—Bank's Administrative Freeze

The United States Supreme Court, in a unanimous opinion, has held that a bank's *temporary hold* on a debtor's deposit account, up to the amount allegedly subject to setoff, while the bank promptly seeks relief from the automatic stay, is not a setoff and, thus, does not violate the automatic stay. [**Citizens Bank of Maryland v. Strumpf,** 516 U.S. 16 (1995)]

h. Tax Court Proceedings

The Code stays the commencement or continuation of a case in the United States Tax Court concerning the tax liability of (i) a corporate debtor for a taxable period that the bankruptcy court may determine or (ii) an individual for a taxable period ending before the order for relief. [B.C. §§ 362(a)(8), 505]

CHECKLIST OF ACTS ENJOINED BY THE AUTOMATIC STAY   **GILBERT**

AFTER THE BANKRUPTCY PETITION HAS BEEN FILED, THE FOLLOWING ACTS ARE ENJOINED BY THE AUTOMATIC STAY:

- ☑ The commencement or continuation of an action against the debtor *to recover a pre-petition claim*

- ☑ The enforcement against the debtor or against property of the estate of a *pre-petition judgment*

- ☑ Any act to *obtain possession of estate property or property in the possession of the estate,* or to exercise *control over estate property*

- ☑ Any act designed to create, perfect, or enforce a *lien against estate property*

- ☑ Any act to create, perfect, or enforce a *lien against property of the debtor to the extent the lien secures a pre-petition claim*

- ☑ Any act to *collect, recover, or assess a pre-petition claim*

- ☑ The *setoff of a pre-petition debt owing to the debtor* against a claim against the debtor

- ☑ The commencement or continuation of a *case in the United States Tax Court concerning the tax liability of (i) a corporate debtor* for a taxable period that the bankruptcy court may determine *or (ii) an individual debtor* for a taxable period prior to the order for relief

3. Exceptions to the Automatic Stay

There is an ever-expanding list of exceptions to the automatic stay. Congress added a number of new exceptions to the stay in 2005. The filing of a bankruptcy petition does not operate as a stay of the following actions. [B.C. § 362(b)]

a. Criminal Proceedings

The commencement or continuation of a criminal action against the debtor is not enjoined by the automatic stay. [B.C. § 362(b)(1)] One issue on which there is a split of authority is whether the exception at § 362(b)(1) excepts from the automatic stay commencement or continuation of a criminal prosecution against a debtor who passed a bad check. [*See In re* **Bibbs**, 282 B.R. 876 (Bankr. E.D. Ark. 2002) (discussing split of authority)] Some courts have examined whether the real reason for prosecuting the debtor for passing bad checks is to exert pressure on the debtor to pay a dischargeable debt. [3 Collier ¶ 362.05(2)(a)] A majority of courts, however, have held that the plain language of § 362(b)(1) creates no "distinction based on a prosecutor's motive" and, thus, the automatic stay does not apply to the prosecution of a debtor on a bad check charge. [*See, e.g.,* **Hutchison-Corbin v. Burton,** 2009 WL 2407698 (W.D. Ky. 2009); *In re* **Caravona,** 347 B.R. 259 (Bankr. N.D. Ohio 2006)]

b. Family Law Matters

BAPCPA significantly expanded the Code's exception for actions taken regarding a number of family law matters, including the collection of domestic support obligations, child custody orders, and the establishment of paternity.

(i) Domestic Support Obligations

The automatic stay now does not apply to any of the following actions related to enforcement or collection of domestic support obligations:

(1) the commencement or continuation of a civil action or proceeding to *establish or modify* a domestic support obligation order [B.C. §§ 362(b)(2)(A)(ii), 101(14A)];

(2) the *collection* of a domestic support obligation from *assets that are not property of the estate,* such as property that is exempt or is acquired post-petition by the debtor [B.C. §§ 362(b)(2)(B), 101(14A)];

(3) the *withholding of income* that is estate property or debtor property to pay a domestic support obligation pursuant to judicial or administrative order or statute [B.C. §§ 362(b)(2)(C), 101(14A)];

(4) the *withholding, suspension, or restriction* of a *driver's license,* a *professional or occupational license,* of a *recreational license* because of past-due support or failure to comply with warrants or subpoenas in child support proceedings, under state law, as provided for in the Social Security Act [B.C. §§ 362(b)(2)(D), 101(14A); 42 U.S.C. § 666(a)(16)];

(5) the *reporting to a consumer reporting agency* of overdue support owed by a parent [B.C. §§ 362(b)(2)(E), 101(14A); 42 U.S.C. §§ 601 *et seq.*];

(6) the *interception of a tax refund* to apply to a past-due domestic support obligation as provided for under 42 U.S.C. §§ 664 and 666(a)(3), or similar state law [B.C. §§ 362(b)(2)(F), 101(14A)]; or

(7) the *enforcement of a medical obligation,* as specified in the Social Security Act. [B.C. §§ 362(b)(2)(G), 101(14A); 42 U.S.C. §§ 601 *et seq.*]

(ii) Paternity and Child Custody and Visitation

The filing of a bankruptcy petition does not stay the commencement or continuation of a civil action or proceeding to *establish paternity* or concerning *child custody or visitation.* [B.C. §§ 362(b)(2)(A)(i), (iii)]

(iii) Domestic Violence

The automatic stay does not apply to the commencement or continuation of any civil action or proceeding regarding domestic violence. [B.C. § 362(b)(2)(A)(v)]

(iv) Dissolution of Marriage

The commencement or continuation of a civil action or proceeding to *dissolve a marriage* is not a violation of the automatic stay. This exception to the stay *does not apply,* however, to the extent that the proceeding seeks to determine a *division of property that is estate property.* [B.C. § 362(b)(2)(A)(iv); *see In re* **Kallabat,** 482 B.R. 563 (Bankr. E.D. Mich. 2012) (holding that while the Code did not stay debtor's divorce proceeding, it was a violation of the automatic stay for attorney of debtor's former spouse to ask the state court judge to "adjudicate property rights in the marital home")]

c. Certain Acts of Perfection

The automatic stay does not prohibit the perfection of an interest in property to the extent that perfection occurs within the 30-day grace period allowed by § 547(e)(2)(A), or to the extent that it would prevail over the trustee's avoiding powers pursuant to § 546(b), such as in the case of retroactive perfection of a purchase-money security interest within the 20-day grace period allowed under U.C.C. § 9–317(e). The filing of a *continuation statement* also is excepted from the automatic stay to the same extent. [B.C. § 362(b)(3); U.C.C. § 9–515]

d. Police or Regulatory Actions: General Principles

The commencement or continuation of a proceeding by a governmental unit to enforce its police or regulatory power is not stayed. [B.C. § 362(b)(4); **Board of Governors of the Federal Reserve System v. MCorp Financial, Inc.,** 502 U.S. 32 (1991) (administrative proceedings against bank holding company by the Board of Governors of the Federal Reserve system were not enjoined, concluding that the Board's action fell "squarely within § 362(b)(4)")] The courts use two tests to determine whether the police or regulatory exception to the stay applies to government action. If the government satisfies *either* test, then the automatic stay does *not* apply to the government's action. [3 Collier ¶ 362.05(5)(a)]

The two tests are the *"pecuniary purpose"* test and the *"public policy"* test. The "pecuniary purpose" test requires the court to determine whether the government's action primarily concerns *public safety and welfare or the government's pecuniary interest.* The stay applies *if* the government's primary concern is protection of its "pecuniary interest in the debtor's property." The public policy test requires the court to " 'distinguish[ ] between government actions that effectuate public policy and those that adjudicate private rights.' " Thus, if the government's conduct *furthers public policy by protecting public safety and welfare,* then the exception at § 362(b)(4) applies. [**United States v. Federal Resources Corp.,** 525 B.R. 759 (Bankr. D. Idaho 2015); *see also* 3 Collier ¶ 362.05(5)(a)]

e.g. **Example:** The Commonwealth of Pennsylvania issued an order to show cause to Debtor Corporation and its nondebtor principal regarding alleged violations of the Pennsylvania Prevailing Wage Act ("PPWA"). Thirty minutes before the show cause hearing, Debtor filed for relief under Chapter 7. The hearing took place, and Debtor filed an adversary complaint alleging violation of the automatic stay. The bankruptcy court "outright" rejected any argument that the Commonwealth was not acting pursuant to its police and regulatory powers. The court also rejected Debtor's argument that the hearing was an invalid exercise of the Commonwealth's police and regulatory powers, because Debtor had permanently ceased operations and, thus, there was no risk of future harm. The court first noted that the bankruptcy court was not the proper forum for determining the risk of future harm. The court also explained that the police and regulatory powers exception to the stay " 'includes actions to fix the amount of damages for past conduct, whether or not that conduct is continuing' because the Code distinguishes 'between entry and enforcement of a money judgment, *allowing entry but not enforcement.*' " Thus, the Commonwealth's conduct in holding the hearing fell within the stay exception at § 362(b)(4). [**Travacomm Communications, Inc. v. Pennsylvania (*In re* Travacomm Communications, Inc.),** 300 B.R. 635 (Bankr. W.D. Penn. 2003)]

e.g. **Example:** The United States filed suit against various defendants under the Comprehensive Environmental Response, Compensation, and Liability Act ("CERCLA") for monies spent on cleaning up hazardous waste at two mines in Idaho. The federal district court granted summary judgment to the United States as to liability and damages on its CERCLA claim. It also ruled in favor of the government on its veil-piercing and Federal Debt Collection Procedures Act ("FDCPA") claims. Before the district court could enter final judgment, however, two defendants filed for bankruptcy. The district court held that it could enter final judgment, without violating the automatic stay, on all three claims: FDCPA, veil piercing, and CERCLA. First, the court relied on Ninth Circuit precedent to conclude that FDCPA claims fell squarely within the government's police and regulatory powers under § 362(b)(4). Second, the court concluded that it could enter final judgment on the veil-piercing claim. The court explained that the purpose of its decision was to prevent fraud, which the Ninth Circuit previously had held fell within the scope of § 362(b)(4)'s exception to the automatic stay. Finally, the court held that the government's action to recover costs under CERCLA satisfied both the "pecuniary purpose" and the "public policy" test and, thus, fell within the scope of § 362(b)(4). While the court held that it could enter final judgment, it stayed *execution* of that judgment against the two parties that had filed for relief under the Bankruptcy Code. [**United States v. Federal Resources Corp.,** *supra*]

e. Police or Regulatory Powers: Enforcement of Judgments

The enforcement of a judgment obtained by a governmental unit in implementing its police or regulatory power is subject to the automatic stay if the judgment is ***a money judgment.*** [B.C. § 362(b)(4)]

e.g. **Example:** Debtor was the chief executive and stockholder of Corporation. Corporation and other business entities operated an industrial and hazardous waste site in State. State sued Debtor, Corporation, and the other companies in state court for violations of various state environmental laws. Debtor subsequently signed a stipulation in his individual capacity and on behalf of Corporation that settled the State's lawsuit. The stipulation, in part, enjoined Debtor and the other businesses from further polluting the air or public waters, prohibited them from bringing more waste onto the site, and required them to remove certain waste products from the site. In addition, the stipulation ordered the payment of $75,000 as compensation to the State for injuries to wildlife. Debtor and the other firms did not comply with the obligations set forth in the stipulation, which resulted in the appointment of a receiver; the state court ordered the receiver to take possession of the assets of the Debtor and the other business entities, and to clean up the site. The receiver took possession of the site, but Debtor filed for relief under Chapter 11 before site cleanup was complete. State argued that the clean-up obligation was not a debt under the Bankruptcy Code. The Supreme Court disagreed. The Court explained that the state court order had "dispossessed" Debtor and eliminated his authority over the site. Thus, the State only sought the payment of money from Debtor. [B.C. § 362(b)(4); *see* **Ohio v. Kovacs,** 469 U.S. 274 (1985) (decision in context of whether clean-up obligation was a debt and, thus, dischargeable under the Code)]

f. Setoffs and Other Contractual Rights: Commodities and Securities Brokers, Repo Participants

Four exceptions to the automatic stay, including one added by BAPCPA, are Congressional reactions to concern for the stability of markets. If the stay applied in cases covered by these exceptions, it would prevent "prompt liquidation of an insolvent's positions [and] because [of] market fluctuations in the securities market [could] create an inordinate risk that the insolvency of one party could trigger a chain reaction of insolvencies of the others." [**Petersen v. Cargill, Inc. (***In re* **G&R Feed & Grain Co.),** 2013 WL 8351982 (Bankr. S.D. Iowa 2013)] Moreover, no court or administrative agency in any bankruptcy proceeding can stay the exercise of rights not subject to the stay pursuant to §§ 362(b)(6), (7), (17), or (27). [B.C. § 362(o); *see In re* **Weinraub,** 361 B.R. 586 (Bankr. S.D. Fla. 2007) ("The only reading of § 362 that gives effect to § 362(o) is to acknowledge that the Court has the power to stay any of the parts of § 362(b) that are not specifically listed in § 362(o)")]

(i) Commodity Brokers, Stockbrokers

The automatic stay does not apply to the exercise by a *commodity broker, forward contract merchant, stockbroker, financial institution, financial participant, or securities clearing agency* of any contractual right, defined in Code §§ 555 or 556, under any security agreement or arrangement or other credit enhancement related to a commodity contract, forward contract or securities contract. [B.C. § 362(b)(6); §§ 101(6), (22), (22A), (25), (48), (50), (53A)] The contractual rights under §§ 555 and 556 are the rights to *liquidate, terminate, or accelerate a securities contract, a commodities contract, or a forward contract.* [B.C. §§ 555, 556] Also excepted from the automatic stay is the exercise of any contractual right by a *commodity broker, forward contract merchant, stockbroker, financial institution, financial participant, or securities clearing agency* to *set off or net out* any termination value, payment amount or other transfer obligation arising under a commodity contract, forward contract, or securities contract, including any master agreement for such contracts. [B.C. § 362(b)(6); §§ 101(6), (22), (22A), (25), (48), (50), (53A)]

(ii) Repurchase Agreements

The automatic stay does not apply to the exercise by a *repo participant or financial participant* of any contractual right, defined in Code § 559, under any security agreement or arrangement or other credit enhancement related to any *repurchase agreement.* [B.C. §§ 362(b)(7), 559; §§ 101(22A), (46), (47), (48), (50)] The contractual rights under § 559 are the rights to *liquidate, terminate, or accelerate* a *repurchase agreement.* [B.C. § 559] Also excepted from the automatic stay is the exercise of any contractual right by a *repo participant or financial participant to set off or net out* any termination value, payment amount or other transfer obligation arising under one or more repurchase agreements, including a master agreement. [B.C. § 362(b)(7); §§ 101(22A), (46), (47), (48), (50)]

(iii) Swap Agreements

The automatic stay does not apply to the exercise by a *swap participant or financial participant* of any contractual right, defined in Code § 560, under any security agreement or arrangement or other credit enhancement related to any *swap agreement.* [B.C. §§ 362(b)(17), 560; §§ 101(22A), (50), (53B), (53C)] The contractual rights under § 560 are the rights to *liquidate, terminate, or accelerate* a *swap agreement.* [B.C. § 560] Also excepted from the automatic stay is the exercise of any contractual right by a *swap participant or financial participant to set off or net out* any termination value, payment amount or other transfer obligation arising under one or more swap agreements, including a master agreement. [B.C. § 362(b)(17); §§ 101(22A), (50), (53B), (53C)]

(iv) Master Netting Agreements

Also excepted from the automatic stay is the exercise by a *master netting arrangement participant* of any contractual right, defined in Code §§ 555, 556, 559, or 560, under any security agreement or arrangement or other credit enhancement related to any *master netting agreement.* [B.C. §§ 362(b)(27), 555, 556, 559, 560; §§ 101(38A), (38B), (50)] The contractual rights under §§ 555, 556, 559, and 560 are the rights to *liquidate, terminate, or accelerate* a *securities contract, a commodities contract, a forward contract, a repurchase agreement, and a swap agreement.* [B.C. §§ 555, 556, 559, 560; §§ 101(25), (47), (53B)] Also excepted from the automatic stay is the exercise of any contractual right by a *master netting arrangement participant to set off or net out* any termination value, payment amount or other transfer obligation arising under one or more master netting agreements. This exception to that automatic stay applies *to the extent* that the *master netting arrangement participant* is *eligible to exercise these rights* under §§ 362(b)(6), (7), or (17) for each individual contract under the master netting arrangement in issue. [B.C. §§ 362(b)(27), (6), (7), (17)]

g. HUD Mortgage Foreclosures

The *commencement* of certain mortgage or deed of trust foreclosure actions by the Secretary of Housing and Urban Development is excepted from the automatic stay. [B.C. § 362(b)(8)]

h. Tax Audits and Assessments

A tax audit, an issuance of a notice of tax deficiency, a demand for tax returns, and an assessment of any tax and issuance of a notice and demand for payment of the assessed tax are excepted from the automatic stay. [B.C. § 362(b)(9)]

(i) Tax Lien

Any tax lien that otherwise would attach to property of the estate as a result of the assessment will *not be effective,* unless the tax debt is nondischargeable and the property or its proceeds are transferred out of the estate to the debtor or otherwise revest in the debtor, which apparently refers to abandoned or exempt property, or revesting of property under Code §§ 1141(b), 1227(b), or 1327(b). [B.C. § 362(b)(9)(D)]

i. Recovery of Property by Certain Lessors

The automatic stay also does not prohibit any act by a debtor's lessor to obtain possession of nonresidential real property if the lease has *terminated by the expiration of its stated term* prior to the filing of the bankruptcy petition or during the case. [B.C. § 362(b)(10)] This exception only applies if the termination occurs because the stated term of the lease expires. The stay prohibits a landlord of nonresidential real property from taking action to obtain possession based on lease termination due to a post-petition default. [3 Collier ¶ 362.05(11)]

(i) Relationship to Estate Property

A debtor's leasehold interest in nonresidential realty for which the lease has terminated at the expiration of its stated term before the start of the bankruptcy case is not included in property of the estate. A lease for nonresidential real property that terminates during the case ceases to be estate property. [B.C. § 541(b)(2)]

j. Certain Actions Relating to Negotiable Instruments

The automatic stay does not stay the presentment of a negotiable instrument, sending notice of dishonor, or protesting dishonor of such instrument. [B.C. § 362(b)(11)]

k. Certain Actions Against Educational Institutions

The automatic stay does not apply to any action by an accrediting agency or state licensing body concerning the accreditation status or licensure of the debtor as an educational institution. [B.C. §§ 362(b)(14), (15)] The stay also does not apply to any action by a guaranty agency or the Secretary of Education concerning the debtor's eligibility to participate in programs under the Higher Education Act of 1965. [B.C. § 362(b)(16); 20 U.S.C. § 1085(j)]

(i) Relationship to Estate Property

A debtor's eligibility to participate in programs authorized under the Higher Education Act of 1964, the debtor's accreditation status, and the State licensure of the debtor as an educational institution are not property of the estate. [B.C. § 541(b)(3)]

l. Repossession of Aircrafts and Vessels

The automatic stay does not apply in a *Chapter 11 case* to certain actions by the Secretary of Transportation or the Secretary of Commerce if the action is commenced, continued, or concluded *more than 90 days* after filing of the petition. [B.C. §§ 362(b)(12), (13)] Actions that fall within this exception to the stay are:

(i) foreclosure of a *preferred ship or fleet mortgage;*

(ii) foreclosure of a security interest in or relating to a *vessel or vessel under construction,* held by the Secretary of Transportation under chapter 537 of title 46, 49 U.S.C. § 109(h), or applicable state law; or

(iii) foreclosure of a mortgage, deed of trust, or other security interest in a *fishing facility* held by the Secretary of Commerce under chapter 537 of title 46.

Congress added these two exceptions to the stay in the Omnibus Budget Reconciliation Act of 1986, which provided that the exceptions applied to cases filed after August 1, 1986 and before December 31, 1989. [Pub. L. No. 99–509 §§ 5001(a), (b), (c)]

m. Ad Valorem Property Tax Liens and Special Assessments on Real Property

Section 362(b)(18) exempts from the automatic stay the creation or perfection of a statutory lien for *ad valorem property taxes,* imposed by a governmental unit, that *become due post-petition.* In 2005, Congress expanded this exception. Thus, § 362(b)(18) now also excepts from the stay *special taxes or special assessments* on real property, regardless of whether ad valorem, imposed by a governmental unit and that *become due post-petition.* [B.C. § 362(b)(18)]

n. Withholding of Income for Pensions

The automatic stay does not apply to the *withholding of income* from a debtor's wages and collection of those amounts withheld pursuant to the debtor's agreement authorizing withholding and collection for the benefit of a *pension, profit-sharing, stock bonus or other plan* established under certain sections of the Internal Revenue Code and sponsored by the debtor's employer, or an affiliate, successor, or predecessor of such employer to the extent that the monies withheld and collected are only used to repay certain loans. [B.C. § 362(b)(19); 26 U.S.C. §§ 401, 403, 408, 408A, 414, 457, 501(c)] The exception applies to loans from: (1) a plan under § 408(b)(1) of the Employee Retirement Security Act of 1974 ("ERISA"); (2) a plan subject to § 72(p) of the Internal Revenue Code; or (3) a thrift savings plan in the Federal Employee's Retirement System that meets the requirements of 5 U.S.C. § 8433(g). [B.C. §§ 362(b)(19)(A), (B); 29 U.S.C. § 1108(b)(1); 26 U.S.C. § 72(p); 5 U.S.C. § 8433(g); *see also* 3 Collier ¶ 362.05(18)] The exception makes clear that no loan under a government plan pursuant to § 414(d), or a contract or account under § 403(b), of the Internal Revenue Code constitutes a claim or debt under the Bankruptcy Code. [B.C. § 362(b)(19); 26 U.S.C. §§ 403(b), 414(d)] Congress added § 362(b)(19) to the Code in 2005.

o. Prior Bankruptcy Cases

In 2005, Congress added two new exceptions to the stay for actions against *real property* based on what took place in a *prior bankruptcy* filing by the debtor.

(i) Scheme to Delay, Hinder, or Defraud

The bankruptcy court may grant relief from the automatic stay to a creditor whose claim is secured by *real property* if the court finds that the debtor's filing for bankruptcy was part of a *scheme to delay, hinder, or defraud* creditors that involved either (1) *the transfer* of part or all of the real property *without the secured creditor's consent* or (2) *multiple bankruptcy filings* affecting such real property. The court's order remains in effect in any *subsequent bankruptcy case* filed within *two years* after entry of the order, if the order is recorded in compliance with applicable state laws for recording real property liens or notices of interest in real property. [B.C. § 362(d)(4)] Section 362(b)(20) provides an exception to the automatic stay, then, for any act to *enforce any lien against or security interest in real property* following entry of an order pursuant to *§ 362(d)(4).* [B.C. § 362(b)(20)] In the later bankruptcy case, the debtor may move for relief from such order based on *changed circumstances* or for other *good cause.* The court may grant debtor relief from the order after notice and a hearing. [B.C. §§ 362(b)(20), (d)(4)]

(ii) Ineligible Debtor Based on Prior Bankruptcy Case

The automatic stay does not apply to any act to enforce a lien against or security interest in real property if the debtor is not eligible under § 109(g) to be a debtor or if the debtor filed the bankruptcy case in violation of an order in a prior case prohibiting the debtor from being a debtor in another bankruptcy case. [B.C. §§ 362(b)(21), 109(g)] Congress created this new exception to curb abusive filings. [H.R. Rep. No. 109–31, at 70]

e.g. **Example:** Debtor filed for relief under Chapter 13. Creditor held the note and deed of trust on Debtor's home, and moved to lift the stay based on Debtor's default on the note. The bankruptcy court granted Creditor's motion, and Creditor noticed a trustee's sale (under state law) of the property. On the day scheduled for the trustee's sale of Debtor's property, Debtor filed a request to dismiss her Chapter 13 case and immediately filed a second bankruptcy case. The trustee's sale occurred after the filing of Debtor's second bankruptcy case, but before Creditor's attorney received notice of that case. The court held that the filing of Debtor's second bankruptcy petition did not stay the trustee's sale of her property. Debtor filed her second bankruptcy case within 180 days of requesting a voluntary dismissal of her prior Chapter 13 case after Creditor had filed a motion for and obtained relief from the stay. As a result, Debtor was not eligible under § 109(g)(2) to be a debtor in her second bankruptcy case. Therefore, the automatic stay did not apply to her second bankruptcy filing, and the trustee's sale of the property did not violate the stay. [*See* **Leafty v. Aussie Sonoran Capital, LLC (*In re* Leafty),** 479 B.R. 545 (B.A.P. 9th Cir. 2012)]

p. Eviction: Residential Real Property

In 2005, Congress added two new exceptions to the stay that affect the ability of a lessor to move forward with eviction proceedings, in certain circumstances, without obtaining relief from the automatic stay. Both subsections are exceptions to § 362(a)(3), which stays any act to obtain possession of or exercise control over estate property. [B.C. §§ 362(a)(3), (a)(22), (a)(23)]

(i) Pre-Petition Judgment for Possession

In 2005, Congress created an exception to the stay for the continuation of any *eviction, unlawful detainer, or similar proceeding* by a lessor of residential real property against a debtor/tenant if the lessor has obtained a *judgment for possession pre-petition.* [B.C. § 362(b)(22)] The exception, however, is subject to § 362(*l*), which keeps the automatic stay in place if the debtor/tenant satisfies certain conditions.

(1) Applicability of the Exception During the First 30 Days

The stay will go into effect (exception will not apply) for *30 days after the filing of the petition* if the debtor (1) files with the petition a *certification,* under penalty of perjury, that she has the right under nonbankruptcy law to *cure the entire monetary default* that gave rise to the judgment for possession; (2) *serves* such certification on the *lessor;* and (3) deposits with the court clerk any *rent that would come due during the 30-day period.* [B.C. § 362(*l*)(1); *see* Official Form 101A]

(2) Applicability of the Exception from Day 31 Forward

If the debtor takes the steps outlined above under (1) and within that 30-day period files with the court and serves on the lessor a *further certification,* under penalty of perjury, that debtor has *cured,* under nonbankruptcy law, the entire monetary default that gave rise to the judgment for possession, then the exception under § 362(b)(22) does not apply. In other words, the automatic stay applies and prevents the lessor from proceeding against the debtor. [B.C. § 362(*l*)(2)]

(3) Objection by Lessor

If the lessor objects to either the debtor's initial certification or her further certification of cure and serves that objection on the debtor, then the court must hold a **hearing within 10 days** after filing and service of the objection to determine whether the debtor's certification is true. [B.C. § 362(*l*)(3)(A)] If the court upholds the lessor's objection, then the exception to the stay at § 362(b)(22) applies immediately; therefore, the lessor need not apply for relief from the stay in order to complete the process of recovering full possession of the property. [B.C. § 362(*l*)(3)(B)(i)] The court clerk must immediately serve upon the debtor and lessor a certified copy of the court's order upholding the lessor's objection. [B.C. § 362(*l*)(3)(B)(ii)]

(4) Debtor's Failure to File Certification

The debtor must indicate on the petition whether there is a judgment for possession of the rental property where she resides, and must provide the lessor's name and address. [B.C. § 362(*l*)(5)] If the debtor indicates on the petition that there is a judgment for possession of her rental premises but fails to file either the initial certification or further certification described above, then the exception at § 362(b)(22) shall apply immediately upon failure to file the certification. The lessor is not required to file a motion to lift the automatic stay in order to complete the process of recovering full possession of the leased property. [B.C. § 362(*l*)(4)(A)] The clerk of the court also must immediately serve on the lessor and the debtor a certified copy of the docket indicating the absence of a filed certification and the applicability of § 362(b)(22). [B.C. § 362(*l*)(4)(B)]

(5) Summary

The lessor may complete the process to recover possession of leased residential premises without moving to lift the automatic stay under § 362(a)(3) if there is a **pre-petition judgment for possession** and:

(1) the debtor/tenant **fails to file the initial certification** under § 362(*l*)(1)(A);

(2) the debtor/tenant **fails to deposit rent** that would become due during the 30-day period after filing of the petition [B.C. § 362(*l*)(1)(B)];

(3) the debtor/tenant, during the 30-day period after filing for bankruptcy, **fails to file the further certification of cure** under § 362(*l*)(2)(A);

(4) the debtor/tenant files the **initial certification** under § 362(*l*)(1)(A), the **lessor objects to such certification,** and the **court upholds** the lessor's objection; *or*

(5) the debtor/tenant files the **further certification of cure** under § 362(*l*)(1)(A), the **lessor objects to such certification,** and the **court upholds** the lessor's objection.

(ii) Property Endangerment or Controlled Substance Use

Congress added this exception to the automatic stay in 2005, and the structure of the exception is similar to that involving a pre-petition judgment for possession under

§ 362(b)(22). Section 362(b)(23), however, allows the lessor, under certain conditions, to **begin or continue an eviction action** without moving to lift the stay.

A lessor of residential real property may commence or continue an eviction action based on **endangerment of the property** or **illegal use of controlled substances on the property.** In order to take advantage of this exception, the lessor must file with the court and serve on the debtor a **certification,** under penalty of perjury, that such an **eviction action has been filed** or that the debtor, during the **30 days prior to filing of the certification,** has **endangered** the property or illegally used or allowed the use of a **controlled substance on the property.** [B.C. § 362(b)(23)] The exception, however, is subject to § 362(m), which keeps the automatic stay in place if the debtor/tenant satisfies certain conditions.

(1) When Exception Applies

The exception at § 362(b)(23), allowing the lessor to move forward with the eviction, applies on the date that is **15 days** after the lessor files and serves the certification. [B.C. § 362(m)(1)] The 15-day period does not apply, however, if the debtor takes certain action in response to the certification. [B.C. § 362(m)(2)]

(2) Debtor Objection

If the debtor files with the court an **objection** to the **truth or legal sufficiency** of the lessor's **certification** and serves that objection on the lessor, then the exception to the stay at § 362(b)(23) does not apply, unless the court orders otherwise. [B.C. § 362(m)(2)(A)] The court must hold a **hearing within 10 days** after the filing and service of debtor's objection in order to determine if the situation giving rise to the lessor's certification existed or has been remedied. [B.C. § 362(m)(2)(B)]

(3) Hearing Determination

If the debtor can **demonstrate,** to the court's satisfaction, that the situation giving rise to lessor's certification either **did not exist or has been remedied,** then the **automatic stay remains in effect** as otherwise provided by § 362. [B.C. §§ 362(a)(3), (m)(2)(C)] If the debtor fails to make such demonstration to the court's satisfaction, then the lessor does not need to move for relief from the stay under § 362(a)(3) in order to proceed with the eviction. [B.C. § 362(m)(2)(D)(i)] The court clerk, then, immediately must serve on the lessor and the debtor a certified copy of the court's order upholding the lessor's certification. [B.C. § 362(m)(2)(D)(ii)]

(4) No Debtor Objection

If the debtor does not object to the lessor's certification within 15 days, then **§ 362(b)(23) immediately applies** and lessor does not have to move for relief from the stay under § 362(a)(3) in order to complete the process of recovering full possession of the leased property. [B.C. § 362(m)(3)(A)] The court clerk then shall immediately serve on the lessor and the debtor a certified copy of the docket indicating debtor's failure to file an objection. [B.C. § 362(m)(3)(B)]

(5) Summary

The lessor may complete the process to recover possession of leased residential premises without moving to lift the automatic stay under § 362(a)(3) if the lessor files with the court and serves on the debtor a *certification,* under penalty of perjury, that it has filed an eviction action based on *endangerment of the property* or *illegal use of controlled substances on the property* or that the debtor, during the *30 days prior to filing of the certification,* has *endangered* the property or illegally used or allowed the use of a *controlled substance on the property* and

   (a) the debtor *fails to object* to lessor's certification within 15 days after lessor filed and served on debtor the certification; or

   (b) the debtor filed an objection but failed to demonstrate to the court's satisfaction that the situation giving rise to lessor's certification either did not exist or had been remedied.

q. Non-Avoidable Transfers

This exception, added to the Code in 2005, provides that the automatic stay does not apply to any transfer that is not avoidable under § 544 and that is not avoidable under § 549. [B.C. § 362(b)(24)] Thus, if the trustee cannot avoid the debtor's post-petition transfer of estate property under § 549, the trustee cannot void that transfer by claiming it violates the automatic stay. The trustee must challenge the transfer under § 549, rather than "side step the limitations found in § 549 by asserting that an unauthorized transfer is also void in violation of the automatic stay." [**Slone v. Anderson (*In re* Anderson),** 511 B.R. 481 (Bankr. S.D. Ohio 2013) (also noting that § 362(b)(24) is " 'one of the oddest and perhaps the most poorly drafted of the BAPCPA provisions dealing with the automatic stay' ")]

r. Securities Self-Regulatory Organizations

In 2005, Congress added another exception to the automatic stay for certain conduct by securities self-regulatory organizations, which it defined as a securities association or a national securities exchange registered with the Securities Exchange Commission. [B.C. §§ 362(b)(25), 101(48A)] The exception covers the following actions:

   (i) the commencement or continuation of an *investigation or action* by a securities self-regulatory organization to enforce the organization's regulatory power [B.C. § 362(b)(25)(A)];

   (ii) the *enforcement* of an *order or a decision*, other than for monetary sanctions, obtained by a securities self-regulatory organization to enforce the organization's regulatory power [B.C. § 362(b)(25)(B)]; or

   (iii) any action taken by a securities self-regulatory organization to *delist, delete,* or *refuse to permit quotation of stock* that fails to meet applicable regulatory standards. [B.C. § 362(b)(25)(C)]

s. Setoff Income Tax Refund

In 2005, Congress added an exception to the stay to permit a governmental unit to setoff, if allowed under nonbankruptcy law, an *income tax refund for a pre-petition taxable period against a pre-petition tax liability.* The income tax refund and the tax liability must be for a pre-petition taxable period. If applicable nonbankruptcy law does not allow the setoff because there is a pending action to determine the amount or legality of a tax liability, then the governmental unit may hold the refund until the pending action is resolved. The trustee, however, may move for turnover of the refund. The court, after notice and a hearing, may order turnover, but only if the court grants the government adequate protection, within the meaning of § 361, for any secured claim that the government unit has under § 506(a) by virtue of its right to setoff. [B.C. § 362(b)(26)]

Example: Debtor filed for relief under Chapter 13 in 2008. The IRS filed a proof of claim in her case for more than $44,000 owed in pre-petition income taxes. The IRS set off Debtor's pre-petition tax liability against $1,500 that Debtor had overpaid on her 2007 pre-petition taxes. Debtor argued that the setoff violated the automatic stay. The bankruptcy court held that there was no stay violation. The court explained that the IRS has the right to set off tax liabilities against tax refunds under nonbankruptcy law, specifically 26 U.S.C. § 6402(a). Because both the tax liability and the tax refund were for pre-petition taxable periods, the IRS's setoff fell "squarely within the exception of § 362(b)(26) and [did] not violate the automatic stay." [**Ewing v. United States (*In re Ewing*),** 400 B.R. 913 (Bankr. N.D. Ga. 2008)]

t. Federal Health Care Programs

It is not a violation of the automatic stay for the Secretary of Health and Human Services to exclude the debtor from participating in the Medicare program or any other federal health care program, as defined in the Social Security Act. [B.C. § 362(b)(28); 42 U.S.C. §§ 1320a–7b(f), 1301 et seq., 1395 et seq.] Congress added this exception in 2005.

u. Small Business Debtor

In 2005, Congress added an exception to the stay to address what it perceived as a problem with serial filing by small business debtors. The stay exception only applies to a *small business case,* which is a term of art defined in the Code. [B.C. §§ 362(n), 101(51C)] This exception to the stay *only applies* if the debtor files a bankruptcy case and

(i) *is a debtor in a small business case pending* at the time debtor files its subsequent bankruptcy case [B.C. § 362(n)(1)(A)];

(ii) *was a debtor in a small business case* that was *dismissed for any reason* by an order that became final in the *two-year period* before the date of the order for relief in the subsequent bankruptcy case [B.C. § 362(n)(1)(B)];

(iii) *was a debtor in a small business case* in which a *plan was confirmed* in the *two-year period* before the date of the order for relief in the subsequent bankruptcy case [B.C. § 362(n)(1)(C)]; or

(iv) is an *entity that acquired substantially all of the assets or business of a small business debtor described above in (i)–(iii),* unless such entity establishes by a preponderance of the evidence that it acquired the assets or business in *good faith and not to evade the restrictions of § 362(n).* [B.C. § 362(n)(1)(D)]

(1) Inapplicability of the Small Business Exception

The Code provides that in certain circumstances, the *exception* to the automatic stay for small business cases *does not apply,* which means that the automatic stay *does* apply. The automatic stay applies

(a) to an *involuntary case,* so long as there is no collusion between the debtor and creditors [B.C. § 362(n)(2)(A)]; or

(b) to the filing of a petition if the debtor proves by a preponderance of the evidence that the filing resulted from *circumstances beyond the debtor's control not foreseeable at the time the case then pending was filed,* and it is more likely than not that the court will *confirm a feasible reorganization, not liquidating, plan within a reasonable time period.* [B.C. § 362(n)(2)(B)]

e.g. **Example:** Debtor owns and operates a boat marina business. She filed for relief under Chapter 11, and filed a reorganization plan and disclosure statement. Debtor was a small business debtor and her Chapter 11 case was a small business case. On April 1, 2010, the bankruptcy court dismissed Debtor's Chapter 11 case, because she failed to comply with the 45-day confirmation requirement at § 1129(e) for small business debtors. On April 9, 2010, Debtor filed a second small business Chapter 11 case. Debtor argued that the exception to the stay at § 362(n) did not apply to her second bankruptcy case, because she satisfied the requirements of § 362(n)(2)(B)(i)—her second bankruptcy filing resulted from circumstances not foreseeable at the time that she filed her first Chapter 11 case. Debtor posited that her first Chapter 11 case was "the case then pending." The bankruptcy court rejected Debtor's argument. It held that the "plain language" of § 362(n)(2)(B)(i) "refers to a separate case that *is* pending at the time that second petition is filed" and because there was no *pending* case at the time that Debtor filed her second bankruptcy case, § 362(n)(2)(B)(i) simply did not apply. Therefore, the court concluded that § 362(n)(1)(B) applied to Debtor's second bankruptcy filing on April 9, 2010, thereby "rendering the automatic stay inapplicable." [**Palmer v. Bank of the West,** 438 B.R. 167 (Bankr. E.D. Wis. 2010)]

CHECKLIST OF EXCEPTIONS TO OR CASES IN WHICH THE AUTOMATIC STAY DOES NOT APPLY **◪GILBERT**

THE AUTOMATIC STAY DOES NOT APPLY TO:

☑ The commencement or continuation of a *criminal action against the debtor*

☑ Various actions related to the collection of *domestic support obligations*

☑ The commencement or continuation of a civil suit to establish *paternity* or concerning *child custody or visitation*

☑ The commencement or continuation of any civil action regarding *domestic violence*

☑ The commencement or continuation of a civil action to *dissolve a marriage*

☑ Certain *acts of perfection or filings of continuation statements* to the extent that they occur within the applicable grace period, or to the extent that they would prevail over the trustee's avoiding powers

☑ Governmental proceedings to *enforce police or regulatory powers* and enforcement of *nonmonetary judgments* resulting from such proceedings

☑ The exercise of certain contractual rights to *liquidate, terminate, or accelerate securities, commodities, or forward contracts; repurchase or swap agreements; or master netting agreements*

☑ Certain setoffs related to *securities, commodities, or forward contracts; repurchase or swap agreements; or master netting agreements*

☑ Certain *HUD mortgage foreclosures*

☑ *Tax audits and assessments*

☑ Actions to recover nonresidential real property under a lease that has **terminated by expiration of the lease's stated term** before or during the case

☑ **Presentment** of a negotiable instrument, sending a **notice of dishonor,** or **protesting dishonor**

☑ Certain actions against **educational institutions** relating to accreditation, licensure, or eligibility to participate in federal programs

☑ Actions by the Secretary of Transportation or the Secretary of Commerce to **foreclose a preferred ship or fleet mortgage,** to **foreclose on a security interest** relating to a **vessel or vessel construction** under applicable state or federal law, or **to foreclose a mortgage, deed of trust, or other security interest in a fishing facility** held by the Secretary of Commerce under federal law

☑ The creation or perfection of a **statutory lien for ad valorem property taxes that become due post-petition**

☑ **Special taxes or special assessments on real property,** regardless of whether ad valorem, imposed by a governmental unit, that **become due post-petition**

☑ **Withholding of income** from a debtor's wages and **collection of the withheld** amounts pursuant to an agreement with debtor authorizing such withholding and collection for the benefit of a **pension, profit-sharing, stock bonus or other plan** established pursuant to provisions of the Internal Revenue Code **to the extent** such monies are withheld and collected only to repay certain loans

☑ Any act to **enforce any lien against or security interest in real property** based on an order lifting the stay in the debtor's **prior bankruptcy case** because debtor engaged in a **scheme to delay, hinder, or defraud creditors** that involved either the transfer of real property without the secured creditor's consent or multiple bankruptcy filings affecting such real property

☑ Any act to **enforce a lien or security interest in real property** if the debtor is **ineligible under § 109(g)** to be a debtor or if the debtor's bankruptcy filing violates an **order entered in a prior bankruptcy case** prohibiting the debtor from filing another bankruptcy case

☑ Under certain circumstances, the **continuation of any eviction, unlawful detainer, or similar proceeding** by a lessor of **residential real property** if the lessor has obtained a **pre-petition judgment for possession** of the leased premises

☑ Under certain circumstances, the **commencement or continuation of an eviction action** based on the debtor's **endangerment of the leased property or illegal use of a controlled substance on the leased property**

☑ Any transfer that is **not avoidable under § 544 and not avoidable under § 549**

☑ A **securities self-regulatory organization's commencement or continuation** of an **investigation or action, enforcement** of an **order or decision** (other than for monetary sanctions), or action to **delist, delete or refuse to permit quotation of a stock** that fails to meet applicable regulatory standards

☑ If allowed under applicable nonbankruptcy law, the **setoff** by a governmental unit, of an **income tax refund for a pre-petition taxable period against a pre-petition tax liability**

☑ The **exclusion by the Secretary of Health and Human Services of the debtor** from participating in the Medicare program or any other federal health care program, as defined in the Social Security Act

☑ The debtor's filing of a bankruptcy case if the debtor is a debtor in a *pending small business case* at the time of the subsequent bankruptcy filing

☑ The debtor's filing of a bankruptcy case if the debtor was a debtor in a *small business case* that was *dismissed for any reason* by an order that became final in the *two years* prior to the date of the order for relief in debtor's subsequent bankruptcy filing

☑ The debtor's filing of a bankruptcy case if the debtor was a debtor in a *small business case in which a plan was confirmed* in the *two years* prior to the date of the order for relief in debtor's subsequent bankruptcy filing

☑ A case in which the debtor is an entity that *acquired substantially all of the assets or business of a small business debtor* described in the three scenarios immediately above, unless the debtor establishes by a preponderance of the evidence that it obtained the assets or business in *good faith* and *not to circumvent the Code's provisions on serial filing*

4. Expiration of Stay

Prior to BAPCPA's enactment, the Code's rules on when the stay expired were relatively simple. In 2005, however, Congress added new rules on stay termination for *personal property* in cases involving *individual Chapter 7 debtors.* [B.C. § 362(h)] Congress also significantly expanded § 362(c) by creating detailed rules about the operation of the stay in cases involving *serial filing by individual debtors.* [B.C. § 362(c)]

a. Individual Chapter 7 Debtors and Personal Property

Section 521(a)(2) of the Code requires an individual Chapter 7 debtor to file a statement of intention and perform that intention within certain time periods with regard to debts secured by property of the estate. [B.C. § 521(a)(2)] In 2005, Congress added § 362(h) to the Code and tied termination of the automatic stay to the debtor's performance of her obligations under § 521 with regard to *personal property of the estate or of the debtor* that secures a claim or that is subject to an unexpired lease. [B.C. § 362(h)(1)]

(i) Stay Termination

In an *individual Chapter 7* case, the automatic stay terminates with respect to *personal property of the estate or of the debtor* that secures a claim or that is subject to a lease and such property is no longer property of the estate if the debtor fails (i) to *timely file a statement of intention* or to indicate on such statement that it will *surrender or redeem, the property, reaffirm the debt secured by the property, or assume such unexpired lease* pursuant to § 365(p); or (ii) *timely take the action* specified in the statement. [B.C. §§ 362(h)(1)(A), (B)] The stay does not terminate if the debtor specifies an intention to reaffirm the debt on the original contract terms and the creditor refuses to agree to reaffirmation on those terms. [B.C. § 362(h)(1)(B); *In re* **Craker,** 337 B.R. 549 Bankr. M.D. N.C. 2006)]

Note: The language of § 362(h) is not limited to Chapter 7 cases, but § 521(a)(2), to which § 362(h) specifically refers, *is* so limited. Thus, a noted commentator contends that "it is clear that an early stay termination under section 362(h) can occur only in a Chapter 7 case in which the debtor is an individual." [3 Collier ¶ 362.11; *see also In re* **Schlitzer,** 332 B.R. 856 (Bankr. W.D. N.Y. 2005) (holding that § 362(h) does not apply in a Chapter 13 case)]

(ii) Exception

The trustee may file a motion *before § 521(a)(2)'s time limits expire* asking the court to stop the operation of § 362(h). The *stay does not terminate* if the court, after notice and a hearing, determines that the *property is of consequential value or benefit* to the estate, orders *adequate protection* of the creditor's interest, and orders the debtor to *deliver to the trustee any collateral in the debtor's possession.* [B.C. § 362(h)(2)] If the court rules against the trustee's motion, however, the stay terminates at the conclusion of the hearing on the motion.

(iii) Comfort Order

Section 362(j) provides that a party in interest may request the court to issue an order that the automatic stay has terminated under § 362(c). Section 362(j) specifically mentions § 362(c), but not § 362(h). Thus, there is disagreement as to whether a court may issue a comfort order that the automatic stay has terminated under § 362(h).

cf. **Compare:** *In re* **Grossi,** 365 B.R. 608 (Bankr. E.D. Va. 2007) ("[e]ntry of a comfort order under 11 U.S.C. § 362(j) is not appropriate when the stay allegedly has been terminated under 11 U.S.C. § 362(h)) *with In re* **Espey,** 347 B.R. 785 (Bankr. M.D. Fla. 2006) (stating that because § 362(c)(1) provides that the stay continues only so long as property is estate property, once property no longer is estate property, e.g., when the stay terminates under § 362(h), "a party in interest may move the Court for an order confirming that the stay is terminated under § 362(j)").

(iv) Compare: Stay Termination § 521(a)(6)

Section 521(a)(6) also contains a stay termination provision, but with regard to *personal property securing a purchase-money security interest.* If a Chapter 7 debtor fails to reaffirm the debt or redeem the property securing the creditor's purchase-money interest within *45 days* after the first meeting of creditors, then the *automatic stay terminates* and the property *no longer is estate property.* [B.C. § 521(a)(6)] Section 521(a)(6) is limited to *purchase-money security interests in personal property,* while § 362(h) "applies to all debts secured by personal property, not just purchase-money debts." [*In re* **Lopez,** 440 B.R. 447 (Bankr. E.D. Va. 2010)]

(v) The Ride-Through

Some jurisdictions, prior to the passage of BAPCPA, recognized what came to be known as the "ride-through." A debtor could continue to make payments on a current debt and keep the collateral securing the debt without redeeming the property or reaffirming the debt. BAPCPA's changes to the Code, e.g., the stay termination provisions at §§ 362(h) and 521(a)(6), limited, but did not eliminate, the ride-through. For example, the stay termination provisions at §§ 362(h) and 521(a)(6) apply to *personal,* not *real,* property. Thus, some courts have held that BAPCPA did not "eliminate the ride-through for debts secured by real property." [**Lopez,** *supra*]

Suppose a debtor who is current on her car payments decides neither to redeem the vehicle nor to reaffirm the debt secured by the car. When the stay lifts, can the creditor repossess the vehicle based on an *ipso facto* clause in the parties' contract? The answer to this question depends on whether a creditor can repossess under state law based on a contractual *ipso facto* clause when the debtor is current on her vehicle payments. [*In re* **Donald,** 343 B.R. 524 (E.C. N.C. 2006) (stating that when the debtor does not act, as required by § 521(a)(6) or § 362(h), § 521(d) merely eliminates the Code's prior limitations "on the operation of ipso facto clauses . . . [and] [c]reditors still must ensure that the contract, and their efforts to enforce the terms in it, do not run afoul of any applicable state laws"); *see, e.g.,* **Hall v. Ford Motor Credit, LLC,** 229 Kan. 176 (Kan. 2011) (affirming lower court holding that even though debtor was current on car payments creditor did not violate the Kansas Uniform Consumer Credit Code by repossessing debtor's vehicle post-bankruptcy based on ipso facto clause in parties' contract)]

b. **Section 362(c): General Rules**

Unless the court grants relief from the automatic stay, it remains operative from the time that the bankruptcy petition is filed until it statutorily terminates as follows.

(i) The stay of an *act against estate property* is effective until the property no longer constitutes property of the estate. [B.C. § 362(c)(1)]

(ii) The stay of *any other act* enjoined under § 362(a) continues until a discharge is granted or denied, the case is dismissed, or the case is closed, whichever occurs first. [B.C. § 362(c)(2)]

e.g. **Example:** Trustee, in compliance with § 363, sells an asset of the estate to Third Party. The automatic stay is terminated with respect to the asset at the time that it ceases to be property of the estate. [B.C. § 362(c)(1)]

e.g. **Example:** Trustee abandons an over-encumbered asset of the estate. Debtor has not been granted or denied a discharge, and the case has neither been closed nor dismissed. Although the asset is no longer property of the estate, it becomes Debtor's property and continues to be protected by the automatic stay. [B.C. §§ 362(a)(5), (c)(2)]

e.g. **Example:** Trustee abandons an over-encumbered asset of the estate. The bankruptcy court subsequently grants Debtor a discharge, which terminates the automatic stay. The secured creditor can proceed to foreclose her lien on the property. [B.C. § 362(c)(2)(C)]

Confirmation of a Chapter 11 plan usually vests all of the property of the estate in the debtor, and also discharges the debtor from pre-confirmation debts. [B.C. §§ 1141(b), (d)(1)(A)] Thus, plan confirmation normally terminates the automatic stay. [B.C. §§ 362(c)(1), (2)(C)]

Remember: Property that the debtor exempts is no longer property of the estate. But, unless the debtor's case is dismissed, exempt property is not liable during or after the case for a debtor's pre-petition debts. [B.C. § 522(c)] There are exceptions, however, to this general rule. For example, exempt property is liable for nondischargeable tax and domestic support obligations. [B.C. §§ 522(c)(1), 523(a)(1), (a)(5)]

c. **Section 362(c): Serial Filers and BAPCPA's Changes**

The Code's provisions on serial filers apply only to *individual debtors,* and only if the debtor's prior case was *dismissed.* [*See* B.C. § 362(c)(3), (4)] The serial filer provisions do not apply, however, if the debtor filed her later case because her prior case was filed under Chapter 7 and dismissed pursuant to § 707(b). [B.C. §§ 362(c)(3), (c)(4)(A)(i)]

(i) Prior Pending Case: 30-Day Rule

If an *individual debtor* files for bankruptcy and there was *pending in the prior year* a Chapter 7, 11, or 13 case that was *dismissed,* § 362(c)(3) provides that the stay in debtor's current bankruptcy case expires after *30 days.* The stay expires, however, only as to a debt, property securing that debt, or a lease *with respect to the debtor.* Therefore, the majority of courts have held that after 30 days, while the automatic stay expires as to *the debtor and property of the debtor,* it remains in place with regard to *estate property.* [**Holcomb v. Hardeman (*In re* Holcomb),** 380 B.R. 813 (B.A.P. 10th Cir. 2008)] This stay-expiration rule does *not* apply to cases under Chapter 12. [B.C. § 362(c)(3)]

(1) What Does *Pending* Mean?

The stay-termination provision at § 362(c)(3) applies to a subsequent bankruptcy filing by an individual debtor if a prior Chapter 7, 11, or 13 case was *pending* during the prior year. The Bankruptcy Code does not define what "pending" means. For example, if the bankruptcy court dismisses the debtor's Chapter 13 case on March 1, 2017, but the clerk of court does not close the case until September 1, 2017, does debtor's filing another Chapter 13 case on June 1, 2018 run afoul of § 362(c)(3)? There is limited case law on the issue, but most courts run the time frame from the order of dismissal, not the administrative case closing. [*See, e.g.,* **In re Linares,** 2010 WL 2788248 (Bankr. S.D. Fla. 2010) (holding that dismissal, not administrative closing, is relevant date from which to run the time period in § 362(c)(3)); *In re* **Easthope,** 2006 WL 851829 (Bankr. D. Utah 2006) (noting that it would be unfair to debtors to run the time period in § 362(c)(3) from the date of case closing because debtors cannot control when the clerk's office closes a case and, thus, holding that "[t]he plain meaning of the word 'pending' as well as policy considerations demonstrate that a case is no longer pending once it has been dismissed"); *In re* **Moore,** 337 B.R. 79, 81 (Bankr. E.D. N.C. 2005) (stating that debtor's prior bankruptcy case was "no longer 'pending' for purposes of § 362(c)(3) as of the date of dismissal, regardless of when the case was closed")]

(2) Request for Stay Continuation: Procedure

A party in interest may file a motion to continue the automatic stay as to any or all creditors. To obtain relief, the party in interest must demonstrate that the filing of the subsequent case was in *good faith* as to the creditors to be stayed. The Code requires notice and a hearing, and that the *hearing be completed within the 30-day period* before the stay expires. [B.C. § 362(c)(3)(B)]

(3) Statutory Presumption: All Creditors

The filing of the subsequent case is *presumed not to be in good faith* as to *all creditors* if:

(a) *more than one prior case* filed by or against the debtor under Chapter 7, 11, or 13 was *pending* within the preceding one-year period [B.C. § 362(c)(3)(C)(i)(I)];

(b) a prior case filed by or against the debtor under Chapter 7, 11, or 13 was *dismissed* within the preceding one-year period because the debtor (i) *without having a substantial excuse* failed to file or amend the petition or other required documents; (ii) *provide adequate protection,* as required by the court; or (iii) *perform the terms of a confirmed plan* [B.C. § 362(c)(3)(C)(i)(II)]; *or*

Note: Mere inadvertence or negligence does not constitute substantial excuse, unless the negligence of debtor's attorney resulted in the prior case's dismissal.

(c)   there has been *no substantial change* in the *debtor's financial or personal affairs since the dismissal* of the next most prior case nor any other reason to conclude that the subsequent case will result in a discharge, if filed under Chapter 7, or a fully performed confirmed plan, if filed under Chapter 11 or 13. [B.C. § 362(c)(3)(C)(i)(III)]

(4) Statutory Presumption: Creditor Moved to Lift Stay

The filing of the subsequent case is *presumed not to be in good faith* as to any creditor that sought relief from the stay in the debtor's prior case and that *motion was pending at the time of dismissal* of the prior case *or* was *resolved by terminating, conditioning, or limiting the stay* as to such creditor's actions. [B.C. § 362(c)(3)(C)(ii)]

(5) Presumption not Applicable

The presumption does not apply to a subsequent bankruptcy filing if the debtor's prior Chapter 7, 11 or 13 case was dismissed due to the creation of a *debt repayment plan.* [B.C. § 362(i)] The Code does not require that the debtor have completed this debt repayment plan in order for the presumption under § 362(c)(3) not to apply.

(6) Rebutting the Presumption

The debtor may rebut the presumption that her subsequent bankruptcy case was not filed in good faith. The debtor must rebut the presumption by *clear and convincing evidence.* [B.C. § 362(c)(3)(C)]

e.g. **Example:** Debtor filed for relief under Chapter 13 on October 23, 2012. That case was dismissed on November 14, 2013, because Debtor failed to make timely payments under his Chapter 13 plan. On August 26, 2014, less than one year from the dismissal of his earlier Chapter 13 case. On August 26, 2014, Debtor filed a motion to continue the automatic stay beyond the 30-day period. The court examined a number of factors, including the debtor's motive and reasons for dismissal of his first bankruptcy case. The court noted that Debtor's first bankruptcy case was dismissed because he could not make the Chapter 13 payments, not because of any improper conduct. At the hearing, Debtor testified that he could not make the Chapter 13 plan payments in his prior case because the business had lost its liquor license. The business, however, had regained the license and while Debtor testified that he had been seriously ill, he had since recovered. The court also concluded that based on the Debtor's credible testimony, Debtor had narrowly met his burden of establishing by clear and convincing evidence that he could fund and perform a plan in his second Chapter 13 case. The bankruptcy court, applying a totality-of-the-circumstances test, concluded that Debtor had established by clear and convincing evidence that his second Chapter 13 case was filed in good faith. Therefore, the court granted the Debtor's motion to extend the automatic stay beyond the 30-day period. [*In re* **Riedy,** 517 B.R. 88 (Bankr. W.D. Mich. 2014)]

(ii) Two or More Prior Pending Cases

If an individual debtor files for bankruptcy and there were *two or more bankruptcy cases pending in the prior year* that were *dismissed,* § 362(c)(4) provides that the automatic stay in debtor's current bankruptcy case does not go into effect. Unlike § 362(c)(3), § 362(c)(4) applies to all prior bankruptcy filings, including those under Chapter 12. [*Compare* B.C. § 362(c)(3) *with* B.C. § 362(c)(4)(A)(i)] On request of a party in interest, the court must promptly enter an order confirming that no stay is in effect in debtor's bankruptcy case. [B.C. § 362(c)(4)(A)(ii)]

(1) Request for Stay to Take Effect

Within *30 days of the filing of the debtor's subsequent bankruptcy case,* a party in interest may request that the court order the stay to take effect as to any or all creditors, subject to any conditions imposed by the court. The court may so order, after notice and a hearing, only if the party in interest demonstrates that the filing of the subsequent case was in *good faith as to the creditors to be stayed.* [B.C. § 362(c)(3)(B)] Unlike the hearing under § 362(c)(3), the hearing under § 362(c)(4) does not have to conclude within 30 days after the filing of the petition. [*Compare* § 362(c)(3)(B) *with* § 362(c)(4)(B)] If the court grants the request, the stay is effective on the date of the court's order allowing the stay to go into effect. [B.C. § 362(c)(4)(C)]

(2) Statutory Presumption: All Creditors

The filing of the subsequent case is *presumed not to be in good faith* as to *all creditors* if:

(a) *two or more prior cases* filed by or against the debtor were *pending* within the preceding one-year period [B.C. § 362(c)(4)(D)(i)(I)];

(b) a prior case filed by or against the debtor was *dismissed* within the preceding one-year period because the debtor (i) *without having a substantial excuse* failed to file or amend the petition or other required documents; (ii) failed to *provide adequate protection,* as required by the court; or (iii) failed to *perform the terms of a confirmed plan* [B.C. § 362(c)(4)(D)(i)(II)]; *or*

Note: Mere inadvertence or negligence do not constitute substantial excuse, unless the negligence of debtor's attorney resulted in the prior case's dismissal.

(c) there has been *no substantial change* in the *debtor's financial or personal affairs since the dismissal* of the next most prior case nor any other reason to conclude that the subsequent case will result in a discharge, if filed under Chapter 7, or a fully performed confirmed plan, if filed under Chapter 11 or 13. [B.C. § 362(c)(4)(D)(i)(III)]

(3) Statutory Presumption: Creditor Moved for Relief of Stay

The filing of the subsequent case is *presumed not to be in good faith* as to any creditor that sought relief from the stay in a prior case and that *motion was pending at the time of dismissal* of the prior case *or* was *resolved by terminating, conditioning, or limiting the stay* as to such creditor's actions. [B.C. § 362(c)(4)(D)(ii)]

(4) Rebutting the Presumption

The debtor may rebut the presumption that her subsequent bankruptcy case was not filed in good faith. The debtor must rebut the presumption by *clear and convincing evidence.* [B.C. § 362(c)(4)(D)]

d. Comfort Orders

Upon the request of a party in interest, the court shall issue an order under § 362(c) that the automatic stay has been terminated. [B.C. § 362(j)]

5. Relief from Stay

Upon request, and after notice and a hearing, the court may grant relief from the automatic stay by *terminating, modifying, annulling, or conditioning* the stay. [B.C. § 362(d)]

e.g. **Example:** Debtor owned a residential real estate development project and defaulted on a construction loan obtained from Bank. Bank foreclosed on the property but before the sheriff's sale Debtor's counsel filed for relief under Chapter 7. Debtor's counsel had intended to file for relief under Chapter 11, and when he learned that he could not withdraw the Chapter 7 petition he filed a Chapter 11 petition less than an hour after filing the Chapter 7 petition. The Chapter 11 case moved forward, and Bank filed a motion to lift the automatic stay. Construction Company, which had recorded a mechanic's lien against the property pre-petition based on its work on the property, had notice of both bankruptcy filings and did not object to Bank's motion. The bankruptcy court granted Bank's motion and the Chapter 11 case was subsequently dismissed. Several days after dismissal of the Chapter 11 case, the Debtor filed a motion to dismiss the Chapter 7 case. Construction Company received notice of the motion to dismiss. Before dismissal of the Chapter 7 case, there was a sheriff's sale of the property, at which Bank bid. Bank then sold the property to a third party. After dismissal of Debtor's Chapter 7 case, Construction Company filed a motion to vacate the foreclosure sale, arguing that at the time of the sale Debtor's Chapter 7 case was still open and, thus, the automatic stay was still in effect. Bank then moved for the bankruptcy court to retroactively annul the Chapter 7 automatic stay and the bankruptcy court granted Bank's motion. The district court affirmed. The court explained that Bank had not willfully violated the stay; no action had taken place in the Chapter 7 case, which had been filed in error. Once the Bank realized that the sale had taken place while the Chapter 7 case was still open, Bank filed its motion to retroactively annul the stay. The court also noted that Construction Company had received all relevant notices, and that vacating the foreclosure sale would prejudice the rights of an alleged bona fide purchaser. The district court affirmed the bankruptcy court's order, which retroactively annulled the automatic stay effective on the date that the court had lifted the stay in Debtor's Chapter 11 case. [**Arrow Road Construction Company v. Bridgeview Bank Group (*In re* Brittwood Creek, LLC),** 450 B.R. 769 (N.D. Ill. 2011)]

a. Grounds for Relief

The Bankruptcy Code spells out several grounds for moving for relief from the automatic stay. Commonly, these motions are filed by a secured creditor for the purpose of recovering its property.

(i) "Cause"

After notice and a hearing, the bankruptcy court must grant relief from the automatic stay to a party in interest if *cause* exists to lift the stay. [B.C. § 362(d)(1)] The Code does not define the term "cause." Thus, the determination of whether cause exists to lift the stay is fact-intensive, and "there is no set formula courts can use to make the determination." [*In re* **Vista International Development,** 2008 Bankr. LEXIS 5139 (Bankr. W.D. Tenn. 2008)]

(1) Lack of Adequate Protection

The debtor's failure to provide adequate protection of an entity's interest in property is sufficient cause for the court to order relief from the stay. [B.C. § 362(d)(1)] Other than a case filed under Chapter 12, adequate protection may constitute cash payments, granting of an additional or replacement lien, or realization of the indubitable equivalent of the party in interest's interest in the property. [B.C. § 361] Adequate protection of an entity's interest in property in a ***Chapter 12 case*** may require cash payments, granting of an additional or replacement lien, or payment of a reasonable rent for use of farmland. [B.C. § 1205] Granting an administrative expense, however, does not constitute adequate protection under any chapter of the Bankruptcy Code. [B.C. §§ 361(3), 1205(b)(4)] Failing to insure collateral also may constitute a failure of adequate protection and, thus, cause to lift the automatic stay. [*In re* **Melincavage,** 2018 WL 3725746 (Bankr. D. N.J. 2018) (holding, in part, that cause existed to lift the stay because "[a]dequate protection includes providing proof of enforceable insurance on collateral")]

e.g. **Example:** Debtor owned real property on which her mother operated a car wash. Debtor failed to pay the real estate taxes, and the property was sold for nonpayment of taxes. Buyer then assigned its certificate of purchase to Waters, who filed a petition for a tax deed under state law. At the time of Debtor's bankruptcy filing, the time period under state law to redeem had not yet expired and Waters' petition for a tax deed was still pending. Debtor filed her Chapter 13 plan, which provided for payment of past-due taxes on the property. Waters moved for lift of the stay to proceed in state court with the tax deed proceeding. Post-petition, Debtor missed a tax payment on the property and failed to demonstrate that her mother could make the tax payments from the revenue from the car wash business. The bankruptcy court explained that the property could be sold again at another tax sale because of missed tax payments. In order to obtain a tax deed, Waters then would have to redeem from that property tax sale. The bankruptcy court concluded that because of the "great risk that another tax buyer [might] intercede, Waters's interest in [Debtor's] property [was] not therefore adequately protected." Therefore, the court granted his motion to lift the stay. [*In re* **Scott,** 449 B.R. 535 (Bankr. N.D. Ill. 2011)]

(2) Lack of Good Faith

The debtor's lack of good faith in filing the bankruptcy petition can constitute cause for granting relief from the automatic stay. [B.C. § 362(d)(1); *see, e.g.,* **Alta Vista, LLC v. Juarez (*In re* Juarez),** 533 B.R. 818 (Bankr. D. Colo. 2015) (Chapter 13); *In re* **Sterling Bluff Investors, LLC,** 515 B.R. 902 (Bankr. S.D. Ga. 2014) (Chapter 11)] Courts have used different tests and factors in their determination of whether a debtor's bankruptcy filing is in bad faith and, thus, constitutes cause to lift the automatic stay. [*See, e.g., In re* **Louchesch, LLC,** 2011 WL 3319891 (Bankr. D. Mass. 2011) (discussing various tests and approaches taken by courts); *In re* **Reyes Ramos,** 2006 WL 3898377 (Bankr. D. P.R. 2006) (same)]; *see also In re* **Boates,** 2006 WL 166569 (E.D. Penn. 2006) (examining seven factors, including debtor's motives, effect on creditors, debtor's pre- and post-petition treatment of creditors, in bad-faith filing analysis)]

Note: A court's order to lift the stay due to bad faith filing of a petition differs from an order entered in a prior case pursuant to § 362(d)(4) based on a scheme to defraud or the debtor's multiple bankruptcy filings. [B.C. § 362(d)(4)]

(3) Judicial Economy and Other Tribunals

The lack of adequate protection is not the only cause for lifting the stay. "[A] desire to permit an action to proceed to completion in another tribunal may provide another cause." [H.R. Rep. No. 95–595, at 343 (1977)] In making the decision whether to lift the stay to allow pending litigation to go forward, courts examine several factors:

(a) whether the litigation involves *only state law issues,* such that it is not necessary to draw upon the expertise of the bankruptcy court;

(b) whether lifting the stay would *promote judicial economy;* and

(c) whether the *estate can be protected* by requiring creditors to seek enforcement of any judgment through the bankruptcy court.

[*See, e.g.,* ***In re*** **Bayou Haven Bed & Breakfast, LLC,** 2018 WL 3956933 (Bankr. E.D. La. 2018)]

(ii) Acts Against Property

The bankruptcy court will grant relief from the stay of an act against property if (i) the debtor has *no equity* in the property and (ii) the property is *not necessary for an effective reorganization.* [B.C. § 362(d)(2)]

(1) No Equity

Most courts view equity as the difference between the total of all liens on the property and the property's value. [B.C. § 362(d)(2)(A); *see, e.g.,* ***In re*** **Madco Products,** 2009 Bankr. LEXIS 5724 (Bankr. W.D. Tenn. 2009)]

Example: Debtor owns certain land encumbered by a $100,000 first mortgage in favor of Bank A, and a $50,000 second mortgage in favor of Bank B. The property has a fair market value of $130,000. Under the definition above, the debtor has no equity in the property because the *total* of all encumbrances ($150,000) exceeds the value of the property.

(2) Not Necessary for an Effective Reorganization

The property at issue also must not be necessary to an effective reorganization. [B.C. § 362(d)(2)(B); *see* ***In re*** **Heritage Oracle, LLC,** 2010 WL 4259772 (Bankr. D. Ariz. 2010) (finding that debtor's brokerage and property management business was a service business that could operate in any location and, thus, debtor did not need the particular commercial real property from which it was currently operating and for which creditor sought relief from stay)] While a Chapter 13 debtor does not reorganize, as does a Chapter 11 entity, the clear weight of authority is that § 362(d)(2) applies to a Chapter 13 case. [***In re*** **Donahue,** 231 B.R. 865 (Bankr. D. Vt. 1998)]

The debtor's prospects for reorganization are relevant to the "necessary to an effective reorganization" prong of the lift-of-stay analysis. Property will be deemed not necessary for an effective reorganization upon a finding that the debtor does not have a reasonable possibility of successfully reorganizing within a reasonable time. [B.C. § 362(d)(2)(B); **United Savings Association of Texas v. Timbers of Inwood Forest Associates, Ltd.,** 484 U.S. 365 (1988)]

e.g. **Example:** Debtor LLC owned ten acres of land on which it was developing a retail shopping center and hotel complex. Secured Creditor filed a complaint in state court seeking judicial foreclosure and appointment of a receiver. The state court granted Creditor's request for relief, but before the receiver took possession of the property Debtor filed for relief under Chapter 11. Secured Creditor filed a motion to lift the stay. Relief from the automatic stay was appropriate under § 362(d)(2). The property was appraised at almost $26 million, but the Secured Creditor's claim alone was approximately $35 million. Therefore, Debtor had no equity in the property. The Debtor also failed to provide evidence that it could reorganize within a reasonable period of time. Debtor would be unable to obtain consent from creditors with impaired claims without making full or near full payment to those impaired claimants, but Debtor had not secured the monies necessary to fund such a full-payment plan. [**FF, LLC v. U.S. Hung Wui Investments, Inc. (*In re* F&F, LLC),** 2010 WL 6452907 (B.A.P. 9th Cir. 2010)]

(iii) Single Asset Real Estate

The Code also contains special rules for stay relief on property that satisfies the definition of "single asset real estate." If a creditor's claim is secured by an interest in single asset real estate, the court must grant relief from the automatic stay if the debtor fails to do either of the following within certain prescribed time frames:

(1) *file a plan of reorganization* that has a *reasonable possibility of being confirmed* within a *reasonable time* [B.C. § 362(d)(3)(A)] or

(2) *starts to make monthly payments* at the current fair market rate, to each creditor with a claim secured by the real estate, other than creditors with a judgment lien or an unmatured statutory lien. [B.C. § 362(d)(4)(B)]

Note: In 2005, Congress added language to § 362(d)(3)(B) that now gives the debtor the discretion to make the monthly payments from *rents or other income generated* before, on, or after the start of the bankruptcy case *from the single asset real estate.* [B.C. § 362(d)(3)(B)(i)]

(a) Action Required

The debtor must take one of these two actions by the *later of:*

- *90 days after the order for relief; or*

- *30 days after the court determines debtor is subject to § 362(d)(3).*

For cause, the court may extend the 90-day period by an order entered within the 90 days. [B.C. § 362(d)(3)]

(b) Single Asset Real Estate Defined

The Code defines "single asset real estate" as "real property constituting a *single property or project,* other than residential real property with fewer than four residential units, which generates *substantially all of the gross income* of a debtor who is not a family farmer and on which no substantial business is being conducted by a debtor other than the business of operating the real property and activities incidental thereto." [B.C.

§ 101(51B)] In 2005, Congress deleted the $4 million secured debt cap previously in the definition and excluded family farmers from the scope of the definition.

(3) Abuse by Debtor: Real Property

In 2005, Congress added a new subsection to § 362(d) to address a perceived problem with abusive filings. Section 362(d)(4) does two things. First, it states that the court must provide relief from the stay of any *act against real property* to a creditor with an interest secured by that property if the court finds that filing of the petition was part of a *scheme to delay, hinder, or defraud creditors* that involved either of the following:

(i) the *transfer* of all or a part of the *real property* without the secured creditor's consent or court approval [B.C. § 362(d)(4)(A)]; or

(ii) *multiple bankruptcy filings* affecting the real property. [B.C. § 362(d)(4)(B)]

Second, if the secured creditor takes certain action, the stay relief entered in the current bankruptcy case may extend for *two years* after entry of that stay relief order. If the stay relief order is *recorded* in such a way as to satisfy applicable state laws on notices of interests or liens on real property, then the order is *binding in any other bankruptcy case* purporting to affect the real property *filed within two years* of the entry of the order. The debtor in the subsequent bankruptcy case, however, may move for relief from the order based on *changed circumstances* or other *good cause* shown, after notice and a hearing. Any governmental unit that accepts notices of interests or liens on real property must accept a certified copy of such a stay relief order for indexing and recording. [B.C. § 362(d)(4)]

(4) Lessors

While Code § 363(e) requires adequate protection of an entity's interest in property that is leased by the trustee or debtor in possession, it also precludes a lessor of *personal property* from seeking relief from the automatic stay under § 362.

b. Procedure for Requesting Relief

To initiate stay litigation, a party in interest files a motion for relief from the stay. [Bankruptcy Rule 4001(a)(1)]

(i) Acts Against Estate Property: Hearing

When the relief sought is from the stay of an act against *property of the estate,* the stay terminates, by operation of law with respect to the party in interest making the request for stay relief, *30 days* after the motion is filed unless, after notice and a hearing, the court orders that the stay remain operative until a final hearing is concluded. The general rule is that "if there is a reasonable likelihood that the party opposing relief from the stay will prevail at the conclusion of such final hearing," the court will order that the stay continue in effect until such time. [B.C. § 362(e)]

(1) Preliminary Hearing

When the court directs that the stay will remain in effect until a final hearing has been concluded, the initial hearing is called a preliminary hearing. The final hearing must *conclude* within 30 days after the conclusion of the preliminary hearing, unless the 30-day period is extended by consent of the parties or by the court, for a specific time, due to compelling circumstances. The parties may agree, or the court may direct, that the preliminary and final hearings be consolidated. [B.C. § 362(e)]

(ii) Individual Chapter 7, 11, or 13 Case

In 2005, Congress added a subsection to § 362(e) to provide special rules that apply to a request for stay relief involving an individual debtor's Chapter 7, 11, or 13 case. In such a case, the automatic stay terminates, by operation of law, *60 days* after a request for relief is made by a party in interest, *unless*

(1) the court renders a *final decision during the 60-day period* starting on the date of the request for stay relief [B.C. § 362(e)(2)(A)]; or

(2) the 60-day period is extended by the *agreement of all parties in interest or* by the court for the time that the court finds is required for cause. [B.C. § 362(e)(2)(B)]

(iii) Burden of Proof

In litigation concerning relief from the stay of *any act* enjoined under § 362(a), the *party seeking relief has* the burden of proof *regarding the debtor's equity* in property; the *party opposing relief* must bear the burden of proof *on all other issues.* [B.C. § 362(g)]

(iv) Ex Parte Relief

In the exceptional case in which *irreparable harm* to an entity's interest in property will occur before there is time for notice and a hearing, the court may grant ex parte relief from the stay to prevent the threatened loss. Ex parte relief should be a measure of last resort, and the court will closely examine the efforts made to notify the adverse party. [B.C. § 362(f); Bankruptcy Rule 4001(a)(2)]

(v) Appeal

A decision to grant or deny relief from the stay is a final order, which may be appealed. Unless the bankruptcy court orders otherwise, the order granting relief from the stay is stayed for *14 days* from entry. [Bankruptcy Rule 4001(a)(3)]

6. Willful Violation of Stay

An individual who is injured by a *willful* violation of the automatic stay may recover actual damages, costs, attorneys' fees, and, when warranted, punitive damages. [B.C. § 362(k)(1)] Several Circuits have held that actual damages under § 362(k) may include emotional distress damages in appropriate cases. [*See* **Lodge v. Kondaur Capital Corp.,** 750 F.3d 1263 (11th Cir. 2014) (stating that it 'join[ed] other circuits in concluding that emotional distress damages fall within the broad term of 'actual damages' in § 362(k)")] Section 362(k)(1) provides for damages to *individuals*, not to entities. Thus, damages for willful violations of the stay should not be available under § 362(k)(1) to corporations or other entities. [*See, e.g.,* **TLB Equipment, LLC v. Quality Car & Truck Leasing, Inc. (***In re* **TLB Equipment, LLC),** 479 B.R. 464 (Bankr. S.D. Ohio 2012); **5th Avenue Real Estate Development, Inc. v. Countrywide Home Loans, Inc. (***In re* **5th Avenue Real Estate Development, Inc.,** 2008 WL 4371336 (Bankr. S.D. Fla. 2008)] Congress could have used the word "entity," as it did in § 362(k)(2), in order to make relief for stay violations more broadly available under § 362(k)(1). Nonetheless, a bankruptcy court may punish stay violations "under § 105 of the Bankruptcy Code and under its inherent equitable powers . . . even when the debtor is a corporation, even though § 362(k)(1) provides a remedy for a stay violation only to 'individuals.' " [***In re* Mirabilis Ventures, Inc.,** 2011 WL 1167880 (Bankr. M.D. Fla. 2011)] Courts are split on whether "a bankruptcy trustee, acting as representative of a bankruptcy estate, is an 'individual' within the meaning of § 362(k)(1)" because the "bankruptcy estate is an entity but not a natural person." [***In re* Sayeh,** 445 B.R. 19 (Bankr. D. Mass 2011)]

In 2005, Congress added a new subsection that provides that if the stay violation is based on an entity's ***good faith belief*** that the stay has terminated pursuant to § 362(h), then recovery is limited to ***actual damages.*** [B.C. §§ 362(k)(2), (h)] This limitation on damages makes sense if § 362(j) does not apply to § 362(h), and an entity is unable to obtain a comfort order that the stay has terminated.

Chapter Eleven

Administrative Powers: §§ 363–366 of the Code

Chapter Approach

This chapter is the second of two that examine the various administrative powers set forth in Chapter 3 of the Bankruptcy Code. Chapter 10 covers the automatic stay, while this chapter covers (1) adequate protection, (2) the use, sale, or lease of property, (3) obtaining credit, (4) executory contracts and unexpired leases, and (5) utility service. Your bankruptcy exam likely will include questions on some or all of these topics. The following questions should help you to focus on the important points for discussion.

1. **Adequate Protection**

    Is an entity's interest in property adequately protected by periodic cash payments, by an additional or replacement lien, by an equity cushion, or by some other manner constituting the indubitable equivalent of the entity's interest? Adequate protection of an entity's interest in property is required for property subject to the *automatic stay;* for property *used, sold, or leased* by the trustee or debtor in possession; or when the court authorizes the trustee or debtor in possession to incur debt or obtain credit secured by an *equal or senior lien* on property of the estate that is already subject to the entity's lien.

2. **Administrative Powers of Trustee or Debtor in Possession**

    a. If the trustee or debtor in possession wants to *use, sell, or lease property* of the estate, will the transaction be in or outside the ordinary course of the debtor's business? Such transactions that are not in the ordinary course of business require notice and a hearing. If the property constitutes *cash collateral,* court authorization, after notice and hearing, or the consent of all entities having an interest in the property is required.

    b. If *post-petition financing* is needed, will it be in or outside the ordinary course of business, and on what basis can financing be obtained? The lender may extend financing in exchange for an *administrative expense,* the grant of *super super-priority* ahead of all administrative expenses, or the grant of a *lien.*

    c. If the debtor is a party to an *executory contract or unexpired lease,* be sure to discuss: (i) whether the trustee or debtor in possession wants to assume, assume and assign, or reject it; (ii) the process for assuming or rejecting the contract or lease; and (iii) the legal consequences of the assumption, assignment, or rejection.

    d. Has the debtor been *denied utility service* because of the bankruptcy case? Has the debtor provided the utility with *adequate assurance of payment* for services rendered after the order for relief?

A. Adequate Protection

1. Interest in Property

The Bankruptcy Code mandates that in certain circumstances a party's interest in property be adequately protected. [B.C. § 361]

a. Property Subject to Automatic Stay

If an entity's interest in property is subject to the automatic stay and the entity moves to lift the automatic stay because of a lack of adequate protection, the court must grant relief from the stay or require that the entity's interest in the property be adequately protected. [B.C. § 362(d)(1)]

b. Property Used, Sold, or Leased

Upon the request of an entity with an interest in property that the trustee or debtor in possession proposes to use, sell, or lease, the bankruptcy court may condition such use, sale, or lease on the provision of adequate protection of the interest. [B.C. § 363(e)]

c. Equal or Senior Lien on Property

If the court authorizes the trustee or the debtor in possession to incur debt or to obtain credit secured by a lien on property of the estate that is equal or senior to a lien held by an entity on the same property, adequate protection of that entity's interest is required. [B.C. § 364(d)(1)(B)]

2. Methods of Providing Adequate Protection

An entity's interest in property may be adequately protected in a variety of ways; the Bankruptcy Code sets forth three *nonexclusive* methods. [B.C. § 361]

a. Cash Payments

The trustee or debtor in possession may provide adequate protection by making *cash or periodic cash payments* to the extent that an entity's interest in the property has decreased in value (i) due to the automatic stay; (ii) as a result of the use, sale, or lease of the property; or (iii) because of the grant of a lien of equal or higher priority on the property. [B.C. § 361(1)]

e.g. **Example:** Creditor has a $100,000 claim against Debtor; the claim is secured by collateral worth $75,000. The collateral is depreciating at a rate of approximately $500 per month. Thus, without adequate protection, Creditor's secured claim shrinks by $500 each month and its unsecured claim grows by $500 per month. One way to provide adequate protection of Creditor's interest in the collateral is to require the trustee or debtor in possession to make monthly cash payments of $500 during the pendency of the bankruptcy case. The adequate protection payments ensure that the value to pay Creditor's secured claim remains constant and that the unsecured claim does not increase by virtue of the Creditor's inability to enforce its rights to the collateral during the bankruptcy case. [*See* 3 Collier ¶ 361.03(2)]

b. Additional or Replacement Lien

The trustee or debtor in possession may provide adequate protection by furnishing an *additional or replacement lien* to the extent of any decrease in value of the entity's interest in the property caused by (i) the automatic stay; (ii) the use, sale, or lease of the property; or (iii) the grant of a senior or equal lien on the property. [B.C. § 361(2)]

c. Indubitable Equivalent

The third method described in § 361 for providing adequate protection is for the bankruptcy court to grant relief constituting the *indubitable equivalent* of the entity's interest in the property. Giving an entity an allowable administrative expense does not constitute the indubitable equivalent of the entity's interest in the property. [B.C. § 361(3)] The term "indubitable equivalent" comes from the phrase "the most indubitable equivalence" in a Learned Hand Bankruptcy Act case. [*In re* **Murel Holding Corp.**, 75 F.2d 941 (2d Cir. 1935)] Bankruptcy courts have not required adequate protection to be of the *most* indubitable equivalent; they do, however, require adequate protection to be completely compensatory. [**Desert Fire Protection v. Fontainebleau Las Vegas Holdings, LLC** (*In re* **Fontainebleau**), 434 B.R. 716 (S.D. Fla. 2010)]

d. Equity Cushion

An **oversecured** creditor often is adequately protected by an equity cushion, which is the amount by which the value of the collateral exceeds the debt owed to the creditor. A substantial equity cushion may adequately protect a secured creditor's interest from depreciation of the collateral that might occur while the property is being used, sold, or leased by the trustee or the debtor in possession, or while the automatic stay precludes the secured party from taking possession.

e.g. **Example:** Debtor, the owner of certain land valued at $100,000, files a Chapter 11 petition. First Mortgagee is owed $50,000, secured by a mortgage on the realty. Second Mortgagee holds a junior lien on the same property in the amount of $80,000. First Mortgagee files a motion to lift the automatic stay, under § 362(d)(1), on the ground of lack of adequate protection. Unless the land is expected to depreciate rapidly, the equity cushion of $50,000 appears to be sufficient to adequately protect First Mortgagee's interest. Therefore, First Mortgagee's motion for relief from the stay probably will be denied.

(i) Method of Determination

In determining whether the **equity cushion** adequately protects First Mortgagee's interest in the property in the example above, the court compares the value of the property to the amount of the secured claim plus all **senior** secured claims. Therefore, the court does not take into consideration Second Mortgagee's **junior** lien of $80,000.

e.g. **Example:** Debtor LLC ("Debtor") filed for relief under Chapter 11 in early September 2017. Creditor Canyon was Debtor's pre-petition lender. Debtor filed a motion for bankruptcy court approval to borrow $22 million post-petition from Ardent Financial. In its motion, Debtor asked the court for a priming lien for Ardent pursuant to § 364(d)(1). The issue was whether there was adequate protection of Canyon's interest if the court granted a priming lien to Ardent. Debtor's expert testified to an "as is" value of approximately $77 million. The value of Canyon's liens ($59.6 million) and the amount of the proposed priming lien ($22 million) totaled $81 million, which *exceeded* the value of the property. Thus, there was no equity cushion under Debtor's "as is" valuation. The court evaluated other valuations provided by Debtor's expert and concluded that Debtor had failed to prove "adequate protection in the form of any equity cushion, let alone an adequate equity cushion, to protect the lien interests of the existing lien holders, including Canyon, if the proposed DIP loan and priming lien are approved." [**In re Packard Square LLC,** 574 B.R. 107 (Bankr. E.D. Mich. 2017)]

(1) Post-Petition Interest Oversecured Creditors

While an oversecured creditor is entitled to the **accrual** of post-petition interest, this allowance does not entitle the oversecured creditor to **present payments** of post-petition interest. [B.C. § 506(b)] Adequate protection protects the secured creditor against a decrease in the collateral securing the creditor's loan. The accrual of post-petition interest increases Creditor's claim, which, in turn, shrinks any existing equity cushion. The shrinkage of the equity cushion, however, is not due to a decrease in the collateral value and should not trigger adequate protection. Thus, a bankruptcy court should not provide adequate protection to a creditor in a case in which post-petition interest payments erode the equity cushion. [3 Collier ¶ 361.03(1); *see* **United Savings Association of Texas v. Timbers of Inwood Forest Associates,** 484 U.S. 365 (1988)]

(2) Undersecured Creditors

The United States Supreme Court has held that the requirement of adequate protection does *not* entitle an undersecured creditor to receive compensation, i.e., interest, for the delay caused by the automatic stay in foreclosing on the creditor's collateral and reinvesting the proceeds. This decision construes adequate protection to mean protection against *depreciation in "the value of the collateral,"* and not protection of "a secured party's right to immediate foreclosure." [**Timbers,** *supra*] The Code provides secured creditors with other remedies to safeguard against unreasonable delay. These other remedies include seeking relief from the automatic stay for the purpose of foreclosure if the debtor has no equity in the collateral and there is no reasonable possibility of a successful reorganization [B.C. § 362(d)(2)], requesting conversion or dismissal of the case [B.C. § 1112(b)], or proposing a Chapter 11 plan of reorganization or liquidation after the debtor's period of exclusivity has expired. [B.C. § 1121(c)] [*In re* **Timbers of Inwood Forest Associates, Ltd.,** 808 F.2d 363 (5th Cir. 1987), *aff'd,* 484 U.S. 365 (1988)]

3. Valuation of Collateral

To determine what constitutes adequate protection in any particular case, it is necessary to ascertain the value of the collateral as accurately as possible. But, Congress did not specify how to determine value, instead leaving the determination to development by the courts. Congress did not anticipate development of a "hard and fast rule" to apply in all cases but rather recognized the importance of flexibility to allow courts to "adapt to varying circumstances and changing modes of financing." Congress also did not expect the courts to "construe the term value to mean, in every case, forced sale liquidation or going concern value", and noted the "wide latitude between those extremes." [H.R. Rep. No. 95–595, at 339 (1977)] Therefore, there is no single valuation standard. Congress anticipated a flexible approach with courts taking account of factors such as the *purpose of the valuation* and the *intended use or disposition of the collateral.* [B.C. § 506(a)]

4. Failure of Adequate Protection

If adequate protection is provided to a creditor whose claim is secured by a lien on property of the debtor, but the "adequate protection" eventually is shown to have been deficient, the secured creditor will receive an administrative expense claim with super-priority, which means priority over all other administrative expenses allowed in the case. [B.C. § 507(b)]

Note: The bankruptcy court may authorize the post-petition obtaining of unsecured credit or incurring of unsecured debt with *super super-priority.* The post-petition lender in such a case has priority over creditors with super-priority claims based on a deficiency in the adequate protection provided to them. [B.C. § 364(c)(1)]

5. Chapter 12 Cases

The adequate protection provisions of § 361 do not apply to a case under Chapter 12 concerning a family farmer or family fisherman. [B.C. § 1205(a)] The Code contains special rules for adequate protection in such cases. [B.C. § 1205(b)]

Adequate protection is a very important concept in bankruptcy. If you encounter an exam question involving adequate protection, remember that it is *within the court's discretion* to approve or disapprove it. Consider *all possible methods* that could protect against depreciation in the value of the creditor's collateral under the particular circumstances.

B. Use, Sale, or Lease of Property

1. In General

The use, sale, or lease of estate property, both in and out of the ordinary course of the debtor's business, is an integral part of the bankruptcy process, such as when the trustee liquidates a Chapter 7 debtor's estate, or when a debtor in possession or trustee is authorized to operate the debtor's business, farm or commercial fishing operation in a case under Chapter 11 or Chapter 12. [B.C. § 363]

a. Debtor in Possession

Ordinarily, a Chapter 11 or 12 debtor in possession has nearly all of the rights, powers, functions, and duties of a Chapter 11 trustee, including the right to use, sell, and lease property of the estate. [B.C. §§ 1107(a), 1203]

b. Chapter 13

There are also special provisions authorizing a debtor or a debtor engaged in business to use, sell, or lease property in a case under Chapter 13. [B.C. §§ 1303, 1304]

2. Out of Ordinary Course of Business

After *notice and a hearing,* a trustee or a debtor in possession may use, sell, or lease property of the estate out of the ordinary course of the debtor's business, unless the sale or lease involves *personally identifiable information,* in which case special rules apply. Whether any individual sale, use, or lease of property is deemed to be outside the ordinary course of business is a question of fact under the circumstances. [B.C. § 363(b)(1)]

a. Personally Identifiable Information

Customer lists and other customer information have value and, thus, a debtor may wish to sell such information during its bankruptcy case. In 2005, however, Congress created special rules for the *sale or lease* of personally identifiable information. The rules do not apply to the trustee's or debtor in possession's *use* of such personally identifiable information.

(i) Definition of Personally Identifiable Information

If an individual obtains a product or service from the debtor primarily for *personal, family, or household purposes,* then any of the following information constitutes *personally identifiable information* if provided in connection with obtaining that product or service:

(1) the individual's first name or initial, and last name [B.C. § 101(41A)(A)(i)];

(2) the address of the individual's residence [B.C. § 101(41A)(A)(ii)];

(3) the individual's electronic address, including an e-mail address [B.C. § 101(41A)(A)(iii)];

(4) a phone number dedicated to contacting the individual at her residence [B.C. § 101(41A)(A)(iv)];

(5) the individual's social security number [B.C. § 101(41A)(A)(v)];

(6) an account number of a credit card issued to the individual [B.C. § 101(41A)(A)(vi)];

(7) a birth date, number of a birth or adoption certificate, or a place of birth, if identified in connection with one or more of the items specified above in 1–6 [B.C. § 101(41A)(B)(i)]; or

(8) any other information about an identified individual that, if disclosed, will result in contacting or identifying such individual physically or electronically. [B.C. § 101(41A)(B)(ii)]

(ii) Requirements for Approving Sale or Lease of Personally Identifiable Information

If the debtor, in connection with offering a product or service, discloses to an individual a *policy prohibiting the transfer of personally identifiable information* to persons not affiliated with the debtor and if that *policy is in effect on the date debtor files for bankruptcy*, then the trustee or debtor in possession *cannot sell or lease personally identifiable information* to any person *unless*

(1) the sale or lease is *consistent with the policy* [B.C. § 363(b)(1)(A)]; or

(2) after appointment of a *consumer privacy ombudsman,* pursuant to § 332, and after notice and a hearing, the *court approves the sale or lease* giving due consideration to the facts, circumstances and conditions of the sale or lease *and* finds that there was no showing that the sale or lease would violate applicable nonbankruptcy law. [B.C. § 363(b)(1)(B)]

b. "Notice and a Hearing"

The Code authorizes the doing of an act *without a hearing* if appropriate notice is provided and no party in interest timely requests a hearing. [B.C. § 102(1)(B)(i); *see* H.R. Rep. No. 95–595, at 315 (1977) (stating that "[i]f there is no objection to the proposed action, the action may go ahead without court action" and noting that "[t]his is a significant change from present law, which requires the affirmative approval of the bankruptcy judge for almost every action")] Thus, for example, following proper notice to creditors in a Chapter 7 case, if no objection is made to a trustee's proposed liquidation of certain assets, the trustee may proceed to sell the property without obtaining a court order approving the sale. [B.C. § 363(b)(1); *see* Bankruptcy Rule 6004] The Bankruptcy Rules relax the notice requirement for small estates. [*See* B.C. § 102(1)(A) ("notice as is appropriate in the particular circumstances")] If the estate's non-exempt property has an aggregate gross value *less than $2,500,* then a *general notice of intent to sell* the property other than in the ordinary course suffices. [Bankruptcy Rule 6004(d)]

c. Business Judgment Test

Courts apply a *business judgment test* to decide whether to approve a use, sale, or lease of estate property outside the ordinary course of business. Under the business judgment test, the court defers to the debtor's decision so long as the decision was a fair and reasonable exercise of the debtor's business judgment. [*See **In re Alpha Natural Resources, Inc.,*** 546 B.R. 348 (Bankr. E.D. Va. 2016); *see also **In re Nine W. Holdings, Inc.,*** 2018 WL 3238695 (Bankr. S.D. N.Y. 2018) (court is not to "second guess" board's business judgment so long as board acted on an informed basis, in good faith, and in the honest belief the decision was in the firm's best interests)] The business judgment test applied by courts under § 363(b) is not the same as the business judgment rule applied outside bankruptcy to corporate law decisions. [3 Collier ¶ 363.02(4)]

d. Chapter 11 Case: Sales of Substantially All Assets

A sale of substantially all of the assets of a Chapter 11 estate raises questions of whether the sale is an effort to circumvent the protections afforded creditors under a Chapter 11 plan, e.g., disclosure, voting, confirmation. The concern is with the sale being the equivalent of a *sub rosa* plan. Such sales, while closely scrutinized by bankruptcy courts, are allowed. [*See **Florida Department of Revenue v. Piccadilly Cafeterias, Inc.,*** 554 U.S. 33 (2008) (stating in a footnote that while a Chapter 11 case normally ends with a confirmed reorganization plan, in some cases the debtor sells substantially all its assets prior to confirmation of a plan of liquidation)] The two most controversial cases of such sales were those in the GM and Chrysler bankruptcies during the height of the Great Recession. [*See **Indiana State Police Pension Trust v. Chrysler LLC (*In re* Chrysler LLC),*** 576 F.3d 108 (2d Cir. 2009), *cert. dismissed* 557 U.S. 961 (2009) (affirming bankruptcy court order approving sale, under § 363, of substantially all of Chrysler's assets and rejecting argument that sale transaction constituted a *sub rosa* plan); ***In re GMC,*** 407 B.R. 463 (Bankr. S.D. N.Y. 2009) (approving GM's motion for an order under § 363 to sell, pursuant to a master purchase and sale agreement, substantially all its assets, free and clear, to a buyer sponsored by the U.S. Treasury)] When there is no "need for speed," the assets are not perishable and value will not be lost waiting for plan confirmation, the plan proponent must demonstrate why "there is a need to sell prior to the plan confirmation hearing." [***In re Gulf Coast Oil, Corp.,*** 404 B.R. 407 (Bankr. S.D. Tex. 2009) (declining to approve sale of substantially all assets under § 363, noting that proponents of transaction sought to avoid the Congressional scheme that required bargaining, voting, and satisfaction of the requirements of § 1129)] Even though a court may approve a sale of substantially all of a debtor's assets, it will scrutinize the proposed transaction and may decline to approve certain portions of the transaction that it considers a *sub rosa* plan of reorganization. [***In re On-Site Sourcing, Inc.,*** 412 B.R. 817 (Bankr. E.D. Va. 2009) (approving motion for sale of substantially all assets because it was the best and only deal available, but excising certain provisions that "all furthered a *sub rosa* plan of reorganization")]

e. Secured Creditor's Right to Bid

Ordinarily, a secured creditor whose lien secures an allowed claim on property sold *outside the ordinary course of business* may "credit bid" at the sale of such property. By doing so, the secured creditor offsets her claim against the purchase price of the property. [B.C. § 363(k)]

3. In Ordinary Course of Business

A trustee or a debtor in possession who is authorized to operate the debtor's business may use, sell, or lease property of the estate in the ordinary course of business *without notice or a hearing,* unless the court orders otherwise. [B.C. § 363(c)(1)]

a. Determining Ordinary Course of Business

In determining whether a particular transaction is in or out of the *ordinary course of business,* the courts apply both of the following tests to the transaction: (i) the *vertical dimension test,* also known as the *reasonable expectations or creditor's expectation test,* and (ii) the *horizontal dimension test.* It is not clear whether *both tests* must be satisfied in order for the transaction to fall within § 364(c)'s ordinary course protection. [**Aalfs v. Wirum (*In re* Straightline Investments,** 525 F.3d 879 (9th Cir. 2008) (applying both tests)]

(i) Vertical Dimension Test

The *vertical dimension test* examines the debtor's normal business practices to determine whether the transaction subjects creditors to risks of a different character than the risks present when credit was extended. [**Crawforth v. Wheeler (*In re* Wheeler),** 444 B.R. 598 (Bankr. D. Idaho 2011)]

(ii) Horizontal Dimension Test

The *horizontal dimension test* compares the debtor's business to similar businesses and asks whether a similar business would enter into a transaction like the one proposed by the debtor's business. [**Aalfs v. Wirum (*In re* Straightline Investments,** 525 F.3d 879 (9th Cir. 2008) (concluding that sale of debtor's accounts did not satisfy the horizontal dimension test because purchaser of accounts "failed to show that the sale of accounts receivable by a custom milling business was the type of transaction 'that other similar businesses would engage in as ordinary business' ")]

b. Exception—Cash Collateral

The trustee or the debtor in possession may use, sell, or lease *cash collateral* in the *ordinary course of business only* if she obtains either *court authorization,* after notice and a hearing, or the *consent* of all entities having an interest in the cash collateral. [B.C. § 363(c)(2)]

(i) Definition

The Code defines "cash collateral" as cash, negotiable instruments, documents of title, securities, deposit accounts, and other cash equivalents in which both the debtor's estate and a third party have an interest. Cash collateral includes proceeds, rents, profits, products, or offspring of property in which an entity has an interest. It also includes fees, charges, accounts or other payments for hotel or motel rooms, or other lodging properties. [B.C. §§ 363(a); 552(b)] The Code's definition of cash collateral is expansive and covers situations that may not involve a security interest. For example, a bank having a right to set off its claim against the debtor's deposit account has a secured claim, by virtue of § 506(a); thus, that deposit account constitutes cash collateral. [3 Collier ¶ 363.03(3)]

(ii) Hearing

When a request is made for authorization to use cash collateral, usually time is of the essence. Thus, the court must act promptly to schedule a hearing *based on the needs of the debtor.* The hearing may be a preliminary hearing or may be consolidated with a hearing on adequate protection. If it is a preliminary hearing, the court may authorize the use, sale, or lease of cash collateral only if there is a *reasonable likelihood* that the trustee or the debtor in possession will prevail at the final hearing on adequate protection. [B.C. § 363(c)(3), (e); *see* Bankruptcy Rule 4001(b)]

(iii) Duty to Segregate

The trustee or the debtor in possession must **segregate and account for any cash collateral** in her possession, custody, or control, except to the extent that the cash collateral has been used, sold, or leased pursuant to court authorization. [B.C. § 363(c)(4)]

EXAM TIP   **GILBERT**

Suppose an exam question asks whether the debtor in possession may use cash collateral to pay the employees in the ordinary course of business. Your answer should explain that *either court authorization* or the secured party's *consent* is required. As a practical matter, the hearing on this issue will be very important, because a Chapter 11 case might abort if wages cannot be paid and the employees quit.

---

4. Automatic Stay

The trustee or debtor in possession may use, sell, or lease property in the ordinary or non-ordinary course only (i) in accordance with nonbankruptcy law governing the transfer of property by a corporation or nonprofit entity, or (ii) to the extent not inconsistent with any relief granted from the automatic stay. [B.C. §§ 363(d), 362(c)–(f); 3 Collier ¶ 363.04]

5. Adequate Protection

Upon the motion of an entity having an interest in property that is, or proposed to be, used, sold, or leased by the trustee or the debtor in possession, the court must **prohibit or condition** the use, sale, or lease in a manner that provides adequate protection of the entity's interest. [B.C. § 363(e); Bankruptcy Rule 4001(b)(1)(B)(iv)] The trustee or debtor in possession has the burden of proof on the issue of adequate protection. [B.C. § 363(p)(1)] In deciding the question of adequate protection, many courts consider the following factors:

- the **value** of the secured party's interest;

- the **risks** to the secured creditor's value that ensue from the use, sale, or lease of the property; and

- whether the adequate protection offered by the debtor protects the value as nearly as is possible against the risks, under the **"indubitable equivalent"** standard.

[*In re* **Puff,** 2010 WL 5018401 (Bankr. N.D. Iowa 2010)]

a. Insurance

Frequently, the use, sale, or lease of property may be **conditioned** on the procurement of insurance as one of the elements of adequate protection. [B.C. § 363(e)]

b. Unexpired Leases of Personal Property

While the Code requires adequate protection of a lessor's interest in personal property that is subject to an unexpired lease, this remedy is to the exclusion of relief from the automatic stay under § 362(d). [B.C. § 363(e)]

6. Ipso Facto or "Bankruptcy" Clauses

Subject to the requirements of § 365, the trustee or debtor in possession may use, sell, or lease property in or out of the ordinary course of business, or under the terms of a Chapter 11, 12, or 13 plan, notwithstanding provisions in a contract, lease, or nonbankruptcy law that otherwise would cause a forfeiture, modification, or termination of the debtor's interest in the property as a result of:

(a) *the insolvency or inadequate financial condition* of the debtor;

(b) *the commencement of a case* under the Bankruptcy Code concerning the debtor;

(c) *the appointment of a bankruptcy trustee or a nonbankruptcy custodian;* or

(d) *the seizure of property* by a bankruptcy trustee or a nonbankruptcy custodian.

[B.C. § 363(*l*)]

The trustee's or debtor in possession's sale, use, or lease of the property, however, is still subject to other restrictions on transfer or use that are unrelated to the debtor's filing for bankruptcy or financial situation. [*See* **Board of Trade v. Johnson,** 264 U.S. 1 (1924) (Bankruptcy Act case in which the Court held that the bankruptcy trustee could sell a seat on the Chicago Board of Trade owned by debtor only if the trustee satisfied the Board's rule that a seat owner could not sell his seat until he had paid debts owed to fellow Board of Trade seat owners)]

7. Sale Free and Clear

The trustee or the debtor in possession may sell property of the estate, either in or out of the ordinary course of business, free and clear of any interest in the property held by an entity other than the estate. The sale may proceed *only if one of the following* statutory requirements is satisfied:

(a) *applicable state or other nonbankruptcy law allows* a free-and-clear sale of the property [B.C. § 363(f)(1)];

(b) the entity holding the interest *consents to the sale* [B.C. § 363(f)(2)];

(c) *if the interest is a lien*, the *sale price for the property is greater than the total value of all liens* on the property [B.C. § 363(f)(3)];

   Note: Courts disagree about the meaning of "aggregate value of all liens." Some courts hold that the phrase means the *economic value* of all liens under § 506(a). Thus, the face amount of a lien held by an out-of-the-money junior lienholder (insufficient collateral value to cover junior lienholder's claim) would not count in determining the "aggregate value of all liens." [*See, e.g.,* **In re Collins,** 180 B.R. 447 (Bankr. E.D. Va. 1995)] Other courts hold that "aggregate value of all liens" means the *face value* of all liens. [*See, e.g.,* **Clear Channel Outdoor, Inc. v. Knupfer (*In re* PW, LLC),** 391 B.R. 25 (B.A.P. 9th Cir. 2008)]

(d) *there is a bona fide dispute* concerning the entity's interest in the property [B.C. § 363(f)(4)]; *or*

(e) *the entity holding the interest could be required to accept a money satisfaction* in a legal or equitable action. [B.C. § 363(f)(5)]

8. Sale Free and Clear Affecting Dower, Curtesy, or Co-Ownership Interests

a. Dower or Curtesy

Notwithstanding the conditions above for a *free and clear sale*, the trustee or the debtor in possession may sell property free and clear of an entity's *vested or contingent right of dower or curtesy.* [B.C. § 363(g)]

b. Co-Owner's Interest

If estate property is co-owned by the debtor and another entity, the trustee or the debtor in possession may *sell the interests of both* the estate *and* a tenant in common, a joint tenant, or a tenant by the entirety *only if all* of the following elements are satisfied:

(i) *it is impracticable to partition* the property between the estate and the co-owner [B.C. § 363(h)(1)];

(ii) *the amount realized* from the sale of the *estate's undivided interest* in the property is *substantially less* than from the sale of the property *free of the co-owner's interest* [B.C. § 363(h)(2)];

(iii) *the benefit to the estate* from a sale free of the co-owner's interest *outweighs any harm to the co-owner* [B.C. § 363(h)(3)]; *and*

(iv) *the property is not used in producing, transmitting, or distributing,* for the purpose of sale, *electric energy or gas* for heat, light, or power. [B.C. § 363(h)(4)]

c. Right of First Refusal

Before the completion of (i) a sale of property free and clear of dower or curtesy rights, (ii) a sale of a co-owner's interest in property, or (iii) a sale of community property, the debtor's spouse or a co-owner of the property may buy the property at the same price for which it is about to be sold. [B.C. §§ 363(i), (g), (h)]

d. Distribution of Proceeds

After a sale of property free and clear of dower or curtesy rights, or a sale of a co-owner's interest in property, the trustee or the debtor in possession must pay the appropriate portion of the proceeds to the debtor's spouse or the co-owner, less costs and expenses but without deducting for any compensation earned by the trustee. [B.C. § 363(j)]

9. Not Free and Clear: Consumer Credit Transactions

In 2005, Congress added a new provision to § 363 that addresses the sale of an interest in a consumer credit transaction or consumer credit contract. The sale of any interest in a consumer credit transaction subject to the Truth in Lending Act or any interest in a consumer credit contract, as defined at 16 C.F.R. § 433.1, is *not free and clear* of any claim or defense related to such consumer credit transaction or consumer credit contract. [B.C. § 363(o)] All claims and defenses that a consumer could raise to the sale outside bankruptcy apply to the buyer in a sale under the Bankruptcy Code.

10. Burden of Proof

In any hearing concerning the use, sale, or lease of property, the trustee or debtor in possession has the burden of proof regarding the question of adequate protection, while the entity claiming an interest in property bears the burden of showing the validity, priority, or extent of that interest. [B.C. § 363(p)]

11. Appeal: Mootness

Section 363(m) provides ***protection***, under certain circumstances, to the buyers or lessees of property ***against the reversal or modification on appeal*** of a sale or lease order. The provision is similar to that at § 364(e).

Absent a stay pending appeal, the validity of an authorization to sell or lease property, in or outside the ordinary course of business, is not affected by a reversal or modification on appeal if the purchaser or lessee acted in ***good faith,*** regardless of the purchaser's or lessee's knowledge of the appeal. [B.C. § 363(m)] Thus, in order to protect its rights, a party seeking to appeal a sale order must obtain a stay of that order pending appeal. A majority of circuits have held that § 363(m) creates "a *per se* rule automatically mooting appeals for failure to obtain a stay of the sale at issue." [**Parker v. Goodman (*In re* Parker),** 499 F.3d 616 (6th Cir. 2007)]

Courts have adopted ***no single definition*** of "good faith." A buyer who shows a lack of integrity during the course of sale proceedings, who engages in fraud or collusion, or who tries to take grossly unfair advantage of other bidders does not act in good faith. [***In re* GMC,** 407 B.R. 463 (Bankr. S.D. N.Y. 2009)]

a. Exceptions to Mootness Doctrine

Some courts have held that even if a stay pending appeal has not been obtained, the appeal will not be moot if (i) real property has been sold to a creditor involved in the appeal subject to a statutory right of redemption, or (ii) the transaction otherwise could be set aside under state law. [***In re* Mann,** 907 F.2d 923 (9th Cir. 1990); ***In re* Fuentes,** 2018 WL 2460283 (C.D. Cal. 2018)]

12. Collusive Sale

If the sale price of the estate property is controlled by an agreement among bidders, the trustee or debtor in possession may avoid the sale, or may recover damages from any of the conspirators equal to the value of the property minus the price paid, plus any costs, attorneys' fees, or expenses of obtaining relief. Moreover, in a case in which a party entered into such an agreement in willful disregard of this Code provision on collusive sales, recovery also may include punitive damages. [B.C. § 363(n)]

13. Sales and Use Taxes Permitted

The United States Supreme Court has held that a bankruptcy liquidation sale is not immune from a nondiscriminatory state sales or use tax. [**California State Board of Equalization v. Sierra Summit, Inc.,** 490 U.S. 844 (1989)]

C. Obtaining Credit

1. In General

A trustee, debtor in possession under Chapters 11 or 12, or a debtor engaged in business under Chapter 13 often needs to obtain credit or incur debt. The Code provides rules for the acquisition of both unsecured and secured credit or the incurring of debt. [B.C. § 364]

a. Chapter 13

A debtor engaged in business in a case under Chapter 13 ordinarily is permitted to operate the business and will be treated, for purposes of her entitlement to obtain credit, as having the rights of a trustee under § 364. [B.C. § 1304(b)]

2. In Ordinary Course of Business

Unless the court orders otherwise, a trustee or debtor in possession authorized to operate the debtor's business may procure *unsecured credit,* e.g., trade credit, and incur *unsecured debt* in the ordinary course of business without notice or a hearing. Such credit or debt is allowable as an *administrative expense.* [B.C. §§ 364(a), 503(b)(1)] Administrative expense claims, if not timely paid, are entitled to second level priority under § 507(a)(2).

3. Out of Ordinary Course of Business

After *notice and a hearing,* the court may approve the request of a trustee or debtor in possession to obtain unsecured credit or to incur unsecured debt *out of the ordinary course of business* as an *allowable expense of administration.* [B.C. § 364(b)] What happens, however, if a creditor fails to obtain court approval before lending money or extending credit to the debtor out of the ordinary course of the debtor's business? The courts have reached different conclusions. Some courts allow for retroactive approval of the creditor's claim as an administrative expense, but normally only under extraordinary circumstances. [*See In re* **Ockerlund Construction Co.,** 308 B.R. 325 (Bankr. N.D. Ill. 2004) (citing cases); *see also* *In re* **Ohio Valley Amusement Co.,** 2008 WL 5062464 (Bankr. N.D. W.Va. 2008) (holding that creditor's loans to debtor were outside the ordinary course of business and denying *nunc pro tunc* approval of two loans made without prior court approval)] Other courts deny the creditor an administrative expense claim priority but treat the creditor's claim as a general unsecured claim. Some courts, however, have gone so far as to find that a creditor that fails to obtain court approval for a post-petition loan or extension of credit has no bankruptcy claim at all and, thus, is not entitled to participate in any distribution during the bankruptcy case. [*See In re* **Ockerlund Construction Co.,** 308 B.R. 325 (Bankr. N.D. Ill. 2004) (holding that the "holder of a post-petition 'claim" that is not entitled to administrative-expense priority cannot be a creditor, cannot file a proof of claim, and, even if he could file one, cannot by definition have an 'allowed' claim as of the petition date"); *see also* 3 Collier ¶ 364.03(2)]

4. Priority or Security

Prospective post-petition lenders may not be satisfied with an administrative expense priority even though it is the second category of unsecured claims to be paid. [B.C. §§ 503(b)(1), 507(a)(2)] Thus, when the trustee or debtor in possession is *unable* to obtain unsecured credit without offering more than an administrative expense, the court, after notice and a hearing, may authorize credit to be acquired or debt to be incurred:

(a) with *super super-priority status* entitling the creditor to payment ahead of not only all administrative expense claims but also any super-priority administrative expense claims resulting from the failure of adequate protection [B.C. §§ 364(c)(1), 361, 507(b)];

(b) secured by a *lien on unencumbered estate property* [B.C. § 364(c)(2)]; *or*

(c) secured by a *junior lien on encumbered estate property.* [B.C. § 364(c)(3)]

The trustee or debtor in possession may ask the court for any combination of the alternatives provided under § 364(c). The trustee or debtor in possession must show "that it has reasonably attempted, but failed, to obtain unsecured credit under sections 364(a) or (b)." [*In re* **Ames Department Stores, Inc.,** 115 B.R. 34 (Bankr. S.D.N.Y. 1990)] Some courts have adopted a three-part test to determine whether to authorize a post-petition loan or extension of credit under § 364(c): (1) Was the debtor unable to obtain unsecured credit with an administrative expense priority? (2) Is the transaction necessary to preserve estate assets? and (3) Are the transaction's terms fair, reasonable, and adequate, given the debtor's circumstances and the proposed lender? [*In re* **L.A. Dodgers LLC,** 457 B.R. 308 (Bankr. D. Del. 2011); *see also In re* **Republic Airways Holdings, Inc.,** 2016 WL 2616717 (Bankr. S.D. N.Y. 2016)] In the motion seeking relief pursuant to § 364(c), the trustee or debtor in possession must "describe the nature and extent" of any provision in the credit or loan agreement that grants priority or a lien on estate property and also identify the location of such a provision in the proposed agreement and order. [Bankruptcy Rule 4002(c)(1)(B)(i)]

5. Priming Lien

If the trustee or the debtor in possession cannot obtain credit on any basis other than by the grant of a senior or equal lien on property that already is encumbered, the court, after notice and a hearing, may approve new credit or debt to be secured by a lien on estate property that will be *senior or equal* to any lien held by another entity on the same property. The trustee or debtor in possession must show that "less burdensome financing is unavailable," but it is not necessary to demonstrate that credit was sought "from every possible lender." [*In re* **Vegt,** 499 B.R. 631 (Bankr. N.D. Iowa 2013) (finding that requirement that credit is unavailable elsewhere was satisfied because financing had been sought unsuccessfully from between 15 to 20 other lenders)] Adequate protection must be provided to the original lienholder, and the trustee or debtor in possession bears the burden of proof on the issue of adequate protection. [B.C. § 364(d)]

EXAM TIP   🔖GILBERT

If you have an exam question concerning (i) a trustee, (ii) a Chapter 11 or Chapter 12 debtor in possession, or (iii) a Chapter 13 debtor engaged in business who needs to obtain credit or incur debt, you will need to remember the following rules.

(a) Generally, the trustee or debtor in possession may obtain *unsecured credit or incur unsecured debt in the ordinary course of business* without notice or a hearing, and it is allowable as an administrative expense.

(b) Obtaining *unsecured credit or incurring unsecured debt that is out of the ordinary course of business* requires prior court approval after notice and the opportunity for a hearing. Otherwise, the creditor's claim may be denied administrative expense status.

(c) In circumstances in which the trustee or debtor in possession can prove that it made a reasonable attempt but was unable to obtain unsecured credit or debt on an administrative expense basis, the court, after notice and opportunity for a hearing, may authorize credit or debt:

   (i) with a super super-priority that is *ahead of all other administrative expenses*, including a super-priority claim for the failure of adequate protection;

   (ii) *secured* by a lien on estate property that is unencumbered; or

   (iii) *secured* by a junior lien on estate property that is encumbered.

(d) If the trustee or debtor in possession cannot obtain credit or incur debt on any basis other than by granting to the creditor a lien that is senior or equal to an existing lien on estate property, the court, after notice and opportunity for a hearing, may authorize a *priming lien,* but only if the original lienholder is given *adequate protection.*

---

6. Certain Other Provisions in Post-Petition Lending Agreements

Post-petition financing agreements may contain controversial provisions that require the court to scrutinize the terms for fairness to the bankruptcy estate. The Bankruptcy Rules provide that a motion to authorize the obtaining of post-petition credit must describe the nature and extent of any of these controversial provisions and identify their specific location in the proposed agreement and order. [Bankruptcy Rule 4001(c)(1)(B)]

a. Cross-Collateralization

Cross-collateralization occurs when a pre-petition lender agrees to lend to the debtor post-petition but wants a security interest in unencumbered estate property to secure not only the post-petition loan but also existing pre-petition unsecured claims against the debtor. The Eleventh Circuit has held that cross-collateralization is an "impermissible means of obtaining post-petition financing" because it is "contrary to the basic priority structure of the Code." [*See In re* **Saybrook Manufacturing Co.**, 963 F.2d 1490 (11th Cir. 1992)] Other courts have found the use of cross-collateralization permissible under certain circumstances. [*See In re* **Ellingsen MacLean Oil Co.**, 834 F.2d 599 (6th Cir. 1987) (noting that while controversial, cross-collateralization "is often used, and even the courts that discourage it have approved its use")] A motion for post-petition financing that includes a cross-collateralization provision must specifically identify the location of such provision in the proposed agreement and order, and describe the nature and extent of the provision. [Bankruptcy Rule 4001(c)(1)(B)(ii)]

b. Roll-Ups

In a roll-up, there is a pre-petition lender with pre-petition debt that agrees to lend to the debtor post-petition. Prior to the post-petition loan, that lender has pre-petition debt and pre-petition collateral securing that debt. The lender agrees to extend credit post-petition secured by post-petition collateral, but "as opposed to segregating the pre-petition collateral and applying it to pre-petition debt and applying post-petition collateral to the post-petition debt, *all* of the cash collateral generated by the debtor is applied first to reduce the pre-petition debt." [*See In re* **Cranberry Growers Cooperative**, 592 B.R. 325 (Bankr. W.D. Wis. 2018)] As a result, the lender's pre-petition debt is "rolled up" into the lender's post-petition debt; the total post-petition debt is the sum of the pre-petition debt and any post-petition extensions of credit made by the lender. [*See In re* **Cranberry Growers**, *supra*] A motion for post-petition financing that includes a "roll up" must specifically identify the location of such provision in the proposed agreement and order, and describe the nature and extent of the provision. [Bankruptcy Rule 4001(c)(1)(B)(ii)]

7. Notice and Hearing

A motion for authority to obtain credit must be accompanied by a copy of the credit agreement and a proposed order. [Bankruptcy Rule 4001(c)(1)(A)] The court ***cannot commence a final hearing*** on the motion ***earlier than 14 days*** after service of the motion. The movant may request that the court conduct a hearing before that 14-day period expires, but the court may authorize the obtaining of credit only to avoid ***immediate and irreparable harm to the estate pending a final hearing.*** [Bankruptcy Rule 4001(c)(2)]

8. Appeal

Absent a stay pending appeal, the validity of the court's order authorizing the debtor to obtain credit or to incur debt, or the validity of any lien or priority granted by the court under § 364, is not affected by a reversal or modification on appeal, so long as the lender acted in ***good faith.*** This rule applies even if the lender knew of the appeal. [B.C. § 364(e)]

D. Executory Contracts and Unexpired Leases

1. Definitions

The Bankruptcy Code does not define the terms "executory contract" or "unexpired lease." Thus, the courts have attempted to construe these terms in the bankruptcy context when applying § 365's provisions on assumption or rejection.

a. Executory Contract

In determining whether a contract is executory, many courts look to see whether the contractual obligations of ***the debtor and the nondebtor party*** are " 'so far unperformed that the failure of either to complete performance would constitute a material breach excusing performance of the other.' " [**Lewis Bros. Bakeries Inc. v. Interstate Brands Corp. (*In re* Interstate Bakeries Corp.),** 751 F.3d 955 (8th Cir. 2014); ***In re* Calpine Corp.,** 2008 WL 3154763 (Bankr. S.D. N.Y. 2008)] Professor Vern Countryman of Harvard Law School developed this "material breach" test. The contract is not executory under the Countryman test if the payment of money is the only remaining obligation. [*See* **Holzer v. Barnard,** 2016 WL 4046767 (E.D. N.Y. 2016)] Some courts, however, use the ***functional approach*** to determine whether a contract is executory. [**Holzer,** *supra* (stating that courts in the Second Circuit had "adopted two different standards as to executory contracts"—the Countryman test and the functional approach)] Under the functional approach, a court may deem a contract executory, even if *only one* party has outstanding material obligations under the contract, if "assumption[ ] [or] rejection would ultimately benefit the estate and its creditors.' " [**Thompkins v. Lil' Joe Records, Inc.,** 476 F.3d 1294 (11th Cir. 2007)] While no Court of Appeals has rejected the Countryman test, the Eleventh Circuit has used the functional test in some cases. [3 Collier ¶ 365.02(2)(a); *see* **Lil' Joe Records,** *supra* (noting that bankruptcy court had used the functional approach, which the Eleventh Circuit had "tacitly approved in [its] precedent")]

(i) Options

Most courts have held that a paid-for but unexercised option is an executory contract. Those courts that have held that such options are not executory contracts have rested their decisions on the fact that the optionor owes no performance unless and until the option is exercised. [*See* **COR Route 5 Co., LLC v. Penn Traffic Co. (*In re* Penn Traffic Co.),** 524 F.3d 373 (2d Cir. 2008) (listing cases)]

b. Unexpired Lease

Under § 365, an unexpired lease must be a true lease, rather than one intended as a secured transaction. The bankruptcy court should use applicable state law in making this determination. [***In re* Montgomery Ward, LLC,** 469 B.R. 522 (Bankr. D. Del. 2012)] Courts look to the economic realities of the transaction, not to the labels that the parties assign to it. [*See* S. Rep. No. 95–989 at 64 (stating, in the context of real property, that "[t]he distinction between a true lease and a financing transaction is based upon the economic substance of the transaction and not, for example, upon the locus of title, the form of the transaction or the fact that the transaction is denominated a lease")]

To distinguish between a true lease and a security agreement, courts often consider the provisions of § 1–203(b) of the Uniform Commercial Code.

(i) If the *lessee can terminate* the transaction, then the transaction is more likely a lease than a secured sale. [**Hitchin Post Steak Co. v. GE Capital Corp. (*In re* HP Distribution, LLP),** 436 B.R. 679 (Bankr. D. Kan. 2010)]

(ii) If the *lessee cannot terminate* the transaction *and* can *renew the lease* for the *remaining economic life* of the goods for *no additional or nominal additional consideration* or has an *option to purchase* for *no additional or nominal additional consideration,* then the transaction is a secured sale, not a lease. [U.C.C. §§ 1–203(b)(3), (4)]

(iii) If the lessee *cannot terminate* the transaction *and* the lease term is equal to or greater than the *remaining economic life of the goods,* then the transaction is a secured sale, not a lease. [U.C.C. § 1–203(b)(1)]

e.g. **Example:** Prior to filing for bankruptcy, Debtor signed an agreement called a "lease" with Creditor for a vehicle. The vehicle has an economic life of 15 years, and the lease is for a five-year term. Debtor can terminate the agreement, but if she decides not to do so she has the option to buy the vehicle at the end of five years for a price that is equal to the reasonably predicted market value at that time. The transaction is a lease; it is structured so that Creditor/Lessor retains a valuable reversionary interest in the vehicle. [*See* U.C.C. § 1–203(c)(6)]

e.g. **Example:** Prior to filing for bankruptcy, Debtor signed an agreement called a "lease" with Creditor for a vehicle. The vehicle has an economic life of 15 years. The lease term is five years, and Debtor cannot terminate the agreement. The reasonably predicted market value of the vehicle in five years is $7,600. The agreement gives Debtor the option to buy the vehicle for $10. The transaction is a disguised sale, not a lease. The transaction is structured so as to give Debtor an enormous incentive to purchase the vehicle in five years; thus, Creditor/Lessor did not expect to receive the vehicle back from Debtor at the time that the parties signed the "lease." [*See* U.C.C. § 1–203(c)(6)]

2. Assumption or Rejection: General Principles

The debtor in possession or trustee, with the court's approval, may assume or reject an executory contract or an unexpired lease of the debtor. [B.C. § 365(a)] A motion is required, as are reasonable notice and an opportunity for a hearing. [Bankruptcy Rules 6006, 9014] In a case under Chapters 11, 12, or 13, assumption or rejection also may occur by a permissive provision in a confirmed plan. [B.C. §§ 1123(b)(2), 1222(b)(6), 1322(b)(7)]

a. Court Approval Mandatory

Assumption or rejection by conduct alone is not valid because the Code requires judicial authorization, except when rejection occurs automatically upon the expiration of certain statutory time limits placed on the power to assume or reject. [B.C. § 365(a); *In re* **Robb & Stucky, Ltd., LLLP,** 2011 WL 3948805 (Bankr. M.D. Fla. 2011)]

e.g. **Example:** Debtor, operating its business as a debtor in possession, made post-petition premium payments to Insurance Agent, pursuant to certain insurance policies. The payments represented both post-petition and pre-petition insurance coverage; no court approval was obtained to assume the agreements. Several months later, Debtor decided to reject the contracts, but Insurance Agent asserted that they had already been assumed by Debtor's post-petition conduct. The court ruled against Insurance Agent and noted that it was the rare case in which a debtor in possession's conduct constitutes assumption of an agreement under § 365. "The more generally followed rule is that acceptance of benefits (i.e. 'conduct') under an executory contract does not in and of itself work an assumption." Therefore, Insurance Agent had to repay the amounts received in payment of the pre-petition portion of the indebtedness. [*In re* **A. H. Robins Co.,** 68 B.R. 705 (Bankr. E.D. Va. 1986)]

b. Business Judgment Rule

A majority of courts apply a ***business judgment*** test to the debtor in possession's or trustee's decision to assume or reject an executory contract or an unexpired lease. The test requires the court to put " 'itself in the position of the trustee or debtor in possession and determin[e] whether assuming the contract would be a good business decision or a bad one.' " The test "presupposes that the estate will assume a contract only where doing so will be to its economic advantage and will reject contracts whose performance would benefit the counterparty at the expense of the estate." [**Cor Route 5 Co., LLC v. Penn Traffic Co. (***In re* **Penn Traffic Co.),** 524 F.3d 373 (2d Cir. 2008)] While the ***business judgment*** test is not identical to the ***business judgment rule*** that courts use to review corporate decisions, it does have "similar factors" to the business judgment rule. [*In re* **The Great Atlantic & Pacific Tea Company, Inc.,** 544 B.R. 43 (Bankr. S.D. N.Y. 2016)]

e.g. **Example:** Debtor has a contract with Creditor to deliver 1,000 widgets for $10,000. Debtor files for bankruptcy and at that time the parties have not performed the contract. If performing the contract will cost $5,000, then the debtor in possession or trustee will assume the contract in order to obtain the benefit for the estate. If, however, it will cost $15,000 to supply the widgets, then there is no benefit to the estate and the debtor in possession or trustee will reject the contract. [*See In re* **Giordano,** 446 B.R.744 (Bankr. E.D. Va. 2010)]

(i) Exception: Collective Bargaining Agreements

In a Chapter 11 case, the rejection of a collective bargaining agreement is governed by the standards set forth in Bankruptcy Code § 1113, not by the business judgment test.

c. Assume or Reject in Entirety

The trustee or debtor in possession may not assume the benefits and reject the burdens of an executory contract or an unexpired lease. The contract or lease must be either assumed or rejected in its entirety. [*In re* **Hagood Reserve, LLC,** 2010 WL 5067444 (Bankr. W.D. N.C. 2010); *In re* **AbitibiBowater Inc.,** 418 B.R. 815 (Bankr. D. Del. 2009)]

d. Pre-Bankruptcy Termination

The trustee or debtor in possession cannot assume a contract or a lease that has been legally terminated prior to the commencement of the bankruptcy case, with no right to cure. [*See, e.g., In re* **DBSI, Inc.,** 407 B.R. 159 (Bankr. D. Del. 2009)]

3. Assumption of Contracts and Leases in Default

If the debtor in possession is not in default of the obligations under an executory contract or an unexpired lease, then the debtor in possession or trustee may assume and, perhaps, assign the contract or lease. In a case in which the debtor in possession is in default, whether the default occurred pre- or post-petition, the trustee or debtor in possession may assume an executory contract or an unexpired lease *only* if the following three requirements are met at the time of assumption. [B.C. § 365(b)(1)]

a. Cure

With certain exceptions, the trustee or debtor in possession must *cure* the default or provide *adequate assurance* that the default will be *cured promptly.* [B.C. § 365(b)(1)(A)] The Code does not define what constitutes a prompt cure. Thus, the issue is whether a debtor may cure over the entire length of the debtor's plan or whether prompt cure requires payment over some shorter period of time. The facts and circumstances of each case shape the court's determination of whether cure is prompt. [*In re* **M. Fine Lumber Co., Inc.,** 383 B.R. 565 (Bankr. E.D. N.Y. 2008)]

e.g. **Example:** Married Debtors filed for relief under Chapter 13. At the time of their bankruptcy filing, they owed approximately $1,400 in pre-petition arrearages on a car lease. Debtors proposed curing the arrearages by making payments over the 51 months of their Chapter 13 plan. Lessor objected and argued that Debtors had to complete their cure prior to the expiration of the vehicle lease. The bankruptcy court agreed with Lessor. The court explained that some courts had held that in a consumer case cure could not extend beyond six months while other courts had held that defaults had to be cured prior to the end of the lease term. The bankruptcy court concluded that it did not have to decide the appropriate time frame, because Lessor had asked that Debtors be required to cure by the lease termination date. The court held that Lessor's request was reasonable and that Debtors had to cure the pre-petition arrearages by the end of the lease's term rather than allowing Debtors to cure over the plan's 51-month period. [*In re* **Coffman,** 339 B.R. 829 (Bankr. S.D. Ohio 2008)]

(i) Exceptions to Requirement of Cure

There are a number of exceptions to the requirement that the debtor in possession or trustee cure any default prior to assumption. The exceptions apply to the breach of any of the following provisions that the parties' contract defines as a default:

(1) the debtor's *financial condition or insolvency* at any time before the bankruptcy case closes [B.C. § 365(b)(2)(A)];

(2) the debtor's *filing for bankruptcy* [B.C. § 365(b)(2)(B)];

(3) the appointment of a *bankruptcy trustee* or a *custodian prior to bankruptcy* [B.C. § 365(b)(2)(C)];

(4) the *taking possession of property* by a bankruptcy trustee or custodian prior to bankruptcy [B.C. § 365(b)(2)(C)];

(5) failure to satisfy a *penalty rate or a penalty provision* arising from the debtor's failure to perform *nonmonetary obligations* under the lease or executory contract [B.C. § 365(b)(2)(D)]; or

(6) except for a penalty rate or penalty provision, the failure to perform *nonmonetary obligations* under an unexpired *lease of real property,* if it is impossible to perform such obligations at or after the time of assumption [B.C. § 365(b)(1)(A)]. *Note:* This exception applies *only* to real property leases.

(ii) Amendments to the Code's Cure Provisions

(1) 1994 Amendments and Cure

In 1994, Congress created an exception to the cure requirement such that the debtor in possession or trustee prior to assumption did not have to satisfy "any penalty rate or provision relating to a default arising from any failure by the debtor to perform nonmonetary obligations under the executory contract or unexpired lease." [Pub. Law 103–394 § 219(a)(3), 108 Stat. 4106] This provision is codified at § 365(b)(1)(D), and with the 2005 amendments now reads "penalty rate or penalty provision."

(2) BAPCPA and Cure

Prior to BAPCPA's passage, § 365(b)(2)(D) excepted from the requirement of cure "any penalty rate or provision relating to a default arising from any failure by the debtor to perform nonmonetary obligations under the executory contract or unexpired lease." [B.C. § 365(b)(2)(D) *pre-BAPCPA*] There was a split of authority as to the meaning of this provision. Some courts interpreted the language to mean that the debtor did not have to cure a penalty rate *or any other provision* relating to a default stemming from the breach of a nonmonetary obligation. Other courts read the word "penalty" as modifying *both* rate and provision, thereby limiting the exception to *penalty rates and penalty provisions* arising from nonmonetary defaults. In 2005, Congress amended § 365(b)(2)(D) by adding the word "penalty" before provision, thereby changing the language from "penalty rate or provision" to "penalty rate or penalty provision." [*See In re* **Empire Equities Capital Corp.,** 405 B.R. 687 (Bankr. S.D. N.Y. 2009)]

In 2005, Congress also amended § 365(b)(1)(A) to provide an exception to the Code's cure requirement for an ***unexpired lease of real property*** if the debtor's ***default*** relates to a ***nonmonetary obligation*** that ***cannot be cured*** at or after the time that the trustee assumes the lease. The exception to the cure requirement in such a case, however, does *not* apply to a penalty rate or penalty provision, which means that the debtor in possession or trustee must cure a breach of a penalty rate or penalty provision prior to assuming an unexpired lease of real property. [3 Collier ¶ 365.06(3)(c)] At the same time, Congress provided that for a nonmonetary default arising from failure to abide by the terms of a commercial real property lease the debtor in possession or trustee may cure by performing according to the lease terms after assumption and by providing compensation for pecuniary losses. [B.C. § 365(b)(1)(A)]

(3) What Does It All Mean?

The amendments to § 365(b), both in 1994 and in 2005, are not models of clarity. There are a few points on which most courts are in agreement, but a number of issues on which there is a split of authority or remaining questions of interpretation.

(a) Courts in Agreement

(i) The debtor in possession or trustee may assume an ***unexpired lease of real property*** without curing a default as to a nonmonetary obligation that is impossible to cure at the time of assumption.

(ii) The debtor in possession or trustee cannot assume an ***executory contract or an unexpired lease of personal property*** if, at the time of assumption, it is impossible to cure the debtor's default of a nonmonetary obligation under the lease or executory contract.

e.g. **Example:** Debtor purchased an option from Capital to buy several loans secured by real property. The option expired on April 30, 2009 at 12 p.m. Debtor filed for relief under Chapter 11 39 minutes prior to expiration of the option, and argued that § 365 provided it with the time necessary to raise the money to purchase the loans and assume the contract. The court held that debtor's default—its failure to exercise the option within the time provided—was material and uncurable. The court noted that the case involved a non-lease executory contract and that BAPCPA's amendments "establish[ed] that a debtor must cure most defaults arising from an executory contract that is not a real property lease." Because debtor's failure to timely exercise the option was not curable, the contract could not be assumed under § 365. (*Note:* The court did hold, however, that § 108(b) extended the option period for 60 days from the bankruptcy filing.) [*In re* **Empire Equities Capital Corp.**, 405 B.R. 687 (Bankr. S.D. N.Y. 2009); *see also* **Quantum Diversified Holdings, Inc. v. Wienheimer (***In re* **Escarent Entities, L.P.**), 423 Fed. Appx. 462 (5th Cir. 2011) (holding that debtor could not assume contract because it could not cure non-monetary, material default in executory contract)]

(iii) The debtor in possession or trustee must cure a default of a penalty rate or penalty provision before assuming an unexpired lease for real property. [B.C. § 365(b)(1)(A); 3 Collier ¶ 365.06(3)(c)]

(b) Questions of Interpretation

The amendments in 1994 and 2005 created some interpretation questions that remain unresolved.

(i) It is unclear whether the Code's language "relating to a default arising from any failure by the debtor to perform nonmonetary obligations" applies to *both* "penalty rate" and "penalty provision" or only to "penalty provision." If the language applies only to "penalty provision," then the debtor need not cure any penalty rate, regardless of whether it arises from a failure by the debtor of a *monetary or nonmonetary* obligation. [B.C. § 365(b)(2)(D); *see, e.g.,* **In re Zamani**, 390 B.R. 680 (Bankr. N.D. Cal. 2008) (holding that § 365(b)(2)(D)'s cure exception, incorporated into § 1124(2), relieved the debtor of satisfying any penalty interest rate related to a monetary or nonmonetary default)]

(ii) The 2005 amendments to § 365(b)(1)(A) provide that if "such default" arises from the failure of the debtor to abide by the terms of a non-residential real property lease, then the trustee may cure by performing according to the lease terms after assumption and providing compensation for pecuniary losses. The problem is that it is unclear what prior default Congress intended to reference when it used "such default:" the default that § 365(b) requires be cured as a condition of assumption *or* the default of a nonmonetary obligation that is impossible to cure. Collier concludes that the words "such default" refer back to nonmonetary obligation as a "substitute for cure of an incurable obligation." [3 Collier ¶ 365.06(3)(c); *see* **In re Patriot Place, Ltd.**, 486 B.R. 773 (Bankr. W.D. Tex. 2013) (holding that in the case of a nonmonetary default of a "nonresidential (commercial) real property lease, as long as [debtor] is not currently committing a nonmonetary default at the time of assumption, then it is performing under the lease and § 365(b)(1)(A) will excuse any previous uncurable nonmonetary defaults")]

b. Compensation

The trustee or debtor in possession must *compensate* or provide adequate assurance of prompt compensation to the non-debtor party for any *monetary loss* caused by the default [B.C. § 365(b)(1)(B)]; and

c. Adequate Assurance of Future Performance

The trustee or debtor in possession must furnish *adequate assurance of future performance* of the executory contract or the unexpired lease. [B.C. § 365(b)(1)(C)]

(i) Criteria

In deciding whether the trustee has provided adequate assurance of future performance, the courts consider a number of factors, including the following: (i) the debtor's payment history; (ii) the debtor's profitability, if in business; (iii) the existence of a guarantee or other monies on deposit or dedicated to payment on the lease or executory contract; and (iv) the overall economic prognosis for the debtor's industry. [*See, e.g., In re* **M. Fine Lumber Co., Inc.,** 383 B.R 565 (Bankr. E.D. N.Y. 2008)]

(ii) Shopping Center Leases

The Bankruptcy Code is more specific with respect to the elements of "adequate assurance of future performance of a lease of real property in a shopping center." [B.C. § 365(b)(3)]

(1) "Shopping Center"

The Code does not define the term "shopping center." The decision as to whether the lease is in a shopping center is made on a case-by-case basis and courts normally consider a number of factors, including "combination of leases, whether all leases are held by [a] single landlord, [the] presence of common parking area, [the] existence of [a] master lease, and [the] contiguity of stores." [**Androse Associations of Allaire, LLC v. A&P (*In re* A&P),** 472 B.R. 666 (Bankr. S.D. N.Y. 2011)] The most important factors likely are " 'a combination of leases held by a single landlord leased to commercial retail distributors of goods, with the presence of a common parking area.' " [*In re* **Ames Department Stores, Inc.,** 348 B.R. 91 (Bankr. S.D. N.Y. 2006) (quoting Collier)]

(2) "Adequate Assurance"

In the context of a shopping center lease, adequate assurance of future performance includes adequate assurance:

(a) of the *source of the rent* due under the lease [B.C. § 365(b)(3)(A)];

(b) if the lease is assumed and assigned, that the *financial condition and operating performance* of the proposed assignee and any guarantors is similar to the financial condition and operating performance of the debtor and any guarantors as of the time that the debtor became the lessee under the lease [B.C. § 365(b)(3)(A)];

    (c) of the *continuation,* without a significant decrease, of any *percentage rent* required by the lease [B.C. § 365(b)(3)(B)];

    (d) that *assumption or assignment* of the lease is *subject to all lease terms,* including provisions concerning location, use, radius, or exclusivity [B.C. § 365(b)(3)(C)]; and

    (e) that *assumption or assignment* will *not disrupt any tenant mix or balance* in the shopping center. [B.C. § 365(b)(3)(D)]

d. Incidental Services and Supplies

Prior to the assumption of an unexpired lease in default, other than a default under § 365(b)(2), the lessor is not obligated to provide incidental services or supplies, unless the trustee or debtor in possession pays, according to the terms of the lease, for any services or supplies furnished before assumption. [B.C. § 365(b)(4)]

4. Assignment

The trustee or debtor in possession may assign an executory contract or an unexpired lease only after assuming the contract or lease and providing adequate assurance of the assignee's future performance, regardless of whether there has been a default. [B.C. § 365(f)(2)] Unless assumption and assignment are provided for under the terms of the debtor's plan, the trustee or debtor in possession must file a motion to assume and assign an executory contract or unexpired lease. Reasonable notice and an opportunity for a hearing must be afforded to the party against whom relief is sought. [Bankruptcy Rules 6006(a), 9014(a)]

a. Ineffectiveness of Restrictions on Assignment

Except as discussed below, an assignment that complies with the requirements of § 365(f)(2) is valid, notwithstanding any provision in the contract or lease or in applicable nonbankruptcy law that prohibits, restricts, or conditions the assignment, or that terminates or modifies the contract or lease because of the assignment. [B.C. §§ 365(f)(1), (3)]

b. Liability of Trustee

The assignment of an executory contract or an unexpired lease has the effect of relieving the trustee and the estate from any liability resulting from a breach occurring after the assignment. [B.C. § 365(k)]

c. Landlord's Deposit

The assignment of an unexpired lease under which the debtor is the lessee entitles the lessor to demand substantially the same deposit or other security that she would have required under the original lease from a comparable tenant. [B.C. § 365(*l*)]

5. Agreements Not Assumable or Assignable

The trustee may not assume or assign certain kinds of executory contracts and unexpired leases. [B.C. § 365(c)]

a. Personal Service Contracts and Government Contracts

If *applicable nonbankruptcy law* excuses the nondebtor party from accepting performance from, or furnishing performance to, an entity other than the debtor or the debtor in possession, the trustee may not assume or assign the contract or lease, unless the nondebtor party consents. [B.C. § 365(c)(1)] The prohibition against assumption and assignment is not limited solely to personal service contracts. [*See, e.g., **In re** **Virgin** **Offshore USA, Inc.,*** 2013 WL 4854312 (E.D. La. 2013) (nonexclusive intellectual property licenses cannot be assigned without the licensor's consent); ***In re* XMH Corp.,** 647 F.3d 690 (7th Cir. 2011) (trademark license not assignable without consent of trademark owner)] Likewise, a debtor in possession is prohibited from assigning such a contract or lease without the other party's consent, although the law is not settled as to whether a debtor in possession may *assume and perform,* rather than *assume and assign,* a contract of this kind.

(i) Hypothetical Versus Actual Performance Test

Can a Chapter 11 debtor in possession *assume and perform* a contract or lease that it could **not** *assume and assign* because of the prohibition at § 365(c)(1)? A majority of the Courts of Appeal to address the issue have adopted the "hypothetical test." Under the hypothetical test, "if the debtor in possession lacks hypothetical authority to assign a contract, then it may not assume it—even if the debtor in possession has no *actual* intention of assigning the contract to another." [**N.C.P. Marketing Group v. B.G. Star Products,** 556 U.S. 1145 (2009) (statement of Justice Kennedy, joined by Justice Breyer, regarding denial of petition for certiorari)] The problem with the hypothetical test, of course, is that the third party originally contracted with the debtor (now the debtor in possession in Chapter 11); thus, the concerns underlying § 365(c)(1) of the Code, e.g., forcing a third party to accept performance of a non-delegable duty, simply do not apply if it is the original contracting party assuming performance of its original contractual obligations.

The First Circuit and most bankruptcy courts faced with the issue have adopted the "actual performance test." Under the "actual performance test," the bankruptcy court must determine whether the debtor in possession intends to assign the contract or lease after assumption. [**Institut Pasteur v. Cambridge Biotech Corp.,** 104 F.3d 489 (1st Cir. 1997)] If not, then the debtor in possession may assume the executory contract or unexpired lease.

b. Contracts to Loan Money or to Issue Securities

The trustee or debtor in possession may not assume or assign an executory contract (i) to make a loan or to grant other debt financing or financial accommodations, e.g., surety or guaranty contracts, to the debtor, or (ii) to issue a security of the debtor. [B.C. §§ 365(c)(2), 1107(a)] This prohibition, however, does not apply to "an ordinary contract to provide goods or services that has incidental financial accommodations or extensions of credit." [3 Collier ¶ 365.07(2)] A credit card merchant agreement between a bank and a merchant does not constitute a financial accommodations contract and, thus, the trustee or debtor in possession may assume such agreement in bankruptcy. [*See, e.g., **In re** **United Airlines, Inc.,*** 368 F.3d 720 (7th Cir. 2004)]

c. Nonresidential Leases Terminated Before Bankruptcy

The trustee or debtor in possession may not assume or assign a lease of nonresidential real property that has terminated under nonbankruptcy law prior to the order for relief. [B.C. § 365(c)(3)] Some courts engage in a two-step analysis to determine whether § 365(c)(3) precludes assumption of a lease of nonresidential real property. The first step is to determine whether the lease was terminated under applicable nonbankruptcy law before the bankruptcy filing. If the lease was terminated, then the court must decide whether the termination was reversible under state anti-forfeiture law or other applicable state law. [***In re* Waterkist Corp.,** 775 F.2d 1089 (9th Cir. 1985); *see **In re** **Sterling** **Mining Co.,*** 2009 WL 1377471 (D. Idaho 2009) (applying test from *Waterkist*)]

6. Rejection Constitutes Breach

The general rule is that a rejection by the trustee or debtor in possession operates as a breach of the executory contract or the unexpired lease. Section 365(g) provides the rules for determining the time that the breach is deemed to have occurred, which, in turn, determines the nature of the non-breacher's claim.

a. No Assumption

If the trustee or debtor in possession has not assumed the contract or the lease under the terms of a confirmed plan or pursuant to the provisions of § 365, then the failure to assume constitutes a rejection and a breach. The breach is deemed to occur *pre-petition,* immediately before the filing of the bankruptcy petition. [B.C. § 365(g)(1)] As a result, the non-breacher's claim is subject to any limitations that normally apply to the kind of pre-petition claim she holds. [B.C. § 502(g); *but compare* **In re Multech Corp.,** 47 B.R. 747 (Bankr. N.D. Iowa 1985) (holding that damages resulting from rejection of a previously assumed lease are an administrative expense and, thus, § 502 does not limit such damages)] Thus, for example, the claim of a lessor that results from the rejection of a real property lease is limited to the amount fixed by § 502(b)(6), and an employee's claim for damages caused by the rejection of an employment contract is limited to the amount allowable under § 502(b)(7).

b. Assumption

Administrative expense status is accorded if the trustee or debtor in possession first assumed but later rejected the contract or lease. In such a case, the breach is deemed to have occurred *at the time of the rejection* if the case was not converted to Chapter 7 prior to the rejection. [B.C. § 365(g)(2)(A)]

(i) Conversion to Chapter 7

If the case was converted to Chapter 7 *before the rejection,* the rules for determining the time of breach depend on when assumption occurred. If the contract or lease was *assumed before the conversion,* the breach is deemed to have occurred *immediately prior to the date of conversion.* [B.C. § 365(g)(2)(B)(i)] If the *assumption took place after the conversion,* the breach is deemed to have occurred *at the time of the rejection.* [B.C. § 365(g)(2)(B)(ii)]

Remember: If a case has been converted to Chapter 7 from Chapter 11, 12, or 13, the administrative expenses of the Chapter 7 case have priority over the administrative expenses of the prior Chapter 11, 12, or 13 case. [B.C. § 726(b)]

Example: On May 1, Debtor/Lessee filed for relief under Chapter 11 petition and, on June 1, obtained court approval to assume an unexpired lease of certain real property. On July 1, Debtor rejected the lease and, on August 1, converted the case to Chapter 7. The rejection of the lease constituted a breach deemed to have occurred on July 1, and for which Lessor is entitled to an administrative expense. [B.C. § 365(g)(2)(A)] Any administrative expenses arising *after conversion* in the Chapter 7 case have priority over Lessor's administrative expense claim, which was incurred prior to conversion. [B.C. § 726(b); *In re* **Multech Corp.,** *supra*]

c. Personal Property Leases and the Stay

Congress added subsection (p) to § 365 with the passage of BAPCPA. Section 365(p) provides rules related to *termination of the automatic stay* upon *rejection or deemed rejection* of a *personal property lease.* [B.C. §§ 365(p)(1), (3)] It also provides a process by which an individual Chapter 7 debtor may assume a lease that has been rejected or deemed rejected. [B.C. § 365(p)(2)]

(i) Not Estate Property

If a personal property lease is *rejected or deemed rejected* because it was not timely assumed under § 365(d), then the leased property *no longer is estate property* and the *automatic stay is automatically terminated.* [B.C. § 365(p)(1)]

(ii) Individual Chapter 7 Debtors

In an individual Chapter 7 case, if the trustee has rejected a personal property lease or the lease has been deemed rejected, the debtor may *notify the creditor in writing* that the debtor *wants to assume* the lease. The lessor, upon receiving such notice, may inform the debtor that it is willing to have the lease assumed and may condition assumption on the cure of any default according to the terms of the parties' contract. The lessor need not agree to assumption. [B.C. § 365(p)(2)(A)] If the debtor, no later than *30 days* after notice is provided, notifies the lessor in writing that the lease is assumed then the *debtor, not the estate, has assumed liability* for the lease. [B.C. § 365(p)(2)(B)] The Code does not specify *which* notice—that of the debtor or the lessor—starts the 30-day clock. The lessor's response to the debtor's notice that she wants to assume the lease violates neither the automatic stay nor the discharge injunction. [B.C. §§ 365(p)(2)(C), 362, 524(a)(2)] There is a split of authority as to whether a lease assumption under § 365(p) is enforceable after discharge if the debtor did not reaffirm the debt under the lease pursuant to § 524(c). [3 Collier ¶ 365.10(6); *see In re* **Bailly**, 522 B.R. 711 (Bankr. M.D. Fla. 2014) (discussing split of authority on issue and holding that debtor could assume his car lease "without separately reaffirming the debt and, indeed, without seeking any approval from the Court")]

(iii) Chapter 13 and Individual Chapter 11 Cases

In a Chapter 13 case or an individual Chapter 11 case in which the debtor is the lessee under a *personal property lease,* the lease is deemed rejected as of the conclusion of the confirmation hearing if the lease is not assumed in the confirmed plan. [B.C. § 365(p)(3)] Upon rejection, the automatic stay and the co-debtor stay are automatically terminated as to the property subject to the lease. [B.C. §§ 365(p)(3), 1301] *Note:* This subsection does not terminate the stay with regard to the debtor or other property of the estate.

7. Time Limitations for Assumption or Rejection

The period within which the trustee or debtor in possession may assume or reject an executory contract or an unexpired lease depends on the chapter under which the case is filed and the nature of the property that is the subject matter of the contract or lease. [B.C. § 365(d)]

a. Chapter 7 Cases: Executory Contracts and Certain Leases

The trustee, in a case under Chapter 7, has *60 days* after the order for relief within which to assume or reject an *executory contract* or an unexpired lease of *personal property or residential real property.* Otherwise, the contract or the lease is deemed rejected. The court, during the 60-day period, may extend the period for cause. [B.C. § 365(d)(1)]

b. Chapter 11, 12, and 13 Cases

Assumption or rejection of an *executory contract* or unexpired lease of *personal property or residential real property* may occur at any time prior to the confirmation of a plan under Chapter 11, 12, or 13. [B.C. § 365(d)(2)]

(i) Expedited Decision

The nondebtor party may request that the court direct the trustee or debtor in possession either to assume or reject an executory contract or an unexpired lease of personal or real property within a fixed period of time. [B.C. § 365(d)(2)]

Note: A nondebtor party may use this provision in a Chapter 11 case in which plan confirmation is not expected in the near future. Bankruptcy courts, however, often are reluctant to order the debtor to decide in a short period of time; thus, the non-debtor party may seek payment from the court for goods or services provided to the debtor during this limbo period.

c. Lease of Nonresidential Real Property Under Any Chapter

If the debtor is a lessee of nonresidential real property, then a trustee in a case under *any chapter,* or the debtor in possession in Chapter 11, has until the *earlier of* the date of the entry of a *plan confirmation order or 120 days after the order for relief* within which to assume or reject an unexpired lease of the property, or else the lease is deemed rejected and the property must be immediately surrendered to the lessor. [B.C. § 365(d)(4)(A)] During the 120-day period, the trustee or the lessor may move for an extension of this time period, and the bankruptcy court, for cause, may *extend* the period for *90 days.* [B.C. § 365(d)(4)(B)(i)] If the bankruptcy court grants such an extension, it only may grant a subsequent additional extension of time if the lessor consents in writing to this subsequent additional time extension. [B.C. § 365(d)(4)(B)(ii)]

Note: Prior to the passage of BAPCPA, the time period was 60 days from the order for relief.

8. Trustee Obligations Prior to Assumption or Rejection

a. Lease of Nonresidential Real Property

The trustee or debtor in possession must timely perform all duties arising under an unexpired lease of nonresidential real property after the order for relief and until assumption or rejection. The only duties excluded are those described in § 365(b)(2). [B.C. § 365(d)(3)] Therefore, all rents due under such a lease during this period must be *timely paid at the rate specified in the lease,* without the necessity of notice or a hearing. [B.C. § 365(d)(3); *see, e.g., In re* **Art & Architecture Books of the 20th Century,** 522 B.R. 249 (Bankr. C.D. Cal. 2014) (Section 365(d)(3) "requires the payment of rent in the *amount required by the lease* (not some other "fair value" amount based on the estate's actual use and occupancy of the premises), *plus* all other obligations of the tenant debtor under the lease (e.g., common area maintenance charges"))]

(i) Failure to Perform

The Bankruptcy Code does not address what happens if the trustee or debtor in possession fails to perform the duties arising under a lease of nonresidential real property prior to assumption or rejection. A *majority of courts* treat the accrued rent as an *administrative expense* equal to the total amount of rent due under the lease during this period, regardless of the extent of use by the trustee or debtor in possession, and independent of the usual requirement of proving the reasonableness of an administrative expense claim under § 503(b)(1). [*See, e.g.,* **Towers v. Chickering & Gregory (***In re* **Pacific-Atlantic Trading Co.),** 27 F.3d 401 (9th Cir. 1994) (holding that "[b]y providing for timely performance of *all* lease obligations, 'notwithstanding *section 503(b)(1),*' the statute has already granted priority payment status to the full amount of rent due under nonresidential leases"); *see also* 3 Collier ¶ 365.04(1)(b)] A *minority of courts* have held that if the trustee fails to perform as required by § 365(d)(3), then the lessor must assert an administrative expense claim under § 503(b)(1) and demonstrate the benefit to the estate—actual and necessary use—and the reasonableness of the rent. These courts conclude that because Congress failed to provide a specific remedy for the trustee's failure to perform, Congress left the remedy determination to the sound discretion of the bankruptcy court. [*See In re* **Simbaki, Ltd.,** 2015 WL 1593888 (Bankr. S.D. Tex. 2015) (discussing courts' approaches to issue)]

b. **Lease of Commercial Personal Property in Chapter 11**

In a Chapter 11 case, the trustee or debtor in possession must timely perform all obligations, except those specified under § 365(b)(2), in a lease of *non-consumer personal property* first arising *from 60 days after the order for relief* until the lease is assumed or rejected. After notice and a hearing, the bankruptcy court, based on the *equities of the case,* may order otherwise with regard to the lease obligations or their timely performance. [B.C. § 365(d)(5)]

This obligation to perform, unlike that in § 365(d)(3), does not apply until *60 days after the order for relief.* Thus, during the first 60 days, the estate pays for use of commercial personal property based on general concepts of benefit to the estate; if the estate does not use the property, then the lessor likely receives no payment for those first 60 days. After 60 days, however, the trustee or debtor in possession must pay at the lease rate for the noncommercial personal property. The most common type of unexpired commercial lease is an *equipment lease.*

c. **Executory Contracts and All Other Leases**

The Bankruptcy Code does not contain specific rules about the trustee's or debtor in possession's obligations to perform prior to assumption or rejection of executory contracts, or leases of residential property or consumer personal property. But, the estate must pay for the benefit it receives from post-petition performance of an executory contract, or an unexpired lease of residential real property or personal property other than in a Chapter 11 case. That benefit is compensated as a priority administrative expense and only to the extent of any *actual benefit to the estate.* [*See* B.C. § 503(b)(1)]

9. Ipso Facto Provisions

With certain exceptions, an executory contract or unexpired lease may not be terminated or modified *after* the filing of a bankruptcy petition solely on account of an *ipso facto* or other bankruptcy termination clause in the contract or lease. Thus, the Code invalidates any contractual provision that terminates or modifies the parties' contract or lease based on:

a. the insolvency or financial state of the debtor [B.C. § 365(e)(1)(A)];

b. the commencement by the debtor of a bankruptcy case [B.C. § 365(e)(1)(B)];

c. the appointment of a bankruptcy trustee or a nonbankruptcy custodian [B.C. § 365(e)(1)(C)]; *or*

d. the seizure of property by a bankruptcy trustee or a nonbankruptcy custodian [B.C. § 365(e)(1)(C)].

e.g. **Example:** The post-petition cancellation of Debtor's insurance policy under an "at will" clause of the contract, solely because of the filing of an involuntary petition against Debtor, is ineffective; thus, the policy continues in force. [B.C. § 365(e)(1)(B); *In re B. Siegel Co.,* 51 B.R. 159 (Bankr. E.D. Mich. 1985)]

cf. **Compare—pre-petition termination:** A pre-bankruptcy termination of an executory contract under an ipso facto clause, for example, solely because of the debtor's insolvency, would not be prohibited. [*In re* **LJP, Inc.,** 22 B.R. 556 (Bankr. S.D. Fla. 1982)]

Exception

The Code provides an exception to the basic rule that *ipso facto* and other bankruptcy termination clauses are not effective post-petition. Such clauses are effective to terminate or modify the parties' agreement, if the non-debtor party invokes the clause, in either of the following two situations:

a. applicable law excuses the non-debtor party from accepting performance from or rendering performance to the trustee or an assignee, e.g., a personal services contract [B.C. § 365(e)(2)(A)]; *or*

b. the contract is one to make a loan or extend other debt or financial accommodations to the debtor, or to issue a security of the debtor. [B.C. § 365(e)(2)(B)]

10. Debtor as Lessor

If the ***debtor is the lessor*** under an unexpired lease of real property, and the lease has been rejected by the trustee or debtor in possession, the lessee either may consider the lease terminated or, ***if the term of the lease has commenced,*** retain rights under the lease for the balance of the current term and for any period of renewal or extension enforceable under nonbankruptcy law. [B.C. § 365(h)(1)] Similarly, a non-debtor timeshare interest purchaser has the choice of treating a rejected timeshare plan as terminated or, if the term of the timeshare interest has commenced, retaining rights in the timeshare interest for the balance of the term and for any period of renewal or extension enforceable under nonbankruptcy law. [B.C. §§ 365(h)(2)(A), 101(53D)]

a. Continued Possession

If the lessee or timeshare interest purchaser elects to retain her rights, she may offset against her post-rejection rent or monies due for the timeshare interest any damages occurring after the date of rejection that flow from the failure of the trustee or debtor in possession to perform its obligations under the lease or the timeshare plan. The right of setoff is the exclusive remedy against the estate or the debtor for post-rejection damages. [B.C. §§ 365(h)(1)(B), (2)(B)] In a shopping center, the rejection of a lease of real property in a case in which the lessee elects to retain its rights does not affect the enforceability of any lease provision related to radius, location, use, exclusivity, or tenant mix or balance. [B.C. § 365(h)(1)(C)]

11. Debtor as Seller

If the debtor is the seller under an executory contract to sell real property or a timeshare interest and the trustee or debtor in possession has rejected the executory contract for sale, the buyer, ***if in possession,*** may treat the contract as terminated or may stay in possession of the real property or timeshare interest. [B.C. § 365(i)(1)]

a. Continued Possession

If the purchaser chooses to remain in possession, she must make all payments required by the contract. However, she may offset against these payments any damages occurring after the date of rejection that result from nonperformance by the trustee or debtor in possession. The right of setoff is the exclusive remedy against the estate for post-rejection damages. [B.C. § 365(i)(2)(A)]

(i) Title

The trustee or debtor in possession must deliver the title to the buyer after all payments have been made or as otherwise provided for in the contract of sale, but is not obligated to perform any other duties under the contract. [B.C. § 365(i)(2)(B)]

b. Termination of Contract

If the buyer treats a rejected executory contract to sell real property as terminated *or* if the buyer is not in possession of the property, then the buyer has a *lien* on the property to the extent of any payments made toward the purchase price. [B.C. § 365(j)]

12. Intellectual Property

If the debtor is the licensor of a right to intellectual property, and the trustee or debtor in possession rejects an executory contract under which the license has been granted, the licensee may consider the contract terminated or may retain its contractual rights to the intellectual property, including any right to exclusivity, but excluding any other right to specific performance of the contract, and use the property for the remaining period of the contract and any rightful extension. [B.C. § 365(n)] Congress added § 365(n) to the Code in response to **Lubrizol Enterprises, Inc. v. Richmond Metal Finishers, Inc.,** 756 F.2d 1043 (4th Cir. 1985), which held that rejection of an intellectual property license terminated the licensee's right to use licensed copyrights, trademarks, and patents.

a. Retention of Rights

If the licensee elects to retain its contractual rights to the property, it continues to be responsible for all royalty payments under the contract, or any extension thereof, but waives any right of setoff concerning the contract and any claim for administrative expenses resulting from performance of the contract. [B.C. § 365(n)(2)(C)] Following rejection, the trustee or debtor in possession is relieved of future obligations under the contract. Upon the licensee's written request, however, the trustee or debtor in possession must do the following:

(i) provide the licensee, to the extent required by the parties' contract or any supplementary agreement, the intellectual property or any embodiment that is held by the trustee or debtor in possession [B.C. § 365(n)(3)(A)]; and

(ii) not interfere with the licensee's rights, as provided in the parties' contract or supplementary agreement, to the intellectual property or any embodiment, including any right to obtain the intellectual property or any embodiment from a third party. [B.C. § 365(n)(3)(B)]

b. "Intellectual Property" Defined

The Bankruptcy Code defines intellectual property as any of the following:

(i) trade secrets [B.C. § 101(35A)(A)];

    (ii) inventions, processes, designs, or plants protected under United States Code title 35 [B.C. § 101(35A)(B)];

    (iii) patent applications [B.C. § 101(35A)(C)];

    (iv) plant varieties [B.C. § 101(35A)(D)];

    (v) works of authorship protected under title 17 of the United States Code [B.C. § 101(35A)(E)]; and

    (vi) mask work (relating to semiconductor chip product) protected under chapter 9 of title 17 of the United States Code, "to the extent protected by applicable nonbankruptcy law." [B.C. § 101(35A)(F)]

The Code's definition of intellectual property does not include trademarks, trade names, or service marks; thus, § 365(n) does not apply to them. Some courts have concluded that this omission meant that Congress intended to codify *Lubrizol* with regard to trademarks, thereby leaving the licensee with no right to use a trademark after rejection of the trademark license. Other courts, however, have pointed to the legislative history of § 365(n), which indicated that "the omission was designed to allow more time for study, not to approve *Lubrizol.*" [**Sunbeam Products v. Chicago American Manufacturing, LLC,** 686 F.3d 372 (7th Cir. 2012) (analyzing rejection of trademark license under § 365(g) and holding that rejection did not end the licensee's right to use trademarks)]

13. Capital Commitment of a Financial Institution

In a Chapter 11 case, the trustee or debtor in possession is deemed to have assumed and must immediately cure any deficiency under any commitment by the debtor to a federal depository institutions regulatory agency, e.g., the FDIC or RTC, to maintain the capital of an insured depository institution. [B.C. §§ 365(o), 101(21B), (35)] Any subsequent breach will result in a claim entitled to ninth priority. [B.C. §§ 365(o), 507(a)(9)]

E. Utility Service

1. Protection for Debtor

A utility may not discontinue, alter, or refuse service to, or discriminate against, the trustee or debtor solely because of the filing of a bankruptcy case or because the debtor failed to timely pay a debt owed for utility services furnished prior to the order for relief. [B.C. § 366(a)]

e.g. **Example:** Married Debtors filed for relief under Chapter 13 on October 26. At the time of their bankruptcy filing, Debtors owed Gas Utility more than $1,200. While Gas Utility could have discontinued Debtors' gas service as of November 16 if Debtors failed to provide adequate assurance of payment, it instead gave Debtors until December 22 to pay a $217 deposit as adequate assurance of payment. Debtors paid the $217, but then accumulated more than $1,100 in unpaid, post-petition gas bills. After providing proper notice under state law, Gas Utility terminated Debtors gas service for failure to pay their post-petition gas bills. Debtors sued for violation of the automatic stay. The bankruptcy court ruled against Debtors, and the district court affirmed. The district court held that "[i]t is well-established that § 366 permits a utility to terminate service to a debtor or trustee who has posted adequate assurance but fails to make post-petition payments on the utility service, and may do so without seeking relief from the automatic stay as long as the utility follows its state law termination procedures." [**Weisel v. Dominion Peoples Gas Co. (*In re* Weisel),** 428 B.R. 185 (W.D. Penn. 2010)]

2. Exception: Insufficient Security

A utility may discontinue, alter, or refuse service if, within *20 days* after the order for relief, neither the debtor nor the trustee provides a deposit or other security constituting *adequate assurance of payment* for post-petition services. [B.C. § 366(b); *In re* **Hanratty,** 907 F.2d 1418 (3d Cir. 1990) (rejecting debtors' contention that a utility's request for a deposit from Chapter 13 debtors constituted discrimination against those debtors because the utility did not request such a deposit from new residential utility customers)]

a. Adequate Assurance of Payment

In BAPCPA, Congress defined what does and does not constitute assurance of payment. An administrative expense priority does *not* constitute assurance of payment. [B.C. § 366(c)(1)(B)] Assurance of payment means any of the following:

(i) a cash deposit [B.C. § 366(c)(1)(B)(i)];

(ii) a letter of credit [B.C. § 366(c)(1)(B)(ii)];

(iii) a certificate of deposit [B.C. § 366(c)(1)(B)(iii)];

(iv) a surety bond [B.C. § 366(c)(1)(B)(iv)];

(v) a prepayment of utility consumption [B.C. § 366(c)(1)(B)(v)]; or

(vi) another form of security on which the utility and debtor or trustee agree. [B.C. § 366(c)(1)(B)(vi)]

b. Modification of Payment

The bankruptcy court, upon the request of a party in interest and after notice and a hearing, may order reasonable modification of the amount of any deposit or security intended as adequate assurance of payment. [B.C. § 366(b)]

3. Exception: Chapter 11

In a Chapter 11 case, a utility may alter, refuse, or discontinue service if during the *30-day period* starting with the filing of the petition the debtor or trustee does not provide *adequate assurance of payment* that is *satisfactory to the utility.* [B.C. § 366(c)(2)] Congress added this provision to the Code in 2005.

a. Modification of Payment

The bankruptcy court, upon request of a party in interest and after notice and a hearing, may order reasonable modification of the amount of any deposit or security intended as adequate assurance of payment. [B.C. § 366(c)(3)(A)]

b. Irrelevant Factors

In making its determination on the adequacy of an assurance of payment in the Chapter 11 context, the bankruptcy court *may not consider* any of the following factors:

(i) the absence of pre-petition security [B.C. § 366(c)(3)(B)(i)];

(ii) the debtor's timely payment of pre-petition charges [B.C. § 366(c)(3)(B)(ii)]; or

(iii) the availability of an administrative expense priority claim. [B.C. § 366(c)(3)(B)(i)]

Congress added this language to the Code in 2005.

4. Pre-Petition Deposit

A utility, without notice or order of the court, may set off or recover a pre-petition deposit provided to the utility by the debtor. [B.C. § 366(c)(4)] Congress added this provision to the Code in 2005.

Chapter Twelve

Bankruptcy Code Chapter 7: Liquidation

Chapter Approach

In a Chapter 7 case, the trustee collects the property of the estate, reduces it to cash, and pays claimants in a prescribed order.

Your professor is likely to ask you to decide whether a debtor may file for relief under Chapter 7. In 2005, Congress enacted the Bankruptcy Abuse Prevention and Consumer Protection Act ("BAPCPA"), which established new eligibility requirements for individual consumer debtors filing for Chapter 7. The new financial eligibility test determines whether a debtor's filing for relief under Chapter 7 creates a presumption of abuse. If the debtor fails to rebut the presumption, then the debtor's Chapter 7 case will be dismissed. The following are some key things for you to keep in mind when answering this type of question.

1. The new eligibility requirements to file for relief under Chapter 7 *only apply to individual debtors with primarily consumer debts.*

2. If a debtor's *annual income is less than the state's median income,* then the Chapter 7 "means test" does not apply.

3. An *above-median income debtor* must "pass" the means test to file for or remain in Chapter 7.

4. The court may still dismiss the Chapter 7 case of a below-median income debtor or of an above-median income debtor who passes the means test if the court determines that the debtor filed the case *in bad faith* or that under the *totality of the circumstances* the filing of the case demonstrates *abuse.*

Another *likely exam question* will ask you to discuss the *order and amount of distribution* to each creditor. The following are some key things for you to consider in answering this type of question.

1. Ordinarily, *secured* creditors are paid out of their collateral.

2. *Unsecured priority* claimants receive distribution ahead of the general unsecured creditors.

3. If there is not enough money to pay all claims at a particular level, claimants within that level take a *pro rata share.*

4. The trustee can *avoid* liens for certain kinds of penalties, and *tax liens* are subject to subordination.

5. If your question concerns a *partnership* debtor, remember that special rules apply if there are insufficient assets to pay all the claims against the partnership.

You professor also may ask you to determine whether the debtor should receive a *discharge* under Chapter 7. Look for any of the grounds for a *global denial* of a discharge, e.g., the debtor transferred property with the intent to hinder, delay, or defraud a creditor. If the facts do not show any of the grounds for denial, a discharge *must* be granted, although under appropriate circumstances, a discharge may be *revoked.* Remember to distinguish between a *global denial* of discharge and the *debt-specific* discharge exceptions in § 523 of the Bankruptcy Code.

Finally, keep in mind that the debtor may *convert* a Chapter 7 case to Chapter 11, 12, or 13, if the case has not been converted earlier and the debtor is eligible under the other chapter. The court also may *dismiss* a case for cause or if a consumer debtor has filed but does not qualify for relief under Chapter 7.

Note: This outline does not cover stockbroker, commodity broker, or clearing bank liquidation cases. [*See* B.C. §§ 741–53, 761–67, 781–84]

A. Introduction

1. Eligibility for Relief

With the following exceptions, a person, i.e., individual, partnership, or corporation, that resides or has a domicile, a place of business, or property in the United States may be a debtor under Chapter 7. [B.C. §§ 109(a), (b)]

a. Exceptions for Certain Entities

The following persons are *not eligible* to be debtors under Chapter 7:

(i) *railroads* [B.C. § 109(b)(1)];

(ii) *domestic banks, insurance companies,* credit unions, savings and loan associations, building and loan associations, homestead associations, cooperative banks, industrial banks, small business investment companies licensed by the Small Business Administration, New Markets Venture Capital companies, and other similar institutions [B.C. § 109(b)(2)];

(iii) *foreign insurance companies* that are *engaged in such business in the United States* [B.C. § 109(b)(3)(A)]; and

(iv) *foreign banks, savings banks, savings and loan associations, credit unions* and other similar financial institutions with a *branch or agency in the United States.* [B.C. § 109(b)(3)(B)]

b. Exceptions: Financial Situation or Pre-Bankruptcy Conduct

The exceptions above are based on *entity type,* e.g., railroads. The Code also provides that certain debtors are not eligible for relief under Chapter 7 based on their *current financial situation* or *pre-bankruptcy conduct.* For this group of debtors, changing the time of the bankruptcy filing may remove the bar to eligibility. The following debtors also are not eligible for relief under Chapter 7:

(i) *an individual or a family farmer* who was a debtor in a case that was *dismissed in the preceding 180 days* because of the debtor's willful failure to obey court orders or to appear before the court, or because of the debtor's request for a voluntary dismissal of the case following a party's request for relief from the automatic stay [B.C. § 109(g)];

Note: This disqualification applies not only to Chapter 7 but also to Chapters 11, 12, and 13.

(ii) *above-median income individual debtors with primarily consumer debts* who fail the "means test" [B.C. § 707(b)]; and

(iii) with certain limited exceptions, an *individual debtor* who has not obtained *credit counseling* during the *180 days* prior to seeking relief under the Bankruptcy Code. [B.C. § 109(h)]

Note: This disqualification applies not only to Chapter 7 but also to Chapters 11, 12, and 13.

2. Chapter 7 Trustee

Immediately after the order for relief, the United States trustee appoints a disinterested member of the panel of private trustees to serve as the interim trustee in a Chapter 7 case. [B.C. § 701(a)(1); 28 U.S.C. § 586(a)(1)] Then, either a trustee is elected at the § 341 meeting of creditors or, as usually occurs, the interim trustee automatically becomes the permanent trustee in the case. [B.C. § 702]

a. Duties of Trustee

In a Chapter 7 case, the trustee's primary responsibilities are to locate and collect property of the estate, convert the property to cash, make distributions to claimants in the order established by the Bankruptcy Code, and close the estate expeditiously. [B.C. §§ 704(a), 726] BAPCPA added a number of new responsibilities for the Chapter 7 trustee, including verifying that individual debtors are eligible for relief under Chapter 7 and providing various notices related to claims for domestic support obligations. [*See* B.C. §§ 704(a)(10), (b), (c)] Bankruptcy Code § 704 provides a full list of the administrative duties of the Chapter 7 trustee.

3. Authority to Operate Debtor's Business

Occasionally, the trustee may receive authorization from the court to operate the debtor's business temporarily, under circumstances in which continuing the business for a while is in the best interest of the estate and will assist in its orderly liquidation. "An example is the operation of a watch company to convert watch movements and cases into completed watches which will bring much higher prices than the component parts would have brought." [H.R. Rep. No. 95–595, at 380 (1977); *see* B.C. § 721]

4. Meeting of Creditors

No earlier than 21 and no later than 40 days after the order for relief, the United States trustee convenes and presides at the § 341 meeting. [B.C. § 341; Bankruptcy Rule 2003(a)]

a. Business Conducted

The business conducted at the § 341 meeting includes the following matters:

(i) *examination of the debtor,* under oath, by creditors, the trustee or an examiner in the case, an indenture trustee, or the United States trustee [B.C. § 343; Bankruptcy Rule 2003(b)(1)];

(ii) *the election of a trustee,* if requested by a sufficient number of unsecured creditors [B.C. § 702]; and

(iii) *election of a creditors' committee,* if desired, consisting of between 3 and 11 unsecured creditors, to act in an advisory role in consultation with the Chapter 7 trustee or the United States trustee. [B.C. § 705; Bankruptcy Rule 2003(b)(1)]

b. Conclusion of § 341 Meeting

Before concluding the § 341 meeting, the trustee must orally examine the debtor to make certain that the debtor is aware of the following matters:

(i) the possible consequences, including the impact on credit history, of obtaining a bankruptcy discharge [B.C. § 341(d)(1)];

(ii) the availability of relief under other chapters of the Bankruptcy Code [B.C. § 341(d)(2)];

(iii) the effect of a discharge of debts [B.C. § 341(d)(3)]; and

(iv) the effect of reaffirming a debt, including the debtor's knowledge of the impact of reaffirmation on discharge. [B.C. §§ 341(d)(1), 524(d)]

B. The Means Test

1. Introduction

BAPCPA created a financial eligibility test for *individual Chapter 7 debtors with primarily consumer debts.* The goal of this financial eligibility test is to force a debtor to file for relief under Chapter 13 instead of Chapter 7 if the debtor has the financial means to pay some threshold amount of money to the debtor's unsecured creditors. BAPCPA provides that filing for relief under Chapter 7 for these "can pay" debtors creates a *presumption of abuse.*

The *first step* of this new financial eligibility test is determining whether the individual debtor's income is *above or below the median income* for the debtor's household size in the state in which the debtor resides. The *means test,* which is the second step, only applies to *above-median income debtors.*

2. The Below-Median Income Debtor

a. The Bankruptcy Code provides that there is no *presumption of abuse* for a *below-median income debtor.* Therefore, no one may file a motion to dismiss the debtor's case on the *sole* ground that the filing for relief under Chapter 7 is an abuse of the bankruptcy system. [B.C. § 707(b)(7)]

b. The below median-income debtor's Chapter 7 case may be dismissed, however, if the court determines that the *petition was filed in bad faith* or *the totality of the debtor's financial situation demonstrates abuse.* [B.C. § 707(b)(3)]

c. Only the *judge, United States trustee, or Bankruptcy Administrator* may move to dismiss the case of a below-median income debtor for *bad faith* or under the *totality-of-the-circumstances* test. [B.C. § 707(b)(6)]

3. The Above-Median Income Debtor

a. An above-median income debtor must do the *means test* in order to determine whether the debtor's filing for relief under Chapter 7 creates a *presumption of abuse.* If there is no presumption of abuse, then the debtor's case may be dismissed only if it was *filed in bad faith* or if the *totality of the debtor's financial situation demonstrates abuse.* [B.C. §§ 707(b)(2), (3)]

b. If there is a presumption of abuse, then the debtor may *rebut the presumption* by showing *special circumstances* that justify additional expenses or adjustments to current monthly income for which there is *no reasonable alternative.* Special circumstances may include *"a serious medical condition or a call or order to active duty in the Armed Forces."* [B.C. § 707(b)(2)(B)]

4. Current Monthly Income

a. All *individual* debtors must determine their *current monthly income,* because this figure determines the debtor's income status as above or below median.

   Note: An *individual debtor whose debts are primarily business in nature* must submit a statement that she is *exempt* from the *presumption of abuse.* [Official Form 122A-1 Supp] The debtor still must complete and submit the statement of current monthly income form. [Official Form 122A-1]

b. *Current monthly income* is the debtor's *average monthly income from all sources* that the debtor receives during the *six-month period* prior to filing for bankruptcy. The six-month period *ends on the last day of the calendar month immediately preceding* the filing of the bankruptcy case. [B.C. § 101(10A)(A)]

> **Example:** Dale files for relief under Chapter 7 on October 20, 2017. Dale's current monthly income is computed by averaging his income for the months of April through September of 2017. Dale's income from October is not included, because the six-month period ends on the last day of the month prior to his filing for bankruptcy.

> **Example:** Dale's income varies by month, because commissions are a large part of his compensation. Dale files for relief under Chapter 7 on October 20, 2017. His gross wages in April and May of 2017 were $2,000; in June and July, his wages increased to $3,000; in August and September, his gross wages were $2,200. Dale's current monthly income is the average over the past 6 months or $2,400 ($14,400/6 months).

(i) What is included in current monthly income?

Current monthly income *includes* (1) non-taxable income or (2) amounts paid by any entity other than the debtor *on a regular basis* for the *household expenses* of the debtor or the debtor's dependents. [B.C. § 101(10A)] Current monthly income *does not include* (1) *Social Security benefits,* (2) payments to *victims of war crimes or crimes against humanity* based on their status as victims of these crimes or (3) payments to *victims of domestic or international terrorism* based on their status as victims of terrorism. [B.C. § 101(10A)(B)]

> **Example:** Debbie is a retired school teacher. She has a modest pension and also collects Social Security benefits, which do not cover all of her household expenses. Debbie's son pays her utility bills each month. Debbie's current monthly income includes her pension payments as well as the amount her son contributes each month toward her utility payments. It does not include her Social Security benefits.

5. Above or Below Median?

a. Once the debtor determines her current monthly income, she *multiplies that number by 12* and compares it with the median income for her household size in the state in which she resides. If her income exceeds the state median, then she is an above-median income debtor and must complete the "means test." If her income is equal to or less than the state median, then she is a *below-median* income debtor and there is *no presumption of abuse.*

> **Example:** Dilbert is single and his current monthly income is $2,000, for an annual income of $24,000. The median income for a single person in the state where Dilbert resides is $32,000. Dilbert is a below-median income debtor; therefore, Dilbert's filing of relief under Chapter 7 does not create a presumption of abuse.

b. The median income by state and household size, as well as the expense amounts that the individual debtor must use for the means test are found at the *Means Testing Information* link on the Department of Justice United States Trustee program website, *available at https://www.justice.gov/ust/means-testing*

c. In determining whether a *married debtor who files alone* is an above- or below-median income debtor, the income of the non-filing spouse is included in the calculation unless the *couple is separated under applicable nonbankruptcy law or* the couple is *living apart* and the debtor files a *statement under penalty of perjury* that attests to the fact the couple *lives apart* and that *discloses payments* from the non-filing spouse attributable to the *filing spouse's current monthly income.* [B.C. § 707(b)(7)(B)]

Example: Donald earns $40,000 per year. His wife Delia earns $30,000 per year. Donald and Delia live together. The median income for a family of two in the state in which Donald and Delia reside is $60,000. Only Donald plans to file for relief under Chapter 7. Donald is an above-median income debtor, because his and Delia's income combined is $70,000, which exceeds the state median.

6. Above-Median Income Debtors and the Chapter 7 Means Test

a. To determine whether there is a presumption of abuse, the above-median income debtor subtracts her *monthly expenses* from her *current monthly income.* The debtor then multiplies the *difference by 60* and compares the *product* with the following numbers.

(i) **$8,175:** If the *product is less than $8,175,* then the debtor's filing for relief under Chapter 7 *does not create* a *presumption of abuse.* [B.C. § 707(b)(2)(A)(i)(I)]

> **Example:** David is single and earns $50,400 per year. He lives in a state with a median income of $45,000 for single people. David's current monthly income is $4200, but his monthly means test expenses are $4,100, which leaves $100 per month for his unsecured creditors. Over 60 months, David has $6,000, which is less than $8,175. Therefore, there is no presumption of abuse.

(ii) **$13,650:** If the *product is greater than $13,650,* then there is a *presumption of abuse.* [B.C. § 707(b)(2)(A)(i)(II)] Unless the debtor can rebut the presumption, the debtor cannot file for relief under Chapter 7.

> **Example:** Debi is single, earns $48,000 per year, and lives in a state with a median income of $45,000 for single people. Debi's current monthly income is $4,000, and her monthly expenses are $3,750. The difference of $250 when multiplied by 60 months equals $15,000, which exceeds $13,650. Therefore, the presumption of abuse arises and unless Debi is able to rebut it, she may not file for relief under Chapter 7.

(iii) **$8,175 ≥ product ≤ $13,650:** If the *product is greater than or equal to $8,175 but also less than or equal to $13,650,* then the debtor must conduct the *secondary abuse test.*

(1) The Secondary Abuse Test

The *secondary abuse test* requires the debtor to compare the product *with* 25% of the debtor's non-priority unsecured claims. [B.C. § 707(b)(2)(A)(i)(I)] If the product *exceeds 25%* of the debtor's non-priority unsecured claims, then the presumption of abuse arises. If the product is *less than 25%* of the debtor's non-priority unsecured claims, then the presumption of abuse does not arise.

> **Example:** Danielle is an above-median income debtor with current monthly income of $4,000 and means test monthly expenses of $3,850, leaving $150 per month. Because $150 x 60 months is $9,000, which falls between $8,175 and $13,650, the secondary abuse test applies. If Danielle's non-priority unsecured debt equals $28,000, then 25% of that amount is $7,000. The presumption of abuse arises, because $9,000 > $7,000. Unless Danielle can rebut the presumption, she cannot file for relief under Chapter 7.

> **Example:** Same facts as in the example above, except Danielle's non-priority unsecured claims equal $40,000; 25% of those claims equal $10,000. The presumption of abuse does not arise, because $9,000 < $10,000.

(2) Rationale

The ***rationale of the secondary abuse test*** is that if the debtor has enough money left over after paying monthly expenses to pay at least 25% of her unsecured claims, then the debtor should file for Chapter 13 and make such payments over time to the debtor's non-priority unsecured creditors.

b. *Note:* The $8,175 and $13,650 figures went into effect on April 1, 2019. They increase every three years. [B.C. § 104(a)] The next increase will take effect on April 1, 2022.

c. **Means Test Expenses**

(i) The Standards

The means test allows the debtor to deduct certain expenses based on ***applicable national and local standards.*** [B.C. § 707(b)(2)(A)(ii)(I)] Thus, regardless of the debtor's ***actual*** expense, the standard expense figure governs.

> **e.g.** **Example:** Donna owns her home and spends approximately $400 per month for homeowners' insurance, maintenance, and home utilities. The local standards provide $450 for such expenses. Donna may deduct $450 from her current monthly income even though she actually pays only $400 per month.

> **e.g.** **Example:** Duane owns his home and spends approximately $490 per month for homeowners' insurance, maintenance, and home utilities. The local standards provide $450 for such expenses. Duane may only deduct $450 from his current monthly income even though he actually pays $490 per month.

But, a debtor ***may not deduct*** the amount provided by the national or local standards if the debtor ***does not incur*** the expense covered by the standard.

> **e.g.** **Example:** Daria owns a car that she paid off two years ago. The local standards provide for a standard ownership expense to cover loan or lease payments, and a standard operating expense to cover gas, insurance, and maintenance. Daria may deduct the standard operating expense from her current monthly income. However, she may not deduct the standard ownership expense, because she no longer makes loan payments on the car. [**Ransom v. FIA Card Services,** 562 U.S. 61 (2011)]

(ii) Secured Debt

The means test allows a debtor to deduct the ***actual amount*** that she pays on her ***secured debt*** *even if* the applicable national or local standard provides a smaller deduction. [B.C. § 707(b)(2)(A)(iii)] As a result, a debtor with high secured debt fares better under the means test than a similarly situated debtor who has been more cautious in her spending.

> **e.g.** **Example:** Dahlia and Denise are both above-median income debtors with current monthly income of $4,500 per month. Dahlia lives in a large home with a monthly mortgage payment of $1,850. Denise's home is more modest; her monthly mortgage payment is only $1,500. The applicable local standard for a debtor's home ownership expense in the state in which Dahlia and Denise reside is $1,500. Dahlia and Denise each have other monthly expenses of $2,600. Dahlia's means test expenses total to $4,450 ($2,600 + home ownership expense of $1,850). Thus, Dahlia passes the means test, because $50 x 60 months = $3,000, which is less than $8,175. Denise, on the other hand, fails the "means test," because her monthly expenses are only $4,100, leaving her with $400 per month or $24,000 over 60 months, which far exceeds the $13,650 figure that triggers a presumption of abuse.

(iii) Other Necessary Expenses

A debtor also may deduct the *actual cost* of *other necessary expenses,* including amounts paid for *federal, state,* and *local taxes, life insurance, alimony, child support,* and *child care.*

(iv) Charitable Contributions

A debtor's monthly expenses may include *charitable contributions to any qualified religious or charitable entity or organization.* [B.C. § 707(b)(1); §§ 548(d)(3) & (4)]

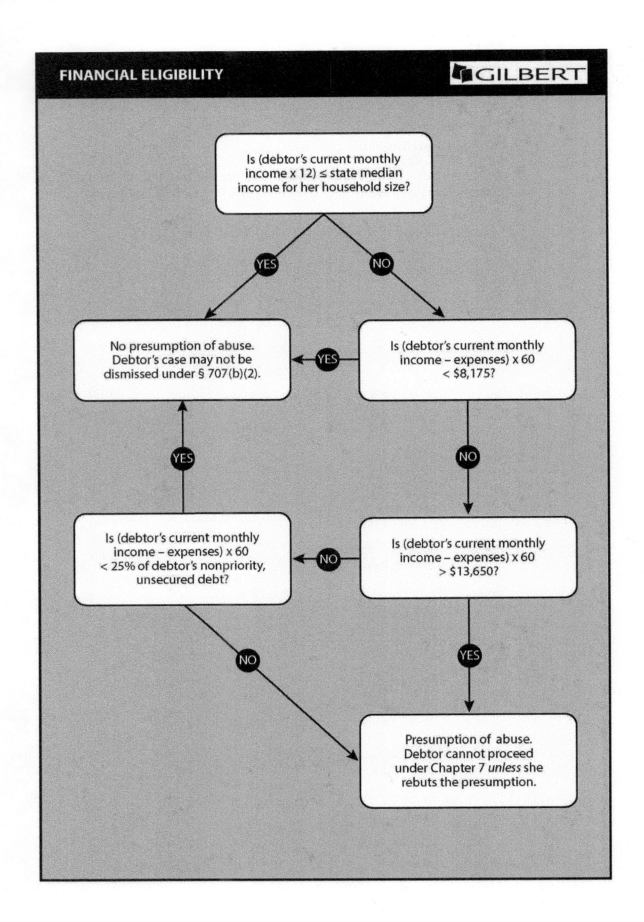

C. Distribution of Property of the Estate

1. Order of Payment

Claimants in a Chapter 7 case receive distribution according to the order prescribed by the Code.

a. Secured Creditors

If the Chapter 7 trustee has sold collateral that secures a claim, the secured creditor is paid from the sale proceeds before there is any distribution to priority or general unsecured creditors. The Chapter 7 trustee, however, does not work for the benefit of secured creditors. If the value of the secured claim exceeds that of the collateral, the trustee may abandon the property under § 554. The bankruptcy court also may have lifted the stay to allow a secured creditor to foreclose on the collateral. If property subject to a lien is not disposed of during the Chapter 7 case, such as by sale, abandonment, or allowing foreclosure by lifting the automatic stay, § 725 authorizes the bankruptcy court to dispose of the collateral by returning it to the secured creditor. [B.C. § 725; H.R. Rep. No. 95–595, at 382 (1977)] Thus, it is possible that the Chapter 7 trustee may sell no collateral during the case, even though there are secured creditors in debtor's case.

b. Priority Claims

Unsecured claims entitled to priority under § 507 are paid before any distribution to the general unsecured creditors and are paid in the order of priority provided by the Code. [*See* B.C. § 507] Timely filed claims or late-filed claims that are filed *on or before the earlier of* the date on which the trustee begins *final distribution or* the date that is *10 days after mailing of the trustee's final report* are the first unsecured claims paid out of any distribution made by the Chapter 7 trustee. [B.C. § 726(a)(1)] Such claims are paid in the following order:

(i)   *administrative expenses of a trustee* to the extent that the trustee administers assets available for payment of *domestic support obligations* [B.C. § 507(a)(1)(C)];

(ii)   *domestic support obligations* [B.C. §§ 507(a)(1)(A), (B)];

(iii)   *administrative expenses* [B.C. § 507(a)(2)]

   Note: A tardy claim for administrative expenses requires *court approval,* for cause, to be filed [B.C. § 503(a)];

(iv)   *involuntary case gap claims* [B.C. § 507(a)(3)];

(v)   *wages, salaries, or commissions* [B.C. § 507(a)(4)];

(vi)   *contributions to employee benefit plans* [B.C. § 507(a)(5)];

(vii)   *claims of grain farmers and United States fishermen* [B.C. § 507(a)(6)];

(viii) *consumer layaway claims* [B.C. § 507(a)(7)];

(ix)   *unsecured pre-petition taxes* [B.C. § 507(a)(8)];

(x)   *capital requirements of insured depository institutions* [B.C. § 507(a)(9)]; and

(xi)   *claims for death or personal injury resulting from debtor's unlawful operation of a motor vehicle or vessel due to intoxication.* [B.C. § 507(a)(10)]

c. General Unsecured Claims

After satisfying all priority unsecured claims, the Chapter 7 trustee pays allowed unsecured claims that are *timely filed* and *justifiably late-filed* claims. [B.C. §§ 726(a)(2)(A), (B)] A late-filed claim will be paid second in the distribution scheme under § 726 if the creditor had *neither notice nor actual knowledge* of the case in time to file a claim on time and the creditor filed its claims in time to permit payment on the claim. [B.C. § 726(a)(2)(C)]

d. Unexcused Tardy Claims

Allowed claims filed late without justification are paid after all timely filed and justifiably late-filed claims. [B.C. § 726(a)(3)]

e. Penalty Claims

Next in the order of distribution are allowed unsecured or secured claims for *punitive, exemplary, or multiple damages,* or for *fines, penalties, or forfeitures* that do not constitute compensation for actual pecuniary loss. [B.C. § 726(a)(4)]

f. Interest

If there are sufficient funds to pay all of the allowed claims above, then the Chapter 7 trustee will pay interest, at the legal rate, that accrued from the date that the petition was filed on all priority and general unsecured claims paid pursuant to § 726(a)(1)–(4). [B.C. § 726(a)(5)]

g. Payment to Debtor

If there is any property of the estate left after payment of post-petition interest on the unsecured claims, it is distributed to the debtor. [B.C. § 726(a)(6)]

2. Pro Rata Payment

The general rule is that priority creditors *within a class* share equally in any distribution. Thus, within a priority class, there is no payment hierarchy.

e.g. **Example:** Debtor Corporation files a voluntary Chapter 7 petition. There are no secured creditors, and the general unsecured claims total $30,000. Administrative expenses are $5,000, and each of 10 employees of Debtor Corporation holds a third priority wage claim in the amount of $1,000. Unsecured pre-petition tax claims, with eighth priority status, total $20,000. If the amount available for distribution is $10,000, the administrative expenses will be paid in full ($5,000), and the 10 employees will receive $500 each. The holders of the priority tax claims and the general unsecured claims will receive nothing. [B.C. § 726(b)]

a. Exceptions

There are several exceptions, however, to this general rule.

(i) Domestic Support Obligations

There is a hierarchy of payment among first priority domestic support obligation claims. The trustee, if she administers assets to pay a domestic support obligation, is paid first, then a spouse, former spouse, or child of the debtor with a domestic support obligation claim, and finally, a governmental unit with a domestic support obligation assigned to it by a spouse, former spouse, or child of the debtor. [B.C. §§ 507(a)(1)(A)–(C)]

(ii) Conversion to Chapter 7

If a case is converted from Chapter 11, 12, or 13 to a case under Chapter 7, the administrative expense claims in the Chapter 7 case *after conversion* have priority over the administrative expenses incurred prior to conversion. [B.C. § 726(b)]

(iii) Super-Priority: Inadequately Protected Secured Creditor

If adequate protection is furnished under §§ 362, 363, or 364 to a creditor whose claim is secured by a lien on the debtor's property, but the adequate protection ultimately proves to be deficient, the creditor will receive an administrative expense claim with *priority over all other administrative expenses* allowed against the debtor's estate. [B.C. § 507(b)]

(iv) Super Super-Priority: Post-Petition Credit

If the trustee or the debtor in possession is unable to obtain unsecured post-petition credit by means of an administrative expense priority, the court may approve new credit or debt with priority over all other administrative expense claims, *including* any super-priority claims arising from the failure of adequate protection. [B.C. § 364(c)(1)]

3. Community Property

If any property of the estate constitutes community property, it must be segregated from other property of the estate. Special rules for distribution apply. For example, allowed claims for administrative expenses are to be paid either from the community property or from the other property of the estate, as justice requires. [B.C. §§ 726(c), 541(a)(2)]

4. Exception: Subordination of Claims

The Chapter 7 payment hierarchy is subject to the Bankruptcy Code's provisions on subordination. Thus, a claim may be subordinated to a lower rank in the distribution if, for example, there is a subordination agreement or the principles of equitable subordination apply. [B.C. §§ 726(a), 510]

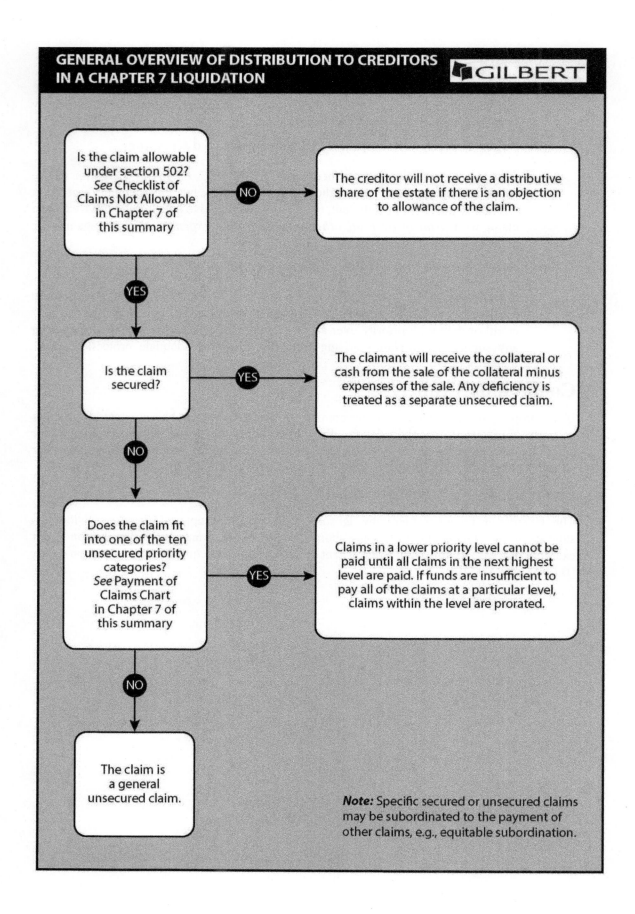

GENERAL OVERVIEW OF DISTRIBUTION TO CREDITORS IN A CHAPTER 7 LIQUIDATION

GILBERT

Is the claim allowable under section 502? *See* Checklist of Claims Not Allowable in Chapter 7 of this summary

NO → The creditor will not receive a distributive share of the estate if there is an objection to allowance of the claim.

YES ↓

Is the claim secured?

YES → The claimant will receive the collateral or cash from the sale of the collateral minus expenses of the sale. Any deficiency is treated as a separate unsecured claim.

NO ↓

Does the claim fit into one of the ten unsecured priority categories? *See* Payment of Claims Chart in Chapter 7 of this summary

YES → Claims in a lower priority level cannot be paid until all claims in the next highest level are paid. If funds are insufficient to pay all of the claims at a particular level, claims within the level are prorated.

NO ↓

The claim is a general unsecured claim.

Note: Specific secured or unsecured claims may be subordinated to the payment of other claims, e.g., equitable subordination.

D. Treatment of Certain Liens in a Chapter 7 Case

1. Avoidance of Liens Securing Penalties

The trustee may avoid a lien securing the type of claim described in § 726(a)(4) for a fine, penalty, or forfeiture, or for punitive, multiple, or exemplary damages that do not constitute compensation for actual pecuniary loss. [B.C. § 724(a)] "The purpose of § 724(a) is to protect unsecured creditors from the debtor's wrongdoing." [**Gill v. Kirresh (*In re* Gill),** 574 B.R. 709 (B.A.P. 9th Cir. 2017)] Paying a creditor that holds a lien on estate property for a penalty or fine does little to punish the debtor; instead, it is unsecured creditors, normally at the bottom of the distribution scheme, that will not be paid and, thus, bear the cost of the penalty or fine.

> **e.g.** **Example:** Debtor files for relief under Chapter 7. Debtor's home is valued at $500,000. Bank has a first lien on the home and has filed a secured proof of claim for $370,000. The IRS has a second lien on the home in the amount of $161,000, of which $50,000 constitutes tax penalties. The Chapter 7 trustee sells the residence and pays off the first lien. The trustee, pursuant to § 724(a), avoids the penalty portion of the IRS lien; § 551 gives the trustee the right to preserve the avoided lien for the benefit of the unsecured creditors. [*See In re* **Gill,** *supra*]

2. Subordination of Tax Liens

The Code provides for the subordination of certain allowed tax claims that are secured by nonavoidable liens, e.g., a perfected tax lien, on estate property. Before subordinating a tax lien on real or personal property, however, the Chapter 7 trustee must first ***exhaust*** the estate's ***unencumbered assets*** and recover from the property securing an allowed secured claim the ***reasonably and necessary costs and expenses*** of disposing of or preserving the property. [B.C. § 724(e)]

Note: With limited exceptions, the subordination rules do not apply to nonavoidable liens for ad valorem taxes on real or personal property. [B.C. §§ 724(b), (e), (f)]

Thus, if there is a tax lien on estate property that otherwise cannot be avoided under the Code, § 724 provides the following rules for distribution of the property or its proceeds. [B.C. § 724(b)]

a. The Chapter 7 trustee's first distribution is to ***any lienholder*** possessing an allowed claim secured by a nonavoidable lien on the collateral that is ***senior to the tax lien.*** [B.C. § 724(b)(1)]

b. Next in the line of distribution are ***the holders of any priority claims*** under §§ 507(a)(1)–(7), with the aggregate of such distributions not to exceed the amount of the allowed secured tax claim. [B.C. § 724(b)(2)] The priority claimants entitled to distribution under § 724(b)(2) ***do not include*** eighth priority unsecured tax claims, ninth priority claims owed to federal depository institutions regulatory agencies, or tenth priority claims for death or personal injury resulting from intoxicated operation of a motor vehicle or vessel. [B.C. §§ 507(a)(8), (9) & (10)]

Exception: As for administrative claims under § 507(a)(2), with one exception, only those administrative claims incurred post-conversion to Chapter 7 from Chapter 11 are included in this distribution. Thus, with the exception of post-petition, pre-conversion administrative claims for wages, salaries, or commissions, the administrative expenses incurred in the Chapter 11 case prior to conversion do not participate in this distribution. [B.C. § 724(b)]

c. Third in the line of distribution is *the tax lienholder, but only* to the extent that its allowed secured tax claim is *greater* than the total of all distributions made under § 724(b)(2) to priority claimants. [B.C. § 724(b)(3)]

d. Fourth in the line of distribution is *any lienholder* possessing an allowed claim secured by a nonavoidable lien on the collateral that is *junior to the tax lien.* [B.C. § 724(b)(4)]

e. Next is *the tax lienholder* to the extent that the allowed secured tax claim is *not satisfied* under § 724(b)(3). [B.C. § 724(b)(5)]

f. Finally, any property or proceeds remaining go to the *Chapter 7 estate.* [B.C. § 724(b)(6)]

e.g. **Example:** Debtor Corporation files a voluntary Chapter 7 petition, and the only property available for distribution is a building that is worth $20,000. The Internal Revenue Service holds an allowed claim for $7,000, secured by a perfected tax lien on the building. Bank A holds a $10,000 claim secured by a nonavoidable lien on the building that is senior to the tax lien. Bank B holds a $2,000 claim secured by a nonavoidable lien on the building that is junior to the tax lien. Administrative expenses in the case total $4,000, and there also are priority claims in the amount of $1,000 for pre-petition wages owed to employees of Debtor Corporation. If the building is sold for a price of $20,000, distribution in the case will be as follows: (i) to Bank A in the amount of $10,000; (ii) to the priority claimants for the expenses of administration ($4,000) and for the employees' wages ($1,000); (iii) to the IRS in the amount of $2,000, which is the extent that its allowed secured tax claim ($7,000) exceeds the total payments to the priority claimants ($5,000); (iv) to Bank B in the amount of $2,000; and (v) to the IRS in the amount of $1,000, which are the only funds remaining. Thus, as a result of the subordination of its tax lien in the Chapter 7 case, the IRS receives a total distribution of only $3,000 on its allowed secured claim. [B.C. § 724(b)]

3. Multiple Claimants

Payment to more than one claimant within any particular level of distribution under § 724(b) is made in the order that would have been required under the Code outside of the provisions for the treatment of tax liens. [B.C. § 724(c)]

4. Similar Statutory Liens

Any statutory lien, e.g., an ERISA lien, whose priority is determined by the same method as that prescribed under 26 U.S.C. § 6323 for the priority of a tax lien, is treated under § 724(b) exactly like a tax lien, and is subordinated accordingly. [B.C. § 724(d)]

5. Ad Valorem Taxes

In 2005, Congress excluded ad valorem taxes from the operation of § 724's subordination rules but, at the same time, carved out two exceptions to that exclusion. A claim for ad valorem taxes secured by a lien on real or personal property may be subordinated to claims for *wages, salaries and commissions* entitled to priority under § 507(a)(4) or claims for *contributions to employee benefit plans* under § 507(a)(5). [B.C. § 724(f)]

E. Partnership Trustee's Claim Against General Partners

1. Deficiency of Partnership Property

If the estate of a Chapter 7 partnership debtor lacks sufficient property to fully satisfy all claims against the partnership, the *trustee* is entitled to a claim for the *deficiency* against any general partner who is personally liable, but only to the extent that the general partner is personally liable under applicable nonbankruptcy law. [B.C. § 723(a)]

a. Nondebtor General Partners

In attempting to recover the deficiency, if practicable, the trustee must first pursue any general partner who is *not a debtor* in a bankruptcy case. Until the amount of the deficiency is determined, the court may require the partner to supply indemnity for or assurance of payment of any deficiency, or may enjoin the partner from disposing of property. [B.C. § 723(b)]

b. General Partners Who Are Debtors

The trustee's claim against the estate of each general partner who is a debtor in a bankruptcy case equals the total of allowed creditors' claims in the partnership's bankruptcy case. The trustee receives distribution with the general partner's individual unsecured creditors. [B.C. § 723(c)]

(i) Disallowance of Claims of Partnership Creditors

A creditor's claim for which both the partnership debtor and a general partner are responsible will be *disallowed in the bankruptcy case of the general partner,* except to the extent that the claim is secured solely by the general partner's property and not by the partnership's assets. [B.C. § 723(c)]

2. Excess Recovery by Trustee

If the trustee in the partnership's bankruptcy case recovers from the general partners who are bankruptcy debtors an amount that exceeds a deficiency remaining after payment by the nondebtor general partners, the surplus will be returned to the general partners' bankruptcy estates in an equitable manner. [B.C. § 723(d)]

F. Chapter 7 Discharge

1. In General

The bankruptcy court must grant the Chapter 7 debtor a discharge unless one of the 11 statutory grounds for denial of a Chapter 7 discharge applies. [B.C. § 727(a)] The effect of the discharge is to discharge the debtor from all debts that arose prior to the order for relief under Chapter 7, as well as from all debts that, under Bankruptcy Code § 502, are treated as prepetition debts. [B.C. § 727(b)]

a. Exception: Nondischargeable Debts

The discharge does not include particular debts that are nondischargeable under § 523. [B.C. § 727(b)] It is important to distinguish between *denial of the entire discharge* under

§ 727 and a determination under § 523 that a ***specific debt is nondischargeable.*** A denial of the entire discharge allows *all* creditors to pursue their claims postbankruptcy. If a discharge is granted, however, only those creditors who are owed debts found to be nondischargeable under § 523 will be free to collect their claims post-bankruptcy.

2. Objection to Discharge

The Chapter 7 trustee, United States trustee, or a creditor may object to the debtor's discharge. [B.C. § 727(c)(1)] If a party in interest makes the request, the bankruptcy court may order the trustee to investigate the debtor's conduct to determine whether there is a basis for denying the discharge. [B.C. § 727(c)(2)]

3. Grounds for Denial of Discharge

The bankruptcy court may deny a discharge to a Chapter 7 debtor for any of the following reasons. [B.C. §§ 727(a)(1)–(12)]

a. Debtor Not an Individual

Under Chapter 7, only an individual may receive a discharge. Therefore, other persons, e.g., corporations and partnerships, are not granted a discharge. [B.C. § 727(a)(1)] The reason for the rule is to "avoid trafficking in corporate shells and in bankruptcy partnerships." [H.R. Rep. No. 95–595, at 384 (1977)] As a practical matter, however, if a corporation liquidates and its owners are not "trafficking in corporate shells," there is no entity to pursue after liquidation of the firm in Chapter 7. In addition, the firm's owners generally are not responsible for the firm's pre-petition debts, unless they guaranteed or were co-signers on corporate obligations, or a creditor successfully pierces the corporate veil.

b. Transfer of Property with Intent to Hinder, Delay, or Defraud Creditors

The debtor will be denied a discharge if with the ***intent to hinder, delay, or defraud*** a creditor or an officer of the estate entitled to possession of the property, she transferred, removed, concealed, mutilated, or destroyed ***property of the debtor,*** within ***one year*** before the filing of the petition, or ***property of the estate,*** after the petition was filed. [B.C. § 727(a)(2)]

(i) Conversion of Nonexempt to Exempt Property on Eve of Bankruptcy

When Congress passed the Bankruptcy Reform Act of 1978, it made clear that pre-bankruptcy planning involving the conversion of non-exempt to exempt property "is not fraudulent as to creditors, and permits the debtor to make full use of the exemptions to which he is entitled under the law." [H.R. Rep. No. 95–595, at 380 (1977); S. Rep. No. 95–989 (1978)] Absent extrinsic evidence of fraud, the mere conversion of non-exempt to exempt property is not fraudulent. The question, however, is what constitutes extrinsic evidence of fraud. As the following two cases—handed down on the same day by the same Circuit—indicate, it is difficult to determine the line between acceptable pre-bankruptcy planning and improper conversion of assets that amounts to an intent to hinder, delay, or defraud creditors.

e.g. **Example:** Prior to filing for bankruptcy, Kenneth and Lucille Hanson ("Debtors") sold various pieces of non-exempt personal property. They undertook this course of action after having consulted an attorney. Debtors sold various vehicles to their son for fair market value. The son stored the vehicles on the Debtors' property while he lived with them. Debtors also sold household goods and furnishings to Kenneth's brother for fair market value. The brother stored these possessions at Debtors' home for some time because he lived out of state at the time of the sale. Debtors used the money from these sales to buy life insurance policies, which were exempt, and to prepay their mortgage, which they exempted as their homestead. In response to a creditor's objection to Debtors' exemptions, the bankruptcy court held that the Debtors' actions did not constitute extrinsic evidence of fraud. The district court affirmed and the Eighth Circuit affirmed, concluding that the bankruptcy court's decision to allow Debtors to claim their full exemptions was not clearly erroneous. The Eighth Circuit rejected creditor's argument that storage of the sold property at Debtors' home was a "badge of fraud." The court observed that the items were sold for fair market value and were not gifts. The court also noted that Debtors' son took out a loan to buy the vehicles, and subsequently sold one of them and kept the money for himself. [**Hanson v. First National Bank,** 848 F.2d 866 (8th Cir. 1988)]

Example: At the time that Dr. Tveten ("Debtor") filed for bankruptcy, he owed $19 million to several creditors because he had guaranteed debt for various real estate investments that had failed. Prior to filing for bankruptcy, Debtor sold almost all his non-exempt property for fair market value, and converted it into exempt property worth about $700,000. Debtor did so after having consulted with an attorney. Creditors objected to Debtor's discharge. The bankruptcy court denied Debtor a discharge, and the district court affirmed. The Eighth Circuit affirmed and held that the bankruptcy court's inference of fraudulent intent on Dr. Tveten's part was not clearly erroneous. The Eighth Circuit acknowledged that the standard governing the permissibility of exemptions and the standard for denial of discharge were the same—whether there is extrinsic evidence of fraud. The court noted, however, that in Dr. Tveten's case the state exemption was unlimited "with the potential for unlimited abuse." The court said that Dr. Tveten had liquidated almost all his property and converted it into exempt assets while owing his creditors $19 million. Doing so, according to the court, went "well beyond the purpose for which exemptions are permitted." The court acknowledged that Dr. Tveten was entitled to retain the property he had exempted, because state law governed the permissibility of his exemptions. But, federal law governed the question of whether he was entitled to a discharge. Allowing Dr. Tveten, "who earns over $60,000 annually, to convert all his major non-exempt assets into sheltered property on the eve of bankruptcy with actual intent to defraud his creditors 'would constitute a perversion of the purposes of the Bankruptcy Code.' " The court concluded by distinguishing the result in *Hanson* on the basis that the bankruptcy court in *Hanson* had found no extrinsic evidence of fraud. [**Norwest Bank Nebraska v. Tveten,** 848 F.3d 871 (8th Cir. 1988)] Judge Arnold dissented in *Tveten* and wrote a concurring opinion in *Hanson* that criticized the court's deference to bankruptcy court findings premised on the amount of money involved. Judge Arnold noted that three things distinguished *Hanson* from *Tveten:* (1) Dr. Tveten was a doctor while the Hansons were farmers; (2) Dr. Tveten exempted $700,000 in property while the Hansons exempted $31,000; and (3) the state exemption Dr. Tveten used had no dollar limit while the state exemption used by the Hansons did. Judge Arnold noted that the Bankruptcy Code allows debtors to exempt property under state law without regard to whether the state exemption contains a monetary cap. Moreover, according to Judge Arnold, the amount of money at issue was irrelevant, because the state exemption statute had "no dollar limit, and for judges to set one involve[d] essentially a legislative decision not suitable for the judicial branch." [**Hanson v. First National Bank,** *supra*]

(ii) Bankruptcy Crimes

Bankruptcy fraud also may result in the conviction of a federal crime, the penalty for which is a fine, imprisonment for a maximum of five years, or both. [18 U.S.C. § 157]

c. Destruction or Concealment of Books or Records

Another ground for denying a discharge to the debtor is her destruction, concealment, mutilation, falsification of, or failure to keep books, records, documents, or other recorded information from which her business transactions or financial state might be determined. [B.C. § 727(a)(3)] Debtors do not have to keep books and records in any particular form, so long as the Chapter 7 trustee and creditors can figure out the reason for debtor's bankruptcy and understand debtor's financial condition. What is expected of a large corporation is not expected of a small business. The inquiry is a fact-intensive one. [6 Collier ¶ 727.03(3)]

d. Perjury, Bribery, Extortion, and Other Fraudulent Acts

The bankruptcy court also will deny a Chapter 7 debtor a discharge if she *knowingly and fraudulently* in or in connection with the bankruptcy case does any of the following:

(i) makes a false oath or account [B.C. § 727(a)(4)(A)];

(ii) submits or uses a false claim [B.C. § 727(a)(4)(B)];

(iii) pays, offers, receives, or obtains money, property, or advantage or a promise of money, property or advantage for acting or forbearing to act, i.e., extortion or bribery, or an attempt at extortion or bribery [B.C. § 727(a)(4)(C)]; or

(iv) withholds any books, records, or other recorded information concerning the debtor's property or finances from an officer of the estate who is entitled to possession. [B.C. § 727(a)(4)(D)]

e. Failure to Account for Loss of Assets

Another basis for denial of the debtor's discharge is her failure to adequately explain any loss of assets or deficiency of assets to meet her liabilities. [B.C. § 727(a)(5)]

Example: Debtor settled a wrongful death suit with Creditors for $100,000. When Debtor subsequently filed for relief under Chapter 7, Creditors filed an adversary proceeding that, among other things, sought to deny Debtor a discharge under § 727(a)(5). As the basis for their § 727(a)(5) claim, Creditors argued that there was an "intentional and unexplained loss of value in Debtor's residence, which Debtor valued at $390,000 in his bankruptcy schedules but which was worth $500,000, according to a valuation done four years earlier. The bankruptcy court granted summary judgment in favor of Debtor. The court concluded that there was "no evidence in the record that an actual loss occurred (requiring an explanation from the Debtor)." The court explained that a drop in value is not a " 'loss' of a tangible asset." [**Thomas v. Roberson (*In re Roberson*),** 2017 WL 2125807 (Bankr. D. V.I. 2017)]

f. Violation of Court Order or Refusal to Respond to Material Question

The debtor also will be denied a discharge if she does any of the following:

(i) refuses to obey a valid court order, other than one directing the debtor to testify or to answer a material question [B.C. § 727(a)(6)(A)];

(ii) refuses, for a reason other than the appropriate use of the Fifth Amendment privilege against self-incrimination, to testify or to answer a material question that the bankruptcy judge has approved [B.C. § 727(a)(6)(C)]; or

(iii) refuses, on the basis of the privilege against self-incrimination, to testify or to answer a judicially approved material question *after she has been granted immunity* regarding the privileged matter. [B.C. § 727(a)(6)(B)]

Example: State probate court appointed Debtor the guardian of various veterans' estates, and Creditor Corporation issued surety bonds in connection with the appointments. Debtor subsequently resigned as guardian when discrepancies were found in the guardianship accounts. The new guardians filed claims against Debtor, who then filed for relief under Chapter 7 with his wife. Creditor Corporation filed an adversary proceeding in Debtors' Chapter 7 case seeking a determination that the debts arising from the surety bonds were not dischargeable. While the adversary proceeding was pending, Debtors were indicted on various criminal charges stemming from the guardianships. Creditor Corporation then filed a motion to compel depositions, and Debtors responded with a motion to quash and for a protective order. The bankruptcy court directed Debtors to sit for the depositions, and Debtors invoked their privilege against self-incrimination. Debtors then filed an appeal of the bankruptcy court's decision and argued, in part, that the bankruptcy court had created a "Hobson's choice" of either having to invoke their Fifth Amendment right against self-incrimination or "suffer[ ] the effects of having an adverse inference drawn against them in the bankruptcy court." The district court, on appeal, affirmed the decision of the bankruptcy court. The district court explained that there was no error "in drawing an adverse inference against a civil litigant for invoking the right to remain silent" because the Fifth Amendment applies to criminal, not civil, proceedings. The bankruptcy court did not compel Debtors to testify, and Debtors invoked their Fifth Amendment right not to testify during the depositions. Thus, there was no risk that their testimony would be used against them in a future criminal proceeding. [**Phillips v. First National Insurance Co.**, 2011 WL 2447954 (S.D. Tex. 2011)]

g. Acts Committed in Insider Case

The bankruptcy court may deny the Chapter 7 debtor a discharge if the debtor commits any act, either during her bankruptcy case or within one year before the petition was filed, described in § 727(a)(2)–(6) in connection with a separate bankruptcy case regarding an insider. [B.C. §§ 727(a)(7), 101(31)]

h. Prior Discharge Obtained Under Chapter 7 or Chapter 11

The bankruptcy court will deny a Chapter 7 debtor a discharge in her *current case* if she previously received a discharge in a Chapter 7 or a Chapter 11 case that was *commenced within eight years* before the date that the petition was filed in the current case. [B.C. § 727(a)(8)]

Example: Debtor filed for relief under Chapter 7 on June 3, 2010, and received a discharge on November 10, 2010. Debtor filed another Chapter 7 case on October 10, 2018. The court may not deny Debtor a discharge under § 727(a)(8), because she filed her *current* bankruptcy case more than eight years from the filing of her 2010 Chapter 7 case.

Example: Debtor filed for relief under Chapter 7 on October 10, 2017, and the bankruptcy court dismissed her case on November 15, 2017. The court did not dismiss Debtor's case under § 707(b). Debtor then filed another Chapter 7 case on December 15, 2017. Section 727(a)(8) does not apply, because Debtor did not receive a discharge in her prior case. Instead, the case was dismissed. But, Debtor may have problems with the automatic stay in her second Chapter 7 case. [B.C. § 362(c)(3)]

i. Prior Discharge Obtained Under Chapter 12 or Chapter 13

Similarly, the bankruptcy court will deny a Chapter 7 debtor a discharge if she previously was granted a discharge in a Chapter 12 or a Chapter 13 case that was *commenced within six years* before the date of the filing of the petition in the *current case, unless:*

(i) all of the allowed unsecured claims in the earlier case were *paid in full* [B.C. § 727(a)(9)(A)]; *or*

(ii) payments under the plan in the earlier case totaled *at least 70%* of the allowed unsecured claims, and the debtor's plan was *proposed in good faith and represented her best effort.* [B.C. § 727(a)(9)(B)]

EXAM TIP   GILBERT

It is important to remember that the six- or eight-year bar to discharge is measured from the date of the *bankruptcy petition* (not from the date of discharge) in the prior case to the date that the *petition* was filed in the current case.

---

j. Waiver

If the debtor has executed a court-approved written waiver of discharge after the Chapter 7 order for relief, a discharge will not be granted. [B.C. § 727(a)(10)]

k. Failure to Complete Instructional Course

The debtor will be denied a discharge if post-petition she fails to complete an instructional course on personal financial management. [B.C. §§ 727(a)(11), 111] The failure to complete such a course is *not grounds* for denial of a discharge in *two situations.* The first is if the court determines, after notice and a hearing, that the debtor cannot complete such a course due to the debtor's *incapacity, disability, or active military service* in a military combat zone. [B.C. §§ 727(a)(11), 109(h)(4)] The second exception applies to debtors who live in a district for which the United States trustee or bankruptcy administrator, if applicable, has determined that the *approved courses are inadequate* to service the individuals who are required to take such courses. [B.C. § 727(a)(11)] BAPCPA added this ground for denial of discharge.

4. Delaying Entry of the Discharge

In 2005, Congress added a provision to the Code that says that the bankruptcy court shall not grant a Chapter 7 debtor a discharge if the court finds, after notice and a hearing held *no more than 10 days* before the entry of the discharge, that *reasonable cause* exists to believe either that *§ 522(q)(1) may apply* to the debtor's case *or* that there is a proceeding pending in which the debtor may be found guilty of a *felony listed in § 522(q)(1)(A)* or liable for a *debt described in § 522(q)(1)(B).* [B.C. § 727(a)(12)] While the new provision is situated in the Code's denial-of-discharge section, the section appears to merely *delay, not deny, the debtor's discharge.* [*See* Bankruptcy Rule 4004(c)(1)(I) (the court may not grant a discharge if "a motion to delay or postpone the discharge under § 727(a)(12) is pending")]

THE FOLLOWING ARE GROUNDS FOR DENYING A DISCHARGE IN A CHAPTER 7 CASE:

☑ The debtor is *not an individual*

☑ The debtor *transferred, concealed, mutilated, or destroyed his property* within a year before the petition, *or estate property* after the petition, with the *intent* to hinder, delay, or defraud a creditor or an officer of the estate

☑ The debtor *destroyed, concealed, mutilated, falsified, or failed to keep records or documents* concerning his business transactions and financial status, unless such conduct was justified

☑ "The debtor knowingly and fraudulently, in or in connection with the case, made a *false oath or account* about a material issue," submitted a *false claim,* committed or attempted to commit *bribery or extortion,* or *withheld records or documents* pertinent to the debtor's property or financial affairs from an officer of the estate

☑ The debtor *failed to adequately explain any loss of assets* or deficiency of assets to meet liabilities

☑ The debtor *refused to obey a valid judicial order or to testify* or answer a material question approved by the court other than on legitimate Fifth Amendment self-incrimination grounds

☑ The debtor *committed any of the above acts in connection with a separate bankruptcy case regarding an insider* during or within a year before the debtor's case

☑ The debtor received a *discharge in a prior Chapter 7 or Chapter 11 case commenced within eight years before the date the petition was filed* in the present case

☑ Subject to two exceptions, the debtor received a *discharge in a prior Chapter 12 or Chapter 13 case commenced within six years before the date the petition was filed* in the present case

☑ The debtor executed a *court-approved written waiver* of discharge *after* the Chapter 7 order for relief

☑ Subject to two exceptions, the debtor *failed to complete a post-petition instruction course on personal financial management*

5. Revocation of Discharge

A creditor, the Chapter 7 trustee, or the United States trustee may request that the court, after notice and a hearing, revoke the debtor's discharge for any of the following reasons:

a. *the debtor obtained the discharge fraudulently,* and the party seeking revocation did not discover the fraud until after the discharge was granted [B.C. § 727(d)(1)];

b. *the debtor acquired or became entitled to acquire property* that would constitute property of the estate, and she *knowingly and fraudulently* failed to disclose this fact or to turn over the property to the trustee [B.C. § 727(d)(2)];

c. *the debtor committed one of the acts of impropriety* described in § 727(a)(6) [B.C. § 727(d)(3)]; or

d. *the debtor failed to satisfactorily explain* (i) *a material misstatement* in an *audit* referred to in 28 U.S.C. § 586(f) *or* (ii) a *failure to make available for inspection* accounts, documents, financial records, papers, files and all other papers, things, or property belonging to the debtor that are requested for *the audit* referred to in 28 U.S.C. § 586(f). [B.C. § 727(d)(4)]

6. Limitations Period for Discharge Revocation

A request to revoke the debtor's discharge under § 727(d)(1) may be filed within *one year* after the granting of the discharge. [B.C. § 727(e)(1)] A request under §§ 727(d)(2) or (d)(3) may be filed within *one year* after granting of the discharge or prior to the date that the *case is closed*, whichever is later. [B.C. § 727(e)(2)] BAPCPA added another ground for revocation of the debtor's discharge based on the debtor's failure to satisfactorily explain either (i) material misstatements in an audit or (ii) the debtor's failure to make various records available for inspection for an audit. [B.C. § 727(d)(4); 28 U.S.C. § 586(f)] Congress, however, did not amend § 727(e) to provide a limitations period for bringing a revocation of discharge proceeding under § 727(d)(4). As a result, there is no limitations period in the Code for bringing revocation of discharge proceedings related to the new audit language contained at § 727(d)(4).

G. Conversion

1. Voluntary Conversion

If a Chapter 7 case has not been converted from Chapter 11, 12, or 13, the debtor has an *absolute nonwaivable right* to convert the case from Chapter 7 to any of such other chapters at any time. [B.C. § 706(a)]

2. Involuntary Conversion

Unless the debtor requests or consents to conversion, the court may *not* convert a Chapter 7 case to one under Chapter 12 or 13. [B.C. § 706(c)] However, the court may convert a Chapter 7 case to one under Chapter 11, upon a request by a party in interest, after notice and a hearing. [B.C. § 706(b)]

3. Eligibility

Conversion of a Chapter 7 case to another chapter of the Code requires that the debtor be eligible for relief under the particular chapter to which the case is being converted. [B.C. § 706(d)]

4. Means Test

If an *individual Chapter 7 debtor with primarily consumer debts* fails the "means test," then a presumption of abuse arises. In such a case, after notice and a hearing, the court, on its own motion or a motion by the Chapter 7 trustee, the United States trustee, the Bankruptcy Administrator in North Carolina or Alabama cases, or any party in interest, may dismiss or convert the debtor's case. The court may only convert the case to Chapter 11 or 13 with the debtor's consent. [B.C. § 707(b)(1)]

H. Dismissal

1. For Cause

After notice and a hearing, the court may dismiss a Chapter 7 case for *cause,* which includes the following circumstances:

a. *the debtor is responsible for an unreasonable delay that is prejudicial to creditors* [B.C. § 707(a)(1)];

b. *the debtor has not paid fees or charges* prescribed by chapter 123 of title 28 [B.C. § 707(a)(2)]; or

c. *the debtor in a voluntary case has not filed a list of creditors and all schedules and statements* required under § 521(a)(1) within *15 days,* or any extension granted by the court, after the petition was filed. [B.C. § 707(a)(3)]

Note: Only the United States trustee may move for dismissal under § 707(a)(3).

2. Abuse of Chapter 7

a. Means Test

If an *individual Chapter 7 debtor with primarily consumer debts* fails the "means test," then a presumption of abuse arises. In such a case, after notice and a hearing, the court, on its own motion or a motion by the Chapter 7 trustee, the United States trustee, the Bankruptcy Administrator in North Carolina or Alabama cases, or any party in interest, may dismiss the debtor's case. [B.C. § 707(b)(1)]

Exception: The court may not dismiss such a case if the debtor establishes by a preponderance of the evidence that filing under Chapter 7 is *necessary* to satisfy a *domestic support obligation.* [B.C. § 707(c)(3)]

b. Bad Faith or Totality of the Circumstances

In determining whether the filing of a Chapter 7 case *by an individual debtor with primarily consumer debts* constitutes abuse, the court must consider:

(i) whether the debtor *filed* the petition in *bad faith; or*

(ii) whether the *totality of the circumstances of debtor's financial situation* demonstrates abuse. The Code specifically includes as part of the evaluation of debtor's circumstances whether debtor plans to reject a personal services contract and the financial need for such rejection. [B.C. § 707(b)(3)]

(1) Criteria: Totality of the Circumstances

Courts use a number of criteria to determine whether the individual debtor's filing for relief under Chapter 7 is an abuse. Courts examine the following factors in evaluating whether debtor's filing was an abuse under the totality of the circumstances:

(a) the debtor's *reason for filing* the Chapter 7 petition, e.g., because of *unemployment, medical expenses, disability, or other misfortune;*

(b) the *excessiveness or extravagance* of the debtor's *anticipated family budget;*

(c) the extent to which the debtor's *statements and schedules accurately represents* her actual financial condition;

(d) debtor's efforts to *repay her debts or negotiate with creditors;*

(e) the availability of *nonbankruptcy remedies;*

(f) whether debtor is *eligible to file for relief under Chapter 13;* and

(g) whether debtor's *expenses* can be *reduced significantly without depriving* her or her dependents of *necessities.*

[*See, e.g.,* **DeAngelis v. Gearhart (*In re* Gearhart),** 2010 WL 4866179 (Bankr. M.D. Penn. 2010); *In re* **Cribbs,** 387 B.R. 324 (Bankr. S.D. Ga. 2008)]

c. **Charitable Contributions**

In making its determination whether to dismiss a Chapter 7 case for abuse, the bankruptcy court *may not consider* the debtor's *charitable contributions* to any qualified religious or charitable entity or organization. [B.C. §§ 707(b)(1), 548(d)(3), (4)]

3. Crimes of Violence

The bankruptcy court may dismiss the case of an individual Chapter 7 debtor who has been convicted of a crime of violence or a drug trafficking crime if the victim of such crime moves for dismissal and the court determines that dismissal is in the best interest of the crime victim. Dismissal may occur only after notice and a hearing. [B.C. § 707(c)(2)] The court may not dismiss the case, however, if filing is necessary to satisfy a domestic support obligation. [§ 707(c)(3)] A "crime of violence" is defined at 18 U.S.C. § 16, and a "drug trafficking crime" is defined at 18 U.S.C. § 924(c)(2). [B.C. § 707(c)(1); 18 U.S.C. §§ 16, 924(c)(2)] Congress added this provision to the Code in 2005 with the passage of BAPCPA.

Chapter Thirteen

Bankruptcy Code Chapter 11: Reorganization

Chapter Approach

A Chapter 11 reorganization case is the means by which a troubled business may continue to operate and rehabilitate itself while also paying creditors and keeping workers employed. In recent years, some large companies have used Chapter 11 as a vehicle for dealing with mass tort liability, e.g., asbestos, *in one forum.*

Chapter 11 is thought of as the *business reorganization* chapter, but it is limited to neither businesses nor reorganization. The Supreme Court has held that individual consumer debtors may file for relief under Chapter 11. In addition, a business may use Chapter 11 to liquidate instead of reorganize. Instead of filing a plan of reorganization, the debtor files a liquidating plan.

In answering an exam question about Chapter 11, keep in mind that the Code provides for the debtor to continue to manage the business as a *debtor in possession* unless the conduct of current management or the interests of creditors, equity security holders, and the estate necessitate the appointment of a *trustee.* However, if a trustee is appointed, note that the debtor then loses the exclusive right to file a plan even if the exclusivity period has not expired. If a trustee has not been appointed, sometimes an *examiner* is appointed to investigate the debtor's operations and financial condition, and to advise whether the business should be continued.

If your professor asks you to evaluate a *reorganization plan,* pay careful attention to the manner in which *claims are classified,* and to the kinds of plan provisions that the Code either requires or permits. While all *mandatory provisions* must be included as part of the plan, those that are *discretionary* generally are left to the ingenuity of the plan's proponent. In addition, pay attention to whether the debtor qualifies as a small business debtor. The Code contains certain plan-proposal and plan-confirmation deadlines applicable only to small business debtors.

A unique feature of Chapter 11 is the right of a partially secured creditor *to elect to have her entire claim treated as secured,* under Bankruptcy Code § 1111(b), but at the cost of forfeiting an unsecured claim for a deficiency. Be prepared to consider the advisability of this election in light of factors such as (i) how much the *unsecured creditors are being offered* under the plan, (ii) whether the plan proposes to *cash out* the secured creditor at the value of her collateral, (iii) whether confirmation will involve application of the Code's *cramdown* provisions with respect to the secured creditor, and (iv) whether her *collateral is likely to appreciate or depreciate* in value.

Of importance, too, is the adequacy of the information contained in the *disclosure statement,* which must be approved by the court prior to the *post-petition solicitation of acceptances or rejections* from creditors and equity security holders. Keep in mind that BAPCPA relaxed the requirements for disclosure statements in small business cases. Your professor may ask you to consider the plan from the perspective of various classes in the case and to determine whether the plan can be confirmed. Your answer will require an understanding of the Code's *requirements for confirmation,* including application of the *absolute priority rule* and the use of the *cramdown* provisions concerning any dissenting classes that are impaired.

Finally, your professor may test you on the rules for Chapter 11 small business cases. The Code provides a longer exclusivity period for proposing a plan and relaxed rules on disclosure statements for small business cases. At the same time, however, there are "drop dead" dates by which a plan must be proposed and confirmed in a small business case; there are no such dates for a Chapter 11 debtor whose case does not qualify as a small business case.

A. Eligibility for Relief

1. In General

Relief under Chapter 11 is available to *any person*—individual, corporation, or partnership—who *qualifies to be a debtor under Chapter 7,* except for a stockbroker or a commodity broker. In addition, *railroads are eligible* for relief under special provisions of Chapter 11. [B.C. § 109(d)] Railroad reorganization, however, is a topic beyond the scope of this book.

2. Business or Consumer Debtors

Chapter 11 is designed primarily for *business reorganizations.* However, the Supreme Court has held that a consumer debtor, i.e., an individual not engaged in business, may qualify for relief under this chapter. [**Toibb v. Radloff,** 501 U.S. 157 (1991)]

B. Administration of Chapter 11 Case

1. Creditors' Committees

The Bankruptcy Code provides that shortly after the order for relief, the United States trustee shall appoint a committee of unsecured creditors, usually consisting of those *persons,* willing to serve, that hold the *seven largest unsecured claims* against the debtor. [B.C §§ 1102(a)(1), (b)(1)] While the Code uses the term "shall," it is not unusual for the United States trustee to be unable to find creditors willing to serve on the unsecured creditors' committee. Thus, in many Chapter 11 cases, there is no official committee of unsecured creditors. *Note:* In a *small business case,* a party in interest may request and the court may order, upon finding cause, that an official committee of unsecured creditors not be appointed. [B.C. § 1102(a)(3)]

a. List of Creditors

The debtor is required to file a list of the creditors holding the 20 largest unsecured claims, excluding insiders. In a voluntary case, the list must be filed with the petition; in an involuntary case, it must be filed within two days after the entry of the order for relief. [Bankruptcy Rule 1007(d); Official Form 204]

b. Membership on Creditors' Committee

Membership on a creditors' committee is not limited to individuals; other persons holding large unsecured claims may be appointed.

(i) Certain Governmental Units

Generally, governmental units are excluded from the definition of the term *person.* For purposes of eligibility to serve on a Chapter 11 creditors' committee, however, "person" includes a governmental unit that:

(1) acquires an asset as a result of a loan guarantee agreement, or as a receiver or liquidating agent of a person, such as the FDIC [B.C. § 101(41)(A)];

(2) is a guarantor of pension benefits, e.g., the Pension Benefit Guaranty Corporation, payable by or for the debtor or an affiliate [B.C. § 101(41)(B)]; or

(3) is the legal or beneficial owner of an asset of a certain type of pension plan, such as a state employee pension fund. [B.C. § 101(41)(C)]

(ii) Pre-Petition Committee

A creditors' committee may consist of the members of a committee created before the petition was filed if the members were selected fairly and exemplify the types of claims to be represented. [B.C. § 1102(b)(1); Bankruptcy Rule 2007(b)]

c. Additional Committees

The bankruptcy court, upon the request of a party in interest, may order the appointment of additional committees of creditors or equity security holders. The United States trustee appoints the committee. [B.C. § 1102(a)(2)] If the United States trustee deems it appropriate, she also may appoint additional committees of creditors or equity security holders to ensure adequate representation. [B.C. § 1102(a)(1)]

(i) Equity Security Holders

If a committee of equity security holders is appointed, it usually will consist of the seven largest holders, in amount, of the type of equity securities represented by the committee. [B.C. § 1102(b)(2)] Unless the court orders otherwise, the debtor must file a list of equity security holders of each class within 14 days after the entry of the order for relief. [Bankruptcy Rule 1007(a)(3)]

d. Change in Committee Composition

Upon the request of a party in interest and after notice and a hearing, the bankruptcy court may order the United States trustee to *change the composition* of a creditors' or equity security holders' committee, because the court has determined that a change is needed in order to *ensure adequate representation.* The court may order the United States trustee to increase the size of a committee in order *to add a creditor that is a small business debtor,* as that term is defined in the Small Business Act. [15 U.S.C. § 632(a)(1)] The court may order the addition of a small business debtor to a committee if such debtor holds claims of the kind represented by the committee and the *aggregate amount of those claims is disproportionately large in relation to the annual gross revenue of the small business.* [B.C. § 1102(a)(4)] Congress added this provision to the Code in 2005 with the passage of BAPCPA.

e. Mandatory Duties

A creditors' committee or equity security holders' committee must provide *access to information* to creditors who are not appointed to the committee but who hold claims of the type represented by the committee. [B.C. § 1102(b)(3)(A)] The committee also must *solicit and receive comments* from such creditors, and is subject to a court order compelling the committee to make any *additional report or disclosure* to such creditors. [B.C. §§ 1103(b)(3)(B), (C)] Congress added these duties to the Code in 2005.

f. Powers and Discretionary Duties

A creditors' committee or an equity security holders' committee may engage in any of the following activities during a Chapter 11 case:

(i) *consult with the debtor in possession* or with the trustee, if one has been appointed [B.C. § 1103(c)(1)];

(ii) *investigate the debtor's conduct, financial condition, assets and liabilities, business operations,* the *desirability of continuing* the debtor's business, and other matters pertinent to the case and to formulation of a plan [B.C. § 1103(c)(2)];

(iii) *participate in the preparation of a reorganization plan* [B.C. § 1103(c)(3)];

(iv) *advise the creditors or equity security holders* it represents of the committee's judgment or conclusions concerning any plan formulated [B.C. § 1103(c)(3)];

(v) *collect and file acceptances or rejections of a plan* [B.C. § 1103(c)(3)];

(vi) *if appropriate, request the appointment of a trustee or an examiner* [B.C. § 1103(c)(4)]; and

(vii) *render any other services* for the benefit of the creditors or equity security holders represented by the committee. [B.C. § 1103(c)(5)]

g. Employment of Attorneys or Accountants

A creditors' committee or an equity security holders' committee may hire attorneys, accountants, or other professionals to represent or perform services for the committee. The committee's hiring decision must be made at a scheduled meeting attended by a *majority of the committee members* and *court approval* is required. [B.C. § 1103(a)]

(i) Limitation: No Adverse Interest

An attorney or an accountant hired by a creditors' committee or an equity security holders' committee is prohibited from representing, during the period of her employment, any entity possessing an adverse interest in connection with the case. The representation of a creditor of the same class as the committee represents is not automatically deemed representation of an adverse interest. [B.C. § 1103(b)]

(ii) Prior Approval

It is important that a lawyer or an accountant employed by a creditors' committee or an equity security holders' committee make certain that she obtains court approval *before* rendering services, because, in many jurisdictions, a court will not retroactively grant approval absent extraordinary or exceptional circumstances.

2. Debtor in Possession

Unless a trustee is appointed in the case, the debtor in possession remains in possession of the property of the estate and has all of the rights, powers, and duties of a trustee, *except* the right to compensation and the duty to investigate the debtor. [B.C. §§ 1101(1), 1107(a)] Unless the court orders otherwise, upon the request of a party in interest and after notice and a hearing, the debtor continues to operate its business. [B.C. § 1108]

a. Business Judgment

Because the debtor is familiar with its business and the industry, the courts will defer to the exercise of the debtor in possession's business judgment absent a showing that the decision is so manifestly unreasonable that the debtor in possession was not exercising sound business judgment but instead was acting in bad faith or on a whim. [*See, e.g., In re* **9 Houston LLC,** 578 B.R. 600 (Bankr. S.D. Tex. 2017) (in context of dispute over whether a part of the estate's sole asset should be sold pursuant to the debtor in possession's emergency motion or pursuant to a plan of reorganization); *In re* **SW Boston Hotel Venture, LLC,** 2010 WL 3396863 (Bankr. D. Mass. 2010) (in context of motion by debtor in possession under § 363 to approve the lease of condo units owned by debtor)]

b. **Employment of Professionals**

Any attorney, accountant, or other professional employed by the debtor in possession must be a *disinterested* person and cannot hold or represent any interest that is *adverse* to the estate. [B.C. §§ 101(14), 327(a)] A professional person is not disqualified from employment *solely* because she was employed by or represented the debtor prior to commencement of the bankruptcy case. [B.C. § 1107(b)]

3. Appointment of Trustee

The debtor in possession usually is considered the most appropriate person to operate its business. Thus, it is well settled that appointment of a trustee is the exception, not the rule. [*In re* **Europark Industries,** 424 B.R. 621 (Bankr. E.D. N.Y. 2010)] In fact, there is a presumption that the debtor should be allowed to remain in possession unless the need for a trustee is shown. [*In re* **China Fishery Group, Ltd.,** 2016 WL 6875903 (Bankr. S.D. N.Y. 2016)]

Nonetheless, after the filing of the petition and prior to confirmation of a plan, a party in interest or the United States trustee may request the appointment of a trustee. The bankruptcy court, after notice and a hearing, may order the appointment of a trustee (i) *for cause,* (ii) if the appointment is in the interests of creditors, equity security holders, and other interests of the estate, or (iii) if the bankruptcy court determines it is in the *best interests* of the creditors and the estate to appoint a trustee rather than *convert or dismiss* the case. [B.C. § 1104(a)(1), (2), (3)] Most courts require that the party requesting appointment of a trustee prove by *clear and convincing evidence* that cause exists under § 1104(a)(1) or the need for a trustee under § 1104(a)(2). [*See In re* **Adelphia Communications Corp.,** 336 B.R. 610 (Bankr. S.D. N.Y. 2006)]

a. **Cause for Appointment**

Cause for appointment of a Chapter 11 trustee includes *fraud, dishonesty, incompetence, or gross mismanagement,* by current management, either before or after the filing of the bankruptcy case. [B.C. § 1104(a)(1)] The court, however, is not limited to fraud, dishonesty, incompetence, or gross mismanagement in establishing cause. While there is no one definitive list, courts have examined some of the following additional factors in making the "cause" determination:

(i) whether the debtor treated *insiders and affiliates better or worse* than its *customers and creditors;*

(ii) whether management's *conflicts of interest* interfered with its ability to satisfy its fiduciary obligations to the debtor;

(iii) whether management *misused or squandered assets and funds;*

(iv) whether management *lacked credibility* and had *lost creditor confidence*; and

(v) whether the misconduct alleged was *material.*

[*See, e.g., In re* **Ashley River Consulting, LLC,** 2015 WL 1540941 (Bankr. S.D. N.Y. 2015); *In re* **LHC, LLC,** 497 B.R. 281 (Bankr. N.D. Ill. 2013)]

b. **Interests of the Estate**

The Code provides that the court shall appoint a trustee if appointment is in the interests of creditors, equity security holders, and other interests of the estate. [B.C. § 1104(a)(2)] Courts examine the following factors in making a decision whether to appoint a trustee pursuant to § 1104(a)(2):

(i) debtor's *trustworthiness;*

(ii) the *past and current performance* of the debtor;

(iii) the *prospects* for debtor's reorganization;

(iv) the business community's and creditors' *confidence in current management;* and

(v) the *benefits* of appointing a trustee weighed against the *costs* of doing so.

[*See, e.g.,* **In re Ashley River Consulting, LLC,** *supra*; **In re Celeritas Technologies, LLC,** 446 B.R. 514 (Bankr. D. Kan. 2011)]

c. Alternative to Conversion or Dismissal

If cause exists to dismiss the case or to convert it to Chapter 7, a bankruptcy court may appoint a Chapter 11 trustee (or examiner) instead, if doing so is in the *best interests of creditors and the estate.* [B.C. § 1112(b)(1)]

d. Mandatory Motion by United States Trustee

The United States trustee must move for the appointment of a Chapter 11 trustee if there are *reasonable grounds to suspect* that current members of the governing body of the debtor, e.g., the board of directors, the chief executive officer, or the chief financial officer, or members of the governing body who selected the CEO or CFO participated in *actual fraud, dishonesty, or criminal conduct* in managing the debtor or the debtor's public financial reporting. [B.C. § 1104(e)] While the United States trustee must file a motion for appointment under such circumstances, the bankruptcy court is not required to appoint a Chapter 11 trustee.

e. Choosing a Trustee

If the court orders the appointment of a trustee, generally the United States trustee consults with parties in interest and then *appoints* a *disinterested person*, other than himself, subject to the court's approval. [B.C. § 1104(d)] Alternatively, in cases other than railroad reorganizations, the Code provides for *election* of the trustee *if* a party in interest requests an election within *30 days after the court orders appointment* of a trustee. The election is held at a meeting of creditors convened by the United States trustee and is conducted in the same manner as the election of a trustee under Chapter 7. [B.C. §§ 1104(b)(1), 702] If an eligible, disinterested person is elected at a meeting of creditors, then the United States trustee must file a report certifying the election. In cases in which an eligible, disinterested person is elected to serve as trustee after the United States trustee has appointed a trustee through consultation, the election terminates the service of the trustee appointed by the United States trustee. [B.C. § 1104(b)(2); *see* Bankruptcy Rule 2007.1]

f. Duties of Trustee

The duties of a Chapter 11 trustee include many of the same duties performed by a Chapter 7 trustee, as well as several additional obligations. The Chapter 11 trustee's duties include the following:

(i) *to account for all property received* [B.C. §§ 1106(a)(1), 704(a)(2)];

(ii) *to examine proofs of claims* and object to the allowance of any improper ones [B.C. §§ 1106(a)(1), 704(a)(5)];

(iii) *to provide information requested by parties in interest* about the estate and the administration of the estate [B.C. §§ 1106(a)(1), 704(a)(7)];

(iv)   *if the court authorizes operation of the debtor's business, to file periodic financial reports,* including a statement of receipts and disbursements, with the court, the United States trustee, and the appropriate taxing authorities [B.C. §§ 1106(a)(1), 704(a)(8)];

(v)   *to prepare and file* with the court and with the United States trustee *a final report and account* concerning the case [B.C. §§ 1106(a)(1), 704(a)(9)];

(vi)   *to provide* the notice required for creditors holding *domestic support obligation claims* [B.C. §§ 1106(a)(1), (8), 704(a)(10)];

(vii)   *to continue to perform* the obligations of an administrator of an *employee benefit plan,* if at the start of the Chapter 11 case the debtor or an entity designated by the debtor served that function [B.C. §§ 1106(a)(1), 704(a)(11); 29 U.S.C. § 1002];

(viii)   *to use reasonable and best efforts* to transfer patients to an appropriate health care business if the debtor is a *health care business* in the process of closing [B.C. §§ 1106(a)(1), 704(a)(12)];

(ix)   *to file any document required* under § 521(a)(1), e.g., list of creditors, schedule of assets and liabilities, that the debtor has not filed [B.C. §§ 1106(a)(2), 521(a)(1)];

(x)   *to investigate the debtor's conduct, financial condition, and business operations,* as well as *the advisability of continuing the debtor's business* [B.C. § 1106(a)(3)];

(xi)   *to file a report of the investigation,* relating any facts evidencing fraud, dishonesty, incompetence, misconduct, or mismanagement, and to send a copy of the findings to any creditors' committee, equity security holders' committee, indenture trustee, or any other entity designated by the bankruptcy court [B.C. § 1106(a)(4)];

(xii)   as soon as is feasible, *to file a Chapter 11 plan,* or *to file a report* as to why the trustee will not file a plan, or *to recommend conversion or dismissal* of the case [B.C. § 1106(a)(5)];

(xiii)   *to provide available information to the taxing authorities* concerning any year for which the debtor failed to file a return [B.C. § 1106(a)(6)]; and

(xiv)   *after a plan has been confirmed, to file any required reports.* [B.C. § 1106(a)(7)]

g. Authority to Operate Business

A trustee who is appointed in a Chapter 11 case is authorized to manage the debtor's business, unless the court rules otherwise. [B.C. § 1108] "If a trustee is appointed, the management is completely ousted, although occasionally a trustee hires former management to handle day-to-day operations." [H.R. Rep. No. 95–595, at 220 (1977)] As a consequence, the trustee replaces the debtor's directors, and they must surrender the corporation's property to the trustee. [**Commodity Futures Trading Commission v. Weintraub,** 471 U.S. 343 (1985)]

h. Termination of Trustee's Appointment

The bankruptcy court may terminate the trustee's appointment at any time before a plan is confirmed. Any party in interest or the United States trustee may make such a request. If the bankruptcy court terminates the Chapter 11 trustee's appointment, after notice and a hearing, the court restores the debtor to possession and management of the estate property and of operation of the debtor's business. [B.C § 1105]

4. Appointment of Examiner

In a Chapter 11 case in which the court has not ordered the appointment of a trustee, the court sometimes will order the appointment of an examiner, prior to confirmation of a plan, *to investigate* any charges of fraud, dishonesty, incompetence, misconduct, mismanagement, or irregularity on the part of the debtor's present or former management. The appointment is made by the United States trustee, who selects a disinterested person other than himself. The debtor in possession, however, retains the estate property and continues to operate the business. [B.C. §§ 1104(c), (d)]

a. Reasons for Appointment

When the appointment of an examiner is requested by a party in interest or the United States trustee, the court, after notice and a hearing, *must order* that an examiner be appointed if the debtor's fixed, liquidated, unsecured debts exceed $5 million, excluding debts for goods, services, or taxes, and any debts owed to an insider. [B.C. § 1104(c)(2); **Loral Stockholders Protective Committee v. Loral Space & Communications, Ltd. (*In re* Loral Space & Communications, Ltd.),** 2004 WL 2979785 (S.D. N.Y. 2004) (stating that § 1104(c)(2) "mandates the appointment of an examiner where a party in interest moves for an examiner and the debtor has $5,000,000 of qualifying debt")] The purpose of § 1104(c)(2) is to give the shareholders of public firms "extra protection" by providing a mechanism for oversight by an independent person. [*See In re* **Loral,** *supra*] The court will also order the appointment of an examiner if the appointment is in the *best interests* of creditors, equity security holders, and the estate. [B.C. § 1104(c)(1)]

b. Duties of Examiner

An examiner's duties include the following:

(i) *to investigate the debtor's conduct, financial condition, assets and liabilities, and business operations, the advisability of continuing the debtor's business,* and other matters pertinent to the case and to formulation of a plan [B.C. § 1106(b), (a)(3)];

(ii) *to file a report of the investigation,* relating any facts evidencing fraud, dishonesty, incompetence, misconduct, or mismanagement, and to send a copy of the findings to any creditors' committee, equity security holders' committee, indenture trustee, or other entities designated by the court [B.C. § 1106(b), (a)(4)]; and

(iii) to perform *any other responsibilities of a trustee* that the judge directs the debtor in possession not to perform. [B.C. § 1106(b)]

5. Right to Be Heard

The Securities and Exchange Commission may raise, and may appear and be heard on, any issue in a Chapter 11 case. The SEC, however, may not appeal from any judgment or order, or decree entered in the case. [B.C. § 1109(a)] While the Commission may not initiate an appeal, it may join or participate in one brought by a true party in interest. [H.R. Rep. No. 95–595, at 404 (1977)] A party in interest also may appear and be heard on any issue in a Chapter 11 case. A party in interest includes but is not limited to the debtor, the trustee, a creditors' committee, an equity security holders' committee, or an indenture trustee. Others asserting the status of a party in interest are determined on a case-by-case basis. [B.C. § 1109(b); **Seraphin v. Morris Publishing Group LLC (*In re* Morris Publishing Group LLC),** 2010 WL 599393 (Bankr. S.D. Ga. 2010) (denying motion of newspaper readers and subscribers to intervene and object to confirmation of plan of debtor newspaper group, because readers and subscribers had "no standing to object as parties in interest" and failed to show cause to allow them to intervene)]

a. Intervention in Adversary Proceeding

There is a split of authority as to whether a party in interest, which includes an unsecured creditors' committee, has an absolute statutory right to intervene in an adversary proceeding. Some courts hold that a party in interest has an absolute right to intervene, because § 1109(b) provides the right to be heard "on any issue" in a Chapter 11 case. [5 Norton § 100.3; B.C. § 1109(b); Bankruptcy Rule 7024] Other courts examine various factors, including whether existing parties can adequately represent the interest of the party seeking intervention, in ruling on a motion to intervene in an adversary proceeding. [*See, e.g.,* **United Methodist Publishing House Inc. v. Family Christian LLC (*In re* Family Christian LLC),** 530 B.R. 517 (Bankr. W.D. Mich. 2015) (denying motion of official creditors' committee to intervene, pursuant to Bankruptcy Rule 7024, after analyzing four-element test established by the Sixth Circuit); *see also* 5 Norton § 100.3 (distinguishing between "Bankruptcy Rule 2018 [which] deals only with general matters within a 'case' [and] 'adversary proceedings [which] are separately governed under Bankruptcy Rule 7024"]

6. Claims and Interests

The filing of proofs of claims or interests and the allowance of secured claims are accorded special treatment in a Chapter 11 case. [B.C. § 1111]

a. Proofs of Claims or Interests

In a Chapter 11 case, the court fixes and sends notice of a *bar date* that operates as a deadline for filing proofs of claims or interests. A claim or interest that is listed in the schedules filed by the debtor is deemed filed, for the scheduled amount, unless it is scheduled as disputed, contingent, or unliquidated. [B.C. § 1111(a); Bankruptcy Rule 3003(b), (c)] Therefore, in a Chapter 11 case, the holder of a correctly scheduled, undisputed, noncontingent, liquidated claim or interest is not required to file a proof of claim or a proof of interest.

b. Secured Claims

In a Chapter 11 case, both recourse and nonrecourse secured claims are treated as recourse claims for the purpose of allowance. [B.C. § 1111(b)(1)(A)] Thus, while an undersecured creditor holding a nonrecourse claim, either under an agreement or under applicable nonbankruptcy law, ordinarily cannot assert a deficiency claim for the portion of her claim exceeding the value of the collateral, the creditor is given recourse status under Chapter 11, with the effect being that the unsecured part of the claim will not be disallowed under Bankruptcy Code § 502(b)(1). [**Bank of America National Trust & Savings Association v. 203 N. LaSalle St. Partnership,** 526 U.S. 434 (1999) (stating in a footnote that § 1111(b) "provides that nonrecourse secured creditors who are undersecured must be treated in Chapter 11 as if they had recourse")]

Note: Outside of bankruptcy, if a claim is recourse, the creditor has a right to seek a personal judgment against the debtor for any deficiency; if a claim is nonrecourse, there is no such right. [*See* **203 N. LaSalle,** *supra* (stating in a footnote that "[a] nonrecourse loan requires the [creditor] to look only to the Debtor's collateral for payment")]

e.g. **Example:** Creditor holds a $500,000 claim secured by a first mortgage on Blackacre, which is valued at $400,000. The agreement between Creditor and Debtor provides that Creditor's claim is nonrecourse. Debtor files a Chapter 11 bankruptcy petition. Under § 1111(b)(1)(A), Creditor's claim is treated as if it were a recourse claim, and, thus, the $100,000 deficiency is allowed as a general unsecured claim. Of course, Creditor also holds an allowed secured claim in the amount of $400,000.

[B.C. § 506(a)] *Note:* Absent this provision, the unsecured portion of Creditor's claim would not be allowable under § 502(b)(1) because of its nonrecourse character.

(i) Exceptions to Conversion of Non-Recourse Into Recourse Claims

There are a few situations in which a claim is *not* treated as if the holder has recourse, thus barring any unsecured claim for a deficiency:

(1) *if the creditor does not have recourse* and the *property is sold* either under Bankruptcy Code § 363 or under the plan of reorganization [B.C. § 1111(b)(1)(A)(ii)];

(2) *if the creditor does not have recourse* and, during the case (i) the *collateral is abandoned or is returned* to the secured creditor, or (ii) the *secured party forecloses* on the property after having been granted relief from the automatic stay [*See, e.g.,* **Mastan v. Salamon (*In re* Salamon),** 854 F.3d 632 (9th Cir. 2017) (holding that junior non-recourse lien was eliminated as a result of non-judicial foreclosure sale and, thus, § 1111(b) did not apply); *In re* **Union Meeting Partners,** 160 B.R. 757 (Bankr. E.D. Penn. 1993) (holding that because non-recourse creditor received property securing its lien, it received benefit of its bargain with debtor and, thus, was not "entitled to an unsecured deficiency claim under § 1111(b) in addition")]; or

(3) *if the class to which the claim belongs makes the § 1111(b) election* by at least two-thirds in amount and more than half in number of allowed claims in the class. [B.C. § 1111(b)(1)(A)(i)] *Note:* Usually, each secured claim is placed alone in a separate class.

c. Section 1111(b) Election

A partially secured creditor may elect to have her claim in a Chapter 11 case treated as *secured to the full extent that the claim is allowed,* even though under § 506(a) it otherwise would be considered secured only up to the value of the collateral. [B.C. § 1111(b)(2)]

e.g. **Example #1:** Debtor owes $500,000 to Creditor pursuant to a nonrecourse loan secured by a first mortgage on Blackacre, which has a fair market value of $400,000. Creditor's claim is classified in a separate class from the other claims in the case, and Creditor makes the election, under § 1111(b), to have her entire $500,000 claim treated as secured. Subsequently, Debtor defaults on payments to Creditor under the confirmed reorganization plan at a time when Blackacre has *appreciated in value* to $500,000. In this instance, the effect of the election will be to enable Creditor to recover the full amount of her claim.

e.g. **Example #2:** Assume the same facts as above, except that Creditor does *not* make the § 1111(b) election. Following Debtor's default, a third-party bidder pays $500,000 for Blackacre at the foreclosure sale. Since Creditor's allowed secured claim was $400,000, the surplus of $100,000 will go to Debtor's estate. Creditor's recovery will be limited to $400,000, plus whatever percentage she is entitled to under the plan on her unsecured claim for a deficiency.

(i) Exceptions: Creditor Cannot Make § 1111(b) Election

Creditors cannot make the § 1111(b) election under either of the following circumstances:

(1) *if the creditor's interest in the property is of inconsequential value,* as in the case of a low priority junior lien that would bring minimal or zero recovery at foreclosure [B.C. § 1111(b)(1)(B)(i)]; or

(2) *if the creditor has recourse and the collateral is sold* under § 363 or under the plan. [B.C. § 1111(b)(1)(B)(ii)] As with the exception for sales pursuant to § 363 or the plan for non-recourse claims, the sale permits the creditor to credit bid under § 363(k), for example, and thereby preserve the benefit of its bargain with the debtor. [7 Collier ¶ 1111.03(2)(a), (3)(b)]

(ii) Waiver of Deficiency Claim

If the § 1111(b) election is made, the secured party forfeits her unsecured claim for any deficiency and also loses the opportunity to affect the decision of the unsecured class to accept or reject the reorganization plan. [B.C. § 1111(b)(2); *see* Bankruptcy Rule 3018(d) (stating that a creditor "whose claim has been allowed in part as a secured claim and in part as an unsecured claim shall be entitled to accept or reject a plan in both capacities")]

e.g. **Example:** Assume the same facts as in Example #1 above, except that the value of Blackacre has *depreciated* to $300,000 at the time of Debtor's default after confirmation. Because Creditor made the § 1111(b) election, she loses her unsecured claim for a deficiency, and her recovery will be only $300,000.

(iii) Preventing a Cash out

The § 1111(b) election sometimes is invoked where the plan proposes no payment to the unsecured creditors and the electing creditor desires to avert a cash out for the value of her collateral. [B.C. § 1111(b)(2); *see, e.g.,* **In re Griffiths,** 27 B.R. 873 (Bankr. D. Kan. 1983)]

(iv) Cramdown

If a secured creditor making the § 1111(b) election rejects the proposed Chapter 11 plan, confirmation can be obtained under the Code's "cramdown" provisions if the plan, in addition to providing for the creditor's retention of her lien, proposes to pay the electing creditor deferred cash payments that equal at least the *full dollar amount* of her allowed claim and that have a *present value,* as of the effective date of the plan, of at least the value of the collateral. [B.C. § 1129(b)(2)(A)(i)]

e.g. **Example:** Creditor loans Debtor $500,000, secured by a first mortgage on Blackacre, which has a value of $600,000. Debtor defaults and then files a Chapter 11 petition. Blackacre has depreciated and is worth $400,000, and Creditor makes the § 1111(b) election. The proposed plan provides for Creditor to retain her lien on Blackacre and to receive deferred cash payments on her claim. Creditor rejects the plan. For the plan to be confirmed over Creditor's rejection, the proposed payments must total at least $500,000 and must have a present value, as of the effective date of the plan, of at least $400,000. [B.C. § 1129(b)(2)(A)(i)]

(v) Time of Election

A creditor may make the § 1111(b) election at any time before the *end of the hearing on the disclosure statement* or within a later time set by the court. [Bankruptcy Rule 3014] In a small business case in which the court conditionally approves but does not conduct a final hearing on the disclosure statement, the creditor must make the § 1111(b) election *no later than the time set for filing objections to the disclosure statement* or some other time set by the bankruptcy court. [Bankruptcy Rules 3014, 3017.1(a)(2)]

---

7. Conversion or Dismissal

In appropriate circumstances, the bankruptcy court may order dismissal or conversion to another chapter of a Chapter 11 case. The debtor must be eligible to file for relief under the chapter to which her Chapter 11 case is converted. [B.C. § 1112] In BAPCPA, Congress made substantial changes to the Code's rules on conversion or dismissal of a Chapter 11 case.

a. Voluntary Conversion to Chapter 7

The debtor may convert a Chapter 11 case to Chapter 7 so long as none of the following apply:

(i) a Chapter 11 trustee has been appointed [B.C. § 1112(a)(1)];

(ii) the case began with the filing of an involuntary Chapter 11 petition [B.C. § 1112(a)(2)]; or

(iii) the case was involuntarily converted to Chapter 11, i.e., on the request of an entity other than the debtor. [B.C. § 1112(a)(3)]

b. Mandatory Conversion to Chapter 7 or Dismissal

With certain exceptions, the bankruptcy court, upon request of a party in interest, must dismiss a Chapter 11 case or convert it to Chapter 7, whichever is better for creditors and the estate, if the party in interest *establishes "cause"* for dismissal or conversion. Notice and a hearing are required. [B.C. § 1112(b)(1)] Prior to the passage of BAPCPA, dismissal or conversion was within the court's discretion. In 2005, however, Congress changed the language of § 1112(b) from "may" to "shall," thereby making dismissal or conversion mandatory, absent some exception, upon a party in interest establishing cause.

(i) "Cause" for Dismissal or Conversion

If a party in interest establishes cause for dismissal or conversion of a Chapter 11 case and none of the relevant exceptions are satisfied, then the bankruptcy court must dismiss the case or convert it to Chapter 7. The Code lists *16 reasons*—a substantial expansion post-BAPCPA—as *sufficient cause* for dismissal or conversion. The list, however, is not exhaustive and a party in interest may raise and the court may find other sufficient cause to dismiss or convert the debtor's Chapter 11 case. The following are the 16 reasons that Congress provided in § 1112(a)(4):

(1) *substantial or continuing loss to or diminution of the estate* and the absence of a *reasonable likelihood of rehabilitation* [B.C. § 1112(b)(4)(A)];

(2) *gross mismanagement of the estate* [B.C. § 1112(b)(4)(B)];

(3) *failure to maintain appropriate insurance* that poses a *risk to the estate or to the public* [B.C. § 1112(b)(4)(C)];

(4) *unauthorized use of cash collateral* that *substantially harms* one or more creditors [B.C. § 1112(b)(4)(D)];

(5) *failure to comply with a court order* [B.C. § 1112(b)(4)(E)];

(6) *unexcused failure* to satisfy in a timely fashion any *filing or reporting requirement* [B.C. § 1112(b)(4)(F)];

(7) *failure* of the debtor without good cause to *attend the § 341 meeting* or a *Rule 2004 examination* [B.C. § 1112(b)(4)(G)];

(8) *failure of the debtor to provide information in a timely fashion or to attend meetings* reasonably requested by the United States trustee or bankruptcy administrator [B.C. § 1112(b)(4)(H)];

(9) *failure to pay taxes or to file tax returns* owed or due after the order for relief [B.C. § 1112(b)(4)(I)];

(10) *failure to file a disclosure statement, or to file or confirm a plan* within the time provided by the Bankruptcy Code or order of the bankruptcy court [B.C. § 1112(b)(4)(J)];

(11) *failure to pay any necessary fees or charges* imposed under chapter 123 of title 28 [B.C. § 1112(b)(4)(K)];

(12) *revocation of an order of confirmation* [B.C. § 1112(b)(4)(L)];

(13) *inability to substantially consummate a confirmed plan* [B.C. § 1112(b)(4)(M)];

(14) *material default* by the debtor with regard to *a confirmed plan* [B.C. § 1112(b)(4)(N)];

(15) *termination of a plan by reason of a condition contained in the plan* [B.C. § 1112(b)(4)(O)]; or

(16) *failure* of the debtor to *pay any domestic support obligation* that first becomes payable after filing of the petition. [B.C. § 1112(b)(4)(P)]

(a) Note on Language

Section 1112(a)(4) uses the word "includes;" thus, the list of reasons provided is not exhaustive. Thus, a debtor's lack of good faith in filing a Chapter 11 petition constitutes sufficient cause to dismiss. [*See, e.g.,* **Daughtrey v. Rivera (*In re* Daughtrey)**, 896 F.3d 1255 (11th Cir. 2018)] In addition, in a voluntary case and upon request of the United States trustee, the court may dismiss or convert a Chapter 11 case to a case under Chapter 7 because of the *debtor's failure to file the information* required by § 521(a)(1), including a list of the creditors holding the 20 largest unsecured claims with their amounts, within *15 days* after the filing of the Chapter 11 petition. [B.C. § 1112(e)]

(ii) Exceptions to Mandatory Dismissal or Conversion

If the party in interest moving for dismissal or conversion of a Chapter 11 case establishes cause, the bankruptcy court is not required to dismiss or convert in certain situations.

(1) Unusual Circumstances

The court does not have to dismiss or convert the Chapter 11 case if it specifically identifies *unusual circumstances* that establish that dismissal or conversion is *not in the best interests of creditors and the estate.* [B.C. § 1112(b)(1)] Congress did not define what constitutes "unusual circumstances," but some courts have found that the term means " 'conditions that are not common in most chapter 11 cases.' " [*In re* **Wallace,** 2010 WL 378351 (Bankr. D. Idaho 2010)]

> **e.g.** **Example:** Debtor filed for relief under Chapter 11, and filed a plan of reorganization, dependent upon a significant infusion of capital, to pay all creditors in full on the plan's effective date. Creditors filed a motion to dismiss or convert Debtor's Chapter 11 case, and the bankruptcy court found that cause existed to dismiss or convert. The bankruptcy court held, however, that neither dismissal nor conversion was in the best interests of creditors and the estate. The court concluded that a plan that would pay creditors in full on the plan's effective date was "an unusual circumstance sufficient to deny conversion or dismissal even in the face of demonstrated cause." [*In re* **Orbit Petroleum, Inc.,** 395 B.R. 145 (Bankr. D. N.M. 2008)]

(2) Farmers and Nonbusiness Corporations

If the debtor is a farmer or a nonbusiness corporation, conversion of the case to Chapter 7 is prohibited unless the debtor requests the conversion. [B.C. §§ 1112(b)(1), (c)]

(3) Appointment of Chapter 11 Trustee or Examiner

Even if grounds exist to dismiss or convert a Chapter 11 case, the bankruptcy court may determine that it is in the *best interests of creditors and the estate* to order the appointment of a trustee or examiner rather than order the dismissal or conversion of the case. [B.C. §§ 1112(b)(1), 1104(a)(2)]

(4) Cause but no Unusual Circumstances

If a party in interest establishes *cause to dismiss or convert* the Chapter 11 case but there are *no unusual circumstances,* the bankruptcy court still may deny the motion to convert or dismiss if the debtor or another party in interest objects to dismissal or conversion *and* the following conditions are satisfied:

(a) there is a *reasonable likelihood* that a plan of reorganization will be *confirmed* within a reasonable period of time or for a small business case within the time frames established by the Code [B.C. §§ 1112(b)(2)(A), 1121(e), 1129(e)];

(b) "cause" for dismissal or conversion is a reason *other than substantial or continuing loss to or diminution of the estate and absence of a reasonable likelihood of rehabilitation* [B.C. §§ 1112(b)(2)(B), 1112(b)(4)(A)]; *and*

(c) there is a *reasonable justification* for the debtor's act or omission and that act or omission will be *cured within a reasonable period of time established by the court.* [B.C. §§ 1112(b)(2)(B)(i), (ii)]

c. Conversion to Chapter 12 or 13

The court may convert a Chapter 11 case to a Chapter 12 or 13 case *only if:*

(i) *the debtor requests the conversion* [B.C. § 1112(d)(1)];

(ii) *the debtor has not received a Chapter 11 discharge* [B.C. §§ 1112(d)(2), 1141(d)]; and

(iii) if the debtor requests *conversion to Chapter 12,* the court finds that conversion is *equitable.* [B.C. § 1112(d)(3)]

C. Rejection of Collective Bargaining Agreements

1. Introduction

Congress added § 1113 on rejection of collective bargaining agreements to the Code with the passage of the Bankruptcy Amendments and Federal Judgeship Act of 1984. Section 1113 is a response to the Supreme Court's decision in **National Labor Relations Board v. Bildisco & Bildisco,** 465 U.S. 513 (1984). A debtor in possession or Chapter 11 trustee that wants to reject a collective bargaining agreement must follow the requirements set forth at § 1113, not those governing rejection of executory contracts under § 365. [B.C. § 1113]

2. Prerequisites for Rejection

Court approval of an application to reject a collective bargaining agreement requires satisfaction of a number of statutory conditions.

a. The debtor has made a *proposal to the union to modify* the collective bargaining agreement. [B.C. § 1113(b)(1)(A)]

b. The proposal is *based on the most complete and reliable information* available at the time of the proposal. [B.C. § 1113(b)(1)(A)]

c. The proposed *modifications are necessary* to permit the reorganization of the debtor. [B.C. § 1113(b)(1)(A)]

d. The proposed modifications treat *all of the affected parties fairly and equitably.* [B.C. § 1113(b)(1)(A)]

e. The debtor *provides to the union such relevant information as is necessary to evaluate* the proposal. [B.C. § 1113(b)(1)(B)]

Note: These first five elements must occur after the filing of the Chapter 11 petition and before the filing of the application to reject. [B.C. § 1113(b)(1)]

f. After making the proposal, the *debtor meets at reasonable times with the union.* [B.C. § 1113(b)(2)]

g. At its meetings with the union, the debtor *negotiates in good faith* in an effort to reach mutually satisfactory modifications of the collective bargaining agreement. [B.C. § 1113(b)(2)]

h. The union *refuses to accept the proposal without good cause.* [B.C. § 1113(c)(2)]

i. The balance of the equities *clearly favors rejection* of the collective bargaining agreement. [B.C. § 1113(c)(3)]

3. Hearing

The bankruptcy court must schedule a hearing on an application to reject a collective bargaining agreement within *14 days* after the application is filed. The court may extend for *7 days* the start of the hearing on the rejection application if the *circumstances* of the case coupled with the *interests of justice* require an extension. The debtor and union representative must agree to any further time extensions. [B.C. § 1114(d)(1)] The court must rule on the issue within *30 days* after the commencement of the hearing, unless the debtor and the union representative agree to an extension of such time period. [B.C. § 1113(d)(2)]

4. Protective Orders

The bankruptcy court may issue protective orders as are needed to prevent disclosure of the information provided to the union representative if disclosure of such information could *compromise the debtor's position* in relation to its *industry competitors.* [B.C. § 1113(d)(3)]

5. Interim Changes

The court may permit the debtor to make temporary interim modifications in the terms of a collective bargaining agreement if such changes are necessary to *continue the debtor's business* or to *avoid irreparable harm* to the estate. Notice and a hearing are required. [B.C. § 1113(e); *In re* **Evans Products Co.,** 55 B.R. 231 (Bankr. S.D. Fla. 1985)]

6. Unilateral Action Prohibited

The debtor may not unilaterally terminate or modify any terms of a collective bargaining agreement before compliance with the provisions set forth in § 1113. [B.C. § 1113(f)]

D. Retiree Benefits

1. Introduction

The Code provides procedural and substantive protections against a Chapter 11 company's modification of retiree benefits. [B.C. § 1114] The Code's provisions cover both union and non-union employees. [*See* B.C. § 1114(b)(1)] The Code's rules on modification of retiree benefits are complex. This summary provides only a brief overview.

a. Exception

Section 1114 does not apply to a retiree or the spouse or any dependent of the retiree if the retiree's *gross income* for the 12 months prior to the bankruptcy filing equals or exceeds *$250,000.* [B.C. § 1114(m)] However, if such a retiree can demonstrate to the court's satisfaction that she cannot obtain health, medical, life, and disability coverage comparable to that provided by the employer on the date of the bankruptcy petition, then the protections of § 1114 apply to such retiree.

2. Definition of Retiree Benefits

The Code defines "retiree benefits" as payments to *retirees and their spouses and dependents* for *medical, surgical, or hospital care,* or *benefits* in the event of *sickness, accident, disability, or death* under a plan maintained or established by the debtor prior to the debtor's bankruptcy filing. [B.C. § 1114(a)]

3. Payment Obligation

The debtor in possession (or Chapter 11 trustee) must *timely pay* retiree benefits, unless an appropriate modification to such benefits has been put into place. [B.C. § 1114(e)] Any payment required to be made prior to plan confirmation has the status of an *allowed administrative expense.* [B.C. §§ 1114(e)(2), 503] Section 502(b)(7)'s limitation on allowable claims for damages for termination of an employment contract *do not apply* to claims for retiree benefits. [B.C. § 1114(j)]

4. Modification of Benefits

There are two basic paths to modify retiree benefits. First, the debtor in possession (or trustee) and the retirees' authorized representative may agree to a modification. [B.C. § 1114(e)(1)(B)] Second, if the debtor in possession and authorized representative cannot agree, then the court, after notice and a hearing, may order modification. [B.C. §§ 1114(e)(1)(A), (g)]

a. Authorized Representative

In the case of retirees covered by a collective bargaining agreement, the *labor union* is the retirees' authorized representative. [B.C. §§ 1114(b)(1), (c)] For non-union retirees, the court, upon motion of any party in interest and after notice and a hearing, must order the *appointment of a committee of retired employees* to serve as the retirees' authorized representative. The United States trustee appoints the committee. [B.C. § 1114(d)]

b. Modification Proposal

Before filing an application to modify retiree benefits, the debtor in possession (or Chapter 11 trustee) first must make a *proposal to the retirees' authorized representative.* The proposal must be based on the *most complete and reliable information* available and treat all of the affected parties *fairly and equitably.* Modification must be *necessary for the debtor's reorganization.* [B.C. § 1114(f)(1)(A)] The debtor in possession (or Chapter 11 trustee) must provide the authorized representative with the information necessary to evaluate the proposal. [B.C. § 1114(f)(1)(B)] After making the proposal but prior to the hearing on the proposal, the debtor in possession (or Chapter 11 trustee) must *meet at reasonable times* with the authorized representative, *confer in good faith,* and attempt to reach a *mutually satisfactory modification.* [B.C. § 1114(f)(2)]

c. Failure to Agree: Final Order

The bankruptcy court must enter a final order modifying retiree benefits if the court finds that *all of the following requirements* are satisfied.

(i) The debtor in possession (or Chapter 11 trustee) *complied with the requirements for making a modification proposal.* [B.C. § 1114(g)(1)]

(ii) The retirees' authorized representative *refused to accept the proposal without good cause.* [B.C. § 1114(g)(2)]

(iii) The modification is *necessary* to permit the *debtor's reorganization.* [B.C. § 1114(g)(3)]

(iv) All affected parties are treated *fairly and equitably.* [B.C. § 1114(g)(3)]

(v) The modification is clearly favored by the *balance of the equities.* [B.C. § 1114(g)(3)]

d. Interim Modifications

Prior to entering a final order on modification, the court may authorize an interim modification in retiree benefits if such interim modification is *essential to continuation of the debtor's business* or in order to *avoid irreparable harm.* Notice and a hearing are required. [B.C. § 1114(h)]

e. Pre-Bankruptcy Modifications

If the debtor, during the *180 days* prior to filing for bankruptcy, *modified retiree benefits while insolvent,* then the court, on the motion of a party in interest and after notice and a hearing, must *reinstate* those benefits, *unless* the court finds that the *balance of the equities favors such modification.* [B.C. § 1114(*l*)] Congress added this provision to the Code in 2005.

E. The Disclosure Statement and Chapter 11 Plan

1. The Disclosure Statement

a. Overview

After filing of the petition, the debtor or other plan proponent may not solicit acceptances or rejections of the plan unless they first have provided a plan (or plan summary) and a *written court-approved disclosure statement* to the holders of the claims or interests whose acceptances or rejections are being sought. After the debtor or plan proponent files the disclosure statement, the bankruptcy court holds a hearing to consider the disclosure statement and any objections or modifications to the disclosure statement. The court must provide at least *28 days' notice* of the hearing to the debtor, creditors, equity security holders, and other parties in interest. [Bankruptcy Rule 3017(a)]

Exception: BAPCPA added special rules for disclosure statements in small business cases. [B.C. § 1125(f), Bankruptcy Rule 3017.1]

b. Adequate Information

Because the purpose of the disclosure statement is to provide information to creditors and equity security holders adequate to evaluate the plan, the Code requires that the disclosure statement contain sufficient information, under the circumstances, to enable a *hypothetical reasonable investor* typical of holders of claims or interests of the relevant class to make an *informed decision* to accept or reject the plan. [B.C. § 1125(a)(1)]

(i) Impact of BAPCPA

Congress amended the definition of *adequate information* in BAPCPA to provide that the disclosure statement should include "a discussion of the potential material Federal tax consequences of the plan to the debtor." [B.C. § 1125(a)(1)] In addition, the bankruptcy court also must consider the *complexity of the case,* the *benefit of additional information* to parties in interest, and *the cost of providing additional information* when evaluating the adequacy of information provided by the disclosure statement. [B.C. § 1125(a)(1)]

(ii) *Metrocraft* Factors

Deciding whether the disclosure statement provides adequate information is a fact-intensive inquiry. Some courts have adopted the factors set forth in *In re* **Metrocraft Publishing Services, Inc.,** 39 B.R. 567 (Bankr. N.D. Ga. 1984). [*See, e.g., In re* **Divine Ripe, L.L.C.,** 554 B.R. 395 (Bankr. S.D. Tex. 2016)] Those factors include:

(1) *the events leading to the filing* of the bankruptcy petition;

(2) *a description of the available assets and their value,*

(3) *the anticipated future of the company;*

(4) *the source of the information* stated in the disclosure statement;

(5) *a disclaimer;*

(6) *the present condition of the debtor* while in Chapter 11;

(7) *the scheduled claims;*

(8) *the estimated return to creditors* under a Chapter 7 liquidation;

(9) *the accounting method* used to produce financial information and the *names of the accountants* responsible for such information;

(10) *the future management* of the debtor;

(11) *the Chapter 11 plan* or a summary thereof;

(12) *the estimated administrative expenses,* including attorneys' and accountants' fees;

(13) *the collectibility of accounts receivable;*

(14) *financial information, data, valuations, or projections* relevant to the creditors' decision to accept or reject the Chapter 11 plan;

(15) *information relevant to the risks* posed to creditors under the plan;

(16) *the actual or projected realizable value from recovery of preferential or otherwise voidable transfers;*

(17) whether *litigation is likely to arise* in a nonbankruptcy context;

(18) *tax attributes* of the debtor; and

(19) *the relationship of the debtor with affiliates.*

c. Distribution of Disclosure Statement

Because the information needed by separate classes of claims or interests may vary in kind and detail, different disclosure statements may be sent to different classes. However, the holders of the claims or interests of any particular class must receive the identical disclosure statement. [B.C. § 1125(c)]

d. Nonbankruptcy Securities Laws, Rules, and Regulations

The adequacy of the information contained in a post-petition disclosure statement is determined without regard to any nonbankruptcy securities law, rule, or regulation that otherwise would apply, although the Securities and Exchange Commission may appear and be heard on the issue of the adequacy of the disclosure statement. [B.C. § 1125(d)] Also, Chapter 11 includes a *safe harbor provision,* insulating from liability for violation of any applicable securities law, rule, or regulation, a person who in good faith and in compliance with the provisions of the Bankruptcy Code solicits acceptances or rejections of a plan, or participates in the offer, issuance, purchase, or sale of a security under a plan. [B.C. § 1125(e)]

e. **Distinguish Pre-Petition Solicitation**

Acceptances or rejections of a plan may be solicited before the filing of a Chapter 11 petition only if the solicitation meets the disclosure requirements of any applicable securities or other nonbankruptcy law or regulation, or in the absence of any such law or regulation, is preceded by the disclosure of adequate information, as defined in Bankruptcy Code section 1125(a). [B.C. § 1126(b)] Adherence to this rule could be of great significance when an attempted extrajudicial "workout" fails, and a Chapter 11 petition subsequently is filed.

2. Filing a Plan

In a voluntary case, the debtor may file a plan of reorganization with the Chapter 11 petition or at any other time. In an involuntary case, the debtor may file a plan at any time. [B.C. § 1121(a)]

a. **Exclusivity Period**

Unless a trustee has been appointed in the case, the *debtor* has the exclusive right to file a plan for the first *120 days after* the order for relief. [B.C. § 1121(b)] A small business debtor has the exclusive right to file a plan for the first *180 days after* the order for relief. [B.C. § 1121(e)]

b. *Extension or Reduction of Exclusivity Period*

A party in interest may request and the court, after notice and hearing, may grant a request to extend or reduce the debtor's exclusivity period. [B.C. § 1121(d)(1)] The Bankruptcy Code, however, places outer limits on the time to which the court may extend the exclusivity period. Thus, the court may not extend the *120-day* period beyond *18 months* after the order for relief. [B.C. § 1121(d)(2)(A)] In a small business case, the court may not extend the *180-day* period beyond *20 months* from the order for relief. [B.C. § 1121(d)(2)(B)]

c. **Other Proponents**

The debtor, the Chapter 11 trustee (if one is appointed), a creditor, a creditors' committee, an equity security holder, an equity security holders' committee, an indenture trustee, or any party in interest, *except the United States trustee* [B.C. § 307], may file a plan *but only if:*

(i) *a Chapter 11 trustee has been appointed* [B.C. § 1121(c)(1)];

(ii) *the debtor has not filed a plan within 120 days* after the order for relief [B.C. § 1121(c)(2)]; *or*

(iii) *the debtor has not filed a plan and obtained the acceptances* of every impaired class of claims or interests within *180 days* after the order for relief. [B.C. § 1121(c)(3)]

3. The Plan's Classification of Claims or Interests

With the exception of administrative, gap, and tax claims, the Bankruptcy Code requires that a Chapter 11 plan classify the claims and the equity interests in the case. [B.C. § 1123(a)(1)] However, the statutory provisions regarding the manner of classification are relatively brief, and much case law has developed in this area. [B.C. § 1122]

a. "Substantially Similar" Claims or Interests

A claim or interest may be placed in a particular class only if it is substantially similar to the other claims or interests included in that class. [B.C. § 1122(a)] The Code, however, does *not require* that all substantially similar claims be placed in the same class.

(i) Majority View

Most courts have held that § 1122(a) does not compel the classification of all substantially similar claims together in one class. Thus, a plan proponent can separately classify substantially similar claims if there is a reasonable or rational justification for the separate classification. [*In re* **Light Squared, Inc.,** 513 B.R. 56 (Bankr. S.D. N.Y. 2014)] Separate classification is proper if the creditors in the two classes have different legal rights or different interests in the plan, or if the plan proponent has a legitimate business reason for the separate classification. [*See In re* **STC, Inc.,** 2016 WL 3884799 (Bankr. S.D. Ill. 2016)]

e.g. **Example:** Debtor Corporation filed a voluntary Chapter 11 petition and a plan of reorganization that put Creditor, a general unsecured creditor, into a separate class from the other general unsecured creditors. Creditor objected to the separate classification, but the bankruptcy court overruled Creditor's objection. The court concluded that Creditor's "non-creditor interests" justified separate classification of Creditor's claim. Creditor was a competitor of Debtor's, had competing rights to a trademark, and was engaged in continuing litigation with the Debtor. The court noted that it was "reasonable to infer" that if Debtor's reorganization failed Creditor would benefit. [*In re* **Thru, Inc.,** 2017 WL 3394506 (Bankr. N.D. Tex. 2017)]

(ii) Minority View

A few courts follow what has been identified as the "strict approach" to separate classification of general unsecured creditors. This approach requires that similar claims be classified together, unless the legal character and status of the separately classified claim differs from the legal character and status of other general unsecured creditors. [B.C. § 1122(a); *see, e.g.,* **Granada Wines, Inc. v. New England Teamsters & Trucking Industry Pension Fund,** 748 F.2d 42 (1st Cir. 1984); *In re* **River Valley Fitness One L.P.,** 2003 WL 22298573 (Bankr. D. N.H. 2003)]

(iii) Gerrymandering

While most courts generally allow separate classification of similar claims, there is an important exception: a plan proponent may not separately classify similar claims in an attempt to gerrymander the plan confirmation vote. [**Mineral Technologies, Inc. v. Novinda Corp. (*In re* Novinda Corp.),** 585 B.R. 145 (B.A.P. 10th Cir. 2018)] If the sole reason for separate classification is to create an impaired class that will accept the plan, then separate classification is not allowed. [B.C. §§ 1122(a), 1129(a)(10); *see, e.g., In re* **STC, Inc.,** 2016 WL 3884799 (Bankr. S.D. Ill. 2016)]

e.g. **Example:** Debtor proposes a plan with four classes. Classes 1 and 2 each contain one secured creditor and are unimpaired. Creditor has a large enough unsecured claim that if she votes with the general unsecured creditors, the plan cannot be confirmed. Creditor plans to vote against the plan, but without Creditor in the general unsecured class the class will vote in favor of the plan. Debtor puts Creditor into Class 3, and the remaining general unsecured creditors into Class 4. Both Class 3 and 4 are impaired. Creditor votes against the plan, but Class 4 votes in favor. Creditor objects to Debtor's plan. The bankruptcy court will not confirm the plan, because Debtor gerrymandered the unsecured classes in order to obtain an impaired class that would vote in favor of plan confirmation. [B.C. §§ 1126(c), 1129(a)(10), 1129(b)(2)(B)]

(iv) Administrative Convenience Claims

A plan proponent may create a separate class of *unsecured claims* with a value less than or reduced to an amount that the court approves as reasonable and necessary for *administrative convenience.* [B.C. § 1122(b)]

e.g. **Example:** Debtor Corporation proposes a Chapter 11 plan with 2 classes of unsecured claims: an administrative convenience class and the class of general unsecured creditors. The administrative convenience class contains general unsecured claims of $500 or less, or claims of those creditors willing to reduce their claim to $500. The plan proposes to pay the administrative convenience claimants in full in cash on the plan's effective date. This type of separation of substantially similar claims into separate classes generally does not pose a problem for plan confirmation.

b. Specific Types of Claims or Interests

(i) Secured Claims

Usually, if secured creditors' liens are in different property or are entitled to different priorities in the same property, each secured claim should be placed alone in a separate class. [*See* 6 Norton § 109:2 ("Each secured claim is treated as a separate class unless there is another secured claimholder having identical and equal rights in the same collateral")]

(ii) Priority Claims

Administrative expenses, involuntary case gap claims, and unsecured, pre-petition tax claims are *excepted* from the requirement of classification because the standards for confirmation require that the plan provide for such claims on an individual, as opposed to a class, basis. [B.C. §§ 1123(a)(1), 1129(a)(9)(A), (C)] However, first, fourth, fifth, sixth, seventh, ninth, and tenth priority claims (i.e., domestic support obligations, wages and commissions, contributions to employee benefit plans, claims of grain farmers and United States fishermen, consumer layaways, capital requirements of an insured depository institution, and claims for death or personal injury due to intoxicated operation of a motor vehicle or vessel) should be placed in separate classes together with claims of equal priority. [B.C. §§ 1123(a)(1), 507(a)(1), (4)–(7), (9), (10)]

(iii) Administrative Convenience Class

The Code permits the plan to designate a separate class of small claims comprised of all unsecured claims that are less than, or by consent decreased to, an amount approved by the court as *reasonable and necessary.* Generally, such claims are paid in full in cash, and the estate benefits by the reduction of administrative expenses associated with "the cost of sending disclosure statements, soliciting votes from the *de minimis* creditors, and making fractional distributions." [*In re* **Autterson,** 547 B.R. 372 (Bankr. D. Colo. 2016); B.C. § 1122(b); 7 Collier ¶ 1122.03(4)]

(iv) Interests

Equity interests in a sole proprietorship, a partnership, or a corporation must be classified separately from creditors' claims. Furthermore, common stock and preferred stock interests should be placed in different classes. [B.C. § 1122(a)]

4. Contents of Plan: Mandatory Provisions

All Chapter 11 plans must do the following:

a. *classify all claims and interests,* other than priority claims for administrative expenses, involuntary case gap claims, or eighth priority taxes [B.C. §§ 1123(a)(1), 507(a)(1), (2), (8)];

b. *specify any class that is not impaired* [B.C. § 1123(a)(2)];

c. *describe the treatment* to be accorded *any impaired class* [B.C. § 1123(a)(3)];

d. *treat every claim or interest within a particular class identically,* unless a holder consents to less favorable treatment [B.C. § 1123(a)(4)];

e. *establish adequate ways to implement the plan,* such as by [B.C. §§ 1123(a)(5)(A)–(J)]:

   (i)   *the debtor's retention* of estate property;

   (ii)   *the transfer of estate property* to another entity;

   (iii) *merger or consolidation* of the debtor with other persons;

   (iv) *the sale of estate property free and clear of liens,* or the *distribution of estate property to the holders* of any interests in the property;

   (v)   *the satisfaction or modification of a lien;*

   (vi) *the cancellation or modification of an indenture;*

   (vii) *curing or waiving a default;*

  (viii) *extending the maturity date,* or altering the interest rate or other terms of outstanding securities;

   (ix) *amending the debtor's charter;* or

   (x)   *issuing securities of the debtor* or a successor to the debtor, or of an entity with whom the debtor has merged or has been consolidated for cash, property, in exchange for claims or interests, or for any other proper purpose;

f. *include, in the charter of a corporate debtor or successor,* or any corporation with which debtor *merged or was consolidated, a provision prohibiting the issuance of nonvoting stock,* and complying with certain other requirements concerning voting powers [B.C. § 1123(a)(6)];

g. *provide for the selection of officers and directors* in a manner consistent with the interests of creditors and equity security holders and that does not violate public policy [B.C. § 1123(a)(7)]; and

h. *provide for payment,* in an *individual Chapter 11 case,* of debtor's post-petition earnings or future income sufficient to execute the plan. [B.C. § 1123(a)(8)]

5. Contents of Plan: Permissive Provisions

In addition to the mandatory items described above, a plan *may:*

a. *impair or leave unimpaired* any class of claims or interests [B.C. § 1123(b)(1)];

b. *assume, reject, or assign executory contracts or unexpired leases* [B.C. § 1123(b)(2)];

c. *settle or adjust any claim or interest* held by the debtor or the estate, or provide for the retention and enforcement of the claim or interest by the debtor, Chapter 11 trustee, or an appointed representative of the estate [B.C. § 1123(b)(3)];

d. *sell all or substantially all of the estate property,* and distribute the proceeds among claim and interest holders [B.C. § 1123(b)(4)];

e. *modify the rights of secured creditors or unsecured creditors, unless* the creditor's claim is secured *solely* by a security interest in real property constituting the debtor's principal residence [B.C. § 1123(b)(5)]; and

> *Note:* The prohibition against modification of home mortgages applies only to an individual Chapter 11 debtor. It prevents an individual Chapter 11 debtor from *stripping down* an undersecured mortgage on his principal residence to the fair market value of the residence. [*See* **Nobelman v. American Savings Bank,** 508 U.S. 324 (1993) (construing language in § 1322(b)(2) identical to that in § 1123(b)(5), and holding that anti-modification language precluded a Chapter 13 debtor from reducing outstanding mortgage principal to the fair market value of debtor's principal residence)]

f. *include any other appropriate measure* that is consistent with the provisions of the Bankruptcy Code. [B.C. § 1123(b)(6)] For example, the Supreme Court has upheld a plan's provision requiring the IRS to allocate a Chapter 11 debtor's tax payments first to *trust fund taxes,* before being applied to non-trust fund tax liabilities, if *necessary for the success of the debtor's reorganization.* [**United States v. Energy Resources Co.,** 495 U.S. 545 (1990)]

6. Contents of Plan: Exempt Property

If the debtor is an individual, any plan proposed by another entity may not include a provision to use, sell, or lease exempt property without the consent of the debtor. [B.C. § 1123(c)]

7. Contents of Plan: Interest on Arrearages

If the plan proposes to cure a default, the Code addresses the issue of interest on interest, e.g., interest on mortgage arrearages that include interest. The amount necessary to cure the default is determined by looking to the underlying contract and applicable nonbankruptcy law. [B.C. § 1123(d)] In addition, if the parties' agreement and relevant nonbankruptcy law allow, the debtor must pay the agreed-upon default rate of interest when curing a default. [**JPMCC 2006-LDP7 Miami Beach Lodging, LLC v. Sagamore Partners, Ltd. (***In re* **Sagamore Partners, Ltd.),** 2015 WL 4170215 (11th Cir. 2015)]

8. Modifying a Plan

Prior to confirmation, a plan may be modified only by its proponent. After confirmation and before substantial consummation of a plan, it may be modified, if warranted, by the proponent *or* by the reorganized debtor. Notice and a hearing are required. Any modification must satisfy the statutory requirements concerning classification of claims or interests [B.C. § 1122], contents of the plan [B.C. § 1123], disclosure [B.C. § 1125], and the requirements for confirmation. [B.C. § 1129] An acceptance or a rejection of a plan before modification will be deemed to apply to the plan as modified unless the vote is changed within the deadline set by the court. [B.C. § 1127] BAPCPA added special rules for plan modification for individual Chapter 11 debtors.

F. Confirmation of Plan

1. Confirmation Hearing

After proper notice, the court conducts a hearing to determine whether a proposed plan satisfies the elements necessary for confirmation. Any party in interest may file an objection to confirmation. [B.C. § 1128; Bankruptcy Rule 3020(b)]

2. Requirements for Confirmation of a Consent Plan

Consensual confirmation of a Chapter 11 plan requires that the plan proponent satisfy all of the following statutory requirements. [B.C. § 1129(a)]

a. Plan Complies with Code Provisions

The plan must comply with the applicable provisions of the Bankruptcy Code, such as the requirements for classification of claims and the mandatory contents of a Chapter 11 plan. [B.C. § 1129(a)(1)]

b. Proponent Complies with Code Provisions

The proponent of the plan must comply with the applicable provisions of the Code, such as those requiring disclosure of adequate information and solicitation of acceptances. [B.C. § 1129(a)(2)]

c. Plan in Good Faith

The plan must be proposed in good faith and not by any means forbidden by law. [B.C. § 1129(a)(3)] [*See In re* **American Capital Equipment, LLC,** 668 F.3d 145 (3d Cir. 2012) ("[a] plan is proposed in good faith only if it will '*fairly* achieve a result consistent with the objectives and purposes of the Bankruptcy Code' "); **Argo Fund Ltd. v. Board of Directors of Telecom Argentina (*In re* Board of Directors of Telecom Argentina),** 528 F.3d 162 (2d Cir. 2008) ("Under § 1129(a)(3), a plan will be found in good faith if it 'was proposed with honesty and good intentions and with a basis for expecting that a reorganization can be effected.' ")]

d. Payment for Services or Expenses Approved

The court must approve as reasonable all payments made by the plan's proponent, the debtor, or a person issuing securities or receiving property under the plan for services or expenses in or in connection with the Chapter 11 case or related to the plan, e.g., attorneys' fees. [B.C. § 1129(a)(4)]

e. Officers, Directors, Insiders Disclosed

The plan must disclose the names and affiliations of all individuals who, after plan confirmation, will serve as officers, directors, or voting trustees of the debtor, a successor to the debtor, or a debtor affiliate participating in a joint plan with the debtor. [B.C. § 1129(a)(5)(A)(i)] Appointment of these individuals or their continuation as officers, directors, or voting trustees must be consistent with the interests of creditors, equity security holders, and public policy. [B.C. § 1129(a)(5)(A)(ii)] The plan proponent must also disclose the names and proposed compensation of all insiders who will be employed or retained by the reorganized debtor. [B.C. § 1129(a)(5)(B)]

f.   Rate Change Approved

If the debtor's rates are regulated by a governmental commission, that commission must approve any rate change proposed by the plan, or the proposed rate change must be expressly conditioned on such approval. [B.C. § 1129(a)(6)]

g.   "Best Interests of Creditors Test" Met

Each holder of a claim or interest of an *impaired class* either must (i) *accept* the plan *or* (ii) *receive* under the plan property having a *present value,* as of the effective date of the plan, of *not less than the amount* that the holder would receive in a *Chapter 7 liquidation.* This element of confirmation usually is called the "best interests of creditors test." [B.C. § 1129(a)(7)(A)] Unlike other confirmation requirements, which apply to the *class* of creditors, the "best interests of creditors test" applies to *each creditor,* even if the creditor objecting to the plan on the basis of the test is part of a class that has voted to accept the plan. If the holder made the § 1111(b) election, however, the exception below applies.

> **e.g.** **Example:** Debtor Company filed for relief under Chapter 11 and proposed a plan. Creditor held an unsecured claim and the class of general unsecured creditors was impaired under the terms of the plan. While Debtor contended that it did not have substantial assets to liquidate, it failed to provide a persuasive liquidation analysis. Debtor also did not provide sufficient financial information for the bankruptcy court to conduct a "best interests of creditors" analysis. Finally, while the plan proposed making payments to creditors from future profits, the court concluded that the payment stream for these payments was "highly speculative." Thus, the bankruptcy court held that the Debtor had not established by a preponderance of the evidence that the plan satisfied the "best interests of creditors" test. [*In re* **Premiere Network Services,** 333 B.R. 130 (Bankr. N.D. Tex. 2005)]

Exception: If a holder has made the *election under § 1111(b),* the plan must provide that she receive property having a present value, as of the effective date of the plan, of at least the value of the collateral securing her claim. [B.C. § 1129(a)(7)(B)]

h.   All Impaired Classes Accept Plan

Each class of claims or interests must have *accepted* the plan *or be unimpaired* under the plan. [B.C. § 1129(a)(8)] If this element is not satisfied, the plan cannot be confirmed under § 1129(a) as a *consent plan.* The plan proponent, however, may move for confirmation under the Code's *cramdown* provisions at § 1129(b).

(i)   What Constitutes Acceptance by a Class?

Any creditor or equity security holder whose claim or interest has been allowed may accept or reject a Chapter 11 plan by a signed writing identifying the plan and conforming to the appropriate Official Form. [B.C. § 1126(a); Bankruptcy Rule 3018(c); Official Form 314]

(1)   Classes of Claims

Acceptance of a plan by a class of claims requires acceptance by creditors holding at least *two-thirds in amount and more than half in number* of the allowed claims actually being voted. [B.C. § 1126(c)]

> **Example:** The debtor Ajax Corporation proposes a plan, if confirmed, that will pay Class 5, its general unsecured creditors, 30 cents on the dollar. There are 50 unsecured creditors in Class 5 with claims totaling

$500,000. Of those 50 unsecured creditors, 25 creditors with claims totaling $250,000 cast ballots to accept or reject the plan. If 20 creditors (more than half in number of claims voting) with claims totaling $200,000 (80% in amount of claims voting) vote in favor of the plan, then Class 5 votes to accept the plan.

Example: The debtor Ajax Corporation proposes a plan, if confirmed, that will pay Class 5, its general unsecured creditors, 30 cents on the dollar. There are 50 unsecured creditors in Class 5 with claims totaling $500,000. Of those 50 unsecured creditors, 25 creditors with claims totaling $250,000 cast ballots to accept or reject the plan. If 12 creditors with claims of $170,000 vote in favor of the plan, then Class 5 has voted to reject the plan. While more than two-thirds in amount of claims voted in favor of the plan ($170,000/$250,000 = 68%), less than half in number of claims (12/25 = 48%) voted "yes" on the plan. The Code requires *both* two-thirds in amount of claims *and* more than half in number of claims to vote to accept the plan.

(2) Classes of Interests

Acceptance of a plan by a class of interests requires acceptance by equity security holders having at least *two-thirds in amount* of the allowed interests actually being voted. [B.C. § 1126(d)]

(3) Bad Faith Votes

The court, after notice and a hearing, may disqualify any acceptance or rejection not made in good faith or that was not solicited in good faith or in compliance with the provisions of the Code. [B.C. § 1126(e)]

Example: The debtor Gamma Company proposes a plan, if confirmed, that will pay Class 6, its general unsecured creditors, 40 cents on the dollar. Thirty of Gamma's unsecured creditors holding claims worth $600,000 vote on the plan. Kappa, Inc., one of Gamma's largest unsecured creditors with a claim of $200,000, votes in favor of the plan. Twenty of Gamma's other unsecured creditors holding claims of $100,000 also vote in favor of the plan, while $300,000 cast ballots rejecting the plan. If the bankruptcy court determines that Kappa's vote was not made or solicited in good faith or in compliance with the Code, then Kappa's vote will not count toward plan confirmation. In such a case, Class 6 will not have voted to approve the plan, because seventy-five percent of claims ($300,000 of the $400,000 of claims remaining after disqualifying Kappa's vote) voted against plan confirmation.

(4) Unimpaired Classes

If a particular class is not impaired under a plan, there is a conclusive presumption that the plan has been accepted by the class and by the holder of each claim or interest in the class. Consequently, it will be unnecessary for the proponent of the plan to solicit their acceptances. [B.C. § 1126(f)]

(5) Classes Receiving no Property

A class that receives or retains no property under a plan is deemed to have rejected the plan. [B.C. § 1126(g)]

(6) Pre-Petition Acceptance or Rejection

If the acceptance or rejection occurs before commencement of the case, it is valid only if:

(a) it was solicited in accordance with the Code's requirements for pre-petition solicitation; *and*

(b) the plan was sent to substantially all creditors and equity security holders of the same class within a reasonable time to accept or reject the plan.

In addition, if the claim of the creditor or equity security holder is based on a ***security of record***, a pre-petition acceptance or rejection is valid *only if* the creditor or equity security holder was the holder of record of the security on the date specified in the solicitation. [B.C. § 1126(b); Bankruptcy Rule 3018(b)]

(ii) What is Impairment and Why is it Important?

If a class is ***not*** impaired, there is a ***conclusive presumption*** that the plan has been accepted by the class and by the holder of each claim or interest in the class. Consequently, it is unnecessary for the proponent of the plan to solicit their acceptances. [B.C. § 1126(f)] A class is ***deemed impaired unless*** the plan provides for all claims or interests of that class to be treated in accordance with either of the following two methods. [B.C. § 1124]

(1) Rights Unmodified

A class is considered ***unimpaired*** if the plan does ***not alter*** the legal, equitable, or contractual rights of the holders of the claims or interests. Any change in a holder's rights, ***even a favorable change,*** constitutes impairment. [B.C. § 1124(1); *see **In re L & J Anaheim Associates**,* 995 F.2d 940 (9th Cir. 1993) (stating a claim is impaired if the claim holder's rights are changed, regardless of the kind or degree of change)]

(2) Cure and Deacceleration

If the Chapter 11 debtor has defaulted on a payment obligation, the contract with the creditor may provide for accelerated payment on the creditor's claim, which means the creditor is entitled to full payment of the obligation upon default. If the debtor files for relief under Chapter 11 and proposes to cure any default and reinstate the terms of the parties' agreement, the creditor could argue that the debtor has impaired the creditor's claim, which was entitled to full payment based on the contract's acceleration clause. But, under § 1124 "a claim or interest is unimpaired by curing the effect of a default and reinstating the original terms of an obligation when maturity was brought on or accelerated by the default. . . . The holder of a claim or interest who under the plan is restored to his original position, when others receive less or get nothing at all, is fortunate indeed and has no cause to complain." [S. Rep. No. 95–989 (1978)]

(3) Deemed Unimpaired

Section 1124(2) provides that a class is deemed ***unimpaired*** if the plan proposes, regardless of any contractual or other legal right to accelerate payment on default, to:

(a) ***cure any default,*** other than one related to an *ipso facto* provision or of a kind that § 365(b)(2) does not require to be cured [B.C. § 1124(2)(A)];

(b) ***reinstate the original maturity date*** of the claim or interest [B.C. § 1124(2)(B)];

(c) ***pay for any damages*** caused by the claimant's or the interest holder's ***reasonable reliance*** on the right to accelerate [B.C. § 1124(2)(C)];

(d) *pay for any damages* caused by the debtor's failure to *perform a nonmonetary obligation,* other than a default arising from a failure to operate a nonresidential real property lease subject to § 365(b)(1)(A) [B.C. § 1124(2)(D)]; and

(e) *not otherwise alter* the legal, equitable, or contractual rights of the holder of the claim or interest. [B.C. § 1124(2)(E)]

(4) Foreclosure Judgments and Cure

If state law does not provide for the merger of a mortgage and foreclosure judgment, the debtor usually is permitted to cure the default and reinstate the obligation at any time *prior to a foreclosure sale.* [*In re* **Madison Hotel Associates,** 749 F.2d 410 (7th Cir. 1984)] But if the mortgage merges into the foreclosure judgment under state law, some courts have held that there is nothing to cure and reinstate. Other courts, however, have concluded that merger is irrelevant, because § 1124(2) evidences Congress's intent to permit deacceleration. [7 Collier ¶ 1124.04(6)]

i. Administrative Expenses and Involuntary Gap Claims

The plan must provide for *payment in full in cash* on the effective date of the plan for each claim that is entitled to priority as an administrative expense or as an involuntary case gap claim, unless the holder of the claim consents to different treatment. [B.C. §§ 1129(a)(9)(A), 507(a)(2), (3)]

j. First, Fourth, Fifth, Sixth, and Seventh Priority Claims

Unless the holder of a particular claim consents to different treatment, the plan must provide the following treatment to *each holder* of a domestic support obligation claim, wage or commission claim, claim for contributions to an employee benefit plan, claim by a grain farmer or United States fisherman, or a claim for a consumer layaway. [B.C. §§ 1129(a)(9)(B), 507(a)(1), (4)–(7)]

(i) *If the class has accepted the plan,* each claimant is entitled to receive deferred cash payments having a present value, as of the effective date of the plan, equal to the allowed amount of her claim. [B.C. § 1129(a)(9)(B)(i)]

(ii) *If the class has rejected the plan,* each claimant must receive total payment of her claim, in cash, on the effective date of the plan. [B.C. § 1129(a)(9)(B)(ii)]

k. Eighth Priority Tax Claims

In BAPCPA, Congress changed the treatment required under the plan for unsecured priority tax claims. Unless it consents to different treatment, each tax claimant entitled to eighth priority must receive *regular installment payments in cash:*

(i) having a present value, as of the effective date of the plan, equal to the allowed amount of the claim [B.C. § 1129(a)(9)(C)(i)];

(ii) over a period of time that ends *no later than 5 years from the order for relief* [B.C. § 1129(a)(9)(C)(ii)]; and

(iii) in a manner *no less favorable* than the plan's treatment—with the exception of a class of creditors under § 1122(b)—of the *most favored non-priority unsecured claim.* [B.C. § 1129(a)(9)(C)(iii)]

(1) Note: Secured Tax Claim

A secured tax claim that but for its secured status would qualify as an unsecured tax claim of a governmental unit entitled to priority under § 507(a)(8) is entitled to cash payments in the same manner and over the same time period as required for other priority tax claims. [B.C. § 1129(a)(9)(D)] Congress added this subsection to § 1129 in BAPCPA.

l. Ninth and Tenth Priority Claims

Section 1129 provides no special rules for the treatment of ninth or tenth priority claims. [*See* B.C. §§ 507(a)(9), (10)]

m. At Least One Impaired Class of Claims Accepts Plan

If the plan *impairs any class of claims,* then the plan must be accepted by *at least one class of claims* that is impaired, excluding any acceptances by insiders of the consenting class. [B.C. § 1129(a)(10)] The purpose of this requirement is to prevent a cramdown, i.e., confirmation under § 1129(b), under circumstances in which none of the impaired classes of claims has accepted the plan.

n. Plan Is Feasible

The plan must be feasible, which means that confirmation of the plan is *not likely* to be followed by the debtor's liquidation or the need for further financial reorganization. [B.C. § 1192(a)(11)] The Code's feasibility test does not require guaranteed success, but the plan must propose a " 'realistic and workable framework.' " [*In re* **American Capital Equipment, LLC,** 688 F.3d 145 (3d Cir. 2011)]

> **e.g.** **Example:** Married debtors filed for relief under Chapter 11. Husband was a solo practitioner, and Wife provided secretarial and clerical help to Husband in his law practice. Debtors proposed a plan that contemplated Husband, who was 68, working for thirty more years at his law practice. The court found that Husband, given his age, could not be expected to practice law full time for another thirty years and that fact "alone doom[ed] the plan as infeasible." [*In re* **Haas,** 162 F.3d 1087 (11th Cir. 1998)]

o. Bankruptcy Fees Paid

All bankruptcy fees required under 28 U.S.C. § 1930 were paid prior to the confirmation hearing, or the plan must provide that they will be paid on the effective date of the plan. [B.C. § 1129(a)(12)]

p. Retiree Insurance Benefits Protected

The plan must provide for the continued payment of all retiree benefits at the level originally provided by the debtor unless (i) the debtor or trustee, if one is appointed, and the authorized representative of the recipients agree to a modification or (ii) the court orders the payments to be modified in accordance with § 1114. The plan must provide for the payment of retiree benefits for the time period that debtor has obligated itself to provide such benefits. [B.C. § 1129(a)(13)]

q. Domestic Support Obligations

In an individual Chapter 11 case, the debtor must have paid all *post-petition domestic support obligations* required by judicial or administrative order, or by statute. [B.C. §§ 1129(a)(14), 101(14A)] Congress added this subsection to § 1129 in 2005. *Pre-*

petition domestic support obligations are first-priority claims and, thus, are paid under the plan according to the requirements of § 1129(a)(9)(B). [B.C. §§ 507(a)(1), 101(14A)]

r. Disposable Income Requirement: Individual Cases

In 2005, Congress added to the requirements for confirmation of a consent plan a *disposable income test* for cases involving *individual Chapter 11 debtors.* The test is similar, but not identical, to Chapter 13's disposable income test. [*Compare* B.C. § 1129(a)(15) *with* § 1325(b)] If the holder of an *allowed unsecured claim objects* to confirmation of the individual debtor's plan, the bankruptcy court cannot confirm the plan unless it provides for one of the following two alternatives:

(i) payment of the *present value,* as of the plan's effective date, of such claim [B.C. § 1129(a)(15)(A)]; or

(ii) payment of the debtor's *projected disposable income* for the *longer* of two time periods: (a) the five-year period starting when the plan's first payment is due or (b) the period of time during which payments are made under the plan. [B.C. §§ 1129(a)(15)(B), 1325(b)(2)]

Example: David files for relief under Chapter 11, and proposes a plan that impairs the class of general unsecured creditors. Craig is a general unsecured creditor, and votes against the plan. The class of general unsecured creditors, however, accepts the plan. Craig may object to plan confirmation. The language of § 1129(a)(15) is like that of § 1129(a)(7); it gives an individual creditor the right to object to plan confirmation even if the class of creditors to which he belongs has voted in favor of the plan under § 1129(a)(8). Therefore, the bankruptcy court cannot confirm David's plan unless it provides for payment *in full* of the general unsecured claims *or* devotes an *amount of money equal* to David's *five-year projected disposable income.*

Note: Section 1129(a)(15) does not *require* that the plan last for five years. There is no applicable commitment period as in Chapter 13. Thus, if an individual Chapter 11 debtor proposes a three-year plan that pays the equivalent of five years of projected disposable income, the debtor should not run afoul of § 1129(a)(15).

s. Property Transfers

Any transfer of property by a non-profit corporation or trust under the plan must be made in accordance with applicable nonbankruptcy law. [B.C. § 1129(a)(16)] Congress added this subsection in 2005 in order to "restrict the authority of a trustee to use, sell, or lease property by a nonprofit corporation or trust." [H.R. No. 109–31, at 145 (2005)]

3. Cramdown

A plan can be confirmed if all of the above requirements have been satisfied *except* § 1129(a)(8), which requires every class of claims or interests to accept the plan or be unimpaired under the plan. Thus, on request by the proponent of a plan, the court will confirm the plan, despite the rejection by one or more impaired classes, if the plan is *not unfairly discriminatory* and *is fair and equitable* with respect to any dissenting impaired classes. [B.C. § 1129(b)(1)]

a. Unfair Discrimination

The Code does not define "unfair discrimination" and provides no statutory guidance, as it does with the "fair and equitable" requirement. [*See* B.C. § 1129(b)(2)] The Code's legislative history makes clear that the "criterion of unfair discrimination is not derived from the fair and equitable rule or from the best interests of creditor test [but] [r]ather preserves just treatment of a dissenting class from the class's own perspective." [H.R. No. 95–595 (1977)] That language, however, provides little substantive guidance as to the contours of the statutory requirement. As a result, courts have grappled with how to determine what constitutes unfair discrimination. There are various tests for unfair discrimination, but most courts "tend to look at the disparity of treatment proposed in the plan, and whether such disparity can be justified under the Code." [7 Collier ¶ 1129.03(3)(a)]

e.g. **Example:** Debtor Corporation files a Chapter 11 plan that separately classifies a large tort claim (Class V) from the remaining general unsecured claims (Class VI), most of which are owed to trade creditors that will continue to supply goods to the reorganized debtor. The plan provides for same percentage payment over time for Class V and Class VI, but Class VI claims are to be paid before payments are made to Class V. The reason for doing so is the size of the tort claim; pro rata payments to *all* unsecured creditors—trade and tort claimants—would result in very small payments to trade creditors due to the size of the tort claim. Because many of the general unsecured creditors will continue to supply goods to the reorganized debtor, it makes sense to pay them before making payments on the large tort claim. If the plan is feasible, however, both sets of creditors will receive the same payout over time. Therefore, while the plan does discriminate between these two classes of creditors, the discrimination is not unfair. [*See* 7 Collier ¶ 1129.03(3)(b)(i)]

Note: It is important to remember that § 1129(b) prohibits unfair discrimination *only* " 'among creditors who have the same level of priority." [*In re* **Greate Bay Hotel & Casino, Inc.,** 251 B.R. 213 (Bankr. D. N.J. 2000) (overruling unfair discrimination objection of intercompany note holders because subordination agreements between debtor and such noteholders "changed the level of priority" of such noteholders)]

b. Fair and Equitable

The Code provides specific guidelines for determining whether a plan is fair and equitable with respect to a particular class. These tests differ according to whether the class is comprised of secured claims, unsecured claims, or equity interests. [B.C. § 1129(b)(2)]

(i) Secured Claims

If a class of secured creditors is *impaired and does not accept the plan,* then the plan's treatment of that class *must be fair and equitable.* (Remember that usually each secured claim is classified in a separate class if the liens are in different property or are entitled to different priorities in the same property.) As to any such impaired class, the plan is fair and equitable if it satisfies *one of the following three conditions.*

(1) Secured Party Retains Lien and Receives Deferred Cash Payments

The plan satisfies the Code's "fair and equitable" requirement if it provides for the creditor to retain her lien on the collateral for the allowed amount of the secured claim, and also to receive payment in deferred *cash* installments that total at least the allowed amount of the secured claim and that have a *present value,* as of the effective date of the plan, of at least the value of the collateral. [B.C. § 1129(b)(2)(A)(i)]

e.g. **Example:** Debtor files for relief under Chapter 11 and proposes a plan that places Creditor into Class 2 by itself. Creditor's claim is for $10,000 and is secured by collateral of the Debtor that is valued at $12,000. Debtor proposes to pay the Class 2 claim $2,000 per year over the course of five years at the market interest rate for such loans. The plan also provides that Creditor will retain its lien to the extent of the allowed amount of its claim. Creditor's claim is impaired, and Creditor votes against Debtor's plan and argues that the plan's treatment of Class is not fair and equitable. The bankruptcy court will rule against Creditor on this ground. First, the plan provides that Creditor retains its lien to the extent of its allowed claim, as required by § 1129(b)(2)(A)(i)(I). Second, Creditor will receive deferred cash payments that equal the allowed amount of the claim ($2,000 per year × 5 years = $10,000). Third, Creditor's interest in the property is $10,000, which is the amount of its claim, and by paying the market interest rate on the claim the plan ensures that Creditor is receiving the present value of its $10,000 claim.

(a) Section 1111(b) Election

Recall that if a partially secured creditor elects, under § 1111(b), to have her entire claim treated as secured, then the deferred cash payments in a cramdown must equal the full dollar amount of her allowed claim and must have a present value of at least the value of the collateral.

e.g. **Example:** Debtor files for relief under Chapter 11 and proposes a plan that places Creditor into Class 2 by itself. Creditor's claim is for $12,000 and is secured by collateral of the Debtor that is valued at $10,000. Creditor makes the § 1111(b) election. Debtor proposes to pay the Class 2 claim $2,000 per year over the course of five years at 5% interest and, to make the calculation simpler, assume that interest does not compound. Also assume that this is the market interest rate. The plan also provides that Creditor will retain its lien to the extent of the allowed amount of its claim. Creditor's claim is impaired, and Creditor votes against Debtor's plan and argues that the plan's treatment of Class is not fair and equitable. The bankruptcy court will rule in favor of Creditor on this ground. The plan payments total $11,500. (For example, in Year 1, Creditor gets $2,000 in principal plus $500 in interest. In Year 2, it's $2,000 in principal but $400 in interest, because the interest payment is 5% of the remaining $8,000 balance. And so on for three more years— $2,000 in principal payments plus a total of $800 in interest, at 5% on the decreasing balance each year.) The problem is that the deferred cash payments of $11,500 do not equal the allowed amount of Creditor's claim, which is $12,000 because of the § 1111(b) election.

(b) Interest Rate

The Supreme Court, in a plurality opinion, held that the interest rate to use in a Chapter 13 cramdown is *prime plus.* The Court explained that the starting point is the *national prime rate,* which the bankruptcy court *adjusts for risk* based on factors such as the length and feasibility of the plan and the nature of the creditor's security. While the plurality did not determine what constitutes a proper risk adjustment, it did note that courts generally had approved 1% to 3% adjustments to the prime rate. *Till* was a Chapter 13 case, but the plurality noted that a number of provisions in the Code, including portions of § 1129(b), required discounting of a stream of payments to present value. Thus, the plurality concluded that Congress likely "intended bankruptcy judges and trustees to follow essentially the same approach when choosing an appropriate interest rate" under any of these other provisions of the Code. [**Till v. SCS Credit Corp.,** 541 U.S.

465 (2004)] Most bankruptcy courts have applied the prime-plus formula from the plurality's opinion in *Till* in Chapter 11 cramdown cases. [*See* **Wells Fargo Bank v. Texas Grand Prairie Hotel Realty, LLC,** 710 F.3d 324 (5th Cir. 2013) (holding that it would not "tie bankruptcy courts to a specific methodology as they assess the appropriate Chapter 11 cramdown interest rate," but noting that the "vast majority of bankruptcy courts" used *Till's* prime-plus formula in Chapter 11 cases)]

(2) Secured Party Receives Indubitable Equivalent

The plan satisfies the "fair and equitable" requirement if it provides the creditor with the ***indubitable equivalent*** of her secured claim. [B.C. § 1129(b)(2)(A)(iii)]

e.g. **Example:** Prior to bankruptcy, Creditor sold Debtor 79 tracts of land for $65 million. Debtor paid $9 million and financed the remainder through Creditor. While Debtor eventually paid Creditor over $60 million for the properties, Debtor failed to repay the debt in full by the maturity date of the loan. Debtor filed for relief under Chapter 11 and proposed a partial dirt-for-debt plan. (In a partial dirt-for-debt plan, the debtor transfers part of the collateral to the secured creditor in satisfaction of the creditor's claim.) The plan impaired Creditor's claim and Creditor voted against it, thereby triggering a cramdown. After conducting valuation hearings, the bankruptcy court concluded that the Debtor's conveyance of 8 of the 79 tracts to Creditor and the payment of cash totaling about $1 million constituted the indubitable equivalent of Creditor's claim. On appeal, the Fourth Circuit rejected Creditor's argument that the uncertainties associated with property valuation make it impossible for *any* partial dirt-for-debt plan to satisfy the indubitable equivalent standard. The court noted that such a holding would "eviscerate" the standard because uncertainty inheres in all disputed valuations. The court affirmed the bankruptcy court's decision and "decline[d] to hold that a partial dirt-for-debt plan can never provide the indubitable equivalent of a secured creditor's claim as a matter of law." [**Bate Land Co. LP v. Bate Land Timber LLC,** 877 F.3d 188 (4th Cir. 2017)]

(3) Collateral Sold and Lien Attaches to Proceeds

The third statutory method for satisfying the "fair and equitable" requirement for secured claims is for the plan to provide for the collateral to be sold free and clear of the creditor's lien, with the lien attaching to the proceeds of the sale. The lien on the sale proceeds must be treated in a manner described in (a) (deferred cash payments) or (b) (indubitable equivalent) above. For example, the debtor may turn over the sale proceeds to the secured creditor, which satisfies the secured creditor's claim. The secured creditor realizes the indubitable equivalent of its claim, and the debtor satisfies the Code's "fair and equitable" requirement.

Note: The sale is subject to the creditor's right, under § 363(k), to bid at the sale, purchase the property, and offset her claim against the purchase price. [B.C. § 1129(b)(2)(A)(ii)]

(ii) Unsecured Claims

If a class of unsecured creditors is *impaired and does not accept the plan,* then the plan's treatment of that class *must be fair and equitable.* As to any such impaired class, the plan is fair and equitable if it satisfies *one of the following two conditions.*

(1) Each Creditor Receives Property Equal to Allowed Claim

The first statutory method for satisfying the "fair and equitable" requirement for a class of unsecured creditors is for the plan to provide that each creditor in the class receive property, e.g., cash notes, stock, or other property of the debtor, having a *present value,* as of the effective date of the plan, equal to the allowed amount of her unsecured claim. [B.C. § 1129(b)(2)(B)(i)]

(2) Senior Classes Fully Paid Before Junior Classes

In many cases, the Chapter 11 debtor will not be able to pay its unsecured creditors in full. Thus, the Code provides the *absolute priority rule* as an alternative method for satisfying the "fair and equitable" requirement if a class of unsecured creditors is impaired and does not vote to approve the plan. The *absolute priority rule* requires that no holder of a claim or an interest that is junior to the impaired unsecured class receive or retain any property on account of the junior claim or interest. In other words, if an impaired unsecured class does not vote to approve the plan and the plan does not pay those claims in full, then the plan may not provide that the debtor's current equity holders retain their interests in the reorganized entity. [B.C. § 1129(b)(2)(B)(ii)]

(a) "New Value Exception"

The courts are split concerning the continuing validity of a pre-Code, judicially created exception allowing equity security holders to retain an interest in cases in which they invest (i) *new capital,* (ii) *in money or money's worth,* that is (iii) *a substantial contribution,* (iv) *reasonably equivalent to the interest received or retained,* and (v) *necessary for a successful reorganization.* [*See* **Case v. Los Angeles Lumber Products Co.,** 308 U.S. 106 (1939) *see, e.g., In re* **Civil Partners Sioux City, LLC,** 2013 WL 5534743 (2013) (holding that $150,000 new value proposal was insufficient while noting that court did not have to "definitely decide the application of the 'new value' exception"] In two opinions, the Supreme Court has dodged the issue of whether there is a "new value" exception to the absolute priority rule. [*See* **Bank of America National Trust and Savings Association v. 203 North LaSalle Street Partnership,** 526 U.S. 434 (1999) (without ruling on whether the new value exception survived enactment of the Bankruptcy Code, holding that plan giving pre-bankruptcy equity holders the sole right to contribute new capital and keep their equity, without consideration of alternatives, could not constitute new value); **Norwest Bank Worthington v. Ahlers,** 485 U.S. 197 (1988) (holding that debtors' promise of future "labor, experience and expertise" did not constitute "money or money's worth" and, thus, was not new value)]

(b) The Absolute Priority Rule in Individual Cases

In BAPCPA, Congress added an exception to the language of § 1129(b)(2)(B)(ii) for *individual debtors.* That exception provides that if the debtor is an individual, she may "retain property included in the estate under section 1115," subject to the Code's disposable income requirement. [B.C. §§ 1129(b)(2)(B)(ii), 1129(a)(14)] Congress also added § 1115, which defines property of the estate in an individual Chapter 11 case to include all property under § 541, all property acquired post-petition of the kind described in § 541, and all of the debtor's post-petition earnings. [B.C. § 1115] The courts have split on whether Congress intended, through these changes to the Code, to repeal the absolute priority rule for cases involving individual Chapter 11 debtors.

1. Narrow View

Most courts have adopted the *narrow* interpretation of the *absolute priority rule* for *individual* Chapter 11 debtors. Courts adopting the narrow view hold that the exception excludes from the operation of the absolute priority rule *only* the debtor's post-petition earnings and acquisitions of property.

e.g. **Example:** Debtor filed for relief under Chapter 13, but his case was converted to Chapter 11, because his debts exceeded the Chapter 13 debt limits. Debtor proposed that he retain valuable, non-exempt, pre-petition assets while paying a small dividend to his unsecured creditors, a majority of which voted to reject his plan. The bankruptcy court denied confirmation on the basis of the absolute priority rule. The Fifth Circuit affirmed. The court explained that with BAPCPA Congress amended both § 1129(b)(2)(B)(ii) and § 1115 in order to coordinate the rules for individuals in Chapter 11 to avoid having more favorable terms for individual debtors in Chapter 11 than in Chapter 13. By including the debtor's post-petition earnings and property in the new definition of estate property at § 1115, however, Congress also "had to modify the absolute priority rule so that a debtor would not be saddled with committing all post-petition property to satisfy creditors' claims." Thus, the court held that Congress did not repeal the absolute priority rule, but instead modified and refined it in order to protect an individual debtor's post-petition earnings and acquisitions of property. [*In re* **Lively,** 717 F.3d 406 (5th Cir. 2013)]

2. Broad View

A minority of courts has adopted the broad view of the absolute priority rule. Courts following the broad view do not apply the absolute priority rule to individual Chapter 11 debtors. They reason that the "except" clause in § 1129(b)(2)(B)(ii) speaks in terms of property under § 1115, and is not limited to post-petition property. Thus, the plain meaning of the statutory provisions leads to the conclusion that "the absolute priority rule no longer applies to prevent individual Chapter 11 debtors from retaining pre- or post-petition property over an unsecured creditor's objection." [**SPCP Group, LLC v. Biggins,** 465 B.R. 316 (M.D. Fla. 2011)]

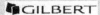

Remember that if an impaired class of **unsecured claims** has rejected the plan, the **"fair and equitable"** element of a cramdown is determined as follows: The plan is fair and equitable with respect to the class if (i) the plan proposes to pay each creditor in the class the full amount of her allowed unsecured claim on a present value basis, or (ii) no holder of a claim or interest that is junior to the class will receive or retain any property, on account of the junior claim or interest, under the plan. This rule is known as **the absolute priority rule.** On an exam, it also could be important for you to note that some courts recognize a **new value exception to the absolute priority rule** if the plan provides for a class of equity security holders to receive or retain an interest in the reorganized debtor, on account of their junior interests, in exchange for a substantial contribution of new capital in money or money's worth that is reasonably equivalent to the interest received or retained and necessary for the reorganization. Your professor also may test you on whether the absolute priority rule applies to an individual Chapter 11 debtor. It is important to understand how the courts have construed the statutory language in the cramdown and estate property sections of the Code in order to arrive at the **narrow and broad interpretations** of the absolute priority rule.

DETERMINING WHETHER A CRAMDOWN IS FAIR AND EQUITABLE  GILBERT		
TO BE FAIR AND EQUITABLE, THE PLAN MUST PROPOSE ONE OF THE ACCEPTABLE TREATMENTS FOR EACH CLASS OF CLAIMS OR INTERESTS THAT IS IMPAIRED AND HAS REJECTED THE PLAN.		
SECURED CLASSES*	**UNSECURED CLASSES**	**CLASSES OF EQUITY INTERESTS**
Creditor retains her lien on the collateral for the allowed amount of the secured claim, and receives deferred **cash** payments totaling at least the allowed amount of her secured claim and having a **present value** of at least the value of the collateral	Each creditor of the class receives property (not necessarily cash) having a **present value** equal to the allowed amount of her unsecured claim	Each interest holder receives or retains property having a **present value** equal to the allowed amount of any fixed liquidation preference or fixed redemption price to which the holder is entitled, or the value of her equity interest, whichever is the **greatest**
or	*or*	*or*
Creditor realizes the **indubitable equivalent** of her secured claim	No creditor or interest holder junior to the class receives or retains any property on account of the junior claim or interest	No interest holder junior to the class receives or retains any property on account of the junior interest
or		
Collateral is **sold free and clear** of creditor's lien, with the lien attaching to the proceeds and treated in one of the ways above		
* Note that usually each secured claim is classified in a separate class.		

(iii) Equity Interests

With respect to a class of interests, the plan must propose one of the two following methods of treatment for such interests in order to satisfy the "fair and equitable" requirement.

(1) Holder Receives or Retains Property Equal to Any Applicable Fixed Liquidation Preference or Fixed Redemption Price, or Value of Equity Interest

Treatment of an impaired class of interests is fair and equitable, notwithstanding the class's vote against the plan, if the plan provides that each interest holder *receive or retain property* having a *present value,* as of the effective date of the plan, equal to the allowed amount of any fixed liquidation preference or fixed redemption price to which the holder is entitled, or the value of her equity interest, *whichever is the greatest.* [B.C. § 1129(b)(2)(C)(i)]

(2) Senior Classes Fully Paid Before Junior Classes

An alternative method of satisfying the "fair and equitable" requirement if no interest holder that is junior to the class receives or retains any property on account of the junior interest. [B.C. § 1129(b)(2)(C)(ii)]

4. Denial of Confirmation

On the request of a governmental unit that is a party in interest, the court must deny confirmation of a plan if it finds that the *plan's principal purpose* is to *avoid taxes* or *registration under § 5 of the Securities Act of 1933.* In any hearing on this issue the governmental unit bears the burden of proof. [B.C. § 1129(d)]

G. Small Business Debtors

1. Introduction

Prior to the passage of the Bankruptcy Abuse Prevention and Consumer Protection Act ("BAPCPA"), the Bankruptcy Code permitted a debtor to elect treatment as a small business debtor. BAPCPA eliminated the election and made the small business provisions of the Bankruptcy Code mandatory for any debtor that satisfied the Code's definition of a small business debtor. The *debtor must designate* its status as either a small or not a small business by *checking the appropriate box* on the voluntary petition. [Official Forms 101, 201] In an involuntary case, the debtor must file a statement within 14 days of the order for relief as to whether it is a small business. The United States trustee or a party in interest may *object* to the debtor's designation within *30 days of the conclusion of the § 341 meeting* or within *30 days of any amendment* to the debtor's designation, whichever is later. Unless an official committee of unsecured creditors forms, the debtor's designation stands unless and until the court enters an order finding that the debtor's designation is incorrect. [Bankruptcy Rule 1020(a)]

2. Definition of a Small Business Debtor

A *small business debtor* is any person *engaged in commercial or business activities,* including any affiliated debtor, whose aggregate *noncontingent unliquidated secured and unsecured debts* are *$2,725,625 or less,* excluding debts owed to *affiliates or insiders,* on the petition filing date. [B.C. § 101(51D)] The liability cutoff adjusts every three years, and will increase again on April 1, 2022. [B.C. § 104(a)] The Code does not require that the debtor be engaged in commercial or business activities at the time of filing the petition. [Collier ¶ 101.51D] The Code also does not require an affiliated debtor to be engaged in commercial or business activities.

Example: Dexter is the sole owner of *Acme, Inc.* Dexter's liabilities are primarily consumer in nature. Dexter and *Acme* file for relief under Chapter 11. Dexter's and *Acme*'s noncontingent unliquidated liabilities total to less than $2.5 million. *Acme* is engaged in commercial or business activities and is a small business debtor. Dexter, as sole owner of *Acme*, is an affiliate of *Acme*. [B.C. § 101(2)(A)] Even if Dexter is a consumer debtor and not engaged in commercial or business activities, he qualifies as a small business debtor because he is an *Acme* affiliate. [5 Norton § 107:1]

A debtor is *not a small business debtor* if any of the following exclusions apply:

a. the debtor's *primary activity* is the business of *owning or operating real property* or activities incidental to such ownership or operation;

b. the United States trustee has appointed an *official committee of unsecured creditors* pursuant to § 1102(a)(1);

c. the United States trustee has appointed an *official committee of unsecured creditors* and the court has determined that the committee is *not sufficiently active and representative* to provide effective oversight of the debtor; or

d. the debtor is a member of a *group of affiliated debtors* with *aggregate noncontingent liquidated liabilities greater than $2,725,625,* excluding debts owed to insiders and affiliates. [B.C. § 101(51D)]

Example: *Burgerz, Inc.* is a small burger restaurant in financial trouble. The firm files for relief under Chapter 11. Its total liabilities are $2.3 million. The United States trustee appoints an official committee of unsecured creditors. *Burgerz* is not a small business debtor.

Example: *Dreamsicle Company* is a specialty ice cream store that files for relief under Chapter 11. *Dreamsicle* has total liabilities of $2.4 million. The United States trustee appoints an official committee of unsecured creditors but subsequently requests a determination that the committee is not sufficiently active and representative. The court enters an order stating that the committee is not sufficiently active and representative to provide effective oversight of *Dreamsicle*. *Dreamsicle*'s Chapter 11 case now will proceed as a small business case upon entry of the court's order. [Bankruptcy Rule 1020(c)]

Example: Dinah is the sole owner of *Atlas, Inc., Bella Corp.,* and *Calypso Company.* *Atlas, Bella,* and *Calypso* file for relief under Chapter 11 on the same day. Each firm's total liabilities range between $1 and $2 million, but the three firms' aggregate noncontingent liquidated liabilities equal $4 million. None of the three firms has insider or affiliate debt. *Atlas, Bella,* and *Calypso* are not small business debtors, because the aggregate of the three affiliated firms' liabilities exceeds $2,725,625.

Example: Dinah is the sole owner and president of *Atlas, Inc., Bella Corp.,* and *Calypso Company. Atlas, Bella,* and *Calypso* file for relief under Chapter 11 on the same day. The United States trustee does not appoint an official committee in any of the three bankruptcy cases, and none of the firms is in the real property business. *Atlas* has $1 million in liabilities, but $500,000 of that amount is a guarantee of a loan owed by *Bella. Bella* is current on the loan, which means that $500,000 of *Atlas*'s debt is contingent. On the petition date, *Bella* and *Calypso* each have $1.5 million in liabilities. Pre-petition, Dinah had loaned $400,000 to *Bella* and $600,000 to *Calypso.* As the president of both firms, Dinah is an insider, which means that in computing liabilities for purposes of the small business debtor definition the $1 million in loans from Dinah to *Bella* and *Calypso* do not count toward the firms' liability totals. While *Atlas, Bella,* and *Calypso* qualify as a group of affiliated debtors, their aggregate noncontingent liquidated liabilities are $2.5 million ($500,000 for *Atlas* and $2 million for *Bella* and *Calypso* combined). Therefore, *Atlas, Bella,* and *Calypso* are small business debtors.

3. Duties of Debtor in Possession or Trustee in Small Business Case

In small business cases, the Bankruptcy Code imposes on the debtor in possession or the Chapter 11 trustee, if one is appointed, additional obligations not applicable to a non-small business case. [B.C. §§ 308, 1116; Bankruptcy Rule 2015(a)(6); Official Form 425C] The *small business debtor* must:

a. file its ***most recent balance sheet, statement of operations, cash-flow statement, and Federal income tax return*** with the petition in a voluntary case or within seven days of the order for relief in an involuntary case, or file a ***statement*** made under ***penalty of perjury*** that such documents do not exist;

b. ***attend an initial debtor interview*** with the United States trustee prior to the § 341 meeting; and

c. ***file monthly reports*** that include:

   (i) the ***debtor's profitability;***

   (ii) reasonable approximations of the ***debtor's projected cash receipts and cash disbursements;***

   (iii) a comparison of ***actual cash receipts and disbursements*** with ***prior projections;***

   (iv) whether the debtor is ***complying with the requirements*** imposed by the ***Bankruptcy Code and the Federal Rules of Bankruptcy Procedure;***

   (v) whether the debtor is ***filing tax returns*** and other required government filings in a ***timely fashion;***

   (vi) whether debtor is ***paying taxes and administrative expenses when due;***

   (vii) the ***steps that debtor intends to make to remedy*** any failure to comply with the requirements of the Bankruptcy Code or Rules, to file tax returns or other government reporting documents, or to pay taxes or other administrative expenses; and

   (viii) any other matter that is in the ***best interests of the debtor and creditors,*** and in the ***public's interest in fair and efficient administration*** of the bankruptcy laws.

4. United States Trustee Duties in Small Business Case

a. The United States trustee has additional oversight obligations in small business cases. [28 U.S.C. § 586(a)(7)] The United States trustee must:

   (i) conduct an ***initial interview with the debtor*** as soon as practicable after the order for relief but ***before the date set for the § 341 meeting;***

   (ii) if appropriate and advisable, ***visit the debtor's business premises,*** ascertain the ***state of the debtor's books and records,*** and verify that the debtor has ***filed its tax returns;*** and

   (iii) ***review and monitor the debtor's activities*** in order to determine as soon as possible whether debtor will be ***unable to confirm a plan.***

b. At the *initial debtor interview,* the United States trustee shall:

    (i) begin to *investigate the debtor's viability;*

    (ii) ask about the *debtor's business plan;*

    (iii) explain the debtor's obligation to *file monthly reports* and other *required reports;*

    (iv) try to develop an *agreed scheduling order;* and

    (v) *inform* the debtor of other *obligations.*

5. The Small Business Debtor's Disclosure Statement and Plan

a. Disclosure Statement

If the court determines that a disclosure statement must be filed, then it must be filed *no later than 300 days after* the order for relief. [B.C. § 1121(e)(2)] The Bankruptcy Code does not provide a deadline for filing the disclosure statement in non-small business cases. Otherwise, the Bankruptcy Code's disclosure-statement requirements are more flexible for small compared with non-small business cases.

(i) The bankruptcy court may determine that a disclosure statement is not needed because the *plan provides adequate information.* [B.C. § 1125(f)(1)]

(ii) The bankruptcy court also may approve a disclosure statement submitted on *standard forms.* [B.C. § 1125(f)(2); Official Form 425B]

(iii) The bankruptcy court may *conditionally approve* the disclosure statement subject to final approval at a hearing after notice. [B.C. § 1125(f)(3)(A)] The debtor may solicit votes on the plan based on a conditionally approved disclosure statement, but the debtor must mail the disclosure statement *no later than 25 days before* the plan confirmation hearing. [B.C. § 1125(f)(3)(B)] The court may combine the final hearing on the disclosure statement with the hearing on plan confirmation. [B.C. § 1125(f)(3)(C)]

b. Exclusivity Period

Unless the court grants an extension or for cause orders otherwise, the *small business debtor* has the exclusive right to file a plan for the first *180 days after* the order for relief. [B.C. § 1121(e)(1)]

c. "Drop Dead" Date

Unless the court grants an extension, the plan and disclosure statement, if any, must be filed no later than *300 days after* the order for relief. [B.C. § 1121(e)(2)] Courts have struggled with how to interpret the 300-day deadline language that BAPCPA added to the Code.

(i) Non-Debtors and the 300-Day Deadline

The Bankruptcy Code does not specifically state that the "debtor" must file a plan within 300 days. Thus, the question has arisen whether the 300-day plan-filing deadline applies to debtors and non-debtors alike. The few courts that have addressed the issue generally have held that the 300-day time limit applies only to the debtor, not to other parties in interest that want to file a plan. [*See, e.g.,* **In re Simbaki, Ltd.,** 522 B.R. 917, 920–24 (Bankr. S.D. Tex. 2017) (holding that 300-day deadline does not apply to non-debtor plan proponents); **In re Florida Coastal Airlines, Inc.,** 361 B.R. 286 (Bankr. S.D. Fla. 2007) (holding that the 300-day plan proposal period in § 1121(e)(2) "applies only to plans filed by the debtor and that there is no statutory deadline for the filing of such a reorganization plan by any party in interest other than the debtor")]

(ii) Plan amendments Outside the 300 days

It is unclear whether the Bankruptcy Code only requires the filing of a plan within 300 days or whether all amendments to the plan also must be filed within the 300-day period. There is very little case law on the issue, but those few courts that have considered the question appear to focus on whether an amendment outside the 300 days is simply a cleaned-up version of the first-filed plan or a fundamentally different plan from the originally filed plan. [*See, e.g., In re* **Castle Horizon Real Estate, LLC,** 2010 WL 3636160 (Bankr. E.D. N.C. 2010) (holding that the 300-day deadline applies to plan that are not "cleaned up version[s] of the original"); *In re* **Florida Coastal Airlines, Inc.,** 361 B.R. 286 (S.D. Fla. 2007) (holding that debtor's amended plan, which was filed more than 300 days after the order for relief, related back to original plan filed within the 300-day period because the amended plan was "fundamentally a cleaned-up version of [debtor's] original plan")]

(iii) Debtor Incorrectly Identifies Itself as *Not* a Small Business Debtor

The small business debtor must identify itself as such on the voluntary petition or must file a statement indicating its status in an involuntary case. If the court later determines that the debtor is a small business, even though debtor had identified as a non-small business, the question arises whether the 300-day deadline for filing a plan runs from the order for relief or from the court's subsequent determination that the debtor is a small business. The few cases that have addressed the issue have held that the 300-day deadline runs from the order for relief, even in a case converted to Chapter 11 from another chapter of the Bankruptcy Code.

e.g. **Example:** Debtor filed for relief under Chapter 11 and checked the box on the petition stating that it was not a small business debtor. Two months later, the United States trustee objected to the debtor's designation on the petition. More than four months after the debtor had filed its voluntary petition, the bankruptcy court determined that the debtor's designation on the petition was incorrect and that the debtor indeed was a small business debtor. The court held that the 300-day plan-proposal deadline ran from the debtor's filing of the petition, leaving the debtor with six, as opposed to ten, months to file a plan. [*In re* **Display Group,** 2010 WL 4777550 (Bankr. E.D. N.Y. 2010)]

e.g. **Example:** Debtor originally filed for relief under Chapter 13 in August of 2011. In December of 2012, the bankruptcy court granted her motion to convert her case to Chapter 11. Debtor filed her Chapter 11 plan approximately four months later and a confirmation hearing was scheduled for June of 2013. When the debtor sought an extension of the confirmation hearing date, the United States trustee objected on the ground that debtor had filed her plan more than 300 days from the order for relief, which was the date that she commenced her bankruptcy case under Chapter 13. The bankruptcy court agreed with the interpretation of the Code advanced by the United States trustee and cited to the language of § 348(a), which provides that conversion to another chapter does not change the date of the order for relief. Because the debtor filed her Chapter 11 plan about 20 months from the commencement of her Chapter 13 case, she failed to satisfy the Code's requirement that a Chapter 11 small business debtor file the plan within 300 days of the order for relief. [*In re* **Rivera,** 2013 WL 3367100 (Bankr. D. P.R. 2013)]

(iv) Debtor Incorrectly Identifies Itself as a Small Business Debtor

If a debtor initially checks the small business debtor box on the petition, then the debtor's Chapter 11 case proceeds as a small business case. [Bankruptcy Rule 1020(a)] If the debtor later seeks to change its designation to a non-small business, the question that arises is whether the debtor may avoid the consequences of not satisfying the Code's small-business deadlines *before* the change of status to a non-small business. There are few cases specifically on the issue of the 300-day deadline. [*See* **In re Swartville, LLC,** 483 B.R. 453 (Bankr. E.D. N.C. 2012) (holding that the debtor's failure to file its second amended plan within the 300-day deadline was excusable and not grounds for dismissal because the debtor had mistakenly and in "good faith" checked the wrong box on the petition and that mistaken designation neither benefitted debtor nor prejudiced creditors)]

d. Plan Confirmation

The bankruptcy court must confirm the small business debtor's plan *no later than 45 days after* the plan is filed, unless the time for confirmation is extended. [B.C. §§ 1129(e), 1121(e)(3)]

e. Time Extensions

The court may extend the small business debtor's (1) *exclusivity period,* (2) *300-day deadline* for filing a plan and disclosure statement, and (3) *45-day period* for plan confirmation, but only if several conditions are satisfied [B.C. § 1121(e)(3)]:

(i) the *small business debtor* provides *notice* to parties in interest, including the United States trustee;

(ii) the *small business debtor* demonstrates by a *preponderance of the evidence* that it is *more likely than not* that the court will *confirm a plan within a reasonable period of time;*

(iii) the court imposes a *new deadline* when it grants the extension; and

(iv) the court *signs the order* extending the deadline *before the existing deadline expires.*

H. Post-Confirmation Matters

1. Effects of Confirmation

The provisions of a confirmed Chapter 11 plan are binding on all creditors and equity security holders, the debtor, any general partner in the debtor, and any entity that issues securities or acquires property under the plan. The fact that the claim or interest of a creditor, equity security holder, or general partner is impaired under the plan and that such creditor, equity security holder, or general partner did not accept the plan is irrelevant; they still are bound by the terms of the plan. [B.C. § 1141(a); *see* **Browning v. Levy,** 283 F.3d 761 (6th Cir. 2002) (discussing res judicata effect of confirmation order)]

a. On Property

Unless the plan or the confirmation order provides otherwise, confirmation causes all property of the estate to vest in the debtor, and all property that is dealt with by the plan to be free and clear of all claims and interests. [B.C. §§ 1141(b), (c)]

(i) Secured Creditors

The general rule is that liens pass through bankruptcy unaffected. But, a number of courts have held that "confirmation of a Chapter 11 plan voids liens on property dealt with by the plan unless they are specifically preserved, if the lien holder participates in the reorganization." [**Elixir Industries v. City Bank & Trust (*In re Ahern Enterprises*),** 507 F.3d 817 (5th Cir. 2007); *see also* **Airadigm Communications, Inc. v. FCC (*In re* Airadigm Communications, Inc.),** 519 F.3d 640 (7th Cir. 2008) (stating that if a "secured creditor participates in the debtor's bankruptcy and the ultimate plan does not preserve the creditor's interest, the interest is gone")] Courts have reached different conclusions on the amount of creditor participation needed to extinguish a lien under the plan. [*In re* **Northern New England Telephone Operations, LLC,** 504 B.R. 372 (Bankr. S.D. N.Y. 2014)] Some courts have held that the mere filing of a proof of claim does not suffice to extinguish a secured creditor's lien. But, if the creditor files a proof of claim, and the reorganization plan provides for payment of the claim but is silent concerning the lien, confirmation extinguishes the lien, because the creditor participated in the case. [*See, e.g.,* **In re Penrod,** 50 F.3d 459 (7th Cir. 1995)] Thus, in a jurisdiction following the *Penrod* interpretation of § 1141(c), a secured creditor should require language in the plan that expressly preserves its lien. Other courts have held that participation requires nothing more than "having been given notice of the proposed plan's terms and the opportunity to object to confirmation of the plan." [*In re* **Regional Building Systems, Inc.,** 251 B.R. 274 (Bankr. D. Md. 2000)]

b. Discharge of Debts

Generally, unless the plan or the confirmation order provides otherwise, confirmation discharges the debtor from ***all pre-confirmation debts,*** as well as from debts arising from (i) the rejection of executory contracts or unexpired leases not assumed by the trustee or debtor in possession; (ii) the recovery of property by the trustee or the debtor under §§ 522, 550, or 553; and (iii) eighth priority tax claims that occasionally arise post-petition. [B.C. §§ 1141(d)(1)(A), 502(g)–(i)] These debts are discharged regardless of whether (i) a proof of claim was filed, (ii) the claim was allowed, or (iii) the holder accepted the plan.

(i) Discharge Not Restricted to Individuals

A Chapter 11 discharge is not restricted to individual debtors, as in Chapter 7; thus, ***corporations and partnerships*** may be discharged as well. [B.C. § 1141(d)(1)(A)] Confirmation terminates all rights and interests of general partners and equity security holders who are dealt with by the plan. [B.C. § 1141(d)(1)(B)]

(ii) Individual Debtors

Prior to the passage of BAPCPA, confirmation of a plan discharged the debtor from its pre-confirmation debts, with the exception of those debts excepted from discharge under § 523. The Code currently provides that an individual Chapter 11 debtor does not receive a discharge until the bankruptcy court grants a discharge upon the debtor's ***completion of all payments under the plan.*** [B.C. § 1142(d)(5)(A)]

(1) Exception to Completion-of-Payments Requirement

After confirmation of the plan and after notice and a hearing, a bankruptcy court may grant an individual debtor who has *not completed her plan payments* a discharge if the following conditions are satisfied:

(a) the *present value* as of the plan's effective date of property distributed to unsecured creditors is equal to or greater than what those creditors would have received in a *Chapter 7 liquidation* [B.C. § 1141(d)(5)(B)(i)];

(b) *modification* of the plan under § 1127 is *not practicable.* [B.C. § 1141(d)(5)(B)(ii)]; and

(c) the exemption limits under § 522(q) do not apply. [B.C. § 1141(d)(5)(B)(iii)]

(2) Exemption Limits Under § 522(q)

The court may not grant the debtor a discharge unless it determines, after notice and a hearing held *no more than 10 days before* the entry of the discharge order, that there is *no reasonable cause to believe* that *§ 522(q)(1)* may apply to the debtor and that there is *no proceeding pending* in which the debtor may be found guilty of a felony described in *§ 522(q)(1)(A)* or a debt described in *§ 522(q)(1)(B).* [B.C. § 1141(d)(5)(C)] It is unclear whether this provision results in a *denial of discharge* or merely a *delay of entry of discharge.*

(iii) Exceptions to Discharge

(1) Individual's Nondischargeable Debts

If the debtor is an individual, a Chapter 11 discharge does not include any debts that are nondischargeable under Bankruptcy Code § 523, e.g., certain taxes, alimony, child support, educational loans. [B.C. § 1141(d)(2)]

(2) Liquidating Plan

The debtor will not receive a discharge if:

(a) the confirmed plan provides for the liquidation of all or substantially all of the estate property [B.C. § 1141(d)(3)(A)];

(b) the debtor does not continue in business after the plan is consummated [B.C. § 1141(d)(3)(B)]; and

(c) the debtor would not be granted a discharge in a Chapter 7 case under § 727(a). [B.C. § 1141(d)(3)(A)]

For example, a corporation or a partnership will not receive a discharge if the court confirms a Chapter 11 liquidating plan and the debtor's business is discontinued.

(iv) Corporate Debtors

In BAPCPA, Congress created several *exceptions* to the discharge received by a *corporate debtor.* Confirmation of a plan does not discharge a corporate debtor from any of the following debts:

(1) debts for *fraud* under §§ 523(a)(2)(A) or (B) that are owed to a *domestic governmental unit* [B.C. § 1141(d)(6)(A)];

    (2) debts owed to a person as a result of an action filed against the United States government under 31 U.S.C. § 3721 *et seq.* or any similar State statute [B.C. § 1142(d)(6)(A)]; or

    (3) any *tax or customs duty* for which the debtor made a *fraudulent return or willfully attempted to evade or defeat.* [B.C. § 1141(d)(6)(B)]

(v) Officers and Directors

Confirmation of a Chapter 11 plan discharges only the debtor; therefore, officers and directors of a debtor corporation are *not* discharged from any liabilities incurred *personally* while associated with the debtor e.g., claims for tortious conduct brought by former shareholders.

(vi) Failure to Give Notice

If the debtor knows of a creditor's claim but fails to schedule it, and the creditor does not receive notice of the bankruptcy proceedings, the principle of due process should prevail over the Code's discharge provisions, and so the debt should not be discharged. But a creditor may not sleep on its rights. Thus, if a creditor that filed a claim in the debtor's bankruptcy case and had actual notice of the debtor's plan, its contents, and the confirmation hearing but failed to object, the creditor cannot complain of an erroneous ruling that is had a "full and fair opportunity to litigate." [**United Student Aid Funds, Inc. v. Espinosa,** 559 U.S. 260 (2010)]

c. Termination of Automatic Stay

Generally, confirmation of a Chapter 11 plan terminates the automatic stay, because property that vests in the debtor is no longer property of the estate and confirmation of a reorganization plan usually discharges the debtor. [B.C. §§ 362(c)(1), (2)(C)] But, BAPCPA changed the time for entry of a discharge in an individual Chapter 11 case. Section 362(c) provides that the stay of any act other than an act against estate property, e.g. an act against the debtor, does not terminate until the earliest of the case closing, dismissal, or entry of or denial of a discharge. [B.C. §§ 362(c)(2)(A)–(C)]

2. Implementation of Plan

Notwithstanding any nonbankruptcy law concerning financial condition, the Bankruptcy Code requires that the debtor and any successor implement the plan and comply with all court orders. Furthermore, the court is authorized to order the debtor and any other necessary party to execute or deliver any instrument required for the transfer of property under the plan and to perform whatever else is needed to consummate the plan. [B.C. § 1142]

3. Distribution

If the plan provides that an entity's participation in distribution is contingent on the entity's surrender or presentment of a security or on the doing of some other act, the entity must perform accordingly within *five years* after the date of the *entry of the confirmation order* or it will forfeit the right to share in distribution under the plan. [B.C. § 1143]

4. Revocation of Confirmation Order

Within *180 days* after the entry of the order confirming the Chapter 11 plan, a party in interest may request that the order be revoked, but only on the ground that it was *procured by fraud.* If, after notice and a hearing, the confirmation order is revoked, the court must provide protection for any rights that have been acquired by an entity's good faith reliance on the confirmation order, and it also must revoke any discharge received by the debtor. [B.C. § 1144;

see **Tenn-Fla Partners v. First Union National Bank (*In re* Tenn-Fla Partners),** 226 F.3d 746 (6th Cir. 2000)]

5. Exemption from Securities Laws

Generally, securities offered or sold by the debtor or its successor under a Chapter 11 plan in exchange for claims against or interests in the debtor or for administrative expense claims are exempt from the registration requirements of § 5 of the 1933 Securities Act and from registration requirements in any state or local securities law. [B.C. § 1145(a)] Furthermore, such an issuance is deemed to be a public offering, thereby escaping the restrictions imposed by Rule 144 of the Securities and Exchange Commission concerning the resale of securities that are part of a private placement. [B.C. § 1145(c)] Congress created this exemption to facilitate reorganizations. At the time that Congress enacted the Code, there was "great uncertainty" about the ability of creditors that received securities in a debtor's reorganization to sell those securities without running afoul of the federal securities laws. "This uncertainty act[ed] as a retarding force on the flexibility of the reorganization process." [H.R. Rep. No. 95–595, at 237 (1977)]

a. Underwriter

At the time that Congress created the securities exemption, the SEC considered any creditors that received 1% of a distribution of securities under a debtor's reorganization plan to be an underwriter. Congress was concerned with the ability of such creditors to resell their shares in the public market without filing a registration statement. "Thus, the resale provisions allow resale by creditors that are not real underwriters. . . . The technical statutory underwriter is excluded because of the restrictive impact on bankruptcy plans." [H.R. No. 95–595, at 238 (1977)]

Thus, a creditor or an equity security holder receiving securities under a Chapter 11 plan normally may resell them, unless she really is an "underwriter," a term which the Code defines in great detail. [B.C. § 1145(b)] An underwriter includes, for example, an entity that purchases a claim against or an interest in the debtor, or an administrative expense claim, with the *intention of distributing securities* that it will acquire under a Chapter 11 plan in exchange for the claim or interest. Similarly, the definition includes an entity that offers to sell securities on behalf of those receiving securities under a plan, or that offers to buy such securities from them for the purpose of resale pursuant to an agreement related to the plan. While the bankruptcy definition of an underwriter also covers an issuer, as used in § 2(11) of the Securities Act of 1933, neither the debtor nor its successor are considered "issuers." However, an issuer does include a controlling person, i.e., a creditor holding 10% or more of the debtor's securities. [H.R. 95–595, at 238 (1977)] Any party considered to be an underwriter must comply with the registration requirements and any resale restrictions of the securities laws.

6. Special Tax Provisions

The issuance, transfer, or exchange of a security *or* the making or delivery of an instrument of transfer under a confirmed plan may not be taxed under any law imposing a stamp tax or similar tax. [B.C. § 1146(a)] The Supreme Court has held that this exemption "does not apply to transfers made before a plan is confirmed under Chapter 11." [**Florida Department of Revenue v. Piccadilly Cafeterias, Inc.,** 554 U.S. 33 (2008)]

The court may authorize a plan proponent to request a determination, from a State or local governmental unit responsible for collecting or determining income tax, of the plan's tax effects. The request must be limited to *questions of law.* [B.C. §§ 1146(b), 346] In the event of an *actual controversy,* the court may declare such effects after the *earlier of* (i) the *date on*

which the governmental unit responds to the request or (ii) *270 days after such request* is made. [B.C. § 1146(b)]

I. *Manville*-Type Trust/ Injunction

1. Used in Chapter 11 Asbestos-Related Cases

Section 524(g) of the Bankruptcy Code authorizes the bankruptcy court to order the type of trust/injunction used in the *Johns-Manville* case. [**Kane v. Johns-Manville Corp.,** 843 F.2d 636 (2d Cir. 1988)] Section 524(g) applies only to cases in Chapter 11 involving *asbestos-related liabilities* of the debtor when an indeterminable number of substantial future demands for payment necessitate use of the trust in order to deal equitably with claims and future demands. [B.C. § 524(g)]

2. Actions Against Debtor Enjoined

This provision permits the court, after notice and a hearing, to enjoin suits against (i) the debtor; (ii) officers, directors, affiliates, and insurance companies of the debtor; (iii) successors to the debtor; and (iv) any other entity directly or indirectly liable for claims or demands against the debtor. [B.C. § 524(g)(4)] Instead of suits being brought against the debtor, or such other entities, *present and future claims and demands will be brought against the trust,* which will be established under the plan of reorganization and will be funded by securities of the debtor and future payments to be made by the debtor. [B.C. § 524(g)(2)(B)]

3. Elements of the Trust/Injunction

The requirements for the trust/injunction include the following:

a. at least 75% of those voting in each class of present claims must approve the plan [B.C. § 524(g)(2)(B)(ii)(IV)(bb)];

b. the trust must own or have the right to become the owner of a majority of the stock of the reorganized debtor [B.C. § 524(g)(2)(B)(i)(III)];

c. a legal representative must be appointed for persons who might assert future demands [B.C. § 524(g)(4)(B)(i)]; and

d. the trust must provide reasonable assurance that it will value, and be able to pay, present claims and future demands that are similar in kind in substantially the same manner. [B.C. § 524(g)(2)(B)(ii)(V)]

4. Note: Rule of Construction

The Bankruptcy Reform Act of 1994, which amended the Code to authorize use of the *Manville-type* trust/injunction, also contains the following rule of construction: "Nothing in [Code section 524(g)] shall be construed to modify, impair, or supersede any other authority the court has to issue injunctions in connection with an order confirming a plan of reorganization." [Bankruptcy Reform Act of 1994, § 111(b), 108 Stat. at 4117]

Chapter Fourteen

Bankruptcy Code Chapter 12: Family Farmer or Fisherman with Regular Annual Income

Chapter Approach

If your exam question involves a farming or fishing operation, consider whether Chapter 12 will apply and, if so, its advantages for the debtor. Study carefully the Bankruptcy Code's definition of a *family farmer* or *family fisherman* [B.C. §§ 101(18) & (19A)], and note that corporations and partnerships, as well as individuals and their spouses may qualify for Chapter 12 relief. Recall that Chapter 12 gives the family farmer or family fisherman access to the bankruptcy court through a speedier, simpler, and less expensive procedure than under Chapter 11, and with higher debt limitations, in particular for family farmers, than those of Chapter 13. In situations in which farmland has depreciated greatly in value, Chapter 12 may offer a good alternative for the family farmer debtor.

Although many of the provisions of Chapter 12 are very similar, or identical, to their counterparts found in Chapter 13, there are some important differences. For example, a *standard discharge* under Chapter 12 differs substantially from a Chapter 13 standard discharge. For an individual debtor, this means that *all* debts that are nondischargeable under § 523(a) are not discharged in a Chapter 12 case. Under a Chapter 13 standard discharge, the debts that are nondischargeable are specified in Code § 1328(a) and include some but not all of the nondischargeable debts described in § 523(a).

As to secured creditors, remember that the § 1111(b) election applies only in Chapter 11 cases and, thus, is *not* available in Chapter 12.

Finally, note that very few debtors file for relief under Chapter 12. For example, in 2017, there were only 501 Chapter 12 cases filed in all 94 U.S. judicial districts. The numbers were similar in prior years: 461 in 2016 and 207 in 2015. That means that across the United States, Chapter 12 cases were less than 1% of all bankruptcy cases filed in calendar years 2015, 2016, and 2017.

A. Eligibility for Relief

1. In General

Chapter 12 relief is available only to a family farmer or family fisherman with regular annual income. [B.C. § 109(f)]

2. Definitions

a. Family Farmer or Family Fisherman with Regular Annual Income

A family farmer or family fisherman with regular annual income is an individual, corporation, or partnership with annual income that is *sufficiently stable and regular* to permit the family farmer or family fisherman to make payments under a Chapter 12 plan. [B.C. §§ 101(19), (19B)]

b. Family Farmer

The Code's definition of a family farmer includes certain *individuals,* or individuals and their spouses, and certain *corporations or partnerships.* The definition varies depending on the nature of the entity. [B.C. § 101(18)]

(i) Individuals

If an individual (or an individual and spouse) satisfies all of the following five requirements, then she is considered a family farmer [B.C. § 101(18)(A)]:

(1) the individual (or individual and spouse) is *engaged in a farming operation;* and

(2) on the date that the Chapter 12 case is filed:

    (a) the individual's (or individual's and spouse's) *total debts do not exceed $4,411,400;*

    (b) at least *50% of the individual (or individual's and spouse's) total noncontingent, liquidated debts comes from a farming operation* owned or operated by the individual (or individual and spouse); *and*

    Note: This 50% figure does *not* include any debt for the individual's (or individual's and spouse's) principal residence, *unless* the debt arises from a farming operation.

    (c) the individual (or individual and spouse) receive from the farming operation *more than 50% of gross income* for *either* of the following time periods:

        (i) the taxable year before the taxable year in which the bankruptcy case is commenced *or*

        (ii) each of the second and third taxable years before the taxable year in which the bankruptcy case is commenced.

        e.g. Example: Debtor owned and operated a rice farm until 2010, when he became disabled. Debtor filed a Chapter 12 case in late 2013. On his 2012 tax return, Debtor listed two sources of income: (1) $20,362.80 from Social Security; and (2) $30,688 from a class action settlement related to crop losses for the years 2006–2008. The Chapter 12 trustee moved to dismiss the case and argued, among other things, that Debtor had not received more than 50% of his gross income from farming operations in 2012, because the settlement money related to farming activities from 2008 and 2009. (There was no issue about 2010 or 2011, the second and third taxable years prior to the bankruptcy filing.) The bankruptcy court disagreed and looked to the Internal Revenue Code, which treats settlement proceeds as income in the year in which they are received. The court explained that the Bankruptcy Code only requires that the debtor *receive* the income during the relevant time frame; it does not require that the debtor *earn* the income during that time frame. Thus, the court held that Debtor had received more than 50% of his gross income from a farming operation in 2012, which was the taxable year preceding the taxable year (2013) in which the Debtor filed for relief under Chapter 12. [*In re* **McLawchlin,** 511 B.R. 422 (Bankr. S.D. Tex. 2014)]

(ii) Corporations and Partnerships

A corporation or a partnership that satisfies *all of the following requirements* is considered a family farmer. [B.C. § 101(18)(B)]

(1) If the entity is a corporation, its *stock is not publicly traded.*

(2) *One family* (or one family and their relatives) *holds more than 50% of the outstanding stock or equity* in the corporation or the partnership.

(3) The *family or the relatives conduct the farming operation.*

(4) *More than 80% of the value of the corporate or partnership assets concerns the farming operation.*

(5) On the date that the Chapter 12 petition is filed:

    (a) the *total debts* of the corporation or the partnership *do not exceed $4,411,400;* and

    (b) *at least 50% of the total noncontingent, liquidated debts* of the corporation or the partnership *come from a farming operation* that it owns or operates.

    Note: This 50% figure does *not* include any debt for a home that the corporation or partnership owns and that constitutes the principal residence of a shareholder or a partner, unless the debt arises from a farming operation.

c. "Farming Operation"

A farming operation "includes farming, tillage of the soil, dairy farming, ranching, production or raising of crops, poultry, or livestock, and production of poultry or livestock products in an unmanufactured state." [B.C. § 101(21)] In determining whether a debtor is engaged in a "farming operation," a majority of courts follow the "totality of the circumstances" test, which examines whether the debtor, at the time of the Chapter 12 filing, "intend[ed] to continue to engage in a 'farming operation.' " [*In re McLawchlin,* 511 B.R. 422 (Bankr. S.D. Tex. 2014)]

d. Family Fisherman

The Code's definition of a family fisherman includes (i) certain individuals, or individuals and their spouses, and (ii) certain corporations or partnerships. The definition varies depending on the nature of the entity. [B.C. § 101(19A)]

(i) Individuals

If an individual (or an individual and spouse) satisfies *all of the following requirements,* then she is considered a family fisherman. [B.C. § 101(19)(A)]

(1) On the date that the Chapter 12 case is filed:

    (a) the individual's (or individual's and spouse's) *total debts do not exceed $2,044,225;* and

    (b) at least *80% of the individual (or individual's and spouse's) total noncontingent, liquidated debts come from a commercial fishing operation* owned or operated by the individual (or individual and spouse); *and*

    Note: This 80% figure does *not* include any debt for the individual's (or individual's and spouse's) principal residence, *unless* the debt arises from a commercial fishing operation.

    (c) the individual (or individual and spouse) receives from the commercial fishing operation *more than 50% of gross income* for the taxable year before the taxable year in which the bankruptcy case is filed.

(ii) Corporations and Partnerships

A corporation or a partnership that satisfies *all of the following requirements* is considered a family fisherman. [B.C. § 101(19)(B)]

(1) If the entity is a corporation, its *stock is not publicly traded.*

(2) *One family* (or one family and the family's relatives) *holds more than 50% of the outstanding stock or equity* in the corporation or the partnership.

(3) The *family or the relatives conduct the commercial fishing operation.*

(4) *More than 80% of the value of the corporate or partnership assets* relate to the *commercial fishing operation.*

(5) On the date that the Chapter 12 petition is filed:

(a) the *total debts* of the corporation or the partnership *do not exceed $2,044,225;* and

(b) *at least 80% of the total noncontingent, liquidated debts* of the corporation or the partnership *come from a commercial fishing operation* that it owns or operates.

Note: This 80% figure does *not* include any debt for a home that the corporation or partnership owns and that constitutes the principal residence of a shareholder or a partner, *unless* the debt arises from a farming operation.

EXAM TIP   ◆GILBERT

It is important to remember that only an individual with regular income is eligible for Chapter 13 relief, but that an individual, a partnership, *or* a corporation can be eligible for Chapter 12 relief if qualified as a *family farmer or family fisherman* with regular *annual* income under Code §§ 101(18), (19), (19A), and (19B).

---

3. Voluntary Petition

A case under Chapter 12 may be commenced only by the filing of a voluntary bankruptcy petition. [B.C. §§ 301, 303(a)]

4. Multiple Petitions

A family farmer is *ineligible* for relief under Chapter 12 if the family farmer was a debtor in a case that was dismissed in the preceding 180 days (i) because of the family farmer's intentional failure to obey court orders or to appear before the court, or (ii) as a result of the family farmer's request for a voluntary dismissal of the case following a party's request for relief from the automatic stay. [B.C. § 109(g)]

Note: In 2005, with the passage of BAPCPA, Congress added family fishermen as eligible debtors under Chapter 12. Congress, however, did not amend § 109(g). Thus, § 109(g)'s prohibition against multiple petitions does not apply to family fishermen.

B. Similarities to Chapter 13

1. Introduction

Pre-BAPCPA, many of the rules and procedures governing Chapter 12 cases paralleled those governing Chapter 13 cases. With BAPCPA, however, Congress changed a number of provisions applicable to both Chapter 12 and Chapter 13 cases. While there are still similarities between the two chapters, there now are fewer than there were before BAPCPA's passage.

2. Filing Petition

As mentioned previously, the Chapter 12 case may be commenced only by the filing of a *voluntary* petition. This is also true of a Chapter 13 case. [B.C. §§ 301, 303(a)]

3. Co-Debtor Stay

As in the Chapter 13 case, in addition to the automatic stay of § 362(a), there is a stay against individuals who are liable with the debtor on consumer debts or who have secured consumer debts of the debtor. [B.C. §§ 1201, 1301]

4. Trustee

The appointment of a trustee, either a standing trustee or one for the particular case, is mandatory, and the trustee's duties in Chapter 12 and Chapter 13 are very similar as long as the debtor continues to be a debtor in possession. [B.C. §§ 1202(a), (b)(1)–(4), 1302] However, if a Chapter 12 debtor is removed from possession, the trustee is charged with several of the duties of a Chapter 11 trustee and also with operation of the debtor's farm or commercial fishing operation. [B.C. §§ 1202(b)(5), 1203] With the enactment of BAPCPA, Congress created new duties for the Chapter 12 trustee in cases in which the debtor owes a *domestic support obligation.* [B.C. §§ 1202(b)(6), (c)] Those duties are the same as the ones imposed on Chapter 13 trustees. [B.C. §§ 1302(b)(6), (d)]

5. Property of Estate

Estate property is the same in a Chapter 12 case as in a Chapter 13 case. [B.C. §§ 1207(a), 1306(a)] Ordinarily, a Chapter 12 debtor remains in possession of property of the estate unless otherwise directed by (i) a court order removing the debtor from possession, (ii) a provision in a confirmed plan, or (iii) the confirmation order. [B.C. §§ 1207(b), 1306(b)] Furthermore, the Code expressly provides for a *Chapter 12 debtor in possession to continue to operate the farm or commercial fishing operation.* [B.C. §§ 1203; 1304(b)]

a. Removal

The bankruptcy court may remove the debtor as debtor in possession for *cause,* including "fraud, dishonesty, incompetence, or gross mismanagement" of the debtor's affairs either prior to or after filing of the Chapter 12 case. [B.C. § 1204(a)] The Code defines *cause* for appointment of a trustee or examiner in a Chapter 11 case in the same way. [*See* B.C. § 1104(a)(1)]

6. The Plan

The debtor has the *exclusive right* to file a plan, even if he is not a debtor in possession. [*Compare* B.C. §§ 1221 and 1321 *with* B.C. §§ 1121(b), (c)]

7. Mandatory Plan Provisions

With the following two exceptions, the mandatory provisions of a Chapter 12 plan are essentially the same as those under Chapter 13. [B.C. §§ 1222(a), 1322(a)]

a. In a Chapter 12 case, the holder of a particular claim or interest may consent to less favorable treatment than others of the same class. [*Compare* B.C. § 1222(a)(3) *with* § 1322(a)(3)]

b. In a Chapter 12 case, the plan must provide for payment of a ***claim owed to a governmental unit*** that arises out of the ***sale, transfer, exchange, or other disposition*** of any farm asset used in the ***debtor's farming operation.*** The claim must be treated as ***unsecured*** and is not entitled to ***priority.*** [B.C. § 1232(a)]

Note: This requirement applies to "any property used in the debtor's farming operation." There is no mention of assets used in commercial fishing operations.

8. Objections to Confirmation

Objections to confirmation are governed by the same rule of procedure as in Chapter 13. [Bankruptcy Rule 3015(f)]

9. Effects of Confirmation

The Chapter 12 provisions concerning the binding nature of a confirmed plan and the vesting of property of the estate in the debtor "free and clear" are similar to those under Chapter 13, but the discharge provisions differ substantially. [B.C. §§ 1227, 1327] Also, as in Chapter 13, confirmation does *not* operate as a discharge. [*See* B.C. §§ 1228, 1328]

10. Modification of Plan

The provisions for pre-confirmation modification of a Chapter 12 plan parallel the respective provisions of Chapter 13. [B.C. §§ 1223, 1323] Congress changed both § 1229 and § 1329 when it enacted BAPCPA and, thus, the provisions for post-confirmation modification of a Chapter 12 plan differ in certain respects from those for post-confirmation modification of a Chapter 13 plan. [B.C. §§ 1229, 1329]

11. Revocation of Confirmation Order

The provisions for revocation of a Chapter 12 confirmation order procured by fraud parallel the corresponding provisions of Chapter 13. [B.C. §§ 1230, 1330]

C. Differences from Chapter 13

1. Eligibility for Relief

The debt ceiling for eligibility under Chapter 12 is $2,044,225 for family fishermen and $4,411,400 for family farmers, both of which are higher than the ceiling under Chapter 13 (unsecured debts less than $419,275, and secured debts less than $1,257,850). [B.C. §§ 101(18), (19A), 109(e)]

2. Filing of Plan

A Chapter 12 debtor must file a plan ***within 90 days*** after the order for relief, unless an extension is granted for cause for which the debtor should not justly be held accountable. Under Chapter 13, the debtor ordinarily must file a plan within 14 days after the filing of the petition (or within 14 days after a case is converted to Chapter 13). [B.C. § 1221; Bankruptcy Rule 3015(a), (b)]

3. Commencement of Payments

In Chapter 13, the debtor must begin making payments by the *earlier* of *30 days* after the *filing of the plan* or the *start of the Chapter 13* case. [B.C. § 1326(a)(1)] The Code provides no specific period in which a Chapter 12 debtor must begin making payments. [B.C. § 1226]

4. Duration of Plan

With the exception of payments on certain long-term debts, payments under the *Chapter 12* plan may not extend beyond *three years,* unless the court for cause approves a longer time period. The court, however, may not approve a plan period that is longer than *five years.* [B.C. § 1222(c)] Pre-BAPCPA, the Code's rules on plan duration were similar for Chapter 12 and Chapter 13 cases. Post-BAPCPA, however, the rules governing plan duration for Chapter 13 cases turn on the debtor's status as an above-median or below-median income debtor. For a debtor whose income is at or *above the median* for her state, plan payments may not extend beyond *five years.* [B.C. § 1322(d)(1)] For below-median income debtors, plan payments may not extend beyond *three years* unless the court finds cause to approve a longer time period. In no event, however, may the court approve a Chapter 13 plan that is longer than five years. [B.C. § 1322(d)(2)]

5. Debtor's Rights and Duties

In addition to permitting the debtor to continue to operate his farm or commercial fishing operation, Chapter 12 confers on a debtor in possession *all of the rights and duties of a Chapter 11 trustee,* except the right to compensation and the duty to investigate the debtor. [B.C. §§ 1203, 1303, 1304]

6. Adequate Protection

The Code expressly states that *§ 361* on adequate protection *does not apply in Chapter 12 cases.* Instead, Congress created § 1205 to address adequate protection in the context of Chapter 12 cases. [B.C. § 1205] Section 1205 provides that adequate protection is designed to protect against a decline in the value of the *property* securing a claim or of an *entity's ownership interest* in the property. [B.C. §§ 1205(b)(1), (2), (4); *compare* **United Savings Association of Texas v. Timbers of Inwood Forest Associates, Ltd.,** 484 U.S. 365 (1988)]

The statute sets forth the following nonexclusive methods of providing adequate protection in a Chapter 12 case:

a. *a cash payment or periodic cash payments* [B.C. § 1205(b)(1)];

b. *an additional or replacement lien* [B.C. § 1205(b)(2)];

c. *if the collateral is farmland, the reasonable rent* prevailing in that locality, taking into account "the rental value, net income, and earning capacity of the property" [B.C. § 1205(b)(3)]; or

d. *other relief* that will protect the value of the collateral securing the claim or of the creditor's ownership interest in the property. Other relief does not include granting the creditor an administrative expense claim. [B.C. § 1205(b)(4)]

Note: Section 361 contains no counterpart to the "reasonable rent" provision at § 1205(b)(3).

7. Sales Free and Clear

To reduce the level of farming or commercial fishing operations, a **Chapter 12 trustee** may sell farmland, farm equipment, or property used to carry out a commercial fishing operation, including a commercial fishing vessel, free and clear of liens or other interests. The proceeds of the sale are subject to the secured creditor's interest. Notice and a hearing are required. [B.C. § 1206]

8. Permissive Provisions of Chapter 12 Plan

The provisions that may be included in a plan under Chapter 12 differ from those allowable in a Chapter 13 plan, as follows.

a. Modifying Rights

The power of a Chapter 12 debtor to modify the rights of secured or unsecured creditors is not subject to the exception found in Chapter 13 that prohibits modification of a **claim secured solely by a security interest in real property constituting the principal residence of the debtor.** [B.C. §§ 1222(b)(2), 1322(b)(2)]

b. Sale or Distribution of Property

A Chapter 12 plan may propose to sell all or any part of estate property or distribute all or any part of estate property among entities having an interest in the property. [B.C. § 1222(b)(8)]

c. Payment of Secured Claims

A Chapter 12 plan may provide for secured creditors to be paid over a longer period than the three or five years referred to in § 1222(c). However, any such provision must be in conformity with the requirement for confirmation contained in § 1225(a)(5). [B.C. § 1222(b)(9)]

9. Confirmation Requirements

The Bankruptcy Code imposes several conditions on confirmation of a Chapter 12 plan that parallel those for confirmation of a Chapter 13 plan. [B.C. §§ 1225(a)(1)–(4), (6), (7), 1325(a)(1)–(4), (6), (8)] For example, both Chapter 12 and Chapter 13 plans must be proposed in good faith and must be feasible. [B.C. §§ 1225(a)(3), (6), 1325(a)(3), (6)] But there are a several differences in confirmation requirements for Chapter 12 and Chapter 13 plans.

a. Chapter 13 requires not only **good faith** in filing the plan, but also good faith in **filing the petition.** Chapter 12 does not expressly require that the debtor filed the petition in good faith as a condition of plan confirmation. [B.C. § 1325(a)(7)]

b. To obtain confirmation of a Chapter 13 plan, the debtor must have filed all pre-petition tax returns. [B.C. §§ 1325(a)(9), 1308] No such requirement exists for confirmation of a Chapter 12 plan. [B.C. § 1225]

c. If the Chapter 13 plan proposes periodic payments for a secured creditor, those payments must be in **equal monthly amount,** unless the creditor has accepted the plan. [B.C. § 1325(a)(5)(B)(iii)(I)] If the secured creditor's collateral is personal property, then the amount of the payments must suffice to provide adequate protection to the creditor over the course of the plan, unless the creditor has accepted the plan. [B.C. § 1325(a)(5)(B)(iii)(II)] Neither requirement is a condition of confirmation for a Chapter 12 plan. [B.C. § 1225(a)(5)]

d. The debtor may *cram down* a secured creditor's claim in both Chapter 12 and Chapter 13 so long as the plan provides for *retention* of the creditor's *lien* and payment of the *present value* of the creditor's *secured claim.* [B.C. §§ 1225(a)(5)(B), 1325(a)(5)(B)] BAPCPA created additional requirements for *cramdown* in a Chapter 13 case; those requirements do not exist for plan confirmation in a Chapter 12 case.

e. There is no *hanging paragraph* in Chapter 12. [*Compare* § 1225(a) *with* § 1325(a)(9) hanging paragraph]

f. If an unsecured creditor or the trustee objects to confirmation of a Chapter 12 plan that does not propose full repayment of the respective allowed claims(s), confirmation will be denied unless the debtor commits (i) to pay all of his expected *projected disposable income* for three years *or for any longer plan period* approved by the court, *not exceeding five years* or (ii) to distribute *property whose present value* is equal to or greater than the debtor's *projected disposable income* for the relevant plan period. [B.C. § 1225(b)(1)] The requirements for treatment of unsecured creditors in Chapter 13 cases differ from those in Chapter 12 cases in several respects.

(i) The *length of the Chapter 13 plan* is determined by whether the debtor's income is *above or below the median* for the state in which she filed her plan. [B.C. § 1325(b)(4)]

(ii) Chapter 13 does not have the option, available in Chapter 12, for the debtor to distribute property whose present value equals the amount of the debtor's disposable income over the plan period.

(iii) The Code defines *"disposable income"* differently for Chapter 12 and Chapter 13 cases.

(1) Chapter 12 does not use the term *current monthly income.* Instead, the Code simply says income received by the debtor. [B.C. § 1225(b)(2)]

(2) A Chapter 12 debtor arrives at her *disposable income* by deducting from her income amounts reasonably necessary to be expended for (1) *maintenance or support* of the debtor or her dependents; (2) a *domestic support obligation* first due after filing of the Chapter 12 case; and (3) expenses needed to *continue, preserve, and operate* the debtor's business. [B.C. § 1225(b)(2)]

(3) Unlike Chapter 13, Chapter 12 has no express exclusion from disposable income for a debtor's *charitable contributions.* [*Compare* B.C. § 1225(b)(2) *with* § 1325(b)(2)(A)(ii)]

(4) The amount of the Chapter 13 debtor's *reasonably necessary expenses* depend on whether the debtor's income is *above or below the median* for the state in which she filed her bankruptcy petition. [B.C. §§ 1325(b)(2), (3)] That is not the case for the Chapter 12 debtor.

10. Confirmation Hearing

In a Chapter 12 case, the court must conclude the confirmation hearing within *45 days* after the plan is filed, "except for cause." In a Chapter 13 case, the confirmation hearing must be held *no earlier than 20* and *no later than 45 days* after the *§ 341 meeting, unless* the court determines that it would be in the *best interests of creditors* to hold the confirmation hearing at an *earlier date* and there is *no objection* to doing so. [B.C. §§ 1224, 1324(b)]

11. Discharge

A standard discharge under Chapter 12 differs significantly from a standard Chapter 13 discharge, in that *all debts that are nondischargeable under § 523(a)* are not discharged in a

Chapter 12 case in which the debtor is an individual. [B.C. § 1228(a)(2)] Under a Chapter 13 standard discharge, the debts that are nondischargeable are specified in Code § 1328(a) and include some but not all of the nondischargeable debts described in § 523(a).

a. Note

If the Chapter 12 plan provides for curing a default within a reasonable time and maintaining payments during the case on a long-term debt with the final payment due after the last plan payment, then that debt is *nondischargeable.* The rule is the same for Chapter 13 cases. [B.C. §§ 1228(a)(1), 1222(b)(5), 1328(a)(1), 1322(b)(5)]

b. Hardship Discharge

In Chapter 12, the debts that are nondischargeable under a standard discharge are nondischargeable under a hardship discharge. [B.C. §§ 1228(b), (c)]

c. The *Enron* Exemption Exception

BAPCPA added a provision to the denial-of-discharge section for *individual Chapter 12 debtors;* the provision is tied to the so-called *Enron* exemption exception at § 522(q). The Code provides that the bankruptcy court may not grant a discharge to an individual Chapter 12 debtor unless it has found *no reasonable cause to believe* that *§ 522(q)(1) may apply* to the debtor *and* there is proceeding pending in which the debtor may be found guilty of a felony described in *§ 522(q)(1)(A)* or liable for a debt described in *§ 522(q)(1)(B).* [B.C. §§ 1228(f), 522(q)] The court's finding must come after *notice and a hearing* held no more than *10 days* before *entry of the discharge order.* It is unclear whether this provision results in a *denial of discharge* or merely a *delay of entry of discharge.*

CHECKLIST OF NONDISCHARGEABLE DEBTS UNDER CHAPTER 12   **GILBERT**

THE FOLLOWING IS A CHECKLIST OF THE DEBTS THAT ARE NOT DISCHARGEABLE UNDER CHAPTER 12:

☑ *Long-term debts* with the final payment due after the last payment under the plan if the Chapter 12 plan provides for curing a default within a reasonable time and maintaining payments during the case

☑ *Debts for secured claims that the Chapter 12 plan has provided to pay over a longer period* than the three or five years referred to in § 1222(c) and in a manner consistent with § 1225(a)(5)'s requirement for confirmation

☑ *If the Chapter 12 debtor is an individual,* all debts that are nondischargeable under § 523(a)

D. Differences from Chapter 11

1. Voluntary Petition Only

Unlike a Chapter 11 case, a Chapter 12 case can be commenced only by the filing of a voluntary petition. [B.C. §§ 301, 303(a)]

2. Trustee

A Chapter 12 trustee (either a standing trustee or one appointed for the particular case) serves in the case even if the family farmer or family fisherman remains a debtor in possession. [B.C. § 1202]

3. Co-Debtor Stay

In a Chapter 12 case, the co-debtor stay applies, while it does not in a case under Chapter 11. [B.C. § 1201]

4. Adequate Protection

Under Chapter 12, adequate protection is determined by Code § 1205, rather than under § 361 as in a Chapter 11 case.

5. No Creditors' Committees

There is no provision in Chapter 12 for the appointment of creditors' committees or equity security holders' committees, as in Chapter 11 cases. [B.C. § 1102]

6. Filing Plan: by Debtor Only

In a Chapter 12 case, only the debtor may file a plan. In a Chapter 11 case, any party in interest may file a plan after the debtor's exclusivity period ends. [B.C. §§ 1121(c), (e), 1221]

7. No Impairment of Classes

The concept of impairment of classes of claims or interests does not apply in a Chapter 12 case; it is unique to Chapter 11. [*See* B.C. § 1124]

8. No Solicitation of Acceptance or Rejection

Under Chapter 12, creditors and equity security holders do not vote to accept or reject the plan, and, thus, the debtor is not burdened by the necessities of preparing and obtaining court approval of a disclosure statement or of soliciting acceptances from the various classes. [*See* B.C. §§ 1125–1126]

9. Earlier Confirmation

The Chapter 12 confirmation hearing is ordinarily concluded much earlier (within 45 days after the plan is filed) than in a Chapter 11 case. [B.C. §§ 1224, 1128]

10. No Absolute Priority Rule

The absolute priority rule does not apply in a Chapter 12 case and, therefore, the debtor is not barred from keeping his property when the plan fails to provide for full satisfaction of the claims of nonconsenting unsecured creditors. [*See* B.C. § 1129(b)(2)(B)(ii)]

11. Confirmation of Plan Not a Discharge

Confirmation of the debtor's plan does not constitute a discharge under Chapter 12. [B.C. § 1228] With the exception of cases filed by individual debtors, confirmation of the debtor's plan in a Chapter 11 case generally does constitute a discharge. [B.C. §§ 1141(d)(1), (5)]

12. No Election by Partially Secured Creditors

Partially secured creditors cannot elect to have their claims treated as fully secured under Chapter 12. This election is a unique feature of Chapter 11. [B.C. § 1111(b)]

13. Trustee Pays Creditors

Ordinarily, the trustee disburses the payments to creditors under a Chapter 12 plan. [B.C. § 1226(c)]

E. Secured Creditors

1. Requirement for Confirmation

The bankruptcy court cannot confirm the debtor's plan unless as to each allowed secured claim:

a.   *the secured creditor accepts the plan* [B.C. § 1225(a)(5)(A)];

b.   *the debtor surrenders the collateral* to the secured creditor [B.C. § 1225(a)(5)(C)]; or

c.   *the plan preserves the creditor's lien* on the collateral and provides for the distribution of *cash or other property* having a present value, on the effective date of the plan, of at least the amount of the creditor's allowed secured claim. [B.C. § 1225(a)(5)(B)]

2. Permissive Plan Provisions

If there has been a large decline in the value of the debtor's farm, Chapter 12 may be used to "write down" a creditor's secured claim to the market value of the collateral, and to provide for payments to be made over a longer period of time and at a lower (but reasonable) rate of interest. [B.C. §§ 1222(b)(2), (9)]

e.g. **Example:** Debtor borrows $1.7 million from Bank, at 8% interest, secured by a 25-year first mortgage on Debtor's farm, which is valued at $2 million. Several years later, Debtor files a Chapter 12 bankruptcy petition. The market value of the farm has decreased to $1 million. Debtor's plan provides for Bank to retain its lien on the farm, and for Bank's claim to be modified by reducing the principal of its allowed secured claim to $1 million (the value of the collateral). The plan also proposes payments, having a present value of $1 million, over 30 years at a discount rate of 7%. The provision satisfies the applicable requirement for confirmation and should be permissible if the terms are found to be reasonable. [B.C. §§ 1222(b), 1225(a)(5)(B)] Note that Bank's total claim of $1.7 million has been bifurcated, and that it now holds an unsecured claim in the amount of $700,000. [B.C. § 506(a)]

F. Unsecured Creditors

1. "Best Interests of Creditors Test"

As in a Chapter 13 case, the Chapter 12 plan must provide that *each unsecured creditor* holding an allowed claim will receive property having a *present value,* as of the effective date of the plan, that is not less than the amount he would receive for his claim in a case under Chapter 7 if the estate were liquidated on that date, taking into account the exemptions that would be available to the individual Chapter 12 debtor. [B.C. § 1225(a)(4)]

2. Best Efforts

If an unsecured creditor or the Chapter 12 trustee objects to confirmation of a plan, the bankruptcy court may not confirm the plan unless *one of the following three conditions* is met.

a.   The plan provides for 100% payment of each unsecured claim. [B.C. § 1225(b)(1)(A)]

b.   The debtor commits all of his *"projected disposable income"* to plan payments for three years or for any longer plan period approved by the court not exceeding five years. [B.C. §§ 1225(b)(1)(B), 1222(c)]

c.   The plan proposes to distribute *property whose present value* is equal to or greater than the debtor's *projected disposable income* for the relevant plan period. [B.C. § 1225(b)(1)(C)]

(i)   Disposable Income

In Chapter 12, disposable income is that portion of the debtor's income that is *not reasonably necessary* to (1) *maintain or support* the debtor or her dependents, (2) pay post-petition *domestic support obligations*, or (3) pay the expenses required for the *continuation, operation, and preservation of the debtor's business.* [B.C. § 1225(b)(2)]

G.   Conversion or Dismissal

1.   Voluntary Conversion to Chapter 7

The debtor has an absolute right to convert the case to Chapter 7, and this right cannot be waived. [B.C. § 1208(a)]

2.   Voluntary Dismissal

The debtor also has the nonwaivable right to dismiss the case if it has not been converted earlier from Chapter 7 or Chapter 11. [B.C. § 1208(b)]

3.   Discretionary Conversion to Chapter 7

The court may convert the case to Chapter 7, on the request of a party in interest, if the debtor has committed *fraud* concerning the case. Notice and a hearing are required. [B.C. § 1208(d)]

4.   Discretionary Dismissal

On the request of a party in interest, the court may dismiss the case for cause. Notice and a hearing are required. [B.C. § 1208(c)]

a.   **"Cause"**

Reasons for which a Chapter 12 case may be dismissed include:

(i)   *gross mismanagement or unreasonable delay by the debtor* that is prejudicial to creditors [B.C. § 1208(c)(1)];

(ii)   *failure to pay any necessary fees* or charges imposed under chapter 123 of title 28 [B.C. § 1208(c)(2)];

(iii)   *failure to file a plan within 90 days* after the filing of the petition, or within any period of extension granted by the court [B.C. §§ 1208(c)(3), 1221];

(iv)   *failure to begin making timely payments* under a confirmed plan [B.C. § 1208(c)(4)];

(v)   *denial of confirmation* of the debtor's plan, and denial of a request for an extension of time to file another plan or to modify the plan [B.C. § 1208(c)(5)];

(vi)   *a material default by the debtor* concerning a provision of a confirmed plan [B.C. § 1208(c)(6)];

(vii) *revocation of a confirmation order that was procured by fraud,* and the court's refusal to confirm a modified plan [B.C. §§ 1208(c)(7), 1230];

(viii) *termination of a confirmed plan because of the happening of a condition* contained in the plan [B.C. § 1208(c)(8)];

(ix) *continuing loss* to or *diminution of* the Chapter 12 estate, and the *absence of a reasonable probability of rehabilitation* [B.C. § 1208(c)(9)];

(x) debtor's failure to pay a *domestic support obligation* that first came due *after filing of the Chapter 12 petition* [B.C. § 1208(c)(10)];

(xi) *lack of good faith* in filing the Chapter 12 petition [**Snider v. Rogers (*In re* Rogers),** 2018 WL 576750 (Bankr. W.D. N.Y. 2018)]; *or*

(xii) *the debtor's fraud* in the case. [B.C. § 1208(d)]

Chapter Fifteen

Bankruptcy Code Chapter 13: Individual with Regular Income

Chapter Approach

Chapter 13 is designed for an *individual debtor,* including a debtor engaged in business, who has a regular source of income and who desires to repay all or a percentage of her debts pursuant to a plan, which she has the *exclusive right* to propose. Post-BAPCPA, however, a debtor who fails the "means test" may have little choice but to file for relief under Chapter 13, because Chapter 7 is unavailable to her and Chapter 11 is too complex and expensive. Keep in mind that a case under Chapter 13 is very different from a Chapter 7 liquidation case, and that BAPCPA's changes to the Bankruptcy Code account for some of those differences.

The following table summarizes some of the differences between a Chapter 7 and a Chapter 13 case for an individual debtor:

	Chapter 7	Chapter 13
Eligibility	1) Below-median income debtor *or* 2) Pass the "means" test	1) Individual with 2) Regular income *and* 3) Secured debts < $1,257,850 *and* 4) Unsecured debts < $419,275
Type of case	Voluntary or involuntary	Only voluntary
Estate Property	*Excludes* debtor's post-petition earnings	*Includes* debtor's post-petition earnings
Automatic Stay	No co-debtor stay	Applies, with limited exceptions, to co-debtors on *consumer* debt
Time in bankruptcy	Varies based on complexity of case	1) 3-year plan for below-median income debtor 2) 5-year plan for above-median income debtor
Valuation of claims secured by personal property	1) *Replacement value* 2) If acquired for *personal, family, household* purposes, then replacement = *retail value*	Same as Chapter 7, *except* claim = *amount of debt if:* 1) *PMSI* in *motor vehicle* acquired for *personal use* within *910 days* of bankruptcy *or* 2) *PMSI* in any other personal property acquired within *one year* of filing for bankruptcy
Lien stripping	No	Yes, so long as not debtor's *principal residence* and last loan payment due *after* last plan payment
How creditors are paid	From liquidation of debtor's non-exempt assets	According to terms of debtor's 3- or 5-year plan based on

	Chapter 7	Chapter 13
		debtor's *projected disposable income*
Discharge	Varies, depending on length of Chapter 7 case, but no requirement that debtor pay a particular amount over a certain time period as in Chapter 13	Normally, only upon completion of plan payments

A. Eligibility for Relief

1. In General

Chapter 13 relief is available to an *individual* (i) who has *regular income,* (ii) whose *unsecured debts* total less than $419,275, and (iii) whose *secured debts* total less than $1,257,850. The indebtedness used in these calculations must be noncontingent and liquidated liabilities, determined as of the date of the filing of the petition. [B.C. § 109(e)] The unsecured and secured debt limits increase every three years with the next increase to occur on April 1, 2022. [B.C. § 104(a)] In determining eligibility in a case in which at least one of the debts is undersecured, the vast majority of courts and all Courts of Appeal that have ruled on the question apply the general rule that a claim is secured only up to the value of the collateral, with the balance constituting an unsecured claim. [*See, e.g.,* **Scovis v. Henrichsen (*In re* Scovis),** 249 F.3d 975 (9th Cir. 2001)]

a. Individual with Regular Income

An individual with regular income is defined as an "individual whose income is sufficiently stable and regular to enable such individual to make payments under a plan under Chapter 13, other than a stockbroker or a commodity broker." [B.C. § 101(30)] In most cases, a Chapter 13 debtor's regular income is generated from her wages or salary, but it may be derived from almost any legitimate source, such as interest income, rental income, a business, a pension, a trust, or even welfare, if it is regular enough to fund the debtor's plan of repayment. The courts have reached different conclusions on whether to consider Social Security benefits as part of a debtor's regular income.

cf. **Compare:** *In re* **Santiago-Monteverde,** 512 B.R. 432 (S.D. N.Y. 2014) ("Social Security income may not be considered in a Chapter 13 eligibility determination.") *with In re* **Patrick,** 2013 WL 168222 (Bankr. S.D. Miss. Jan. 16, 2013) ("[I]t is well settled that chapter 13 relief is available even to an individual who receives only Social Security benefits.")

Remember: The Bankruptcy Code specifically excludes Social Security benefits from the calculation of *current monthly income.* [B.C. § 101(10A)(B)]

b. Voluntary Petition Only

A Chapter 13 case may be commenced only by the filing of a voluntary petition. [B.C. §§ 301, 303(a)]

c. Joint Case

An individual with regular income and her spouse may file a joint petition, in which case the debt limitations of $419,275 and $1,257,850 apply to their *aggregate* indebtedness. [B.C. §§ 302(a), 109(e)]

2. Individuals Ineligible for Chapter 13 Relief

Stockbrokers and commodity brokers are not eligible for relief under Chapter 13. [B.C. § 109(e)] Also, an individual debtor in a case that was *dismissed in the preceding 180 days* is not eligible if the dismissal was due to the debtor's willful failure to obey court orders or appear before the court to prosecute her case, or was a result of the debtor's request for a voluntary dismissal of the case following a party's request for relief from the automatic stay. [B.C. § 109(g)]

B. Co-Debtor Stay

1. Stay in Favor of Certain Individuals

The filing of a Chapter 13 petition operates not only as a stay of actions against the debtor under § 362, but also as a stay against any civil action or other act by a creditor to collect a *consumer debt from an individual who has guaranteed or secured that debt* or who is otherwise *liable on that consumer debt with the debtor.* [B.C. § 1301(a)]

2. Consumer Debt

The Code defines a consumer debt as one "incurred by an individual primarily for a *personal, family, or household purpose.*" [B.C. § 101(8)]

3. Exceptions to Co-Debtor Stay

The co-debtor stay does not apply in two situations:

(a) the Chapter 13 case has been closed, dismissed, or converted to Chapter 7 or 11; or

(b) the co-debtor's liability was incurred in the ordinary course of *his* business. [B.C. §§ 1301(a)(1), (2)]

4. Grounds for Relief from Stay

A creditor may be granted relief from the co-debtor stay under any of the following circumstances. [B.C. § 1301(c)]

a. Co-Debtor Received Consideration

To the extent that the co-debtor, not the Chapter 13 debtor, was the actual recipient of the consideration for the claim, the creditor may be granted relief from the stay. [B.C. § 1301(c)(1)] If the Chapter 13 debtor is nothing more than a co-signer or guarantor of an obligation, then it is the co-debtor who received the benefit and the creditor should be able to obtain recover from the co-debtor. [8 Collier ¶ 1301.03(a)]

e.g. **Example:** Nancy, T.J., and Katherine purchased property together. They borrowed money from Bank for the purchase, and signed a promissory note payable to Bank. The note was secured by a deed of trust on the real property. Bank assigned the note and deed to trust to Third Party. Nancy, T.J., and Katherine lived on the property until Third Party foreclosed on the property. Nancy filed for relief under Chapter 13, and Third Party moved to lift the stay against T.J. and Katherine. The bankruptcy court noted that Debtor received some of the consideration for the loan because she had lived in the home with non-debtors T.J. and Katherine. In other words, Nancy was not a mere co-signer with the consideration flowing only to non-debtors T.J. and Katherine. The court in *dicta* stated that in such a case, Third Party would fail to meet its burden to lift the co-debtor stay against T.J. and Katherine. [*See **In re** Williams*, 374 B.R. 713 (W.D. Mo. 2007); B.C. § 1301(c)(1)]

b. Creditor's Claim Unpaid Under Plan

To the extent that the creditor's claim will not be paid under the debtor's proposed Chapter 13 plan, the creditor may receive relief from the stay. [B.C. § 1301(c)(2)] A creditor who receives no dividend under the debtor's plan because the creditor failed to file a proof of claim is not entitled to relief from the co-debtor stay.

e.g. **Example:** Arbors of Oregon ("Arbors") provided care to Diann Grace at its residential nursing facility. Willie, Diann's husband, signed a promissory note related to Diann's care from Arbors of Oregon. Willie subsequently filed for relief under Chapter 13 and proposed a plan that would pay 24.5% of Arbors' claim for the cost of Diann's care. Arbors of Oregon moved to lift the co-debtor stay in order to pursue Diann Grace, because Debtor's plan failed to pay Arbors in full for its claim. The bankruptcy court ruled to lift the stay to allow Arbors to pursue Diann for the debt. The court noted, that the statutory language "to the extent" limited Arbors to collect from Dian only what was not paid to Arbors in Debtor's Chapter 13 case. [*In re* **Grace**, 2015 WL 912532 (Bankr. N.D. Ohio 2015); B.C. § 1301(c)(2)]

(i) Note

If a motion for relief from the co-debtor stay is filed on this basis [B.C. § 1301(c)(2)], the stay automatically terminates with respect to the movant 20 days later if a written objection has not been filed by the debtor or the co-debtor. [B.C. § 1301(d)]

c. Irreparable Harm to Creditor

Under circumstances in which the creditor will be irreparably harmed if the stay remains in effect, relief from the stay will be granted. [B.C. § 1301(c)(3)]

e.g. **Example:** Debtor borrows $3,000 from Credit Union and executes a consumer promissory note, which Friend co-signs as a favor. Subsequently, Debtor files a Chapter 13 petition and a proposed plan. Friend purchases a one-way ticket to Switzerland with the stated intention of permanently residing there beginning next week. Credit Union should be justified in making a prompt request for relief from the co-debtor stay under § 1301(c)(3).

C. Administration of Chapter 13 Case

1. Appointment of Chapter 13 Trustee

In regions where many Chapter 13 cases are filed, the United States trustee ordinarily appoints a qualified individual to serve as a ***standing trustee.*** Otherwise, the United States trustee appoints a disinterested person as the trustee for a particular case, or the United States trustee may serve as the trustee in the case. [B.C. § 1302(a); 28 U.S.C. § 586(b)]

a. Duties of Trustee

The duties of a Chapter 13 trustee include the following:

(i) *to account for all property received* [B.C. §§ 1302(b)(1), 704(a)(2)];

(ii) *to make sure that the debtor performs* her intention regarding debts secured by estate property [B.C. §§ 1302(b)(1), 704(a)(3), 521(a)(2)(B)];

(iii) *to investigate* the debtor's financial affairs [B.C. §§ 1302(b)(1), 704(a)(4)];

(iv) *to examine proofs of claims* and object to the allowance of any improper ones [B.C. §§ 1302(b)(1), 704(a)(5)];

(v) *if circumstances warrant,* to *object to* the debtor's discharge [B.C. §§ 1302(b)(1), 704(a)(6)];

(vi) *to provide information requested by parties in interest* about the estate and the administration of the estate [B.C. §§ 1302(b)(1), 704(a)(7)];

(vii) *to prepare and file* with the court and with the United States trustee a *final report and account* concerning the case [B.C. §§ 1302(b)(1), 704(a)(9)];

(viii) *to appear and be heard at any hearing* regarding (i) valuation of property on which there is a lien, (ii) confirmation of a Chapter 13 plan, or (iii) post-confirmation modification of a plan [B.C. § 1302(b)(2)];

(ix) *to furnish nonlegal advice and assistance* to the debtor in implementing the plan [B.C. § 1302(b)(4)];

(x) *to ensure that the debtor begins making the payments* proposed by the plan within the *earlier of 30 days* from filing of the Chapter 13 petition or the Chapter 13 plan [B.C. §§ 1302(b)(5), 1326(a)(1)];

(xi) if there is a *domestic support obligation claim, to provide the notice* required by § 1302(d) [B.C. §§ 1302(b)(6), (d)];

(xii) *if the debtor is engaged in business*:

    (1) *to investigate* the debtor's conduct, financial condition, and business operations, as well as the *advisability of continuing* the debtor's business [B.C. §§ 1302(c), 1106(a)(3)]; and

    (2) *to file a report* of the investigation that states whether:

        (a) there are any facts evidencing fraud, dishonesty, incompetence, misconduct, mismanagement, or irregularity in management of debtor's affairs [B.C. §§ 1302(c), 1106(a)(4)]; or

        (b) any causes of action are available to the estate [B.C. §§ 1302(c), 1106(a)(4)]; and

(xiii) if the debtor owes a *domestic support obligation:*

    (1) *to provide written notice* to the holder of *the domestic support obligation* of the right to use the services of the State child support enforcement agency for the State in which the claim holder resides to help with *collecting child support* during and after the Chapter 13 case. [B.C. § 1302(d)(1)(A)(i); 42 U.S.C. §§ 664, 666] The written notice must include the State agency's address and phone number. [B.C. § 1302(a)(1)(A)(ii)];

    (2) *to provide written notice* to the relevant *State child support enforcement agency* that includes the name, address, and phone number of the holder of the domestic support obligation claim [B.C. § 1032(d)(1)(B)]; and

(3) if the court grants the *debtor a discharge* under § 1328, to *provide written notice* to both the holder of the domestic support obligation claim and the relevant State child support enforcement agency of [B.C. § 1302(d)(1)(C)]:

(a) the debtor's discharge;

(b) the debtor's most recent address;

(c) the name and address of the debtor's most recent employer; and

(d) the name of each creditor holding nondischargeable claims under § 523(a)(4) or (6), or holding claims that the debtor reaffirmed under § 524(c); and

(xiv) unless the plan or plan confirmation order provides to the contrary, *to disburse the payments* to creditors under the confirmed plan. [B.C. § 1326(c)]

Note: Duties (i) through (vii) are also duties of a Chapter 7 trustee.

2. Rights and Powers of Debtor

In a Chapter 13 case, the *debtor has the exclusive right* to use, sell, or lease estate property under §§ 363(b), (d), (e), (f), or (*l*). Thus, for example, a debtor may use, sell, or lease property out of the ordinary course of business, in accordance with § 363(b). [B.C. § 1303]

a. Debtor Engaged in Business

A debtor engaged in business is a *self-employed individual* who incurs trade credit in producing income from her business, which she is *entitled to operate unless the court orders otherwise.* Usually, a Chapter 13 debtor engaged in business, in addition to the rights described in the preceding paragraph, has the exclusive right to use, sell, or lease property in the ordinary course of business [B.C. § 363(c)] and to obtain credit. [B.C. § 364] However, these rights are subject to any limitations specified in those sections, as well as to any restrictions or conditions imposed by the court. [B.C. §§ 1304(a), (b)]

(i) Duties

A debtor engaged in business must file periodic financial reports (including a statement of receipts and disbursements) with the court, the United States trustee, and the appropriate taxing authorities. [B.C. §§ 1304(c), 704(a)(8)]

3. Post-Petition Claims

Certain kinds of post-petition claims may be filed in a Chapter 13 case. One is for *taxes* that become due during the pendency of the case, and another is for *consumer debts* incurred by the debtor after the order for relief for property or services that the debtor needs to carry out the plan. [B.C. § 1305(a)]

a. Allowance

Post-petition claims for such taxes and necessary consumer debts are treated as pre-petition claims for the purpose of allowance, but they are determined as of the date that they arise. [B.C. § 1305(b)]

b. Exception: Failure to Obtain Approval

A post-petition claim for necessary consumer debts will be disallowed if the claimant knew or should have known that prior approval of the debt by the trustee was practicable and was not procured. [B.C. § 1305(c)]

4. Property of Estate

The Chapter 13 estate consists of (i) all property specified in § 541; (ii) all § 541 property acquired by the debtor post-petition, but before the earliest of the closing, dismissal, or conversion of the case; and (iii) all of the debtor's earnings from services performed post-petition, but before the earliest of the closing, dismissal, or conversion of the case. [B.C. § 1306(a)] The *debtor retains possession* of all property of the Chapter 13 estate *unless a confirmed plan or confirmation order provides otherwise.* [B.C. § 1306(b)]

5. Conversion or Dismissal

In appropriate circumstances, a Chapter 13 case may be dismissed or converted to another chapter of the Bankruptcy Code under which the debtor is eligible. [B.C. § 1307]

a. Voluntary Conversion to Chapter 7

The debtor has an absolute right to convert the case to Chapter 7, and this right cannot be waived. [B.C. § 1307(a)]

b. Voluntary Dismissal

The debtor also has the nonwaivable right to dismiss the case if it has not been converted earlier from Chapter 7, 11, or 12. [B.C. § 1307(b)] There is a split of authority, however, as to whether the debtor's right to dismiss is absolute or subject to a bad faith or fraud exception. [*See In re* **Ross,** 2017 WL 2470594 (3d Cir. 2017); *compare In re* **Barbieri,** 199 F.3d 616 (2d Cir. 1999) (holding that debtor has absolute right to dismiss) *with* **Jacobsen v. Moser (*In re* Jacobsen),** 609 F.3d 647 (5th Cir. 2010) (holding that debtor's right to dismiss under § 1307(b) is subject to a "bad faith" exception, "at least when the debtor's request for dismissal is made in response to a motion to convert under § 1307(c)")]

c. Discretionary Dismissal or Conversion to Chapter 7

Upon a request by a party in interest or the United States trustee, the court, *for cause,* may dismiss the case or convert it to Chapter 7, whichever is better for creditors and the estate. The Code specifies numerous examples of cause. Even if one or more grounds exist, however, conversion or dismissal of the case is within the court's discretion and not a matter of right. Notice and a hearing are required. [B.C. § 1307(c)]

(i) "Cause"

Reasons for dismissal of the case or conversion to Chapter 7 include the following [B.C. § 1307(c)]:

(1) *unreasonable and prejudicial delay* on the part of the debtor [B.C. § 1307(c)(1)];

(2) *failure to pay any necessary fees or charges* imposed under chapter 123 of title 28 [B.C. § 1307(c)(2)];

(3) *failure to file a plan* within 14 days after the filing of the petition (or within 14 days after conversion to Chapter 13), unless an extension is granted for cause [B.C. § 1307(c)(3); Bankruptcy Rule 3015(b)];

(4) *failure to begin making payments* under the proposed plan within *the earlier of 30 days* of filing the plan or filing the Chapter 13 petition [B.C. §§ 1307(c)(4), 1326(a)(1)];

(5) *denial of confirmation of the debtor's plan,* and denial of a request for an extension of time to file another plan or to modify the plan [B.C. § 1307(c)(5)];

(6) *a material default* by the debtor concerning a provision of a confirmed plan [B.C. § 1307(c)(6)];

(7) *revocation of a confirmation order procured by fraud,* and the court's refusal to confirm a modified plan [B.C. §§ 1307(c)(7), 1330];

(8) *termination of a confirmed plan because of the happening of a condition contained in the plan* (other than completing all payments) [B.C. § 1307(c)(8)];

(9) *failure to file* within 15 days (or any court-ordered extension) after the filing of the petition the following information [B.C. §§ 1307(c)(9), 521(a)(1)]:

(a) a list of creditors;

(b) a schedule of assets and liabilities;

(c) a schedule of current income and current expenditures;

(d) a statement of the debtor's financial affairs;

(e) a certificate signed by the debtor's attorney or by the debtor if not represented by an attorney that the debtor received the notices required by § 342(b), but only if the debtor's liabilities are primarily consumer in nature;

(f) all payment advices received by the debtor from any employer within 60 days before filing the petition;

(g) a statement of monthly net income itemized to show how such income was calculated; and

(h) a statement disclosing any reasonably anticipated increase in income or expenditures over the 12-month period following the filing of the petition;

But note: Only the United States trustee may request conversion or dismissal for the debtor's failure to file the above information.

(10) *failure to timely file the statement of intention* required by Bankruptcy Code § 521(a)(2);

But note: This ground applies to a request for conversion or dismissal made by the United States trustee. [B.C. §§ 1307(c)(10), 521(a)(2)]

(11) *failure by the debtor to pay any domestic support obligation* that first becomes payable after filing of the petition; or

(12) *lack of good faith* in filing the Chapter 13 petition.

(ii) Pre-petition Tax Returns

If the debtor fails to file her pre-petition tax returns, as required by § 1308, and upon a request by a party in interest or the United States trustee, the court may dismiss the case or convert it to Chapter 7, whichever is better for creditors and the estate. [B.C. § 1307(e)]

d. Conversion to Chapter 11 or 12

Before a Chapter 13 plan is confirmed, the court may convert the case to Chapter 11 or 12 upon a request by a party in interest (including the debtor) or the United States trustee. Notice and a hearing are required to determine if the alternative chapter would be more suitable, and the court also must find that the debtor is eligible for relief under that chapter. [B.C. §§ 1307(d), (g)]

e. Exception for Farmers

If the debtor is a farmer, a Chapter 13 case cannot be converted to Chapter 7, 11, or 12 *unless* the debtor requests conversion. [B.C. § 1307(f)]

f. Property of Estate in Converted Case

If a case is converted from Chapter 13 to another chapter of the Code, property of the estate in the converted case consists of property of the estate on the *date of the Chapter 13 filing* that remains in the possession or control of the debtor on the date of conversion. [B.C. §§ 348(f)(1)(A), (B)] The Supreme Court, in a unanimous opinion, has held that if the debtor converts the case to Chapter 7 after confirmation of her plan, any post-petition wages that the Chapter 13 trustee has received but not yet disbursed to creditors must be returned to the debtor. [**Harris v. Viegalahn,** 135 S.Ct. 1829 (2015)]

If the debtor converts the case in *bad faith*, property of the estate in the converted case will consist of the estate property on the date of conversion. [B.C. § 348(f)(2)]

6. Filing Pre-Petition Tax Returns

If the debtor has not filed *tax returns* for any taxable period ending during the *four years prior to filing of the petition,* the debtor shall file those returns with the appropriate tax authorities no later than the day before the *date first scheduled for the § 341 meeting.* [B.C. § 1308(a)]

a. Time Extension—Chapter 13 Trustee

If the debtor *fails to file her tax returns* by the day before the date first scheduled for the § 341 meeting, the Chapter 13 trustee may hold open that meeting for an additional period of time to allow the debtor to file her returns. [B.C. § 1308(b)(1)] With the limited exception explained below, the *additional time period* cannot extend:

(i) *beyond 120 days after the § 341* meeting if the debtor's return was past due on the petition filing date [B.C. § 1308(b)(1)(A)]; *or*

(ii) beyond the *later of 120 days after the § 341 meeting or* the *date on which the return is due* under the last automatic extension requested by the debtor if the debtor's return was not past due on the petition filing date. [B.C. § 1308(b)(1)(B)]

b. Time Extension—Court Order

The bankruptcy court may *extend the time period* for the debtor to file her returns if the debtor demonstrates by a preponderance of the evidence that the failure to file is attributable to *circumstances beyond the debtor's control.* The court may only do so after notice and a hearing and by an order entered prior to expiration of the time period described above. The court may extend the time period established by the trustee but not for

(i) *more than 30 days* for returns that were past due on the petition filing date [B.C. § 1308(b)(2)(A)]; *or*

(ii) a period beyond the applicable extended due date for returns that were not past due on the petition filing date. [B.C. § 1308(b)(2)(B)]

D. Chapter 13 Plan: Contents and Confirmation

1. Filing a Plan

Only the *debtor* may file a Chapter 13 plan. She must file the plan with the *petition or within 14 days thereafter* (or within 14 days after conversion to Chapter 13), unless the court grants an extension for cause. [B.C. § 1321; Bankruptcy Rule 3015(b)]

2. Confirmation Hearing

After proper notice, the court conducts a hearing to determine whether a proposed plan satisfies the elements necessary for confirmation. Any party in interest may file an objection to the plan. Unless the court orders otherwise, *objections* must be filed at *least seven days before the confirmation hearing.* The confirmation hearing may be held *no earlier than 20 days nor later than 45 days* after the date set for the § 341 meeting, unless the court determines that it is in the best interests of the creditors and the estate to hold the confirmation hearing at an earlier date and no party objects to doing so. [B.C. § 1324; Bankruptcy Rule 3015]

3. Requirements for Plan Confirmation

The bankruptcy court cannot confirm the debtor's plan unless the plan satisfies a number of requirements, including payment of various fees, the "best interests of the creditors test," and the Code's provisions for payment of secured, unsecured priority, and general unsecured creditors. A Chapter 13 plan must satisfy *all of the following requirements.* [B.C. §§ 1322(a), 1325]

a. Plan Complies with Code Provisions

The plan must comply with the provisions of Chapter 13, as well as with the other applicable provisions of the Code. [B.C. § 1325(a)(1)] For example, the court may not confirm a plan for an individual debtor who is ineligible for relief under Chapter 13. A plan filed by an individual who was a debtor in a case that was dismissed in the preceding 180 days because of the debtor's willful failure to obey court orders cannot be confirmed. [*In re Smith*, 286 B.R. 104 (Bankr. W.D. Ark. 2002); B.C. § 109(g)]

(i) Sufficient Income to be Turned over to Trustee

The plan must provide that such amount of the debtor's future earnings or other future income as is required for the implementation of the plan will be turned over to the Chapter 13 trustee. [B.C. § 1322(a)(1)]

(ii) Same Treatment for Claims of a Class

If the plan designates classes of claims, it must provide identical treatment for all claims within any one class. [B.C. § 1322(a)(3)]

(iii) Full Payment of Priority Claims

With one exception, the plan must provide that all priority claims will be paid fully in deferred cash payments, unless a particular creditor consents to different treatment. [B.C. § 1322(a)(2); *In re Monahan,* 497 B.R. 642 (B.A.P. 1st Cir. 2013)]

(1) Exception

The plan may provide for less than full payment of *domestic support obligations* that as of the filing of the petition had been assigned to a *governmental unit* or were owed directly to or recoverable by a governmental unit so long as the plan provides that all of the *debtor's projected disposable income* is applied to make plan payments for the *five-year period* starting when the first plan payment is due. [B.C. §§ 1322(a)(4), 507(a)(1)(B)]

(2) Interest on Priority Claims

While priority claimants in a Chapter 13 case are entitled to receive payments totaling the full amount of their claims, the payments need not equal the *present value* of their claims. The one *exception* is a priority unsecured debt for a *domestic support obligation.* The Code's definition of a *domestic support obligation* specifically includes interest accruing on the underlying debt under applicable nonbankruptcy law. [B.C. § 101(14A)] The Code does permit the payment of interest on priority unsecured claims that are *not dischargeable* but only in the rare case in which the debtor otherwise has *disposable income* sufficient to pay *all allowed claims in full.* [B.C. § 1322(b)(10); *In re Monahan,* 497 B.R. 642 (B.A.P. 1st Cir. 2013)]

(iv) Plan Length

The time period during which the debtor must make payments under her plan varies depending on whether she is an *above- or below-median income debtor.* [B.C. § 1325(b)(4)] But, the Bankruptcy Code also states that the plan may not provide for payments over a period that exceeds *five years.* [B.C. §§ 1322(d)(1), (2)]

(1) When Does the Plan's Term Begin?

The Chapter 13 debtor files the plan either with the petition or within 14 days thereafter. The Code requires the debtor to start making *plan payments* no later than *30 days after filing the plan* or the *order for relief,* whichever comes first. [B.C. § 1326(a)(1)] Some courts hold that this first payment, which occurs prior to plan confirmation, starts the five-year period for plan payments. [*In re Humes,* 579 B.R. 557 (Bankr. D. Colo. 2018)] Other courts start the plan-payments clock with the first payment made post-confirmation. [*In re Morris,* 2014 WL 3818947 (Bankr. E.D. N.C. 2014)]

e.g. **Example:** Darren is an above-median income debtor. On March 5, 2018, he filed his Chapter 13 plan at the same time that he filed his petition for relief under Chapter 13. Darren makes his first plan payment on April 3, 2018. [B.C. § 1326(a)(1); Bankruptcy Rule 9006(a)(1)] He confirms his plan on June 13, 2018. In a jurisdiction that follows the rule used in *In re Humes,* Darren would make his final plan payment in April of 2023. In a jurisdiction that follows the rule in *In re Morris,* Darren would make his final plan payment in June of 2023.

b. Fees Paid

All fees, e.g., the filing fee, charges, or amounts required to be paid prior to confirmation by chapter 123 of title 28, or by the plan, must have been paid. [B.C. § 1325(a)(2)]

c. Plan Filed in Good Faith

The plan must be proposed in *good faith* and not by any means forbidden by law. [B.C. § 1325(a)(3)] The test for good faith is fact-intensive and a majority of courts take a " 'case-by-case' approach" in evaluating whether the plan was proposed in good faith. [*In re* **Banks**, 545 B.R. 241 (Bankr. N.D. Ill. 2016)] Absent "serious debtor misconduct or abuse," a Chapter 13 plan should satisfy the good faith test. [8 Collier ¶ 1325.04(2)] If no objection to confirmation is filed, the court may determine that the plan was proposed in good faith and not by any means forbidden by law without receiving evidence on this issue. [Bankruptcy Rule 3015(f)]

(i) Comparison of Plan Versus Petition

The consequences of a finding that the plan was not filed in good faith under § 1325(a)(3) may differ from those of a finding that the debtor did not file the petition in good faith under § 1325(a)(7). If the debtor did not file the petition in good faith, the court likely will dismiss the case. A bankruptcy court, however, may give the debtor another opportunity to file a plan if the court concludes that the debtor did not propose her original plan in good faith. [*See In re* **McCreary**, 2009 WL 5215587 (Bankr. C.D. Ill. 2009)]

d. Best Interests of the Creditors

Each unsecured creditor must receive *property whose present value* at least equals what the creditor would receive in a *Chapter 7 liquidation* case. [B.C. § 1325(a)(4)]

e. Plan Is Feasible

The plan must be *feasible,* which means that the bankruptcy court must find that the debtor will be able to make all plan payments. The debtor need not prove that the plan is guaranteed to be successful, but she must show that the plan has a *reasonable chance of success.* [B.C. § 1325(a)(6); *In re* **Ewing,** 2018 WL 1137611 (Bankr. D. Mont. 2018); *In re* **Merhi,** 518 B.R. 705 (Bankr. E.D. N.Y. 2014)]

f. Debtor Filed for Bankruptcy in Good Faith

The debtor must have filed the *Chapter 13 petition in good faith.* [B.C. § 1325(a)(7)]

g. Domestic Support Obligations

Debtor must pay all *domestic support obligations* required by judicial or administrative order, or by statute, that came *due after filing* of the petition. [B.C. §§ 101(14A), 1325(a)(8)]

h. Tax Returns

Debtor must have filed all *pre-petition* federal, state, and local *tax returns,* as required by § 1308. [B.C. §§ 1308, 1325(a)(9)]

i. No Material Alteration of Certain Retirement Fund Loans

The plan may *not materially alter* the terms of a loan taken by the debtor from any of the following *retirement plans:* (1) a plan under § 408(b)(1) of the Employee Retirement Income Security Act ("ERISA"); (2) a plan subject to § 72(p) of the Internal Revenue Code; or (3) a thrift savings plan in the Federal Employee's Retirement System that meets the requirements of 5 U.S.C. § 8422(g). [B.C. §§ 1322(f), 362(b)(19); *see* 3 Collier ¶ 362.05(18)]

j. Payments to Chapter 7 Trustee in Converted or Dismissed Case

If the debtor's Chapter 7 case was converted to Chapter 13 or dismissed and re-filed under Chapter 13, then the Chapter 13 plan must provide for the payment of unpaid but allowed compensation to the Chapter 7 trustee. The Chapter 7 trustee must have been allowed compensation, which remained unpaid, due to the conversion or dismissal of the debtor's Chapter 7 case pursuant to § 707(b). [B.C. § 1326(b)(3)] In such a case, the plan must provide for *monthly* payments to the Chapter 7 trustee by *pro rating* the amount owed over the *term of the Chapter 13 plan.* [B.C. § 1326(b)(3)(A); *In re* **Kuhn,** 337 B.R. 668 (Bankr. N.D. Ind. 2006)] The *monthly payment cannot exceed* the *greater of $25 or* the *total amount payable to the general unsecured creditors* over the term of the plan *multiplied by 5%* and then *divided by the number of months* in the plan. [B.C. § 1326(b)(3)(B)]

k. Treatment of Secured Creditors' Claims

The plan must satisfy *one of the following three* requirements for *each allowed secured claim:* (1) the secured creditor *accepted the plan;* (2) the debtor *surrendered the collateral;* or (3) the debtor *complied* with the Code's *cramdown requirements.* [B.C. § 1325(a)(5)]

(i) Plan Acceptance

A secured creditor may *accept its treatment* under the plan. [B.C. § 1325(a)(5)(A)] A secured creditor's failure to object to the treatment of its claim in the plan may constitute acceptance of the plan. [*In re Flynn,* 402 B.R. 437 (B.A.P. 1st Cir. 2009)]

(ii) Surrender

The debtor may *surrender the collateral* to the secured creditor. [B.C. § 1325(a)(5)(C)] Surrender of the collateral does not extinguish the creditor's unsecured claim for any deficiency resulting from sale of the surrendered collateral. [**AmeriCredit Fin. Servs. v. Tompkins,** 604 F.3d 753 (2d Cir. 2010)]

(iii) Cramdown

The debtor may *cram down* a non-consenting secured creditor's claim so long as the plan *preserves the creditor's lien* on the collateral and distributes to the creditor *cash or other property* with a *present value,* on the plan's effective date, of at least the *amount of the creditor's allowed secured claim.* [B.C. § 1325(a)(5)(B)]

Cramdown means that the debtor has modified the secured creditor's rights over its objection. [**DaimlerChrysler Servs. N. Am. LLC v. Taranto,** 365 B.R. 85 (B.A.P. 6th Cir. 2007)] Typically, debtors cram down on a secured creditor by bifurcating the secured creditor's claim into a secured claim and an unsecured claim.

Example: Daphne owns a piece of collateral valued at $80,000. Bank5 has a valid security interest in the collateral to secure a loan of $90,000. Bank5 has an $80,000 secured claim and an unsecured claim of $10,000. The $10,000 portion of Bank5's undersecured claim is *not* treated as a secured claim under § 1325(a)(5).

(1) Lien

The plan must preserve the creditor's lien until the *earlier* of payment of the *underlying debt* or *discharge.* The Chapter 13 debtor's discharge, however, does not include the discharge of a debt for which the last payment is due *after* the last payment under the plan is due. [B.C. §§ 1322(b)(5), 1328(a)(1)]

Example: Darlene purchased a vacation home five years ago. Fifteen years remain on the mortgage held by Bank3. The balance on the mortgage is $100,000. Bank3's mortgage on Darlene's vacation home remains even after Darlene completes her plan payments and obtains a discharge, because Darlene did not pay off the mortgage during her plan and the Bankruptcy Code excepts from discharge long-term debts in which the final payment on the secured loan is due after the final plan payment. [B.C. §§ 1322(b)(5), 1328(a)(1)]

(2) Present Value

The plan must pay secured creditors the ***present value*** of their secured claims. That means that the plan must provide for the payment of interest on secured claims over the course of the debtor's three- or five-year plan. The interest rate is the *Till* rate, which the Supreme Court defined as the ***national prime rate adjusted for risk.*** The Supreme Court in *Till* did not decide the proper risk adjustment but did note that courts had "generally approved adjustments of 1% to 3%." [**Till v. SCS Credit Corporation,** 541 U.S. 465 (2004)]

(3) Valuing the Secured Creditor's Claim

A claim is secured to the extent of the creditor's interest in the collateral. The bankruptcy court should determine the value "in light of the purpose of the valuation" and "the proposed use or disposition" of the collateral. [B.C. § 506(a)(1)] In a Chapter 13 case, the value of ***personal property*** is ***replacement value.*** [**Associates Commercial Corp. v. Rash,** 520 U.S. 953 (1997); B.C. § 506(a)(2)] ***Replacement value,*** however, varies depending on the ***purpose*** for which the debtor acquired the property.

(a) Personal, Family, Household Purposes

If the debtor acquired the property for ***personal, family, or household purposes,*** then ***replacement value*** is the ***retail price*** considering the age and condition of the property at the time of valuation. [B.C. § 506(a)(2)]

Example: Delilah purchased a minivan for her family on August 5, 2014. She financed the vehicle through *Carz 'R Us*. Delilah filed for relief under Chapter 13 on September 2, 2017. Delilah still owes $15,000 on the minivan. Retail price for a three-year-old van of that condition is $12,000; wholesale price is $10,500. Even though *Carz 'R Us* has a purchase-money security interest in a motor vehicle acquired for personal use, the hanging paragraph does not apply because Delilah purchased the minivan more than 910 days prior to filing for bankruptcy. Because Delilah acquired the minivan for family purposes, the van's value is $12,000, which is the retail price. *Carz 'R Us* has a secured claim for $12,000, and an unsecured claim for $3,000.

(b) Not for Personal, Family, Household Purposes

If the debtor did not acquire the property for ***personal, family, or household purposes,*** then the value is ***replacement value without deduction for costs of sale or marketing.*** [B.C. § 506(a)(2)] Section 506(a)(2) does not specify what figure to use for replacement value when the collateral was not acquired for personal, family, or household use. But, § 506(a) supposedly codified the Supreme Court's decision in *Rash.* In *Rash,* the Supreme Court described replacement value as "the cost the debtor would incur to obtain a like asset for the same proposed use," and it indicated that ascertaining such value would "depend on the type of debtor and the nature of the property." [**Rash,** *supra*]

(iv) Cramdown Exception: The Hanging Paragraph

With BAPCPA, Congress added an unnumbered paragraph, which courts have labeled the "hanging paragraph," to the end of § 1325(a). Most courts have held that if the hanging paragraph applies to a secured creditor's claim, then the debtor may not bifurcate the creditor's claim into a secured and an unsecured claim. [*See, e.g.,* **Nuvell Credit Co., LLC v. Dean,** 537 F.3d 1315 (11 Cir. 2008); **Wachovia Dealer Servs. v. Jones,** 503 F.3d 1284 (10th Cir. 2008); **DaimlerChrysler,** *supra*] If the hanging paragraph applies, the creditor's *secured claim equals the amount that the debtor owes the secured creditor,* regardless of the actual value of the collateral. The hanging paragraph applies in two situations.

(1) Creditor has a *purchase-money security interest* in a *motor vehicle* that the debtor *acquired for personal use* within *910 days* of filing for bankruptcy. [B.C. § 1325(a)(9) hanging paragraph]

e.g. **Example:** On May 1, 2016, Darren purchased a car on credit from *Cal's Cars* for personal use. *Cal's Cars* has a purchase-money security interest in the vehicle. Darren filed for relief under chapter 13 on July 1, 2017. Darren owes $25,000 on the car, which is worth $20,000. Without the hanging paragraph, *Cal's Cars* would have a secured claim for $20,000, and an unsecured claim for $5,000. Because the hanging paragraph applies, however, *Cal's Cars* has a secured claim for $25,000, which is the amount of Darren's indebtedness.

(2) Creditor has a *purchase-money security interest* in *any other thing of value* if the debt was incurred *within one year of the bankruptcy filing.* [B.C. § 1325(a)(9) hanging paragraph] Most courts have held that the one-year provision does *not* apply to motor vehicles because the hanging paragraph creates two categories of collateral—motor vehicles and any *other* thing of value.

e.g. **Example:** Debtor acquired a motor vehicle for business use within one year of filing for relief under Chapter 13. DaimlerChrysler has a purchase-money security interest in the car. At the time that he filed for bankruptcy, Debtor owed more than $43,000 on the car, which was worth $22,000. Because debtor acquired and used the vehicle for business, not personal, use, the 910-day provision in the hanging paragraph did not apply. The one-year provision in the hanging paragraph also did not apply because that provision was limited to "anything of value *other than a motor vehicle.*" [*In re* **Horton,** 398 B.R. 73 (Bankr. S.D. Fla. 2008); *but see In re* **Littlefield,** 388 B.R. 1 (Bankr. D. Me. 2008) (holding that one-year provision in the hanging paragraph applied to purchase-money security interest in motor vehicle acquired for business use within one year of bankruptcy)]

(v) Cramdown Exception: Debtor's Principal Residence

(1) Bifurcation of Home Mortgage

Bankruptcy Code § 1322(b)(2) *prohibits* a Chapter 13 debtor from *stripping down* an undersecured mortgage on the *debtor's principal residence* to the fair market value of the home, notwithstanding § 506(a), if the last payment on the secured creditor's claim is due after the final plan payment. [**Nobelman v. American Savings Bank,** 508 U.S. 324 (1993); B.C. § 1322(b)(2); *but see In re* **Hammond,** 27 F.3d 52 (3d Cir. 1994) (allowing bifurcation of a home mortgage that also created security interests in *personal property*)]

e.g. **Example:** Dannie purchased his home seven years ago. The home is Dannie's principal residence. Dannie obtained financing from Local Bank, which holds the 30-year mortgage. The balance on the home loan is $150,000, but Dannie's home is worth only $110,000. The Code's anti-modification provision does not allow bifurcation of Local Bank's claim into a $110,000 secured claim and a $40,000 unsecured claim. Instead, Dannie must pay Local Bank according to the terms of the original loan agreement with the bank.

(2) Permissible Modification of Home Mortgage Payments

If the final payment on a debt secured solely by a security interest in real property constituting the debtor's principal residence is due *before* the last payment under the plan, it is permissible for the plan to modify payment of the debt in accordance with Code § 1325(a)(5). [B.C. § 1322(c)(2)]

(3) "Unsecured" Junior Mortgage

Although there is a split of authority, the majority view holds that a junior mortgage that is *wholly unsecured* is not protected from modification and, therefore, can be "stripped off" and treated as a general unsecured claim. [*See, e.g.,* **Branigan v. Davis,** 716 F.3d 331 (4th Cir. 2013) (explaining that under § 506(a) valueless liens are unsecured claims and finding that "the Bankruptcy Code permits the stripping off of valueless liens in Chapter 13 proceedings"); *but see In re Frame,* 2009 WL 8725111 (Bankr. D. Minn. 2009) (finding that debtor cannot strip off valueless lien on debtor's principal residence)]

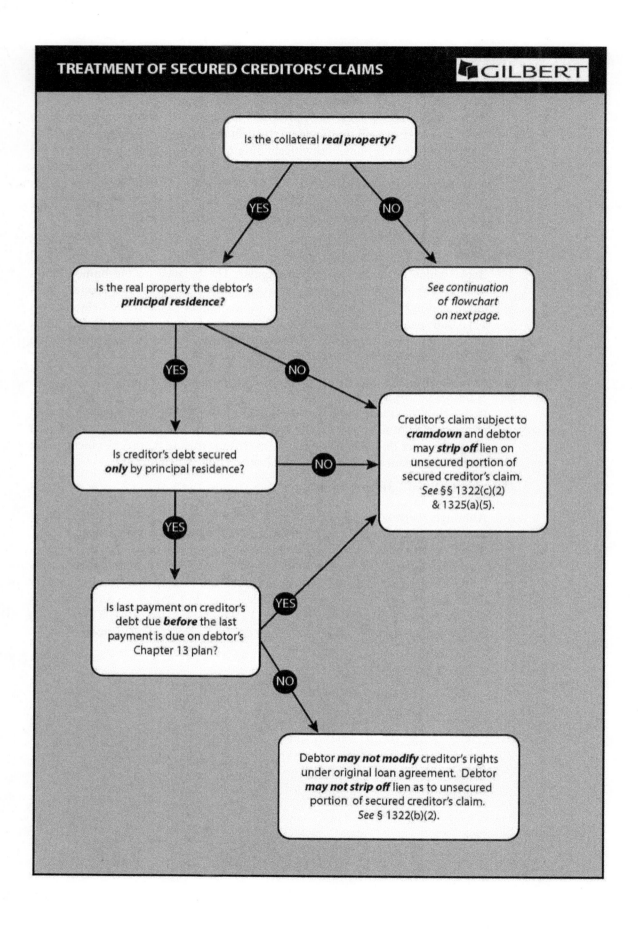

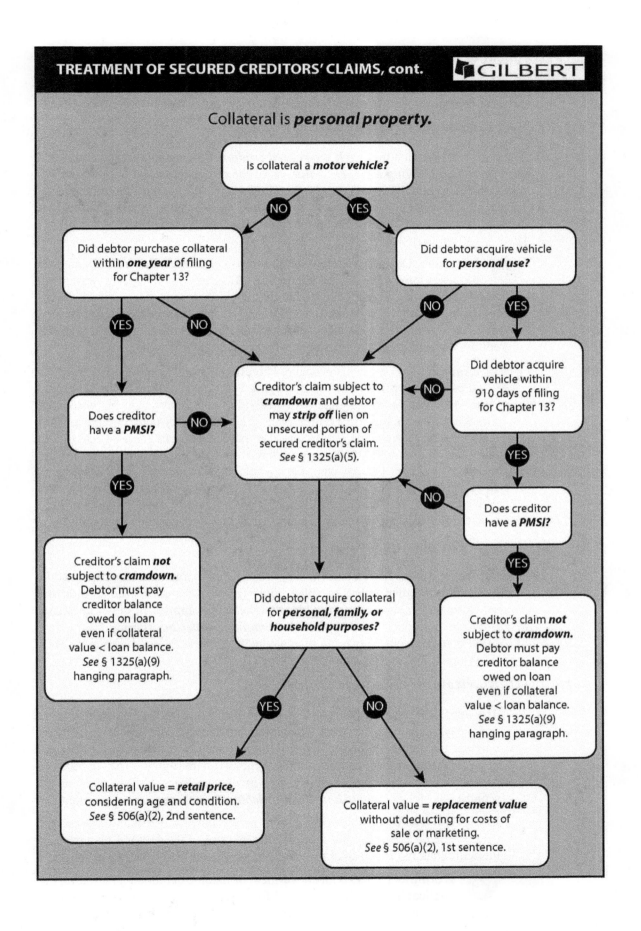

Collateral is *personal property.*

Is collateral a *motor vehicle?*

NO → **Did debtor purchase collateral within *one year* of filing for Chapter 13?**

YES → **Did debtor acquire vehicle for *personal use?***

Did debtor purchase collateral within *one year* of filing for Chapter 13?
- YES → **Does creditor have a *PMSI?***
- NO → Creditor's claim subject to *cramdown*...

Does creditor have a *PMSI?*
- NO → Creditor's claim subject to *cramdown* and debtor may *strip off* lien on unsecured portion of secured creditor's claim. *See* § 1325(a)(5).
- YES → **Creditor's claim *not* subject to *cramdown.* Debtor must pay creditor balance owed on loan even if collateral value < loan balance. *See* § 1325(a)(9) hanging paragraph.**

Did debtor acquire vehicle for *personal use?*
- NO → Creditor's claim subject to *cramdown*...
- YES → **Did debtor acquire vehicle within 910 days of filing for Chapter 13?**

Did debtor acquire vehicle within 910 days of filing for Chapter 13?
- NO → Creditor's claim subject to *cramdown*...
- YES → **Does creditor have a *PMSI?***

Does creditor have a *PMSI?*
- NO → Creditor's claim subject to *cramdown*...
- YES → **Creditor's claim *not* subject to *cramdown.* Debtor must pay creditor balance owed on loan even if collateral value < loan balance. *See* § 1325(a)(9) hanging paragraph.**

Creditor's claim subject to *cramdown* and debtor may *strip off* lien on unsecured portion of secured creditor's claim. *See* § 1325(a)(5).
→ **Did debtor acquire collateral for *personal, family, or household purposes?***

Did debtor acquire collateral for *personal, family, or household purposes?*
- YES → **Collateral value = *retail price,* considering age and condition. *See* § 506(a)(2), 2nd sentence.**
- NO → **Collateral value = *replacement value* without deducting for costs of sale or marketing. *See* § 506(a)(2), 1st sentence.**

l. Treatment of Unsecured Creditors' Claims

The debtor's plan must satisfy the *best interests of the creditors* test and, if the trustee or an unsecured creditor objects to plan confirmation, the *projected disposable income* test.

(i) Best Interests of Creditors Test

The plan must provide that *each unsecured creditor* holding an allowed claim will receive property having a *present value,* as of the effective date of the plan, of *not less* than the amount he would *receive* for his claim in a *Chapter 7* case on that date, taking into account the exemptions that would be available to the debtor. This element of confirmation usually is referred to as the "best interests of creditors test." [B.C. § 1325(a)(4)]

e.g. **Example:** Debi is a below-median-income debtor. Her three-year plan proposes to pay her unsecured creditors $100 per month, which amounts to a 10% dividend to Debi's unsecured creditors. Debi, however, has a valuable non-exempt asset, which if liquidated, would provide her unsecured creditors in a Chapter 7 case with a 15% dividend. Debi's plan does not satisfy the best interests of creditors test and, thus, the bankruptcy court cannot confirm the plan.

e.g. **Example:** Dell owes his unsecured creditors $30,000 and his plan proposes to pay those creditors in full by paying $500 per month over the 60-month plan. Had Dell filed for relief under Chapter 7, he would have paid his unsecured creditors $30,000 from his non-exempt assets. The bankruptcy court cannot confirm Dell's plan, because the Code requires Dell to pay the *present value* of $30,000 to his unsecured creditors. Without paying interest on the $30,000, Dell is not paying his unsecured creditors at least what they would have recovered under Chapter 7. [*See In re* **Hardy,** 755 F.2d 75 (6th Cir. 1985) ("When liquidation will result in full payment of all allowed unsecured claims, a debtor cannot defer payment of the claims without providing interest payments to the creditors")]

(ii) Projected Disposable Income Test

If the *trustee* or an *unsecured creditor* objects to the plan, then the bankruptcy court cannot confirm the plan unless the plan *either* (a) pays the unsecured creditor the *present value of its claim or* (b) provides that the debtor applies all of her *projected disposable income* during the *applicable commitment period,* starting on the date of the first plan payment, to making plan payments to her unsecured creditors. [B.C. § 1325(b)(1)]

(1) Applicable Commitment Period

The *applicable commitment period* is the length of time that the debtor must make payments under her plan. The applicable commitment period depends on whether the debtor's annual income is above or below the median for the state in which the debtor resides at the time of bankruptcy. The *applicable commitment period for above-median-income debtors* is five years or 60 months, and for *below-median-income debtors* it is three years or 36 months.

Exception: The applicable commitment period may be less than three or five years, whichever time period is applicable, but *only if* the debtor's plan pays all unsecured claims in full over the shorter time period. [B.C. § 1325(a)(4)]

e.g. **Example:** Denise is an above-median-income debtor and, therefore, the applicable commitment period for her plan is five years or 60 months. Denise may propose and the bankruptcy court may approve a plan with an applicable commitment period of four years or 48 months if the plan provides for payment in full to all of Denise's unsecured creditors over the plan's 48-month period.

(2) Disposable Income

Disposable income is *current monthly income* minus *reasonably necessary expenses,* including *domestic support obligations, charitable contributions,* and amounts to repay certain *pension loans.* [B.C. §§ 1325(b)(2), 1322(f)]

(a) Reasonably Necessary Expenses

For *above-median* income debtors, reasonably necessary expenses are the *"means test"* expense amounts. [B.C. § 1325(b)(3)] For *below-median* income debtors, the bankruptcy court determines the reasonableness of the debtor's expenses.

(b) Charitable Contributions

The debtor may deduct from her current monthly income *charitable contributions* to a *qualified religious or charitable entity or organization* in an amount not to exceed *15%* of the debtor's *gross income* for the year in which the contributions are made. [B.C. § 1325(b)(2)(A)(ii)] The Code defines a *qualified religious or charitable entity or organization* as an entity described in § 170(c)(1) or an entity or organization described in § 170(c)(2) of the Internal Revenue Code. [B.C. § 548(d)(4)]

e.g. **Example:** Diane has current monthly income of $4,000, and is an above-median income debtor. Her $3,900 of monthly expenses includes $400 that Diane tithes each month to her church. Diane's charitable contributions are 10% of her gross income; therefore, she may include them in the calculation of her disposable income.

(c) Certain Retirement Plan Loans

Amounts that the debtor is required to repay certain retirement plan loans are not considered part of the debtor's disposable income. [B.C. §§ 1322(f), 362(b)(19)]

(3) Projected Disposable Income

The Bankruptcy Code defines *disposable income* but not *projected disposable income.* Because the calculation of *current monthly income* is backward looking—at the six months prior to filing for bankruptcy—a debtor whose financial circumstances change prior to bankruptcy may have less (or more) actual income to commit to a Chapter 13 plan than the disposable income calculation shows. The Supreme Court has held that in determining a debtor's *projected disposable income,* the bankruptcy court "may account for changes in the debtor's income or expenses that are known or virtually certain at the time of confirmation." [**Hamilton v. Lanning,** 560 U.S. 505 (2010)]

e.g. **Example:** During the six months prior to filing for bankruptcy, Dominique, a single person, received a one-time buyout from her employer, which significantly increased her gross income for several months. As a result, Dominique's current monthly income is $5,000 (making her an above-median income debtor) and her disposable income is $1,200 per month. But, Dominique cannot afford to pay her unsecured creditors $1,200 per month, because the actual income from her new job, is only $2,000 per month. Her actual monthly expenses are $1,830, leaving her $170 per month in actual disposable income. The bankruptcy court may take account of the known changes to Dominique's income and confirm a plan in which she pays $155 per month to her unsecured creditors.

Note: A debtor may commit less than her full disposable income to plan payments to her unsecured creditors. The reason is to provide the debtor with a cushion or reserve to take account of unexpected changes in monthly expenses. [Collier ¶ 1325.11]

4. Permissive Provisions

A Chapter 13 plan *may include* any of the following provisions. [B.C. § 1322(b)]

a. Classification of Claims

The plan may specify various *classes of unsecured claims* in accordance with Bankruptcy Code § 1122, provided that it does not discriminate unfairly against any particular class. [B.C. § 1322(b)(1)] In 1984, Congress amended § 1322(b)(1) to allow a Chapter 13 plan to provide different treatment for a consumer debt on which an individual co-debtor is also liable than for other unsecured claims. [B.C. § 1322(b)(1)] The amendment, which courts call the "however clause," has been the subject of much debate. Some courts hold that the "however clause" creates an exception to the unfair discrimination requirement for co-debtor consumer claims and, thus, there is no unfair discrimination analysis for plans treating co-debtor consumer claims differently from other unsecured claims. The majority of courts, however, hold that the clause qualifies the unfair discrimination analysis although the courts struggle with the degree of qualification. [**Meyer v. Renteria (*In re* Renteria),** 470 B.R. 838 (B.A.P. 9th Cir. 2012)]

(i) "Unfair Discrimination"

The courts have developed a number of tests for determining unfair discrimination, including The Balance Approach, The Bright-line Approach, and the Reasonableness Approach. [*In re* **Engen,** 561 B.R. 523 (Bankr. D. Kan. 2016] In determining whether discrimination against a class is fair, many courts use the following four-part test:

(1) whether there is a *reasonable basis* for the discriminatory treatment;

(2) whether the plan could be implemented *without* the discrimination;

(3) the presence or absence of *good faith;* and

(4) whether the degree of discrimination is directly related to the basis or rationale for the discrimination.

[*In re* **Engen,** *supra*]

Example: Married debtors filed for relief under Chapter 13 and proposed a plan that separately classified their delinquent tax debts, some of which were non-dischargeable. The proposed plan would have resulted in full payment of the nondischargeable tax debt with no payment for the remaining unsecured non-priority creditors. The Chapter 13 trustee objected to the plan, and the debtors amended it to delete the special classification for their tax creditors. Subsequently, however, debtors objected to their own amended plan and claimed that the Bankruptcy Code allowed them to prefer their tax creditors in the plan. The bankruptcy court overruled the objection and confirmed the plan without special treatment for the tax creditors.

The debtors appealed and the Eighth Circuit affirmed the bankruptcy court's decision. The Eighth Circuit found that the debtors had failed to satisfy the four-part test for unfair discrimination. For example, the court concluded that the plan lacked good faith because the debtors "propose[d] to 'protect' those creditors least in need of protection, at the expense of the most vulnerable." [**Copeland v. Fink (*In re Copeland*),** 742 F.3d 811 (8th Cir. 2013)]

e.g. **Example:** Debtor filed for relief under Chapter 13. At the § 341 meeting, she stated her intention to pay the unsecured part of Car Company's claim in full to prevent Car Company from seeking relief from the co-debtor stay and pursuing co-debtor for payment. Debtor, however, failed to amend her Chapter 13 plan to so provide, and Car Company objected to confirmation of the plan because it failed to give Car Company preferential treatment of its unsecured claim. The Chapter 13 trustee opposed preferential treatment for Car Company's unsecured claim. The bankruptcy court held that "the language of § 1322(b)(1) creates an exception to the unfair discrimination test in cases involving co-signed debt" and that "Congress intended to permit debtors to specially classify co-debtor claims without convincing a court that the classification is not unfairly discriminatory." Thus, as long as Debtor satisfied the other requirements for confirmation of her Chapter 13 plan, preferential treatment of Car Company's unsecured claim compared with other unsecured claims would not preclude confirmation of the plan. [*In re* **Monroe,** 281 B.R. 398 (Bankr. N.D. Ga. 2002)]

b. Modification of Creditors' Rights

With one exception, the plan may modify the rights of secured creditors or unsecured creditors, e.g., by changing the size and timing of installment payments.

(i) Principal Residence

The plan *may not modify* the rights of a creditor whose claim is secured *solely* by a security interest in real property constituting the *debtor's principal residence.* [B.C. § 1322(b)(2)] The Code defines a security interest as a *lien created by an agreement.* [B.C. § 101(51)] Thus, § 1322(b)(2)'s anti-modification provision prevents the debtor from doing such things as reducing the amount of the loan's monthly payments, converting a variable to a fixed interest rate, or extending the term of the loan. [*See* **Anderson v. Hancock,** 820 F.3d 670 (4th Cir. 2016)] A majority of courts use the petition date as the date for determining debtor's principal residence. [*In re* **Brinkley,** 505 B.R. 207 (Bankr. E.D. Mich. 2013)]

e.g. **Example:** Debtor filed for relief under Chapter 13, and listed a doublewide mobile home on her Schedule B of personal property. Debtor listed no real property on Schedule A. In her Chapter 13 plan, Debtor proposed to modify the rights of Green Tree, which held the security interest in her mobile home. Green Tree argued that because Debtor used the mobile home as her principal residence, § 1322(b)(2) precluded her from modifying its rights. The bankruptcy court disagreed. The court held that while the mobile home was Debtor's principal residence, it was personal, not real, property under Alabama law. As a result, § 1322(b)(2) did not apply. [*In re* **Manning,** 2007 WL 2220454 (Bankr. N.D. Ala. 2007)]

(ii) Hybrid Properties

Most courts use one of three tests to decide whether § 1322(b)(2) applies to real property that serves not only as the debtor's principal residence but also as the location for some commercial activity. Courts using the ***case-by-case approach*** look to the ***totality of the circumstances*** to determine whether the parties' predominant intent was to enter into a primarily residence or commercial transaction. Courts using the ***bright-line test,*** by comparison, only apply § 1322(b)(2) if the real property serves any other function besides the debtor's principal residence. Finally, courts using the third approach focus on the fact that the word "only" in § 1322(b)(2) does not modify "debtor's principal residence." These courts apply § 1322(b)(2) to real property that serves as the only security for the debt so long as the debtor "principally resides in *some portion* of the real property." [***In re* Hutsler,** 2016 WL 7984348 (Bankr. W.D. Mo. 2016)]

> **Example:** Debtors filed for relief under Chapter 13. Prior to bankruptcy, they had purchased three tracts of land on which sat two houses. The Debtors lived on the residence on one tract of land; the father of one of the debtors ("Father") lived in the second home on one of the other three tracts of land. Father also farmed some of the acreage. The Debtors financed the purchase through WFO Investments. The purchase-money note provided for $1,500 monthly payments and bore a 10% annual interest rate. The note had a balloon payment due approximately one year after Debtors filed for bankruptcy. The Debtors' plan provided for payment to WFO of $2,000 per month for 48 months, at 4.55% interest, with the balloon payment due at the end of the 48-month payment period. WFO objected to the Debtors' plan on the basis of § 1322(b)(2). Debtors argued that only one of the three tracts of land contained *their* principal residence, and that Father farmed some of the other land. Thus, they argued that § 1322(b)(2) did not apply, because WFO's claim was secured *not only* by real property that was a principal residence. The court applied each of the three tests used by most courts in cases involving hybrid use of the real property on which sits the debtor's principal residence. The court found that under any of the three tests, WFO's claim was secured by real property that was the debtor's principal residence. Thus, the court held that Debtors could not modify WFO's rights under the loan documents. [***In re* Hutsler,** *supra*]

c. Cure or Waiver of Default

The plan may cure or waive any default. [B.C. § 1322(b)(3)]

d. Order of Payments

The plan may provide for any general unsecured claim to be paid concurrently with any secured claim or with any unsecured priority claim. [B.C. § 1322(b)(4)]

e. Long-Term Debts

Sometimes a debtor has a long-term debt for which the last payment is due after the due date of the final payment required by the Chapter 13 plan. If such a debt is in default—whether secured or unsecured—the Chapter 13 plan may provide for ***curing the default*** within a reasonable time and ***maintaining payments*** while the case is pending. [B.C. § 1322(b)(5)] This section, by specific statutory authorization, frequently is applied with respect to claims secured solely by real property constituting the principal residence of the debtor, notwithstanding the exception contained in § 1322(b)(2) concerning non-modification of home mortgages. Cure, however, does not permit the debtor to modify the rights of a creditor whose claim is secured by real property that is the debtor's principal residence.

If your exam question asks you to determine whether Chapter 7 or Chapter 13 would provide optimal relief for the debtor, often an important factor will be the debtor's desire to keep her home. Section 1322(b)(3) allows the Chapter 13 plan to include a provision to cure any default. But suppose that the final mortgage payment will be due after the due date of the last payment required by the Chapter 13 plan. Under these circumstances, the debtor may use § 1322(b)(5) to include a provision in the plan to *cure the default within a reasonable time* and *maintain the payments* while the case is pending, with the balance of the mortgage payments to be made after completion of the payments under the plan. In this way, the debtor can retain her home, but the long-term mortgage debt will not be discharged in the debtor's Chapter 13 bankruptcy case. You might note in your answer that, if keeping her home is the debtor's main goal, Chapter 7 probably will not be as attractive an option, because many mortgagees require the debtor to get current before reaffirming. In Chapter 13, the debtor has a reasonable time to cure.

(i) Cure

If the debtor seeks to cure a default with respect to a lien on her principal residence, cure is permitted until a foreclosure sale conducted according to applicable nonbankruptcy law has occurred. [B.C. § 1322(c)(1)] Cure focuses on the debtor's ability to "decelerate and continue paying a loan, thereby avoiding foreclosure." [**Anderson v. Hancock,** 820 F.3d 670 (4th Cir. 2016)]

(ii) "Reasonable Time"

What constitutes a reasonable time to cure a default depends on the circumstances of the particular case. Courts examine various factors in making the "reasonable time" determination but "primary consideration to whether the cure period is the debtor's best effort and is the most that the debtor can reasonably be expected to pay considering his income." [**Hence v. Indian Cave P'ship** (*In re* **Hence**), 2007 WL 1176787 (S.D. Tex. 2007)]

(iii) Interest on Arrearages

If the plan proposes to cure a default, the amount necessary to cure the default is determined by looking to the underlying contract and applicable nonbankruptcy law. [B.C. § 1322(e)] Therefore, a creditor will be entitled to interest on interest only if it was agreed to by the parties and is permissible under state law, or alternatively if it is required by state law.

f. Post-Petition Tax Claims or Necessary Consumer Debts

The plan may provide for the payment of any allowed post-petition claims for taxes that become due during the pendency of the case, or for certain necessary consumer debts incurred after the order for relief. [B.C. §§ 1322(b)(6), 1305]

g. Assumption or Rejection of Executory Contracts or Unexpired Leases

The plan may provide for any previously unrejected executory contract or unexpired lease to be assumed, rejected, or assigned in accordance with § 365. [B.C. § 1322(b)(7)]

h.   Property Used to Pay Claims

The plan may provide for particular claims to be paid from property of the estate or from the debtor's property. [B.C. § 1322(b)(8)]

i.   Vesting of Property

The plan may provide for property of the estate to vest in the debtor or in another entity when the plan is confirmed or at a subsequent time. [B.C. § 1322(b)(9)]

j.   Interest on Nondischargeable Debts

The plan may provide for the payment of interest accruing post-petition on unsecured nondischargeable debts *but only if* the debtor has disposable income available to pay interest after providing for full payment of all allowed claims. [B.C. §§ 1322(b)(10), 1328(a)]

k.   Miscellaneous Provisions

The plan also may contain any other provisions that are appropriate and consistent with the Bankruptcy Code. [B.C. § 1322(b)(11)]

5.   Modification of Plan

The debtor has the *exclusive right* to modify a plan *prior to confirmation.* The modified plan must satisfy the requirements of § 1322. [B.C. § 1323]

E.   Payments

1.   Commencement of Payments

Unless the court orders otherwise, the debtor must begin making payments under a proposed plan no later than *30 days* after the earlier of the order for relief or the date that the plan is filed. [B.C. § 1326(a)(1)]

2.   To Whom Are Payments Made?

The debtor must remit *plan payments* to the trustee. [B.C. § 1326(a)(1)(A)] In the following two situations, however, the debtor's payment goes directly to the creditor.

a.   Personal Property Lease

The debtor directly pays the lessor for scheduled post-petition payments on a lease of personal property. [B.C. § 1326(a)(1)(B)]

b.   Adequate Protection

The debtor makes *adequate protection* payments directly to a creditor with a *PMSI in personal property* but only with respect to the post-petition obligation. [B.C. § 1326(a)(1)(C)]

Note: The debtor reduces the amount owed to the trustee by the amounts paid directly to the personal property lessor and for adequate protection payments described above. The debtor must provide the *trustee* with *evidence of the payment,* including the amount and date of the payment. [B.C. § 1325(a)(1)(B), (C)]

Note: No later than *60 days* after filing the petition, the debtor who retains *personal property* must provide to the *lessor* of such property or to a creditor with a *PMSI* in such property evidence that the debtor is maintaining required *insurance coverage* on the property. The debtor's obligation continues as long as the debtor retains possession of the property.

3. Pre-Confirmation Payments to Trustee

Prior to confirmation, the court, after notice and hearing, may increase or decrease the payments required of the debtor. The trustee retains any payment made before confirmation until the confirmation hearing. If the plan is confirmed, the trustee makes distributions as provided for by the plan as soon as practicable. However, if confirmation is denied, the money must be returned to the debtor, less any unpaid administrative expenses that have been allowed. [B.C. § 1326(a)(2)]

4. Payment Orders

After a plan has been confirmed, the court may order the debtor's employer, or any other entity providing income to the debtor, to make direct payments to the Chapter 13 trustee. The Social Security Administration, however, is not subject to such income deduction orders concerning the debtor's social security benefits. [B.C. § 1325(c); 8 Collier ¶ 1325.12(2)]

5. Distribution

Ordinarily, the payments under a confirmed plan are sent to creditors *by the trustee* unless the plan or the confirmation order provides otherwise, such as where a debtor engaged in business is allowed to perform this function. [B.C. § 1326(c)]

6. Administrative Expenses

Prior to or concurrent with each payment to creditors under a Chapter 13 plan, the trustee is required to pay any unpaid administrative expenses or bankruptcy fees or charges, as well as the percentage fee set for a standing trustee, if one has been appointed. [B.C. § 1326(b)] In addition, BAPCPA amended the Bankruptcy Code to provide for the payment of compensation to a Chapter 7 trustee in a debtor's subsequent Chapter 13 case. The trustee must have been allowed compensation, which remained unpaid, due to the conversion or dismissal of the debtor's prior case pursuant to the § 707(b) abuse test. [B.C. § 1326(b)(3)] In such a case, the plan must provide for *monthly* payments to the Chapter 7 trustee by *pro rating* the amount owed over the *term of the Chapter 13 plan.* [B.C. § 1326(b)(3)(A); *In re* **Kuhn,** 337 B.R. 668 (Bankr. N.D. Ind. 2006)] The *monthly payment cannot exceed* the *greater of $25 or* the *total amount payable to the general unsecured creditors* over the term of the plan *multiplied by 5%* and then *divided by the number of months* in the plan. [B.C. § 1326(b)(3)(B)]

7. Filing Fee

The debtor may apply to pay the Chapter 13 filing fee in installments. [Bankruptcy Rule 1006(b)(1)] The deadline for paying the entire filing fee for the Chapter 13 petition is the time of the first payment to creditors. [8 Collier ¶ 1326.03(1)]

F. Post-Confirmation Matters

1. Effects of Confirmation

A confirmed plan *binds the debtor and every creditor,* regardless of whether a creditor has accepted or rejected the plan or has objected to confirmation of the plan, or whether the creditor's claim is provided for by the plan. [B.C. § 1327(a)]

e.g. **Example:** Debtor filed for relief under Chapter 13, and proposed a plan that provided for payment of only the principal of his outstanding student loans and discharge of that debt once he paid off the principal through the plan. Debtor owed United Student Aid Funds ("United") $17,832.15, which represented both the principal and interest on his student loans. United filed a proof of claim and received a copy of Debtor's plan but failed to object to the plan. The bankruptcy court confirmed the plan, even though Debtor had filed no adversary proceeding to determine dischargeability of the debt and the court had made no findings on undue hardship. After completing plan payments on the principal on his student loans, Debtor obtained a discharge on the interest due on the loans. When collection efforts were undertaken for the loan interest, Debtor filed a motion with the bankruptcy court asking for enforcement of the earlier discharge order. United opposed the motion and filed a cross-motion under Federal Rule of Civil Procedure 60(b)(4) to set aside as void the bankruptcy court's order confirming Debtor's plan. The bankruptcy court denied United's cross-motion and ordered that collection activities stop. The district court reversed the bankruptcy court, but the Tenth Circuit reversed the district court's order. The United States Supreme Court affirmed the decision of the Tenth Circuit and held that Rule 60(b)(4) did not provide United with a basis for voiding the bankruptcy court's confirmation order. Thus, the bankruptcy court's confirmation order stood. While affirming the Tenth Circuit's decision, the Supreme Court faulted the Tenth Circuit for concluding that unless a creditor timely objects to confirmation a bankruptcy court *must* confirm the plan, even if the plan provides for the discharge of student loan debt without an undue hardship determination. The Supreme Court noted that the Bankruptcy Code "makes plain that bankruptcy courts have the authority—indeed, the obligation—to direct a debtor to conform his plan to the requirements of §§ 1328(a)(2) and 523(a)(8)." [**United Student Aid Funds, Inc. v. Espinosa,** 559 U.S. 260 (2010)]

a. Property

Unless the Chapter 13 plan or the confirmation order provides otherwise, confirmation causes all property of the estate to vest in the debtor "free and clear of any claim or interest of any creditor provided for by the plan." [B.C. § 1327(b), (c)] The debtor may request in the plan a determination of the amount of a creditor's secured claim. With the exception of a secured claim held by a governmental unit, any determination in the plan about the amount of a secured claim binds the holder of that claim, even if the holder files a contrary proof of claim or the debtor schedules the claim, or a claim objection was filed. [Bankruptcy Rule 3015(g), 3012] In order to bind the secured claim holder, however, the plan containing a request to determine the amount of the secured claim must be served on the holder of that claim and any other party designated by the bankruptcy court in the manner required for service of a summons and complaint. [Bankruptcy Rules 3012(b), 7004] Therefore, notice to the secured creditor is critical. If the creditor receives proper notice of the valuation of its claim in the plan and fails to object, then it is bound by confirmation of the Chapter 13 plan.

e.g. **Example:** Debtor owns a vehicle that is not subject to the hanging paragraph following § 1325(a)(9). The car is worth $9,500 but Debtor still owes Car Company $16,000 for the vehicle. Debtor filed for relief under Chapter 13 and filed a plan that proposed stripping off Car Company's lien once Debtor completed plan payments on Car Company's $9,500 secured claim. Car Company received proper notice of Debtor's plan, but failed to object to the lien-stripping provision in the plan. The bankruptcy court confirmed Debtor's plan. Car Company is bound by the terms of the plan. Therefore, when Debtor completes plan payments on the $9,500 secured claim, Car Company no longer has a lien on Debtor's vehicle. [For a pre-BAPCPA case with similar facts, *see In re* **Harvey,** 213 F.3d 318 (7th Cir. 2000)]

(i) Note on Notice

Official Form 113—the Chapter 13 Plan—contains a check box on the first page of the plan to inform secured creditors whether the plan places a "limit on the amount of the secured claim, [ ] which may result in a partial payment or no payment at all to the secured creditor." [Official Form 113 § 1.1] If a district uses its own Local Form Chapter 13 Plan, then the Local Form must include an initial paragraph that includes a statement as to whether the plan "limit[s] the amount of a secured claim based on a valuation of the collateral for the claim." [Bankruptcy Rules 3015(c), 3015.1(c)(2)]

b. Debts

In a Chapter 13 case, confirmation does *not* operate as a discharge of the debtor's debts. [B.C. § 1328]

2. Post-Confirmation Modification

The debtor, the trustee, or an unsecured creditor may request a modification of a plan at any time after it has been confirmed but before all payments have been made. Generally, a request for post-confirmation modification of a plan occurs under circumstances in which the income or expenses of the debtor have *changed materially and unexpectedly.* [B.C. § 1329(a); 8 Collier ¶ 1329.03] The modification cannot result in a plan that provides for payments for a period longer than five years. [B.C. § 1329(c)] Modification may be requested for the following reasons:

a. to *increase or reduce the amount of payments* to a particular class [B.C. § 1329(a)(1)];

b. to provide for a *longer or shorter payout* period [B.C. § 1329(a)(2)];

c. to change the amount to be paid to a creditor to *adjust for any payment obtained* from a third party or from property outside of the plan [B.C. § 1329(a)(3)]; or

d. to *reduce amounts* to be paid under the plan to the *actual amount spent for health insurance* for the debtor and any dependent not covered by health insurance. [B.C. § 1329(a)(4)] The debtor must document the cost of the insurance and show the following:

(i) the expenses are *reasonable and necessary;*

(ii) for a debtor who previously paid for health insurance, the amount is *not materially larger* than what it *previously cost* the debtor for health insurance or to maintain the lapsed policy;

(iii) for a debtor who did not previously have health insurance, the amount is *not materially larger* than the cost for a *similarly situated debtor;*

(iv) the amount is *not otherwise accounted for in determining disposable income* under § 1325(b); and

(v) if any party in interest requests proof that insurance was purchased, the debtor will file such proof.

e.g. **Example:** Married debtors filed for relief under Chapter 13. The bankruptcy court confirmed debtors' plan. Three years later, the Chapter 13 trustee moved to modify the plan under § 1329 to increase debtors' monthly payments by $746. The trustee showed that the debtors' income had increased by $50,000 since plan confirmation. Both the bankruptcy court and the district court concluded that they lacked authority to grant the trustee's motion because § 1329 did not specifically provide for modifications to the plan based on post-confirmation increases in debtors' income. The Seventh Circuit acknowledged that no provision in the Bankruptcy Code specifically authorized a post-confirmation plan modification based on a change in debtors' income. But the court explained that both the purposes of Chapter 13—to allow debtors a fresh start without the need to liquidate assets and to ensure that debtors devoted all disposable income to repaying creditors—and the legislative history of the 1984 amendments, which provided that the trustee or unsecured creditors, not simply the debtor, could seek a post-confirmation modification of the plan supported the trustee's position. The Seventh Circuit held that a bankruptcy court may permit a post-confirmation modification to increase plan payments if the court determines that debtors can afford the increase in payments. [**Germeraad v. Powers,** 826 F.3d 962 (7th Cir. 2016)]

3. Revocation of Confirmation Order

Within *180 days after an order confirming* a Chapter 13 plan has been entered, a party in interest may request that the order be revoked on the ground that it was *procured by fraud.* Revocation is discretionary. If after notice and a hearing the confirmation order is revoked, the court may grant the debtor time to propose and obtain confirmation of a modified plan. Otherwise, the court must convert or dismiss the case under § 1307. [B.C. § 1330]

4. Debtor's Failure to Make Payments

If the debtor fails to make all payments under the plan, a party in interest or the United States trustee may move for dismissal of the case or conversion to Chapter 7. Alternatively, the debtor may request a hardship discharge if the circumstances warrant.

G. Discharge

1. Overview of the Chapter 13 Discharge

The Bankruptcy Code, as originally enacted, provided the Chapter 13 debtor with a broader discharge of debts than the Chapter 7 debtor. But Congress, most recently with the enactment of BAPCPA, has increased the number of debts for which the Chapter 13 debtor does not receive a discharge.

With the exceptions listed below, a standard Chapter 13 discharge includes all debts that are provided for by the plan or that have been disallowed by the court under § 502. Unless the debtor has executed a court-approved written waiver of discharge subsequent to the order for relief, the debtor will be granted a discharge under Chapter 13 after:

a. she has made *all payments* under the plan; and

b. she has *certified* that she has *paid all domestic support obligations* required by *judicial or administrative order, or by statute* and due prior to the date of the certification. [B.C. § 1328(a)]

2. Cases to Which Discharge Does Not Apply

The Code provides that the Chapter 13 debtor will not receive a discharge in certain situations. Make sure to distinguish between this *global denial of discharge* and the nondischargeability of specific debts discussed below.

a. Instructional Course

A Chapter 13 debtor will not receive a discharge if she fails to complete the *instructional course on personal financial management* mandated by § 111 of the Bankruptcy Code. [B.C. §§ 1328(g), 111]

(i)   Exception #1: Incapacity, Disability, Active Military Duty

A debtor need not complete the instructional course if she is unable to do so due to *incapacity, disability,* or *active military duty in a military combat zone.* [B.C. §§ 1328(g)(2), 109(h)(4)]

(ii)   Exception #2: Inadequate Service

A debtor need not complete the instructional course if the United States trustee determines that the instructional courses in the *district in which she resides* are *inadequate* to service individuals in need of such services. [B.C. § 1328(g)(2)]

b.   Prior Bankruptcy Cases

The debtor will not receive a discharge in her current Chapter 13 case if she has received a discharge within a certain time period in a prior bankruptcy case. The time between the filing of the earlier case and the current Chapter 13 case varies depending on the chapter under which the debtor filed her prior case.

(i)   Prior Chapter 7, 11, or 12 Case

The debtor will not receive a discharge in her current Chapter 13 case if she received a discharge in a case filed under *Chapters 7, 11, or 12* during the *four years prior to the filing* of her current Chapter 13 case. [B.C. § 1328(f)(1)] The time period runs from the *filing date* of the prior case to the *filing date* of the current Chapter 13 case.

> **e.g.**   **Example:** Debtor filed for relief under Chapter 7 on July 29, 2002; he received a discharge on February 5, 2003. Debtor filed for relief under Chapter 13 on January 5, 2007. Because Debtor filed his Chapter 7 case more than four years before his later Chapter 13 case, he is entitled to a discharge in the later Chapter 13 case. The four-year time period runs from the *filing date* of the prior Chapter 7 case, not the date on which Debtor received his discharge. [**Carroll v. Sanders (*In re* Sanders),** 551 F.3d 397 (6th Cir. 2008)]

(ii)   Prior Chapter 13 Case

The debtor will not receive a discharge in her current Chapter 13 case if she received a discharge in a case filed under *Chapter 13* during the *two years* prior to the filing of her current Chapter 13 case. [B.C. § 1328(f)(2)] The time period runs from the *filing date* of the prior case to the *filing date* of the current Chapter 13 case.

c.   Exemption Issue Under § 522(q)

The bankruptcy court may not grant a discharge unless it has determined, after notice and a hearing held *no more than 10 days* before the discharge order that there is *no reasonable cause to believe* that:

(i)   the Bankruptcy Code's limitation on state-law exemption rights pursuant to § 522(q)(1) may apply to the debtor [B.C. §§ 1328(h)(1), 522(q)(1)]; *and*

(ii)   there is a pending proceeding in which the debtor may be found guilty of one of the *felonies listed in § 522(q)(1)(A)* or liable for a *debt described in § 522(q)(1)(B).* [B.C. §§ 1328(h)(2), 522(q)(1)]

This provision of the Code should operate to *delay* rather than *permanently deny* the debtor a discharge. The reason for the delay is to allow time to determine whether the debtor's homestead exemption should be limited under § 522(q). "Once that determination is made, and the nonbankruptcy proceeding is no longer pending, the chapter 13 discharge can be granted." [8 Collier ¶ 1328.09]

3. Nondischargeable Debts

The following *debts* are *not dischargeable* in Chapter 13.

a. Long-Term Debts

Debts for which the last payment is due after the due date of the final payment required by the Chapter 13 plan are not dischargeable, if the plan provides for curing any default within a reasonable time and maintaining payments while the case is pending. [B.C. §§ 1328(a)(1), 1322(b)(5)]

b. Certain Taxes

The following types of taxes are not dischargeable:

(i) a tax required to be collected or withheld and for which the debtor is liable in any capacity [B.C. §§ 1328(a)(2), 507(a)(8)(C)];

(ii) a tax for which a *return, or equivalent report or notice,* if required, was *not filed or given or* was filed or given but *after the date on which it was due and* within the *two year-period prior to filing* of the bankruptcy petition [B.C. §§ 1328(a)(2), 523(a)(1)(B)]; and

(iii) a tax for which the debtor either made a *fraudulent return or willfully attempted* to *evade or defeat* the tax. [B.C. §§ 1328(a)(2), 523(a)(1)(C)]

c. Fraud

Debts for money, property, services, or extensions, renewals, or refinancing of credit obtained by *fraud, consumer debts* exceeding *$725* incurred within *90 days* of bankruptcy for *luxury goods,* or *cash advances* exceeding *$1,000* obtained within *70 days* of bankruptcy are not dischargeable. [B.C. §§ 1328(a)(2), 523(a)(2)]

d. Unscheduled Debts

Debts that the debtor did not *list or schedule* in time for the creditor to *timely file a proof of claim* are not dischargeable, unless the creditor had *notice or actual knowledge* in time to make a timely filing. [B.C. § 523(a)(3)(A)]

e. Section 523(a)(2), (4), and (6)

Debts that are potentially nondischargeable under *§ 523(a)(2), (4), or (6),* and that the debtor neither *listed nor scheduled* in time for the creditor to *timely file a proof of claim* and *timely request a determination of dischargeability* are not dischargeable, unless the creditor had *notice or actual knowledge* in time to make a timely filing. [B.C. § 523(a)(3)(B)]

f. Embezzlement

Debts owed for *embezzlement, larceny,* or *fraud or defalcation in a fiduciary capacity* are not dischargeable. [B.C. § 523(a)(4)]

g. Domestic Support Obligations

Domestic support obligations are not dischargeable. [B.C. §§ 1328(a)(2), 523(a)(5)] *Debts for support* owed under state law to a *state or municipality* that are enforceable under the Social Security Act are not dischargeable. [42 U.S.C. § 656(b)]

h. Student Loans

Unless excepting the debt from discharge will constitute an ***undue hardship*** on the debtor and her dependents, ***student loan debt*** is nondischargeable. [B.C. §§ 1328(a)(2), 523(a)(8)] ***Health Education Assistance Loans*** ("HEAL"), in cases in which the three conditions for discharge required by the applicable federal nonbankruptcy statute have not been satisfied also are not dischargeable. [42 U.S.C. § 292f(g); **United States v. Beams,** 2008 WL 1774423 (S.D. Ind. 2008) (noting that discharge is even more difficult than for general student loans because the debtor must satisfy "the more stringent standard of unconscionability")]

i. Certain Personal Injury Debts

Liability for death or personal injury caused by the debtor's operation of a ***motor vehicle, vessel, or aircraft*** while ***intoxicated*** from using ***alcohol, drugs, or another substance*** is not dischargeable. [B.C. §§ 1328(a)(2), 523(a)(9)]

j. Restitution

A debt for ***restitution,*** or a ***criminal fine,*** that is included in the debtor's sentence for ***conviction of a crime*** is not dischargeable. [B.C. § 1328(a)(3)] A debt for ***restitution*** or ***damages awarded in a civil action*** against the debtor as a result of ***willful*** or ***malicious injury*** that caused ***death or personal injury*** also is nondischargeable. [B.C. § 1328(a)(4)]

k. Certain Consumer Debts

Post-petition consumer debts for property or services necessary for the debtor to perform the plan are not dischargeable, if the corresponding claims were allowed, and if the trustee's prior approval to incur the debt was practicable but was not obtained. [B.C. §§ 1328(d), 1305(a)(2)]

(i) Distinguish § 523(a)

Only the categories of debts described above are nondischargeable. Any other debts that would be nondischargeable under the general dischargeability provisions of § 523(a) ***are discharged*** by a standard Chapter 13 discharge.

EXAM TIP

If you encounter an exam question that asks you to decide whether the debtor should file for relief under Chapter 7 or Chapter 13, one factor to consider is the difference in the ***kinds of debts that can be discharged*** under each chapter.

---

4. Hardship Discharge

a. Requirements

If the debtor has not made all payments under the plan, the court, after notice and a hearing, may award a hardship discharge if the following three conditions exist:

(i) ***the reason for the debtor's failure*** to complete the payments under the plan is not one for which, in fairness, she should be held accountable [B.C. § 1328(b)(1)];

(ii) ***each unsecured creditor holding an allowed claim has received property*** under the plan, having a present value as of the effective date of the plan, of not less than the amount that he would have received for his claim in a case under Chapter 7 if the estate had been liquidated (i.e., the "best interests of creditors test") [B.C. § 1328(b)(2)]; and

(iii) *modification of the plan is not practicable.* [B.C. § 1328(b)(3)]

b. Debts Discharged in Hardship Case

A Chapter 13 hardship discharge includes the unsecured debts that discharged under a standard Chapter 13 discharge, *except* the following:

(i) debts that are *nondischargeable under § 523(a)* [B.C. § 1328(c)(2)];

(ii) *Health Education Assistance Loans ("HEAL")* not meeting the three conditions for discharge under the applicable federal nonbankruptcy statute;

(iii) *long-term debts* provided for under the *cure provision of Code § 1322(b)(5)* [B.C. § 1328(c)(1)];

(iv) *post-petition consumer debts for property or services necessary for the debtor to perform the plan,* if the corresponding claims were allowed, and if the trustee's prior approval to incur the debt was practicable but was not obtained. [B.C. §§ 1328(d), 1305(a)(2)]

5. Revocation of Discharge

The court may revoke a Chapter 13 discharge that was *obtained by the debtor's fraud* if the party in interest seeking the revocation *did not discover* the fraud until *after the discharge* was awarded. The party seeking revocation must make its request for revocation no later than *one year* from the *date the discharge was granted.* Notice and a hearing are required. [B.C. § 1328(e)]

GILBERT

CHECKLIST OF NONDISCHARGEABLE DEBTS UNDER CHAPTER 13

THE FOLLOWING IS A CHECKLIST OF THE DEBTS THAT ARE NOT DISCHARGEABLE UNDER CHAPTER 13:

STANDARD DISCHARGE

☑ *Long-term debts* if the plan provides for curing any default within a reasonable time and maintaining payments during the case, with the final payment due after the due date of the final payment required by the plan

☑ A *tax* required to be collected or withheld and for which the debtor is liable in any capacity

☑ A *tax* for which a *return, or equivalent report or notice,* if required, was *not filed or given* or was filed or given but *after the date on which it was due* and within the *two year-period prior to filing for bankruptcy*

☑ A *tax* for which the debtor either made a *fraudulent return or willfully attempted to evade or defeat* the tax

☑ Debts for money, property, services, or extensions, renewals, or refinancing of credit obtained by *fraud, consumer debts* exceeding *$725* incurred within *90 days* of bankruptcy for *luxury goods,* or *cash advances* exceeding *$1,000* obtained within *70 days* of bankruptcy

☑ Debts that the debtor did not **list or schedule** in time for the creditor to **timely file a proof of claim,** unless the creditor had **notice or actual knowledge** in time to make a timely filing

☑ Debts that are potentially nondischargeable pursuant to **§ 523(a)(2), (4), or (6)** that the debtor neither **listed nor scheduled** in time for the creditor to **timely file a proof of claim** and **timely request a determination of dischargeability,** unless the creditor had **notice or actual knowledge** in time to make a timely filing

☑ Debts owed for **embezzlement, larceny,** or **fraud or defalcation in a fiduciary capacity**

☑ **Domestic support obligations** and **debts for support** owed under state law to a state or municipality that are enforceable under the Social Security Act

☑ **Student loans** absent undue hardship for the debtor and her dependents

☑ **Health Education Assistance Loans** ("HEAL") for which debtor fails to satisfy the discharge requirements of 42 U.S.C. § 292f(g)

☑ Debts **for death or personal injury** caused by the debtor's operation of a **motor vehicle, vessel, or aircraft** while **intoxicated** from using **alcohol, drugs, or another substance**

☑ **Restitution or a criminal fine** that is included in the debtor's sentence upon conviction of a crime

☑ **Restitution** or **damages awarded in a civil action** against the debtor as a result of **willful** or **malicious injury** that caused **death or personal injury**

☑ **Post-petition consumer debts for property or services necessary for the debtor to perform the plan,** if the corresponding claims were allowed, and if the trustee's prior approval to incur the debt was practicable but was not obtained

HARDSHIP DISCHARGE

☑ **Long-term debts** if the plan provides for curing any default within a reasonable time and maintaining payments during the case, with the final payment due after the due date of the final payment required by the plan

☑ **All debts that are nondischargeable under § 523(a)**

☑ **Health Education Assistance Loans** ("HEAL") for which debtor fails to satisfy the discharge requirements of 42 U.S.C. § 292f(g)

☑ **Post-petition consumer debts for property or services necessary for the debtor to perform the plan,** if the corresponding claims were allowed, and if the trustee's prior approval to incur the debt was practicable but was not obtained

Review Questions
and Answers

Review Questions: Short Answer

CHAPTER ONE. INTRODUCTION

1. Debtor files for relief under Chapter 7 on February 1, 2018. Debtor's monthly income varies, because she works on commission. Debtor's gross income in 2018 was $34,000. Debtor earned $3,000 in August and September of 2017, $2,500 in October, $3,500 in November, $4,000 in December of 2017, and $2,000 in January of 2018. Is Debtor's current monthly income $2,833.33?

2. Debtor files for relief under Chapter 7. Prior to bankruptcy, Acme performed services for Debtor, but Debtor has not yet paid Acme. Debtor claims that Acme did not perform according to the terms of the parties' contract and, thus, Debtor does not owe Acme for its work. Does Acme have a claim in Debtor's Chapter 7 case?

3. Does the United States trustee program operate in all 94 judicial districts in the United States?

4. Can a bankruptcy petition preparer offer a potential debtor legal advice?

CHAPTER TWO. JURISDICTION AND PROCEDURE; SOVEREIGN IMMUNITY

5. Several months before bankruptcy, Debtor was involved in an automobile accident in which Victim, the driver of the other car, was seriously injured when Debtor failed to stop at a red light. Victim files a claim for personal injury in Debtor's bankruptcy case. Will Victim's claim be tried in the bankruptcy court?

6. Do bankruptcy judges have lifetime tenure?

7. Acme Company files for relief under Chapter 11. The same day, Zed Corporation, an affiliate of Acme's, also files a Chapter 11 petition. The bankruptcy court grants Acme's motion for joint administration of its case with Zed Corporation. Does the order for joint administration mean that Acme's and Zed's assets, debts, and causes of action are pooled?

8. Does the United States district court have original and exclusive jurisdiction over bankruptcy cases?

9. Can the bankruptcy court enter a final judgment or order in a core proceeding?

10. Debtor files for relief under Chapter 11 and Creditor files an adversary proceeding complaint to determine the priority of certain security interests in a commercial building owned by Debtor. Creditor's complaint included claims against Debtor and the County Clerk, whom Creditor alleged had improperly indexed Creditor's deed of trust. After the bankruptcy court dismissed several counts of Creditor's complaint, Creditor moved to sever and withdraw the reference of its claims against County Clerk. Must the reference be withdrawn? _____

11. Debtor obtained a divorce and the state court ordered him to pay alimony to his wife. Debtor failed to make the payments, and the state court eventually awarded Debtor's ex-wife more than $1 million in past-due payments and interest. Debtor then filed for bankruptcy. The bankruptcy court dismissed Debtor's bankruptcy case, concluding that it was simply a two-party dispute between Debtor and his ex-wife and served no bankruptcy purpose. The bankruptcy court found that the state court was the more appropriate forum for resolving family law issues, such as those presented in the case. Is the bankruptcy court's decision correct? _____

12. Debtor operates his law practice in Kansas City, Missouri, which is in Missouri's Western District, but Debtor maintains his residence and is domiciled in the State of Kansas. Debtor filed for bankruptcy in the Western District of Missouri. Debtor's principal assets are located in Kansas, but his principal place of business (his law practice) is located in the Western District of Missouri. Creditor files a motion to dismiss the case for improper venue. Will the bankruptcy court grant Creditor's motion? _____

13. Debtor is in default on an installment note, and Creditor files a motion requesting relief from the automatic stay in order to foreclose on certain collateral securing the note. The bankruptcy court denies relief from the stay. Can Creditor appeal the decision? _____

14. Debtor filed for relief under Chapter 13 and proposed a plan that provided for payment of Creditor's claim. Creditor objected to its treatment under Debtor's plan. The bankruptcy court denied confirmation of the plan and ordered Debtor to propose a new plan. Can the Debtor immediately appeal the bankruptcy court's order denying confirmation of her plan? _____

CHAPTER THREE. COMMENCEMENT AND ADMINISTRATION

15. Debtor, a solvent individual residing in Maryland, is undergoing financial difficulties and is thinking about filing a voluntary bankruptcy petition. Will the fact that she is not insolvent preclude Debtor from being eligible for relief under the Bankruptcy Code? _____

16. Debtor, an individual, filed for relief under Chapter 7. Two weeks prior to filing for bankruptcy, Debtor obtained credit counseling over the phone from one of the nonprofit budget and credit counseling service on the list approved by the United States trustee. Has the Debtor satisfied the Code's credit counseling requirement? _____

17. In January, Debtor, an individual, files a Chapter 13 petition, which is dismissed in March because of Debtor's intentional failure to obey certain orders of the bankruptcy court. In June, Debtor seeks to file another Chapter 13 petition. Is she eligible? _____

18. Debtor is a consumer. She files for relief under Chapter 11. Is Debtor eligible for relief under Chapter 11? _____

19. Debtor, who is an accountant, inherited his family's farm several years ago when his parents passed away. Debtor's aggregate noncontingent, liquidated debts are $1 million. Debtor does weekend farming so only 10–20% of his gross income each year comes from his weekend farming operation. Is Debtor eligible to file for relief under Chapter 12? _____

20. Debtor is employed and earns $3,000 per week. She owes $500,000 in unsecured debts and $600,000 in secured debts. Is she eligible for relief under Chapter 13? _____

21. Debtor owes $90,000 in unsecured debts, owes no secured debts, and earns a salary of $2,000 per week. Three creditors file an involuntary Chapter 13 petition against Debtor. If Debtor is generally not paying his debts as they become due, will an order for relief be entered? _____

22. Debtor is engaged in a multistate manufacturing business and is indebted to hundreds of creditors. Since Debtor very consistently is not paying its debts as they become due, three creditors holding unsecured claims totaling $3,000 file an involuntary petition against Debtor. Will an order for relief be entered? _____

23. Chapter 7 Debtor owes a $10,000 consumer loan that is secured by her car. Creditor wants to know whether Debtor plans to retain the car or surrender it. Is Debtor required to disclose her intention? _____

24. May the bankruptcy court waive a debtor's attendance at the § 341 meeting? _____

25. Debtor files for relief under Chapter 7. Debtor converts her case to Chapter 13. Must Debtor file her Chapter 13 plan within 14 days of conversion to Chapter 13? _____

26. Debtor files for relief under Chapter 13. She files some of her schedules, but fails to file (i) copies of all her pay stubs for the 60-day period prior to bankruptcy, (ii) a statement of financial affairs, and (iii) a statement of her monthly income. On Day 46 of her bankruptcy case, is Debtor's bankruptcy case automatically dismissed?

_____

CHAPTER FOUR. CASE ADMINISTRATION: OFFICERS OF THE ESTATE

27. An involuntary Chapter 11 petition is filed against Debtor Corporation, a nationwide marketing firm, and an order for relief is entered in the case. Because of the incompetence of current management, Trustee is appointed under § 1104. Does Trustee have the authority to operate the Debtor's business?

_____

28. Is a trustee normally appointed in a Chapter 11 case?

_____

29. Acme Corporation files for relief under Chapter 11. There are reasonable grounds to suspect that current members of Acme's board and the CEO have engaged in actual fraud in managing Acme. Must the United States trustee move for appointment of a Chapter 11 trustee?

_____

30. Debtor files for relief under Chapter 7. The Chapter 7 trustee ("Trustee") sells estate property to Buyer. After sale to Buyer, Trustee discovers that Debtor was not the sole owner of the property. Buyer sues Trustee. Is Trustee personally liable for breach of her duties?

_____

31. Assume the same facts as in Question 29, above. Does Trustee have the authority to waive Debtor Corporation's attorney-client privilege concerning communications made by the former officers and directors to Debtor Corporation's attorney prior to bankruptcy?

_____

32. Debtor files a voluntary Chapter 11 petition, and allegations of fraud and dishonesty are made against Debtor's management. If the court does not order the appointment of a trustee, are there any means by which the charges against Debtor's management can be investigated appropriately?

_____

33. Debtor files a voluntary Chapter 7 petition, and a trustee is appointed. Because of the complicated financial and legal issues in the case, the trustee wants to hire an attorney and an accountant. Should court approval of their employment be obtained before any professional services are rendered?

_____

34. Acme Health Care Company operates an assisted living facility for the elderly. Acme files for relief under Chapter 11. Must the bankruptcy court order the appointment of a patient care ombudsman?

_____

35. Debtor is an individual and hires Lawyer to file her Chapter 7 petition. Is Lawyer entitled to have her fees paid from Debtor's Chapter 7 estate?

CHAPTER FIVE. THE BANKRUPTCY ESTATE

36. Debtor, an individual, files a Chapter 7 petition. Are the wages that Debtor earns post-petition included in property of the estate?

37. Lessee leases 10 computers from Lessor, with the term of the lease beginning on January 1 and ending on December 31. The lease contains a provision that causes a termination of the lease and a forfeiture of Lessee's interest in the computers if and when Lessee becomes a debtor in a case under the Bankruptcy Code. On June 1, Lessee files a voluntary Chapter 11 petition. Is Lessee's leasehold interest in the computers included in property of the estate?

38. Debtor files for relief under Chapter 7. She has worked for Acme Company for 25 years and has vested in the company's ERISA-qualified pension plan. Are the monies in Debtor's pension plan part of her bankruptcy estate?

39. Debtor files for relief under Chapter 13. Shortly before bankruptcy, Big Bank lawfully repossessed Debtor's car. Big Bank had a perfected security interest in the vehicle, and Debtor had missed several monthly payments on the car. Debtor's attorney notified Big Bank of Debtor's bankruptcy filing, but Big Bank did not return the vehicle; it retained it. Does Big Bank's retention of Debtor's car violate the automatic stay?

40. Debtor, who owes $10,000 to Bank, files for relief under Chapter 7. Bank receives notice of the filing. Debtor has $5,000 in an account with Bank. Can Bank temporarily freeze the $5,000 in Debtor's account without being in violation of the automatic stay?

41. Acme Company filed for relief under Chapter 11. At the time of bankruptcy filing, Bank had an account at Big Bank with a balance of $50,000. Prior to bankruptcy, Trade Creditor had performed services for Acme worth $40,000. Acme failed to pay Trade Creditor. Two months prior to Acme's bankruptcy filing Big Bank purchased Trade Creditor's claim for $25,000. Does Big Bank have a right of setoff against Acme?

42. Debtor Company filed for relief under Chapter 11. Big Bank is one of Debtor's secured creditors. A year ago, Big Bank made a working capital loan to Debtor, and Debtor granted Big Bank a security interest in its inventory, whether now owned or hereafter acquired. Big Bank properly perfected its security interest. After filing for bankruptcy, Debtor purchased new inventory for its business. Does Big Bank's security interest attach to the new inventory?

CHAPTER SIX. THE BANKRUPTCY ESTATE: THE TRUSTEE'S AVOIDING POWERS

43. Debtor purchases office equipment on credit, granting Seller a security interest in the equipment. Six months later, Debtor files a Chapter 7 petition and Seller has failed to perfect his security interest. Can Trustee avoid Seller's security interest in the equipment?

_____

44. Every month for the past 10 years, Debtor has purchased goods on credit from Supplier, always remitting full payment within 30 days after receipt of the goods, in accordance with the agreement between the parties and consistent with the norm in Supplier's industry. If Debtor receives goods from Supplier on June 1, pays for them in full on July 1 in the ordinary course of business, and files a Chapter 7 petition on August 1, can the bankruptcy trustee avoid the payment to Supplier as a preferential transfer?

_____

45. Debtor, an individual, has suffered numerous financial reverses and decides to file a voluntary Chapter 7 petition. Ten days before filing, Debtor forms a corporation solely for the purpose of sheltering assets that otherwise would be used to satisfy creditors. On the day before bankruptcy, Debtor transfers her $250,000 house to the corporation for no consideration. Is the transfer voidable by the bankruptcy trustee?

_____

46. Debtor is in default to Creditor on a $40,000 debt, and Creditor forecloses on its collateral, a building. The foreclosure sale occurs on February 1, when Debtor is insolvent. The sale has been advertised appropriately and is conducted regularly and in compliance with "all the requirements of the state's foreclosure law," proper notice has been given, and there is no evidence of any collusion. Creditor purchases the building for a price of $40,000. The fair market value of the building is $90,000. On July 1, Debtor files a Chapter 7 petition. Is the transfer voidable by the bankruptcy trustee?

_____

47. On March 1, Debtor buys and takes possession of new office furniture, while granting Seller a purchase-money security interest in the furniture. On March 5, Debtor files a voluntary Chapter 7 petition. Applicable state law provides that a purchase-money security interest perfected within 20 days after the debtor receives possession of the collateral has priority over an intervening lien creditor. [U.C.C. § 9–317(e)] On March 8, Seller perfects its security interest.

    a. Will Seller's security interest have priority over the bankruptcy trustee's rights and avoiding powers under the strong arm clause?

    _____

    b. Does Seller's post-petition perfection of its security interest violate the automatic stay?

    _____

48. Debtor purchases goods on credit from Seller and is insolvent when she receives the merchandise on June 1. The sale was in the ordinary course of the Seller's business. On June 2, Debtor files a voluntary bankruptcy petition. Can Seller reclaim the goods from Debtor? _____

49. A year prior to bankruptcy, Debtor borrowed $20,000 from Friend. As Debtor's financial situation deteriorated, he realized that he had to file for bankruptcy. Prior to filing, Debtor scraped together $1,000 and paid Friend $1,000 of the $20,000 that he still owed Friend. Debtor then filed for relief under Chapter 7. Debtor's unsecured creditors will receive a 5% dividend in the bankruptcy case. Is the payment to Friend a preference? _____

50. A month before filing for bankruptcy, Debtor, who is insolvent, transfers property to Amy for less than reasonably equivalent value. Amy sells the property to Ben, who takes in good faith, pays fair value for the property, and is unaware of the transaction between Amy and Debtor. Debtor files for bankruptcy. Can the trustee recover the property from Ben? _____

CHAPTER SEVEN. CLAIMS OF CREDITORS

51. Debtor, an insolvent corporation, files a Chapter 7 petition. Creditor holds an unsecured claim evidenced by a promissory note bearing an interest rate of 10%. Is Creditor entitled to post-petition interest on his claim? _____

52. Debtor files a Chapter 11 petition, and thousands of tort victims file unliquidated personal injury claims arising from certain defective products sold by Debtor. May the bankruptcy court estimate the claims for the purpose of allowance? _____

53. Debtor files a Chapter 7 petition. She owes Bank $100,000 pursuant to an 8% mortgage note secured by land that has a fair market value of $90,000. Is Bank's claim fully secured? _____

54. Assume the same facts as in Question 53, above, except that Bank has a $100,000 first mortgage on the land and Bank Two has a $50,000 second mortgage on the land. May Debtor strip off Bank Two's mortgage on the land? _____

55. Assume the same facts as in Question 53 above, except that the value of the land is $120,000. Is Bank entitled to post-petition interest on its claim? _____

56. Debtor files a Chapter 11 petition in an attempt to reorganize its business. Will the wages to be paid to its employees for post-petition services be classified as administrative expenses in the case? _____

57. Debtor files a Chapter 7 petition and owes $50,000 in unsecured pre-petition federal income taxes for the taxable year preceding bankruptcy. Will the tax claim be treated as a general unsecured claim? _____

58. Debtor files a Chapter 11 petition. Creditor's claim is fully secured by a lien on Debtor's equipment, which is depreciating rapidly. Creditor requests and is denied relief from the automatic stay, but the court orders Debtor to provide Creditor with an additional lien on other property as adequate protection. If the additional lien ultimately proves to be deficient, causing Creditor to be undersecured to the extent of $20,000, will the undersecured portion of Creditor's claim be treated as a general unsecured claim? _____

59. Debtor files a Chapter 7 petition. Debtor has $8,000 in assets to pay her unsecured priority and general unsecured creditors. Administrative expenses are $4,000. Debtor owes property taxes of $2,000 for the year prior to the date of filing her bankruptcy petition. She also owes $6,000 in federal income taxes for the two years prior to filing her bankruptcy petition. Unsecured creditors' claims total $30,000. Will the unsecured creditors receive a dividend in Debtor's bankruptcy case? _____

60. Debtor files for relief under Chapter 7. Debtor owes Creditor $100,000, which is secured by a security interest on $110,000 worth of Debtor's property.

   a. Must Creditor file a proof of claim in order to have an allowed claim? _____

   b. Would the answer change if Debtor had filed for relief under Chapter 11? _____

61. If Creditor in Question 60 above fails to file a proof of claim in Debtor's Chapter 7 case, is Creditor's security interest on Debtor's property void? _____

62. Acme Company signed a five-year lease with Landlord at a monthly rental of $8,000. Acme repudiates the lease and immediately files for bankruptcy. At the time of bankruptcy filing, there are four years remaining on the lease, and Acme is current on rent. Landlord is able to re-rent the property but for only $5,000 per month. Landlord files a claim for $144,000 (48 months x $3,000 monthly rent differential). Will Landlord's claim be allowed for $144,000? _____

CHAPTER EIGHT. DEBTOR'S EXEMPTIONS

63. Husband and Wife file a joint Chapter 7 petition. If the State in which Husband and Wife file their joint petition has not opted out of the federal exemption scheme, may Husband elect the federal exemptions while Wife elects the state exemptions? _____

64. Debtor files a Chapter 7 petition. Prior to bankruptcy, Debtor had bought household goods on credit, granting to Seller a purchase-money security interest in all of the items purchased. Can Debtor avoid Seller's security interest, under Bankruptcy Code § 522(f), to the extent that it impairs an exemption? _____

65. Debtor files a Chapter 7 petition. Prior to bankruptcy, Debtor had purchased a home financed by Bank Two, which holds the mortgage on the property. Can Debtor avoid Bank Two's mortgage, under Bankruptcy Code § 522(f), to the extent that it impairs an exemption? _____

66. Husband and Wife ("Debtors") file a joint petition for relief under Chapter 7. Debtors own a home valued at $150,000. Debtors borrowed the money to purchase the home from Big Bank, which holds the mortgage. The outstanding balance on the loan is $110,000. If Debtors use the federal exemptions, can they exempt all the equity in their home? _____

67. Debtor files for relief under Chapter 7 on February 1, 2019, in the Eastern District of Michigan. Debtor grew up in Toledo, Ohio, but changed his domicile to Novi, Michigan, on June 30, 2018. If Debtor had planned on taking state law exemptions, do Michigan's exemptions apply in Debtor's Chapter 7 case? _____

68. Does the "mansion loophole" exception to exemptions in § 522(p) and (q) apply to debtors in opt-out states? _____

69. Debtor files for relief under Chapter 7. Prior to filing for bankruptcy, Debtor inherited her mother's Roth IRA. Debtor wants to exempt the monies in the Roth IRA under § 522(b)(3)(C). Can she do so? _____

70. Debtor, an individual, files for relief under Chapter 7. Debtor owns a small plot of land worth about $10,000. Pre-petition, Debtor took out a small loan of $3,000 from Bank in order to do some work on the land before building a small home on the plot. Can Debtor redeem the property from Bank's lien by paying Bank $3,000? _____

CHAPTER NINE. DISCHARGE OF INDEBTEDNESS

71. Debtor, an individual, files a *Chapter 7* petition. Would the following debts be dischargeable in his case?

    a. A judgment for $1,500 arising from Debtor's fraudulent sale of an automobile to his neighbor. _____

    b. A debt for $5,000, which Debtor borrowed from Creditor six months prior to bankruptcy. Debtor fails to list or schedule the debt, and Creditor has neither notice nor actual knowledge of the bankruptcy case and, thus, is unable to timely file a proof of claim. _____

c. A debt owed for misappropriation of $50,000 in Debtor's capacity as a bank officer. (Assume that the act did not constitute larceny or embezzlement.) _____

d. A debt for $25,000 that was intended to constitute a property settlement arising out of a separation agreement with Debtor's first spouse. _____

e. A debt in the amount of $10,000 for alimony owed to Debtor's second spouse, arising out of a separation and property settlement agreement. _____

72. Debtor owes Creditor $5,000 and files a Chapter 7 petition. All of her debts are discharged (including the debt owed to Creditor), and she does not reaffirm any debts. May Debtor voluntarily repay the debt owed to Creditor following her discharge in bankruptcy? _____

73. Debtor, an individual, desires to reaffirm a consumer debt secured by personal property. All of the elements of an enforceable reaffirmation agreement are satisfied, and Debtor is represented by an attorney during the negotiation of the agreement. Is it necessary to obtain independent court approval of the agreement? _____

74. Debtor files a Chapter 7 petition and does not desire to reaffirm any of his debts. Is the court required to hold a discharge hearing? _____

75. Is post-petition interest on a nondischargeable tax debt also not dischargeable? _____

76. Debtor files for relief under Chapter 13. Prior to bankruptcy, Neighbor obtained a judgment for damages against Debtor for willful and malicious injury to Neighbor's property. Is Neighbor's debt for damages dischargeable in Debtor's bankruptcy case? _____

77. Debtor filed for relief under Chapter 11. Prior to bankruptcy, Creditor had obtained a fraud judgment against Debtor. Creditor filed an adversary proceeding in Debtor's bankruptcy case and alleged that its claim against Debtor for fraud was not dischargeable under § 523(a). Debtor argued that collateral estoppel did not apply to the adversary proceeding, because the standard of proof in the state court trial was preponderance of the evidence while § 523 required proof by clear and convincing evidence. Is Debtor correct? _____

78. Debtor borrowed $10,000 from Bank. Mother signed as guarantor on the loan. Debtor filed for relief under Chapter 7 and obtained a discharge of her debts, including the $10,000 debt owed to Bank. Is Mother's debt to Bank also discharged? _____

CHAPTER TEN. ADMINISTRATIVE POWERS: THE AUTOMATIC STAY

79. Debtor files a voluntary Chapter 7 petition. Would the following post-petition actions be enjoined by the automatic stay? In each instance, assume that the non-debtor party has received notice of Debtor's bankruptcy filing. _____

    a. Creditor's commencement of a lawsuit against Debtor in a state court to recover a pre-petition claim. _____

    b. Bank's repossession of Debtor's automobile, which constitutes collateral securing Bank's pre-petition claim. _____

    c. Telephone calls and letters from Appliance Store's credit department demanding payment of a pre-petition claim. _____

    d. Continuation of an administrative proceeding by the National Labor Relations Board to determine whether Debtor's pre-petition termination of a collective bargaining agreement constituted an unfair labor practice. _____

80. Debtor files a Chapter 7 petition and desires to retain possession of her car, which has a fair market value of $5,000. The car was financed by Bank, which holds a purchase-money security interest in the car. The debt owed to Bank is $7,000. Debtor is current on her car payments. Can Debtor retain possession of the car without redeeming it or reaffirming the debt? _____

81. Debtor files a Chapter 7 petition. Creditor requests relief from the automatic stay, under § 362(d)(2), to foreclose on certain real property securing a pre-petition debt that is in default. The debt is $50,000, and the collateral has a fair market value of $25,000. Will the court grant relief from the stay? _____

82. Debtor filed for relief under Chapter 13. The IRS filed a proof of claim in Debtor's case for $20,000 that Debtor owed in pre-petition federal income taxes. Debtor was entitled to a $2,000 tax refund for the prior, pre-petition tax year, but the IRS set off that refund against Debtor's $20,000 pre-petition tax liability. Debtor claims that the IRS violated the automatic stay. Is he correct? _____

83. Debtor files a Chapter 7 petition. Before filing for bankruptcy, Debtor passed a bad check and the local prosecutor had begun criminal proceedings against Debtor. Can the state court criminal proceeding on the bad check charge continue post-petition? _____

84. Debtor filed for relief under Chapter 7. Prior to bankruptcy, Landlord had obtained a judgment of possession against Debtor for her failure to pay rent. Debtor filed for bankruptcy before the actual eviction and currently resides in the residential apartment. State law gives Debtor the right to cure the entire monetary default. When Debtor filed for bankruptcy, she also filed a certification under penalty of perjury that she had the right to cure the default and deposited with the court clerk the rent due for the 30 days following the date she filed her bankruptcy petition. Debtor served the certification on Landlord. Can Landlord proceed with eviction of Debtor?

85. Debtor, a small business, files for relief under Chapter 11. This is Debtor's second bankruptcy filing. Debtor's prior Chapter 11 small business case was filed two years ago and dismissed one year ago. Does the automatic stay apply in Debtor's current small business case?

CHAPTER ELEVEN. ADMINISTRATIVE POWERS: §§ 363–366

86. Debtor owes Creditor $100,000 pursuant to a mortgage note secured by a building that has a fair market value of $90,000. Creditor seeks relief from the automatic stay, under § 362(d)(1), alleging that his interest in the building is not adequately protected unless he receives interest payments for the delay caused by the automatic stay in exercising his right to foreclose on the building and reinvest the proceeds. Is Creditor entitled to interest payments on his collateral as adequate protection?

87. Debtor Corporation files a Chapter 7 petition and Trustee seeks to sell the company's factory building to a willing buyer. Is a hearing required regarding the proposed sale?

88. Debtor files a Chapter 11 petition and has $100,000 on deposit in a checking account at Bank, which serves as collateral for a debt owed to Secured Creditor. May Debtor use the money in the account in the ordinary course of business?

89. Debtor files for relief under Chapter 11. Debtor owns a piece of land worth $200,000. Debtor borrowed against the land and owes $250,000 to various banks; Debtor used the land as collateral for the loans. Bank1 is first in line, and is owed $100,000. Bank2 has a second mortgage on the property, and is owed $75,000. Bank3 has a third mortgage on the land, and also is owed $75,000. Bank1 files a motion to lift the automatic stay for cause under § 362(d)(1), claiming that its interest in the land is not adequately protected. Will the court grant Bank1's motion?

90. Debtor files a Chapter 11 petition and is unable to obtain unsecured post-petition financing without offering more than an administrative expense priority. May the court authorize an unsecured loan from Bank that will have priority over all administrative expense claims in the case, as well as over any super-priority administrative expense claims that might result from the failure of adequate protection? _____

91. Acme Company files for relief under Chapter 11. Acme's customer list is valuable property that contains personally identifiable information, e.g., names, mailing and e-mail addresses, social security numbers. At the time of bankruptcy, Acme had in place a policy prohibiting the transfer of such personally identifiable information to anyone not affiliated with Acme Company. Acme, as debtor in possession, wants to sell the list, but the sale is not consistent with Acme's policy. Can Acme do so? _____

92. Debtor leases industrial equipment pursuant to a lease that begins on January 1 and ends on December 31. After defaulting on the payments due under the lease for June, July, and August, Debtor files a Chapter 11 petition on August 15. May Debtor (now the debtor in possession) assume the lease? _____

93. On October 1, Debtor, a professional singer, enters into a binding agreement with Variety, Inc. to perform in a series of concerts to be held the following summer. Her compensation will be $25,000. On March 1, Debtor files a voluntary Chapter 11 petition and a trustee is appointed for cause. May the trustee assume the contract? _____

94. Debtor is the tenant of certain nonresidential real property and has defaulted on the monthly rental payments for six consecutive months. Landlord terminates the lease in accordance with terms of the agreement and notifies Debtor in writing. Under applicable state law, all steps necessary to terminate the lease have occurred, and there is no state anti-forfeiture law under which the termination could be reversed. Debtor then files a Chapter 11 petition. Can Debtor (now debtor in possession) assume the lease? _____

95. Debtor is the lessee under an unexpired lease of residential real property, and she files a voluntary Chapter 11 petition. May she assume the lease three months after the order for relief if the court has not yet confirmed a Chapter 11 plan? _____

CHAPTER TWELVE. CHAPTER 7—LIQUIDATION

96. Debtor files a voluntary Chapter 7 petition on July 1. Debtor works several jobs, so her monthly income varies. For the months of January and February, Debtor earned $2,500 each month. In March, Debtor earned $2,700, while in April and May she earned $2,000 each month. In June, Debtor earned $3,500. Debtor resides in a state with an annual median income of $30,000. Is Debtor an above-median income debtor? _____

97. Debtor files a voluntary Chapter 7 petition. She earns $24,000 per year; the median annual income in her state is $40,000. Does Debtor qualify for relief under Chapter 7? _____

98. Same facts as Question 97 above, except Debtor now earns $48,000 per year. Does Debtor's filing for relief under Chapter 7 create a presumption of abuse? _____

99. Debtor files a voluntary Chapter 7 petition. She earns $4,000 each month and has done so for the past two years. The median state income is $40,000 per year. Debtor's monthly means test expenses total $3,900. Does Debtor's filing for relief under Chapter 7 create a presumption of abuse? _____

100. Same facts as Question 99 above, except Debtor's monthly means test expenses total $3,800, and her total unsecured debt equals $40,000. Does Debtor's filing for relief under Chapter 7 create a presumption of abuse? _____

101. Debtor files a voluntary Chapter 7 petition in the bankruptcy court for the Eastern District of Michigan. Debtor is an above-median income debtor. She owns a 2012 Honda Accord that is paid off. Can Debtor include the national standard for owning a vehicle in her monthly means test expenses? _____

102. Creditor is a general unsecured creditor of Debtor, who recently filed for relief under Chapter 7. After payment is made to priority unsecured creditors, $5,000 remains for Debtor's general unsecured creditors. Creditor tardily files its claim for $5,000. General unsecured creditors (including Creditor's $5,000 claim) hold claims worth $50,000 in Debtor's Chapter 7 case. Will Creditor receive $500 in Debtor's Chapter 7 case? _____

103. Debtor files for relief under Chapter 7. There is $6,000 available for distribution to unsecured creditors. Administrative expenses equal $2,000. Debtor has no other priority creditors. General unsecured creditors hold allowed claims that equal $40,000. Creditor A has a claim for $1,000. Will Creditor A receive $400 in Debtor's Chapter 7 case? _____

104. Debtor files a voluntary Chapter 7 petition on January 10, 2018. This is not Debtor's first bankruptcy filing. On March 20, 2010, Debtor received a discharge in a Chapter 7 case that she had filed on December 15, 2009. Is Debtor eligible for a discharge in her current Chapter 7 case? _____

105. Acme Corporation files a voluntary Chapter 7 petition. Is Acme entitled to a discharge? _____

106. About six months prior to filing for bankruptcy, Debtor transfers his home, his only asset with any significant value, to his sister for $100, in an attempt to protect his home from his creditors. Debtor owns the home free and clear; it is worth approximately $100,000. Debtor files a voluntary Chapter 7 petition. Will Debtor receive a discharge in his Chapter 7 case? _____

107. Debtor files a voluntary Chapter 7 petition. Shortly thereafter, she decides that Chapter 13 would be more appropriate and seeks to convert the case to one under that chapter. Creditor objects. May Debtor convert the case to Chapter 13? _____

CHAPTER THIRTEEN. CHAPTER 11—REORGANIZATION

108. Debtor files a Chapter 11 petition, and a committee of unsecured creditors is appointed. Can Attorney be hired by the creditors' committee if Attorney also represents an unsecured creditor in the case? _____

109. Debtor files a Chapter 11 petition. Although the company shows a loss for the past two years, it hopes to reorganize under the Bankruptcy Code. Will a trustee automatically be appointed in the case? _____

110. Debtor files for relief under Chapter 11. If there is insufficient interest among Debtor's unsecured creditors, must the United States trustee still appoint an official committee of unsecured creditors? _____

111. Acme Company files for relief under Chapter 11. Creditor files a motion to convert or dismiss Acme's Chapter 11 case. After notice and a hearing, the bankruptcy court determines that cause exists to convert the case to Chapter 7 the case. Can the bankruptcy court order the appointment of a Chapter 11 trustee instead of granting Creditor's motion to convert? _____

112. Debtor files a Chapter 11 petition. Creditor holds an allowed claim in the amount of $100,000, secured by collateral having a fair market value of $75,000. Can Creditor elect to have his claim treated as secured to the extent of $100,000? _____

113. Farmer files for relief under Chapter 11. Creditor files a motion to convert Farmer's case to Chapter 7. Farmer objects to conversion. Can the bankruptcy court convert Farmer's Chapter 11 case to Chapter 7? _____

114. On February 1, Debtor, a corporation with liabilities in excess of $10 million, files a voluntary Chapter 11 petition and continues to operate the business as a debtor in possession. Under normal circumstances, may Creditor file a proposed plan on April 1? _____

115. *Diner, Inc.* is a small restaurant with assets of approximately $1 million and liabilities of approximately $1.5 million. On February 1, *Diner* files for relief under Chapter 11, and there is insufficient interest among creditors to form an official committee of unsecured creditors. May Creditor file a proposed plan on June 2?

   _____

116. Acme Corporation files for relief under Chapter 11. Prior to bankruptcy, Acme had negotiated a collective bargaining agreement with its employees. Acme wants to reject that collective bargaining agreement in its Chapter 11 case. Does Acme follow the rules for rejection of executory contracts under § 365 of the Bankruptcy Code?

   _____

117. Debtor files a Chapter 11 petition and subsequently files a proposed plan designating a separate class for all unsecured claims that are less than $100. Is this classification permissible?

   _____

118. Debtor files a Chapter 11 petition and subsequently files a proposed plan. May Debtor begin to solicit acceptances from the various classes even though his disclosure statement has not yet been approved by the court?

   _____

119. Debtor files a Chapter 11 petition and subsequently files a plan that proposes to pay Debtor's general unsecured creditors 10 cents on the dollar. Debtor has 10 general unsecured creditors, 9 of which hold claims of $5,000. Creditor X holds a $55,000 claim. All 10 creditors cast ballots on Creditor's plan; 9 of the 10 creditors vote in favor but Creditor X casts a "no" vote on the plan. Ignoring the possibility of confirmation by cramdown, can Debtor obtain confirmation of its plan?

   _____

120. An involuntary Chapter 11 petition is filed against Debtor Corporation, and an order for relief is entered in the case. Debtor Corporation files a proposed plan of reorganization that is accepted by all classes and confirmed by the court. Does confirmation operate as a discharge with respect to Debtor Corporation?

   _____

121. Acme Corporation files a voluntary Chapter 11 petition. Acme owes $10,000 in pre-petition tax claims to the IRS; the claims are entitled to eighth priority. The IRS has not agreed to any treatment that differs from the Code's requirements. Acme proposes a Chapter 11 plan that pays the IRS equal cash installments that equal the present value of its claim over five years from the plan's effective date. Can the bankruptcy court confirm Acme's plan?

   _____

122. Debtor, an individual, files for relief under Chapter 11. Debtor proposes a five-year plan under which his general unsecured creditors will receive approximately 25% of the face value of their claims. Debtor is devoting his projected disposable income to plan payments over the plan's five-year period. While the class of general unsecured creditors votes to approve Debtor's plan, Creditor X objects to the plan. If Debtor otherwise satisfies the requirements of § 1129(a) for plan confirmation, will Debtor obtain confirmation of his plan?

_____

123. Debtor, an individual, files for relief under Chapter 11. Debtor proposes a plan that proposes to pay the class of general unsecured creditors approximately 25% of the face value of their claims. The class of general unsecured creditors votes to reject Debtor's plan. Under the plan, Debtor proposes to retain valuable, non-exempt, pre-petition assets. If Debtor's plan otherwise satisfies the other requirements for confirmation under § 1129(a), can the bankruptcy court confirm the plan?

_____

CHAPTER FOURTEEN. CHAPTER 12—FAMILY FARMERS AND FAMILY FISHERMEN

124. Farmer, who meets the eligibility requirements, files a Chapter 12 petition. The standing Chapter 12 trustee proceeds to serve in the case. May Farmer continue to operate his farm?

_____

125. Farmer files for relief under Chapter 12 but then decides that he should have filed for relief under Chapter 7. Creditor objects to conversion to Chapter 7, but Farmer claims that he has an absolute right to convert. Is Farmer correct?

_____

126. Farmer files a Chapter 12 petition. Creditor holds a mortgage on the farm. Can the requirement of adequate protection be satisfied by reasonable rental payments even if they are substantially less than the normal interest payments under the farm mortgage?

_____

127. Farmer's Chapter 12 plan is confirmed and after making all payments under the plan, she is granted a standard Chapter 12 discharge. Will a pre-petition debt for Debtor's fraud while acting in a fiduciary capacity be discharged if it was provided for in Debtor's plan?

_____

CHAPTER FIFTEEN. CHAPTER 13—INDIVIDUAL WITH REGULAR INCOME

128. Debtor files a Chapter 13 petition accompanied by a plan proposing to pay all unsecured creditors in full over a period of three years. One of his liabilities is an unsecured consumer loan from Bank that was co-signed by Fellow Employee. Can Bank sue Fellow Employee while the Chapter 13 case is pending?

_____

129. Debtor is an individual with regular income. Debtor has two secured debts—on her home and car, and owes a total of $60,000 to two unsecured creditors. Debtor has fallen on hard times financially, and struggles to pay her monthly bills. Creditor X is Debtor's largest unsecured creditor. Can Creditor X file an involuntary Chapter 13 petition against Debtor? _____

130. Debtor files a Chapter 13 petition. She operates her own business as a sole proprietor and incurs trade credit in the operation of her business. Debtor has regular income from the business, and her debts do not exceed the limitations for eligibility established under § 109(e). Is she considered to be a "debtor engaged in business?" _____

131. Debtor files a Chapter 13 petition.

    a.   May Debtor retain possession of property of the estate? _____

    b.   Will Debtor's wages from post-petition services be included in property of the estate? _____

132. Debtor filed for relief under Chapter 13, but now wants to dismiss her case. Does she have an absolute right to do so? _____

133. Debtor files a Chapter 13 petition accompanied by a plan that proposes to pay her creditors over 36 months or three years. Debtor earns a steady $3,500 per month and has done so for the past two years. The annual median income in the state in which Debtor resides is $40,000. Does Debtor's proposed plan comply with the Code's requirements for confirmation? _____

134. Debtor files a Chapter 13 petition accompanied by a plan that proposes to pay Car Creditor the present value of $20,000 over the five-year duration of the plan. (Debtor is an above-median income Debtor.) A year before filing for relief under Chapter 13, Debtor purchased the car that Car Creditor financed. Debtor bought the car for personal use. The car is valued at $20,000, but Debtor owes Car Creditor $25,000 on the vehicle. Does Debtor's proposed plan comply with the Code's requirements for confirmation? _____

135. Debtor files a Chapter 13 petition. She owes $10,000 in unsecured federal income taxes for the taxable year prior to bankruptcy. May her Chapter 13 plan provide for the IRS to be paid 70% of its claim over a period of three years if the IRS does not consent to such treatment? _____

136. Debtor files a Chapter 13 petition accompanied by a proposed plan that is confirmed by the court. Does confirmation operate as a discharge of Debtor's debts? _____

137. Debtor's Chapter 13 plan is confirmed and after making all payments under the plan, she is granted a standard Chapter 13 discharge. Will a pre-petition debt for Debtor's willful (but not malicious) injury to Neighbor's property be discharged if it was provided for in Debtor's plan?

_____

138. Debtor files for relief under Chapter 13 on February 1, 2019, and files a Chapter 13 plan with her petition. She is an above-median income debtor. Debtor makes her first plan payment to the Chapter 13 trustee on March 1, 2019, which is within 30 days of her filing for bankruptcy. Does the five-year period of payments under her plan begin on March 1?

_____

139. Debtor files for relief under Chapter 13 and files her plan with her petition. Debtor is an above-median income debtor. Debtor proposes a five-year plan that pays Car Creditor, which holds a perfected security interest in a car that Debtor purchased three years ago, the remaining principal balance on the car loan in equal monthly installments. Car Creditor objects, claiming it is entitled to interest. Debtor says that Car Creditor is not entitled to interest on its plan payments, because Car Creditor is undersecured. Is Debtor correct?

_____

Answers to Short-Answer Review Questions

1. **NO**   Current monthly income is the average monthly income from all sources that the debtor receives in the six-month period ending on the last day of the month immediately preceding the debtor's bankruptcy filing. Debtor filed for relief on February 1, 2018, which means Debtor's current monthly income is $3,000. The income earned from August of 2017 through the end of January of 2018 is $18,000. That figure divided by six months results in a monthly average of $3,000. Debtor's gross annual income divided by 12 results in $2,833.33. If the Debtor earns the exact same amount each month, then dividing annual gross income by 12 works. If the Debtor's income varies by month—because she works on commissions, her salary increases or decreases, or her work hours increase or decrease—using annual gross income results in an incorrect figure. You use current monthly income to determine the debtor's eligibility for Chapter 7; the figure also is important for determining the amount that the debtor must pay unsecured creditors pursuant to her Chapter 13 plan.

2. **YES**   A claim is a right to payment, even if it is unliquidated, unmatured, disputed, or contingent. Even though Debtor disputes Acme's right to payment, Acme has a claim. Having a claim does *not* mean that Acme will be paid out of the Chapter 7 estate. Only allowed claims are paid, and Debtor likely will object to Acme's claim. [B.C. § 502]

3. **NO**   The United States trustee program does not operate in the six judicial districts in Alabama and North Carolina. In those districts, the bankruptcy administrator performs many of the same functions performed by the United States trustee.

4. **NO**   A bankruptcy petition preparer cannot offer legal advice, including the appropriate chapter under which the debtor should file for relief, whether debts will be discharged, and whether debtor will be able to keep her home, car, or other property. A bankruptcy petition preparer cannot use the word "legal" or any similar word in advertising its services and cannot advertise under any category that includes the word "legal" or any similar term.

5. **NO**   Personal injury tort and wrongful death claims must be tried in the district court.

6. **NO**   Bankruptcy judges do not have lifetime tenure, because they are not Article III judges. They serve for 14-year terms as judicial officers of the United States district court. [28 U.S.C. § 152]

7.	**NO**	Joint administration or procedural consolidation allows the use of a single docket for administrative matters. Thus, if Acme is designated the "lead" case, the court clerk would docket on Acme's docket rather than docketing the same matter twice—once on Acme's and once on Zed's case docket. Had the court granted a motion for substantive consolidation, Acme's and Zed's assets, debts, and causes of action would be pooled. Substantive consolidation is far less common than procedural consolidation or joint administration.
8.	**YES**	The district courts have original and exclusive jurisdiction over bankruptcy cases and are vested with exclusive jurisdiction over all of the debtor's property, regardless of its location, as of the filing of the bankruptcy petition. The district courts also have exclusive jurisdiction over all property of the estate. [28 U.S.C. § 1334(a), (e)]
9.	**DEPENDS**	If the core proceeding is not a *Stern* claim, then the bankruptcy court may enter a final judgment or order. If the core proceeding is a *Stern* claim, then the bankruptcy court may enter a final judgment or order only with the parties' consent. If the core proceeding is a *Stern* claim but the parties do not consent to the bankruptcy court entering a final order or judgment, then the bankruptcy court must submit proposed findings of fact and conclusions of law to the district court to review *de novo*.
10.	**NO**	The district court must withdraw a proceeding from the bankruptcy court if resolution of the proceeding requires substantial and material consideration of a nonbankruptcy federal statute and that statute has more than a *de minimis* impact on interstate commerce. Mandatory withdrawal, however, is not implicated if the dispute requires resolution only of state, not nonbankruptcy federal, law. Creditor's claims involve a determination of the validity and priority of liens under state law. The claims do not involve nonbankruptcy federal law and, therefore, mandatory withdrawal is not applicable. [28 U.S.C. § 157(d)] *Note:* The district court may exercise its discretion to grant permissive withdrawal under 28 U.S.C. § 157(d).
11.	**YES**	A bankruptcy court may abstain from hearing a case by dismissing the entire case or suspending all proceedings in the case if the interests of creditors and the debtor are better served by dismissal or suspension. [B.C. § 305(a)(1)] A significant factor weighing in favor of dismissal under § 305(a)(1) is the absence of a true bankruptcy purpose, especially in a case that is little more than a dispute between the debtor and a single creditor. Because Debtor's bankruptcy case was nothing more than the continuation of his dispute over alimony payments to his ex-wife, no bankruptcy purpose was served. State court was a better forum for resolving such state law issues.

12.	NO	A debtor may file for bankruptcy in any district in which his domicile, residence, principal assets, or principal place of business is located. [28 U.S.C. § 1408(1)] The venue statute provides four alternative bases for venue. Because Debtor's principal place of business is located in the Western District of Missouri, venue is proper there and the bankruptcy court will deny Creditor's motion.
13.	YES	The circuits that have addressed the issue all have held that a bankruptcy court order lifting the automatic stay is a final order. The vast majority of courts also have ruled that a bankruptcy court order refusing to the lift the automatic stay is a final order.
14.	NO	The Supreme Court has held that the relevant proceeding from which an immediate appeal may be taken in the context of consideration of a Chapter 13 plan is "the process of attempting to arrive at an approved plan that would allow the bankruptcy to move forward." Because to Debtor is free to propose a revised plan, the bankruptcy court's order denying confirmation did not terminate the relevant proceeding. Thus, Debtor may not immediately appeal the bankruptcy court's order. [**Bullard v. Blue Hills Bank**, 135 S.Ct. 1686 (2015)]
15.	NO	Insolvency is not a prerequisite for relief under the Bankruptcy Code. If Debtor is eligible under Chapter 7, 11, 12, or 13, she will not be denied relief merely because she is solvent.
16.	YES	The Code requires Debtor to obtain credit counseling services within 180 days of filing for bankruptcy. Debtor received credit counseling two weeks before filing for relief under Chapter 7. She received counseling from a service approved by the United States trustee. Credit counseling may occur over the phone, in person, or on the Internet, and may be done in individual or group sessions. [B.C. § 109(h)]
17.	NO	Debtor is ineligible for relief because she was a debtor in a case that was dismissed in the preceding 180 days due to her willful failure to obey the court's orders. [B.C. § 109(g)(1)]
18.	YES	While Chapter 11 is often referred to as the business reorganization chapter, the Supreme Court has held that an individual consumer debtor may file for relief under Chapter 11. [**Toibb v. Radloff,** 501 U.S. 157 (1991)]
19.	NO	Only a family farmer or family fisherman with regular income may file for relief under Chapter 12. [B.C. § 109(f)] The Code defines a family farmer as an individual whose aggregate noncontingent, liquidated debts do not exceed $4,411,400 and who receives more than 50% of his gross income for the tax year preceding bankruptcy or each of the second and third years prior to bankruptcy from his farming operation. [B.C. § 101(18)] Debtor's debts fall below the debt limit, but he does not earn more than 50% of his gross income from farming. If he wishes to reorganize, Debtor must file for relief under Chapter 11 or 13.

20.	**NO**	Chapter 13 relief is available only to an individual who has regular income, whose unsecured debts total less than $419,275, and whose secured debts total less than $1,257,850. Here, Debtor's unsecured debts of $500,000 exceed the statutory limitation and, thus, make her ineligible for Chapter 13 relief. [B.C. § 109(e)]
21.	**NO**	A Chapter 13 case may be commenced only by the filing of a voluntary petition. Therefore, the involuntary petition against Debtor will be dismissed. [B.C. § 303]
22.	**NO**	Because Debtor has more than 12 creditors, the filing of an involuntary petition against Debtor requires at least three petitioning entities holding noncontingent, undisputed claims, at least $16,750 of which, in the aggregate, are unsecured. Here, the combined unsecured claims of the petitioning creditors total only $3,000. Therefore, the petition will be dismissed. [B.C. § 303(b)(1)]
23.	**YES**	In a Chapter 7 case, an individual debtor with property subject to a security interest must within the earlier of 30 days from the petition or on or before the § 341 meeting state her intention to (1) surrender the property; (2) redeem the property; or (3) reaffirm the debt that the property secures. [B.C. § 521(a)(2)(A); Official Form 108] Within 30 days of the date set for the § 341 meeting, the debtor must perform her intention with regard to the property as to which she filed her statement of intention. [B.C. § 521(a)(2)(B)]
24.	**DEPENDS**	The courts are divided about whether a bankruptcy court has the discretion under § 343 to waive the debtor's attendance at the § 341 meeting. A majority of courts, however, waive physical attendance at the § 341 meeting for good cause.
25.	**YES**	Debtor must file her Chapter 13 plan within 14 days of conversion of her case to Chapter 13. The 14-day period may only be extended for cause and on notice as the bankruptcy court directs. [Bankruptcy Rule 3015(b)]
26.	**YES**	If an individual in a voluntary Chapter 7 or Chapter 13 case fails to file all the information required by § 521(a)(1) within 45 days of filing her petition, then her case is automatically dismissed on Day 46. [B.C. § 521(i)(1)] Debtor failed to file the documents required by § 512(a)(1)(B)(iii)–(v); therefore, the Code provides for automatic dismissal of the case. It is unclear, however, how that happens, and it is possible, notwithstanding the "automatic dismissal" language that a court order is needed.
27.	**YES**	When a trustee is appointed in a Chapter 11 case, she has the authority to operate the debtor's business unless the court orders otherwise. [B.C. § 1108]
28.	**NO**	The debtor normally stays in possession of estate property and continues to manage its business. The debtor is called the debtor in possession in a Chapter 11 case. The bankruptcy court may appoint a trustee, but such appointment is the exception to the rule.

29.	**YES**	Congress amended the Bankruptcy Code in 2005 to require the United States trustee to file a motion for appointment of a Chapter 11 trustee under certain circumstances. Because reasonable grounds exist to suspect that Acme's board and its CEO have engaged in actual fraud in managing Acme, the United States trustee must file a motion for appointment of a trustee. [B.C. § 1104(e)]
30.	**DEPENDS**	The Circuits are split on the type of conduct that gives rise to liability on the part of the trustee. Some courts hold trustees personally liable for *either* intentional or negligent violations of their fiduciary duties, while others impose personal liability only for intentional violations of the trustee's duties.
31.	**YES**	On appointment, Trustee effectively becomes Debtor Corporation's new management and, therefore, the corporate attorney-client privilege passes from former management to Trustee. Thus, Trustee has the power to waive Debtor Corporation's attorney-client privilege concerning communications made by former officers and directors to Debtor Corporation's attorney before bankruptcy. [**Commodity Futures Trading Commission v. Weintraub,** 471 U.S. 343 (1985]
32.	**YES**	In a Chapter 11 case in which appointment of a trustee has not been ordered, the court sometimes will order the appointment of an examiner prior to confirmation of a plan to investigate any charges of fraud, dishonesty, incompetence, mismanagement, or irregularity in the management of the debtor's affairs on the part of the debtor's present or former management. The appointment is made by the United States trustee, who selects a disinterested person other than himself. The debtor in possession, however, retains possession of his property and continues to operate the business. [B.C. § 1104(c)]
33.	**YES**	It is important that court approval of employment of the attorney and accountant be obtained prior to their rendering professional services. Otherwise, their applications for compensation may be denied since many courts will not grant approval retroactively in the absence of extraordinary circumstances. Also, they must be disinterested persons who do not have an interest adverse to the estate.
34.	**YES**	An assisted living facility is a long-term care facility, and a long-term care facility is a health care business. [B.C. § 101(27A)(B)] In the Chapter 7, 9, or 11 bankruptcy case of a health care business, the court must order the appointment of a patient care ombudsman unless the court decides that such appointment is not necessary for patient protection. This requirement is new to the Code with the passage of BAPCPA. The court must order the appointment within 30 days of the commencement of the case. The ombudsman monitors the quality of patient care and represents patients' interests. [B.C. § 333]

35. **NO**   The Supreme Court has held that § 330(a)(1) does not authorize payment of estate funds to the debtor's lawyer for the lawyer's work representing the debtor in debtor's bankruptcy case. Therefore, Lawyer must obtain her fee upfront from Debtor and not rely on compensation from estate funds under § 330(a)(1). [**Lamie v. United States Trustee,** 540 U.S. 526 (2004)]

36. **NO**   An individual debtor's earnings from services performed post-petition are specifically excluded from "§ 541 property" and, thus, are not part of the bankruptcy estate. ***But note:*** An individual debtor's post-petition wages are part of the bankruptcy estate in Chapters 11, 12, and 13. [B.C. §§ 1115(a)(2), 1207(a)(2), 1306(a)(2)]

37. **YES**   The forfeiture clause in the lease is an example of an ipso facto or "bankruptcy" clause, which is not enforceable under § 541(c)(1). Consequently, Lessee's leasehold interest in the computers is included in property of the estate notwithstanding the termination provision in the agreement. With respect to assumption or rejection of the unexpired lease, § 365 controls.

38. **NO**   Section 541(c)(2) of the Code provides that a restriction on the transfer of the debtor's beneficial interest in a trust is enforceable in bankruptcy if that restriction is enforceable under applicable nonbankruptcy law. The Supreme Court has held that § 541(c)(2) covers ERISA-qualified pension plans. [**Patterson v. Shumate,** 504 U.S. 753 (1992)] Therefore, Debtor's interest in the trust of her ERISA plan is excluded from property of her bankruptcy estate.

39. **DEPENDS**   There is a split of authority as to whether a creditor that fails to turn over estate property and merely continues to hold it violates the automatic stay under § 362(a)(3). In other words, is the obligation to turn over estate property self-effectuating, such that a failure to turn over property upon notice of the bankruptcy filing constitutes a violation of the automatic stay? Or, is the stay only violated if the court, after notice and a hearing, compels turnover and the creditor fails to comply with the court's order? Most courts that have addressed the issue have held that failure to turn over estate property, even without a court order, violates the automatic stay.

40. **YES**   The Supreme Court has held that a bank's temporary administrative freeze of a Debtor's checking account is not in violation of the automatic stay. The Court explained that § 542(b)'s setoff exception coupled with the general setoff rules in § 553(a) justify a temporary hold on the debtor's account up to the amount subject to setoff while the bank seeks relief from the automatic stay and the court's determination of the bank's right to setoff. Therefore, Bank can place a temporary administrative freeze on Debtor's account, but also should promptly request relief from the stay and a determination of its right of setoff. [**Citizens Bank v. Strumpf**, 516 U.S. 16 (1995)]

41. **NO** Trade Creditor transferred the claim to Big Bank during the 90 days prior to Acme's bankruptcy filing and Acme was presumed insolvent for that 90-day period. Therefore, Big Bank has no right of setoff. [B.C. § 553(a)(2), (c)]

42. **DEPENDS** The general rule is that an after-acquired property clause in a pre-petition security agreement is not effective to create a security interest in property acquired by the debtor or the estate after the bankruptcy filing. [B.C. § 552(a)] But if the parties' security agreement extends to pre-petition collateral and its proceeds, profits, products, and offspring, then the creditor's security interest attaches to post-petition collateral that constitutes the proceeds, profits, products, or offspring that are traceable to pre-petition collateral. [B.C. § 552(b)(1)]

43. **YES** As a hypothetical judicial lien creditor at the time the bankruptcy case is commenced, Trustee has the power to avoid Seller's unperfected security interest in the office equipment. Under U.C.C. § 9–317(a)(2), a judicial lien has priority over an unperfected security interest.

44. **NO** Even if all of the elements of a voidable preference under § 547(b) are present, this case comes within the "ordinary course of business" exception. Debtor incurred the debt in the ordinary course of its business and paid for the goods in the ordinary course of the parties' business, i.e., parties' course of dealing over past 10 years. [B.C. § 547(c)(2)] Therefore, the transfer cannot be avoided by the trustee.

45. **YES** The conveyance constitutes a fraudulent transfer made with the actual intent to hinder, delay, or defraud creditors. It occurred within two years of the debtor's filing for bankruptcy and, therefore, is voidable by the trustee under § 548(a)(1)(A).

46. **NO** A transfer is any *voluntary or involuntary* disposition of property, including a foreclosure sale of collateral. Here, the foreclosure sale occurred within two years before bankruptcy at a time when Debtor was insolvent. However, under these facts, the proceeds derived from the sale should constitute *reasonably equivalent value.* [§ 548(a)(1)(B)(i), (ii)(I)] The Supreme Court has held that the sale price received at a *noncollusive* foreclosure sale establishes reasonably equivalent value if all the requirements of state foreclosure law are complied with. [**BFP v. Resolution Trust Corporation**, 511 U.S. 531 (1994)] Therefore, the trustee should not be able to avoid the transfer.

47.a. **YES** The trustee's avoiding powers under the strong arm clause are subject to any applicable nonbankruptcy law that permits retroactive perfection of a security interest. Thus, Seller's post-petition perfection within the 20-day period allowed under state law will relate back and will prevail over the bankruptcy trustee's intervening rights as a hypothetical judicial lien creditor.

b. **NO** Seller's post-petition perfection under these circumstances comes within an exception to the automatic stay. [B.C. § 362(b)(3)]

48.	**YES**	With certain exceptions not relevant to this fact pattern, Seller can reclaim the goods from Debtor if she makes a proper reclamation demand, because the (i) the sale was in the ordinary course of Seller's business; (ii) Debtor received the goods while insolvent; and (iii) Debtor received the goods within 45 days of the bankruptcy filing. A proper demand for reclamation must be in writing and done (i) no later than 45 days after Debtor received the goods; or (ii) no later than 20 days after the start of the bankruptcy case, if the 45-day period has expired.
49.	**YES**	The $1,000 payment is a transfer to Friend, an unsecured creditor, within 90 days of bankruptcy when Debtor is presumed insolvent, and Friend obtains more than she would obtain had the transfer not occurred. Without the transfer, Friend would have received $1,000 (5% of $20,000) from Debtor's bankruptcy case. With the transfer, however, Debtor receives $1,950: $1,000 plus another $950 (5% of $19,000 remaining on the debt).
50.	**NO**	The transfer to Amy was a fraudulent transfer. It was made for less than reasonably equivalent value while Debtor was insolvent. Thus, the trustee may avoid the transfer under § 548(a)(1)(B)(i), (ii)(I). But, the trustee may not recover the property from Ben, because Ben is not the initial transferee and, thus, has a defense to a recovery action. Because Ben took in good faith, without knowledge of the voidability of the transfer, and paid value, the trustee may not recover from Ben. [B.C. § 550(b)(1)] The trustee may recover the value of the property from Amy, however, because she was the initial transferee. [B.C. § 550(a)(1)]
51.	**NO**	Unless the estate is solvent, holders of unsecured claims are not entitled to post-petition interest. [B.C. § 506; **United Savings Association of Texas v. Timbers of Inwood Forest Associates**, 484 U.S. 365 (1988) (stating that the "substantive effect" of § 506 is to deny "undersecured creditors post-petition interest on their claims")]
52.	**YES**	While personal injury tort claims must be tried in the district court for the purpose of distribution, if the fixing or liquidation of a contingent or unliquidated claim would cause undue delay in the administration of the case, the bankruptcy court is required to estimate the claim for the purpose of allowance.
53.	**NO**	Bank's claim is secured only to the extent of the value of its collateral ($90,000), and the balance of its claim ($10,000) is treated as an unsecured claim. Absent avoidance, a lien on real property passes through bankruptcy unaffected. The Debtor, however, may not strip down Bank's lien to the value of the land. [**Dewsnup v. Timm**, 502 U.S. 410 (1992)]

54.	NO	Bank Two has an unsecured claim in Debtor's bankruptcy case, because the land is worth $100,000 and Bank's claim is worth $100,000. Thus, there is no value left in the land to cover Bank Two's claim. But, Debtor may not strip off Bank Two's lien on the property. If the property appreciates in value post-petition, Bank Two will receive the benefit of that appreciation, not the Debtor. [**Bank of America v. Caulkett**, 135 S.Ct. 1995 (2015) (declining to limit *Dewsnup* to "partially—as opposed to wholly—underwater liens")]
55.	**YES**	To the extent that Bank is oversecured, it is entitled to the allowance of post-petition interest, and also to any reasonable fees, costs, or other charges agreed to in the mortgage contract. [B.C. § 506]
56.	**YES**	Actual and necessary post-petition costs of preserving the estate, including wages and salaries for post-petition services, are allowable as administrative expenses. [B.C. § 503(b)]
57.	NO	An unsecured pre-petition tax claim of this kind is accorded eighth priority status. While it is an unsecured claim, it is an unsecured claim with eighth priority status in terms of payment from the Chapter 7 estate. In a Chapter 7 case, the priority claims are paid in full before any distribution is made to the general unsecured creditors. [B.C. § 507(a)(8)]
58.	NO	Since the adequate protection furnished to Creditor proved to be deficient, Creditor will receive an administrative expense claim ($20,000) with *super-priority* over all other administrative expenses allowed in the case. [*See* B.C. § 507(b)] ***But note:*** Creditor's super-priority claim will not prevail over a *super super*-priority claim approved under § 364(c)(1) for post-petition credit.
59.	NO	Priority claimants are paid in the order of priority in the Code. Administrative expenses are second priority claims; therefore, they are paid before tax claims and, in this example, are paid in full. After paying the administrative claims, there is $4,000 left to pay the $8,000 in tax claims. Tax claimants share *pro rata* in remaining funds, if there are insufficient funds to pay them in full. The federal taxing authorities are 75% of the remaining tax claims ($6,000 of $8,000), which means that they get 75% of the $4,000 remaining or $3,000. The property tax claimant gets $1,000 or 25% of the $4,000 remaining. After paying the tax claimants, there is no money available to pay a dividend to the general unsecured creditors.
60.a.	**YES**	In a Chapter 7, 12, or 13 case, a secured creditor must file a proof of claim in order to have an allowed claim. [Bankruptcy Rule 3002(a)]
b.	**DEPENDS**	In a Chapter 11 case, however, the secured creditor need not file a proof of claim form if the debtor correctly schedules the creditor's debt and does not list the debt as contingent, unliquidated, or disputed. [Bankruptcy Rule 3003(c)(2)]
61.	**NO**	A secured creditor's lien is not void simply because the creditor fails to file a proof of claim. [Bankruptcy Rule 3002(a)]

62.	**NO**	The time remaining on the lease is less than 80 months, which means that Landlord's allowed claim is no more than one year's rental, which is $96,000. Landlord's claim for the remaining $48,000 ($144,000 − $96,000) is disallowed. [B.C. § 502(b)(6)]
63.	**NO**	In a case filed or administered jointly, both spouses must elect the same exemption plan, either state or federal. If the debtors are unable to agree, they will be deemed to have chosen the federal exemptions.
64.	**NO**	The security interest must be nonpossessory and *nonpurchase-money* for Debtor to be able to avoid it. Here, the Seller's security interest is purchase-money and, therefore, cannot be avoided by Debtor.
65.	**NO**	Section 522(f)(1) allows avoidance of *judicial liens* and nonpossessory, nonpurchase-money security interests in *household furnishings, household goods, wearing apparel, appliances, books, animals, crops, musical instruments, or jewelry.* A mortgage is a consensual lien; a judicial lien is not. *Compare* B.C. § 101(36) (judicial lien) *with* B.C. § 101(37) (lien). A mortgage is a consensual lien on real property, and not in one of the categories of property listed in § 522(f)(1)(B).
66.	**YES**	Husband and Wife each can take the homestead exemption in § 522(d)(1), which means that each can exempt $25,150 in value, or a total of $50,300. [B.C. § 522(m)] Debtors have $40,000 in equity in their home; therefore, they can exempt all of the home's equity.
67.	**NO**	Debtor has not been domiciled in Michigan for the 730 days prior to filing his bankruptcy petition in the Eastern District of Michigan. Therefore, Debtor must use the exemptions for the State where he was domiciled for the longer portion of the 180 days *prior* to the 730 days before his bankruptcy filing. Two and a half years ago, Debtor was domiciled in Ohio; therefore, the Ohio state exemptions apply to his Chapter 7 case. [B.C. § 522(b)(3)(A)]
68.	**DEPENDS BUT LIKELY YES**	Section 522(p) and (q) apply "as a result of [the debtor's] electing" the state law exemptions. The issue is whether these limitations on state law exemptions apply *only* to non-opt-out states, because only in non-opt-out states may debtors *elect* the state law exemptions. The majority rule is that §§ 522(p) and (q) apply in both opt-out and non-opt-out states.
69.	**NO**	In a unanimous opinion, the Supreme Court has held that monies in an inherited IRA do not qualify for exemption under § 522(b)(3)(C), because the monies do not constitute retirement funds. [**Clark v. Rameker,** 573 U.S. 122 (2014)]
70.	**NO**	The individual debtor's right of redemption under Chapter 7 only applies to tangible personal property, not real property. Therefore, Debtor cannot redeem the land from Bank's lien. [B.C. § 722]

71.a.   **NO**   The Code provides that debts for money, property, services, or credit obtained by false representation or fraud are not dischargeable. If the creditor fails to bring an adversary proceeding in the bankruptcy case to determine dischargeability of the debt, however, the debt will be discharged. [B.C. § 523(c), Fed. R. Bankr. P. 7001(6)]

   b.   **NO**   Debtor's failure to list or schedule the debt makes it nondischargeable because Creditor, lacking notice or actual knowledge of the bankruptcy case, was precluded from timely filing a proof of claim.

   c.   **NO**   Because the debt arose from Debtor's defalcation while acting in a fiduciary capacity, it is not dischargeable. If the creditor fails to bring an adversary proceeding in the bankruptcy case to determine dischargeability of the debt, however, the debt will be discharged. [B.C. § 523(c), Fed. R. Bankr. P. 7001(6)]

   d.   **NO**   A debt owed to a former spouse that is *not* a domestic support obligation but that is incurred by the debtor in connection with a separation agreement is not dischargeable. [B.C. § 523(a)(15)]

   e.   **NO**   This debt is a domestic support obligation and is not dischargeable. [B.C. §§ 101(14A), 523(a)(5)]

72.   **YES**   While Debtor has no personal obligation to repay the discharged debt that was owed to Creditor, the Code expressly permits Debtor to voluntarily repay any debt if she so desires.

73.   **NO**   If Debtor had not been represented by an attorney during the negotiation of the reaffirmation agreement, it would be necessary to obtain court approval, which requires a finding that the agreement is in Debtor's best interest and does not impose an undue hardship on Debtor or any of his dependents. However, here, Debtor was represented by an attorney, and, according to the facts, all of the elements of an enforceable reaffirmation agreement were met, one of which is the attorney's filing of an affidavit or a declaration stating that: (i) Debtor has been fully informed; (ii) Debtor has entered into the agreement voluntarily; (iii) the reaffirmation does not impose an undue hardship on Debtor or any of his dependents; and (iv) the attorney has fully advised Debtor of the legal effects of the reaffirmation and of any subsequent default. Therefore, independent court approval is not necessary in this case. [B.C. § 524(c)(3)]

74.	**NO**	If Debtor does not reaffirm any debts, the holding of a discharge hearing is within the court's discretion. On the other hand, if Debtor desires to reaffirm one or more debts negotiated *without* attorney representation, the court must conduct a discharge hearing, at which time the judge must do several things. First, the judge must explain to Debtor the legal effect and consequences of a reaffirmation agreement and of default under such an agreement. [B.C. § 524(d)(1)(B)] Second, the judge must advise Debtor that he is not required to enter into an reaffirmation agreement. [B.C. § 524(d)(1)(A)] Finally, because Debtor wants to reaffirm a consumer debt secured by personal, not real, property, the court must determine that the reaffirmation agreement does not impose an undue hardship on Debtor or his dependents, and is in Debtor's best interest. [B.C. § 524(a)(6), (d)(2)]
75.	**YES**	The great weight of authority is that post-petition interest on a nondischargeable tax debt also is not dischargeable.
76.	**YES**	Section 1328(a)(4) excepts from the standard Chapter 13 discharge any debt for damages resulting from willful or malicious injury that causes personal injury to or death of an individual. Neighbor's debt is for injury to property; therefore, it is dischargeable. Section 523(a)(6), by comparison, covers both injury to persons and to property.
77.	**NO**	The Supreme Court has held that the preponderance-of-the-evidence standard is the standard of proof for the discharge exceptions at § 523(a). [**Grogan v. Garner**, 498 U.S. 279 (1991)]
78.	**NO**	With certain limited exceptions that do not apply to this fact pattern, the discharge of a debtor's debt does not affect the liability of other entities, such as sureties or guarantors. Thus, while Debtor's debt to Bank is discharged, Mother's is not. [B.C. § 524(e)]
79.a.	**YES**	The commencement or continuation of a judicial, administrative, or other action against Debtor to recover a pre-petition claim is enjoined by the automatic stay.
b.	**YES**	Any act to obtain possession of property of the estate, or property in the possession of the estate, is prohibited by the automatic stay. Also enjoined is any act to enforce a lien against property of the estate. Even if the trustee abandons the vehicle to the Debtor, the stay would enjoin Bank's repossession because the vehicle is property of the Debtor and the stay continues until the time that the case is closed, dismissed, or Debtor receives her discharge. [B.C. § 362(c)(2)]
c.	**YES**	Any act to collect, recover, or assess a pre-petition claim against Debtor is enjoined. Here, Appliance Store's telephone calls and letters are clearly in violation of the automatic stay.

d.   **NO**   The commencement or continuation of a proceeding by a governmental unit (here, the NLRB) to enforce its police or regulatory power is excepted from the automatic stay. [B.C. § 362(b)(4)] The NLRB's action satisfies both the public policy test and the pecuniary purpose test that courts employ to determine whether the police or regulatory power exception to the automatic stay applies.

80.   **DEPENDS**   Prior to the passage of BAPCPA, some courts allowed the Debtor to ride through bankruptcy, so long as she was current on her car payments, without redeeming the vehicle or reaffirming the debt. The Code now contains a stay termination provision, which provides if an individual Chapter 7 debtor fails to reaffirm the debt or redeem the property securing the creditor's purchase-money interest within 45 days after the first meeting of creditors, then the automatic stay terminates and the property is no longer estate property. [B.C. § 521(a)(6)] Some jurisdictions do not allow repossession of a vehicle based solely on an *ipso facto* clause in the parties' contract. In these jurisdictions, if Debtor is current on her car payments, then termination of the automatic stay has no effect on her ability to retain possession of her vehicle.

81.   **YES**   Under § 362(d)(2), Creditor is entitled to relief from the stay of an act against the property, because there is no equity in the property and it is not necessary for an effective reorganization.

82.   **NO**   In 2005, Congress added an exception to the automatic stay to cover this fact scenario. A governmental unit may offset an income tax refund for a pre-petition taxable period against a pre-petition tax liability, if offset is allowed under nonbankruptcy law. Nonbankruptcy law (26 U.S.C. § 6402(a)) allows the IRS to set off tax liabilities against tax refunds. Debtor's tax liability and tax refund were for pre-petition taxable periods. Therefore, the IRS did not violate the automatic stay.

83.   **DEPENDS, BUT LIKELY**   The Bankruptcy Code provides an exception to the stay for the commencement or continuation of a criminal action against the debtor. [B.C. § 362(b)(2)] The courts are split as to whether this exception applies to a criminal proceeding for passing a bad check. The concern is that prosecution puts pressure on the debtor to pay a debt that is dischargeable; other creditors do not enjoy the benefit of the state as a collection agent. The majority of courts, however, have held that § 362(b)(2)'s plain language does not distinguish between criminal proceedings based on the prosecutor's motive; therefore, the automatic stay does not apply to the commencement or continuation of a prosecution against the debtor for passing a bad check.

84.	**NO**	The automatic stay is in effect for 30 days from the date of the petition, because Debtor filed and served the required certification, and deposited 30 days' worth of rent with the court clerk. [B.C. § 362(*l*)(1)] If during the 30 days following Debtor's filing of the petition, Debtor pays the past-due rental, and files with the court and serves on Landlord a further certification that she has cured the entire default that led to the judgment for possession, then the automatic stay applies and prevents Landlord from taking further action to evict Debtor from her apartment. [B.C. § 362(d)(2)]
85.	**NO**	Congress amended § 362 in 2005 in an effort to deal with what it considered abusive serial filings by small business debtors. Because Debtor's current case is a small business case and Debtor's prior Chapter 11 case was a small business case dismissed within two years of the filing of Debtor's current case, the automatic stay does not apply in Debtor's current case. [B.C. §§ 362(n)(1)(B), 101(51C), (51D)]
86.	**NO**	Adequate protection does not entitle an undersecured creditor to compensation (i.e., interest) for the delay in foreclosure on his collateral and reinvestment of the proceeds. The United States Supreme Court has held that adequate protection means protection against depreciation in "the value of the collateral," and not protection of "a secured party's right to immediate foreclosure." [**United Savings Association of Texas v. Timbers of Inwood Forest Associates, Ltd.**, 484 U.S. 365 (1988)]
87.	**DEPENDS**	The sale of the factory building is out of the ordinary course of Debtor's business, and therefore requires proper notice and the opportunity for a hearing. If no party in interest timely objects, however, the building may be sold without a hearing.
88.	**DEPENDS**	The checking account constitutes cash collateral, which the Debtor may not use in the ordinary course of business without either Secured Creditor's consent or, after notice and a hearing, court approval. [B.C. § 363(a), (c)(2)]
89.	**NO**	Bank1 is adequately protected by the $100,000 equity cushion that it has in Debtor's land. In determining the equity cushion, the bankruptcy court will compare the value of the property ($200,000) to the amount of Bank1's secured claim and any other *senior* secured claims ($100,000). Therefore, Bank1 has a $100,000 equity cushion in the land.
90.	**YES**	If Debtor is unable to obtain unsecured post-petition financing as an administrative expense, one of the permissible alternatives is for the court to authorize the obtaining of credit or the incurring of debt that will have priority over all administrative expense claims in the case, and also over any super-priority administrative expense claims arising from the failure of adequate protection. The lender will have a super super-priority claim. Notice and a hearing are required. [B.C. § 364(c)(1)]

91. **DEPENDS**   Acme can sell the list, but only after appointment of a consumer privacy ombudsman and court approval, after notice and a hearing, of the sale. The bankruptcy court must take account of the facts, circumstances, and conditions of the sale and find that no showing was made that the sale would violate nonbankruptcy law. [B.C. § 363(b)(1)]

92. **DEPENDS**   For Debtor (now debtor in possession) to assume the unexpired lease of the equipment, she must at the time of assumption: (i) cure the default for June, July, and August or provide adequate assurance that it will be cured promptly; (ii) compensate the lessor for any monetary loss caused by the default (or provide adequate assurance of prompt compensation); and (iii) furnish adequate assurance of future performance of the lease. Court approval is required. [B.C. § 365(b)(1)]

93. **NO**   The question concerns the assumption of a personal services contract. Unless Variety, Inc. consents, which is highly unlikely, the trustee may not assume or assign the executory contract to sing because, as a general rule, applicable nonbankruptcy law would excuse Variety, Inc. from accepting performance from, or furnishing performance to, an entity other than Debtor (or the debtor in possession). Had a trustee not been appointed, there is a split of authority as to whether the debtor in possession could assume and perform the contract. [B.C. § 365(c)(1)]

94. **NO**   A trustee or a debtor in possession may not assume or assign a lease of non-residential real property that has been terminated under applicable nonbankruptcy law prior to the order for relief. [B.C. § 365(c)(3)]

95. **YES**   In a Chapter 11 case, assumption or rejection of an executory contract or an unexpired lease of personal property or residential real property may occur at any time prior to the confirmation of a plan. However, the nondebtor party may request that the court, in its discretion, direct the trustee or the debtor in possession to assume or reject within a fixed period of time. [B.C. § 365(d)(2)]

96. **YES**   You determine whether a debtor is an above- or below-median income debtor by figuring out the debtor's current monthly income, multiplying that number by 12, and comparing it with the state's annual median income. Current monthly income is the average monthly income from all sources for the six-month period prior to the debtor's filing for bankruptcy. During the months of January through June, Debtor earned $5,000 (January and February) + $2,700 (March) + $4,000 (April and May) + $3,500 (June) *or* $15,200, which results in current monthly income of $2,533 ($15,200/6). The result, when annualized, is $30,400 (rounding up product of $2,533 × 12), which is $400 higher than the state median.

97.	**YES**	Debtor is a below-median income debtor; therefore, there is no presumption of abuse. [B.C. § 707(b)(2)] Her case may be dismissed only if it was filed in bad faith or the granting of relief would be an abuse of discretion under a totality of the circumstances. [B.C. § 707(b)]
98.	**DEPENDS**	The mere fact that Debtor's annual income exceeds the state's median income does *not* create a presumption of abuse. The "means test" determines whether Debtor's filing for relief under Chapter 7 creates a presumption of abuse.
99.	**NO**	Debtor is an above-median income debtor, whose current monthly income is $4,000. Her means test expenses are $3,900, leaving $100 per month disposable income. That means disposable income over 60 months (because Debtor is an above-median income debtor) of $6,000, which is below $8,175. Thus, there is no presumption of abuse. [B.C. § 707(b)(2)(A)(i)(I)]
100.	**YES**	Debtor is an above-median income debtor, whose current monthly income is $4,000. Her means test expenses are $3,800, leaving $200 per month disposable income. That means disposable income over 60 months (because Debtor is an above-median income debtor) of $12,000, which is between $8,175 and $13,650. Thus, Debtor must perform the secondary abuse test, which compares her disposable income over 60 months with 25% of her unsecured debt. Because $12,000 is greater than $10,000 (25% of Debtor's unsecured debt), there is a presumption of abuse. Debtor has sufficient disposable income to pay at least 25% of her unsecured debt in a Chapter 13 case. Unless Debtor can rebut the presumption of abuse, her Chapter 7 case will be dismissed.
101.	**NO**	Debtor owns her car free and clear, so she is not making any car payments. She may not deduct the national standard for a car ownership expense as a monthly means test expense. Because the current national standard in the Midwest Census Region is $497, Debtor's disposable income, for purposes of the means test, is $497 higher than if she had a current car payment. [**Ransom v. FIA Card Services**, 562 U.S. 61 (2011)]
102.	**NO**	Creditor filed its claim late and, therefore, is only paid *after* all the timely filed general unsecured claims. Because there is not enough money to pay all the timely filed claims (recovery is approximately 11% per creditor—$5,000 assets/$45,000 in claims), Creditor receives nothing in Debtor's Chapter 7 case. [B.C. §§ 726(a)(2), (3)]
103.	**NO**	Administrative expenses have second priority of payment and, therefore, are paid before any general unsecured creditors. [B.C. § 507(a)(2)] After paying the administrative expenses, there is $4,000 available to pay $40,000 worth of general unsecured claims. That means that each general unsecured creditor receives a 10% dividend ($4,000 assets/$40,000 claims). Ten percent of Creditor A's $1,000 claim is $100 (10% × $1,000), not $400.

104. **YES** An individual Chapter 7 debtor will not receive a discharge of her debts if she files her current Chapter 7 case within 8 years of having filed a prior Chapter 7 case. The dates run from filing, not from discharge. While Debtor received her discharge within the 8-year period, her earlier Chapter 7 case was filed more than 8 years ago. Therefore, Debtor is entitled to a discharge in her current Chapter 7 case. [B.C. § 727(a)(8)]

105. **NO** The Code provides no discharge to a Chapter 7 debtor that is not an individual. [B.C. § 727(a)(1)] But Chapter 7 is the liquidation chapter, which means that Acme is going out of business. As a practical matter, the fact that the corporate entity does not receive a discharge does not matter if the corporate entity no longer exists for creditors to sue.

106. **NO** Debtor transferred valuable property—his home worth $100,000—to his sister, an insider, for nominal consideration in an effort to hinder, delay, or defraud his creditors. He did so within one year of filing for bankruptcy. Thus, he will not receive a discharge in his Chapter 7 case. [B.C. § 727(a)(2)] In addition, the Chapter 7 trustee likely will file an adversary proceeding in the bankruptcy case to recover the home from Debtor's sister because it was a fraudulent transfer. [B.C. § 548(a)(1)(A)] *Note:* The time period for Chapter 7's denial-of-discharge provision is one year, while the time period for fraudulent conveyances is two years.

107. **YES** Because the Chapter 7 case has not been converted previously from Chapter 11, 12, or 13, Debtor has an absolute non-waivable right to convert the case from Chapter 7 to any of the other chapters at any time, provided that Debtor meets the eligibility requirements for that chapter.

108. **DEPENDS** Attorney may be hired by the creditors' committee if he does not "represent any other entity having an *adverse interest*" in connection with the case" during his employment. [B.C. § 1103(b)] Representation of a creditor of the same class as the committee represents is not automatically deemed representation of an adverse interest.

109. **NO** Because the debtor in possession usually is considered to be the most appropriate one to conduct the operations of the business, appointment of a Chapter 11 trustee is the exception to the rule. There is a presumption that the debtor should be allowed to remain in possession. Nonetheless, after the filing of the petition and prior to confirmation of a plan, a party in interest or the United States trustee may request the appointment of a trustee, either *for cause* or in the interest of creditors, equity security holders, and the estate. Examples of cause are fraud, dishonesty, incompetence, or gross mismanagement by current management. The court generally requires evidence showing more than simple mismanagement, and some courts have used a cost-benefit analysis, taking into account the administrative expenses that are likely to ensue from the appointment of a trustee. [B.C. § 1104]

110. **NO** The Bankruptcy Code provides that as soon as practicable after the order for relief, the United States trustee *shall* appoint an official committee of unsecured creditors. [B.C. § 1102(a)] It is not unusual, however, for the United States trustee to be unable to find creditors willing to serve on the unsecured creditors' committee. Thus, in many Chapter 11 cases, there is no official committee of unsecured creditors.

111. **YES** The bankruptcy court may order the appointment of a Chapter 11 trustee instead of converting the case if the court determines that appointment of a trustee is in the best interests of the estate and of creditors. [B.C. § 1112(b)(1)]

112. **YES** By making the election under § 1111(b), Creditor can have his claim treated as secured to the full extent that the claim is allowed ($100,000), even though ordinarily it would be deemed secured only up to the value of the collateral ($75,000). However, by making the election, which is available only in a Chapter 11 case, Creditor forfeits his unsecured claim for any deficiency. [B.C. § 1111(b)(2)]

113. **NO** The Code does not permit a bankruptcy court to convert a farmer's Chapter 11 case to Chapter 7 if the farmer does not request conversion. [B.C. § 1112(c)] Therefore, the bankruptcy court cannot convert Farmer's case to Chapter 7, because Farmer objects to such conversion.

114. **NO** As long as a trustee has not been appointed in the case, Debtor has the exclusive right to file a plan for the first 120 days after the order for relief. *Note:* The rule differs for small business debtors.

115. **NO** *Diner* is a small business debtor, because (i) it is engaged in business activities, (ii) its primary activity is not the business of owning or operating real property, (iii) its liabilities are less than $2,725,625, and (iv) the United States trustee has not appointed an official committee of unsecured creditors. [B.C. § 101(51D)(A)] The exclusivity period for a small business debtor is 180, not 120, days. [B.C. § 1121(e)] Therefore, Creditor may not file a plan within 120 days of *Diner's* bankruptcy filing.

116. **NO** Section 1113 contains a number of conditions that the debtor in possession must satisfy in order to reject its collective bargaining agreement For example, the Code mandates that before filing an application to reject the collective bargaining agreement, the debtor in possession must make a proposal to the union to modify the agreement. [B.C. § 1113(b)(1)(A)] Therefore, Acme cannot reject its collective bargaining agreement by using the rules under § 365 of the Code.

117. **YES** The Code permits the plan to designate a separate class of small claims comprised of all unsecured claims that are less than, or by consent are decreased to, an amount approved by the court as reasonable and necessary. Generally, such administrative convenience claims are paid in full (in cash), and the estate benefits by the reduction of administrative expenses. [B.C. § 1122(b)]

118.	**NO**	Debtor may solicit post-petition acceptances only at or after the time the plan (or a summary of it) and a written court-approved disclosure statement have been sent to the holders of the claims or interests whose acceptances are sought. [B.C. § 1125(b)] *But note:* In a small business case, the bankruptcy court may determine that the plan provides adequate information and a separate disclosure statement is not needed. The court may conditionally approve a disclosure statement that can be used to solicit acceptances if it contains adequate information and is mailed at least 25 days before the confirmation hearing. In such a case, the court may combine the hearing on the disclosure statement with the hearing on confirmation. [B.C. § 1125(f)]
119.	**NO**	The court will not confirm a consent plan unless each class of claims is either unimpaired or accepts the plan. [B.C. § 1129(a)(8)] The class of general unsecured creditors is impaired under the plan, because creditors are receiving less than full payment on their claims. [B.C. § 1124(1)] A class of claims accepts the plan if at least two-thirds in amount and more than half in number of claims vote in favor of the plan. [B.C. § 1126(c)] While 9 of 10 unsecured claimants voted "yes," thereby satisfying the "more than half in number" requirement, only 45% in amount voted in favor. Because Creditor X holds such a large claim, its "no" vote meant that Debtor could not satisfy the two-thirds in amount requirement.
120.	**YES**	In a Chapter 11 case, a discharge is not limited to an individual debtor as it is in Chapter 7. Unless the plan or the confirmation order provides otherwise, *confirmation* discharges Debtor Corporation from all pre-confirmation debts, as well as from certain other debts specified in § 1141(d)(1)(A). *Note:* The result would differ if the confirmed plan were a liquidating plan and Debtor Corporation—which would be denied a discharge under Chapter 7—did not engage in business after consummation of the plan. [B.C. § 1141(d)(3)]
121.	**NO**	The Code requires that an eighth priority tax creditor be paid regular cash installments that equal the present value of its claim over a period of time that does not exceed five years from the order of relief, not the plan's effective date. [B.C. § 1129(b)(9)(C)] The IRS has not agreed to different treatment, which means that the bankruptcy court cannot confirm Acme's plan.
122.	**YES**	If a general unsecured creditor objects to confirmation of an individual debtor's plan, the court cannot confirm the plan unless (i) it pays the present value of the creditor's claim; or (ii) the debtor pays at least his projected disposable income over five years from the first plan payment or the time during which plan payments are made, whichever time period is longer. [B.C. § 1129(a)(15)] Debtor is paying his projected disposable income over a five-year period, which also is the time during which plan payments are being made. Therefore, Debtor's plan satisfies § 1129(a)(15), and the bankruptcy court can confirm the plan.

123. **DEPENDS** If the court follows the narrow interpretation of the absolute priority rule, then the court cannot confirm Debtor's plan. The class of general unsecured creditors has voted to reject Debtor's plan, which means that the court cannot confirm as a consent plan because the unsecured creditors are impaired (receiving only 25% of their claims). [B.C. § 1129(a)(8)] The court could confirm using the Code's cramdown rules, but the absolute priority rule is an issue. Courts following the majority narrow interpretation of the absolute priority rule hold that *only* the debtor's post-petition earnings and acquisitions of property are excluded from operation of the absolute priority rule. That means that Debtor cannot retain valuable, non-exempt pre-petition property that could be used to pay more than a 25% dividend to his general unsecured creditors. If the court follows the broad interpretation of the absolute priority rule, which is the minority position, then the court could confirm Debtor's plan.

124. **YES** Section 1203 authorizes Farmer to continue to operate his farm, unless he is removed as a debtor in possession. The causes for removal of a debtor in possession parallel those in a Chapter 11 case.

125. **YES** A Chapter 12 debtor may convert the case to Chapter 7 at any time. [B.C. § 1208(a)]

126. **YES** In a Chapter 12 case, the issue of adequate protection is governed by § 1205, not by § 361. If the creditor's collateral is farmland, the Code provides that adequate protection includes the payment of the reasonable rent prevailing in that locality, taking into account "the rental value, net income, and earning capacity of the property." [B.C. § 1205(b)(3)]

127. **NO** The standard discharge in Chapter 12 does not discharge any debts of a kind specified in § 523(a). [B.C. § 1228(a)(2)] Section 523(a)(4) provides that a debt for fraud while acting in a fiduciary capacity is not dischargeable. *Note:* A creditor with a claim under §§ 523(a)(2), (4), or (6) must initiate an adversary proceeding in the bankruptcy case for a determination of whether the creditor's claim is not dischargeable. If the creditor fails to do so, the creditor's claim will be discharged. [B.C. § 523(c)]

128. **NO** Fellow Employee is protected by the Chapter 13 co-debtor stay, which became effective when Debtor filed his Chapter 13 petition. Fellow Employee did not become liable on the debt in the ordinary course of Fellow Employee's business. Therefore, during the pendency of Debtor's Chapter 13 case, the Code enjoins the Bank from commencing or continuing any civil action or taking any other act to collect the consumer debt from Fellow Employee. [B.C. § 1301(a)]

129. **NO** An involuntary petition may only be filed against an individual under Chapter 7 or Chapter 11 of the Code. [B.C. § 303(a)]

130. **YES** Debtor is a self-employed individual who incurs trade credit in producing income from her business. Therefore, she is a "debtor engaged in business." As such, Debtor will be permitted to continue to operate her business, unless the court directs otherwise. [B.C. § 1304]

131.a. **YES** In a Chapter 13 case, ordinarily the debtor retains possession of all property of the estate unless a confirmed plan or confirmation order provides otherwise.

b. **YES** The Chapter 13 estate consists not only of all § 541 property, but also of all § 541 property acquired by Debtor post-petition and all of Debtor's earnings from post-petition services performed prior to the earliest of the closing, dismissal, or conversion of the case. [B.C. § 1306]

132. **DEPENDS** Some courts hold that a Chapter 13 debtor has the absolute right to dismiss her case. Other courts hold that the debtor's right to dismiss under § 1307 is subject to a bad faith or fraud exception.

133. **NO** Debtor is an above-median income debtor, because she earns $42,000 per year (current monthly income of $3,500 × 12) and the median income in her state is $40,000. Therefore, Debtor's plan must be 60 months long. [B.C. § 1325(b)(4)]

134. **NO** Car Creditor has a purchase-money security interest in Debtor's vehicle, which was purchased for personal use within 910 days of Debtor's bankruptcy filing. Therefore, the hanging paragraph under § 1325(a)(9) applies, which means that Car Creditor's claim is not bifurcated into a secured ($20,000) and unsecured ($5,000) claim under § 1325(a)(5). Instead, Debtor must treat the entire $25,000 as a secured claim in order to satisfy the Code's requirements for confirmation.

135. **NO** One of the mandatory provisions of a Chapter 13 plan is that all priority claims must be paid in full in deferred cash payments, unless a particular creditor consents to different treatment. Because the claim of the IRS is an eighth priority claim, Debtor's plan must provide for full repayment of the federal tax claim, although not on a present-value basis. [B.C. § 1322(a)(2)]

136. **NO** A standard Chapter 13 discharge occurs only after the debtor has made all payments under the plan. [B.C. § 1328(a)] Therefore, confirmation of Debtor's Chapter 13 plan does not operate as a discharge of her debts.

137. **YES** A standard Chapter 13 discharge includes all debts that are provided for by the plan or that have been disallowed by the court under § 502, *except* a debt (i) provided for under § 1322(b)(5), (ii) for trust fund taxes under § 507(a)(8)(C), (iii) that is not dischargeable under §§ 523(a)(1)(B), (C), 523(a)(2)–(5), 523(a)(8)–(9), (iv) for restitution or a criminal fine included in a sentence on debtor's conviction of a crime, (v) for HEAL loans with respect to which the three conditions of 42 U.S.C. § 292f(g) have not been satisfied, or (vi) for restitution or damages awarded against the debtor in a civil action because of the debtor's willful or malicious injury that caused personal injury to or death of an individual. [B.C. § 1328(a)] While Debtor's conduct was willful and malicious, it resulted in property damage, not personal injury to an individual. Thus, the debt is dischargeable. *Note:* Had Debtor filed for relief under Chapter 7, the debt also would have been discharged. While § 523(a)(6), which applies to Chapter 7 cases, covers injury to *both* persons and property, it requires a willful *and* malicious injury. Section 1328(a)(4) requires only a willful *or* malicious injury.

138. **DEPENDS** There is a split of authority on the question of when the five-year plan period begins. Some courts hold that the five-year period starts to run with the debtor's first plan payment, which normally occurs within 30 days of the filing of the petition. [B.C. § 1326(a)(1)] Other courts start the five-year period with the first payment that the debtor makes under the plan post-confirmation.

139. **NO** Debtor is incorrect and is confusing § 506(b)'s requirement of interest on an oversecured claim with § 1325(a)(5)'s requirement that a Chapter 13 plan pay secured creditors the present value of their claims. In order to give Car Creditor its present value, Debtor must pay interest on Car Creditor's claim. The interest rate paid on secured claims over the term of the plan is the *Till* rate, named after the Supreme Court's decision in **Till v. SCS Credit Corporation**, 541 U.S. 465 (2004). The *Till* rate is the national prime rate adjusted for risk; the risk adjustment generally means an additional 1–3% added to the national prime rate.

Essay Questions and Answers

QUESTION I

Apex, Inc. filed for relief under chapter 11 in late 2016. Bell Bank is Apex's largest secured creditor. Several years ago, Bell made a loan to Apex. The balance on the loan is $1.2 million; the loan is secured by a mortgage on Apex's plant, which is valued at $1.5 million. Apex's second largest secured creditor is Crafty Financial, which extended Apex a loan whose outstanding balance is $500,000. Crafty has a perfected security interest in Apex's inventory and accounts receivable, which are valued at $450,000. Apex has 10 unsecured creditors; the ten include Crafty. Apex's three largest unsecured creditors (apart from Crafty) are Daft Company, Enigma Corporation, and Flighty, Inc. Apex owes Daft $60,000; Enigma $70,000; and Flighty $100,000. The remaining six unsecured creditors are owed claims of $2,000 or less. Total unsecured claims (Classes 3 & 4 below) equal $290,000.

Apex proposes the following plan:

1) Class #1: Bell. Apex continues to pay Bell according to the terms of the parties' original contract.

2) Class #2: Crafty. Apex proposes to extend the loan repayment period on Crafty's loan by five years.

3) Class #3: Unsecured claims of $2,000 or less or creditors with larger claims willing to reduce their claims to $2,000 will be paid in full in cash on the plan's effective date.

4) Class #4: Unsecured claims in excess of $2,000 will be paid in five annual installments with 5% interest; the first payment will be made on the effective date of the plan. Total payout over five years = 20% of creditor's claim.

5) The four family members who currently own the firm will retain their ownership interests in Apex.

Apex knows that Bell and Crafty will vote in favor of the plan. Crafty, Daft, Enigma, and Flighty do not intend to reduce their claims to $2,000 in order to participate in Class #3. The other six unsecured creditors in Class #3 will vote in favor of the plan. Apex also knows that Daft and Enigma will vote "yes" on the plan. The problem is Flighty. If Flighty votes "no" on the plan, can Apex obtain confirmation? Assume all creditors will cast votes.

QUESTION II

Darlene has come to your law office for advice. She wants to file for bankruptcy, and you determine that she qualifies for relief under Chapter 7. While talking with Darlene, you discover the following facts:

- Darlene rents an apartment for $650 per month. Her landlord has obtained a judgment for possession of the apartment against her, which he likely is going to execute on within the next few days. Darlene wants to remain in her current apartment.

- Darlene purchased a car about a year ago. She financed the car through *Carl's Cars* ("CC"). The contract with CC contains an *ipso facto clause* that provides, among other things, that filing for bankruptcy is a default under the contract. Darlene needs the car to get back and forth to her job. She is current on her car payments and, in fact, always has made her car payment on time.

1. If Darlene files for bankruptcy before execution of the judgment for possession, will she be able to stay in the apartment during the pendency of the bankruptcy case? Explain what needs to happen to keep Darlene in her apartment.

2. Darlene cannot afford to redeem her car and does not want to reaffirm the debt with CC. Explain to Darlene what happens if she fails to redeem or enter into a reaffirmation agreement, as provided for under § 521(a)(6) of the Bankruptcy Code?

QUESTION III

Dorothy and Ed are in their late fifties and have been married for 25 years. They have come to your law office because creditors are hounding them "night and day" to pay delinquent medical and credit card bills. Dorothy and Ed want to jointly file for bankruptcy. They ask about Chapter 7 and tell you that their neighbor, who is a lawyer, told them that they do not qualify based on their income. You ask Dorothy and Ed some basic questions about their income and expenses, and they tell you the following:

Dorothy's and Ed's financial situation has been rocky for some time. Three years ago, Dorothy was in a serious car accident. Dorothy is covered by Ed's health insurance, but the plan has a high deductible and did not cover some of Dorothy's care. As a result, the couple has $87,000 in unpaid medical bills. Dorothy had to take an unpaid leave from her job, which put a further strain on the couple's finances. They maxed out their credit cards; the card balances are: (1) $25,000 on Master Card; (2) $30,000 on Visa; and (3) $15,000 on Discover.

Dorothy and Ed purchased their home fifteen years ago. *Local Bank* holds the mortgage on the home. The current balance on the home loan is $113,150, and there are fifteen years left on the loan. Dorothy and Ed recently had the home appraised, because they considered taking out an equity line to pay off their credit cards. The appraiser valued their home at $175,000. The home is not entireties property.

Dorothy's and Ed's household goods and clothes are valued at approximately $26,000; no item of clothing or household furnishings exceeds $625 in value. Ed owns a valuable watch worth about $1,700. Dorothy also has several pieces of fine jewelry worth approximately $1,700. Dorothy and Ed own two cars, both of which were purchased for personal use from (and financed by) *New Motors*. Dorothy owes $21,000 on her car, which is valued at $21,000 at retail. Ed owes $25,000 on his vehicle, which is valued at retail at approximately $22,000.

Ed has an ERISA-qualified pension plan currently valued at $150,000. Dorothy works but has no pension benefits through her job.

Dorothy and Ed gross $5,000 per month from their respective jobs. Median income for a two-person family in their state is $59,000. Their *actual* monthly expenses and deductions are $4,700. Their *means* test monthly expenses and deductions are $4,850.

Assume that Dorothy and Ed have been ***insolvent for the past year***.

1. After a few quick calculations, you realize that Dorothy's and Ed's neighbor was wrong; Dorothy and Ed do qualify for relief under Chapter 7. Explain to Dorothy and Ed *why* they qualify. Be specific.

2. Explain to Dorothy and Ed what property they can protect from their creditors and what property, if any, they cannot protect if they file for relief under Chapter 7. If they file, Dorothy and Ed will use the federal exemptions. Remember: Dorothy and Ed plan to file a joint petition.

QUESTION IV

The past few years have been hard on Darius. A few years ago, he was hospitalized due to complications from diabetes. Darius could not afford the bill, but had worked out an arrangement to pay off the hospital bill in monthly installments. Unfortunately, Darius lost his well-paying job, stopped paying the hospital, and has ignored the hospital's efforts to work out a payment plan. About a year ago, the hospital turned the $45,000 outstanding bill over to a collection agency. Around the same time, Darius gave his sister Jade a New England Tall Case Clock (circa 1820) that had been in their family for generations. The clock had been left to Darius by his grandfather who passed away 10 years ago. Darius gave Jade the clock for "safekeeping;" she paid nothing for it. The clock is valued at $25,800.

Darius files for relief under Chapter 13. Darius has been insolvent for the past 18 months. Can the Chapter 13 trustee recover the New England Tall Case Clock from Jade? Explain why, and evaluate all relevant theories.

QUESTION V

Debi Duncan is an aspiring clothing designer who grew up in southeastern Michigan. Over the past few years, she has tried to jump start her career by auditioning for and, in some cases, appearing on several reality shows for new designers.

Duncan moved to New York City in 2010 to attend design school. After graduating in April of 2013, Duncan moved to Los Angeles, where she appeared on *It's in the Bag,* a new reality show about fashion accessories. Duncan was eliminated in the early rounds of the competition, but earned a reputation as the "bad girl" on the show. Unable to find work in Los Angeles, Duncan moved to New York City in December of 2016, because she was offered a spot as the "design consultant" on *The Alarm,* an unconventional local morning television show. Unfortunately, in early 2018, Duncan received news that her mother was dying. Duncan gave up her job in New York City and on March 1, 2018, flew home to Michigan to care for her mother. Duncan's mother passed away in April of 2018, leaving Duncan a small inheritance. Duncan decided to open her own design business, and on July 1, 2018, signed a ten-year lease at a rental of $5,000 per month for a large, commercial space in a fashionable neighborhood. (As Duncan tells it, the lease was a "steal" because it was in a prime location and by agreeing to sign for ten years she got a lower rental.) Duncan, however, does not have a head for business and at the end of October 2018, she moved out of the commercial space and notified her landlord that she would not return. Duncan paid no rent after the end of October. Her landlord had some trouble re-letting the premises, which sat vacant for November and December. Landlord found a tenant who signed a ten-year, lease effective January 2, 2019, but the new tenant refused to pay more than $4,000 for the space.

1. If Duncan has been domiciled in Michigan since March 1, 2018, can she use the Michigan exemptions if she files for bankruptcy on February 1, 2019? If not, what state exemptions must she take?

2. Duncan files for relief under Chapter 7 on January 2, 2019. The Chapter 7 trustee rejects the lease of the commercial property, and Landlord files a proof of claim for $124,000—$10,000 for the two months the property sat vacant and 114 months (9.5 years) when the rental is $1,000 less. The Chapter 7 trustee objects to Landlord's proof of claim. What is the basis for the trustee's objection?

ANSWERS TO QUESTION I

Classes #2 & #4 are impaired, because their contractual rights were changed. For Crafty, Apex changed the payment period while for the general unsecured creditors Apex agreed to pay only 20% of what was owed. In order to obtain confirmation under § 1129(a) as a consent plan, each class of claims must *either* be unimpaired (Classes 1 & 3) *or* accept the plan. Class #4 contains $280,000 in claims, including Crafty. The problem is that Flighty's claim is $100,000 of the total $280,000 in Class #4, or about 36% of the total amount of claims. In order for a class of claims to accept the plan, more than half in number (3 of the 4 will vote "yes") and at least two-thirds in amount must accept. *See* § 1126(c). Without Flighty's claim as a "yes," the two-thirds in amount requirement is not met. Thus, there can be no consent plan.

But, if at least one impaired class votes "yes," Apex may proceed to cramdown. Crafty is an impaired "yes" class, so § 1129(a)(10) is met and Apex may try unsecured creditor cramdown. Section 1129(b)(2) requires that the plan not discriminate unfairly. The separation of the administrative convenience creditors into Class #3 is proper under § 1122(b). The plan also must be fair and equitable. For a plan to be fair and equitable with regard to a non-accepting unsecured class (§ 1129(b)(2)(B)), the plan either must pay the unsecured claims in full (which it does not do) *or* not allow any junior claimant to receive or retain property. This is the absolute priority rule, and the plan violates it by allowing the owners of the firm to retain their interests in the firm if Class #4 votes "no." (***Note:*** There is no *new value* proposed in the plan.) Therefore, if Flighty votes "no," then Apex cannot confirm its proposed plan.

ANSWERS TO QUESTION II

1. First, when Darlene files for bankruptcy she must deposit the next month's rent of $650 with the clerk of the court. Her state allows her to cure the default that gave rise to the judgment for possession, so she must file a certification to that effect with the petition and serve the certification on the landlord. *See* § 362(*l*)(1). Second, Darlene must pay the past-due rental owed (cure) within 30 days of the filing of the petition. She also must file a certification that she has cured with the bankruptcy court and serve that certification on the landlord. If she does so, then the stay will not lift under § 362(b)(22). That means that the landlord cannot evict her because the stay would prohibit the landlord from doing so.

2. Section 521(a)(6) provides that the car will no longer be estate property and that the automatic stay will terminate as to the stay on day 45 after the § 341 meeting, unless Darlene either redeems or signs a reaffirmation agreement. Because the contract contains an *ipso facto* clause CC could argue that the bankruptcy filing was an event of default and that once the stay is gone CC may repossess the car. Darlene needs the car for work. Section 521(a)(6) states that the creditor may take action as allowed by "applicable nonbankruptcy law." But, state law here does not allow repossession when the debtor is paying on the vehicle. Therefore, if Darlene does nothing, the stay will lift but CC cannot repossess the car because Darlene is paying on the vehicle and, thus, there is no event of default apart from filing for bankruptcy, which this jurisdiction does not recognize as an event of default. ***Note:*** State law varies on the legal effect of ipso facto clauses.

ANSWERS TO QUESTION III

1. Dorothy and Ed are above-median income debtors, because they earn $60,000 per year and median income is $59,000. Their means test expenses leave $150 per month, which multiplied by 60 equals $9,000. Because $9,000 is above $8,175 (no presumption of abuse) but below $13,650 (presumption of abuse), the secondary abuse test must be done. Dorothy and Ed have $160,000 in unsecured debt—$87,000 in medical bills, $70,000 in credit card debt, and $3,000 on Ed's car. [*New Motors'* secured claim is $22,000. Ed is an individual in a Chapter 7 case, so replacement value for property acquired for personal use is the price charged by a retail merchant. *See* § 506(a)(2)] Twenty-five percent of $160,000 = $40,000. Because the amount

that they have left over each month x 60 = $9,000, which is significantly less than 25% of their unsecured debt, there is no presumption of abuse. Dorothy and Ed simply do not have the financial resources to pay even 25% of their unsecured creditors' claims. They may file for Chapter 7.

2. Because Dorothy and Ed are married and filing jointly, they can double the federal exemptions. § 522(m)

    1) Homestead: $25,150 × 2 = $50,300. The problem is that after taking account of the mortgage of $113,150, there is still $11,550 in equity.

    2) Vehicles: The value of the vehicles is determined by § 506(a)(2), because Dorothy and Ed are individuals contemplating a Chapter 7 case, and the cars were acquired for personal use. Thus, the values are $21,000 for Dorothy's and $22,000 for Ed's. Neither Dorothy nor Ed has any equity to exempt.

    3) Jewelry: Dorothy and Ed each may fully exempt their jewelry, because each has jewelry worth $1700 or less. *See* § 522(d)(4).

    4) Household goods: All may be exempted, because the total value of $26,000is less than the maximum allowed for a married couple. § 522(d)(3). In addition, each item of clothing or household good is valued at $625 or less.

    5) Pension: an ERISA-qualified pension is not property of the estate under § 541(c)'s spendthrift trust clause.

    6) Wildcard: they have exhausted the homestead exemption, so they only have $2650 left ($1325 each), which they can apply to their home.

Conclusion: Dorothy and Ed can protect everything except all the equity in their home. After taking the homestead exemption and adding the $1,325 (2x) from the wildcard and taking account of the bank's mortgage, there still is $8,900 in equity for which there is no exemption. Calculation = $175,000 (home value) − $113,150 (mortgage on house) − $50,300 (homestead exemption) − $2,650 (wildcard exemption) = $8.900.

ANSWERS TO QUESTION IV

The transfer of the clock is avoidable by the Chapter 13 trustee using either § 548 and/or § 544(b) with the Uniform Fraudulent Transfer Act (UFTA) or the Uniform Voidable Transactions Act (UVTA), whichever applies in the jurisdiction. The trustee can argue either constructive fraud, which is easier, or actual fraud.

On the constructive fraud issue under § 548(a)(1)(B)(i) & (ii)(I), Darius was insolvent on the date of the transfer (past 18 months and transfer happened a little over a year ago) and the transfer was for less than reasonably equivalent value as Jade paid nothing for it. The same is true under § 544(b)(1) using § 5 of the UFTA or UVTA. The only difference between § 548 and § 5 of both the UFTA and UVTA is that § 5 applies only to present creditors; the Bankruptcy Code does not distinguish between present and future creditors. In this case, however, the hospital was a present creditor at the time of the transfer. The statute of limitations has not run yet on either § 548 (2 years) or the UFTA or UVTA (4 years; *see* § 9).

The Chapter 13 trustee also has a decent case for actual fraud under both § 548 and § 544 (pulling in § 4 of the UFTA or UVTA). There are several badges of fraud: (1) a transfer for less than reasonably equivalent; (2) to an insider—the sister Jade; (3) while debtor was insolvent; and (4) around the same time as the hospital turned over his case for collection.

In terms of recovery from Jade, the trustee would move under § 550. Jade does not have a defense here since she is the initial transferee. Section 548(c) does not help her with regard to a lien as she did not give value. The same is true for § 550(e)—she made no improvements. In fact, Jade has no claim at all since she was never a creditor—she paid nothing for the clock.

ANSWERS TO QUESTION V

1. No, Duncan may not use the Michigan exemptions. While Michigan is not an opt-out state, thereby allowing Duncan to take the Michigan exemptions, under § 522(b)(3)(A) Duncan had to have been domiciled in Michigan for 730 days prior to filing for bankruptcy. She lived in Michigan for less than one year prior to filing, so the statute then requires an examination of the 6 months prior to that two-year period, which is August of 2016 through the end of January of 2017. Duncan lived in New York City and Los Angeles during that time period. She spent about 4 months in L.A. and 2 months in New York City. If the debtor is domiciled in more than one state during the 6-month period, the state in which debtor is domiciled for the "longer portion of the 180-day period than in any other place" is the state whose exemptions govern. Therefore, Duncan must take the California exemptions if she plans to take state exemptions. Because Michigan is not an opt-out state, however, Duncan may elect the federal exemptions instead.

2. Under § 502(b)(6), the claim of a lessor resulting from the termination of a lease of real property is rent reserved by the lease for the *greater* of one year *or* 15% of the remaining term, not to exceed three years, plus any unpaid rent on the petition filing date. One year's rent is $60,000 (12 months × $5,000). The term remaining on the lease is 9.5 years or 114 months; 15% of that remaining term is a little over 17 months for $85,500. Either way, Landlord does not recover $124,000. Instead, Landlord gets $85,500, because it is the greater of one year's rent *or* rent for 15% of the lease's remaining term, *plus* past-due rent for November and December. Remember that § 502(b)(6)'s limitation does not apply to unpaid rent on the date of the petition. Therefore, Landlord is limited to a total claim of $95,500 rather than a total claim of $124,000. *Note:* If the term remaining on the lease is greater than 80 months but less than 240, then the Landlord recovers rent for 15% of the lease's remaining term.

Table of Cases

Table of Statutes

Table of Rules